FALLEN FORESTS

EST. 75 1938
YEARS
THE UNIVERSITY OF GEORGIA PRESS 2013

Fallen Forests

EMOTION, EMBODIMENT, AND ETHICS

IN AMERICAN WOMEN'S

ENVIRONMENTAL WRITING,

1781 – 1924

Karen L. Kilcup

THE UNIVERSITY OF GEORGIA PRESS

ATHENS AND LONDON

© 2013 by the University of Georgia Press
Athens, Georgia 30602
www.ugapress.org
All rights reserved

Designed by April Leidig
Set in Caslon by Copperline Book Services, Inc.
Manufactured by Sheridan Books

The paper in this book meets the guidelines for
permanence and durability of the Committee on
Production Guidelines for Book Longevity of the
Council on Library Resources.

Printed in the United States of America
14 15 16 17 18 P 6 5 4 3 2

Library of Congress Cataloging-in-Publication Data
Kilcup, Karen L.
Fallen forests : emotion, embodiment, and ethics in American
women's environmental writing, 1781–1924 / Karen L. Kilcup.
pages cm
ISBN-13: 978-0-8203-3286-4 (hardback)
ISBN-10: 0-8203-3286-0 (hardcover)
ISBN-13: 978-0-8203-4500-0 (paperback)
1. American literature—Women authors—History and criticism.
2. Environmental protection in literature. 3. Nature conservation in
literature. 4. Ecology in literature. 5. Nature in literature. I. Title.
PS152K55 2013
810.9'9287—dc23   2012043938

British Library Cataloging-in-Publication Data available

FRONTIS
"The trvve picture of a vvomen." From Thomas Harriot, *A Briefe
and True Report of the New Found Land of Virginia: of the commodities
and of the nature and manners of the natural inhabitants. . . .*
(1590; reprinted 1871). Courtesy of the North Carolina Collection,
University of North Carolina Library at Chapel Hill.

FOR FOUR BELOVED MEN

my great-uncle, Leonard Ilsley (1896–1982)

my grandfather, Lauris M. Gove (1904–1986)

my father, Richard S. Kilcup (1931–1997)

and my husband, Chris Chimera

The great tree is a protection to a thousand lesser interests, a central force which keeps in motion and urges on a thousand activities.

SARAH ORNE JEWETT

The elm-tree had his field to himself. He stood alone in a wide and deep expanse of wind-swept grass which once a year surged round him in foaming billows crested with the rose of clover and the whiteness of daisies and the gold of buttercups. The rest of the time the field was green with an even slant of lush grass, or else it was a dun surface, or else a glittering level of snow; but always there stood the tree, with his green branches in the summer, his gold ones in the autumn, his tender, gold-green ones in the spring, and his branches of naked grace in the winter, but always he was superb. There was not in the whole country-side another tree which could compare with him. He was matchless.

MARY WILKINS FREEMAN

Contents

Illustrations

Acknowledgments

FALLEN FORESTS HAS SO many roots that I can only hope to remember a few.

My colleagues at the University of North Carolina at Greensboro have provided a solid and fruitful ground from which to work. All of my Americanist colleagues, among them Tony Cuda, SallyAnn Ferguson, Christian Moraru, and Noelle Morrissette, helped cover my teaching responsibilities during the time I was on leave to finish drafting and revising, and I am grateful for their support. Some colleagues also read chapter drafts: Mark Rifkin, María Sánchez, and Hepsie Roskelly helped me prune excess and encouraged growth in other areas. Karen Weyler and Mary Ellis Gibson deserve many helpings of chocolate cake for reading multiple drafts of the entire manuscript—and for knowing when to cheer and when to chide. The weekly writing group as a whole have my warm thanks for providing a scholarly environment that feeds both mind and body—perceptive criticism accompanied by cream scones and marmalade, lemon pound cake, and strawberry rhubarb pie.

I am grateful for the continuing support of the University of North Carolina at Greensboro. The College of Arts and Sciences, especially Dean Timothy Johnston, provided a research assignment to enable me to draft the manuscript and, with the unexpected arrival of an NEH Fellowship, another to enable me to complete the book. I have been fortunate to have had the best of department heads, Anne Wallace, who has been both encouraging and supportive. The library at the university has, as always, provided outstanding assistance; special thanks to Gaylor Callahan and the interlibrary loan staff. My UNCG students, particularly my graduate students, have energized me toward completion.

Outside my home institution, other institutions, colleagues, and friends have fostered this project in different ways. Several librarians, archivists, and institutions' staff helped with obtaining the book's images: Karen Jania at the Bentley Historical Library of the University of Michigan, Terry Zinn at the Oklahoma Historical Society, Kevin Wilks of the Center for Research

Libraries, Erin Clements Rushing at the Smithsonian Institution Libraries, Jane Winton at the Boston Public Library, Maryellen Tinsley at the Louis Round Special Collections Library at the University of North Carolina at Chapel Hill, and Jackie Maman at the Art Institute of Chicago. Rachel Cooke at Florida Gulf Coast University's library provided capable help in a time of immediate need. At various stages, colleagues Annette Kolodny, Rochelle Johnson, and Melody Graulich provided essential encouragement. Claire and Larry Morse and Christian and Camelia Moraru are kind and generous friends who help keep me moving forward. My in-laws, Rick and Judy Chimera, offered a sunny winter home and a quiet office. My cousin, Clint Gove, has patiently tended home and animals when I could not. Special thanks to Cheryl Walker and John Elder for their crucial enthusiasm and support, without which this project would have taken even longer to complete.

I am profoundly appreciative of the detailed feedback offered by Annie Ingram and Tina Gianquitto, the manuscript readers for the University of Georgia Press; I have seldom seen such care and thoughtfulness given to readers' reports. The final product is much better because of their help, though they are not responsible for its shortcomings. Thanks to the press's efficient production, design, and marketing staff; its helpful managing editor, Jon Davies; and my excellent copyeditor, Joy Margheim. My editor, Nancy Grayson, deserves a medal (or at least a pleasant dinner) for her support and patience.

A few people merit special mention, not only for specific help with the project but also for their support over the past twenty years. Paul Lauter has provided encouragement, fellowship, and mentoring that exceed my ability to thank him. Paula Bernat Bennett read the manuscript carefully and provided characteristically incisive criticism; her encouragement and support always make my work better and mean more than I can say.

My husband, Chris Chimera, is no mythological creature but an enduring, essential supporter. With him, home is "something you somehow haven't to deserve."

Fallen Forests has been made possible in part by a fellowship award from the National Endowment for the Humanities; I am grateful for this support and for recognition of the project as part of the "We the People" initiative. Any views, findings, conclusions, or recommendations expressed in *Fallen*

Forests do not necessarily represent those of the National Endowment for the Humanities.

Some of the material from *Fallen Forests* appeared elsewhere in earlier form. Grateful acknowledgement is made to the following journals and presses:

"Celia Thaxter, 1835–1894," in *Nineteenth-Century American Women Writers: A Bio-Bibliographical Critical Sourcebook*, ed. Denise D. Knight (Westport: Greenwood Press, 1997), 174–79.

"The Domestic Abroad: Cross-Class (Re)Visions of Europe and America," *Legacy: A Journal of American Women Writers* 16, no. 1 (1999): 22–36. Copyright © 1999 by the University of Nebraska Press.

"Frado Taught a Naughty Ram: Animal and Human Natures in *Our Nig*." Copyright © 2012 The Johns Hopkins University Press. This article first appeared in *ELH* 79, no. 2 (Summer 2012): 341–68.

"'I Like These Plants That You Call Weeds': Historicizing American Women's Nature Writing," *Nineteenth-Century Literature* 58, no. 1 (June 2003): 42–74. Copyright © 2003 by the University of California Press.

"Introduction: A Working-Class Woman's View of Europe," in *From Beacon Hill to the Crystal Palace*, ed. Karen L. Kilcup (Iowa City: University of Iowa Press, 2002), 1–49. Copyright © 2002 by the University of Iowa Press.

"Lucy Larcom," *American Writers: A Collection of Literary Biographies*, ed. Jay Parini (New York: Scribner's, 2003), 131–51.

"'We planted, tended, and harvested our corn': Gender, Ethnicity, and Transculturation in *A Narrative of the Life of Mrs. Mary Jemison*," *Women and Language* 18, no. 1 (Spring 1995): 45–51.

"Writing against Wilderness: María Amparo Ruiz de Burton's Elite Environmental Justice," *Western American Literature* 47, no. 4 (Winter 2013): 361–85. Copyright © 2013 Western Literature Association.

Quascacunquen (Newbury, Massachusetts) marshes and
drumlin at dusk, near First Settlers' landing.
Courtesy of Christopher R. Chimera.

Grounding the Texts

An Introduction

There arose a sudden gust at N.W. so violent for half an hour, as it blew down multitudes of trees. It lifted up their meeting house at Newbury, the people being in it. It darkened the air with dust, yet through God's great mercy it did no hurt, but only killed one Indian with the fall of a tree.

—JOHN WINTHROP's journal, 5 July 1643

Humans no longer believe food comes from dirt.

—BARBARA KINGSOLVER

FALLEN FORESTS BEGINS in the dirt.

Or, more accurately, it starts with my hands in the black earth of my grandfather's garden. A carpenter by day but a horticulturalist by desire, he enlists me as his accomplice in planting:

> Corn, beans, squash.
> Potatoes.
> Pumpkins, peppers.
> Tomatoes.[1]

When winter breaks, we harvest sap for maple syrup; in the spring, set strawberries and onions. Come fall, we fill his battered Chevy station wagon so full with squash and pumpkins that I have to lie spread-eagled across the tailgate as we creep across the street to where we'll heap our treasure for sorting in the back yard: golden butternuts, crenellated acorns, huge Blue Hubbards. To bring me home to Quascacunquen, which English settlers renamed Newbury, he has crossed the wide mouth of the Merrimack River, "swift water place."[2] In 1635, our ancestors landed nearby, where the Quascacunquen River uncoils toward the dark Atlantic.[3]

The New World's poem was written well before Europeans arrived in Quascacunquen. Or in Greenland, Jamestown, Plymouth, St. Augustine, the Caribbean, Mexico. The New World's wealth encompassed vegetable, animal, mineral, and liquid gold: food, timber, fur, human labor, water. Founded through resource wars with European colonial powers and indigenous nations, the emergent United States quickly began to expand its earliest borders. Although often elided from written history, women participated, indirectly and directly, on both sides of transnational encounters. An indication of their presence is the question posed by the distinguished Cherokee chief Attakullakulla, for whom women were central to cultural, spiritual, and political balance. Negotiating with English colonial representatives shortly before the American Revolution, he inquired pointedly, "Where are your women?"[4]

Among those who figured significantly in Cherokee and U.S. national affairs was Attakullakulla's niece, Nancy Ward (Nanye-hi, c. 1738–c. 1822), whose oratory concerning resource preservation and peaceful cooperation is one of my touchstones in *Fallen Forests*.[5] As the nineteenth century advanced, increasing numbers of North American women joined energetically in debates about resources and consumption; Ward was only one among many American women writers of the long nineteenth century who, from various perspectives, addressed issues that we would now deem environmental and that should engage our greatest energies.[6] How did nineteenth-century American women's literature (broadly construed to include oratory and as-told-to texts) understand and portray the relationship between women and nature? How did women writers respond to or share in environmental activism, also broadly construed? Why have we forgotten these writers' lessons? What are their perspectives' limitations? What productive analogies, as well as instructive contrasts, emerge when we read earlier writers against their twentieth- and twenty-first-century counterparts? How does their work speak to current environmental concerns and environmental rhetoric? These are some of the questions that I explore in *Fallen Forests*.

Such questions may seem tangential to much of the writing that I discuss. Unlike male writers such as Thoreau, who regarded nature as a means to individual self-development, or painters such as Thomas Cole, who understood it as an object for contemplating the sublime, women in this period more often perceived "nature" and "the environment" within a complex framework of embodied and social experiences. Nineteenth-century

American women writers not only apprehended nature differently, they represented it dissimilarly; for example, they frequently developed hybrid genres less legible today as nature writing than Thoreau's nonfiction and more coherently situated within the framework of environmental writing. Evincing what I will call *literary emotional intelligence*, they also used diverse affective approaches, including a putatively feminine sentimental rhetoric, to accomplish their aims. *Fallen Forests* expands the literary, historical, and theoretical contexts for some of our most pressing environmental debates, explaining how women writers enlisted genre to promote social change and how their rhetorical strategies—appeals to logic, ethics, and, particularly, emotion—engendered awareness of environmental concerns and sometimes propelled action.

Even as I restore these earlier women's voices to audibility, I also critique some ecocritics' idealizing tendency, which has obscured women's complicity in perspectives and agendas that complicate or even depart from today's environmental orthodoxies. This idealizing tendency has particularly obscured working-class, ethnic, and otherwise outsidered women's perspectives on the dominant culture's goals and beliefs. As Susan Kollin points out, "Ecocriticism often uncritically positions wilderness and nature writing as its primary objects of study and in the process celebrates nature as a restorative and regenerative force."[7] Although some earlier women writers express affirmative connections with the natural environment, others dissent from this attitude.[8] We need not only to appreciate their contributions but also to analyze the problems they pose.

Thus, while *Fallen Forests* contributes to the reshaping of American literary history, it also connects historical perceptions to those of the present. Today, ecocritics, environmental historians, and ordinary Americans, among others, contend over such concerns as sustainability, green Christianity, resource depletion and resource wars, globalization and relocalization, voluntary simplicity, and environmental justice. This volume establishes how some nineteenth-century women writers anticipated these debates and how revisiting their work helps us complicate our perception of contemporary issues.[9] More particularly, by highlighting these writers' rhetoric, ethos, and forms, it underscores how their failures and successes both caution us toward self-examination and model potentially productive strategies for engagement with current environmental challenges.

The Lay of the Land: Touchstones

Fallen Forests inhabits the unmapped terrain where nineteenth-century American women's writing converges with such fields as ecocriticism, ecofeminism, and feminist rhetoric.[10] Each of these areas enjoys a rich critical history, in some cases developed over nearly five decades. Scholarship on nineteenth-century American women's writing has been particularly fruitful; nevertheless, even touchstone studies characteristically comprise a single genre (Nina Baym's *American Women of Letters and the Nineteenth-Century Sciences: Styles of Affiliation*; Paula Bennett's *Poets in the Public Sphere: The Emancipatory Project of American Women's Poetry, 1800–1900*), period (Judith Fetterley and Marjorie Pryse's *Writing Out of Place: Regionalism, Women, and American Literary Culture* and Baym's *American Women Writers and the Work of History, 1790–1860*), or identity group (Carla Peterson's *Doers of the Word: African American Women Speakers and Writers in the North [1830–1880]*, Rosemarie Garland Thomson's *Extraordinary Bodies: Figuring Disability in American Culture and Literature*, and Frances Smith Foster's *'Til Death or Distance Do Us Part: Love and Marriage in African America*).[11] Such discussions have characteristically focused on the domestic novel and/or on sentimentalism's ability to challenge or integrate ostensibly separate (male) public and (female) private spheres.[12] Almost without exception — and I mention some below — such studies omit an ecocritical perspective; they do not evaluate, for example, sentimentalism's potential as an environmental discourse, particularly in multicultural women's writing.

Another area to which *Fallen Forests* contributes is women's rhetoric, or what has come to be called *rhetorica*, as scholars have reconstructed a Western female tradition stretching from the ancient Athenian Aspasia to Minnie Bruce Pratt; such projects include Joy Ritchie and Kate Ronald's *Available Means: An Anthology of Women's Rhetoric(s)*. Paralleled and reinforced by critical essays such as those collected in Andrea A. Lunsford's *Reclaiming Rhetorica: Women in the Rhetorical Tradition*, this scholarship has only infrequently considered nineteenth-century American women rhetors. Most work in this area studies issues that particularly concerned women, such as temperance, dress reform, and woman suffrage. I expand rhetorica's substance and its genre scope, including — but going beyond — writing that seeks "most often to persuade or inform" and reviewing texts that envision an imagined as well as actual audience. As Ritchie and Ronald remind us, women writers and rhetors often contended with the right to speak in public at all. *Fallen Forests* demonstrates that many women, especially outsidered writers, resisted and circumvented such confinement as they delineated their environments. The texts that I consider here offer an opportunity for thinking holistically about how American women reiterate familiar terms and forms and how they invented new ones that, as Lunsford puts it, stress "understanding, exploration, connection, and conversation."[13]

Fallen Forests certainly lies within the province of literary ecocriticism, which specifies a polymorphous field and encompasses heterogeneous texts. Traditionally defined as the "critical and pedagogical broadening of literary studies to include texts that deal with the nonhuman world and our relationship to it," ecocriticism extends beyond textual analysis to study literature's social and political consequences, particularly its ethical inflections.[14] Yet assessments of nature writing and environmental literature have, with few exceptions, neglected nineteenth-century women authors' hybrid genres and complicated rhetorical strategies, reflecting on only a tiny group of white nonfiction writers such as Susan Fenimore Cooper, Celia Thaxter, and Mary Austin. I share many ecocritics' premise that we should enlarge the field by period, genre, and culture, and in this spirit, I extend backward ecocriticism's characteristic period emphasis on twentieth-century and contemporary texts. Moving beyond white middle-class women's writing, I analyze work by women of color, working-class women, and non-Protestant women, and I enlarge the traditional genre domain, addressing texts ranging from Cherokee oratory to travel writing, the slave narrative, diaries, polemical texts, sketches, novels, and exposés.[15]

In this endeavor I hope to enrich the three ecocritical modes that Cheryll Glotfelty has identified: considering representations, enlarging the tradition of American nature writing (here, environmental writing), and broadening its theoretical grounds.[16] I concur with Astrid Bracke's observation that "[a] mature ecocritical practice should not dismiss images or texts for not being environmentally sound. Instead, it needs to question what such problematic texts reveal about our experience and perceptions of the (natural) environment."[17] Such a practice fosters greater self-examination, requiring that we reassess what constitute problematic texts and why. Yet even as academic ecocriticism and related activist endeavors continue to flourish, we may often feel unbalanced, that we occupy shifting grounds.

Even definitions present a conundrum: how we perceive *nature*, for example, depends on the viewer's culture and experience, time period, and place. Contemporary philosophers, historians, biological ecologists, and literary critics have variously adopted social constructionist and realist perspectives. The first assumes that nature is mediated through culture, particularly through language, while the second apprehends it as a material presence. Advocates of both stances recognize humans' simultaneous membership in and detachment from nature. I share the view of Noël Sturgeon, who writes, "Humans are inside, coexisting, and interdependent with nature rather than outside and independent of it."[18] Even within categories differences can emerge: one person may regard Central Park as nature, and another may see it as pseudo-nature within a concrete wilderness. Having grown up on a New England farm, I understand the park as a constructed environment—though someone who has lived all her life in Utah's Canyonlands area may see my family farm as artificial. When communities come to blows, definitional differences often propel them.

The terms *nature writing* and *environmental literature* spark similar debates. Merely separating these forms indicates a distinctively Western (rather than, say, Native American) conceptual framework, but a few distinctions will nevertheless be helpful. As Daniel Philippon suggests, the question of how to define nature writing actually incorporates three inquiries: "what to call the genre, how to define its contents, and whether its boundaries change over time."[19] Sometimes denominated "natural history," the term usually denotes nonfiction prose, often in first person, though it also references some (mostly romantic-pastoral) poetry.[20] Pointing toward behavior, H. Lewis Ulman has proposed that nature writing "accommodates natural history but *foregrounds* the construction of writers' personae and ethos in light of ethical judgments about how to be and act at home (i.e., *ecologically*) in the natural world."[21] Such definitions, because they conceptualize nature as a separate or primary concern and they elide gendered concepts of nature, have a relatively limited applicability to many of the writers whose work I analyze in *Fallen Forests*.

If delimiting nature writing has proven difficult, terms such as *the environment* and *environmental writing* pose analogous definitional obstacles. Bill McKibben argues that environmental writing considers collisions and conflicts between humans and "the rest of the world"; it raises difficulties and challenges readers' conventions, and it—sometimes—propounds solutions.[22] Treating concerns related to humans' physical and social environments, I take a similarly broad view toward *Fallen Forests'* writers. Because I survey principally nineteenth-century texts, these environments are more often rural than urban. Again, earlier American women's environmental writing may not always conform to contemporary activists' definitions or standards, but those unsettling instances offer important insights into our own blind spots.

In my reading, nineteenth-century women's environmental literature does not necessarily express an explicitly political or polemical component; to participate in so-called public-sphere concerns or to investigate embodiment, some women writers necessarily coded their dissenting observations. Given this indirection, Scott Slovic's continuum for nature writing seems particularly salient. His epistemological mode proffers ways of understanding the relationship between humans and the natural world, while the political mode attempts to enlighten and prompt action.[23] Exemplified in two examples of literary form, these attitudes correspond to the pastoral rhapsody and the jeremiad, although hybrid forms occur.[24] Noting that "excessive stridency" may alienate readers, Slovic favors pastoral's more "literary" approach because it may "promote concern and attentiveness without necessarily stipulating unanimous agreement."[25]

This continuum provides leverage for appreciating nineteenth-century American women writers' hybrid genres and multiple ambitions. In their hands, for example, the jeremiad sometimes becomes a maternal sermon or, in its milder aspect, advice writing. Alternatively, as Slovic maintains, pastoral can eclipse political content or be readily co-opted into celebration.[26] It becomes vulnerable, my analysis will suggest, to later reinterpretation as mere sentimentalism. As M. Jimmie Killingsworth and Jacqueline S. Palmer contend, however, "genre, medium, or 'form' of any kind is never innocent of meaning."[27] Thus even ostensibly neutral pastoral can have political impact, depending on such variables as speaker, audience, and context. Because nineteenth-century American society associated women with nature, pastoral may have seemed "natural" to some, but they did not necessarily emphasize its celebratory mode, instead sometimes constructing a more political elaboration.

In light of this taxonomical complexity, I endeavor throughout *Fallen Forests* to situate terms such as *nature*, *wilderness*, and *the environmental* in historical moments and social contexts. For example, various Native American nations' and African Americans' experiences of nature diverge dramatically from each other and from Euramericans'. These differences also occur *within* communities, even when writers realized that cohering *as* a community offered sources of cultural power.[28] Although my central argument frames various terms and concepts historically, I draw out analogies to or alliances with contemporary terms, such as *resource wars* and *clear-cutting* (again defined as needed and in context). When I distinguish between humans and nature, I characteristically use such language as *nonhuman nature* or *nonhuman animals*. The phrase *environmental justice* appears regularly, and I define the term in individual chapters, reemphasizing that *Fallen Forests* aims to foster discussion of current challenges while revisiting earlier American engagements with analogous problems. Finally, although taxonomical questions recur, I am less immediately concerned with authenticating an individual author's work as nature writing or environmental literature than with investigating particular texts' rhetorical functions and effects.[29]

Theoretical Grounds

Responding to so many different voices necessitates a capacious and flexible theoretical approach. One term with popular currency requires more substantial comment because it resonates with historical and critical paradigms for nineteenth-century American women's writing: *emotional intelligence*. Popularized by psychologist-journalist Daniel Goleman, the concept of emotional intelligence (EI) has its foundations in Darwinian theories of adaptation and in early twentieth-century intelligence and learning theories.[30] Goleman's model draws from contemporary brain science to contend that EI possesses several principal characteristics—self-awareness, self-management, self-motivation, empathy, and relationship management—and that emotional competencies can be learned.[31] It seems intuitively obvious that writing is one important form through which to exercise emotional intelligence and possibly extend this competence to others.

In its attention to sympathy, literary scholars' work on sentimentalism has paralleled recent brain science. Whole forests have been transmogrified into books relating to nineteenth-century literary and cultural sentimentalism. Given its philosophical origins, however, sentiment should involve much more than sympathy and tears, and, as I have maintained earlier, attending only to this emotional bandwidth constricts our comprehension of both written and spoken communication.[32] Appreciating rhetoric's potentially persuasive power, many nineteenth-century American women writers constructed sentimental appeals supplemented with—or counterbalanced by—humor and accusation or logical and legal arguments. While such projects did not necessarily embrace goals we would today call environmental, some did; some were consciously activist, whereas others advanced social critiques that nudged readers toward better behavior, articulating indirect forms of advice writing.[33] These sophisticated interplays enlist readers' sympathy, encourage their (sometimes outraged) laughter, impugn their integrity, and propel them to action.

Explaining that empathy is biologically hardwired, Goleman observes, "Empathy underlies many facets of moral judgment and action" and "emotions are contagious."[34] More significantly, he adds, "all emotions are . . . impulses to act," part of our evolutionary biology. Hence empathy is only one motivator; anger, fear, happiness, love, surprise, disgust, and sadness encompass some other important affective responses that generate physiological effects.[35] In Western culture "being emotional" has been consistently feminized and considered dangerous, yet humans constantly balance and integrate emotional and rational systems for negotiating the world.[36]

The text/reader dynamic has substantial potential for intervening in this balance, if only by proxy: "When two people interact, the direction of mood transfer is from the one who is more forceful in expressing feelings to the one who is more passive. But some people are particularly susceptible to emotional contagion; their innate sensitivity makes their autonomic nervous system . . . more easily triggered."[37] This directionality implies that a writer expressing strong emotion—or advancing images that create a strong affective response—is more likely to influence readers, especially those sensitive to emotion. However, such a writer might alienate individuals governed principally by intellect, as the metaphor of "contagion"—and Slovic's reference to "excessive stridency," which certainly has contemporary resonances—forecasts.[38]

Just as many EI researchers assume that affective skills can be learned, many nineteenth-century women (and men) believed, analogously, that they could help their readers (in Harriet Beecher Stowe's famous phrase) to "feel right." In *Fallen Forests* I examine rhetoric and form as primary resources for literary emotional intelligence. I unpack how women writers' affective appeals, juxtaposed to or synthesized with logic and ethics, elicit

and educate readers' emotional intelligence. Sometimes those appeals energize readers to such actions as changing personal behavior or investing in
larger social transformations.

In addition to drawing from contemporary emotional intelligence theories, *Fallen Forests* is grounded in ecofeminist theory, a diverse set of critical practices in and across the traditional academic disciplines that also
possesses activist elements (with the two modes not always mutually
congenial); *ecofeminisms* more accurately designates this diversity.[39] Noël
Sturgeon's economical description of unifying features concludes, "Basi-
cally, ecofeminism claims that the oppression, inequality, and exploitation of certain groups (people of color, women, poor people, LGBT people,
Global South people, animals) are theoretically and structurally related to
the degradation and overexploitation of the environment."[40] Emerging unevenly from second-wave feminisms, ecofeminisms share a commitment
to nonhuman nature, which enables a particularly valuable analysis (and
dissolution) of the nature/culture dualism that dominates Western societies.[41] Ecofeminisms, which underline postcolonial and transnational considerations, embodiment, and activism, provide an important interpretive
framework here.[42]

What counts as activism is another matter. Our twenty-first-century
perspective too often occludes one crucial point: for nineteenth-century
Americans, especially women, writing and activism were virtually inseparable.[43] Assessing their texts may help bridge the theory/praxis divide that
contemporary ecocritics and ecofeminists have sought to repair. Greta
Gaard has pointed out that although "literature has not been perceived
as factual data and hence is seen as lacking in persuasive power," some
ecofeminists have considered literature both as data and "as an effective
rhetorical mode."[44] Literary scholars have long valued the persuasive force
and social agency of nineteenth-century American women's writing. My
literary-rhetorical-cultural ecofeminist analysis in *Fallen Forests* highlights
earlier writers' contributions to representations of the environment and their
affective and effective responses to material, social, and political realities.

I build on robust foundations, including Annette Kolodny's pathbreak-
ing *The Land Before Her: Fantasy and Experience of the American Frontiers,
1630–1860*, Vera Norwood's *Made from This Earth: American Women and
Nature*, Carolyn Merchant's *Earthcare: Women and the Environment*, Stacy
Alaimo's *Undomesticated Ground: Recasting Nature as Feminist Space*, Tina

Gianquitto's *"Good Observers of Nature": American Women and the Scientific Study of the Natural World, 1820–1885*, Rochelle Johnson's *Passions for Nature: Nineteenth-Century America's Aesthetics of Alienation*, Sturgeon's *Environmentalism in Popular Culture: Gender, Race, Sexuality, and the Politics of the Natural*, and Kimberly N. Ruffin's *Black on Earth: African American Eco-literary Traditions*.[45] Sturgeon's *"critique of naturalization,"* more specifically, her *"critical approach to any claims to the natural,"* possesses particular salience for *Fallen Forests* (original emphasis).[46]

Another important thread in contemporary ecocriticism also informs my account: the attentiveness to metaphor's role in shaping attitudes toward nature (Johnson) and effecting agency (Daniel Philippon, in *Conserving Words: How American Nature Writers Shaped the Environmental Movement*). While Johnson and Philippon focus on logos, I emphasize ethos and pathos. Certainly, nineteenth-century American women writers understood nature through many of the interlinked and historically mutable metaphors that Philippon names, including frontier, garden, park, and wilderness, as well as savage and mother.[47] But because they themselves were associated with nature, sometimes (particularly for women of color) on multiple grounds, they revised such terms, sometimes dramatically. In *Fallen Forests* I attend to both figure and ground, returning the women writers' imaginative language to its roots in their lived experience. Augmenting the last fifty years' recovery work of primary texts by earlier American women writers, these ecocritical texts form the foundation from which my narrative substantially departs.

My project also extends these recent critics' efforts to return literary studies to earth. Many non-ecocritical scholars of nineteenth-century American women's writing, even many feminists, assume an essentially disembodied stance. The historical reasons for this positioning are too complex to detail here, but one factor has particular significance. Since Ann Douglas's landmark text associating earlier women's literature with weakening sentimentalism—and despite Jane Tompkins–inflected efforts to elevate the genre's cultural work—female critics have, to obtain legitimacy, often distanced ourselves from a literary endeavor problematically associated with (emotional) women. We have studied that tradition dispassionately and "objectively," often prioritizing theory. That is, paradoxically, to recoup sentimentalism's intellectual respectability, we have needed to present ourselves as detached and rational, minds rather than bodies.[48] Such disembodiment has almost certainly been accelerated by most critics'—

female and male, feminist and otherwise—increasingly urban personal and educational experiences. Accompanying the difficulty of conveying our views through language, such contingencies virtually ensure cognitive and emotional distance, a problem multiplied in studying nineteenth-century American women's writing by our temporal belatedness.

If *Fallen Forests* represents a joint venture between ecofeminism and literary ecocriticism, the writers themselves—however unevenly—articulate proto-ecofeminist perspectives as they explore relationships among nature, culture, and women, particularly women's bodies. While they often use the dominant society's language and metaphors, they sometimes remake that language or reinterpret those metaphors as they express material relationships with nature that frequently involve spiritual connections. These writers also evince protoenvironmental concerns, sometimes attempting to correct concrete problems. Although their focus may be local, their reach is often far wider, both national and transnational. Their varied perspectives open opportunities for today's readers to reassess how we formulate contemporary terms and theories, to rework these grounds and grow in new directions.

Cultural and Historical Obstacles

The women writers I treat in *Fallen Forests* faced a range of challenges, depending on their identities and their political investments. In a social environment that first prohibited, then merely discouraged, women's public-sphere participation, those who overtly remarked on reform subjects, including environmental ones, could be censured and excluded. Consequently, many writers express themselves indirectly or in compressed or oblique fashion. Another obstacle was (gendered) Christianity's role as the dominant U.S. spiritual system, even though its influence declined over the century. M. Jimmie Killingsworth and Jacqueline S. Palmer point out that "in traditional Western thought, wilderness is the enemy of civilization."[49] Although by the early nineteenth century attitudes toward wilderness had become less fearful, metamorphosing into appreciation of nature, Christian society remained rooted in the language of savage and civilized. This rhetoric encoded the persistent nature/culture dichotomy to which the writers in *Fallen Forests* directly or indirectly respond.[50]

A related challenge inhered in women's association with nature and embodiment, each differentially defined by such variables as individual history, place, and age. In Native American societies this association was often esteemed, but Indian speakers and writers addressing dominant-culture audiences still had to negotiate its Euramerican affiliations. Women's experiences of themselves and their "natural" bodies were both culturally superimposed and subjectively experienced, not necessarily in identical ways or with consonant valences. For women of color, older women, the disabled, and other outsidered individuals, these connections were intensified, sometimes synergistically. Hence, depending on their background, location, status, attitude toward "respectability," and literary or political ambitions, writers' approaches varied; some elided corporeality, whereas others focused almost forensically on material selfhood. Describing contemporary feminists' flight from corporeality, Alaimo has recently encouraged feminist efforts to "make space for materiality," but I will demonstrate how some of these earlier women successfully, though sometimes painfully, negotiated this troubled territory, creating an embodied rhetoric that encouraged complementarily embodied reading.[51]

Allied to these obstacles were women's attitudes toward progress and technology. If control of nature—and, by extension, the body—meant modernity and "American" advancement, then disparaging progress meant attacking, in Killingsworth and Palmer's phrase, "the master narrative of liberal democracy in use since the Enlightenment."[52] Yet as Kolodny argued long ago, it is "imperative that we recognize at least some part of our urge to progress, and our historical commitment to conquer, master, and alter the continent as another side of the pastoral impulse."[53] Women writers assumed many different positions on progress, which engendered debates that ranged from the proper use of "waste" land and species extinction to (in today's terms) environmental racism. Protesting nature's exploitation rendered women vulnerable to charges of feminine sentimentalism and nostalgia, unenlightened childishness, and antiprogressiveness. Liberal democracy also increasingly privileged individual achievement, and women writers of all ethnicities who operated within the dominant society struggled to negotiate their place and formulate their ethos, even as the ostensible separation between public and private spheres became more tenuous. Minority writers were more likely to invest in a larger community and speak on that community's behalf in response to environmental concerns, but they were not alone.

However circumscribed by factors that included inherited concepts of nature and wilderness, earlier women writers benefited from the absence of established environmental discourse, the "ecospeak" that Killingsworth and Palmer claim constrains contemporary writers and speakers. When disciplinary boundaries were nebulous (early) or blurred (later), women could test and practice a greater range of rhetorical strategies than they now do. Discussing rhetoric's significance to contemporary environmental issues, Killingsworth and Palmer define it as "the production and interpretation of signs and the use of logical, ethical, and emotional appeals in deliberations about public action," and they remind us that it is "both a theory and a practical art."[54] Whether or not nineteenth-century American women were formally educated in classical rhetoric, they drew liberally from its elements, while emphasizing ethics and emotion. A cultural contradiction may have propelled some in this direction. Though associated with savage nature, middle-class white women—Republican Mothers and their descendants—were paradoxically expected to be moral exemplars as the production of goods moved into the public sphere and social classes consolidated. We should not be surprised that much of their rhetoric prioritized ethics or feeling.

These women writers' challenges bespeak the obstacles confronting my own intellectual project, not least of which is the difficulty of generalizing about rhetoric or genre over a large field encompassing writers of different ethnicities, races, ages, religions, and locations. To say that genre per se neither guarantees nor forecloses natural investments, or that it neither ensures nor obstructs political intervention, is *not* to say that it remains innocent of associations and attachments. Genre, sometimes affiliated with gender, matters, although evaluating a particular form may mean eliding the synergies of hybrid genres. Ultimately, what we learn from nineteenth-century American women writers is that how an individual or group performs genre, in what context, for whom, and when, matters more, sometimes much more, than a particular form.[55] Much as readers might prefer that I establish a master narrative that hierarchizes rhetorical practices and formal choices, such a narrative would be myopic at best.

Mapping the Route

In addition to sketching an intellectual framework, every book requires some housekeeping. Beyond certain basic limits, defining the author's standpoint becomes self-indulgent and distracting, but an outline will indicate my own affective affiliations. Having lived and worked abroad for several years, I nevertheless write, in the first instance, as a New Englander transplanted to the South, surrounded by lovely, unfamiliar flora and fauna. The Merrimack River, which formed the lifeblood of early American trade and industry—and which, as the poet Lucy Larcom underscores, powered the mills that processed slave-harvested cotton—appeared as a daily presence during my earlier life. As a relatively privileged Anglo-American-identified reader, I attempt to be as respectful and as informed as possible about the Native American, African American, and Mexican American authors whom I review.[56] As a class migrant with deep working-class roots particularly attached to my carpenter-mason grandfather, I appreciate the complexity of social class in the nineteenth-century United States. These roots, coupled with a rural upbringing marvelously peopled with animals, underwrite my constant awareness of embodied nature. That is, despite the theorizing surrounding the concrete world, and despite recognizing that nature signifies human imagination and desire, I believe not only that it exists but that discerning and describing our relationships to it are profoundly important activities.[57]

In accordance with this belief, one of my oblique projects in *Fallen Forests* is to reground textual study in physical reality, even while realizing the widely varying meanings of materiality. I understand metaphor's power yet remain concerned, like many ecocritics, about its potential to detach us from concrete experience. Having milked cows, shingled barns, planted potatoes, and mucked out stalls, I hope to counterbalance the urbanist perspective that frames much mainstream, contemporary academic criticism, enabling a more grounded view of writers and texts. Not least, I aspire to the humility assumed by many of the women whom this project embraces.[58]

Borrowed from Lydia Sigourney's 1844 poem, the title *Fallen Forests: Emotion, Embodiment, and Ethics in American Women's Environmental Writing, 1781–1924* suggests my ambitions from another angle. Emphasizing the book's principal analytical strands, the subtitle foregrounds three recurrent concerns in the authors' works. I appreciate these women because virtually all invest in changing minds as a means of transforming lives, not just for themselves but often for a larger community. I read them because they puzzle, engage, and, in every sense, move me. Finally, I share Elizabeth Ammons's belief, articulated in *Brave New Words: How Literature Will Save the Planet*, that literature possesses the ability to energize change. Thus, while granting environmental destruction, my title nevertheless signals an unapologetically optimistic endeavor. The message bears repeating: for many women whom I treat, and many of their peers, writing equaled activism.

The title also gestures toward the predominantly Christian context for most of *Fallen Forests'* writers. Although not religiously inflected, my project acknowledges directly and indirectly the power of consumption that sucks spiritual values from most Americans' lives, as it comprehends that not everyone—not even all Americans—enjoys purchasing privileges. But as recent public intellectuals have argued, such "privileges" have ceased to provide meaning, as the stuff we buy piles up, creating a sense of dis-ease or "affluenza."[59] Bill McKibben, for example, has maintained that we must now choose between "More" and "Better"; he concludes that the "key questions will change from whether the economy produces an ever larger pile of stuff to whether it builds or undermines community, for community . . . is the key to physical survival in our environmental predicament and also to human satisfaction."[60] Because I share with theologian George E. "Tink" Tinker (Osage) (whose work I treat in chapter 1) the view that our current crisis is largely owing to a dominant Western social model that privileges individual over common interests, the theme of community (and the tension between an individual and a community ethos) figures significantly.[61]

A map will help readers navigate the sizable territory ahead more efficiently. Beginning in the east and ending in the west, the project moves in overlapping chronological order from the late eighteenth century to the early twentieth century.[62] Chapter 1 begins by surveying America's early resource wars and their religious foundation. Ecocritics have cited Christianity as a source for our current environmental predicament, and I examine that claim in two contexts: the resistance to Cherokee removal in the Southeast and the responses to white incursions in Haudenosaunee (Iroquois) homelands in the Northeast. Comparing Native and Euramerican spiritual perspectives as they relate to gender, the natural world, and representations of that world, I explore how late eighteenth- and early nineteenth-century writers such as Nancy Ward (Cherokee) and Mary Jemison (Seneca) highlight their gendered investment in the environment while (with Lydia Sigourney) they expose the resource wars driving Indian removal, wars that parallel the contemporary battles over mining and extraction in Native lands in Alaska, the Southwest, West Virginia, and North Carolina. Chapter 1 investigates how Christian ideology and affiliated sentimental rhetoric contributed to or helped resolve such conflicts.[63]

In the early nineteenth century, resource pressures propelled white settlers west in droves; they increasingly appropriated Native Americans' traditional homelands, which often faced radical transformation. One such transformation was the deforestation that moved west as the United States grew. Continuing the focus on affective rhetoric, chapter 2 probes how Caroline Kirkland's humorously realistic narratives and Lydia Sigourney's sentimental strategies manifest an ecological intelligence that counters the nineteenth century's extractive ethos, even as it reveals how Harriet Jacobs's disparate view of nature promotes an alternative agenda. With wry descriptions of insect swarms invading domestic space, Kirkland's *Forest Life* punctures the notion of humans as apart from nature and mocks efforts to control it: "[I]f you kill one fly, ten will be sure to come to his funeral." Observing that "Man's warfare on the trees is terrible," Sigourney intimates how masculine economic values motivate clear-cutting in New England and the (Mid)west; her work advocates what she believes are authentic Christian principles as an antidote and proposes a biocentric, intergenerational perspective that contemporary environmental critics invoke.[64] Anticipating laboring women's investment in embodiment, Jacobs's more ambivalent knowledge of nature's resources and her affirmation of her environmental place illuminate how her contemporaries occupy very different grounds.

Ecocritics have frequently ignored working-class writers, especially from the nineteenth century. Chapter 3 addresses this omission with its discussion of midcentury laboring women's texts. Progress and economic growth have meant the exploitation of women's bodies and labor, both conceptualized as expendable natural resources. Illustrating how gender, social class, and race interact in this economy, Harriet Wilson and Lorenza Stevens Berbineau complicate their privileged peers' views of nature as refuge; instead, they sometimes escape into culture. Their genres—an autobiographical novel and domestic servant's diary, respectively—also transform our notions of Thoreauvian nature writing, as do texts such as Lucy Larcom's poem "Weaving," which connects affluent and working women, northern and southern, black and white. Though the setting has changed dramatically, such problematic links continue, as multinational corporations' sweatshops flourish. The writers in chapter 3 reveal the limitations, then and now, of sentimental rhetoric and accounts of female interdependence given substantial class, race, and place differences among women.

Chapter 4 shifts the focus from producers to consumers. Critiques of consumption develop more indirectly in earlier American women's writing than in their male counterparts' work, often emerging in hybrid fictional form illegible as environmental writing. Moving to the later nineteenth century, I continue to focus on embodiment, beginning with versions of "green fashion," promoted today on websites proliferating like kudzu. Resisting species extinction and commercial bird hunting, Celia Thaxter would have bemoaned women's continuing overinvestment in style. Nineteenth-century Paris Hiltons happily wore furs and feathers; beyond advertising their affluence, the feathers of Thaxter's antagonists both concealed and revealed women as erotic natural objects. Thaxter argues for simplicity, but work by Mary Wilkins Freeman, Sarah Orne Jewett, and Pauline Hopkins variously instructs how *involuntary* simplicity and conspicuous consumption are equally troublesome neighbors. Fashion, respectability, and sexuality are intimately intertwined, but their interaction differs depending on ethnicity and social class. Stressing gendered rhetoric concerned with consumption, chapter 4 speaks to the challenges of sustainability from both ends of the economic spectrum.

What we now call environmental justice resonates powerfully for many earlier American women, engendering Sarah Winnemucca's accusation "Hell is full of just such Christians as you!" to the Indian agent stealing her tribe's food. Working with white women and men of conscience, nineteenth-century women of color were particularly active, pointedly underscoring race- and ethnicity-based resource scarcity. María Amparo Ruiz de Burton testified to the theft of Mexican Americans' land in mid- to late nineteenth-century California, while Gertrude Bonnin (Zitkala-Ša [Sioux]) coauthored *Oklahoma's Poor Rich Indians*, exposing, as her subtitle announces, *An Orgy of Graft and Exploitation of the Five Civilized Tribes, Legalized Robbery*. Encompassing the period between the early 1880s and the 1920s, chapter 5 explores how their work depicts an America continuously invested in resource wars, and it highlights their effective, eclectic mixture of sentimental, Christian, legal, humorous, and apocalyptic rhetoric. It also indicates how situating environmental justice in historical contexts might enable a more nuanced grasp of contemporary problems.

Meant to be appreciative and suggestive rather than analytical, *Fallen Forests'* afterword links contemporary women writers' subjects and rhetoric with those of their earlier counterparts, who not only recognized the connections between women's oppression and the mistreatment of nature but also understood that "these two forms of domination are bound with class exploitation, racism, and colonialism and neocolonialism."[65] Barbara Kingsolver warns against industrial farming and celebrates relocalization via a hilarious account of turkey sex, Jamaica Kincaid offers provocative ruminations about imperialism in her Vermont garden, Annie Dillard invites readers to reconnect the environment with spiritual values, and Winona LaDuke powerfully combines sentiment and science. Together they demonstrate that environmental activists — many of them skilled rhetors — continue to employ every available means, including evoking readers' and listeners' emotional intelligence, to achieve their reform goals.

Global environmental crises have generated numerous responses, from Wangari Maathai's 2004 Nobel Peace Prize to environmental justice films like *Blue Vinyl*.[66] Written in this context, *Fallen Forests* provides historical background to complicate discussions of women's rhetoric. It illuminates women's diverse, material relationships to the environment in the United States and beyond, and it investigates socially transformative communication strategies. Tracing some rhetorical roots of interventions into our current crisis, I aim to speak both to those who "no longer believe that food comes from dirt" and those who, with Celia Thaxter, would tell a sandpiper, "I wouldn't hurt you or your nest for the world."[67]

"The Blueish Green Snake." By Mark Catesby, from *The Natural History of Carolina, Florida, and the Bahama Islands*, vol. 2, 1771. The American beautyberry (pictured) and the snake are Carolina natives. Courtesy of the North Carolina Collection, University of North Carolina Library at Chapel Hill.

Chapter 1

"We planted, tended, and harvested our corn"

Native Mothers, Resource Wars, and Conversion Narratives

Many spacious tracts of meadowland are confined by these rugged hills [of Carolina], burdened with grass six feet high. Other of these valleys are replenished with brooks and rivulets of clear water, whose banks are covered with spacious tracts of canes, which retaining their leaves year round, are an excellent food for horses and cattle.

— MARK CATESBY, "Of the Soil of Carolina"

Brother, I am in hopes my Brothers and the Beloved men near the water side will heare from me. . . . I am in hopes if you rightly consider it that woman is the mother of All—and that woman Does not pull Children out of Trees or Stumps nor out of old Logs, but out of their Bodies, so that they ought to mind what a woman says, and look upon her as a mother—and I have taken the privelage to Speak to you as my own children, and the same as if you had sucked my Breast.

— KATTEUHA, The Beloved Woman of Chota, 8 September 1787

WITH ITS SPACIOUS MEADOWS and clear water, the New World was a place worth fighting over. Seeking peaceful interactions between Cherokees and Euramericans, the pointed and affecting letter by the unnamed "Katteuha," or Beloved Woman, to Benjamin Franklin reveals the material and gendered ground on which interethnic resource conflicts were too often fought. Emerging from an ethical framework in which "woman is the mother of All," Katteuha highlights positively valued, embodied resources for human survival while she attempts to restore interpersonal relations to a more appropriate standard of respectful attentiveness and complementarity.

Peace and world security expert Michael T. Klare observes that "[h]uman
history has been marked by a long series of resource wars—stretching all
the way back to the earliest agrarian civilizations." The women whose work
I explore in this chapter—Nancy Ward (Nanye-hi; Cherokee), Margaret
(Peggy) Ann Scott (Cherokee), unnamed Cherokee women, Lydia Sigourney, and Mary Jemison (Seneca)—illuminate this observation's significance
in the early American national context. Klare's *Resource Wars: The New
Landscape of Global Conflict* concisely defines the recently formulated title
term: "conflict over vital materials."[1] Like other contemporary commentators
—including geographers, political scientists, sociologists, and military
historians—Klare addresses current struggles for oil and water that preoc-
cupy nation-states, but he also discusses internal wars over gold, diamonds,
minerals, and timber.[2] Recently Al Gedicks has pointed toward different
kinds of struggles: contemporary conflicts between Native Americans and
multinational corporations reflecting what he calls "resource colonialism."[3]

These commentators' descriptions resonate in colonial America, where
resource competition accelerated with Europeans' arrival. We should consider the treaty-based, juridical confiscation of Native lands—with their
various extractable natural resources, including gold and timber—as resource warfare. Between about 1781 and 1840, Ward and her successors
articulated varying, and gendered, concepts of nature as they intervened
in America's early resource wars. In this chapter, I investigate how these
women's spiritual and religious perspectives affected their activism, how
that activism took shape, and how effectively their rhetoric helped resolve
conflicts. Emotional intelligence features centrally in their approaches and
in what their environmental writing accomplished.[4] As the introduction
stresses, such affective virtuosity incorporates not only emotions—such as
sympathy, anger, fear, and frustration—but also ethical appeals, a rhetorical mode traditionally denied to women in Western societies.[5] The often-
synergistic rhetoric of motherhood and spirituality, even when disparate
social contexts define each term differently, has particular potential to be
politically efficacious.

Some of the writers I examine below have enjoyed considerable scholarly
attention, but that attention has focused principally on historical concerns
(with the Cherokee women) or on issues of gender or ethnicity (both the
Cherokee women and Sigourney).[6] To those conversations I add a dimension of rhetorical analysis: although the Cherokee women's speeches and

some of Sigourney's texts parallel traditional rhetorical forms—nonfiction prose intended to persuade—Sigourney's poetry and Jemison's as-told-to narrative also perform persuasively. In an uneven but coherent manner responding to ongoing resource wars conducted against indigenous peoples, women in early America were engaged in projects we should now recognize as environmental. They were particularly concerned with environmental justice.[7]

We need briefly to define *environmental justice*. In 1991 the First National People of Color Environmental Leadership Summit outlined seventeen principles of environmental justice. The preamble to these principles cites the group's intention "to begin to build a national and international movement of all peoples of color to fight the destruction and taking of our lands and communities" and affirms "our spiritual interdependence to the sacredness of our Mother Earth." The principles prioritize "mutual respect" among peoples; the "ethical, balanced and responsible uses of land and renewable resources in the interest of a sustainable planet for humans and other living things"; and the "fundamental right to political, economic, cultural and environmental self-determination of all peoples."[8] These principles have clear continuities with Ward's and her cohort's concerns.

As they acknowledge the relationship among the exploitation of Native peoples, women, and the environment, the women rhetors whose work I analyze below anticipate contemporary environmental justice and ecofeminist analyses. All, including the white women, recognized that environmental justice involved not only moral, spiritual, or economic issues but also legal and political ones relating specifically to Indian sovereignty. Ward's oratory is the only example among this group that explicitly shares contemporary ecofeminists' concern with nonhuman nature, but all the Native writers express affirmative connections between women and nature, providing a useful critique of contemporary theorists' depreciation of those connections as unsophisticated and "essentialized." Showing how Western ecofeminists' obsession with essentialism represents a conceptually blinkered distraction from efforts to gain environmental agency, I explain how the writers here model powerful gendered affective, ethical, and spiritual appeals, especially when collectively authored, that should undergird contemporary activists' efforts to build and sustain alliances for progressive environmental work.

By connecting Indian women to environmental justice concerns, I am not conjuring the "Ecological Indian," a romanticized and homogenized image that elides the complex, concrete, and diverse "histories, spiritual traditions, and cosmologies" of the many indigenous nations that inhabited early America.[9] We should not idealize the women discussed below: for example, many elite Cherokee women were slaveholders; Jemison participated in Seneca land cessions; Sigourney and Scott supported Indian assimilation, including religious conversion; and Christian missionaries' destructive roles in forced assimilation have been well documented. Moreover, Native American and Euramerican women participated in the same project, antiremoval efforts, for different reasons and with different rationales. Though their rhetoric sometimes appears cognate, its resonances sometimes differ radically; in particular, their grasp of women's relationship to nature and the environment, and even their definitions of *nature* and *women*, sometimes diverged. Nevertheless, alliances were possible despite the challenge of incompatible social and ethical systems. If we wish to understand the interlocking forces that shaped early America's gendered and racialized approach to the environment, examining these writers provides some key perspectives on such topics as the meaning of nature, womanhood, land ownership and resource conflicts, and environmental justice.

Julie Sze emphasizes that contemporary environmental justice is concerned not only with public policy but also with "issues of ideology and representation."[10] This assertion has historical reverberations: *how* these precursors express themselves is often as important as what they say, and so I explore how they worked—what genres and language they used and what affective stances they assumed. Their forms, which include petitions, letters, poems, and conduct writing, suggest that today's readers interested in environmental writing should look well beyond traditional Thoreauvian nature writing—individualistic, reflective, first-person narrative. However, their diverse genres share an oral component—literal for the Cherokee women, figurative in Sigourney, and mediated in Jemison. This orality enhances the impression of an authorial presence that insists on auditors' ethical responsibility to act. Often privileging community over individual well-being, these writers resist the emerging "American" obsession with profit and the ethic of exploitation that too frequently accompanies it.[11]

Despite their differences, Ward, Scott, their cohort, and Sigourney engaged in what we might today call consciousness-raising: all revealed the ongoing resource wars between the early American government and indigenous peoples, all attempted to change minds and behavior, and (with varying emphases and levels of explicitness) all linked gender to these resource wars.[12] Their rhetorical and political strategies arguing for Native agency or sovereignty augured contemporary movements for environmental justice.

"Our cry is all for peace": Cherokee Women, Gold, and Land Ethics

At a meeting with U.S. treaty commissioners in 1785, the Cherokee Beloved Woman Nancy Ward observed, "I am fond of hearing that there is a peace, and I hope that you have now taken us by the hand in friendship. . . . I look on you and the red people as my children." Resource wars framed this period, of which Ward states, "I have seen much trouble," concluding, "we hope the chain of friendship will never more be broke."[13] Notwithstanding energetic efforts by her and many other American women, friendship and peace remained hopes rather than realities.

While many male writers—among them William Bartram, Thomas Jefferson, Lewis and Clark, and Timothy Dwight—often prioritized cataloguing and admiring the natural world, many of their female counterparts, both individually and in groups, sought to preserve Native American lands, sovereignty, and people. These women faced a mountainous rhetorical problem: how to convince the American public and political leaders that removal was wrong. In a dominant society that distinguished between humans and nature, to adequately contend that Indians were people—not animals, not part of nature—advocates had to characterize them as civilized.[14] As Wilma Mankiller (Cherokee) relates, "To the frontiersman, Indians were a dangerous and fierce presence. . . . Hordes of white settlers grew eager to 'conquer the wilderness' and 'civilize' the land. They were anxious to grab up all the salt licks, deposits of gold, stands of old-growth timber, rivers and streams, seas of lush prairie grass, beaver pelts, and buffalo hides. They wished to *own* the land. . . . Nothing and no one— especially 'heathen savages'—would stand in their way."[15]

Even white women, as events proved.

Mankiller's observations anticipate and concretize Philippe Le Billon's framework for interpreting recent conflicts: "Resources have specific historic, geographic, and social qualities participating in shaping the patterns of conflicts and violences."[16] For early Europeans, land, its products, and its inhabitants all stood for means of survival and sources of economic wealth. The very concepts of ownership and resources imply a worldview: the Earth and its inhabitants are objectified and available for consumption.[17] With its image of mother's milk, Katteuha's letter—addressing Benjamin Franklin but certainly encompassing a wider audience—critiques and transforms this perspective. For traditional Native Americans, such objectification of resources problematically eclipses the natural world's spiritual and psychological valences. Indeed, in the Indian polities of early America, distinctions between the spiritual and the physical would have been puzzling if not incomprehensible, because the land and its inhabitants, from the four-footed (animals) to the standing people (trees) formed the web of life. Unlike in Euramerican society, where association with the body linked women to the animal world, such a connection with materiality and embodiment did not mean degradation but, as Katteuha suggests, empowerment.[18] Maintaining this web required careful attention to balance, as well as equal respect for all its elements. For the Cherokee, the language of gender, spirituality, and sovereignty were interconnected.

The Christian ecological theologians Whitney A. Bauman, Richard R. Bohannon II, and Kevin J. O'Brien argue that "[r]eligions do not simply appear . . . on their own . . . but evolve in conversation with other social and natural forces. Religions and other cultural systems, in turn, shape how human beings choose to think about, relate to, and treat the natural world."[19] To assess nineteenth-century women writers' responses to resource conflict, we need to sketch the spiritual systems from which their work emerged and to which it responded. Yet any such outline necessitates caution in the application that follows, because in the period I describe below both sets of traditional beliefs were rapidly changing, as some Christians reinterpreted patriarchal mandates and as elite Cherokees converted to Christianity and Euramerican lifeways.

The Christian creation story, which establishes the relationships between humans and nonhuman nature and between men and women, possesses special significance for our discussion. The King James translation of Genesis 1:26 declares, "And God said, Let us make man in our image, after our likeness: and let them have dominion over the fish of the sea, and over the fowl of the air, and over the cattle, and over all the earth, and over every creeping thing that creepeth upon the earth." Surmounting the creation hierarchy, men seem godlike, an understanding reiterated in verse 28. Not only does it assign man with power over nature, the Genesis story also authorizes gender hierarchy: in the second chapter Eve is created from Adam's rib.[20] In nineteenth-century America, these interpretations enjoyed wide acceptance but, as we will see in Sigourney's work, they sometimes received a different accent.

In contrast to this belief system, traditional Cherokee (and members of other Native nations) apprehend God as "a spiritual force that permeates the whole of the world and is manifest in countless ways in the world around us at any given moment and especially in any given place." According to the theologian George "Tink" Tinker (Osage), these forces have "no inherent or ultimate gender" and are knowable "only in the necessary reciprocal dualism of male and female."[21] Unlike the Genesis story, creation invokes the interdependence "of all the nations other than the two-leggeds—the four-leggeds, the wingeds, and the living-moving things."[22] This sense of "interrelatedness . . . balance, and mutual respect among the different species in the world" indicates indigenous peoples' emphasis on community, broadly conceived, rather than Christian individualism and hierarchy.[23]

Two additional, related principles of a Native perspective are reciprocity and spatiality. Reciprocity obliges compensation for human actions, which may unbalance the world: "Animals, birds, crops, and medicines are all living relatives and must be treated with respect if they are to be genuinely efficacious for the people."[24] Such an attitude, Tinker avers, represents an ethic of sustainability. Spatiality complements reciprocity.[25] While Western societies promote such linear and temporal ideas as progress, history, development, and evolution, Indians comprehend place as foundational to spirituality and identity itself. Thus, Tinker affirms, "conquest and removal from our lands and contemporary ecological destruction of our lands have been and continue to be culturally and genocidally destructive to Indian peoples as peoples."[26] Land thus has a radically different meaning in Indian than in Western societies, and permanency and rootedness signify fundamental values.[27] This conceptual framework helps illuminate the environmental inflections of texts not only by Cherokee women but also by Euramerican women such as Sigourney.

The Cherokee, who had traded with Europeans since at least the late seventeenth century, became entangled in whites' national and imperial ambitions in the period that preceded the American Revolution.[28] Siding with the British proved disastrous, and the Cherokee nation was decimated by starvation and disease as well as warfare.[29] Every element of Cherokee society was in flux, including its land holdings, religious beliefs, and complementarily gendered labor and political systems. Well before the 1830s removal crisis, U.S. presidents George Washington and Thomas Jefferson supported programs to civilize the Cherokee, with Jefferson associating land cessions with progress.[30] Such attitudes accelerated the impetus for cessions and, eventually, removal.

Anti-removal activists like Ward and Sigourney encountered several challenges. First, as women, they themselves were associated with nature— positively in Cherokee terms but negatively in Anglo society. As Stacy Alaimo observes (of white women), "If woman's perceived proximity to nature is responsible for her oppression, then her liberation . . . is contingent upon her distance from nature."[31] Cherokee women faced the dominant society's doubly disabling association of Indians with nature, while white women confronted the nature/culture binary from a different position.[32] Superadded to these obstacles, reformers faced multiple audiences. Speaking to internal and external auditors, Cherokee women like Ward addressed white federal government agents and Cherokee men representing their nation in peace talks; they also spoke separately to the Cherokee National Council. White advocates like Sigourney aimed at other women, political leaders, literate Native Americans, and the U.S. public.

Second, white women expressing themselves in the public sphere rattled white patriarchal norms, whereas traditional Cherokee women needed no apology for such intervention. Another obstacle for these reformers also related to gender: as Roy Harvey Pearce explains, white concepts of Indianness and savagery were based upon examination of Indian *men*; hunting and warfare provided the analytical and philosophical basis for constructing Indians as precivilized or noncivilized.[33] Thus a certain measure of civility and modernity, Christianity, and especially Christian motherhood became desiderata for many anti-removal advocates, Cherokee and white. Both groups of activists deployed the female figure for emotional and ethical ends, but *woman* and *mother* possessed entirely different resonances in Anglo and traditional Cherokee societies, though even within the latter they were rapidly changing due to whites' assimilation efforts. The women's rhetoric, forms, and portrayals of nature reflect such differences and have rendered these early feminine voices inaudible to ecocritics.

Christianity proved to be an important factor not only across societies but also within them: the following discussion on Cherokee women traces women's and mothers' diminished consequence in the Cherokee nation, a diminishment that compromised their traditional verbal authority, including not only *what* they said, but *how* they said it. Unlike in Euramerican society, where women rhetors had to claim validity and space to speak, Cherokee women were socially empowered, and their complementary, balancing role required public participation.[34] Over the time period from Ward's first recorded speech shortly after the declaration of American independence to Margaret Ann Scott's communal address to the men of the Cherokee National Council, Cherokee women's identities, status, and rhetorical position transformed to more closely approximate those of their white counterparts. We might be skeptical about the precise content of the women's speeches, given their recording and transmission by literate white men — though Ward and Scott spoke in English — but studying their rhetoric over a roughly forty-year period reveals the women's increasing acculturation, particularly their Christianization, and its far-reaching social and political consequences.

AROUND 1738, Nanye-hi ("One Who Goes About"), known as Nancy Ward, was born in the Cherokee town of Chota.[35] With a life span that extended to about 1822 and encompassed colonial wars, American independence, and debates about Indian removal, Ward offers an exemplary figure and a cautionary tale. Through speeches to federal officials and to the Cherokee council, Ward fought to retain Cherokee land, the foundation of Cherokee identity, resisting Euramerican domination as she mediated between her people and the U.S. government.[36] Ward's personal prestige enhanced her words' weight in Cherokee society: having joined a battle against her nation's established enemies the Creeks when her husband was killed, she received the title of War Woman and hence was doubly empowered.[37] Such a denomination, accorded to those who had distinguished themselves in battle, authorized the recipient to join ceremonies ordinarily restricted to men and to speak in council, among other honors; the title also acknowledged the special (admirable and fearful) energies embodied in a woman who enjoyed both female and male power.[38] In maturity she received the title of Beloved Woman, an honor typically accorded to respected elders, and she used this authority in trying to prevent land cessions and their affiliated wars and to press for Cherokee sovereignty.

Resource conflicts—over land and, eventually, over gold—propelled Ward and her cohort of Cherokee women into rhetorical prominence.[39] Ward was among the Cherokee principals during treaty negotiations in 1781 with U.S. federal commissioners in Holston (now in Tennessee). In 1791, the Cherokee nation concluded a treaty with the U.S. government, which begins with the declaration that "[t]here shall be perpetual peace and friendship between all the citizens of the United States of America, and all the individuals composing the whole Cherokee nation of Indians" and includes the assertion that "[t]he United States solemnly guarantee to the Cherokee nation, all their lands not hereby ceded."[40] Such "guarantees" were merely temporary. Ward and other Cherokee women spoke to the Cherokee National Council urging their men to resist land cessions, and for a time their efforts were successful. Yet pressure from the state of Georgia and other factors led President Andrew Jackson in 1830 to push through Congress the Indian Removal Act, eventually resulting in the forced march west of eastern Indians; those who wished to remain would become legally subject to the state they inhabited. The Cherokee, among other nations, resisted, and in response the U.S. government worked with unauthorized tribal representatives to obtain the 1835 Treaty of New Echota, which traded Cherokee territory in the southeast for western land and putatively authorized the tribe's removal.[41]

Contemporary historians have recently confirmed Ward's and other Cherokee women's significance in the early nineteenth century's antiremoval campaigns. Tiya Miles, for example, asserts that efforts by white women such as Catharine Beecher and Lydia Sigourney signified "a high point, rather than a starting point, of an ongoing tradition of activism launched by indigenous women in defense of themselves."[42] Beyond appreciating the Cherokee women's agency and activism, we should value their specifically environmental discourse, particularly their interventions into the resource wars that shaped Cherokee-U.S. relations during the early national period and their efforts toward environmental justice. Jace Weaver tenders a salient perspective: "[A]ny Native defense of the environment . . . presupposes a recognition of Native sovereignty. . . . Without question, Native control over their lands and resources is a matter of sovereignty."[43]

Ward and her cohort played a visible role in conflicts that threatened inter-linked Cherokee identity and spirituality, gender, and land.

Presented in Holston to the U.S. treaty commissioners, Ward's first known speech in 1781 employs traditional oratory's formal rhetoric and stance while it demonstrates how she perceptively negotiates Anglo society's attitudes toward women: "You know that women are always looked upon as nothing; but we are your mothers; you are our sons. Our cry is all for peace; let it continue. This peace must last forever. Let your women's sons be ours; our sons be yours. Let your women hear our words."[44] Her dual-voiced petition to whites and Cherokees could express submission, irony, or simply forthrightness. Offering an ostensibly sentimental and submissive appeal, Ward's first sentence disarms her interlocutors by engaging with the so-called negotiators on their conceptual territory. For Euramericans, *woman* and *mother* conjured individuals of subordinate, dependent status, lacking many legal and political rights and more closely connected to animal nature than their male counterparts. As a white woman, Ward would at best have possessed only the power of influence as a type of Republican Mother.[45]

As a Cherokee mother, however, she embodied enviable authority: "Admission to a Cherokee clan derived from birth or adoption, and both depended on women"; unlike in white society, according to the historian Theda Perdue, "motherhood was not a trite sentimentality to Cherokees. Cherokee women invoked motherhood as the source of their power and used their status as women to make public appeals."[46] Invoking the matri-lineal, kinship-centered relationship fundamental to her nation's identity, Ward's speech skillfully redefines her position, situating the assembled white men in an unfamiliar public role—"you are our sons"—and declaring her moral and political authority.[47] By the end she has reinvented the discursive terms, envisioning not only the men but also the Anglo women who should, she suggests, have power to decide momentous matters of war and peace, as she herself had done.[48]

Ward also exemplified another traditional form of Cherokee women's power: the authority of the women's council.[49] Addressing the Cherokee National Council, her later speech on behalf of a group of Cherokee women exhibits the same rhetorical dexterity and conveys a similar perspective on women's appropriate roles. Here, ironically, Ward activates her considerable powers toward the preservation of Cherokee lands from the improvident and short-sighted actions of the council's Cherokee men, rather than, as was common in Indian oratory, from the U.S. government's depredations. Federal representatives sought treaties to superimpose their standards of land tenure; such treaties not only physically displaced the Cherokee nation but also undermined its governance structure and sovereignty.[50] Some Cherokees, fearing whites' increasing incursions into their homeland, favored movement west.

In 1817, joined by twelve other women, Ward made the following plea:

> We have raised all of you on the land which we now have, which God gave us to inhabit and raise provisions. We know that our country has once been extensive, but by repeated sales has become circumscribed to a small track, and [we] never have thought it our duty to interfere in the disposition of it till now. If a father or mother was to sell all their lands which they had to depend on, which their children had to raise their living on, [it] would be bad indeed & [so would it be] to be removed to another country. We do not wish to go to an unknown country which we have understood some of our children wish to go [to] over the Mississippi, but this act of our children would be like destroying your mothers.[51]

This speech suggests the women's authority and responsibility for the land while it intimates the shame that council members' lack of respect should engender. Ward's concern that ceding land and moving west "would be like destroying your mothers" reemerges in the next paragraph: "Your mothers, your sisters ask and beg of you not to part with any more of our lands." Ward and her associates feared that further cessions, "akin to matricide," would destroy the balance, including the gender balance, upon which Cherokee spiritual and material well-being depended.[52]

Such destruction was the product of resource wars initiated by Euramericans unable to apprehend the land as anything more than a place to farm or property from which they might extract objects of economic value—such as, in Mankiller's satirical language, "salt licks, deposits of gold, stands of old-growth timber." Signaling the interconnection of spirituality and spatiality, Ward's plea demonstrates a profound emotional intelligence. Indicating its oral delivery to "a live group of listeners," the petition emphasizes collective presence. At the same time, it articulates an ethical approach that the contemporary rhetoricians Joy Ritchie and Kate Ronald aver has "been historically denied to women" but that Cherokee women clearly had no problem advancing.[53]

This council speech underscores the link between women and nature, but its valences diverged from its Euramerican parallel, enabling a potential critique: contemporary ecofeminists' reductive assessment of this link as essentialized. Among the Cherokee, women were regarded as connected to nature like all humans, but this connection was not depreciated; instead, it was regarded as fundamental to the world's creative balance. In Cherokee society, the women were the horticulturalists, raising the crops that sustained the community, which is, Weaver stresses, "the highest value among Native persons"; "fidelity to it is the highest responsibility."[54] Women's horticultural role complemented men's hunting activities; differentiated gender roles meant that, except for help clearing fields and planting in the spring, men ordinarily did not participate in women's activities. To contemporary Americans, such categorical separation may seem severe and inflexible, but in fact, as Perdue remarks, the Cherokee's "concern with balance made hierarchy, which often serves to oppress women, untenable. Men did not dominate women, and women were not subservient to men." In fact, each group knew little about the other's activities, and men "had no power over women and no control over women's activities. Women had their own arena of power."[55] As the persons responsible for the land and the harvest, they were invested with an important interest in its disposition, as Ward's speeches illustrate.

The story of Selu, Grandmother Corn, and Kana'tī (her husband, the hunter) shaped the Cherokee women's concepts of interpersonal relations as well as relations between human and nonhuman worlds.[56] As the contemporary writer Marilou Awiakta affirms, "'Grandmother' connotes 'Mother of Us All,' a spirit being who is eternally wise"; her name expresses "the indivisibility of body and spirit . . . for both are spelled s-e-l-u. Saying one evokes the other."[57] According to Perdue, "the Cherokees believed that they had always lived [in the fertile valleys of the central Appalachians] and that their ancestral mother, Selu, had given them the corn on which they depended for subsistence."[58] The narrative explains how Selu gave her life to feed her family and why corn must be tended for half the year. The connection between women and corn, notes Perdue, "gave women considerable status and economic power," in part because they "controlled the fruits of their labor, the crops; the means of production, the land; and ultimately,

the result of production, the children."[59] Thus, unlike the metaphoric connection between Euramerican women and nature, especially the concept of
"virgin land," Cherokee women enjoyed a concrete, literally productive (and
reproductive) relationship with nature on which community well-being depended. For Cherokee women—again unlike their Euramerican counterparts, who frequently linked Indians with wilderness and "waste" land—an
association with nature was not only *not* debilitating (or essentialist) but
actively empowering.[60] Regarded from this angle, Ward's speech encodes a
different, and enabling, ecofeminist discourse.

Land cessions threatened the Cherokee nation's increasingly precarious
gender balance. Compounding the internal pressures from some relatively
assimilated elite Cherokees—whose understanding of ownership and
whose religious values often corresponded to their white counterparts'—
"civilization" campaigns by whites sought to make men farmers and women
housewives, transforming the relationships among nature, nation, and
gender. Missionaries and government agents had specific goals, including Christianization and the establishment of patriarchal family relations,
additional manifestations of resource wars to undermine Cherokee sovereignty. As the influential chief John Ridge described the consequences for
Cherokee women, "They sew, they spin, they cook our meals and act well
the duties assigned them by Nature as mothers."[61] Like its many counterparts, the Moravian Springplace Mission, one of the most important Christian schools for the Cherokee, followed the mandate that came in an 1819
letter from the U.S. secretary of war, John C. Calhoun. To contribute to
"the civilization of the Indian" involved, for boys, "the practical knowledge of agriculture and such mechanical arts as are suited to the condition
of the Indian; . . . [for] the girls, spinning, weaving, and sewing."[62] In effect, when Ridge articulated how the meaning of *woman* had changed, he
underscored, however indirectly, the loss of Cherokee women's spiritual,
rhetorical, and political authority.

NANCY WARD'S DESCENDANT, baptized Margaret Ann Scott (later Peggy
Scott Vann Crutchfield), was closely associated with Springplace and, according to Miles, much admired "as a supreme example of the cultural and
spiritual heights that Indians could attain."[63] A second petition by a group
of Cherokee women, including Scott, addresses Cherokee "national affairs"

Margaret Ann Scott Vann's home, near the Moravian mission at Springplace
in northwest Georgia. Known as the Chief James Clement Vann House of
Diamond Hill Plantation, it was often called "the showplace of the Cherokee
nation." Image from 7 April 1962. Courtesy of the Library of Congress.

and presses strongly for land retention, but it also reveals how the definitions of womanhood and motherhood were shifting. Speaking to "Beloved
Children," the petition opens,

> We have heard with painful feelings that the bounds of the land we
> now possess are to be drawn into very narrow limits. The land was
> given to us by the Great Spirit above as our common right, to raise
> our children upon, & to make support for our rising generations. We
> therefore humbly petition our beloved children, the head men & war-
> riors, to hold out to the last in support of our common rights, as the
> Cherokee nation have been the first settlers of this land; we therefore
> claim the right of the soil.
>
> We well remember that our country was formerly very extensive, but
> by repeated sales it has become circumscribed to the very narrow limits
> we have at present. Our Father the President advised us to become
> farmers, to manufacture our own clothes, & to have our children

instructed. To this advice we have attended in every thing as far as we were able. Now the thought of us being compelled to remove [to] the other side of the Mississippi is dreadful to us, because it appears to us that we, by this removal, shall be brought to a savage state again, for we have, by the endeavor of our Father the President, become too much enlightened to throw aside the privileges of a civilized life.

We therefore unanimously join in our meeting to hold our country in common as hitherto.

As in the earlier petition, the language prioritizes community survival rather than individualistic achievement, and it seeks to retain common landownership.[64] Both the first and second petitions invoke the rhetoric of motherhood, but, as Miles point out, the second assumes a more supplicant tone. In addition, the second petition differs substantially by pointing to "Christian authority in the fight against removal" instead of basing its authority on "indigenous motherhood" as the Beloved/War Woman Ward and her cohort had done.[65] In accepting whites' religion, Ward's Christianized relative Scott also accepted their belief that proper females should merely exercise feminine influence over males.

The petition continues, "Some of our children have become Christians. We have missionary schools among us. We have heard the gospel in our nation. We have become civilized & enlightened, & are in hopes that in a few years our nation will be prepared for instruction in other branches of sciences & arts, which are both useful & necessary in civilized society."[66] This section aims not only at the Cherokee men but also at the missionary and government officials who might hear it; and its emotionally intelligent rhetoric, noteworthy for the repeated and fluctuating "we," stresses the tribe's continued assimilation to Euramerica's standards, including its gender norms.[67] Like the 1817 appeal, it forwards a plea ("humbly petition"), but, with its emphasis on progress toward "a civilized life" and rejection of an earlier "savage state," this petition reflects a fundamental transformation from a spatial to a temporal worldview.

We must thus evaluate this petition within a different framework, including the hierarchical Christian gender relations undergirding the apologetic tone that implies anxiety about public voicing and the need to maintain authority to do so. This shift entailed significant legal and political consequences: Scott's group diminishes the insistence of Ward and her colleagues on women's complementary governance and Cherokee sovereignty. Delivering their oratory and petitions during a revolutionary period for the Cherokee, which included huge land cessions to the U.S. government, Ward and her contemporaries encouraged traditional respect for land and women.[68] The council petitions argued against additional sales to the United States and land allotment to individuals, both of which, they asserted, would not only rend the communal social fabric but threaten the Cherokee nation's sovereignty. Some land was ceded in 1817 and 1819, but, although the women's efforts were not entirely successful, the council avoided allotment, retaining common ownership. It ultimately declared an end to cessions.[69]

Nevertheless, in the period encompassing Ward's address to the U.S. treaty commissioners and the petitions to the Cherokee National Council, the loss of Cherokee women's social and political power was essentially complete. Originally the holders of property and respected horticulturalists who owned the fruits of their labor, women were gradually replaced by men as heads of household, landowners, and active participants in Cherokee national government. Perdue observes, "The political organization that existed in the Cherokee Nation in 1817 and 1818 had made it possible for women to voice their opinion. . . . The protests of the women to the National Council in 1817 and 1818 were, however, the last time women presented a collective position to the Cherokee governing body."[70] As Awiakta concludes, "In a final effort at reconciliation, the Cherokee changed to a patriarchal, republican form of government."[71] Notably, in all the treaty meetings and other encounters with the federal government, no white woman was present, an absence questioned by Ward's uncle, the great chief and negotiator Attakullakulla.[72]

Acknowledging the Cherokee as a sovereign nation, the federal government established a "Bureau of Indian Affairs" in 1824; its location in the U.S. Department of War indicated the federal government's stance toward Native peoples. The Cherokee nation continued to adapt to Euramerican norms—developing a constitution and schools, learning English and creating a written language, adopting "civilized" dress and living arrangements, and, as we have seen, converting to Christianity—to protect itself against white depredations. Soon after missionaries' arrival in the early nineteenth century, the Cherokee grasped the practical value of literacy in such self-protection. With Sequoyah's invention of the Cherokee syllabary, bilingual education became the norm in missionary schools. According to some missionary estimates, by 1833, "60% of the Cherokee were literate in their native language and . . . about 20% were English literate." By the 1850s, this rate may have reached over 90 percent.[73] By these measures, Margaret Ann Scott represented the vanguard. Ironically, because of the Cherokee's traditional gender-role complementarity, she benefited from egalitarian access to education (and, hence, to literacy)—a Christian education that ultimately redefined and disempowered women.[74]

The Cherokee also developed public demonstrations of literacy to advance their anti-imperialist project. Elias Boudinot, who would later be assassinated for agreeing to removal, edited the first Native newspaper, the *Cherokee Phoenix*, created as an act of the Cherokee National Council and published simultaneously in English and Cherokee. Beginning in the initial issue of 21 February 1828, the *Phoenix* published the Cherokee Nation's Constitution, among whose provisions is "Article V, Sec. 15. The people shall be secure in their persons, houses, papers, and possessions from unreasonable seizures, and searches, and no warrant to search any place or to seize any person or things, shall issue without describing them as nearly as may be, nor without good cause, supported by oath or affirmation."[75] Articles about land, Cherokee rights to their historical territories, and violence between Native Americans and whites dominate from the *Phoenix's* inception.

But intensifying white settlers' land lust during the early national period was the discovery of gold in Georgia.[76] One of the most striking items in a contemporaneous Milledgeville newspaper ran as follows:

> GOLD.—A gentleman of the first respectability in Habersham county, writes us thus under date of 22d July: "Two gold mines have just been discovered in this county, and preparations are making to bring these hidden treasures of the earth to use." So it appears that what we long anticipated has come to pass at last, namely, that the gold region of North and South Carolina, would be found to extend into Georgia.[77]

This discovery ensured that traditional lands would be increasingly pressured until finally the Cherokee were "removed"—like an inconvenient boulder. Alisse Portnoy points out that "[n]ational Indian removal debates commanded less attention after the Indian removal bill was signed into law, and they ended when the United States federal government forced remaining Cherokees to move west."[78] The emotional, familial, and economic costs of the Cherokee Trail of Tears have been thoroughly documented; the environmental consequences were equally severe. Their words tragically prophetic, Ward and other Cherokee women intervened in public affairs using a language grounded—literally and figuratively—in the land they inhabited. Invocations of traditional motherhood, familial relations, and land meant little—or at least meant differently—to the white Christians commanding these resource wars.[79] Equally importantly, however, Cherokee sovereignty eroded from within, as elites like Scott and Boudinot converted to Christianity, gained a Euramerican education, and adopted white gender roles.

The presentations by Ward, Scott, and their Cherokee sisters expand the scope of Bill McKibben's contemporary definition of environmental literature: beyond considering collisions and conflicts between humans and nonhuman nature or challenging readers' conventions, it assumes an activist stance.[80] These Cherokee women engaged in what Weaver has called "communitist" discourse, combining activism with a commitment to community well-being. Their voices have been excluded from ecocritical discussions for many reasons, including perhaps their oral or orally inflected expressive forms and their appeals to an unfamiliar, gendered ethos. The earlier Cherokee women's speeches—those by Ward and her contemporaries—exemplify how women used environmental rhetoric to perform political work, in particular, to urge respect for the natural world, restore gender balance, and preserve the Cherokee polity.

For these women, nature was not simply a metaphor; it afforded the means of survival. It was not a howling wilderness, as it was for early European settlers, nor was it a place from which to escape urban life or a pastoral ideal, as it was becoming for early nineteenth-century Euramericans; it was central to life, both secular and sacred.[81] Rather than essentializing them, Cherokee women's affiliation with nature supplied crucial social, material, and spiritual balance. Given this intricate interrelationship, we should consider Ward's encounters with the U.S. treaty commissioners and her group's petition to the Cherokee National Council as innovative contributions to early ecofeminism and as expansive forms of environmental justice discourse.[82] Elite "progressives" like Scott, who converted to Christianity and Euramerican lifeways, also contributed to communitist rhetoric. But in relinquishing traditional Cherokee womanhood, they were compelled to seek alliances, and justice, on different grounds.

"Their name is on your waters": Sigourney and the White Fight over Indian Lands

In her 1831 poem "The Cherokee Mother," published amid the ferment over Indian removal, Lydia Sigourney's eponymous speaker laments, "Our hands have till'd these corn-clad grounds, — / Our children's birth these homes have blest."[83] Notably, the poem was published in the *Cherokee Phoenix*, the Cherokee nation's periodical, where it reached an audience of educated Native Americans and their white allies. Courting readers' sympathies via conventional images of motherhood and home, Sigourney confirms her (and their) bond with Cherokee women through shared maternal experience. At the same time, she acknowledges her Indian counterparts' productive role as horticulturalists rather than, as many white contemporaries would do, regarding that role as mere physical drudgery. Acutely sensitive to America's ongoing resource wars, Sigourney exploits the synergistic rhetorics of motherhood and spirituality in her emotionally intelligent fight for environmental justice. Even more strikingly, her work reprises her Cherokee counterparts' understanding of how communally based speech could contribute to that effort.

Perhaps it was Sigourney's obviously broad sympathies that led Ward's younger relative Margaret Ann Scott to approach the poet. The Cherokee women's anti-removal petitions contributed to what Miles calls a "transnational, multigenerational antiremoval project" that pursued a tripartite strategy: "lobbying the Cherokee national government, lobbying the U.S. government, and influencing a U.S. culture maker of note."[84] Scott not only transformed Cherokee women's rhetoric for her immediate audiences, white and Cherokee men, she also solicited the assistance of reformist white women, including Sigourney, employing a nascent version of Andrea Smith's "alliance politics" to enlist the poet's (and Catharine Beecher's) help.[85]

An important foundation for this appeal was Scott's Christian faith. Scott and Sigourney worked in an era of religious revivalism; between the 1790s and the 1840s, Protestant evangelicalism rocked the United States. The Second Great Awakening transfigured the conception of God and individuals' relationship to divinity: no longer seen as severe, even vengeful, God became a benevolent entity.[86] At the same time, Christians rejected the Calvinist emphasis on predestination, the doctrine that humans had no influence on their own salvation, and embraced free will: believers could, through their own good actions, affect their fate. Because the United States fostered ideals that included equality and political and economic mobility, it proved a fertile ground for this movement.[87]

American women were profoundly involved in American Protestantism's revitalization. The new model encouraged women's investment in activist projects, including Native land rights and anti-removal efforts. Early nineteenth-century Christianity provided bourgeois women like Sigourney with an opening, and she plunged through it. Eve may have provoked the Fall, but successors like Sigourney and Stowe were determined to right human wrongs, and the Second Great Awakening seemingly authorized them to do so. Such interventions, as Mary Jemison's narrative indicates, often had unintended consequences for Native nations and for their land. But Sigourney, presaging contemporary liberal Christian ecology, indirectly or directly links nature, justice, and peace.[88] She tackled a daunting lifetime project: promoting Native rights, she sought to redeem both Cherokee and American nations.

MANY WHITE WOMEN were politically engaged, but perhaps none was more sympathetic to Indians' claims than Sigourney. Born to an estate manager in Hartford, Connecticut, in 1791, the writer superseded her humble background and became a household name, perhaps the best-known poet of the early nineteenth century, writing relentlessly and angrily about U.S. treatment of Native Americans throughout her fifty-year career. Unlike such contemporaries as William Cullen Bryant, whose nature poetry characteristically elided or romanticized the continent's first inhabitants, Sigourney constructed an environmental oeuvre that persistently focused attention on America's resource wars against indigenous peoples.[89] Beginning with *Moral Pieces in Prose and Verse* (1815) and encompassing more than fifty volumes in various genres, including over twenty-five editions of her *Select Poems* (the first, titled *Poems*, in 1834), she devoted significant portions of her personal and professional life to improving U.S. treatment of Native Americans.[90]

We may be surprised today that Sigourney's poetry embraced activism so energetically, but in the nineteenth century, especially before the Civil War, poetry was a profoundly popular genre.[91] Mainstream poetry at its strongest went beyond celebrating bourgeois values or engaging readers' sentimental sympathies; it also offered, as Nina Baym explains vis-à-vis Sigourney, a forum for historical and political debates.[92] Employing candid history to provoke action, Sigourney's work "enacted womanly behavior that in many ways nullified the distinction between public and private that operated so crucially in other contexts."[93] Sigourney refuses what Paul Lauter characterizes as "salvage anthropology, the assumptions that have long justified a kind of looting of native cultures around the world"; he argues that she actively "contests this kind of easy nostalgia, which came to support the politics of removal."[94] The writer's activist poetry and affiliated texts have been invisible to ecocritics for many reasons; among them, she complicates traditional pastoral, promotes explicitly Christian ideals, and implements an emotionally intelligent feminine rhetoric that seeks readers' complementary, affective responses.

Epitomizing Sigourney's earliest activist efforts was the 1822 epic *Traits of the Aborigines of America*, a five-canto, four-thousand-line blank verse poem "structured from the Indian point of view" that in Baym's opinion "ought to be considered a belated entry in the competition for 'the' American epic."[95] Here Sigourney articulates a stance that her later writing on Native Americans repeatedly, and sternly, underlines: that Indians and whites were "all of one blood," that (*pace* Columbus) whites' Christianity required them to convert the Indians, and that it was uncertain whether Indians would assimilate into the American nation or be extinguished.[96] Sigourney seemingly assumes that whiteness is the norm into which all difference must be incorporated, an assumption that Baym and Sandra Zagarell apparently accept.[97] Because the writer became increasingly pessimistic about Native American survival—as her publication of *Zinzendorff* (1835) and *Pocahontas, and Other Poems* (1841) after the Trail of Tears reveals—we might presume that she perpetuated the myth of the Vanishing American, which represented, in Brian W. Dippie's formulation, "a perfect fusion of the nostalgic with the progressive impulse."[98]

On the other hand, although Sigourney's Christian investment is unquestionable, because of her considerable rhetorical skill and her regular contact with Native Americans in Connecticut and through her Cherokee correspondence, we might reasonably inquire if the vanishing motif en-coded a strategy for sparking white Americans' activism as much as an ac-tual belief. Like her contemporary Catharine Maria Sedgwick, Sigourney described the depredations on Native Americans by whites; this interest is not surprising, given her residence in the Pequods' and Mohegans' tradi-tional homeland. In contrast to her contemporary Bryant, Sigourney ap-proaches Native Americans with far greater affect as well as an intensified form. Bryant's "The Prairies," for example, both romanticizes indigenous mound builders and erases their names. Sigourney's arguments, configured as more intense elegies that shade into jeremiad, promote Native presence, sovereignty, and environmental justice.

Baym observes that the writer devotes considerable effort to exploring how "the establishment of the Christian American community that [she] extolled in the *Sketch of Connecticut* and elsewhere depended directly on white access to Indian land," concluding that "the Anglo-American na-tional character was defined by how whites acquired the land they needed and what happened to the Indians afterwards." To obtain this land, repub-licanism discarded "its commitments to civic virtue and to the amelioration of the lot of the needy by the fortunate; Christians neglected its imperatives of charity and of taking all souls as equals before God."[99] Whites' unchris-tian land theft was at issue. While *Traits of the Aborigines* highlighted the Christian mission to Native Americans, it indicted Christian hypocrisy; as Sigourney remarks in a sarcastic footnote, "While we urge that the just claims which our aborigines have on us for religious instruction should no longer be slighted, can it be thought of inferior importance, that those christians [*sic*] who have intercourse with them, should strive to exemplify the moral virtues which their faith enjoins?"[100]

The writer's attitudes reemerge in her autobiography, *Letters of Life*, which offers a retrospective on her early epic:

> An early acquaintance with the Mohegan tribe of Indians, who resided a few miles from Norwich, and a taste for searching out the historic legends of our forest-people, deepened my interest in their native lin-eaments of character, and my sympathy for their degraded condition. In the notes of the volume, much information is concentrated respect-ing them, derived from various sources, in the revision of which I

gratefully received the aid of the acute and discriminating mind of my husband. The work was singularly unpopular, there existing in the community no reciprocity with the subject.

Indeed, our injustice and hard-hearted policy with regard to the original owners of the soil has ever seemed to me one of our greatest national sins.[101]

Acerbically noting the community's lack of reciprocal feelings regarding indigenous peoples, Sigourney also foregrounds her peers' failed Christianity: the reference to "one of our greatest national sins" includes unethical resource wars.

Traits of the Aborigines only inaugurated Sigourney's activism.[102] The *Cherokee Phoenix* often reprinted the author's shorter poems, which confirms that Native Americans, including the Cherokee, valued her perspective and her support.[103] Although we lack documentation of Sigourney's correspondence with Elias Boudinot, the *Phoenix*'s editor, such correspondence seems virtually certain, since Boudinot was educated at the American Board of Commissioners for Foreign Missions school in Cornwall, Connecticut, near Sigourney's Hartford home. We do know that Sigourney corresponded with Scott. Strongly moved after hearing a draft of *Traits of the Aborigines*, Scott saw an opportunity for an alliance, eventually exchanging regular letters with the poet and forming a connection that likely helped propel Sigourney's coauthorship of what we today call the "Ladies Circular."[104]

Addressed to the "benevolent Ladies of the U. States" and published in the *Christian Advocate and Journal and Zion's Herald*, this document was the brainchild of Catharine Beecher, Harriet Beecher Stowe's sister, who, energized by nationwide protests, organized a campaign that sent the document to women friends and acquaintances across the country.[105] Representing, in Lauter's assessment, "an unprecedented women's petition against removal," the "Ladies Circular" was signed by thousands of American women "and became a crucial tool for organizing anti-removal sentiment, especially in the religious community, into a potent political force."[106] The circular energized those we would now call progressive Christians to participate in political action, including diverse forms of writing. For women in particular, activism and literary activity were integrally connected.

If we examine the circular's rhetoric and goals, Sigourney's influence seems obvious. The collectively authored petition's language underscores the United States' continuing land wars and the document's own Christian framework. In the first half, the authors emphasize land loss. Urging immediate action, the petition cites as its first "fact" that "[t]his continent was once possessed only by the Indians," then invokes the vanishing Indian, of whom "it is said [he] often comes to the borders of his limited retreat to gaze on the beautiful country no longer his own." In the period's Anglo-American rhetoric, this passage constructs nature as sublime and, for its former inhabitants, unreachable. It also intimates a theme that emerges more and more forcefully: Native sovereignty.

Although one argument for intervention is paternalistic — or more accurately, as the argument evolves, suggests maternal care — the authors drive home the Indians' sovereign status: "Ever since the existence of this nation, our general government . . . have acknowledged these people as free and independent nations, and has protected them in the quiet possession of their lands." The petition charges that treaties signed "by the hands of the most distinguished statesmen, after purchasing the greater part of their host lands, have *promised* them '*to continue the guarantee of the remainder of their country* FOR EVER'" (original emphasis). If Georgia's new laws take effect, the petition warns, "the Indians are no longer independent nations, but are slaves, at the sovereign disposal of the whites, who will legislate for them"; and if they suffer removal from their cultivated (i.e., civilized) homelands, they will become "wandering emigrants." Their intended destination is a "wild and uncultivated land," "a territory . . . deficient both in wood and water. . . . To this wild and unpromising resort it is proposed to remove 60,000 people, of all ages, sexes, and condition." Confronting the masculine, dominant-society frontier myth and advocating that Indians must have access to resources, the authors reenvision, literally and figuratively, the place of indigenous peoples.[107] "Wild" counters the Indians' civilized status, as the authors privilege Westernized land ownership, and temporally based progress, in an ethical and emotional appeal that rejects removal.

The circular parallels the joint authorship and collective voice of the earlier Cherokee women's petitions and epitomizes the community ethos that Ritchie and Ronald specify as characteristic of women's rhetoric. It also juxtaposes the (masculine) legal status of treaties with the (feminine) moral status of promises, substituting an inseparable connection that might have been more familiar to Cherokee women than to their Euramerican counterparts. Moreover, the petition assumes transnational negotiations between the United States and indigenous peoples; that is, it presupposes Indian sovereignty. For the authors, dispossession denotes war on "independent nations," and they remind readers that the U.S. Constitution empowers the president to protect the Indians' land and rights: "to command *the whole military force of our nation* to protect and sustain the Indian in his right" (original emphasis). Equally, they imply that the president can assert U.S. ownership of indigenous lands by war, joining with Georgia's immoral—and according to the U.S. Supreme Court illegal—land seizure. Removing the Indians would decivilize tribes that had made substantial progress adopting white ways; and, the authors assert sarcastically, "when they have made their lands valuable by cultivation, they again must [will] be driven into still more distant wilds."

Conjuring the Israelites wandering in the desert, the authors again separate the Indians from wilderness. Their address—actually an exposé—argues that economics and politics drive the removal project, not, as the government and its allies professed, regard for the Indians' safety from jealous and marauding white settlers: "But the lands of this people are *claimed* to be embraced within the limits of some of our southern states, and as they are fertile and valuable they are demanded by the whites as their own possessions, and efforts are making to dispossess the Indians of their native soil. . . . [I]t has become almost a certainty that these people are to have their lands torn from them, and to be driven into western wilds and to final annihilation, unless the feelings of a humane and Christian nation shall be aroused to prevent the unhallowed sacrifice" (original emphasis). Offering a sentimental reference to "home" and another romantic nod to the image of the Vanishing American, this passage reasserts Indians' independent status and their ownership (in the legalistic, Euramerican sense) of their "possessions." Access to "valuable" mineral rights, the authors indicate, is secondary; green gold is the problem.

As the circular develops, religious language increasingly subsumes the initial, juridical rhetoric of treaties and land rights. The petition ultimately transforms into a sermon or even a jeremiad—an orally inflected lament for the loss of social morals. But it usurps the sermon's and jeremiad's traditional male speech, articulating a rhetorica that asserts female and Christian moral authority. The authors up the ante as the narrative develops, pressing their readers repeatedly with uncomfortable questions ("Why should they not stand, the cherished relic of antiquity, protected and sustained in their rights, and becoming a free and Christian people, under their own laws and governments?") and quoting an Indian chief leaving council: "We do not wish to sell our lands and remove. This land our great Father above gave us. We stand on it. We stood on it before the white man came to the edge of the American land. We stand on it still. It belongs to us. Our land is no borrowed land." The petition leaves unclear to which "great Father" the chief refers, but it underlines the Indians' divinely granted right to their homelands.

Even more significantly, the maternal sermon-jeremiad is delivered on Christmas: the circular was published in the *Advocate* on December 25, 1829. By invoking the image of Christ's "sacrifice" and attempting to "arouse" "the feelings of a humane and Christian nation," the "ladies" might prevent the devilish, "unhallowed" slaughter of innocents. Ultimately, beyond the petitioners' explicit recourse to feeling—sentiment—the circular's Christian rhetoric and its authoritatively oral, sermon-like cast clearly militate for responsibility and ethical action.[108] Anticipating contemporary Christian ecology's social justice thrust, the circular gives voice to Native Americans, arguing for Native sovereignty, confirming indigenous people's humanity, and promoting environmental justice.

FAITHFUL AMERICANS of both genders joined the anti-removal movement. Mary Hershberger details American Christians' passionate commitment to the cause; their influential publications, including the *Advocate*, energized the nation. Perhaps unsurprisingly, given the circular's appropriation of traditionally male authority, pro-removal forces relentlessly feminized Christian men who supported the movement. Coming from various denominations, these anti-removal individuals promoted the moral value of justice and benevolence, and they regarded removal as "a portentous triumph of the market values of aggressive acquisitiveness that placed a monetary value on everything and encouraged human exploitation for commercial gain." As Hershberger also points out, "Between 1802 and 1819, federal treaties with the southern Indians transferred 20 million acres of land to white settlers, a greater expansion of the territory open to slaveholding than the Missouri Compromise had promised."[109] Indian removal was thus explicitly linked to expanded slave territories; as more land opened for white settlement, working this land would require more labor. The environmental justice issues of Native dispossession and removal were thus inextricably interconnected with chattel slavery—and also African colonization, another form of removal.[110]

Demonstrating Sigourney's continuing anti-removal activism, "The Cherokee Mother" was published in the *Phoenix* on 12 March 1831, accompanied by an introduction and a "Letter to the Delegation of the State of Connecticut" from an "Association of Ladies."[111] This letter, which was intended for the Connecticut congressional delegation, assumed a more feminized approach to the problem than the circular, perhaps reflecting the authors' fears of removal's inevitability. It begins apologetically, acknowledging that the women authors appear to have "unwarrantably transgressed the bounds of the subordinate sphere." Its tone of supplication—and appeal to the moral high ground as it seeks "your pity for your Indian brethren in the name of our common Redeemer"—couples with unabashedly sentimental evocations of home and family: "It will probably be alleged that we have viewed this subject solely through the medium of *feeling*. This was our intention." Twenty years before Harriet Beecher Stowe showcased feeling in *Uncle Tom's Cabin* as the spark for ethical behavior, Sigourney and her activist colleagues established a feminine rhetorical authority that effectively combined accommodation and subversion.[112]

As Paula Bennett reminds us, the letter invites emotion as a means to engage white citizens in action.[113] Yet as she insists elsewhere, "With her poem and with the memorial itself, Sigourney is not just trying to get her readers to weep over the Indians' unhappy (if noble) fate; she is asking that, having been made aware of Cherokee suffering, legislators change their votes."[114] As I noted earlier, Sigourney's accompanying poem imagines Cherokee losses, and she foregrounds the charged image of the mother. As in the circular and the letter, she again critiques her white readers' unchristian and anti-American behavior; the framing letter's collective weight propels the poem and advances its authority. The eponymous speaker observes bitterly, "*Ye call us brethren*," and her lament concludes,

> Will a crush'd nation's deep despair,
>   *Your broken faith*,—our tear-wet sod,
> The babe's appeal,—the chieftain's prayer,
>   Find no memorial with our God? (original emphasis)[115]

"The Cherokee Mother" cannot be construed as traditional nature writing. But because whites saw Indians, especially women, as natural—and hence silent—the poem indirectly contests this view, giving voice to the natural world while it humanizes the Cherokee. Stephen Brandon suggests, "As in *Sketch of Connecticut*, Sigourney challenges the myth that Indians are mere objects to be removed or annihilated; it does so by conveying the Native American's experience from the subjective point of view of the Cherokee mother—a position maintained throughout the poem."[116] Indeed, through what Brandon calls its "rhetoric of inclusion," the poem takes pains to establish Indians' and whites' identity, their shared humanity.[117] Sigourney also attributes separate nationhood to the Cherokee, finally mourning "a crush'd nation's deep despair."[118] The "nation" could double as America itself, as the poet gestures toward Americans' unforeseen response to removal, not only its human costs but its debilitating moral consequences for national history and memory.

To help validate the Cherokee's humanity for her Euramerican audience, Sigourney necessarily "whitens" the mother, Christianizing her much as Scott had done in her petition to the (itself increasingly Westernized) Cherokee National Council. Although Sigourney's speaker purports to be the Cherokee mother, the author's almost comically classical rhetoric ("our light shallops," "midnight harms, / And baleful dews, and tempests hoarse") is carefully calibrated to pierce readers' protective shield of racial and ethnic superiority.[119] Unlike Ward's dual-voiced maternal speech to the Holston commissioners and her male Cherokee counterparts, Sigourney's mother epitomizes Christian ethics and articulates a temporal and patriarchal—though in the poet's view not necessarily progressive—worldview. Like Ward's oratory, the poem assumes a posture of presence and an immediate audience, and it asserts that land and place (the "consecrated woods" and "corn-clad grounds") hold spiritual resonance. Again complexly combining accommodation and subversion, Sigourney represents the mother as the speaking woman of traditional Cherokee society, though she is Christianized, and, hence, supposedly silenced by Pauline doctrine.

Imagined disappearance figures centrally in Sigourney's most famous poem today, "Indian Names," which similarly establishes a rhetorical posture of immediacy and authorial presence. The poem's proto-ecofeminist perspective lays bare Euramerican land appropriation and accentuates the interconnection between humans and nature and (as in "The Cherokee

Mother") between peoples.[120] Lauter calls it "a poem of the mid 1830s, precisely the time when Cherokee removal would lead to the Trail of Tears, the forced removal of most Cherokees from Georgia to the Oklahoma territory."[121] "Indian Names" opens:

> Ye say they all have passed away,
>   That noble race and brave;
> That their light canoes have vanishéd
>   From off the crested wave;
> That, mid the forests where they roamed,
>   There rings no hunter's shout:
> But their name is on your waters—
>   Ye may not wash it out.[122]

Again conjuring the Vanishing American, the poem contemplates connections between Native Americans and nature.[123] On the one hand, such an association was, like the women-nature link, reductive and ultimately silencing. On the other, deploying the rhetoric of disrupted pastoral, Sigourney prods readers' consciences, exposing what she regards as America's destructive roots.[124] As she examines the relationships among language, place, and power, she reasserts for Native Americans an important form of social power.

In "The Prairies," William Cullen Bryant invokes the unnamed Indians as objects that inspire philosophical reflections on man's ephemeral existence: "Thus change the forms of being." Races arise and decline according to God's will. Bryant depicts the Indians' departure to the west as voluntary and portrays them in manly terms. In contrast, Sigourney's jeremiad locates agency where it belongs, confronting her Euramerican counterparts' rhetorical obfuscation. The poem continues,

> 'Tis where Ontario's billow
>   Like Ocean's surge is curled;
> Where strong Niagara's thunders wake
>   The echo of the world;
> Where red Missouri bringeth
>   Rich tribute from the west;
> And Rappahannock sweetly sleeps
>   On green Virginia's breast.

Ye say their conelike cabins,
　　That cluster'd o'er the vale,
Have disappeared, as withered leaves
　　Before the autumn's gale:
But their memory liveth on your hills,
　　Their baptism on your shore,
Your everlasting rivers speak
　　Their dialect of yore.

Old Massachusetts wears it
　　Within her lordly crown,
And broad Ohio bears it
　　Amid his young renown;
Connecticut has wreathed it
　　Where her quiet foliage waves,
And bold Kentucky breathes it hoarse
　　Through all her ancient caves.

Wachusett hides its lingering voice
　　Within its rocky heart,
And Allegany graves its tone
　　Throughout his lofty chart.
Monadnock, on his forehead hoar,
　　Doth seal the sacred trust:
Your mountains build their monument,
　　Though ye destroy their dust.

Sigourney's apostrophe highlights language's complicity in the Indians' erasure: "*Ye say* they all have passed away"; "*Ye say* their conelike cabins . . . Have disappeared" (emphasis added). Her transformative Christian rhetoric ("baptism," "sacred," "dust") appropriates for Native Americans the Adamic authority to name, as she enumerates sites where the Indians' names have predominated: Niagara, Rappahannock, Massachusetts, Monadnock. The landscape inescapably incorporates Indians' language.

Ultimately, Sigourney offers a jeremiad that indicts Americans' urge toward empire.[125] When she emphasizes that "Your everlasting rivers speak / Their dialect of yore," the concluding pun mocks Euramericans' attempts to silence, for what is "their" language will never be extinct, "of yore," but has become "your" language, eternally present in a Christianized world. Equally important, her natural images materialize Native Americans' and European Americans' inevitable interconnection, for nature prohibits the segregation entailed by white social norms: "Rappahanock sweetly sleeps / On green Virginia's breast" (lines 15–16). Embedded in a more detached, formal address, this sentimental image is particularly telling, for it intimates Sigourney's larger project of human interconnection through maternal love, a project profoundly enabled by Christian reform rhetoric and exemplified in the image of the Republican Mother. Ending with an apocalyptic curse, "Indian Names" is an elegy, a tribute, and an intensely political lyric arguing that Euramerican invaders must fully apprehend—and assume responsibility for—their unjust actions toward indigenous peoples.[126]

While the poem mourns the losses, and the potential future losses, of and for Native Americans, it rejects mere sentimental sympathy and guilt, insisting on a responsibility that indicts Christian hypocrisy. Lauter insists, "'Indian Names' directly challenges that form of casual, nostalgic consciousness, which saw the disappearance of Native peoples as a kind of natural phenomenon—like the turning of leaves in the fall, or the displaced activities of the beaver, presented as functionally akin to those of Indians."[127] Regarded from this angle, Sigourney's work, which manipulates conventional images to promote activist goals, resonates for current ecofeminist discussions about the woman-nature association. "Indian Names" affirms, rather than critiques, the connections among Indianness, femininity, and nature and, like "The Cherokee Mother," it links control of nature and neocolonialism. It also demonstrates how the natural and the cultural converse in earlier white American women's writing.

In one light, we could read Sigourney's core Christian value of equality as mere stewardship, but such a perspective diminishes her long-term connections with individual Cherokees. Following Ward and her affiliates, and working in tandem with Scott, Sigourney participated in environmental justice activism to prevent Native land loss and establish Native Americans' sovereign rights. Her Christian rhetoric—citing women's weaker status—contrasts with earlier Cherokee counterparts' assumption of women's traditional authority, but both stances address their listeners' ethical and moral sensibilities with emotional intelligence. Ultimately Sigourney's power and authority as an environmental writer derive from her affectively charged engagement with contentious political, public-sphere issues.

Although nothing Sigourney did finally prevented removal, she continued writing on Native Americans' behalf, clearly feeling keenly her inability to influence national events. Again using the dominant society's romantic connection of Indians with nature to indict itself, her late poem "The Indian Summer" (1854) replaces the stern judgment of "Indian Names" with haunted nostalgia:

> "Gorgeous was the time,
> Yet brief as gorgeous. Beautiful to thee,
> Our brother hunter, but to us replete
> With musing thoughts in melancholy train.
> Our joys, alas! too oft were woe to thee.
> Yet ah, poor Indian! whom we fain would drive
> Both from our hearts, and from thy father's lands,
> The perfect year doth bear thee on its crown,
> And when we would forget, repeat thy name."[128]

As a poet—and woman—with limited political agency, Sigourney can only "repeat thy name." Yet, despite the melancholy tone, she intimates the more aggressive stance of "Indian Names": however much whites—the most powerful, men—might be "fain" to do so, they ultimately cannot drive Indians "from our hearts, and from [their] father's lands."

"We planted, tended and harvested our corn": Mary Jemison's Narrative Conversions

Mary Jemison concludes her life story in a manner that reconfirms her matrilineal Seneca identity: "I have been the mother of eight children . . . and I have at this time thirty-nine grand children, and fourteen great-grand children, all living in the neighborhood of Genessee River, and at Buffalo."[129] Not surprisingly, maternity figures centrally, but so does geographical home; she links identity with place. Jemison's important Seneca voice emerged amid intense, continuing Euramerican pressure on Indian resources. Such pressures were unusually intense in the Northeast, where the Seneca, members of the Haudenosaunee Confederacy, had already survived two centuries of invasion. Whites' lust for resources such as timber— which I handle in chapter 2—and upstate New York's increasing industrialization provoked regular clashes. Though heavily mediated through a white

Savagery to "Civilization." Image by Udo J[oseph] Keppler; published in *Puck* magazine, 16 May 1914. Courtesy of the Library of Congress. The text under the image reads: "The Indian Women: We whom you pity as drudges reached centuries ago the goal that you are now nearing." The image insert reads,

WE, THE WOMEN OF THE IROQUOIS:
Own the land, the lodge, the children.
Ours is the right of adoption, of life or death;
Ours the right to raise up and depose chiefs;
Ours the right of representation at all councils;
Ours the right to make and abrogate treaties;
Ours the supervision over domestic and foreign policies;
Ours the trusteeship of the tribal property;
Our lives are valued again as high as man's.

intermediary, *A Narrative of the Life of Mrs. Mary Jemison* augments Ward's and her cohort's Cherokee perspectives from a northern vantage point.

Immensely popular for decades after its 1824 original publication—and embroidered by subsequent editors for multiple purposes—*A Narrative of the Life of Mrs. Mary Jemison* advanced all the spectacle that early American audiences might desire: Jemison's abduction, early in her teens, with her Pennsylvania family, by a group of Delaware Indians; her family's murder; her eventual transportation to western New York State; her adoption by a Seneca family; her successive interracial marriages to two Indian men and the resulting children; and her rebuff of multiple opportunities to return to white society.[130] As Annette Kolodny has observed, Jemison's life story, which she related orally in English at about the age of eighty to the white American James Seaver, circumvents her editor's designs, "evading the narrative conventions of captivity and sentimental romance alike and becoming, instead, the story of a woman who, in the forested wilderness of upstate New York, knew how to 'take my children and look out for myself.'"[131] Yet, more than a story of what Mark Rifkin calls "individual adversity," Jemison's tale develops an anticaptivity narrative, avowing the moral nature of Indian behavior—even violent behavior—and underscoring white cruelty and corruption, while exposing the latter's relentless resource wars and offering an oblique brief for Native sovereignty.[132]

Many contemporary commentators have asserted, both of Jemison's narrative and of Indian autobiography in general, that such as-told-to stories pose complex problems of authorial voice, given their origins in collaborations between European American "authors," "editors," transcribers, translators, and Native American speakers.[133] Jemison's editor, James Seaver, has an explicit agenda—to characterize the Indians as savages by their own admission—but she resists his intentions, revealing Seneca kindness, loyalty, and generosity. Seaver's introduction avers, "The vices of the Indians, she appeared disposed not to aggravate, and seemed to take pride in extoling [*sic*] their virtues."[134] Despite the necessarily speculative endeavor to separate the speaker's and editor's voices, we must, as Susan Walsh urges, try to locate moments at which their "perspectives and agendas . . . are in clearest conflict."[135] In Jemison's story these moments emerge in orally inflected language that expresses, through content and structure, a female Seneca perspective. Most significantly here, she implicitly names herself by structuring her narrative around the planting and harvesting of corn.

While this image ostensibly confirms stereotypical associations (both historical and contemporary) between Indians, especially Indian women, and
nature, corn possesses more complex resonances in Iroquois, as in Cherokee, cosmology, and its frequent reiteration helps Jemison assert equally her
identity and narrative control.[136]

Unlike the Cherokee women's and Sigourney's work, Jemison's text is
not explicitly activist; it does not attempt to intervene in land cession and
removal debates. But it does engage in environmental work through its
focus on land retention, its attentiveness to place, and its insistence on the
cyclical organization of experience, particularly through corn cultivation.
As with her Cherokee predecessors and Sigourney, Christianity plays an
important—though much less affirmative—role in transforming Seneca
society in the late eighteenth and early nineteenth centuries. As a whole,
Jemison's compelling story encapsulates several themes prominent in the
present context: her own connection to the land, her long-term efforts to
retain traditional lands that the Seneca granted her, her negative attitudes
toward Christianity, and her resistance to the loss of Iroquois women's traditional roles and authority. Unlike Ward's efforts at mediation, her nature-
centered language, embedded in stories of conflict and daily life, describes
her era's relentless resource wars and, anticipating contemporary activists,
makes an implicit demand for environmental justice by valuing Indian
agency and sovereignty.

LIKE HER CONTEMPORARY Ward, Jemison inherited a world ravaged by
two centuries of warfare, including the American Revolution (in which the
Seneca, like the Cherokee, had sided with the British and suffered similarly
severe consequences). Jemison was captured in the 1750s during the French
and Indian Wars as her parents settled in western Pennsylvania. By the
time that she related her story, Iroquois holdings had already been severely
diminished. One important treaty, finalized at a meeting that Jemison and
other clan mothers attended, was the Treaty of Big Tree, signed on 15 September 1797, which established eleven Seneca reservations and preserved
perpetual hunting and fishing rights on traditional lands.[137] This sale had
fractured the Indian leadership. The great chief Red Jacket generally opposed such sales, arguing that they diminished the tribe's "consequence"
and that once the proceeds were spent, the Indians would have nothing,

while others, such as the distinguished leaders Cornplanter and Farmer's Brother, were resigned to a more confined existence on reservations.[138]

Because the chiefs could not agree, the white negotiators turned to the Iroquois matrons—who had the authority to override the sachems' decision—pressuring them, via promises of increased resources to relieve their people's poverty, to accept the land transfer. The matrons urged the sachems to continue negotiations, and despite these considerable internal and external frictions, an agreement was finally reached that reserved about 337 square miles and included a payment of $100,000 invested in federal bank stock with a sizable annual dividend for the Seneca. Although the white negotiator, Tom Morris (acting for his speculator father, Robert), expected that this grant to whites would be about 150 acres, when later surveyed, the land encompassed about 18,000 acres—a triumph of resource colonialism.[139] Unscrupulous settlers and speculators subsequently extracted a substantial majority of the remaining Seneca acreage. Jemison's narrative manifests her profound concern with the potential loss of the lands she oversees and her anger at individuals trying to gain control, for too often those who pretended to protect her interests merely forwarded their own.[140]

The narrative documents resource warfare against both individuals and the Seneca nation. Although by this time the Seneca had been granted reservations, land was traditionally held in common, and the clan mothers controlled its use. Personal allotments were occasionally provided to a few, such as Cornplanter, who received a grant from the Commonwealth of Pennsylvania. Jemison's relative Farmer's Brother enabled her to receive the Gardeau Reservation at the time of the Treaty of Big Tree. As Seaver suggests, "Her efforts as intermediary between the Seneca and the whites and her refusal to return to her white family when accorded the opportunity warranted this honor."[141] Jemison struggled repeatedly to retain control over her holdings, battling unscrupulous whites such as George Jemison, who masqueraded as her cousin and persuaded her to deed him and a co-conspirator a significant share.

The episode detailing these events, which ends with an ironic reference to "the friendly disposition of my cousin towards me," represents only the beginning of such land-grab efforts.[142] Chapter 15 tells of her complex dealings with white lawyers and land speculators that result in the transfer of several thousand acres to two whites. The language in this section mixes legalistic white diction with Jemison's concern for her family and her tribe, reminding us of her account's complexly mediated status. Nevertheless, in keeping with matrilineal Seneca tradition, we learn that she has "consulted my daughters on the subject" (122). When her remaining land is sold, "the income . . . is to be equally divided amongst the members of the Seneca nation, without any reference to tribes or families" (124). Perhaps because she appreciated her nation's embattled circumstances and struggle for survival, she planned to distribute these proceeds to the nation rather than, as was customary, to her clan.

Jemison's resource struggle was hardly unique.[143] On numerous occasions, she portrays violent encounters between whites and Indians. During her capture, Jemison tells how the group "passed a Shawnee town, where I saw a number of heads, arms, legs, and other fragments of the bodies of some white people who had just been burnt" (19). In a different passage that evokes Jemison's voice, she insists that such actions constitute fair retribution for others' violence: "Notwithstanding all that has been said against the Indians, in consequence of their cruelties to their enemies—cruelties that I have witnessed, and had abundant proof of—it is a fact that they are naturally kind, tender, and peaceable towards their friends, and strictly honest; and that those cruelties have been practised, only upon their enemies, according to their idea of justice" (33). Like Sarah Winnemucca's account more than five decades later, much of Jemison's narrative is devoted to accounts of war, first between the French (with whom the Seneca were allied) and the British and later between the British (with whom the Seneca then sided) and the Americans.[144] Jemison regards skeptically British efforts to involve her people in the Revolutionary War, because their services are hired rather than informed by a just cause (see 49–52).

The latter alliance was disastrous for the Seneca, as Jemison's references to corn reveal. General George Washington ordered a concerted attack on the Iroquois that focused on complete destruction of their resources.[145] Led by General John Sullivan, in the fall of 1779 the American army "was making rapid progress toward our settlement, burning and destroying the huts and corn-fields; killing the cattle, hogs and horses, and cutting down the fruit trees belonging to the Indians throughout the country" (54). She follows this description with an encounter between Indian brothers who served on opposite sides in the war and then (after she mentions a good corn harvest) a later incursion in which Sullivan and his troops "destroyed every article of the food kind they could lay their hands on. A part of our corn they burnt, and threw the remainder into the river. They burnt our houses, killed what few cattle and horses they could find, destroyed our fruit trees, and left nothing but the bare soil and timber" (58). Jemison's seemingly abrupt linguistic transitions from war to daily life highlight everyday women's events, signaled by the image of corn that gives them weight equal to or greater than the "special," or men's, events. She also reestablishes narrative control.[146]

Although the Indians escape this "work of destruction"—a phrase that Jemison repeats—they are driven away until the army "concluded that there could be no risk in our once more taking possession of our lands. . . . but what were our feelings when we found that there was not a mouthful of any kind of sustenance left, not even enough to keep a child one day from perishing with hunger" (54, 58–59). Conjuring Jemison's own interrupted childhood, the rhetoric of the dying child invokes (Seaver's) Euramerican sentimentalism, but the substance may well register her acerbic perspective. At this point, having five children, Jemison carries the two smallest and leads the others to the Gardeau Reserve.[147] The narrative clearly exposes Europeans' resource warfare. By destroying the seasonal food supplies and housing as well as the long-term provisions that the orchards signified, the invaders sought to eradicate the Seneca as part of what many now call an American genocide.[148]

BECAUSE OF THEIR theological myopia, Euramericans were also, unwittingly or not, erasing Seneca spiritual traditions and rejecting the spiritual connection to the land that defined their identity. As Jemison indicates, Christian missionaries had by this time made significant inroads into Seneca society, attracting converts and threatening the nation's social, political, and spiritual integrity. Unlike white Christian belief systems, which bifurcated and hierarchized the relationship between human and nonhuman nature, traditionalist Senecas, like their Cherokee counterparts, had an integrated, holistic, and gender-balanced worldview. A foundational myth, often known as "The Woman Who Fell from the Sky," tells how, with the animals' essential, complementary aid, a woman creates a new world. In an earlier world "there grew one stately tree that branched beyond the range of vision. Perpetually laden with fruit and blossoms, the air was fragrant with its perfume, and the people gathered to its shade where councils were held." The Great Ruler commands the tree to be uprooted, and Ata-en-sic, who is pregnant, descends through the hole, "wrapp[ing] around her a great ray of light." "Dazzled by the descending light enveloping Ata-en-sic," the animals below fear that the falling object will destroy their homes unless the "*oeh-da* (earth)," "which lies at the bottom of our waters," is brought to the surface. The Beaver, the Duck, and many other divers try and fail, but "the Muskrat, knowing the way, volunteers to obtain it and soon returns bearing a small portion in his paw." The Turtle volunteers to carry the growing earth, and "the water birds, guided by its glow, flew upward, and receiving the woman on their widespread wings, bore her down to the Turtle's back."[149]

As in the Genesis origin story, nature—water, trees, and animals—figures significantly. However, reflecting the egalitarian worldview that George Tinker describes, in the Iroquois narrative the courageous and self-sacrificing animals not only enjoy prominence as individuals equal to humans, but they enable humans to survive. Unlike Genesis, "The Woman Who Fell from the Sky" expresses no gender hierarchy, and creation depends on a woman and the animals that share her responsibility. As Lisa Brooks (Abenaki) writes, "The thinking that results in creation is cooperative, drawing on the insights and abilities of all members of the group to solve the problem at hand."[150] Equally important, "falling" symbolizes no moral condemnation.

When Sky Woman falls, she is pregnant with a daughter, who eventually becomes pregnant herself and dies giving birth to twin sons. Sky Woman buries her and from her grave grow the Three Sisters, the sacred plants of corn, beans, and squash. Living "together in a field," the sisters "were quite different from one another in their size and way of dressing":

> The little sister was so young that she could only crawl at first, and she was dressed in green.
>
> The second sister wore a bright yellow dress, and she had a way of running off by herself when the sun shone and the soft wind blew in her face.
>
> The third was the eldest sister, standing always very straight and tall above the other sisters and trying to protect them. She wore a pale green shawl, and she had long, yellow hair that tossed about her head in the breeze.

There was one way the sisters were all alike, though. They loved each other dearly, and they always stayed together. This made them very strong.

A Mohawk boy arrives, and the two younger sisters disappear, but when he sees that the Elder Sister misses them, "he brought them all back together and they became stronger together, again."[151] This story stresses the sisters' interdependence and their centrality to Iroquois society. Like "The Woman Who Fell from the Sky," "The Three Sisters" reveals the respect accorded to women and the profound spiritual and physical connections between women and nature.[152] Like Ward's oratory to the Cherokee National Council, it illuminates the spiritual and gendered thrust of Euramericans' ongoing resource wars.

Misapprehending or disregarding the integrity of Native spiritual and material life, the invaders advanced hierarchical gender norms that conflicted with Iroquois tradition. In the Euramerican legal system only widows or single adult women (as "femes soles") could own property, and women, though technically citizens, were unable, for example, to vote, hold public office, or testify in court. Their children belonged to their husbands, however brutal or abusive those partners might be, and divorce was difficult and uncommon. Many women endured lives of exhausting physical labor. In contrast, like the Cherokee, the Seneca were matrilineal and matrilocal, and women enjoyed considerable social power and authority.[153] Traditionally the farmers, like their Cherokee counterparts, Seneca women acquired their high status partly because of their horticultural virtuosity, which ensured a high survival rate during famines.

As a Seneca matron or clan mother, Jemison would have shared such responsibilities as the power to appoint and depose chiefs and to regulate wars by providing or withholding food; she would also have possessed the right to control her property and children. Standard Euramerican accounts, even by Indians' early supporters, frequently erased the traditional gender role complementarity of male hunters/warriors and female horticulturalists, partly, as the historian Martha Harroun Foster observes, for imperial purposes: "The theory that Indians wasted valuable farm land by maintaining hunting grounds and persisting in woman-dominated, hoe horticulture, had been used since the seventeenth century to justify the acquisition of Indian land."[154] Thus, as with the Cherokee, transforming traditional

gender roles comprised an important strategy in the settlers' ongoing resource wars and efforts to deny Native American sovereignty.

Given such drastic social differences in gender roles and rights, Jemison's
comparisons between her experiences among the Seneca and the expectations for Euramerican women must have astonished her white readers.
Describing women's work, she affirms that Native women's "task is probably not harder than that of white women . . . and *their cares certainly are not
half as numerous, nor as great*" (31; emphasis added). As a white woman in
European society, she would have had to participate in "spinning, weaving, sewing, stocking knitting, and the like" (31–32)—activities noted by
Cherokee leader John Ridge and the Cherokee women in their second petition to the Cherokee National Council. The passage's outspokenness and
the descriptions that follow offer contemporary readers echoes, however
faint, of Jemison's original oral account.

Jemison avers that, unlike white women's responsibilities, "our labor was
not severe" and that her community of women workers "had no master to
oversee or drive us, so that we could work as leisurely as we pleased" (31).[155]
She tells Seaver that "[a]fter the revolutionary war, I learned to sew, so that
I could make my own clothing after a poor fashion; but the other domestic
arts I have been wholly ignorant of the application of, since my captivity,"
concluding, "[i]n that manner we lived, without any of the jealousies, quar-
rels, and revengeful battles between families and individuals, which have
been common in the Indian tribes since the introduction of ardent spirits
among them" (32). As Kolodny comments, "[C]ontradicting then current
notions of the arduousness of the Indian woman's life, Jemison described
a world that—at least until the horrific disruptions of the Revolutionary
War—appeared almost idyllic in its repeated seasonal routines."[156] Her
straightforward description prioritizes Seneca ethical standards over Euramerican ones; only the introduction of alcohol promotes conflicts. Although
the language seems heavily mediated, her candor suggests an intense conversation and a forceful rhetorical presence. In obliquely disparaging white
women's responsibilities, she reasserts her Native identity and, indirectly,
Seneca sovereignty.

Jemison conveys her Seneca identification and her connection to the land
most notably by structuring her account with repeated references to corn.
These references function on individual and narrative, everyday and sacred
levels.[157] The seasons of corn signify Seneca female identity in practical

and spiritual terms, invoking not only daily survival but also "The Three Sisters."[158] Immediately after she depicts her adoption and her kind Seneca sisters, she emphasizes her connection with nature, and particularly with corn: "The town where they lived was pleasantly situated on the Ohio, at the mouth of the Shenanjee: the land produced good corn; the woods furnished plenty of game, and the waters abounded with fish. Another river emptied itself into the Ohio, directly opposite the mouth of the Shenanjee. We spent the summer at that place, where we planted, hoed, and harvested a large crop of corn, of an excellent quality." As if to reinforce her authority, she continues, "About the time of corn harvest, Fort Pitt was taken from the French by the English" (24–25). Alluding to the women's collective labor, Jemison highlights its importance by noting the corn harvest's size and quality. In this integrated worldview, natural cycles frame political events, such as the capture of Fort Pitt.

In another such cycle, the seasons circumscribe her first child's birth: "In the second summer of my living at Wiishto, I had a child at the time that the kernels of corn first appeared on the cob." She became ill but recovered "by the time that the corn was ripe" (29). Describing her work, she states, "In the summer season, we planted, tended and harvested our corn, and generally had all our children with us" (31). Ultimately, her Seneca gender role defines her life: "I have planted, hoed, and harvested corn every season but one since I was taken prisoner" (127).[159] Even a perfunctory count yields more than two dozen references to corn; as significantly, one of the chapters to which we know Jemison herself contributed little or nothing, the lengthy eleventh chapter on her husband Hiokatoo, has no such allusions. These references form a recurring rhetorical pattern that informally structures the narrative as a whole, disrupting the linear and logical, "progressive" Euramerican norms of temporal and narrative order that Tinker outlines and substituting a seasonal, cyclical, embodied, and place-based reorganization that merits recognition for its contributions to environmental literature.[160]

THESE CYCLES, and the women's central position, were interrupted and transformed by the resource wars waged on a spiritual as well as literal battleground. Iroquois women's significant roles, complementary to men's in spiritual and religious matters, had been changing rapidly during Jemison's lifetime. As with the Cherokee women, rhetoric and metaphors mattered.

For white Americans, nature and wilderness had often been connected, and Jemison's published narrative emerged within specific literary and religious conventions that drew from this connection.[161] In its earliest, Puritan forms the captivity narrative dictated that the captive, usually female, underwent a period of physical and psychic testing in the wilderness, literal and metaphorical. Representing Puritan society's sinful whole, she was tempted to fall from innocent (English) grace into sinful "marriage"—which could be literal—with the diabolical "natural" Indian. Eunice Williams's story reinforced such fears. Captured in 1704 at age seven, she repeatedly chose, despite efforts by her Puritan minister father to ransom her, to remain with her Mohawk husband and family until she died in 1785.

In the captivity narrative's approved variant, the heroine, suffering intense fear and bodily privation, was rescued from her ordeal by God's grace; her rescue emblematized the prospect of Christian salvation for the larger Puritan community. Richard Slotkin notes, "Through the captive's proxy, the promise of a similar salvation could be offered to the faithful among the reading public, while the captive's torments remained to harrow the hearts of those not yet awakened to their fallen nature."[162] The environmental historian Carolyn Merchant underscores the theological foundation for land wars: "The wilderness provided symbolic justification for Puritan land conversion. . . . They could take over the wilderness from the Indians and transform it into a garden through their own ecological additions, even as they transformed the spiritual wilderness in their own souls."[163] Late in the eighteenth century, as the idea of wilderness began to change and the nation's forests were leveled, Americans started to understand "untamed" nature as sublime, "now cathedral, temple, and Bible" and also as "a land of useful commodities, to be extracted from nature by human labor."[164] This extractive ethos, alien to Seneca traditionalists, figured significantly in resource wars for control of water and, as chapter 2 of *Fallen Forests* explores, timber.

The rationale for war and appropriation of Indian lands in the 1820s and 1830s was thus often religious, and Seaver's appendix expresses this motive. Acknowledging the Seneca's faithfulness to their own, "pagan" religious practices and then describing Christian missionaries' arrival, Seaver relates the Seneca perspective: "They say it is highly probable that Jesus Christ came into the world in old times, to establish a religion that would *promote the happiness of the white people*, on the other side of the great water (meaning the sea,) and that he died for the sins of his people, *as the missionaries have informed them*" (emphasis added).[165] The Seneca are skeptical: "But, they say that Jesus Christ had nothing to do with them, and that the Christian religion was not designed for their benefit; but rather, should they embrace it, they are confident it would make them worse, and consequently do them an injury."[166] Professing their own religion, which "is better adapted to their circumstances, situation, and habits, and to the promotion of their present comfort and ultimate happiness, than any system that ever has or can be devised," the Indians reject Christianity, because "they . . . believe that the Christian religion is better calculated for the good of white people than theirs is; and wonder that those who have embraced it, do not attend more strictly to its precepts, and feel more engaged for its support and diffusion among themselves."[167] However unwittingly, Seaver conveys the Seneca's sense that whites are only nominal Christians, believers of convenience.[168]

The narrative proper's account of Jemison's family history intimates her connection with traditional Christian readers' backgrounds. Her Irish parents "were strict observers of religious duties; for it was the daily practice of my father, morning and evening, to attend, in his family, to the worship of God" (2). When the family arrived in America, Jemison received some education typical for women, becoming literate primarily so that she could read the Bible. Despite her early Christian upbringing, the elderly Jemison confides that "my reading, Catechism and prayers, I have long since forgotten; though for a number of the first years that I lived with the Indians, I repeated the prayers as often as I had an opportunity." She also tells how a missionary had recently given her a Bible, which she enjoys hearing read aloud (7–8). We should pause again to consider the difficulty of distinguishing between Jemison's account and Seaver's interpolations. Given his explicit purpose to prove Indians savage (and hence legitimize white land grabs), this account seems contradictory, for it potentially civilizes Jemison for her white readers. But, as Mark Rifkin argues, Jemison's relatively civilized status, along with her whiteness, may have allowed Euramericans to justify her legal authority to cede communally held Seneca lands.[169] These descriptions also rely on sentimental language that would have been atypical for an Indian woman; Seaver may have imported such language, which would have enabled him to reach a broad, popular audience.[170]

Elsewhere Jemison's narrative expresses a dissenting perspective on Christian virtue, for she grimly depicts Christianity as directly responsible for the Indians' national and individual demise. Her directness and her attitude reflect a candid communication in her own voice: "The use of ardent spirits amongst the Indians and the attempts which have been made to civilize and christianize them by the white people, has constantly made them worse and worse; increased their vices, and robbed them of many of their virtues; and will ultimately produce their extermination" (32).[171] Ironically, she equates (or at least couples) the introduction of religion with that of alcohol. Although we never learn why Christian education has these effects, the message is clear: Indians must live by traditional spiritual values or die, both individually and collectively. From this perspective, as an environmental justice text, Jemison's is more radical than Scott's or even Ward's. Mary Rowlandson's captivity narrative, the genre's foundational text, emphasizes the author's spiritual awakening and how her faith preserved her life and redeemed her from Indian captivity; Biblical verses and praise for God's kindness pepper the narrative, even though her captors showed her kindness. Readers accustomed to traditional captivity narratives must have found Jemison's views shocking.

Jemison's castigation of Christianity would have been even more scandalous because, like Sigourney's poetry, her narrative appeared during the Second Great Awakening. Although missionaries—especially Jesuits— had long sought to convert the Iroquois' constituent tribes, including the Seneca, such pressures intensified in the early nineteenth century with western New York State's increasing industrialization. As with the Cherokee, these pressures possessed a specifically gendered component.[172] The emergence of the Seneca leader Handsome Lake (1735–1815) in the early nineteenth century diminished Iroquois women's power and caused significant internal conflict.[173] An influential political leader, Handsome Lake assumed the role of a prophet and, supported by Thomas Jefferson and the U.S. federal government, sought to convert the Iroquois to a syncretic, visionary Christianity that co-opted traditional beliefs under the rubric of monotheistic, patriarchal religious norms.[174] For Iroquois women this movement translated into huge losses of power and prestige and ruptured their historical connection with the land. Handsome Lake's visions included some highly critical of Columbus and orthodox Christianity, such as "How America Was Discovered," but his translations of Christianity advanced a conscious antiwoman agenda, paralleling the pattern that Tinker cites as colonialist efforts to divide the Native community and undercut sovereignty.[175] The Iroquois men, relinquishing traditional roles as hunters and warriors, were to assume women's positions as the farmers and heads of household. No longer valued as sustainers and important spiritual leaders, the women were, like their Cherokee counterparts, relegated to limited domestic roles.

Handsome Lake's emergence had other devastating environmental consequences for Iroquois women. Nancy C. Unger points to Indian women's crucial role in sustainable living; they controlled their own fertility through prolonged lactation, as well as abortion and infanticide: "By carefully controlling their populations, keeping them below the land's 'carrying capacity,' Indian women made a crucial contribution to their peoples' ability to live easily sustainable lifestyles."[176] According to Foster, three of Handsome Lake's four principal mandates, which prohibited "whiskey, witchcraft, love magic, and abortion-and-sterility medicine," responded directly to women's influence.[177] "Love magic" references women's sexual power (a common practice had been for women to collectively withhold sex when wishing, for example, to end a war); "abortion-and-sterility medicine" includes women's fertility control through abortifacients and birth control measures; and "witchcraft" alludes to women's overall power. At least some women elders apprehended clearly how Handsome Lake's leadership threatened to diminish their spiritual, social, and political authority.

Handsome Lake himself had several women killed for witchcraft, and some of his more ardent followers reportedly murdered "other clan mothers who resisted his 'reforms.'"[178] When Jemison observes that "it was believed for a long time, by some of our people, that I was a great witch; but they were unable to prove my guilt, and consequently I escaped the certain doom of those who are convicted of that crime" (128), she was referring not only to the Iroquois' traditional belief system but also to its innovative deployment by Handsome Lake's followers to eliminate strong dissenting, often female, voices. The turn to Europeanized religions eroded the Iroquois' respect for an interdependent natural world and women's authority. Thus, while Handsome Lake's efforts to synthesize Iroquois and Christian belief systems ostensibly reasserted Native sovereignty, they simultaneously eroded that sovereignty by undermining traditionally gendered spiritual (and, thus, political) complementarity.

What do we ultimately learn about the environment from Jemison's narrative? Clearly, any claims vis-à-vis proto-ecofeminism must be relatively modest, given the narrative's heavily mediated quality, Seaver's explicit agenda, and the Iroquois struggle for survival. While sustainability may have featured prominently in earlier Seneca society, merely preventing further Native land losses figured largely on Jemison's agenda. As important as the actions she describes, the older Haudenosaunee worldview, in which women played central spiritual, political, and social roles, emerges through Seaver's screening. These moments arrive in language or structural features — often registering her dissent from her editor's complex agenda — that suggest Jemison's immediate presence. Jemison's perspective seems clearest when she affiliates herself with the Seneca and, sometimes passionately, defends indigenous ethical standards and behavior. Anticipating contemporary claims for environmental justice, Jemison conveys the savagery of Euramericans' early resource wars via her community-based ethos.

Perhaps the story's most striking rhetorical feature, which reveals its oral roots, is the corn-centered language, based in a spatialized worldview, that grounds her narrative, providing cyclical coherence and obliquely but powerfully resisting white society. Her white contemporaries probably believed that this focus indicated her natural, uncivilized status as a laborer doing men's work rather than symbolizing her empowerment. But in affirming her own and Seneca women's connection to the natural world, she denies white ideologies that specify her as savage and parallels the work of women like Ward, Sigourney, and their associates, who variously undercut or inverted the dominant society's negative association of women with nature. Jemison's determination, if not her narrative, ultimately helped to preserve a portion of traditional Iroquois landholdings in upstate New York, on which her descendants still reside.

LAND, NATURE, WOMEN, AND MOTHER: these words held no universal significations in North America during the period encompassing Nancy Ward's speeches and Lydia Sigourney's last Indian poems. With different audiences and belief systems, the women considered here sometimes used similar language with widely different meanings and resonances. Expressing an emotional intelligence more likely to enlist feeling and ethics than logic, this chapter's texts demonstrate that the listeners and the context determine the effects of invoking motherhood and womanhood—sentimental or otherwise. Ward and other Cherokee women addressed audiences ranging from U.S. government representatives to the Cherokee National Council. Their words survive principally through white mediation, and we can only imagine the consequences of immediacy, how voice and tone combined with a responsive audience. Jemison's narrative appears through Seaver's muffling filter, as he liberally supplemented and interpreted her conversational account. Sigourney endeavored, through various (and sometimes collaborative) literary forms, including poetry, sermons, letters, and petitions, to influence both the federal government and white Americans, especially women and Christians.

Although these women's occasions for public speech varied widely, their approaches were sometimes parallel. In particular, literally or figuratively oral speech often reinforced collective authorship and enhanced their authority. The women rhetors share two concerns that often animate their work. The first is Native sovereignty. One of the seventeen principles of contemporary environmental justice is the "fundamental right to political, economic, cultural and environmental self-determination of all peoples."[179] The women in this chapter expose the resource wars against Native nations that dominated early American history, and they contend for Indian agency over resources defined in political and spiritual as well as material terms. But these early Cherokee and white American women also—though very differently—illuminate the problem of erasing land-based identity itself. Whether articulating a traditional Cherokee perspective, a progressive Cherokee stance, or a Christian vision, they believed that removal was not merely unethical, it was murderous, perhaps even genocidal.

Gender, and their sense of themselves as women in their respective societies, inflected their rhetoric powerfully. Their concrete and spiritual association with nature assured Indian women authority and power, not essentialized diminishment. Ward and her traditional contemporaries comprehended that white Americans' resource wars were waged on a gendered front and, while using the dominant society's language, privilege the traditional gender balance, expressed in the Selu and Kana'tī story that was foundational to Cherokee identity. Elites like Scott and her companions may have understood this framework, but, adopting the rhetoric of Christian motherhood, they unintentionally undermine it even as they plead to retain traditional lands. Seeking readers' emotionally intelligent response, Sigourney and her coauthors deploy that same gendered rhetoric to invoke their ethical authority and establish Indian humanity and sovereignty. More nearly coinciding with Ward's approach, Jemison rejects Christian motherhood altogether, asserting her status as a Seneca woman to unmask resource wars and, indirectly, to argue for Native sovereignty.

Perhaps predictably, within a dominant society privileging literacy and a transforming Cherokee society in which women's authority was increasingly diminished, the Cherokee women's oratories proved only temporarily effective. Political alliances between Indian progressives like Scott and the influential Sigourney fostered massive public support and recognition, in this case, of removal's potentially genocidal consequences. Jemison's editor subdued her political message; only by reading against the grain of Seaver's interventions are we now able to perceive Jemison's environmental perspective. But, ultimately, Beloved Women or republican women, Christians or non-Christians were unable to prevent the holocaust of Indian removals and land seizure by convincing the audience that mattered most: the politically powerful men who controlled the U.S. government. Such alliances and rhetorical experiments nevertheless provided foundational experience for later successes, most notably in the antislavery movement. Many earlier women, both Native and white, clearly absorbed the anti-removal project's transnational scope, including the connections between removal and the expansion of slavery.

In this extraordinary period, Native American women—traditionalists and progressives—articulated an ethos of environmental justice, advocating for Native land tenure and sovereignty. Their practices highlight for us the potential risks and benefits of using Christian or spiritual rhetoric to engage in environmental arguments, especially when those arguments emerge from different histories, cultures, and polities. Beyond their differences, the early nineteenth-century women cited above contributed to ecofeminist activism: all raised consciousness about America's historical and ongoing resource wars, all attempted to transform perceptions and behavior, and all underlined gender's prime significance in these resource wars. Their speeches and narratives make forceful, emotionally intelligent appeals that presage the perspectives and goals of today's environmental justice movement and that model potential strategies for progressive change.

Coda: "Songs of Survival"

I am descending into Syracuse airport, near the traditional Haudenosaunee homelands. As we circle the runway, I look down at Onondaga Lake. From one angle the water sparkles, but it slowly turns murky and sickish, orange-brown. On the shores of this lake, Dekanawida, the Great Peacemaker, assembled the Iroquois tribes to form the Haudenosaunee Confederacy in the mid-fifteenth century. With the opening of the Erie Canal, the area's population expanded dramatically and industry boomed.[180] Today this sacred lake, encompassing 4.6 square miles, is a Superfund site, debased by soda ash and limestone mining, polluted by decades of sewage, and contaminated with PCBs, dioxin, and mercury.[181]

Native American health, land, and sovereignty remain under attack. Although many challenges are new, many reprise those faced by earlier activists. Yet much current rhetoric echoes earlier women's priorities of respect, community, and motherhood as the means to achieve environmental justice. Two contemporary Cherokee women, Maria Gunnoe and Marilou Awiakta, take varied approaches to environmental activism, including the maternal jeremiad and the maternal pastoral. These women reprise—and demonstrate the continuing effectiveness of—their predecessors' gendered environmental rhetoric.[182]

Recently awarded the Goldman Prize, also known as the "Green Nobel," Gunnoe has advocated ending mountaintop removal coal mining, which has caused the flooding of her family's ancestral home seven times and severely polluted its water. As the Goldman Prize citation underscores, Gunnoe's home region of West Virginia is environmentally rich, including "some of the most important forest ecosystems in North America." The area also contains huge coal reserves, the region's black gold. Underground mining has long delivered jobs for the region's residents, but mountaintop removal uses machines, blasting "an average of 800 feet off the top of the mountain" to access underlying coal deposits. The explosions circulate dangerous dust, and the rubble and other waste, often toxic, is dumped in adjacent streams and valleys, contaminating air and water supplies.[183]

Withstanding intimidation that includes death threats, Gunnoe has been instrumental in community organizing and condemning this polluting practice of extraction for economic gain.[184] When asked about her activism in a recent interview, she responded, "It had more to do with the fact that I'm a mother than anything else. I started looking into what my children's future was going to look like, and it didn't look good. The best thing I can do for my children is to educate them and to see to it that they have a healthy world to bring their grandchildren into. And it's not that way right now." The third West Virginia woman to be awarded the Goldman Prize, Gunnoe attributes this leadership to family: "Well, we're fierce mothers. That's the only way I know to explain it. Appalachian women are very concerned about the wellbeing of their children, their grandchildren, and their great grandchildren, because the things that sustain life in Appalachia are being destroyed. The water, air, land, the plant life— everything."[185] Like her predecessors, Gunnoe highlights mothers' ability to assume a long-term perspective. Like them, she emphasizes community and people's interconnectedness with the natural environment. And like them, she defines herself as a "fierce mother" contending for environmental justice.

Approaching activism differently, Marilou Awiakta invites readers to join her journey of spiritual reconnection in her multigenre autobiography, *Selu: Seeking the Corn Mother's Wisdom*. In some sense, she reprises Katteuha's perspective: "I have taken the privelage to Speak to you as my own children, and the same as if you had sucked my Breast." Valuing elders' wisdom, Awiakta describes Ward's difficult intermediary position between Cherokees and whites, and she points out that her predecessor not only counsels her tribe to seek peace but, perhaps most importantly, repeatedly tells her people, "Do not sell your land."[186] Land, place, form the basis for identity.

But it is only a foundation. Combining Christian and Cherokee perspectives, Awiakta suggests that patriarchal narratives of domination over nature distort the balance that enables humans and their environment to flourish. In "When Earth Becomes an 'It,'" Awiakta describes how, because people consume her, the female earth warms and can provide no milk. The result, the poem warns, will be self-destruction:

She is taking all green
into her heart
and will not turn back
until we call her
by her name.[187]

Like her nineteenth-century predecessors, Awiakta foregrounds the mother, presenting the earth as an unsentimental and resolute being who requires reciprocity, respect, and humility. The real Cherokee gold, mother's milk, is green.

The Washington Elm, Cambridge, Massachusetts.
Taken on the anniversary of the Battle of Bunker Hill, 17 June 1875, by
James Wallace Black. Though clearly diminished in this photo, which
was snapped three decades after Sigourney celebrated it in *Scenes in
My Native Land*, the elm's massive presence remains evident.
Courtesy of the Trustees of the Boston Public Library.

Chapter 2

"Such Progress in Civilization"

Forest Life and Mushroom Growth,
East, West, and South

Often we beheld the prostrate form of some old sylvan giant which had fallen and crushed down smaller trees under its immense ruin. In spots where destruction had been riotous, the lanterns showed perhaps a hundred trunks, erect, half overthrown, extended along the ground, resting on their shattered limbs or tossing them desperately into the darkness, but all of one ashy white, all naked together, in desolate confusion. . . . The wild nature of America had been driven to this desert-place by the encroachments of civilized man.

—NATHANIEL HAWTHORNE

Friends at home! I charge you to spare, preserve and cherish some portion of your primitive forest; for when these are cut away I apprehend they will not easily be replaced.

—HORACE GREELEY

IN *SCENES IN MY NATIVE LAND*, Lydia Sigourney observes, "The wild elephant, when death approaches, moves slowly to seek the shadow of lofty trees, and there resigns his breath. Intelligent man, like the most sagacious of animals, might surely spare a few, as a shelter for his weary head, and a patrimony for an unborn race."[1] Like many of her contemporaries, she witnessed with dismay the United States' diminishing forest heritage. Unlike many, she comprehended the interconnection between zealous forestry practices and the potential for Native American genocide.[2]

This is a chapter about trees. But it also encompasses forests and the American landscape. More precisely, I will examine women writers' concern for aesthetic, material, and historic appreciation and conservation of the sylvan environment. The intranational resource wars between Indian

75

nations and Euramericans reappear here with a different inflection. Before
the American republic was founded, the British state and colonial communities represented opposed international interests striving for maritime
dominance that depended on wood.[3] This economic motive for conflict
persisted in the new nation, but it paralleled an emergent battle on intellectual and aesthetic grounds, as Americans struggled to conceptualize how
humans and nonhuman nature were related. Women writers in the early
part of the nineteenth century fought resource depletion (such as clear-
cutting), but they—and some male counterparts—understood that the
loss was psychological, mythical, and genealogical as well as concrete. That
is, "resources" were not merely extractable, salable objects, they were also
crucial symbolic assets.

Nathaniel Hawthorne and Horace Greeley's elegiac remarks about
American forests conjure not just the woods but the inhabitants of its "wild
nature"—primitive and endangered "by the encroachments of civilized
man." Such perspectives implicitly counter the nation's ethos of growth
and rhetoric of progress, partly defined as technological advancement and
productively using otherwise "empty" or "waste" land, including Cherokee
and Haudenosaunee homelands. Ralph Waldo Emerson's iconic exhorta-
tions express an analogous mindset. In "The Progress of Culture," an address to Harvard's Phi Beta Kappa Society in 1867, he articulates what had
been a common attitude since well before the Civil War. Lauding American science, he cites its attractions for immigrants who fly "from crowded,
antiquated kingdoms" pursuing material opportunity: "Land without price
is offered to the settler, cheap education to his children. The temper of our
people delights in this whirl of life. Who would live in the stone age, or
the bronze, or the iron, or the lacustrine? Who does not prefer the age of
steel, of gold, of coal, petroleum, cotton, steam, electricity, and the spectro-
scope?"[4] Growth and progress depended on the extraction and consumption of natural resources.

Chapter 1 explored the disparate meanings of *nature*, *woman*, and *mother*
for Euramericans and Native Americans by examining relationships among
landownership, agency, gender, and environmental justice. I argued that
using an oral or orally inflected hybrid rhetoric, early nineteenth-century
women writers leveraged their status as literal or figurative mothers to so-
licit readers' intervention into resource wars against Native Americans.
This chapter shows how travel writing—paradoxically, in its emphasis on

home, whether individual, regional, or national—can constitute environmental writing.[5] Three antebellum American women's texts covering the Northeast, the upper Midwest, and the mid-Atlantic South provide my paradigms; I attend particularly to trees' "tall gold." Often speaking directly to an imagined audience, Lydia Sigourney, Caroline Kirkland, and Harriet Jacobs incorporate traditional masculine rhetorical objectives, such as persuasion, but they also embrace what Andrea Lunsford defines as rhetorica's goals: "understanding, exploration, connection, and conversation."[6] As their narratives move among aesthetic, figurative, and corporeal modes, women travel writers generate such affective responses as sympathetic respect, awe, fear, anger, and amusement, urging readers toward resource conservation.

Anticipating women's involvement in the contemporary forest defense movement and that movement's debates about gendered rhetorical strategies, nineteenth-century American women writers pondered such concerns as forests' ability to create community, aesthetics' significance for humans, ecosystem preservation, and the advancement of national identity.[7] Although they have different emphases, Sigourney and Kirkland's works predate by two decades George Perkins Marsh's visionary account in *Man and Nature* (1864) of deforestation's effects on the environment. By admiring and elevating America's historic trees, Lydia Sigourney's *Scenes in My Native Land* propounds a Christian stewardship ethic that forecasts contemporary Christian ecology, while through embedded humor Caroline Kirkland's *Forest Life* promotes a realistic environmental standpoint that shares many of Sigourney's values, including her appreciation of natural monuments as national monuments. They also articulate an innovative conception of time, juxtaposing "tree-time" with the human life span; Sigourney especially advocates a transgenerational outlook. More akin to Native American worldviews prioritizing community and continuity than to the masculine Euramerican ethos that privileged individualism and progress, Sigourney's and Kirkland's viewpoint of elongated temporality underwrites their affective appeals for environmental responsibility.

Harriet Jacobs's *Incidents in the Life of a Slave Girl* reflects on enslaved persons' different—both highly metaphorical and intensely embodied—relationship to nature's resources. Ecocritics who focus on traditional nature writing necessarily elide the complex environmental experiences of writers of color. Less concerned with resource extraction and the stewardship of America's aesthetic and material legacy than Sigourney and Kirkland, Jacobs supplies essential balance as we contemplate such questions as property ownership and resource exploitation. Like their Native American counterparts, enslaved—and, as chapter 3 explores, free—African Americans were denied environmental agency. For enslaved persons, however, nature represented a potential refuge and means of self-affirmation *and* a place of dehumanization and danger. Jacobs negotiates this fraught territory with a delicate emotional intelligence that carefully calibrates affective overtures; she uses covert strategies that encompass indirection and reticence as well as overt engagement with readers. Offering personal evidence for her moving and ethical project and rejecting a focus only on nonhuman nature, Jacobs's narrative suggests that any understanding of the environment must include human resources.

Traveling, Writing, and the Environment

"Natural resources" encode more than tangible contributions to economic advancement; they also—then and now—incorporate romantic concepts of national identity and history. Lydia Sigourney begins her celebration of America's monumental trees, *Scenes in My Native Land*, by visiting Niagara Falls, a symbolic, contested site for both whites and Native Americans. During the early national period, Niagara Falls had become, as David Stradling acknowledges, "the leading tourist destination in North America"; by the 1830s, "a Niagara visit was almost requisite for the American middle class."[8] We should begin our tour of Sigourney, Kirkland, and Jacobs's work by pausing at this iconic location, then review some generic features of women-authored travel writing.

Even today's tourist propaganda indirectly grants Niagara Falls' status in historical resource conflicts. The official *Maid of the Mist* tour boat homepage opens with an encouragement: "Explore the Roar" (subtitled "Adventure Guide"). "Maid History" flags 1650, when "Niagara Falls [was] under control of [the] Seneca Nation of Native Americans." Within the next two decades, Europeans arrived and eventually dominated the area. In 1846, the *Maid in the Mist*, a "sidewheel steamboat ferry with twin smokestacks," took its maiden voyage.[9] The tour boat's name invokes a mythical Maid of the Mist: a young Indian woman who commits suicide because her family insists she marry an older man whom she does not love. Given the Haudenosaunees' matrilineality and marriage practices—and their women's empowerment—the story is almost certainly fiction, contributing to European imaginings featuring the Indian princess, the noble savage, and the Vanishing American.[10] Still a popular honeymoon destination, Niagara Falls symbolizes romantic love. In this context, progress signifies an expensive vacation and the civilized right to choose one's life partner and, indirectly, to shape a future home. Visitors—whether Sigourney's peers or our contemporaries—thus value Niagara as a psychological resource. The tour boat's name satisfyingly tames wilderness, but the vessel itself ironically embodies one of deforestation's principal causes: steamboats' voracious appetite for wood.

To Sigourney, such concrete reality appears less important than access to the sublime. As wilderness was transformed into farm and garden and old anxieties surrendered to romantic visions, poets such as William Cullen Bryant and Sigourney commemorated America's beauty.[11] A year before Emerson published *Nature* (1836), Sigourney expressed a transcendentalist admiration for Niagara's wonders:

> Every leaf
> That lifts itself within thy wide domain,
> Doth gather greenness from thy living spray,
> Yet tremble at the baptism.—Lo!—yon birds
> Do boldly venture near, and bathe their wing
> Amid thy mist and foam. 'Tis meet for them,
> To touch thy garment's hem, and lightly stir
> The snowy leaflets of thy vapour wreath,
> For they may sport unharmed amid the cloud,
> Or listen at the echoing gate of heaven,
> Without reproof. But as for us, it seems
> Scarce lawful, with our broken tones, to speak
> Familiarly of thee.—Methinks, to tint
> Thy glorious features with our pencil's point,
> Or woo thee to the tablet of a song
> Were profanation.[12]

Natural—ecological—systems interconnect; the leaves are sensitive to the falls' redemptive power and the birds rise closer to "heaven" than humans can safely approach. The "garment's hem," which evokes Christ's healing abilities, implies the reverence with which we should approach the divine falls.[13] Niagara's sublime power renders human speech at once sacrilegious and utterly inefficacious. Transforming the traditional Christian perspective that affirmed humans' domination over nature, substituting a Christian ecological ethos, Sigourney urges restraint and foregrounds humans' relative insignificance. With their spectacular "terror and beauty," the falls incarnate distant sublimity and symbolize a powerful natural home.

When "Niagara" appeared, Americans were engaging in intense national self-examination that included discussions about the importance of wilderness. We have seen how especially potent nationalist discourses surrounded ideas about the appropriate place in America for Native Americans.[14] Ecocritics could interpret "Niagara" as a poem that claims supremacy for the land's Christian conquerors; as Lawrence Buell observes, "American pastoral has simultaneously been counterinstitutional and institutionally sponsored."[15] But such a normative reading ignores the broader environmental vision that Sigourney's lifelong activism on behalf of Native Americans demonstrated.

Sigourney's poem may acknowledge, however obliquely, the falls' symbolic, if not literal, meaning for her Native American counterparts. Niagara was part of the Haudenosaunee homeland.[16] Although Jemison's narrative does not explicitly state how the Iroquois regarded Niagara, it (like Seaver's appendix) describes many nearby conflicts; major battles surrounded Fort Niagara, which she calls by its Seneca name, Fort Ne-a-gaw or Neagaw.[17] During the Seven Years' War, the powerful Seneca helped the British capture the fort from the French, but during the American Revolution this alliance proved disastrous, leading to General Sullivan's destructive campaign, which Jemison documents. Both a military outpost and a sacred site, Niagara Falls prompted conflict and elicited myth for the Seneca, who respected the falls' power.[18]

The chasm between Sigourney's and Jemison's presentations emerges from their ethnicity and their respective genres. Certain forms, such as Sigourney's romantic poetry, are more legible as nature writing (or environmental writing) than others.[19] But "Niagara" is also a form of travel literature. First published in *Zinzendorff* in 1835, the poem was composed in "an album kept at the Falls," according to one of the writer's contemporaries.[20] Moreover, Sigourney herself underlines poetry's contribution to the genre: she opens *Scenes in My Native Land* with another Niagara poem, which prefaced an entire chapter on the falls.[21] The paragraph following the poem recurs to a perennial theme: "Simple and significant . . . was [the falls'] Indian appellation, the 'water-thunderer.' To the wandering son of the forest . . . it forcibly suggested the image of that Great Spirit, who in darkness and storm sends forth from the skies a mighty voice." Connecting the spiritual and the literal, the next paragraph descends to a realistic report intended to ground the "casual visitant" so "transfixed by his emotions" that "he forgets he sees the surplus waters of these vast inland seas, Superior, Huron, Michigan, and Erie, arrested in their rushing passage to the Ocean, by a fearful barrier of rock, 160 feet in height" (7). Emotional intelligence, Sigourney insists, demands variegated responses to this complex environment, and these responses require different aesthetic forms.

Early travel writing has appeared relatively recently and briefly in ecocritical conversations. Matthew Wynn Sivils argues that William Bartram's *Travels* incorporates "the rhetoric of ecological communities," and Thomas Hallock contends that Bartram anticipates the American Adam myth, but neither study addresses genre per se.[22] Except for some late nineteenth- and early twentieth-century western and Alaska narratives and Margaret Fuller's *Summer on the Lakes*, ecocritics have neglected earlier women's travel writing.[23] Sigourney, Kirkland, and Jacobs construct environmental texts that explore—and deplore—resource depletion. Their work also reflects their specifically gendered travel experiences. Much travel literature parallels the normative nature-writing genre, the (usually male-authored) autobiographical essay, but women writers often transformed the travel genre by diminishing its self-assertiveness or diluting its focus.[24] For middle-class women—and, as chapter 3 discusses, for Lorenza Stevens Berbineau—travel represented, or was supposed to represent, an opportunity for self-betterment, which ostensibly rendered the traveler a more sophisticated wife and mother. While, as Mary Suzanne Schriber explains, many nineteenth-century American women describe travel abroad, a substantial number of narratives depict U.S.-based travel or, if we extend the genre, survey the American landscape.[25]

Embodiment and its consequences feature prominently in American women's travel literature. I take up the subject more fully in chapter 3 relative to working-class women, but here we should recall that the dominant society superimposed on *all* women disempowering associations with nature, though women of color endured an extreme version. As we have seen, some early Native American women, like Nancy Ward, rejected their white contemporaries' status, instead regarding women's corporeal place in the environment affirmatively.[26] Sigourney, Kirkland, and Jacobs's contributions illustrate that whether such meshing is liberatory or confining depends on an individual woman's time period, location, culture, status, and body. But travel—movement from home—posed particular challenges, even as it produced potential opportunities, such as freedom from demanding domestic labor.

Given the writers' early to mid-nineteenth-century contexts, travel's material circumstances mattered. Derived from the French *travail*, or work, all travel was arduous and uncomfortable. Although many men, such as Thoreau, initiated travel for personal development (as in *The Maine Woods*), many women were at best reluctant travelers, Margaret Fuller's example notwithstanding. This unwillingness may generate a more critical, less idealistic perspective than the travel genre characteristically exemplifies, engendering a similarly critical view of how men used nature to formulate concepts of home and national identity. At the same time, Susan Kollin's astringent observation merits our attention: "[F]eminists themselves are not exempt from obscuring women's agency and authority in nation-building projects." Nevertheless, as she submits, "[s]tudies of white women's travel writing . . . enable us to raise important questions about cultural authority and projects of conquest, and about gender and environmental rhetoric, that can steer us away from notions of female exceptionalism."[27] By juxtaposing white and African American women's travel writing—and later adding a working-class view—we can complicate how we understand earlier women's assessments of natural resources.

Those with leisure and financial means to travel, such as Lydia Sigourney, could more easily than their working counterparts appreciate nature's aesthetics and the sublime. They were thus more likely to seek readers' pleasure—and invest, however ambivalently, in nation-building projects—through a romantic-sentimental idiom. For the well-educated Caroline Kirkland, reluctantly following her husband west, travel sparked a sometimes humorous, sometimes acerbic idiom, as she contemplated her own and others' embodiment in rougher surroundings. In such instances, the natural sublime was much less available than it was to leisured metropolitans, not because nature was absent but because it was only too immediate. For Harriet Jacobs, travel meant danger and freedom, and although she occasionally voices aesthetic enjoyment, her journey is grounded in her body and more often, though not always, deadly serious. Ultimately, overt advocacy on nature's behalf, such as Sigourney (and, to a lesser degree, Kirkland) conveys, is a luxury when the stakes are survival.

"Warfare on the Trees": Felling the Sacred Groves

On 15 September 1897, over a half-century after Sigourney lauded America's monumental trees in *Scenes in My Native Land*, the *New York Times* published a revealing notice, headed "Big Tree Centennial." Merely twelve lines long, it acknowledges the Treaty of Big Tree at Geneseo, New York, "by which nearly 1,000,000 acres of land was deeded to Mr. Morris and afterward transferred to the Wadsworth family." The occasion "was celebrated . . . by the historical societies of Western New York." In a telling detail, although "several of the Seneca chiefs and their wives were present . . . [they] took no prominent part in the ceremonies."[28] The announcement does not reveal whether the festivities occurred indoors or outside, under a tree.

Iroquois society and history feature many sacred and symbolic trees, as the Sky Woman story exemplifies; and even before colonial times peace trees figured significantly. Dekanawida planted the Tree of Great Peace, also known as the Tree of the Great Long Leaves, at the Haudenosaunee Confederacy's founding.[29] For Jemison and her Seneca community, the woods had practical as well as symbolic consequence; she repeatedly mentions them as a place of refuge and source of food.[30] Jemison's account also indicates that trees resonated differently for the Seneca than for European settlers. As the environmental historian David Stradling points out, "Since native belief systems required a deep respect for other living things, ecologically destructive behavior was limited. Just as important, since native cultures did not place special value on the accumulation of wealth, in the form of either land or objects, prior to European contact indigenous peoples had no cultural incentive to exploit natural resources beyond ensuring their own survival."[31]

America's green lands held mineral wealth—like Cherokee gold—as well as another resource worth fighting over: wood. From white settlers' perspective, as Lisa Brooks (Abenaki) reminds us, "[c]learing the land of its trees was deemed necessary not only for the products that land might provide, but for the progress of 'civilization.' Forested land was unused space in need of improvement."[32] Though settlers frequently clashed with Indians, inter-Anglo conflicts over tall gold erupted from the earliest colonial days, when the King's Mark was engraved on the largest eastern white pine trees, which were reserved by the crown, particularly for ship masts. The 1691 Massachusetts Bay Charter cites some specifications: "For better providing and furnishing of Masts for our Royal Navy wee do hereby reserve to us Our Heires and Successors ALL trees of the diameter of 24 inches and upward of 12 inches from the ground, growing upon any soils or tracts of land within our said Province or Territory not heretofore granted to any private persons." Felling such trees without a license meant a potential fine of £100 per tree—equivalent to more than $20,000 today.[33]

The environmental historian Carolyn Merchant notes that among the items traded during early European settlement, perhaps "the most important forest product was the white pine used in the mast trade."[34] These trees extended "from Maine to Minnesota . . . [in] a vast coniferous forest."[35] Ostensibly "limitless," the forest represented "a means of survival," "a deliverer from the privations of Europe and a liberator of attitudes [regarding land and resources] as well."[36] Commercial ships were not the trees' only destination; warships were central, as the leading European nations each sought naval supremacy.[37] Historicizing today's international resource wars over timber, Philippe Le Billon observes, "Since sea power . . . rested on access to timber, naval timber supply became a major preoccupation for major European powers from the seventeenth century onwards."[38]

Early New Englanders realized the forests' economic importance—the Puritans prohibited "indiscreet fyring of the woods"—and they depended on the trees for both personal comfort and income.[39] As early as 1656, indiscriminate cutting in the seacoast region of present-day Maine and New Hampshire necessitated regulations limiting individuals' consumption.[40] Enormous contributions of manpower were required to cut and process masts and other wood product; "by 1700, along the New Hampshire and Maine coasts, there were ninety sawmills and thirty teams of oxen" as well as cutters, barkers, swampers, drivers, raftsmen, scalers, and sawyers.[41] By this time, the New England ecology had already been irretrievably altered, with climate changes, species depletion, and soil erosion.[42] The human community had also transformed, increasingly divided between laborers and capital ownership, not only in their respective wealth but also in the conceptual division between those who performed punishing manual labor and those who did not—often corresponding to rural and urban dwellers. This distinction remains today, proving a barrier to environmental understanding.

IN 1844, the indefatigable Lydia Sigourney published *Scenes in My Native Land*. Surveying her native Hartford, Connecticut, and the United States more broadly, the author ruminates on spiritual life and national identity in culturally resonant material contexts. The volume followed Sigourney's popular *Pleasant Memories of Pleasant Lands* (1842), which details her travels in England and France. She concludes the earlier volume insisting that "[t]ravelling should incite to a warmer and more enduring patriotism," and *Scenes in My Native Land* takes that advice, extolling America's beauties.[43] The circumstances of the two volumes' composition are unknown, but we can reasonably speculate that after the anti-removal struggle ended—and she had published *Pocahontas, and Other Poems* (1841)—Sigourney needed a physical and psychological break.

Scenes in My Native Land seems determined to recapture her earlier idealism about a nation that she regarded as increasingly corrupted by materialism and arrogance; although the volume addresses some continuing problems—she describes the American Asylum for the Deaf and Dumb near Hartford—its overall mood is celebratory and optimistic, perhaps determinedly so. *Scenes in My Native Land* contributed to a vibrant American literary scene. Despite national conflicts over slavery and continued Indian wars (with the Seminoles), Sigourney's literary contemporaries were imagining the American experiment hopefully.[44] Though sometimes ambivalently, *Scenes in My Native Land*'s narrative participated in nation-building projects, envisioning America as home.[45] Through this travel text—which is not unproblematic in how it treats Native Americans—the author elaborated an ethos of environmental conservation based in a transgenerational perspective, and she sought to enlist her readers' assistance.[46]

Scenes in My Native Land contributed to an emerging cultural tradition: "the American Grand Tour." As Stradling notes, "Tourism and literature worked hand in hand to change the way Americans thought about their nation's landscape."[47] As commercial activity increased, Sigourney's remarkable book attempts to preserve, in print if not literal form, her homeland's natural wonders while it ambivalently lauds American progress and, however tentatively, tries to conceptualize that progress more authentically. The volume's most astonishing chapter, "Fallen Forests," opens with a poem that requires full quotation:

Fallen Forests.

Man's warfare on the trees is terrible.
He lifts his rude hut in the wilderness,
And lo! the loftiest trunks, that age on age
Were nurtured to nobility, and bore
Their summer coronets so gloriously,
Fall with a thunder-sound, to rise no more.
He toucheth flame unto them, and they lie
A blackened wreck, their tracery and wealth
Of sky-fed emerald, madly spent to feed
An arch of brilliance for a single night,
And scaring thence the wild deer and the fox,
And the lithe squirrel from the nut-strewn home,
So long enjoyed.
               He lifts his puny arm,
And every echo of the axe doth hew
The iron heart of centuries away.
He entereth boldly to the solemn groves
On whose green altar-tops, since time was young,
The winged birds have poured their incense strain
Of praise and love, within whose mighty nave
The wearied cattle from a thousand hills
Have found their shelter 'mid the heat of day;
Perchance, in their mute worship pleasing Him
Who careth for the meanest He hath made.
I said he entereth to the sacred groves
Where Nature in her beauty bends to God,
And lo! their temple-arch is desecrate;
Sinks the sweet hymn, the ancient ritual fades,
And uptorn roots, and prostrate columns mark
The invader's footsteps.

> Silent years roll on,
> His babes are men. His ant-heap dwelling grows
> Too narrow, for his hand hath gotten wealth.
> He builds a stately mansion, but it stands
> Unblessed by trees. He smote them recklessly,
> When their green arms were round him, as a guard
> Of tutelary deities, and feels
> Their maledictions, now the burning noon
> Maketh his spirit faint. With anxious care
> He casteth acorns in the earth, and woos
> Sunbeam and rain; he planteth the young shoot,
> And props it from the storm, but neither he,
> Nor yet his children's children, shall behold
> What he hath swept away.
>   Methinks 't were well,
> Not as a spoiler or a thief, to roam
> O'er Nature's bosom, that sweet, gentle nurse
> Who loveth us, and spreads a sheltering couch
> When our brief task is o'er. On that green mound
> Affection's hand may set the willow-tree,
> Or train the cypress, and let none profane
> Her pious care.
>   Oh Father! grant us grace
> In all life's toils, so, with a steadfast hand
> Evil and good to poise, as not to mark
> Our way with wrecks, nor when the sands of time
> Run low, with saddened eye the past survey,
> And mourn the rashness time can ne'er restore.[48]

Countering the elegiac apostrophe in William Cullen Bryant's "Among the Trees"—a paean to male-authored progress—"Fallen Forests" also contrasts with the distinguished travel writer Timothy Dwight's celebration of domestic improvements. Americans, he enthuses, have translated forests into "fruitful fields, covered with houses, schools, and churches, and filled with inhabitants, possessing not only the necessaries and comforts, but also the conveniences of life, and devoted to the worship of JEHOVAH."[49] Unlike Dwight, Sigourney disparages civilization's advance. Comparing humans' "rude huts" with nature's grandeur ("loftiest trunks," "sky-fed emerald"), she bluntly exposes humans' oblivious violence: they thoughtlessly hack down the forest "nobility," burning them into "blackened wreck[s]" and frightening the animals that depend on the tree for livelihood and shelter. Ironically, man's "puny arm" equipped with an "axe" can easily "hew / The iron heart of centuries away." Sigourney's emotionally intelligent, romantic rhetoric seeks readers' sympathy, anger, and humility, as the poet laments the loss of the ancient, heroic tree and its essential ecosystem.

Inserting a hybrid of pastoral and jeremiad into traditional travel writing, Sigourney's observations are more than mere hyperbole. English settlers brought their long, straight-handled axes to America, but these tools proved limited against the dense, old-growth forest.[50] Americans developed a more appropriate technology, with a curved, more balanced product that matched the user's height. The historian Brooke Hindle points out that "[t]rials demonstrated that an American with his axe could fell three times as many trees in a given time as someone with a European axe."[51] Axe manufacture also advanced rapidly, with makers such as Elisha K. Root of Connecticut's Collins & Co. developing technologies that enhanced production—and, Sigourney might add, destruction.[52] According to the National Resources Defense Council, *clear-cutting* denotes "the felling and removal of all trees from a given tract of forest," and it "can destroy an area's ecological integrity."[53] Although the motive today might be more directly economic than in the early nineteenth century, when westering settlers cleared forest land to build homes and develop fields and pastures, the environmental consequences were commensurate. Paralleling Horace Greeley's admonitions to Americans from Europe, Sigourney's poem reflects the terrible impact that these "advancements" registered on the country's forests.

As Sigourney envisions future generations of axemen, she contemplates the mid-nineteenth-century's rage for progress and questions its definition.[54] Her axeman defines it concretely; he moves from an "ant-heap dwelling" to "a stately mansion." The poet believes such wealth is barren: instead of providing a motherly support, "green arms . . . round him," the trees cast "maledictions," so that "now the burning noon maketh his spirit faint." Anyone today who has watched a forest being bulldozed flat for a housing development and then entered one of the new houses, especially in the South, can appreciate the blasting heat that such landscapes magnify. Although our woodsman plants trees and tends "the young shoot," trees' life spans far exceed humans', and a day's damage cannot be remedied even in two generations. The author insists that we think long term, so that regret does not force us to "with saddened eye the past survey, / And mourn the rashness time can ne'er restore."

In this vanishing pastoral scene, several rhetorical strategies stand out. First, rendering humans in miniature terms and trees in monumental ones augments the devastation. The trees "[f]all with a thunder-sound, to rise no more"; creating a "blackened wreck" out of "nobility" with "glorious" "summer coronets," the axeman destroys "their tracery and wealth / Of sky-fed emerald" to create "an arch of brilliance," a fire lasting merely "a single night." Such images may seem overwrought today, but to her contemporaries Sigourney's mode would have signified awe. Sublimity couples with sentimentality; the trees' obliteration means homeless squirrels, exposed cattle, and the woodsman's impoverished children, who will suffer physically and psychically for their father's sins. In this vision, foresters level the national home. Recalling Ward's earlier assertion about continued Cherokee land cessions, "Fallen Forests" suggests that felling ancient trees is akin to matricide and, ultimately, suicide.

The poem's most audacious rhetoric likens the trees' felling to a religious desecration, as the forester, who should reverently encounter such "solemn groves" with their "green altar-tops" instead "entereth boldly" where even cattle know better. Humans "desecrate" "the sacred groves / Where Nature in her beauty bends to God." Sigourney's contemporaries would not have missed the reference to Psalms 49, which illustrates the folly of valuing worldly riches. The title ironically references not just the trees' but their destroyers' spiritual state, and the poem ends with an explicit prayer. Sigourney regards nature as sacred, a divine blessing, and she assumes the posture of stewardship, rather than consumption, that today's followers of Christian ecology would endorse.[55] Her battle extends beyond resource protection; she interrogates readers' interpretation of the Bible and asks them what it means to be a good Christian—and good American citizen.[56]

The "Fallen Forests" chapter proper ponders the nation's trees, as Sigourney invites us to share her travels, beginning with "the more recently settled regions of New York" and continuing to "the far Western States," in the process "bemoaning the recklessness with which the ancient glory of the forest is sacrificed." Although she accepts that some trees must be felled to build homes and establish gardens, she criticizes the human

shortsightedness that demonstrates humans' own "fallen" natures. Attempting to evoke audience members' emotional intelligence, she compares
the devastation that clear-cutting causes to war's ruin: "Hills and vales are
seen covered with stately and immense trunks, blackened with flame, and
smitten down in every form and variety of misery. They lie like soldiers,
when the battle is done, in the waters, among the ashes, wounded, be-
headed, denuded of their limbs, their exhumed roots . . . glaring on the
astonished eye. . . . Cromwell advanced not more surely from Naseby to
the throne, than the axe-armed settler to the destruction of the kingly
trees of Heaven's anointing" (119). This scene seems particularly violent because the anthropomorphized trees are not merely cut down, they are also
tortured and dismembered. The axemen blasphemously battle God rather
than nature.[57] Thus, the author contends, "[i]t seems almost a wickedness,
wantonly to smite down a vigorous, healthful tree. It was of God's planting:
in its veins are circulating the life which He has given. Its green and mighty
arch is full of his beauty and power" (120).[58]

Sigourney also reemphasizes trees' longevity: they have individual histories, but they also stand as witnesses to history: "War may have swept
away armies, revolution overturned thrones, time engulphed whole races
of men, but there it stood, unmoved, unfaded, a chronicler of history, a
benefactor to the traveler, a monument of the goodness of the Almighty"
(113). Again, such language may seem overheated and archaic, and it is.
In fact, we may have a sense of being preached at, if not by a minister, at
least by a chastising mother; Sigourney's feeling rhetoric stresses belief and
conveys certainty.[59] From her viewpoint, not so far removed from Ward's
ethos, trees represent far more than economic or material resources: they
also embody aesthetic, spiritual, and historical resources.

Yet Sigourney's stance toward progress assumes an uneven trajectory.
Scenes in My Native Land as a whole acknowledges American accomplishments while it deplores the environmental and cultural damage that inevitably accompanies them. After the opening section of "Fallen Forests" that
preaches restraint and reverence for the trees, Sigourney takes a different
strategy as she portrays her travels across New York by railroad and boat.
She compares "the too entire extinction of some of the lovely works of creation" to "the rapid growth and prosperity of the works of man, in some of
the new sections of our country" (122); she depicts Indians in Buffalo and

the prison in Auburn (122–24, 124–26). The chapter intermittently approves and critiques development. Ironically, the passages that follow the opening requiem for the trees undercut Sigourney's effort at natural preservation; for example, Buffalo has "all the marks of an enterprising, commercial city" (122).

Counterpointing this depiction, the author admires the numerous Seneca and Tuscarora Indians who people the city streets. She appears to tell a declensionist tale in which "the Chief of the Senecas" "expressed a cunning and adroitness, the fruit of intercourse with the whites, rather than that Roman dignity and taciturnity, which of old marked the rulers of the forest, or that tendency to sarcastic eloquence, which distinguished his immediate predecessor." But this perspective elevates rather than degrades, like the succeeding anecdote in which Indian women sell beadwork at a train station. When one passenger, presumably a white woman, inquires of one mother "what sum would be demanded for [her] child," the mother snatches her baby to safety (123–24). Although Sigourney does not explicitly remark on this encounter, the white woman's savage behavior and the Indian mother's civilized response communicate the author's skepticism about American progress.

"FALLEN FORESTS" is not the first—or last—chapter devoted to trees. Several that focus on personified individuals honor the trees' age and contributions to American history. "The Charter-Oak at Hartford," dedicated to a prominent resident of Sigourney's home community, bespeaks the need to balance pride in human achievements and a humble, multigenerational standpoint that contemporary environmental writing also prioritizes.[60] "The Great Oak of Geneseo" opens with a poem; the eponymous tree addresses the Charter-Oak.[61] The ancient speaker celebrates its counterpart's contributions to the nation's founding, as Sigourney foregrounds the connection between humans and nonhuman nature.

Peering into the past, the Geneseo tree remembers pre–white settlement days, when "[s]tern, lofty chiefs the various clans controlled" (83). Ironically, the Great Oak is the individual that the 1787 Treaty of Big Tree—relinquishing Haudenosaunee lands—describes. Informed by a Christian (and romantic) outlook, Sigourney's vision reinforces stereotypes of the

Vanishing American and conjures a sensational past, simultaneously erasing the clan mothers' influence on Seneca society. Unlike this American
prehistory is the "change" that "a pale-browed race have wrought" (83):

> They came, new blossoms sprang, new fountains flowed,
> . . . .
> Fair herds and flocks o'er velvet meadows stray,
> Where erst the wolf and panther prowled for prey,
> While broad canals unite with giant chain
> The wondering inland to the mighty main. (83–84)

In this vision, whites civilize land, cultivating and transforming it through
massive technological projects such as the so-called Eighth Wonder of the
World, the Erie Canal. Pastoral succumbs to scientific advancement.[62]
Chapter two's first epigraph reveals Nathaniel Hawthorne's response to
this marvel as he strolled the canal's banks. Such transformations meant
the Indians' loss of power, and the writer points to an unnamed chief who,

> While speechless anguish heaved his ample breast,
> Gazed till deep midnight veiled his favorite shore,
> Then westward journeyed, to return no more. (84)

The poem apparently laments the disappearance of an earlier American
home rather than elegizing Native Americans' appropriated homelands.

Why, given the poet's firsthand knowledge—and her admiring description of actual Indians in "Fallen Forests"—does she mythologize Indian
absence? There was some truth to the declensionist claim, for as Stradling
notes, "by the early 1790s . . . indigenous people constituted a small frac-
tion of the state's [New York] population. Altogether the Iroquois tribes
had declined to just 3,500 people in 1794."[63] But Sigourney may have been
mourning disappearing "Indianness" rather than Native Americans' actual
absence and, through that disappearance, also mourning a lost American
past, though without the accusation that poems such as "Indian Names"
and "The Cherokee Mother" propound. Deeply conflicted here, on the
one hand she affirms all humans' powerlessness and eventual death; on
the other, she continues a nation-building project that corresponded with
eastern woodlands destruction: by the time the Erie Canal opened in 1825,
"New Yorkers had cleared more than 7 million acres of forest."[64]

Sigourney resumes in prose, recounting the Wadsworth brothers' settlement of the Geneseo (now Genesee) region, their foresight, and their benevolence, including their "establishment of schools," before returning to the "Great Western Tree, so celebrated for its antiquity and magnificence."[65] Awesomely large, with "massy foliage," it has "a trunk seventy feet in height, ere the profusion of the branches, and thirty in circumference, so that seven persons are scarcely able to clasp it, with arms extended to their utmost length" (87). The tree possesses a presence that exceeds human scale, and to make it comprehensible, Sigourney situates it imaginatively in a "park" setting along the riverbank and among other trees. So significant and durable that "in the old Maps of New York, the surrounding region bears the appellation of *'Big Tree,'* . . . it housed an Indian chieftain of the same name" and his tribe, who held councils, enjoyed athletic activities, and worshipped beneath its canopy (87). Comparing it with a much smaller tree, which when cut down "revealed three hundred annual circles," Sigourney proposes a mythical age—"This majestic Oak is supposed to have attained the age of at least 1000 and possibly 1500 years"—and observes, "The neighboring aborigines were accustomed of old to regard it with veneration, as a sort of intelligent or tutelary being" (87, 88). Consciously or not, the author echoes Native Americans' ethos of respect for an animate natural world. She also uses the travel writing convention of visiting landmarks to advance an environmental ethos, herself regarding the tree as a historic, superhuman presence that should generate emotions of delight, awe, and reverence.[66]

The chapter closes with an encounter between James Wadsworth and an Indian chief, whose small tribe "had made such progress in civilization, as to be able to speak a little English, to read imperfectly, and to sing psalms very well" (88); the tribe met regularly for worship beneath the tree's canopy. The chief mourns what he portrays as his people's inevitable disappearance. Sigourney's conclusion intimates the eradication not just of the Indians but also of the trees and, perhaps, nature itself. In recounting the Great Oak's history and the Native people affiliated with it, she attempts to conserve America's history, which comprises losses as well as gains. Ironically, she elides the names of the chief and his tribe, in effect advancing their disappearance, while she immortalizes the tree itself. The Great Oak achieves the status of a silent, helpful statesman or Biblical elder, since it oversees so many occasions central to two peoples' political and religious history. At the same time, the writer's romantic focus on a single tree merits contextualization: "In the early 1800s, as surveyors measured the former Seneca territory in western New York, they found few areas that were obviously Native American clearings—less than 1 percent of the region. . . . [O]bservers determined that altogether the Iroquois had lived in a world dominated by forests."[67] Within this context, Sigourney's magnificent oak commemorates and suggests the costs of American progress to the natural and human environment.

Later chapters revisit important trees. David Watters's remark about "the cultural practice of making trees icons of Revolutionary War history" mentions the figure in *Scenes in My Native Land*'s penultimate chapter, "The Washington Elm" (subtitled "at Cambridge, Massachusetts").[68] Legend holds that General Washington first convened the Continental Army beneath its branches; the Cambridge Historical Society's website features a monument marking the tree's location and numerous associated artifacts—mugs, decorative plates, and a chunk of the tree itself.[69] The introductory poem apostrophizes the tree, and it becomes first the poet's muse and then her avatar. By communicating through and with this incarnation of ancient wisdom, Sigourney professes power and knowledge that many of her white female contemporaries would be loath to assert, as she moves beyond Republican Motherhood and speaks as a masculine sage and precursor.

Sigourney's successive prose account envisions how Washington "first drew his sword" beneath the tree. Witnessing the Revolution's historic events, it "has a heritage of glory," even superseding the status of Washington, whom it has outlived (314). By picturing the tree as already an elder when the Revolution occurred, Sigourney elongates the young republic's history. The remainder of the brief chapter applauds "the most ancient University in the United States" and appreciates "the efforts made by our ancestors, to secure the means of education for their descendants, while themselves enduring the hardships and privations attendant on colonial life." Education, she affirms, forms the nation's cornerstone and the greatest insurance for its longevity. The elm whose "foliage almost sweeps the walls" of that unnamed university (Harvard) unites American history, as the chapter promulgates a proud nationalism (315).[70] Participating in broader observances, Sigourney's chapter represents another monument: the poet's audacious contention that she embodies and voices American history. Her feminine ethos of community transforms a natural monument into a national one.

Scenes in My Native Land lauds ancient trees, but it also underlines attractions not usually on tourists' itineraries. As John F. Sears points out, Sigourney visits prisons and asylums, reflecting a new spirit of reform. Moreover, as he adds, "religious apprehension [of scenes such as Niagara Falls] and souvenir shopping were [not] incompatible."[71] *Scenes in My Native Land* describes a vacation of sorts, but it adheres much more closely to conventional travel writing than *Summer on the Lakes*, for it includes geographical, historical, and topographical details as well as individual experiences. Unlike many women travel writers, Sigourney does not diminish her self-assertiveness, instead claiming maternal wisdom. In the concluding chapter, she articulates her ambition: "You will not, I hope, count it a deception, that while its title announces a description of *scenes*, its page so often presents those who have peopled them. I felt that a landscape was improved by figures" (319). Thus she humanizes the landscape in ways familiar to her contemporaries; she registers a traditional view of natural history and invokes painterly picturesqueness as well as sublime images of nature untouched by humans. In his "Essay on American Scenery" (1835) the painter Thomas Cole had bemoaned "the destruction of America's abundant and virgin forests," not because of the trees' historical witness but because of their value to art and the aesthetic.[72] Sigourney shares this aesthetic vision, and as a faithful Christian she repeatedly affiliates the nation's magnificent trees with religious sentiment.[73] But she enlarges nature's role in American history, urging recognition that with the devastation of trees, especially the most ancient forest "citizens," America was losing a critical part of its heritage.[74]

Through its rhetoric and genre hybridity, *Scenes in My Native Land* offers readers—then and now—opportunities for varied responses to the environment and specifically to humans' relations with nonhuman nature: awe, horror, admiration, shame, comfort, humility, and respect. Her book encompasses poetry, with which each chapter begins, and narrative prose. But the prose itself incorporates many modes, ranging among natural history, social analysis, sermonistic appeals, and eulogy.[75] In this heterogeneous text Sigourney activates her emotional intelligence to ignite our own. Because she uses several points of view and various forms, she can implement multiple affective strategies (and hence influence more and different people than a single genre would permit).

With its gratitude for the nation's historic trees, *Scenes in My Native*

Land contributes—we must add some caveats—to an American environmental writing tradition. Looking back, we can see that Sigourney anticipated problems such as what we now call clear-cutting (though she did not use that term) and resource depletion. She understands that resources are historical, spiritual, and psychological as well as material. Although her volume articulates a conservative (and conservationist) rather than radical position, she provides a strong antecedent for contemporary Christian ecology. Though frequently in romanticized terms, Sigourney imagines the workings of ecosystems, and she articulates the continuities between human and nonhuman nature. As significantly, she foregrounds a transgenerational standpoint, stretching time well beyond individual human life spans.

On the other hand, Sigourney sometimes hails technological innovation predicated on Native Americans' putative disappearance. *Scenes in My Native Land* typically discusses indigenous peoples in conventional, stereotypical terms, such as *savage*, and it overwrites Native history with the colonizers'.[76] Despite her explicit links between trees and white heroes, however, we could argue that her monumental forest dwellers are figurative reminders of Native American ethnocide and, hence, that Sigourney encodes a criticism of American nation building at indigenous peoples' expense. Perhaps she wrote the book partly to salve her conscience or to compensate for the losses she felt, both as an individual and a citizen, owing to removal. Unquestionably, her colonial history endeavors to honor her patron's family and thus necessitates a skewed treatment of indigenous history. Whatever its compositional rationale, the volume expresses ambivalence about the costs of progress, and the writer struggles to articulate a consistent environmental ethos. *Scenes in My Native Land* exemplifies the mixed character, in form and intention, of earlier American environmental literature. Despite its imperfections from a twenty-first-century perspective, it elaborates passionate, serious, and sometimes forward-thinking representations of Americans' relationships with the environment.

SCENES IN MY NATIVE LAND was warmly reviewed in the United States and abroad, but only Margaret Fuller observed the author's critical response to "the love of ravage which distinguishes the American settler and which makes the marks of his first passage over this land, like those of corrosive acid upon the cheek of beauty."[77] Based at least partially in the belief of virtually limitless abundance, this ravage was partly public policy.[78] Prohibitions against felling, first by the English Crown and then by colonialists themselves, were gradually superseded. In 1786, the Massachusetts Legislature abandoned its long-standing policy of protecting the White Pine and, to divest itself of public lands, formulated a lottery system that eventually distributed three million acres to private owners.[79] New saw technologies hastened the demise of New England's old-growth forests.[80] Although Maine continued to supply important timber resources in the early nineteenth century, the industry began moving west; "by 1840, upstate New York and Pennsylvania had supplanted northern New England as the largest producers of lumber."[81]

Another technology dovetailed with the forestry industry to accelerate woodland destruction: the steamboat. After years of experimentation by inventors Robert Fulton and Robert (Chancellor) Livingston, the first commercial steamship carried passengers between New York City and Albany in 1807. Fulton's biographer, Cynthia Owen Philip, estimates that by 1814, "his steamboats alone burned 17,000 loads of wood annually."[82] The steamboat engine's inefficiency, as well as "the relatively low cost of wood, and the pioneer habit of making prodigal use of seemingly unlimited timber resources all contributed to the high consumption of fuel."[83] One source estimates that smaller vessels daily consumed between twelve and twenty-four cords, while larger ships at midcentury devoured between fifty and seventy-five cords.[84] Andrew Eisenberg has demonstrated that "consumption of firewood by steamboats was probably the primary cause of riparian deforestation in the United States in the first half of the nineteenth century."[85] The country's tall gold, its "standing people" in Marilou Awiakta's phrasing, could not withstand such advances.

In *Scenes in My Native Land*, Sigourney highlights both the beautiful pastoral landscape and the commercial progress that characterized early nineteenth-century America; the more concrete and quotidian sketches that follow each chapter's long framing poem reflect her ambivalence. She casually notes the infrastructure at Buffalo enabling "the regular steam-navigation of the lakes" as well as the use of steam for Pennsylvania coal mining (122, 220–21). Her fullest account of steam engines, however, is "The First Steamboat," which appeared in the *Atlantic Souvenir* in 1832. The poem delineates the invention's "monster" menace, as it travels the Hudson

River "with a hissing sound like a serpent sprite," leaving a "demon-wake."[86] To "the gazing Indian's thought" "She seem'd like the prophet bird of death" (lines 42, 41). Although the poet seems to praise Robert Fulton's invention, Sigourney remains profoundly conflicted, as the closing stanzas—which deliberately confuse Fulton with God—underscore:[87]

> But where is the mighty hand that taught
> This wingless bird to fly?
> Say, where is the breast whose inventive thought
> This mine of wealth for the world hath wrought?
> Land of his birth, reply.
>
> He hath fallen, The lofty tree is dead:
> But it hath a living stem;
> O'er its roots young saplings their verdure spread,
> And the golden fruits which on us it shed,
> We may render it back to them. (lines 46–60)

Paula Bennett argues that, "as in other poems Sigourney wrote on environmental concerns, [she] enlists pastoral nostalgia's sentimental conventions to lament changes in the nation's economic and social structure that she believed were undermining its agrarian foundations." The vital last metaphor connects the tree with Fulton/God himself. Conjuring the notion of a "family tree," Sigourney conveys caustically this technological enterprise's self-consuming nature: steamboats require vast quantities of wood fuel, and hence in "render[ing]" "the golden fruits" "back to them," they perform a violent self-erasure. As Bennett remarks, the poem's rhetoric self-consciously combats its own sentimentalism, concluding with bitter, visionary irony that rebuts Emersonian optimism about technological advancement.

One word—*render*—is particularly trenchant, simultaneously conveying "to perform or depict," "to present or bestow," "to melt down or extract," "to deliver a verdict," and "to relinquish or surrender." Its references may include Matthew 22:21: "Render therefore unto Caesar the things which are Caesar's; and unto God the things that are God's."[88] The poet suggests the invention's blasphemous quality and intimates that only divinity *should* possess this fearsome creative-destructive power. Moreover, the reference questions the economics of creation, for Christ's statement responds to a Roman tax collector; hence Sigourney critiques not just progress but the self-consuming profit ("golden fruits") from the invention. Her bitterness and her irony reemerge full-fledged thirteen years later in "Fallen Forests" and *Scenes in My Native Land* more generally, as she surveys America's changing environment. A successful, self-made woman, the writer could focus on travel's pleasures; as a strong Christian, she could assume an assertive posture that sought her readers' and her country's self-betterment, not simply—as was women travelers' purported goal—her own. Finally, Sigourney praises progress, celebrates America's inventiveness, and enjoys technology's benefits, but she keeps her eyes wide open to the costs, for both humans and the natural environment.[89]

"The total extirpation of the forest": Tall Gold in the West

The warfare on the trees had already moved from east to west by the time Sigourney published *Scenes in My Native Land*, as Margaret Fuller's stern reflection in *Summer on the Lakes* reveals: "I come to the west prepared for the distaste I must experience at its mushroom growth. . . . The march of peaceful is scarce less wanton than that of warlike invasion. The old landmarks are broken down, and the land, for a season, bears none, except of the rudeness of conquest and the needs of the day, whose bivouac fires blacken the sweetest forest glades."[90] Andrew Jackson's 1830 inaugural speech presaged the annihilation of midwestern forests: "[W]hat good man would prefer a country covered with forests and ranged by a few thousand wild savages to our extensive Republic studded with cities, towns, and prosperous farms, embellished with all the improvements which art can devise or industry execute?"[91] David Stairs comments that although "logging of Michigan's pineries did not begin for another decade [after Alexis de Tocqueville's 1831 visit] . . . once commenced, the combination of fire and axe reduced them in a brief 50 years."[92]

As we have seen, technology accelerated the clear-cutting of America's old-growth forests. Better saws led in 1833 to labor-saving balloon frame building techniques—far superior to earlier mortise and tenon construction—still common today.[93] To encourage settlement of the Michigan territory, the federal government began to offer land for $1.25 per acre. This action hastened settlers' movement west and old-growth forests' decline in the 1830s, as lumber graders staked enormous claims for timber speculators.[94]

Grand Rapids, Michigan, log drive, late nineteenth century.
From the Samuel Trask Dana Collection, Courtesy of the
Bentley Historical Library, University of Michigan.

Michigan was granted statehood in 1837, and speculation fever gained momentum until Michigan's pine forests were depleted and logging firms again moved west.[95] David Stairs comments that an estimated "160 billion board feet of timber was harvested from Michigan's pine forests, enough to either construct 10 million six-room houses or fuel the hubris of empire."[96] Put somewhat differently, tall gold powered America's progress.

One witness to Michigan's mushroom growth was an important early writer whose work combines the autobiographical essay, the travel narrative, and the sketch. Caroline Stansbury Kirkland's innovative *A New Home, Who'll Follow?; or, Glimpses of Western Life* (1839) satirizes "a range of habits, conventions, and states of mind" in both east and west.[97] The title indicates the author's dual emphasis on the individual and national home, and her account of moving to the western frontier provocatively juxtaposes nature and culture. Her opening chapter, for example, measures the dimensions of a Michigan "mud-hole":

In the "settlements," a mud-hole is considered as apt to occasion an unpleasant jolt—a breaking of the thread of one's reverie—or in extreme cases, a temporary stand-still or even an overturn of the rash or unwary. Here, on approaching one of these characteristic features of the "West"—(How much does that expression mean to include? I never have been able to discover its limits)—the driver stops—alights—walks up to the dark gulf—and around it if he can get round it. He then seeks a long pole and sounds it, measures it across to ascertain how its width compares with the length of his wagon—tries whether its sides are perpendicular, as is usually the case if the road is much used. If he finds it is not more than three feet deep, he remounts cheerily, encourages his team, and in they go, with a plunge and a shock rather apt to damp the courage of the inexperienced.[98]

With its concreteness counteracting what Lawrence Buell has termed "the aesthetics of the not-there," Kirkland's description delivers readers from metaphor as she deconstructs the boundaries between "settlement" and "frontier" and "east" and "west."[99] Moreover, using stylistic stops and starts—figured by generous dashes—Kirkland performs a bodily encounter with an apparently boundless nature.

Rather than being awed, Kirkland adopts a posture of humorous inquiry, in the process, as Sandra Zagarell explains, dismantling "Romantic clichés and tropes" and "an eastern-based vision of the West as unspoiled 'nature,'" while establishing "the existence of an indigenous western culture."[100] Kirkland's humor frequently contests artificial divisions between humans and nature and questions American society's idealization of nature.[101] Like Sigourney, Kirkland apprehended the transgenerational consequences of "development"; unlike Sigourney, she assumes a characteristically ironic stance, though that irony ranges between sly and overt. While she, too, appreciated nature's and the environment's symbolic resonances, Kirkland was more concerned than her contemporary with the material than with the sublime. Thus in *Forest Life* she uses embodied rhetoric to promote embodied reading and hence more self-aware, ethical behavior.

THE ELDEST OF eleven children, Kirkland was born in New York City in 1801. Her affluent, educated parents fostered an intellectual home environment and challenged their talented daughter in a time when women seldom enjoyed educational opportunities. Attending her paternal aunt's Quaker school beginning at age eight, Kirkland encountered reform sentiments outside as well as inside her home. After completing her education, Kirkland became a teacher, marrying Hamilton College classics instructor William Kirkland, who would take her, with their children (who finally totaled seven), to the west. They founded a girls' school in Geneva, New York, before moving to head the Detroit Female Seminary in 1835. The couple became part of the Michigan land boom a few years later, eventually buying nearly thirteen hundred acres and founding the town of Pinckney sixty miles west of Detroit. As Caroline Gebhard reminds us, the Kirklands' purchase followed considerable resistance from the Ottawas and other Indians who ultimately ceded land to the U.S. government.[102] In 1839, Kirkland published a fictionalized version of her village life in *A New Home*. Although today's critics often categorize it as a novel, *A New Home* would reside comfortably today among Barnes and Noble's creative nonfiction titles.[103] With caustic humor, irony, and affection, Kirkland unsettled easterners' romantic notions of western frontier life, angering her Michigan neighbors. Perhaps partly because of this reaction, Kirkland shifted her direction in *Forest Life* (1842) and *Western Clearings* (1845) to the land itself, but she retained her satirical edge, regularly disparaging the disenfranchisement and exploitation of women, Native Americans, and African Americans by land-hungry male settlers.[104]

Three years after the Kirklands' return to New York City in 1843, William drowned, leaving his wife with a large family, which she maintained by teaching, writing, and editing.[105] In fact, however, Kirkland had been supporting the family for some time, for William was visually impaired and partially deaf, disabilities that may have made him more vulnerable to predatory land speculators and dreamy, idealistic plans.[106] A well-known literary figure, Kirkland edited a highly esteemed periodical, the *Union Magazine of Literature and Art*, where she privileged realistic contributions over the sentimental and romantic texts more popular at the time. Kirkland was deeply invested in America's political and cultural future, supporting activist causes such as women's rights and abolition, and she counted as her friends other progressive women activists, such as Lydia Maria Child and Sigourney.[107]

Although recent critics have focused principally on gender and realism in her work, Kirkland deserves further attention for her attitudes toward the environment and her emotionally intelligent rhetoric, which features satirical and affectionate humor. *Forest Life* investigates the ethos of land development and speculation, "simple living," resource management, realistic vs. romantic views of nature, religion and nature, gender and nature, and American identity and nature. Structurally innovative, the hybrid volume merges realism and satire, blurs the lines between fiction and nonfiction, and explicitly urges readers to assume various viewpoints.[108] The image of the stereoscope, which symbolizes Kirkland's dual vision of romantic idealism and painful reality, frames her narrative. Her transgenerational vision, coupled with her proto-preservationist views, makes *Forest Life* at least as engaging as her better-known *A New Home*.[109]

Unlike Sigourney's romantic appeal to aesthetics, *Forest Life* humorously highlights humans' corporeality, as, for example, when Kirkland discusses western insects. She parodies the academic inclination — possibly thinking of naturalists such as William Bartram — toward taxonomy and collection:

> One may observe, *en passant*, that ours is a rare region for the study of entomology. Those virtuosi who expend their amiable propensities in transfixing butterflies and impaling gnats would here find ample employment from May till November. Indeed they might at times encounter more specimens than they could manage comfortably and without undue precipitation. First, in early April, appear, few and far between, the huge blue-bottle flies, slow-motioned and buzzy, as if they felt the dignity of their position as ancestors. Next in order, if I forget not, come the most minute of midges, silent and stealthy, pretending insignificance in order than they may sting the more securely.[110]

Kirkland's barbed episode contrasts sharply with Bartram's romantic report of mayflies.[111] Undermining idealized notions of the west and wilderness, Kirkland simultaneously assumes and mocks an intellectual distance from bugs. Nature cannot be avoided, easily "transfixed," or "impaled"; indeed, the human impalers become the impaled. The writer emphasizes the necessary, sometimes painful connection between humans and nature while elsewhere she values the latter's beauty, even sublimity. Her dual position as insider and outsider, traveler and native—and her gender—enables this multiple perspective.

Humans' vulnerability and ingenuity emerge when Kirkland describes how people cope with these swarms of insects in the western wilderness. Initially she gives ironic hints about how the "refined" deal with swarms that render "black . . . the prevailing color of ceilings," and then she reveals more gruesome measures:

> Less fanciful people, frugal housewives and hard-hearted old bachelors, —place a large tumbler, partly filled with molasses, and covered with an innocent-looking piece of pasteboard having in the centre a hole large enough for a blue-bottle to enter *toute deployée*, but affording a poor chance for escape after he has clogged his feet and wings in the too eager pursuit of pleasure. . . . And again those of us who may by some chance have attended a course of chemistry, show our superior advantages by using a little water impregnated with cobalt, which carries swift destruction in every sip; and having at least the recommendation of not being sticky, answers to a very good purpose, unless the children happen to drink it.
>
> Yet this ingenious variety of deaths makes no palpable diminution in the number of our tormentors, and I have heard a good old lady exclaim against such contrivances altogether, saying that if you kill one fly, ten will be sure to come to his funeral. (1:146–47)

As Joseph W. Meeker observes, "To evolution and to comedy, nothing is sacred but life itself," and "the lesson of comedy is humility and endurance."[112] Kirkland's self-conscious style indicates how some nineteenth-century American women imagined the conversation between human beings and nature. Kirkland's tone is witty and her language elevated—the French phrases in these passages are an especially nice touch—but her topic is mundane. Her embodied, feminine rhetoric situates readers within a community (of sufferers) via pointed gallows humor.[113] In this environment, which she invites us to perceive with humble clarity, humans are only too close to nature.

Kirkland calls attention to her feminine outlook, for she contextualizes her discussion of insects within female domesticity. She invokes and departs from the travel-writing genre, implicitly inviting us to reassess what home means.[114] The natural west cannot be domesticated, she suggests, and she materializes this insistence through her narrative's restless movement and ironic voice. Among the first American women to use humor as a vehicle for consciousness-raising about the environment, Kirkland deserves prominence in a tradition of American women's environmental literature. Her wit forecasts that of the contemporary writers in *Fallen Forests'* coda, whose humor illuminates humans' complex relationships to nature and enables them to tell unpleasant truths.[115]

Kirkland's drollery permeates *Forest Life* from its opening pages, but her constantly shifting point of view makes analyzing her stance difficult. She is somewhat disingenuous; she rarely hesitates to state her opinions, but she does so through her characters' country voices and her own urbane irony. While her preface apologizes for the furor that *A New Home* provoked, Kirkland boldly states, "I shall not readily renounce my privilege of remarking freely on all subjects of general interest. In matters of opinion I claim the freedom which is my birthright as an American, and still further, the plainness of speech which is a striking characteristic of this Western country, the land of my adoption" (1:4–5). Many female readers would have understood the irony of birthright claims to freedom in an America where women were just nominal citizens—and, if they symbolized culture, also embodied nature.

Continuing in the same vein, the preface intimates that *Forest Life* will reinforce the longstanding civilized/savage dichotomy: "[W]hat I profess to delineate is the scarce reclaimed wilderness,—the forest,—the pioneers,—the settlers,—the people who, coming here of their own free will,—each with his own individual views of profit or advancement,—have, as a mass, been the mighty instrument in the hands of Providence of preparing the way for civilization, for intelligence, for advancement, for refinement, for religion" (1:5). Kirkland expresses an essentially conventional and masculine view of nature as "wilderness" that requires taming. We must accept such assertions with a tablespoonful of salt. Coupled with an abrupt, even halting style, her fluctuating standpoint ironizes the fact that "free will" applied to the male settler, not his female counterpart, who like Kirkland was frequently a reluctant transplant. She demonstrates later, however, that the wild west exposes both men and women to bodily contingencies.

Ultimately Kirkland declares her independence from romantic modes and affirms her own, indigenous method of conveying "some of the very ordinary scenes, manners, and customs of Western Life" (1:10). Wryly humorous, she values realism: "A painter would show his skill but poorly, who, in his zeal for beautifying his subject, should leave out a wart, even though it grew upon the tip of one's nose" (1:14). This putatively pedestrian method depends on the author's gender. Kirkland maintains that her "rambling impressions" will not compete with men's texts and that she will not lose women's "precious privilege of irresponsibility," promising instead to "adhere deliberately to fiddle-faddle and its immunities" (1:14–15). Alert readers, she ironically cautions, will have to delve below the surface. That is, her emotional intelligence, which offers complex, sometimes contradictory versions of the environment, demands our own.

Kirkland's witty and ironic style, and her implicit criticism of those who despite her warnings still seek a romantic vision of western life, blossoms in chapter 2, where she pictures her journey to her new home. We can regard nature, she implies, realistically or romantically, as she first raises then lowers the "magic glasses" that (again ironically) a politician friend has supplied (1:17):

> We were passing over Snake Hill,—an elevation which had always before appeared to me covered with stunted oak bushes, relieved at intervals by a huge stump or a girdled tree. What was my surprise to find its gently-swelling sides planted with luxurious sugar-maples and lofty elms, with fantastic arbors formed here and there amid their stately trunks by garlands of honey-suckle and eglantine, so closely interlaced, that no ray of the fervid sun penetrated their flowery depths, even at high noon! The only vestige I could discover of the wild-oak growth which I had supposed to characterize this region, was to be found in the most delicately-fancied garden-chairs, which abounded in these shady bowers. (1:19–20)

To girdle a tree is to cut through the bark and cambium, the soft layer of tissue that separates the inner bark and the wood, around the tree's circumference; the girdled tree slowly dies. By larding the passage with adjectives and imagining fabulously domesticated garden settings, Kirkland warns against romantic travel writers, who sugarcoat destructive practices and physical challenges. The pastoral mode clashes with western realities.[116]

Should we miss or ignore her message, Kirkland heightens the hyperbole. "The more settled part of the country" appears luxurious: "On every side pillared palaces of painted pine lined the thronged thoroughfares, while marble and mosaic marked the mansions of the more wealthy. Gorgeous peacocks unfurled their flagrant fans in courts musical with the murmur of magnificent fountains. Ladies lovelier than light reclined on lawns of emerald velvet, or loitered languidly at gilded lattices, lily-hung and lace-shaded, inhaling delicious perfumes, and listening to lays of love, warbled to thrilling lutes and silver-voiced lyres" (1:20). She enjoys this silly alliterative vein for several more pages, finally bringing us back down to earth with a thud: she encounters a local woman who asks if her daughter can use Kirkland's magic glasses, and when the child drops them, the writer's romantic vision is "scattered in a million fragments on the ground." Reality's jolt leaves Kirkland "speechless": "Why should I describe the dingy locks,—the check-apron,—the shoeless feet of the object of my admiration! Why picture anew the tumble-down log-house, with its appropriate perfumes of milk-emptins, bread, and fried onions?" She concludes finally that "it would be better to content myself with seeing with my own eyes" rather than envisioning "a dream" (1:23, 24).

With this warning, we are better prepared for the realities that follow, and Kirkland creates an explicit "league" with readers—implicitly female—to forestall "unfriendly criticism" (1:26). In the subsequent pages, Kirkland reveals the foolhardy, speculative land schemes and dreams of the men on whom women depend. Throughout the narrative, *Forest Life* argues forcefully, if sometimes indirectly, against such speculation, with its "ceaseless transit," "blundering search after happiness," and loss of "all local attachments and neighborly sympathies" in "the rapid settlement of the wilds." Not least among her criticisms is how men haphazardly despoil the land: "They purchase a lot or two of 'government land;' they build a log-house, fence a dozen acres or so, plough half of them, girdle the trees, and then sell out to a new comer" (1:27). The thoughtless process repeats itself: "The pioneer is then ready for a new purchase, a new clearing, and a new sale. How his wife and children enjoy themselves meanwhile is a matter of small doubt, but this is a trifle for the present" (1:28).[117] Kirkland's gendered economic and environmental reality diverges from Sigourney's romantic, aestheticized portrayal of clear-cutting and resource depletion.

At first, Kirkland observes, this "flitting plan" was profitable, and "land—the grand object of ambition—was easily tripled by those who were able to turn their strength and hardihood to account" (1:28). Men are motivated not by an ethos emphasizing the land's inherent value or its ostensible improvement but solely by financial gain. Written shortly after the financial panic of 1837 that followed Michigan land speculation, *Forest Life* highlights how nature's permanence contrasts with financial gain's uncertainty: "Every thing but the outpouring of abundance of mother Earth has dwindled and looked blighted since the great commercial revulsion which succeeded the land-mania" (1:30). As María Carla Sánchez recounts concerning fiction in the panic era, writers demonstrated a "profound suspicion" of "everything unreal, unreliable, dishonest—everything made up."[118] Kirkland shares this view, for her plain, realistic rhetoric—actually more familiar to women than to men—insists that the romantic perspective on nature is inherently suspect. Her western experiences thus form a bracing counterpoint to Sigourney's idealized nation-building.

KIRKLAND'S COMPLEX VIEW of nature and natural resources emerges most interestingly when she considers trees' practical and symbolic significance in frontier society. She explains the controversy over the village's "public square," which has been neglected because of the financial crisis and citizens' "indifference to ornament and amusement." Had the area been "neatly fenced, provided with seats and planted with trees"—civilized— the area might have become, as intended, "the glory of our village"; instead, it boasts a thick crop of Canada thistles sown by sheep (1:42). Because the villagers "cannot approach unanimity in deciding what kinds [of shade trees] we shall select, in what order they shall be placed, or in what manner protected . . . blackened stumps are likely to continue the sole ornaments of our Prado" (1:42–43). Politics trump aesthetics. This sketch meditates on settlers' attitudes:

> Would I could hope that the fine remnants of the original forest that still remain to us, were to be allowed foothold on this roomy earth. . . . The Western settler looks upon these earth-born columns and the verdant roofs and towers which they support as "heavy timber,"— nothing more. He sees in them only obstacles which must be removed, at whatever sacrifice, to make way for mills, stores, blacksmiths' shops,—perhaps churches,—certainly taverns. "Clearing" is his daily thought and nightly dream; and so literally does he act upon this guiding idea, that not one tree, not so much as a bush, of natural

growth, must be suffered to cumber the ground, or he fancies his work incomplete. The very notion of advancement, of civilization, of prosperity, seems incomparably connected with the total extirpation of the forest. (1:43)

Like Sigourney, Kirkland deprecates the thoughtless destruction of nature's bounty; like her contemporary, she believes that the forest constitutes America's noneconomic wealth. Although Sigourney appreciates trees for their contributions to the country's cultural and natural history, both authors consider the "fine remnants of the original forest" as an inheritance for future generations.[119]

Also like Sigourney, Kirkland draws upon Biblical parallels. Trees "cumber[ing]" the ground references Luke 13:6–9, Christ's parable about productivity, patience, and redemption:

He spake also this parable; A certain *man* had a fig tree planted in his vineyard; and he came and sought fruit thereon, and found none. Then said he unto the dresser of his vineyard, Behold, these three years I come seeking fruit on this fig tree, and find none: cut it down; why cumbereth it the ground? And he answering said unto him, Lord, let it alone this year also, till I shall dig about it, and dung *it*. And if it bear fruit, *well*: and if not, *then* after that thou shalt cut it down. (original emphasis)[120]

Standard interpretations suggest that the fig tree stands for Israel and the vineyard represents a place where the fig might be expected to fruit within three years. The dresser advises following a natural order abetted by human wisdom (fertilizing the trees). Christ's willingness to delay felling the tree symbolizes God's patience—which nevertheless has limits. Even late repentance will generate forgiveness and salvation, but if spiritual fruit does not appear within that time, then any punishment is justified. Invoking the parable, Kirkland adds an ominous message: the settlers themselves assume the role of gods, leveling trees before their fruition. They break God's commandments, and they risk his wrath, for they too are "cumberers of the ground." For her as for today's Christian ecologists, stewardship of America's natural resources is an important spiritual as well as cultural and aesthetic principle.

Like Sigourney, Kirkland attempts to redefine civilization and progress, but she genders this redefinition more explicitly than her contemporary. Men approach nature with no regard for spiritual or aesthetic values; to the contrary, everything is measured by money (and, as her acerbic reference to "taverns" insinuates, pleasure). To foreground this attitude's shortsightedness, Kirkland translates Talleyrand's observation on "the backwoodsman," whom he disparages for his failure to grasp beauty and feel appropriate "sentiment," concluding that "he has never planted—he knows not the pleasure of planting. A tree which he should plant would be good for nothing to him, for it would never grow large enough to be felled by his hand" (1:44n1). To such men, economic gain is paramount. Kirkland laments how, as settlers clear space "for a residence in the wilderness it is really ludicrous to observe the warm opposition made by *every strong-armed agent* of one's plans, against leaving a scattered remnant of the forest by way of shelter to the rude dwelling. So inveterate is the prejudice that an angry battle must be fought for every tree."[121] Using Talleyrand's male authority, the author heightens the conservationist emphasis. Here warfare translates to gendered domestic internecine conflict.

Sarcasm gives way to sentiment as the chapter continues, with Kirkland prizing how the "feathered tribes" and "multitudes of pretty flutterers of all hues and sizes" that the trees shelter provide "ever-new delight" (1:45). She shows the trees' position in the larger ecosystem, paying particular attention to the red-headed woodpecker. This reflection about country life's pleasures turns painfully to "one darling tree,—a giant oak . . . the grandfather of the forest" that "we thought we had saved" (1:46). The Kirklands loan some land on which the tree resides to a newly arrived, indigent family; the husband immediately girdles the tree—which the author embraces as a family member—and believes the Kirklands should be grateful. She acknowledges that "the felling of a great tree has something of the sublime in it. When the axe first falls on the trunk of a stately oak laden with the green wealth of a century, or a pine whose aspiring peak might look down on a moderate church steeple, the contrast between puny instrument and the gigantic result to be accomplished approaches the ridiculous" (1:48). Nature's majesty and size dwarf humans and their ostensibly civilized human constructions. Countering the rhetoric and ethos of profit and progress, Kirkland anticipates Sigourney's aesthetic language in "Fallen Forests."

This encounter is not a heroic one between David and Goliath. Paralleling the annihilation of Sigourney's ancient trees, the felling represents a violent murder (1:47–48). The "leaf-crowned monarch of the wood has no small reason to quiver" at "a long-armed Yankee approaching his deep-rooted trunk with an awkward axe." But death comes tortuously: "One blow seems to accomplish nothing: not even a chip falls. But with another stroke comes a broad slice of the bark, leaving an ominous, gaping wound. Another pair of blows extends the gash, and when twenty such have fallen, behold a girdled tree." Although girdling "would suffice to kill, and a melancholy death it is," felling the tree is more arduous. Painfully for the reader, Kirkland draws out her sketch of the "destroyer" and the tree, which "trembles," "waves," and emits a "groaning sound": "Yet another stroke is necessary. It is given with desperate force, and the tall peak leaves its place with an easy sailing motion accelerated every instant till it crashes prone on the earth, sending far and wide its scattered branches, and letting in the sunlight upon the cool, damp, mossy earth, for the first time perhaps in half a century" (1:48). Unlike Sigourney, Kirkland explicitly refuses to moralize at the chapter's conclusion, which coincides with the tree's death. By personifying the tree, depicting its destruction in brutal, embodied terms, and imagining the history of sunlight, she doesn't have to admonish. The lesson is obvious: Thou shalt not kill.

Although such a passage may suggest that Kirkland idealizes nature and romanticizes wilderness life, her admiration does not blind her to forest life's material realities and dangers. The book's title embeds her subject's contradictions and complexities, variously indicating people living in the woods, individual trees, forests as living beings, and nonhuman woodland inhabitants. Like the narrative itself, this title simultaneously underscores and erases the differences between human and nonhuman nature. Asking what is tame and what is wild, Kirkland complicates such terms as *nature*, *wilderness*, and *the picturesque*. She also privileges everyday beauty, for example, commenting, with a deliciously ironic juxtaposition, on "the *picturesque*, which we are all *wild* about" (emphasis added)—the Swiss Alps, personified as an "Italian improvisatrice with her wild black eyes and her soul of fire"—and comparing Michigan's quotidian beauty to that of a farmer's daughter, who is "the most comfortable person to live with, though she will attract no tourists to her *soirées*" (1:130–31). Such comparisons, which accentuate the female, the domestic, and the American, criticize romanticizing conceptions of wilderness and Mother Earth.

Returning to practical matters, Kirkland discusses soil quality and its relation to timber and water resources. She describes "the prodigious amount of wet prairie or 'marsh,'" which "is said to promise magnificent resources of wealth for—our great-grandchildren." In response to the land's economic valuation and its romanticization, Kirkland states wryly, "At present it yields, in the first place, agues [malarial fevers] of the first quality, and, secondly, very tolerable wild grass for the cattle of the emigrant" (1:132). In this environment, survival comes first. But she also envisions humans despoiling and depleting this resource: "As to future days, inexhaustible beds of peat and marl—the former to use as fuel when we shall have burned all the oaks, the latter to restore the exhausted soil to its pristine fertility—are to compensate to our descendants for the loss of energy and enterprise which we ancestors shall undoubtedly suffer through agues" (1:132–33). Human stewardship is imperfect at best, culminating not in riches but in death: "We reap the advantages of the rich virgin soil; our hereafter is to find boundless wealth beneath its surface" (1:133). In the end, Kirkland caustically enjoins, people must play by nature's rules; monetary gain bows to mortality.

An encounter with local farmer Seth Mallory illustrates humans' physical vulnerability. Chapter 20 opens by admiring the Michigan sky's beauty: "[T]he stars were beginning to be visible, like specks of chaste silver in the dazzling but shaded gold of the western sky" (1:159). But reality interrupts the idyllic vision, for the family arrives at a dwelling that sits in the middle of a large clearing; its trees have been eradicated. Mallory's lack of foresight forecasts his demise, for they find him ("a stout farmer of forty") dying in bed, surrounded by his wife, "large family of children," and some neighbors. The cause: "The poor man had been crushed by a falling tree. He had been an adventurous and successful bee-hunter, and the pillars which had attracted our attention were the trophies of his triumphs in that line" (1:160). The resource that symbolized his skill, which the author praises and admires, also kills him. Mallory's parlous state rouses her to contemplate "the perils and trials of the unhewn wilderness" and the "stern realities" of life in the woods and "incredible toil" on "the field of battle" (1:162). To enable forest life, some clearing was necessary to erect homes and grow food. But Kirkland insists that trees demand not only admiration and reverence but also respect and humility, for they possess power over human life.[122] The war metaphor acquires an inverted valence: if man destroys nature, he is himself an all-too-vulnerable part of that nature.[123]

IN ASSESSING forest life, Kirkland regularly introduces a version of "simple living" (which I take up more fully in chapter 4): discarding unnecessary belongings, emphasizing spiritual development, and behaving respectfully toward the environment. Writing before Thoreau, she expresses a democratic perspective on wealth and acquisition. Although she underlines "grace, delicacy, beauty, elegance, and even splendor, as gratifications of taste, and aids to mental refinement," she derides acquisitiveness as a means of creating social hierarchies (1:59). Through emotionally intelligent rhetoric, she tries to help her affluent and urban readers comprehend wilderness plainness. Practicing "Republican simplicity" can be challenging, but she avers that "no republic has ever survived the universal prevalence of luxurious habits and the blind and weak pride, which seems to be their inevitable consequence" (1:59). Here Kirkland reverts—without apparent irony—to an earlier model of virtue, prioritizing a community value system over Americans' increasing individualism.[124] As with the natural environment, humility (or at least modesty) toward one's fellow citizens is essential for the nation's survival.

Following republican principles is easier "in the woods": "So great has been the power of habit in simplifying our wants and reducing their number, that many things which are considered essential to comfort among those who make modes of life a study and a science, appeared to us absolutely cumbersome and harassing" (1:63). Country life encourages people to "simplify, simplify" as Thoreau would urge. Kirkland foregrounds the paradox of labor-saving devices that merely require different kinds of work, citing "some of our city friends," who "have secured so many of the comforts and luxuries of life, that life itself is expended in the solicitudes attendant upon such extensive and costly arrangements." She concludes, "every new necessity for the aid of such people seems to entail a new slavery" (1:63). Like Sigourney, Kirkland interrogates American character, celebrates its past, and appraises its prospects—but she is more skeptical about a national identity based on unnecessary consumption.

Kirkland contrasts wealthy city dwellers' luxury to many western settlers' humble conditions; the latter live simply by necessity, not—as simple living advocates today do—by choice. She particularly disparages speculators' folly and greed, depreciating men who leave comfortable eastern homes, "coming to the West to get rich," as a Mr. Gaston does, impoverishing his family (1:91). She also scorns the idle rich, "jewelled [*sic*] bosoms" who "sip their ice-cream" and complain of want, ignorant of physical hardship or deprivation. Material plainness does not mean abjection, however, for Mrs. Gaston's "Republican simplicity" creates a welcoming home: "This log-cabin with its civil and respectable inhabitants would furnish a lesson for such economists, if indeed they were willing to learn of the poor to appreciate the over-abounding comforts of their lot" (1:92). Throughout *Forest Life* Kirkland approves of the hospitality of country people, who, however disparate their circumstances, depend on one another. Critiquing excess, she advocates balance, living appropriately for one's finances and location.

We could misinterpret her scorn as puritanical, but although the Gaston chapter (11) rather grimly chastises profligate Americans, Kirkland frequently uses humor to deflate people's pretensions and reaffirm their connection to animal nature.[125] As we will see with Mary Wilkins Freeman in chapter 4, this humor coalesces around food. One of the most effective — and funniest — chapters explains the superstition that malarial fever ("the ague") causes "an affection for pork": "Pork, the *beau ideal* of good cheer every where in this region, bears also the highest reputation as an abracadabra. Those who are already shaking will often ascribe their low estate to a lack of this indispensable luxury, and expect certain relief to be the consequence of a fresh supply."[126] Not just pork, but pork in quantity, assures relief: "They have no faith in infinitesimal doses. As much as can be swallowed, three times per diem, is the usual prescription; whether intended as a preventive or as cure; — as a relief for present ills or a talisman against those which may come" (1:74–75). People thus "take excellent care of these greasy treasures. Their privileges among us are unlimited — indeed they are generally preferred to their human dependants [*sic*]. . . . Not the sacred cow of Isis was the subject of more reverential attention" (1:76). Allowed free range, pigs provoke regular conversation.

Creating community through feminine rhetoric — we should note that she includes herself as a pork aficionado — Kirkland's humorous hyperbole reemphasizes humility in matters of national identity. Americans are so entirely dependent on pigs that they give them almost human liberty:

Far from being content with the grovelling [*sic*] habits and coarse fare which satisfy their brethren, in those countries where man, under the benighted prejudices of civilization, denies them their true place in society, our porkers will leap a garden fence with the agility, if not the grace of an antelope. Once in, they show their refined taste by banqueting upon tidbits selected here and there from your tomatoes and cauliflowers, your bulbs and your grape-vines; resembling the butterfly in one respect at least, inasmuch as they never complete their feast upon one or two varieties, but rather choose to try every thing in the garden. (1:76–77)

Unlike William Byrd's straightforward disdain in his account of the North Carolina backcountry—for him pigs signify laziness, because they will fend for themselves—Kirkland affectionately anthropomorphizes them. She thus entertains her supposedly superior metropolitan audience and, vulnerable to porcine invasion, shares her neighbors' woes.[127] Elevating pigs to citizen status, Kirkland mock-celebrates their independence.

This romping passage sparks a meditation on Americanness: "Some people have professed to find a connection between national character and national food. They have imagined the waveless calm of the German to have some mysterious affinity with the cool and heavy nature of his beloved cabbage; the mercurial agility of the Frenchman with the salutatory propensities of the frog." Such people connect the Englishman and "blushing red . . . half-cooked beef" and link the Indians' "tameless wildness" with venison. Protesting these associations, she calls those who make them "illiberal pseudo-philosophers" (1:77). She does, however—again with tongue in cheek—assert that Americans and their pigs share one characteristic: "The bristly citizen,—(I speak of him whose nature has been exalted by his privileges,)—when he once fixes his keen eye upon a desirable object,—be it corn, be it cabbage,—is indomitable in perseverance. 'Go ahead' is his motto, whatever be the obstacles in the way. He may get dozens of knocks over the pate, but none the less forces his nose into the pail" (1:78). Naming the pig as a citizen intimates a less than savory affiliation; persistence may be a virtue, but greed is not. Again, humor—here, through exaggeration and association—conveys Kirkland's point more effectively than direct admonition or romantic flights of fancy.[128] But a serious message lurks behind the humor: land speculators—American men—who consume like pigs warrant their ultimate end.

CRITICS PRAISED Kirkland's book-length works.[129] Comparing the later volume with *A New Home*, Edgar Allan Poe reviewed *Forest Life* favorably, noting that it "was read with equal interest. It gives us, perhaps, more of the philosophy of western life, but has the same freshness, freedom, piquancy." He contends, "Unquestionably, she is one of our best writers, has a province all her own, and in that province has very few equals" and lauds her "*freshness* of style" and "species of *wit*, approximating humor, and so interspersed with pure *fun*, that 'wit,' after all, is nothing like a definition of it."[130] Knowing Kirkland's contemporary popularity and fame, her accessibility, her realism, and her timeliness, we might reasonably ask why the book disappeared after only a few American editions and one English edition between its original 1842 publication and 1850. Although less popular than her bestselling *A New Home*, *Forest Life* responds to Emerson's philosophy—although probably not as he might have liked, given its mundane realism—and it anticipates Thoreau's *Walden*.

But in 1842, women writers—especially humorous ones—had difficulty being taken seriously, as Kirkland's elaborate mock apologies, hyperbole, and irony in *Forest Life* indirectly acknowledge.[131] Difficult to categorize, and still challenging readers, the book combined elements of fiction, advice writing, philosophy, travel narrative, and autobiography. But in the 1840s, novels, specifically romantic and sentimental novels, were increasingly popular. As the west became more familiar, Kirkland's themes may have seemed dated or unrealistic, and her ostensibly self-disparaging and unserious voice may have contributed to the book's disappearance. Like her friend Sigourney, she advocated an ethos of humility and stewardship toward the natural world, and much more than Sigourney she represented the physical continuity between humans and their natural environment. Understanding their interconnected but sometimes antagonistic relationship, she presented people as all-too-vulnerable embodied beings—a theme that recurs in Jacobs's *Incidents in the Life of a Slave Girl*.

But porcine citizens may finally have rejected its message. *Forest Life* is a different kind of travel book because it focuses on Kirkland's reluctant transplantation due to her husband's ambition. Where Sigourney commonly uses romantic enticements and an elevated style to encourage readers' environmental conservation, Kirkland more regularly assumes an acerbic and realistic —or, alternatively, humorous—perspective. Less overtly self-assertive than Sigourney in *Scenes in My Native Land*, Kirkland wins by charming rather than correcting. Her story engenders various responses, enabling us to enjoy the west's pleasures and hazards by proxy, and persuading readers to entertain her philosophy of grounded, community-oriented living. She shares with Sigourney trepidation about the clear-cutting of America's old-growth forests and distress about the loss of its most venerable residents, as well as an ambivalence about development. More explicitly interested in human ecology and humans' relationship to the environment, Kirkland also makes important contributions to a tradition of American women's environmental writing.

Realistically, neither Sigourney nor Kirkland could prevent or delay deforestation—they affirm that it is *men*, eager to earn their fortunes in the west, who engage in rampant natural destruction, transforming both individual homes and the national homeland. Whether used for firewood or building materials, trees could not withstand the onslaught of male settlers, well equipped with axes and saws, heading for fortune or, as Kirkland suggests, for ruin. The authors accept that some woodland clearing was necessary, but they question American progress and excess; both, though in different ways and with varying intensities, mourn the passing of prized American cultural and natural history. Ultimately, in this expansionist era neither sentiment nor humor, nor appeals to God, conservation, or aesthetics, would be successful rhetorical weapons to counter humans' arrogant war on the environment. As Harriet Jacobs's *Incidents in the Life of a Slave Girl* demonstrates, this war encompassed not only trees, but people.

"In Woods and Swamps": Southern Natures

"Notwithstanding my grandmother's long and faithful service to her owners, not one of her children escaped the auction block. These God-breathing machines are no more, in the sight of their masters, than the cotton they plant, or the horses they tend."[132] Harriet Jacobs concludes her first chapter with this sardonic statement that juxtaposes her emphasis on

Masthead for the *Liberator*, 23 April 1831. Sign in middle reads "Horse-Market" and
caption on lecturn reads "Slaves Horses & Other Cattle to Be Sold at 12 oc."

enslaved persons' divine humanity with slaveholders' objectification. Enslaved persons are merely resources, animals or "machines." In such an
economy, nature is at once inaccessible and all too present.

Access to and agency in nature continue to concern African Americans.[133] The forest may have meant profit to nineteenth-century speculators and progress to westering settlers, but to enslaved persons it had very
different, and frequently conflicting, resonances. For enslaved women like
Jacobs, trees possessed no special significance as national monuments, and
preserving human resources was the urgent priority. The generic complexity of Kirkland's text invites us to consider Jacobs's *Incidents in the Life of
a Slave Girl*, another narrative that may seem even further outside travel
writing or, indeed, the environmental writing genre. We should thus attend
to Kimberly N. Ruffin's question—clearly relevant for Kirkland—"What
does it mean when work, rather than leisure, is your central ecological
experience?"[134]

Over the past two decades, literary critics have explored questions of
slavery, motherhood, gender, sexuality, and authorship in *Incidents in the
Life of a Slave Girl*, but ecocritics have neglected Jacobs's narrative and similar works. As Ian Frederick Finseth observes, discussions of antislavery literature have, "for understandable reasons, concentrated on the *social* sphere
in examining the rise and eventual triumph of British, and then American,
abolitionist writing" and have elided considerations of "natural philosophy,
natural history, and literary representations of nature."[135] But such considerations are crucial in a slaveholding context in which, as Jacobs asserts,
"Women are considered of no value, unless they continually increase their
owner's stock. They are put on a par with animals" (76). Enslaved women
particularly struggled to acquire agency. To address environmental issues,

Jacob faced barriers to self-expression more forbidding than those her counterparts encountered: like many working-class women and women of color, she had first to establish the right to speak in public.[136]

As we contemplate how nineteenth-century texts by women of color connect to a tradition of American women's environmental writing, our customary categories' narrowness becomes clear.[137] Writers such as Frances Harper, Sarah Winnemucca, and Jacobs, to name just three well-known examples, concern themselves more intensely with cultural ecologies than with nature; they are not interested in "losing the humans," to use Randall Roorda's phrase.[138] I share Ruffin's view that "now is the time for the recovery of key texts and critical frameworks that help describe the power of [African American ecoliterary] traditions."[139] We can appreciate Jacobs anew by assessing her tripartite travels: geographical (from South to North), psychological (from slave to free person), and physiological (from girl to mother).[140] As she pictures these relocations, her experience of the natural world helps complicate our comprehension of white authors, the period's social activism, and environmental literature.

Intensely aware of the multifaceted relationship between nature and black women, Jacobs constructs a moving narrative that invites us to reconsider the artificial boundaries between culture and nature, as well as between environmental writing and other forms. *Incidents in the Life of a Slave Girl* hybridizes several genres, most prominently autobiography and the sentimental novel, and it incorporates multiple rhetorical modes, ranging from petition to accusation. These modes are peopled; as the environmental historian Mart A. Stewart explains, "Slave experiences with the environment were profoundly social ones: slaves moved into nature to enact social meanings, although they did not make the sharp distinctions between the human and nonhuman worlds that were common for whites. For African Americans, nature was negotiated, it was kin, and it was community."[141] When scholars define nature writing as exclusively or principally focused on nature, we reinscribe racial and ethnic boundaries.[142] Reading Jacobs's story as an environmental narrative reestablishes essential missing links and requires of us a more capacious environmental ethos.[143]

Analyzing the relationship between geography and identity in African American literature, Melvin Dixon notes, "Slaves knew that as chattel they were considered part of the property and wilds of nature, which a smoothly functioning plantation could restrain. The nearby woods contained enough

birds and roaming animals to provide slaves with geographical and naturalistic references for freedom."[144] Nevertheless, nature presented a dual
aspect of hindrance and support.[145] When Jacobs flees young Mr. Flint's
plantation, her encounter with nature is hardly elevating: "I . . . concealed
myself in a thicket of bushes. There I remained in an agony of fear for two
hours. Suddenly, a reptile of some kind seized my leg. In my fright, I struck
a blow which loosened its hold, but I could not tell whether I had killed it; it
was so dark, I could not see what it was; I only knew it was something cold
and slimy. The pain I felt soon indicated that the bite was poisonous" (150).
Although darkness promises concealment, it magnifies nature's dangers,
which she must brave to liberate herself. Emphasizing African Americans'
grounding in Christian religious traditions, Dixon affirms slaves' reliance
on three metaphors: "The wilderness, the underground, and the mountaintop are broad geographical metaphors for the search, discovery, and
achievement of self."[146] As Jacobs invokes the serpent, she may be symbolizing herself as an American Eve traveling through a wilderness—spiritual
as well as physical—that brings painful knowledge but may also afford
deliverance. Her feminine rhetoric, which reproduces feelings of anticipation and fear, conveys the forbidding proximity of the human body to the
environment.

Rather than affording Jacobs a promising metaphor of freedom, nature
often presents literal, concrete hazards even more stringent than the dis-
comforts and dangers that Kirkland catalogues. For the escaping woman
slave, Snaky Swamp is terrifying, filled with reptiles, noises, and potential
disease. As the environmental historian Jack Temple Kirby describes them,
pocosins, the areas *Incidents in the Life of a Slave Girl* portrays, "are leg-
endarily snaky places, provoking the aversive dread forever associated with
venomous serpents." These "little studied" "swamps-on-a-hill" "almost certainly [nurture] moccasins, rattlesnakes, and a host of nonpoisonous snakes."
At the same time, they "seem to function as refuges . . . for bears and other
animals harried by human depredations on their habitats"; with a "fearsome
capacity to protect mystery," they should engender respect.[147] Though Jacobs draws on romantic traditions to depict Snaky Swamp, she discards the
sublime when confronted with material dangers.

Herself hunted like an animal in her second escape attempt, Jacobs confirms her increased apprehension owing to the earlier snake bite; nevertheless, she endures another encounter with wildness. Notwithstanding her

friend Peter's help, there is little comfort: "[W]ith a large knife [Peter] cut a path through bamboos and briers of all descriptions. He came back, took me in his arms, and carried me to a seat made among the bamboos. Before we reached it, we were covered with hundreds of mosquitos. In an hour's time they had so poisoned my flesh that I was a pitiful sight to behold. As the light increased, I saw snake after snake crawling round us" (171). Engaging her emotional intelligence to heighten the story's realism, Jacobs offers an apprehensive and anxiety-provoking episode that demands embodied reading. She enlarges her contemporaries' view that humans require humility when faced with the natural world.

With its subtle, ironic rendering of male chivalry and its bald sketch of painful insect bites, this scene parallels Kirkland's indoor sophistication as she recounts the west's entomological plenitude. The writers rely on similar *and* different responses. Jacobs translates Kirkland's amusement at shared hardship into fear, pain, and—paradoxically—hope for deliverance. Aimed at northern white women, Jacobs's sentimental appeal counterpoints Kirkland's urbane humor, enabled by her ethnicity, class, and dual position as insider and outsider. In contrast, Jacobs's oblique ridicule of male gallantry speaks eloquently to African American (and alert white) audience members about the racial double standard: Peter's best efforts merely make her less miserable. As Glenda Carpio remarks, "[M]uch of the satire and wit in nineteenth-century texts by African American women is not conducive to laughter. But this should not lead us to dismiss a powerful aspect of their texts."[148] The swamp episodes imply that we must acknowledge nature's separateness from and hostility toward humans. These moments suggest both Jacobs's necessary alienation from her own body and her imprisonment in it. The environment becomes a way station, a refuge, and a painful obstacle between a hellish, oppressive South and an ostensibly civilized North.

Like Kirkland, Jacobs explores the woman-nature connection through her corporeality, a touchstone issue for chapter 3's working-class women.[149] Jacobs subjectifies her enslaved female body, resisting social imperatives that demand submission to the slave master. She intimates that her body is weak, conventionally feminine—as when she suffers illness and paralysis during her seven-year self-confinement in her grandmother's tiny attic. But it is also strong, traditionally masculine: she weathers this confinement, a prelude to self-birth; she resists Dr. Flint through a sexual alliance with another white man; and she survives a perilous escape. Indeed, sharing the vantage point established in the chapter "The Loophole of Retreat," readers can appreciate Jacobs's grimly humorous stories of the ignorant white men whom she regularly outwits. Her dry account of writing Dr. Flint a letter that erroneously propels him North to bring home his ostensibly repentant possession is particularly amusing.[150] Unlike Kirkland, whose cultural authority as an educated, cosmopolitan white woman permits her considerable expansiveness in ironic and witty self-expression, Jacobs expresses a much more inconspicuous humor. Her acute calibration of affective effects through strategic reticence and understatement underscores her emotional intelligence.

Jacobs's sketches repeatedly underline the charged linkage between her enslaved body and the environment. She figures the passage from South to North, slavery to imagined freedom, in a natural, concrete image. Sailing north, she feels the wind upon her face: "I shall never forget that night. The balmy air of spring was so refreshing! And how shall I describe my sensations when we were fairly sailing on Chesapeake Bay? O, the beautiful sunshine! the exhilarating breeze! and I could enjoy them without fear or restraint. I had never realized what grand things air and sunlight are till I had been deprived of them" (163).[151] This moment acquires ironic weight when we learn that the ostensibly free air holds a false promise: the (delicately implied) menace of the Fugitive Slave Law compromises a lovely sunrise: "The next morning I was on deck as soon as the day dawned. I called Fanny to see the sunrise, for the first time in our lives, on free soil; for such I *then* believed it to be. We watched the reddening sky, and saw the great orb come up slowly out of the water, as it seemed. Soon the waves began to sparkle, and every thing caught the beautiful glow" (241). Although the natural scene may be lovely, Jacobs cautions that it is contingent upon the viewer's situation. She appeals simultaneously to our aesthetic and embodied awareness to generate delight and longing. But careful readers' attention snags on the italicized word, which sparks anxiety that clouds the ensuing narrative.

Geographical travel affords Jacobs no necessary self-improvement or release from gendered activities; it portends only a re-placement of legal or social constraints. Although she is an unwilling traveler, Kirkland is free to observe her various environments with ironic and humorous distance that invokes a shared female perspective, including a comic community of sufferers. While Jacobs is keenly aware of the irony that North and South handle black women's bodies virtually interchangeably, her "distance" must negotiate with an audience conceived of as the same (women) and different (*white* women). Asserting that for the enslaved woman nature is hardly an idealized, feminized object to be conquered (as it was for men) but instead an obstacle to, means toward, and symbol of freedom, Jacobs's environmental text deconstructs the normative associations between women, particularly women of color, and the environment. More explicitly and consciously than Sigourney's "Indian Names," it links the environment's domestication and internal colonialism.

QUESTIONING THESE racial and ethnic boundaries enables a clearer view of other, literal and historical connections. Chapter 1 referenced one important motivation for Indian removal: the potential for slavery's expansion into traditional Native lands. Jacobs's volume follows the early nineteenth century's Indian removal crisis. By 1819, the Cherokee held just five million acres, and when gold was discovered on their land, removal—and thus increased demand for slave labor—seemed to many inevitable, despite the well-organized protests by Christian benevolent individuals and organizations, many of which were managed by women. The experience that these anti-removal activists gained prepared them for abolitionist activity, while it diminished enthusiasm for African colonization, which provoked obvious parallels: how could a good Christian renounce removal and advocate such colonization?[152]

Spokesmen such as William Lloyd Garrison made these links explicit, and they supported antislavery efforts with articles and illustrations, such as the *Liberator*'s revised masthead on 23 April 1831. The abolitionist James Birney also articulated the hypocrisy that "supposed it was easier to remove from the country those who were the subjects of this degradation, than to successfully combat and overthrow the prejudices and false principles which produced it."[153] An ardent abolitionist, Lydia Maria Child was among those who first backed and then, in 1833, rejected colonization.[154] Immediate emancipation, which second-generation abolitionists advocated, necessitated finding a home place for freed slaves, acknowledged by William T. Sherman's Special Field Order No. 15, with its provision of forty acres and—sometimes—a mule, the basis of a family farm. In other words, landownership was an issue of environmental justice for enslaved and emancipated persons, just as it was for Native Americans.[155]

Though few enslaved persons actually enjoyed such ownership, the cultivated landscape was lifted from the forests and swamps literally on their backs.[156] This experience, among many others, ensured that African Americans articulated different attitudes toward nature than Native Americans dispossessed of land originally theirs, though both groups were denied agency and access to nature's benefits.[157] Recent environmental historians have foregrounded African Americans' centrality in the construction of the United States, especially the South; Stewart notes that by "the mid-eighteenth century, colonists in British America had created a characteristic landscape of plantations, villages, small farms, and cowpens in Virginia, North Carolina, South Carolina, and Georgia."[158] The concepts of resource wars and environmental agency thus reverberated very differently for America's diverse ethnicities.

Jacobs's narrative, in her descriptions of the forest in general and trees in particular, encodes this different understanding. In "Sketches of Neighboring Slaveholders," trees figure as antagonists that summon the specter of brutal lynchings, as vicious Mr. Conant ties his body servant to a tree in front of his house during a stormy winter night (73). When she prepares to confess her pregnancy to her grandmother, Jacobs "sat down in the shade of a tree at her door and began to sew" (87). After Jacobs's grandmother learns that Harriet is pregnant and casts her out, she wanders away until "fatigue compelled me to stop. I sat down on the stump of an old tree. The stars were shining through the boughs above me. How they mocked me, with their bright, calm light!" (88). Here the trees—alive and dead—furnish shelter and a resting place, but nature as a whole is indifferent to human suffering. But nature occasionally provides a refuge. When Jacobs returns to the Flints' plantation after a stolen visit to her son, she hides "behind a large tree" (134). Nevertheless, the plantation's rural remoteness shields her master's murderous crimes from public comment. Though Jacobs does not explicitly say so, such remoteness was enhanced by many plantations' forested locations.

Even though it sometimes buffers slaveholders from public condemnation, the forest also gives enslaved persons succor. It allows one individual a temporary escape after "a severe whipping" and another to conceal his children; after Nat Turner's Rebellion, when bands of marauding whites sweep the countryside, many women hide in the woods. Jacobs also depicts a refuge, "their little church in the woods, with their burying-ground around it. It was built by the colored people, and they had no higher happiness than to meet there and sing hymns together, and pour out their hearts in spontaneous prayer" (75, 78, 99).[159] In "Scenes at the Plantation," as she plans her escape Jacobs visits her parents' graves, gathering strength for an impending trial: "The graveyard was in the woods, and twilight was coming on. Nothing broke the death-like stillness except the occasional twitter of a bird. My spirit was overawed by the solemnity of the scene" (138). Mingling natural and cultural realms, Jacobs does not flee into nature but enlists it to help her negotiate her emotions about a harsh, racialized landscape.[160] As Stewart reminds us, "For African Americans, 'wilderness' was not a place in which the preservation of the world could be found, but a site of healing, a highway to kinship, a place where a decisive edge of resources could be added to meager plantation rations, and a place where salvation could be gained, either through worship in the holler, through the strengthening of kin connections, or through stealing oneself away permanently."[161] Ultimately, the forest represented a profoundly complex physical and psychic location for enslaved persons.

Such complexity was founded partly by the forests' historical relationship to work. Ruffin's question emphasizing the ecological experience that labor entails resonates for Jacobs's peers (as well as for Kirkland's foresters).[162] Concrete resources that symbolized such labor were a key issue not only for Euramericans and Native Americans but also, though very differently, for African Americans. The South shared with the Northeast and Midwest a potential fortune in timber. As Timothy Silver points out, "The forests promised to create a lucrative market in timber products. Unlike the gold and silver the Spanish retrieved from the New World, trees could be procured with the most basic tools and a comparatively small labor force."[163] The South Atlantic lumber industry developed principally as an offshoot of clearing fields for such agricultural uses as building fences and turpentine production.[164] From the colonial period onward, great forest reserves were exploited not simply for home construction, where "pine was king," but also for the manufacture of barrels, carts, boats, furniture, and coffins.[165] Tobacco production required drying barns. English colonists waxed eloquent about southern timber's plenitude and quality, but because transportation was challenging and shipping costs expensive, products were manufactured principally for local use: "Throughout the colonial period, much lumber was prepared on plantations, where specially trained slaves sawed planks by hand." Because the best pine grew in sandy soil unsuitable for agriculture, wealthy planters established temporary camps manned by slaves that produced finished pine lumber.[166] In early colonial America, carpenters were generalists and often unskilled, and at the end of the eighteenth century, it was still difficult to locate skilled carpenters, especially in rural areas.[167]

The land around Edenton, North Carolina, Jacobs's birth community, possessed important resources for early Americans, most notably longleaf pine. Kirby observes that "[a]s late as the spring of 1806, Edenton was still the last outpost of civility before a raw hinterland to the north."[168] By the time that Jacobs wrote her life story, the South Atlantic longleaf forests were substantially diminished, including in her own region. Silver comments that by the mid-nineteenth century, "the formerly pure longleaf forests of northeastern North Carolina had given way to small tracts of oak mingled with stands of loblolly pine."[169] Edenton was a commercial center for distributing turpentine, frequently produced with enslaved persons' labor.[170] Forestry and its affiliated occupations provided African Americans valuable sources of income and offered opportunities for gaining independence. According to John Saillant, the free black Nova Scotian John Marrant, known as the "free Carpenter," "contracted to work on a plantation outside Charleston sometime in the early to mid-1770s."[171]

Wood remained an indispensable resource in the mid-nineteenth century, and woodworking skills supplied Jacobs herself with a vital source of status that she conveys with subtle pride. In a passage that parallels the interrupted childhoods portrayed by writers such as Harriet Wilson, Lucy Larcom, Sarah Winnemucca, and Zitkala-Ša, Jacobs begins, "I was born a slave; but I never knew it till six years of happy childhood had passed away. My father was a carpenter, and considered so intelligent and skilful in his trade, that, when buildings out of the common line were to be erected, he was sent for from long distances, to be head workman. On condition of paying his mistress two hundred dollars a year, and supporting himself, he was allowed to work at this trade, and manage his own affairs" (11). Jacobs's understated emphasis on her father's occupation is easily lost on today's readers. In this self-made woman's autobiography, her father's work with wood proposes a crucial model for excellence and self-sufficiency. In a key feminine rhetorical strategy incorporating reticence and indirection, she locates her father's vocation at her narrative's, and her life's, beginning.

Carpentry subtly structures *Incidents in the Life of a Slave Girl* as a whole. We learn, for example, that the man whom Jacobs loves and hopes to marry is "a young colored carpenter; a free born man" (58). Most significantly, her most important living relative after her grandmother, her uncle Phillip, was a skilled carpenter, and she associates him with freedom. A model for Jacobs, he helps his brother Ben to escape, and he is Jacobs's trusted consultant and facilitator as she plans and executes her own escape, suffering imprisonment for his assistance.[172] Even Dr. Flint recognizes Phillip's influence (195). Among his central accomplishments is constructing the garret access, "a concealed trap door," which leads to the metaphoric underground where Jacobs discovers her strength and prepares for departure to a new world and new self (173). Jacobs's identification of this profession bears dual significance: first, carpentry symbolizes the talent, ability, and intelligence needed to succeed in a profoundly hostile environment; and second, it intimates the affiliation of these cherished men with Christ.

Jacobs is hardly a conventional Christian.[173] She excoriates slaveholders' false Christianity, remarking acerbically on the Flints' hypocrisy and commenting of a neighboring slaveholder who gruesomely tortures a slave that "the master who did these things . . . boasted the name and standing of a Christian, though Satan never had a truer follower" (77). When Mrs. Bruce purchases her freedom, Jacobs comments satirically, "A human being *sold* in the free city of New York! The bill of sale is on record, and future generations will learn from it that women were articles of traffic in New York, late in the nineteenth century of the Christian religion" (300). She protests the unethical treatment of women as property in a Christian nation, and she is skeptical about her grandmother's advice of cheek-turning acceptance of her enslavement. And she laments slaves' unconscious acceptance of whites' insincere religious views (108–9). Nevertheless, she acknowledges that her community needs spiritual consolation and honors the genuinely Christian behavior of the men and women who give her strength—such as her grandmother—and enable her freedom.[174] Paralleling Sigourney's arguments for Indian rights, Jacobs contends that Christian stewardship begins with human beings, in Haki Madhubuti's formulation, "the most precious of natural resources."[175]

In the Bible, Christ tells Philip, "Let not your heart be troubled: ye believe in God, believe also in me. In my Father's house are many mansions," and he promises relief: "And whatsoever ye shall ask in my name, that I will do. . . . I will not leave you comfortless."[176] Evoking Christ's promise of a home and her uncle Phillip's own power to free and comfort, Jacobs quietly celebrates his accomplishments in *Incidents in the Life of a Slave Girl*. Just as she has begun her narrative, Jacobs frames its conclusion by referring to a beloved carpenter. Her penultimate paragraph, describing her uncle's death and obituary, suggests understated irony and quiet pride: "So they called a colored man a *citizen!* Strange words to be uttered in that region!" (302). Refusing sentimentality, Jacobs assumes a resolutely realistic perspective as she illuminates the "resources" that provide her with the necessary means, indirect and direct, psychological and material, to liberate her. Human beings, family members, not trees, signify her transgenerational standpoint. Writing beyond family interests, she expresses skepticism about an American project of progress, of nation building, that excludes African Americans.

LIKE SIGOURNEY and Kirkland, Jacobs travels; her journey is more complex and more fraught, and problems of choice loom much larger in *Incidents in the Life of a Slave Girl* than in *Forest Life* or *Scenes in My Native Land*. As a genre, travel literature enabled these writers to show readers their own views' limitations and to rethink the meanings of home and the environment, broadly construed. For all three, home comprised not only the household and family, but America itself. Yet the nation's psychological and physical terrain encompassed settlements and wildernesses with various resonances for different inhabitants in different locations. From fallen forests to snaky swamps, the environment tendered a metaphor and grounded reality from which to appeal, in particular to women, for investments in place, community, and people — for more attention to the moral economy, sometimes explicitly Christian, than to the market economy. While Sigourney and Kirkland explore resource depletion in symbolic and concrete terms, Jacobs addresses the depletion of human resources and, through family pride about skilled carpentry, establishes her environmental agency.

For both Euramerican and African American women, such agency was often contingent. "Who can be sentimental and hungry?" Kirkland's narrator exclaims in *A New Home*.[177] As the working-class writers in chapter 3 demonstrate, the human animal is ultimately subject to her body. Like Sigourney and Jacobs, Kirkland values nature's beauty, and like Jacobs she conveys the limits of rose-tinted glasses. She too critiques the romantic/aesthetic perspective that traditional nature writing by male counterparts such as Dwight and Bryant more habitually assumes. Though Jacobs's aesthetic appreciation is visual, it is also embodied, and its necessary antecedent is physical and psychic freedom. Kirkland and Jacobs present realistic and even raw images of nonhuman nature and human animals, but Jacobs's narrative explicitly recognizes emotional rhetoric's potentially transformative power. Her reliance on the language of motherhood allies her with the environmental justice writers whom I discuss in chapters 1 and 5. Moving sentiments, she moves bodies to action. In the process, she creates a transracial community, demanding an expanded definition of womanhood.[178]

But not all affective accounts invite sympathy: some spark fear, while others engender anger and seek justice or morality. Where Sigourney and Jacobs more frequently urge sentimental sympathy, Kirkland uses ironic humor, privileging intellect over emotion. In Jacobs's hands, humor is also ironic but much more carefully guarded and marshaled. If their rhetorical weapons differ, so do their goals, which depend on their class status, their location, and their ethnicity. Their aesthetic, moral, and spiritual standards meant that forest preservation was important to Sigourney and Kirkland. Depicting clearly the conflict between the dominant society's understanding of nature—place for recreation, emblem of the sublime—and her "American" experience, Jacobs argues for equal environmental access and agency. Finally, all three writers emphasize the humility with which humans must face the natural world. All investigate and question, in varying ways and with different definitions, the concept of American progress, and all participate in the conversation about what the nation should become. But while Sigourney and Kirkland castigate deforestation and the greed and blindness that propel it, Jacobs asserts that humans' initial environment is the body, and her first project must be to possess herself.

Coda: Working the Maine Woods

In "A Winter Drive," Sarah Orne Jewett reflects, "I believe that there are few persons who cannot remember some trees which are as much connected with their own lives as people are. When they stand beside them there is at once a feeling of very great affection. It seems as if the tree remembered what we remember; it is something more than the fact of it having been associated with our past." Jewett foregrounds trees' and humans' mutual fondness and highlights the former's consciousness and character. She also ponders tree illnesses, many of which have been caused by thoughtless forestry practices that propel local climate changes, and insists, "It is a very short-sighted person who looks at the wholesale slaughter of the American forests without dismay, especially in the Eastern States."[179]

Huge swaths of Jewett's native Maine had been cleared by the time that she published "A Winter Drive"; according to the anthropologist James M. Acheson, "The amount of land in [Maine] agriculture reached its apex in 1880," just a year before her essay was published.[180] By the late nineteenth century, the destruction of American forests was largely complete. Unlike John Muir's expansive and nationalist scope in "The American Forests," but modeling an affective rhetoric that he too would use, Jewett focuses on the local and intimate.[181] Envisioning the trees as members of an ecological family, her whimsical humor and vivid detail elicit responses that include affection, nostalgia, anger, thoughtfulness, guilt, awe, and responsibility.

Concerns about deforestation continue.[182] According to the U.S. Forest Service, Maine remains the principal source of American sugar maples and other timber resources; the state has traditionally supplied multinational companies with large quantities of pulp for paper. Not surprisingly, given the state's huge hardwood forests, these companies are heavily invested in Maine real estate, and they are eager to clear-cut Maine's ten-million-acre North Woods. In 1995 the Maine Green Party, along with environmental activists and the Natural Resources Council of Maine, introduced a bill in the state legislature that outlined clear-cutting standards, but corporations successfully lobbied to prevent the bill's passage.[183]

The Maine Green Party described the clear-cutting practices as "the hemorrhaging of Maine's woods." Concerned not only with the environment but also with Maine losing jobs due to globalization, the party gathered together citizens representing many interests—"loggers, mill workers, hunters, fishermen and women, snowmobilers, town officials, hikers"— who "all joined with the activists in a heroic attempt to preserve Maine's last great remaining resource—a forest for future generations that everyone can have a stake in, for jobs and recreation." The *New York Times* reported that the timber industry employed "32,000 people and generat[ed] pulp for paper and lumber valued at $5.5 billion a year. It makes paper for *Time* and *National Geographic* magazines and for *The New York Times Magazine*, as well as for lottery tickets."[184] In the process, according to Nancy Allen, the Green Party's media coordinator, the industry devastates Maine's forests like "the horrors of war. . . . As far as the eye can see, there is nothing—no trees, no birds, no wildlife." She cites the loss of canopy protecting smaller vegetation and widespread herbicide use, concluding, "The paper companies are leaving Maine right now. And leaving it dead."[185] Allen's language echoes Sigourney's and Kirkland's, and it ups the ante, using what Buell calls "toxic discourse."[186]

Clear-cutting is expensive in many ways, not least the $25,000 cost per mile of access roads, which in the mid-1990s were growing at the rate of around one thousand miles annually. The ballot initiative prohibiting clear-cutting enjoyed enormous, diverse public support, but voters eventually rejected the measure. They also denied Governor Angus King's alternative of limited clear-cutting—which was supported by (and in part developed with) the forest industry—despite the $1.8 million budget for television advertising supporting the alternative initiative (compared to $0 for the Green coalition initiative).[187] The Green candidate for governor argued that the clear-cutting ban was intended not to prevent logging but to ensure its sustainability and to maintain employment.[188] The intensity of the debates on the topic spotlighted the disjunction between northern and southern Mainers; as one northerner pointedly stated, "They have clear-cuts down there, but they call them shopping malls."[189]

Humor notwithstanding, as the environmental justice movement underlines (and *Forest Life* and *Incidents in the Life of a Slave Girl* differentially depict), the disparity between working-class people and owners, manual workers and intellectuals, is reflected everywhere in contemporary American society. The heated rhetoric surrounding the forestry industry in the American Northwest, the preservation of the spotted owl, and job retention for loggers indicate this gap; Richard White underscores such fractures in the title of his 1996 essay "Are You an Environmentalist or Do You Work for a Living?"[190] The question of environmental stewardship prompts others: who is the steward, and what is being protected? As they explore the complex meaning of resources, the working women of chapter 3 propose some unsettling answers with continuing echoes.

Nursemaid with her charge, c. 1855. The young woman
pictured appears older than Harriet Wilson was when
she was indentured to the Hayward family.
Courtesy of the Library of Congress.

Chapter 3

Golden Hands

Weaving America

The dwellings of the colored people, unless they happened to be protected by some influential white person, who was nigh at hand, were robbed of clothing and every thing else the marauders thought worth carrying away. All day long these unfeeling wretches went round, like a troop of demons, terrifying and tormenting the helpless. At night, they formed themselves into patrol bands, and went wherever they chose among the colored people, acting out their brutal will. Many women hid themselves in woods and swamps, to keep out of their way.

—HARRIET JACOBS, *Incidents in the Life of a Slave Girl*

DESCRIBING INCURSIONS that "low whites" made into blacks' homes after Nat Turner's insurrection, Harriet Jacobs recounts the physical tortures that the African American community endured. Her grandmother received a visit from one such "pack of hungry wolves," who "snatched at every thing within their reach." Mob members were particularly incensed by letters to Jacobs—evidence of her literacy—and by valuable household items, such as "some silver spoons which ornamented an old-fashioned buffet." Jacobs's rhetoric portrays the invaders as savages, animals contained only by "the better class of the community," and she distinguishes between African Americans' civilized environment and their antagonists' hungry and violent bodies. While protesting that African Americans lack agency in controlling access to their homes, Jacobs acknowledges that alliances with "influential" white community members buffer some, among them her own relatively comfortable family, from the "brutal" marauders' worst abuses.[1]

Often combined with other forms of social advantage and disadvantage, class has always distinguished among Americans, and those who "work for a living" have viewed nature and the environment differently than those who do not. The slaves on antebellum turpentine plantations regarded the pines from which they collected resin differently than the plantation owners who sequestered them in the woods and extracted their labor, while the female slaves with indoor duties had yet another attitude.[2] As we have seen, Sigourney, Kirkland, and Jacobs value nature's beauty, but they also recognize what we might grimly call the aesthetics of poverty and racism. The lexicon of civilized and savage, which establishes social hierarchies, extends beyond the ethnic and racial divisions that I have explored in earlier chapters; it also features in depictions of—and by—working-class writers, whose voices have been almost entirely eclipsed in studies of nineteenth-century American women's writing, American women's rhetoric, and environmental literature.[3]

America was built not only by its founders' ideological efforts but also by its working people's golden hands. Owning one's body—to recall Haki Madhubuti, "the most precious of natural resources"—and one's labor precedes property ownership or resource management, aspects of which I have mapped in the preceding chapters.[4] This chapter develops the theme of embodiment I touched upon in relation to Kirkland and Jacobs. Working-class voices require us to reconceptualize resource wars, for dominant-culture individuals consumed resources that included women's labor and laboring women's bodies. How working women responded to that understanding depended upon such variables as their race, place, and environmental agency. Such women faced numerous obstacles to writing (let alone publication), not least of which were the acquisition of literacy and leisure time. Here I foreground three mid-nineteenth-century workers' writing, paying particular attention to how they envisage their irregular and contingent access to nonhuman nature and the corporeal ramifications of that access. The paid domestic servant Lorenza Stevens Berbineau, the indentured servant and entrepreneur Harriet Wilson, and the factory worker–teacher Lucy Larcom variously circumvent or appreciate their physical presence and claim material, spiritual, and cultural agency, in their individual homes and in America itself. These working-class women's complex representations of embodiment and their negotiations for access and agency encode examples of environmental writing and early environmental justice literature.[5]

Despite significant differences, the writers' experiences overlap: the rural-born Berbineau became a city-based servant; Wilson performed both domestic and agricultural tasks in a rural setting; and Larcom moved from a seafaring community, to a factory town, to the west, and then back to the Boston area. All three women received some education: Wilson and Larcom attended school briefly as children and then gained further education as adults. All wrote out of 1850s New England, although Berbineau came from an earlier generation than the exact contemporaries Wilson and Larcom. Larcom's publications also extended much later into the century, offering a retrospective view of the antebellum period the others describe. I treat Berbineau first because her 1851 diaries show how ideas about nature change in travel writing by a working woman. Continuing with Wilson's 1859 autobiographical novel *Our Nig*, the chapter shifts emphasis from indoor to outdoor labor; that movement illuminates how Wilson characterizes her place in the environment beyond domesticity. Indirectly underscoring the fluidity of class, Larcom's narrative and poetry convey the perspective of a middle-class girl turned factory worker and then teacher and professional author; of the three, her writing is the most intentionally and explicitly political, a stance that her higher social status and relative financial security enabled. Each author grounds her project in concepts of home—individual and national—but home variously symbolizes a refuge, an ideal, or (for Wilson) a toxic, degraded, and potentially dangerous reality.

Notwithstanding their commonalities as New England working-class women, Berbineau, Wilson, and Larcom articulate substantially different outlooks on labor.[6] Because individuals' experiences differed widely and class status was fluid in nineteenth-century America, making generalizations poses challenges. Definitions determined principally by reference to industrial labor are inapplicable, and we should accept E. P. Thompson's still-persuasive argument that class is best understood through relationships.[7] Nevertheless, appreciating the range of their responsibilities entails outlining some discursive trajectories. First, I move from Berbineau's relative lack of literacy to Wilson's terse experiment to Larcom's multiple, professional publications. Simultaneously, I range across genres (and, by extension, audiences) from less to more public: from Berbineau's travel diaries to Wilson's autobiographical novel to Larcom's autobiography and poetry. Connected to genre, another narrative arc encompasses Berbineau's individualist attitude, Wilson's individual (but representative) history, and

Larcom's more community-oriented assessment. Finally, I move from most to least explicitly embodied.

Despite such differences, these working women all practice (though very differently) an aesthetic of genre compression that employs rhetorical indirection and elision. This expressive form reflects their struggles to gain environmental agency and control over their physical resources. Thus humor, a discourse of power, is normally coded or indirect, if it emerges at all. Similarly, their terse and sometimes elliptical aesthetics suggest the limits of sympathy and sentimentalism. My discussion attends particularly to their embodied rhetoric, the textual moments when materiality looms large, because such moments speak most forcefully to the contingencies of achieving environmental justice.[8]

Laboring women afford an important touchstone for exploring the relationship between gender and the environment; while their experience parallels women's generally, it magnifies salient features of that relationship and reminds us that the body is women's first environment. The dominant society of the nineteenth century connected all women with nature, animals, disabled people, and children, but it intensified those associations for some groups.[9] Unlike middle-class white women, who were the putative purveyors of morality (and hence civilization), women of color and working women were both naturalized and sexualized. Harriet Wilson's *Our Nig* reveals the heroine Frado's stepfather contemplating how to dispose of his stepdaughter when he and her mother plan to leave the town: "There's Frado's six years old, and pretty, . . . and white folks'll say so. She'd be a prize somewhere."[10] Laboring women represented resources, including embodied and sexual resources, for the more affluent. In contrast, men like Wilson's slightly older contemporary Thoreau possessed agency over their home and physical self and enjoyed wide access to natural and cultural resources such as books. Thoreau may have wrestled with weeds and woodchucks during his Walden sojourn, but he had the means to alleviate his garden's scanty yields. He also had the leisure to contemplate the pond's "perfect forest mirror" and a partridge's wisdom.[11] Stewardship, this contrast implies, requires a sense of ownership, itself a prerequisite for agency. For midcentury working-class women like Berbineau, Wilson, and Larcom, frequently unable to control their own bodies or determine their homes, nature and the environment in their positive incarnations were too often inaccessible and in their negative ramifications only too immediate.

"The whole face of the Country was perfect Emerald"

As Lorenza Stevens Berbineau recounts the sights from her Grand Tour, she juxtaposes American landscapes with their European counterparts. Traveling to Chester from Liverpool, she observes, "We saw various Gardens with Hawthorn hedges nothing very beautiful the grass did not look as well as in America perhaps this was not a specimen." In Paris nearly a month later, she ponders, "I dont think most of the people work very hard the[y] seem easy and contented they are not like the Americans in many things an American could not live as some of the french do."[12]

Does Berbineau disparage English gardens or elevate American landscapes? Is she praising the French and damning the Americans, or vice versa? The compression of her 1851 European travel diary sometimes makes distinguishing her attitudes difficult. Such attitudes appear not only in her accounts of natural and cultural landscapes but also when she describes her responsibilities as a servant responding to seasick employers, children with dysentery, and her own physical ailments. Questions of access and agency underwrite her narrative as she negotiates embodiment and cultural pleasures in an environment combining domestic employments and foreign excitements. During her visit to Switzerland, Berbineau affirms, "I am neither Painter nor Poet" (79), yet she creates an American working-class woman's depiction of Europe—possibly unique in the period. Berbineau's diary details travel's delights and difficulties, religious differences, Europe's aesthetic pleasures and oddities, and most important for our purposes, working people and the environment. The discussion below provides personal and historical contexts, outlines her views of traveling, investigates how European travel inflected her appreciation of America as home, and analyzes her relationship to nature and the environment, variously rendered through gardens, agricultural labor, and her own embodiment. Her diary submits a tacit if unconscious brief for environmental justice and suggests why ecocritical analysis should attend to class-based as well as gendered material experience.

In the antebellum United States, leisure travel was principally a perquisite of wealth and privilege.[13] Financial success preceded the perambulations Sigourney portrayed in *Scenes in My Native Land*, as it did her earlier volume about Europe, *Pleasant Memories of Pleasant Lands*. Servants may have accompanied their families to Europe, but they were characteristically

too busy or lacked the education to record their experiences. Unlike the
many nineteenth-century American women writers who became literary
laborers because family fortunes reversed, Berbineau was a lifelong member
of the working class, serving as household manager for the wealthy Francis
Cabot Lowell II family of Beacon Hill in Boston. In July 1851, Lowell jour-
neyed to Europe with his household, which consisted of his wife and their
daughters, eighteen-year-old Mary and fifteen-year-old Georgina, and
their six-year-old son, Edward Jackson. One of more than thirty thousand
Americans who annually traveled abroad by midcentury, Berbineau stayed
with the Lowells in grand hotels, caring for her young charge Eddie and
commenting in a series of travel diaries about the people, places, and things
she saw in England, France, Switzerland, Germany, and again in Paris before her departure for New England.[14] Writing hastily, Berbineau reveals a
discerning perspective as appealing and informative to today's readers as it
no doubt was to her fellow domestics, to whom she read parts of her diaries
on her return home. We can imagine the servants' excitement if we consider
Berbineau's managerial role in the household, which at various times encompassed a "coachman, footman, governess, cook . . . and probably three
maids (usually with Irish names) in addition to Lorenza herself." She also
supervised regular visits by outside help. Hence, her leadership role as what
Philip Taylor calls "a trusted veteran" would likely have meant that her
reading generated an atmosphere of anticipation for a memorable event.[15]

Biographical details for Berbineau remain minimal; Taylor's sketch relates virtually all we know. A devout Congregationalist, she joined the
Lowell household in 1830, working there for essentially her entire career
until her 1869 death. She married a Henri Berbineau in 1842, possibly hoping, like many of her peers, to escape service, but her husband has disappeared from historical records. Although we know that she oversaw other
servants and cared for the Lowell children (and, later, their children), we
know only imprecisely how much she was paid.[16] Like most of her peers she
probably lived in an unheated attic in the Lowells' Boston house. Like them
she shared a close connection, emotional and financial, with her Maine
family, visiting them as regularly as possible and, "just as if she had been
a European immigrant sending home remittances," frequently sending
money to those relatives.[17]

In many respects, however, Berbineau's life and career departed radically
from her counterparts'.[18] Her lengthy service with one family was extremely

rare; many servants departed after a few weeks or months, whether because they were dissatisfied with their wages (or received a better offer elsewhere) or due to their employers' excessive expectations, desire for cheaper labor, or unhappiness with their efforts.[19] Berbineau enjoyed a relationship of unusual trust and affection with the Lowells. Francis Lowell not only supported her long after her useful career was done and her health was failing, he also showed magnanimity toward her relatives after her death.[20] Even during the European journey, when she became ill, he assured a physician's attendance and later sent her back to America early, first class, due to continued concerns about her health. Though she clearly worked hard, the family arranged numerous opportunities for her enjoyment, perhaps partly because she and her labor were vital resources upon which many people depended.

Berbineau's affectionate diary entries about and letters to the Lowells furnish the most striking evidence for her distinctive status. She was especially devoted to Eddie as he moved through childhood, Harvard enrollment, marriage (in 1868), and fatherhood; both her later diaries and the European travel narratives contain recurrent references, including notes about presents she bought him. Not only did Berbineau attend Eddie's wedding, he also, as Taylor observes, "wrote to her while on his honeymoon in New York City."[21] In addition to her surviving diaries, we have Berbineau's letters to various Lowell family members, written during her periodic trips to visit her relatives in Maine or during a Lowell absence. As remarkable as the diaries' and letters' content is the fact that the family preserved them. Because of her relative household authority, we might regard Berbineau as a professional or manager, but we need merely turn to the diaries to grasp such definitions' potential limitations. For example, her own health exigencies do not release her from wage labor's demands.

In apprehending Berbineau's complex working-class status, we must finally contemplate her unique position as Francis Cabot Lowell II's employee. Lowell's father was one of the founders of the textile mills in the city bearing his name; Berbineau's employer was thus a major shareholder in the corporations that held the mills and determined management policies. Berbineau assumed her responsibilities for the Lowells in October 1830, so she managed the household during a turbulent time of strikes and protests about long working hours.[22] We have no record of her attitudes toward these events, but her diaries disclose that her own class standpoint shares much with the earlier generation of independent New England "help" and her self-assertive millworker counterparts.[23] In this complicated cultural, historical, and personal environment, Berbineau's relatively close and affectionate relation to the Lowells appears even more extraordinary. Reflecting a flexible class and gender identity, her diaries record an intricate negotiation of femininity, domesticity, and leisure and, consequently, her access to culture's and nature's pleasures.

TRAVEL LITERATURE is a useful medium through which to explore class complexities, because home features centrally in the travel writing genre and in working-class women's experience.[24] For the travel writer, Mary Suzanne Schriber argues, "'home' and 'abroad' are the polarities from which travelers construct meaning."[25] As Kirkland's *Forest Life* cautions, U.S.-based travel to the west—where many New Englanders sought their fortunes—leveled class distinctions; survival trumped middle-class attitudes. For bourgeois antebellum woman leisure travelers, their movement outside the home often permitted (explicitly or implicitly) an increased scope of activity and influence.[26] For working-class women like Berbineau, the idea and reality of home was more tenuous, not necessarily the imagined middle-class haven. A woman domestic, who helped make another woman's home, sometimes resided with her employer or lived in pinched rented accommodations either alone or with her own family.[27] Because they included Berbineau in their educational pursuits, the Lowells obviously subscribed to the popular nineteenth-century philanthropic model that believed exposing the working class to high culture would enable them to better themselves.[28] Berbineau clearly valued such access, but she seems to have possessed a double vision, enjoying the privileges of the wealthy while she documented her position's occasionally onerous responsibilities.[29]

Berbineau's remarks on the European countryside synthesize the disparate perspectives of her rural Maine upbringing and years of service to an elite, intellectual Boston family; these remarks also signal the imperative for all American travelers, especially women, for self-improvement. She concerns herself repeatedly with food production and agriculture. Traveling between Chester and Leamington, England, she comments, "I saw fields of Potatoes & turnips they looked very nice" (60). Riding from Calais to Paris, she remarks, "[Y]ou would see for many miles one vast plain squares planted with different things a good deal of grain & then you would see a patch of potatoes & a spot of mustard and another of Popies and so on with different sorts of vegitables hop fields" (72). She applauds gardens throughout Europe, but she finds the economical agricultural arrangements impressive. Near Berne, she notes, "[T]he plains are all cultivated not an inch of land wasted" (93–94). Addressed to an imagined "you," her rhetoric appeals to a work ethos that she would have shared with her potential audience of friends and fellow servants, male and female.

Her narrative also conjures the labor needed to achieve such beautiful cultivation. Recent feminist theories that distinguish between idealized woman-nature links and a recognition of embodiment have provided an important corrective to charges of essentialism leveled against ecofeminists.[30] As Stacy Alaimo and Susan Hekman point out in *Material Feminisms*, "Women *have* bodies; these bodies have pain as well as pleasure. . . . We need to find a way to talk about these bodies and the materiality they inhabit. Focusing exclusively on representations, ideology, and discourse excludes lived experience, corporeal practice, and biological substance from consideration."[31] This admonition does not require us to ignore representations — especially since working-class women have long struggled to enter public and private discourse — but it suggests that we should particularly concentrate on the bodily experience expressed in and underwriting those representations. Berbineau's description of fruitful English gardens combines her visceral appreciation of the effort they entailed with delight in their aesthetic attractiveness. That is, she unites the rural dweller's pragmatism and the affluent urbanite's admiration of a lovely landscape.

Yankee economy probably fueled her approval, but another part derived from her belief, mirroring her privileged peers', that "cultivation"—a word that recurs—symbolizes improvement according with American ideas of progress. As we saw earlier, undergirding nationalist ideals, such progress in the United States paralleled the environmental injustice and destruction that Jemison's, Sigourney's, and Kirkland's writing reveals. Agricultural improvements denoted social advancement, and Berbineau demonstrates interest in technology when she visits the Great Exhibition: "[S]aw things from the Unted States handsome lamps mechinery farming emplements" (66). Technology benefits domestics: if travel demands effort for affluent travelers, for servants such labor multiplies. Nineteenth-century women regarded laundry as particularly loathsome. Hence, when Berbineau records that "the sides of the [Liverpool] streets are paved & the centre is Mackadamized the cross walks are flag stone" (56), she does so partly because paving meant that travelers' clothes would remain clean longer. A few days later in Chester she repeats this observation, noting the paved streets were "very Broad & Clean." Her next remark indicates from another angle how her class-based experience informs her perceptions: "I have seen some miserable looking objects every now and then a beggar comeing to me for something but as a people they seem very happy" (60). Here and elsewhere, material life and the body remain obstacles and overcoming them betokens progress.

Although she depicts impoverished bodies—called "objects" before they transform into "people"—like her wealthy employers Berbineau esteems beauty.[32] Inside Warwick Castle, she comments, "[I]n looking from the window there was a beautiful view the river ran throug the lawn there was a beautif arch bridge built over it Grand forest of trees va[r]ious kinds very fine oaks & Cedars of Lebenon I cannot describe the place well" (62). Wild nature is also lovely, and one journey elicits extended praise:

> [W]e had a very pleasent day we had some Beautiful views to day in rideing over the Jura Mountains . . . it was a beautiful winding road round the mountains they were covered with balsom firs beautiful shape when on the mountain the plain below was beautiful well cultivated we had a beautiful view of Mont Blanc while changeing horses at Faueille we got out and walked a little way I picked a few flowers we saw the Lake of Geneve when on the Jura Mountain there was a beautiful plain below and many Villages at the sides of that was the Lake then beyond that were the Mountains again above them all arose Mont Blanc they were white with snow then the sun being bright they looked splendid it may well be called the Monarch of Mountains I cannot describe the beauty we saw. (82)[33]

Beauty piles upon beauty, and she concludes that even superlatives are inadequate.[34] Idealized portrayals of the landscape featured significantly in much middle-class women's travel writing. These accounts conveyed their cultivation and their leisure for aesthetic study, just as gardening was beginning to signify affluence at home.[35] Participating in America's fascination with the picturesque and the sublime much like Sigourney in "Niagara,"

Warwick Castle. Engraving by J. C. Bentley, after
George Cattermole, 1834. The image shows the arched
bridge and landscape that Berbineau admires.

Berbineau becomes a representative traveler, and class, with its corporeal contingencies, is momentarily elided.

As with the episode at Chester, however, an eye for class differences and work tempers Berbineau's emphasis on beauty; she cannot see the beautiful in splendid isolation from the material circumstances that engender it. Near Simplon in the Alps, she notices that "the people look very poor & work very hard they raise a good deal Maiz like our Indian corn" (87). The recurrence of such reports intimates sympathy for the laboring poor. She repeatedly juxtaposes the sublime with the real, recounting how the houses near Mont Blanc "looked very poor many houses were built of stone and clay thatched roofs not any windows sometimes little holes in the side of the house." A scene of toiling women seems to reinforce this poverty: "[T]he women were at work as hard as the men their skin was a perfect brown I dont think the women of America could work so" (79).[36] It is unclear whether Berbineau intentionally draws upon aesthetic language only to undercut it. But her embodied rhetoric sparks listeners'/readers' emotional intelligence and creates sympathy for these laboring women. At the same time, her nationalist perspective recalls Sigourney's *Scenes in My Native Land*, where the environment—and here, its affecting inhabitants—promotes a progressive vision of America.

Given Berbineau's Maine roots, it is unlikely that she would be surprised or dismayed to see women doing hard agricultural tasks, but her ambivalence persists. Her text, like Kirkland's, undermines romantic pictures with jolts of realism. Going up the Albus, she notes, "[W]e had a fine view the fields looked so pretty and the spruces were very Beautiful the people look very healthy they live out of doors the women & children work as hard as the men & the Cows as hard as the Oxen they shoe the Cows as they do the Oxen" (92). Near Mount Splugen, she offers a stronger counterpastoral: "[T]his morning in rideing through many places we saw the women mowing not very long grass we saw several women driveing Cows tackeled into a Cart they look very funny nothing on their heads their skin perfect Brown they are very poor looking" (90). Berbineau focuses here and elsewhere on the people in the landscape—including beggars and other "Objects of Charity"—rather than on the landscape itself, revealing the middle-class and sentimental inflection of most American women travelers' writing.[37] Berbineau's voice assumes a sentimental tone only when she has the leisure to do so; sentimentality appears to be a luxury.

In several passages, Berbineau associates women employed outdoors with draft animals. Coupling potential sympathy for Europe's working women with dismay, her descriptions imply a gendered division of labor that may mirror middle-class expectations about women's appropriate responsibilities and standards of respectability that ensured distance from potentially degrading material life. For example, which women are "the women of America"? Her tone and position are difficult to interpret; does she mean that American women are superior? The portrait of the women's skin as a "perfect Brown" suggests an affirmative response: in Europe, women have become like men (or, worse, like animals). Her move to detach herself from these agricultural laborers illuminates the variegated and fraught conceptualizations of the working class in the nineteenth century as well as Berbineau's efforts to assert her humanity. Her work speaks to contemporary ecofeminists' analogies between the exploitation of women and of animals, and it rejects any essentialist affiliation between women and nature. At the same time, it anticipates Alaimo and Hekman's insistence that "Nature is agentic—it acts, and those actions have consequences for both the human and nonhuman world."[38]

Perhaps Berbineau refuses commonality with these brutish women because her duties are domestic, indoors. She seems to evoke the stereotype applied to Native American women as beasts of burden as well as to reference an association between women and slaves in a time when the Fugitive Slave Law was very much on Americans' minds and early feminist activists like Margaret Fuller were drawing precisely this comparison.[39] Rather than empathizing, Berbineau's embodied rhetoric "others" the foreign woman as surely as her middle- and upper-class American counterparts' would do.[40] Rita Felski underscores how "working-class women, in particular, often have a powerful interest and investment in respectability, as a means of distancing themselves from sexualized images of lower-class women's bodies."[41] Sexuality may not have figured in Berbineau's calculus, but respectability certainly did. As we will see for the elite Mexican American author María Amparo Ruiz de Burton in chapter 5, progress, from Berbineau's perspective, entails her separation from (degraded, uncivilized, dehumanized) material existence.

Finally, she decides that England and America are more alike than dissimilar, and she comments with apparent relief in Lucerne, "[T]here are several English familys here with their Maids I find very agreable company" (93). Although Berbineau resituates herself in the company of domestics, she apparently locates them (and herself) on a much higher social scale than the brown-skinned rural workers, just as her counterparts in the Lowell mills of the 1840s and 1850s frequently regarded themselves as superior to the Irish laborers coming to dominate the workplace.[42] Informed by ethnocentrism and by urban prejudice against outdoor activities, Harriet Beecher Stowe's remark about affluent English women makes explicit the occupational and ethnic hierarchy that Berbineau articulates: "They do not, like us, fade their cheeks lying awake nights ruminating the awful question who shall do the washing next week. . . . They are not obliged to choose between washing their own dishes, or having their cut glass, silver, and china left to the mercy of a foreigner, who has never done any thing but field work."[43] Berbineau's opinions may also be inflected by native-born U.S. servants' attitude that claimed equality with their "betters." Employers, in fact, were dismayed by their domestics' independent and equal self-concept; many servants, especially earlier in the nineteenth century when they were considered "help," worked because they chose to do so.[44] Environmental agency matters; in Stowe's account, as in Berbineau's, wealthy women profit materially—not just economically, but in their own bodies—because of servants' and workers' all-too-corporeal labor.

Poverty and toil recur in Berbineau's diary as important narrative threads.[45] The Swiss appear "to be a very Industrious people," and the Dutch are "very neat they are very independent the poorest of them look clean," in contrast, as various passages insinuate, to Germans and Italians (84, 103). Failure in religious observance draws the harshest criticism, and when she discovers the French people working and playing on Sundays, Berbineau is severely nationalist: "[T]he women were at work in the fields cutting grain they look very poor nothwithstanding it was sabbath day th[e]y were at work or at play give me my own Country for the quiet sabbath where man & beast can rest and think of their Maker" (72; see 76). Ambivalently combining judgment and gratitude, inviting potential listeners to feel similarly, her remarks complicate the concept of leisure and may result partly from her faithful Congregationalism. Here she responds indirectly to the continuing debate in the United States and abroad about weekly work hours. Although U.S. factory workers might drudge for as much as seventy-two hours and live-in domestics were virtually always on call, they expected to have Sundays free.[46]

But Berbineau's remarks also signal the city-based employee who elides the seasonal necessities of manual agricultural responsibilities. A conversation with an unnamed German, however, ultimately suppresses such comments on Sunday labor: "I was talking with a person about working on the sabbath he said the people that are poor if they dont work they cant eat they earn so small a sum they were Obliged to work" (98). Her subsequent silence on the subject implies compassion if not agreement with the workers. The realities of European laboring life reveal her own relative privilege, but she is willing to modify even profoundly held beliefs when she encounters concrete experience that complicates those beliefs. Here embodied rhetoric generates terse sympathy rather than distance.[47]

Although her preceding comments ostensibly separate nature from religion, Berbineau shares with Sigourney and her more affluent peers a transcendental understanding of the natural world. Her description of the Lausanne region's vineyards concludes, "I cannot describe the beauty of this great sheet of water with a ripple it was a palish green sometim it shaded like the colours of the rainbow the tops of the moutains were white with snow the reflection of the Sun on the mountain and on the water was Beautiful & the Silver Clouds as it were on the mountains we can truly say God is the maker of them all. while admireing his works may we have hearts to love and serve him" (84–85). The "beauty" with which she infuses her diaries indicates human activity—agriculture and gardening—but nature's sublimity manifests divine creativity. The Lucerne mountains resonate similarly: "[O]ne would think they were in Paradise in looking out of the Back window you see the mountains the well cultivated Gardens which looks so pretty in looking out the front window you see the Beautiful Lake as far as you can see beyond the mountains whose tops are covered with snow the whole prospect is a beautiful view how much we see in the works of nature how much we ought to love & Praise God who made every thing & gave us eyes to behold them" (92). Invoking Eden, Berbineau stresses her gratitude; as for Sigourney, nature becomes an occasion for celebration. Recalling Thoreau's evocations of Walden Pond, such passages perform songs of praise, intended to inspire and awe later listeners and readers, whether friends or the writer herself.

IN BERBINEAU'S DIARY Christian rhetoric serves not to reform, as it did for the authors in chapter 1, but to elevate; she reprises Sigourney's tourist's perspective in *Scenes in My Native Land* and her transcendental vision in "Niagara." Such moments are punctuated by others, more immediate and unpleasantly embodied. Not only did Berbineau attend to the seasick Mrs. Lowell and Nina on the Atlantic voyage, while on the continent she cared for ill family members such as Eddie, supplying skilled nursing that prevented her from enjoying either cultural pursuits or outdoor pleasures. Her own recurring illnesses caused great suffering and meant remaining in the hotel. One such occasion occurred after the household's arrival in Paris, where she remarks, "I felt quite sick when I went to bed." Because Eddie too became very unwell, her labor increased proportionately, despite her own misery. Her diary entries for 10–20 August reflect intense concern for him and her hard work feeding and watching him and preparing medicine: "Pleasent very warm not well I have a bad diherea. as soon as it was light I got up took 20 drops of Laudnum Edie is quite sick he is very feverish has not been dress to day I gave him some oil the rest of the family gone out to walk or ride unfortunate for Edie & me" (73).[48] Her sense of confinement is palpable the next morning, as she notes, "Pleasent very warm Edie quite sick rather more comfortable than yesterday the Dr left me some medicene it was liquid to day he left some powders I cannot realize I am in Paris I have not been out I see many Curious things in looking out the window" (73). Confined and repeatedly disabled by her own illness and her physical labor, Berbineau hints at disappointment and elicits sympathy. Here and elsewhere, her emotional intelligence grounds itself in embodied experience, as she expresses frustration that she lacks environmental agency.

Even when Berbineau is sick, she focuses on her duties cooking and making medicine in the family's elegant accommodations: "[T]here is a kitchen attached to [the dining room] with a little convenient range it is curious in its structure I had a Charcoal fire made up to day I have been cooking arrowroot & gruel & cataplasms for Edie It is rather Inconvient to cook little messes in down stairs as you go out the door pass by one door to get to the kitchen." Despite approving of the elegant "satin damask" and "velvet" furnishings, she remains confined to the rooms, nursing Eddie and his sister: "[V]ery warm Edie quite poorly though Dr [Tusole?] thinks him quite well had an other Doctor this eve he has ordred him some more medicine two powdres of calomile 2 grains each also a dose of medecine Castor Oil for nourishment beef tea arrow root & toast water Nina not well this afternoon diherea they think the water very bad I have used a little brandy in my water for diner very warm day I feel the heat I feel languid very little strength" (74). Caring for the Lowell children means ignoring her own weakness and misery. Questions arise: given her potential audience of fellow servants, why did she enter such remarks in her diary? Did she wish to have a record encompassing the full range of her experiences? Did she anticipate sympathy, or did she simply skip the unpleasant details when she read them aloud? "Nature"—bodily distress—intrudes on work and leisure, as she becomes a domestic workhorse. Regardless of how much she loved the children, the Lowells profit from her care.

Remaining indoors compounds Berbineau's unhappiness, for the diary comments with repeated longing on the sights beyond her window. When she and Eddie are finally able to get outdoors, her diary conveys excitement and relief at diminished domestic cares: "I have Just been out to ride with Mrs Lowell we rode through the Bolevard. it looked very pretty the buildings are very high Beautiful lighted with gass splended Cafe houses Elegantly furnished the shops looked very pretty the Bolevards thronged with people thousands of people walking they walk so every night" (75). We rarely glimpse explicit complaints about the restrictions that her position imposed; rather, such restrictions seem to enhance her appreciation of her limited freedom and erratic pleasure. She attempts to make the best of her situation, enjoying the scene through her window and minimizing her pain from ailments ranging from "dyspepsia" to toothache. Despite her efforts to ignore discomfort, however, family members' and her own illnesses, a constant refrain, curtail her access to outdoor pleasures.[49] In this context, embodiment is too immediate and access to aesthetic and material pleasures too remote.

For Harriet Wilson's Frado, disability is externally superimposed by an employer's demands for superhuman labor and by beatings; for Berbineau, it occurs as a temporary and "natural" event. Nevertheless, it is worth noticing that her health improved dramatically when she boarded the steamer alone to return to America, bespeaking a complex and evocative form of homesickness. For her, class and gender form a matrix in which home travels—responsibilities and relationships, while altered abroad, do not disappear. Home also acquires a nationalist inflection. In addition, labor expectations sometimes undercut cultural gender norms, in effect "ungendering" her.[50] Her occupation not only inflects what she sees and experiences, including nature and the environment, it also affects her writing's form: in a contingent aesthetic of compression, she composes brief, usually telegraphic diary entries whose elisions signal her material constraints. As she struggles for ownership of her resources—her body, her time, her imagination—she translates that struggle into her text's concrete shape.

Although Berbineau extends the travel writing genre, her diary resides at the opposite end of the public-private continuum from Sigourney's, Kirkland's, and Jacobs's narratives, public documents seeking to intervene in readers' worldview. Yet, more than a private project intended to record self-improvement or memorialize a special journey, the diary frames the author's experiences explicitly for the implied "you"—friends, family, and fellow servants—who occasionally emerge.[51] Nature and the environment evoked practical sustenance (the potatoes and "vegitibles" she carefully catalogues), confirmations of faith, physical obstacles, sometimes-inaccessible pleasures, and reminders of status. Berbineau's account is simultaneously antiromantic, in its chronicles of ailments, and romantic, in its spiritually inflected moments. The former, however, outweigh the latter both in number and descriptive precision. Locating realistic details of suffering adjacent to romantic sketches of nature's beauties, Berbineau approximates Kirkland's literate juxtapositions, though she does so unsatirically, if not uncritically. At the same time, her indoor confinement reprises Jacobs's much more stringent self-imprisonment in her grandmother's attic. Despite the Lowells' benevolence, Berbineau could not exceed her status as a working woman, and her diaries alternate between frustration about her enclosure and delight in outdoor pleasures and indoor cultural opportunities.

While Berbineau's rhetoric periodically concedes disappointment, vexation, and longing, it stops short of claiming injustice; but her repetitive reports of illnesses and her emphasis on the constraints that her embodied labor imposed allow us to understand her diary more generously. Berbineau substantiates for us material feminism's insights about the coagency of bodies and nature and what Alaimo and Hekman call "the often obdurate substance and unexpected exigencies of corporeality."[52] However indirectly, her diary propels questions about environmental ethics and environmental justice that are still more urgent in Wilson's work: for example, whose labor, and whose bodies, underwrite leisure or progress?

Berbineau never asks such questions, though the diary genre's potential privacy permits her a degree of frank expression. Combined with her faithful Congregationalism, the conventions of travel writing and the imperative for self-improvement, particularly for women, may have subdued potential criticism of the Lowells or her status. Ultimately, Berbineau's environmental agency and her access to middle- and upper-class culture depended on her employers' largesse, but she apparently privileged their standards, enacting such standards in her observations and even in her interactions with other domestic servants.[53] Similarly, although she acknowledges bodily realities, she more eagerly—or perhaps more resolutely—depicts her admission to high culture and elevated nature, at once echoing and enabling the Lowells' leisure and pleasure. She frequently represents nature according to middle-class conceptions of the picturesque, the romantic, the sublime, and the transcendental, and her diary entries mirror popular narratives of progress and American exceptionalism. For Harriet Wilson, nominally a free black woman but enduring far more severe labor than Berbineau, nature and "the environment" were something else.

Frado Taught a Naughty Ram: Animal and Human Natures in *Our Nig*

Traveling to The Hague on 6 October 1851, Berbineau writes, "[W]e crossed many Dyks & Canals we see many cows and sheep the Dutch put blankets on their cows as we do on horses. neat little stations we stoped at the rail roads are graveled in Holand It is a very pleasent place were we are now." The pastoral landscape impresses her, especially "a large Park belonging to the King of Holland." The next morning, visiting a museum with Mrs. Lowell, she admires "some fine paintings one of a Bull as large as life" (103).

On that same day in 1851, Harriet Adams of Milford, New Hampshire, married Thomas Wilson of Virginia in her hometown.[54] Her movements in subsequent days remain unknown, but her son, George Mason, was born approximately nine months later. Wilson concludes the autobiographical *Our Nig* with a description of the heroine Frado's future husband: "Young, well-formed, and very handsome, he said he had been a *house*-servant, which seemed to account in some measure for his gentlemanly manners and pleasing address. The meeting was entirely accidental; but it was a sad occurrence for poor Alfrado, as her own sequel tells."[55] Paralleling Wilson's own experiences, the sequel involves desertion and recourse to the county poorhouse; the brief return of her profligate, "faithless husband" after her son's birth; and her husband's repeated, and finally permanent, desertion. The letters of support in the book's appendix state that the author herself faced "severe" "struggles with poverty and sickness," alleviated briefly by "a kind gentleman and lady" who tended the child while his mother attempted to support him and herself by "writing an Autobiography" (136–37).

The differences in Berbineau's and Wilson's activities on the same day underscore their disparate status. Although each is a servant, one garners respect and responsibility—and the privileges of a European Grand

Tour—while the other marries, possibly hoping to gain love and security that might help compensate for her childhood regime of scorn, beatings, and home confinement. Home possessed a complex associative matrix for nineteenth-century domestics, but perhaps more so for Wilson than any of the period's other working-class authors.[56] Place as well as race matters: the urbanized Berbineau's experience differed profoundly from that of the young Wilson, who composed a powerful, compressed narrative grounded in Milford's rural New Hampshire environment.[57]

To be sure, the different ages at which they wrote partly explain the disparity in their accounts. Wilson was more than twenty years younger, and *Our Nig* reports retrospectively and imaginatively on her alter ego's childhood. But in contrast to Berbineau's experience, Wilson's book illustrates Frado's quintuply, and sometimes sextuply, outsidered position: black, female, indentured, rural, child, and physically disabled; as such, the novel performs a tour-de-force analysis of synergistic prejudice.[58] If, recalling Jacobs's remark of slaves, "[w]omen are considered of no value, unless they continually increase their owner's stock. They are put on a par with animals," then Frado, Wilson's heroine and alter ego, appears even less than an animal in *Our Nig*, for not only do all these identities share a historical identification with nonhuman animals, their conjunction multiplies the association.[59] As Ian Frederick Finseth remarks more generally, "In talking about race or nature . . . we are always talking, at some level, about the other, and we are always working within and against the conceptual legacies of the eighteenth and nineteenth centuries." Those legacies were particularly complex in relation to Wilson's writing. They include the opposing, pre-Darwinist discourses of developmentalism—which, seeking to establish human beings' relation to animals, posited a hierarchical version of the natural world in which humans occupied the apex—and polygenesis, which argued for distinct (and unequal) branches of human development, determined principally by race, that justified social inequalities.[60]

Although recent ecocriticism has begun to take seriously African Americans' literary production, scholarship has neglected *Our Nig*'s environmental dimensions.[61] Especially relevant for Wilson is Kimberly Ruffin's challenge to "the legitimacy of binaries such as human/animal" and her question, "What does it mean when work, rather than leisure, is your central ecological experience?" Work connects African Americans positively with nonhuman nature, and nonhuman nature serves "to coauthorize their value."[62] Earlier generations of criticism on *Our Nig* variously ponder such questions as gender concerns, racial disadvantage, and labor.[63] Most salient for my discussion is scholars' stress on Wilson's portrayals of embodiment. Assessing Frado's suffering and its effects, Cynthia J. Davis maintains that the narration in *Our Nig* "subverts the muting effects of pain, [and] it also functions to undermine the dehumanizing effects of torture." Dehumanization has specific associations: the torturer must define the object as alien, "'other,' less than human, even as a beast."[64] Wilson foregrounds Frado's mother's "beastliness"; as Gabrielle Foreman notes, "*Our Nig* casts Mag as lowly and animalistic."[65] And Cassandra Jackson contends that Wilson experienced same-sex sexual abuse.[66] Almost forensically focused on corporeality, this criticism collectively gestures toward an obvious conclusion: Frado grows up in a toxic, dangerous home environment, and we can appreciate the novel as an environmental justice analysis.

As chapter 1 outlined, environmental justice refers to the equal treatment of individuals and communities in relation to resources, benefits, and responsibilities. Agency, or the ability to influence decisions and shape one's environment, forms a foundational tenet. Environmental justice also recognizes "the interdependence of all species"; "mandates the right to ethical, balanced and responsible uses of land and renewable resources in the interest of a sustainable planet for humans and other living things"; and "opposes military occupation, repression and exploitation of lands, peoples and cultures, and other life forms."[67] Wilson's work suggests that we need to think about the concept and practice more expansively. Environmental justice concerns not only minoritized communities' agency and avoidance of pollution but also the prevention of dislocation, the choice of a safe home, and access to the resources required to be self-sustaining, healthy, and happy, including nature and nonhuman animals. And it entails the right to control and benefit from one's employment. In *Our Nig*, though Frado is technically not enslaved, both her labor and her body itself represent consumable resources. Wilson emphasizes this point repeatedly, describing Frado's unceasing chores and her exhaustion: "Nig would work while she could remain erect, then sink down upon the floor, or a chair, till she could rally for a fresh effort. Mary would look in upon her, chide her for her laziness, threaten to tell mother when she came home" (64). "Home" clearly possesses different significance for Frado and her employers, the Bellmonts.

This section of the chapter conducts a preliminary ecocritical examination of *Our Nig* from several different perspectives that constellate around the heroine's embodiment. An impediment to reading nineteenth-century working-class women, but especially Wilson, is comprehending their rural experience, a particularly difficult task for today's scholars, most of whom have been educated in cities and whose personal experience remains remote from farm life's concrete realities. Such distance increases the potential for us to elide the internal conflicts — as well as the affirmations — in the writers' experiences of place. The Maine-born Berbineau reflects her employers' mobility, but because she remained in Boston for most of her adult life, her travel diaries convey a relatively urban viewpoint, unlike her younger counterparts Wilson and Larcom. Again relying on material feminism, I will investigate Wilson's accounts of Frado's rural physical labor, her relationship with animals, and her masterful analysis of multiple identity classifications that are sometimes self-reinforcing and sometimes mutually deconstructing. Hence, while my discussion studies rhetoric and representations, it frames that language and those images in the concrete, lived, "natural" experience within which Frado, and Wilson herself, sought environmental justice.

THE RACIALLY MIXED Wilson, believed to have been born in New Hampshire in 1825 to a white mother and black father, was abandoned by her mother and informally indentured to a white family with abolitionist connections, the Nehemiah Haywards.[68] After completing her indenture at eighteen, like Frado she sought independent employment, but after years of overwork and beatings her fragile health permitted only sporadic self-sufficiency, and she married Samuel, an African American man who may, like Frado's husband, have pretended to be an escaped slave. Abandoning Wilson and their son, who was born the next year, Samuel died, and his wife and son were forced to seek town charity. Wilson faced bleak choices. Although some towns maintained public poorhouses, others "auctioned" the care of the poor to the lowest bidder after the annual town meeting; occasionally, the two systems functioned in tandem.[69] Wilson apparently depended on both options, but gruesome circumstances at the county poor farm in Hillsborough propelled her to compose her book in an effort to regain care of her son, who lived at the farm while Wilson attempted to earn enough to support them independently.[70] In a cruel irony, George died a few months after it was published, and Wilson's racial identity was confirmed via his death certificate.[71] Scholarly findings indicate that, as Barbara White acknowledges, "many of Wilson's stories in *Our Nig* are literally true," although Wilson's strategic alterations and omissions radically complicate any assertions that it is merely autobiography.[72]

Part of Frado's hardship is her inability to travel, to leave home, except creatively through play and, ultimately, through education; another part is her isolation and lack of community.[73] Frado's race, gender, poverty, and indentured status enable Mrs. Bellmont's exploitation of her as merely a profitable set of hands. As I explained earlier, employers distinguished dramatically between servants and "help." The latter, often neighbors' sons or daughters who chose such occupations, were regarded as equals and ate with the family, while servants were distanced.[74] Ethnicity and race counted: with the influx of immigrant labor, by midcentury paid domestics replaced local help, and one problem for native-born Americans was distinguishing themselves from such foreign labor.[75] Free black children in Wilson's time were normally indentured. Valerie Cunningham puts the situation bluntly: "White America defined servants as Negroes and Negroes as servants."[76] Hence, when Frado's abusive employer Mrs. Bellmont declares, "I don't mind the nigger in the child. I should like a dozen better than one. . . . I have so much trouble with the girls I hire, I am almost persuaded if I have one to train up in my way from a child, I shall be able to keep them awhile. I am tired of changing every few months" (26), her preference was ordinary, not extraordinary, and her experience displayed only the extreme of mobility pursued by dissatisfied servants.

Wilson's portrait of Frado and Mrs. Bellmont enters the cultural scene with the emergence of industrial capitalism and the separate spheres ideology that specified ideal (white middle-class) womanhood as "essentially idle, frail, and beautiful"—all characteristics foreign to Wilson's heroine.[77] In Wilson's critique of the sentimental pattern in which suffering ignites sympathy—Stowe's Tom is the obvious example—neither Frado's blackness, nor femaleness, nor youth, nor sporadic disability, nor grinding domestic servitude generates meaningful sympathy among the Bellmonts.[78] Given Mrs. Bellmont's vicious cruelty and Frado's misery, it is understandable that readers would wish to dissociate the heroine (and the author) from embodiment, but Wilson's account of the body is more intricate than we have granted.[79] It differs substantially from Berbineau's and Jacobs's, partly because of Frado's rural location, the type of work that she performs, and especially her complex relations with animals.[80] In *Our Nig*, alliances between humans and animals, positive and negative, help reveal the matrices of environmental (in)justice.

Most critics of *Our Nig*, when they consider nonhuman animals, assume that they are subordinate or inferior, but Wilson complicates this hierarchy. On the one hand, she deconstructs the association between Frado and nonhuman animals (such as Fido), and on the other, she reconstructs humans (like Mrs. Bellmont) as beasts. It is, as Davis avers, easier to other the already silenced: "By speaking, [Frado] effectively protests Mrs. Bellmont's definition of her as beast and asserts instead—through protesting torture, not sexualization—that she is a thinking, feeling *human* being, and that it is the white woman who, because of her cruel actions, is inhuman(e)."[81] Such polarized interpretations, however, relegate cruelty and brutality to nonhuman animals, a reading that the novel insistently rejects. Indeed, Wilson portrays animals as having their own forms of subjectivity; however "mute" they may be, animals are able to think, plan, feel, and respond to human distress and loneliness; and, she shows, an alliance with them can be lifesaving.[82]

Wilson's skillful use of animals to satirize her white employers' vices and prejudices revises the associations proposed by proslavery advocates and decried by abolitionists between nonhuman animals and African Americans (and women, children, servants, and the disabled) as well as the assumption that black people were hardier than whites.[83] Wilson ironizes and complicates such assumptions when she has Mrs. Bellmont jeer, in one discussion with her husband, "[Y]ou know these niggers are just like black snakes; you *can't* kill them. If she wasn't tough she would have been killed long ago. There was never one of my girls could do half the work" (88–89). Recalling Berbineau's remark that American women could not do the heavy labor that female European farmworkers performed, Mrs. Bellmont reinforces her daughters' whiteness. The image also evokes Jacobs's horrific account of being surrounded and bitten by snakes, a response that Jacobs's principally domestic, indoor responsibilities intensify. There is a literal resonance in *Our Nig* as well, but Wilson provides a different perspective. Common in southern New Hampshire, black snakes were appreciated by farm families as rat catchers and general varmint removers. Large (sometimes more than five feet long) and speedy (commonly known as the black racer), this reptile typically avoids danger but will fight aggressively when cornered.[84] By placing this comparison in Mrs. Bellmont's mouth, Wilson at once underscores Frado's value and forecasts her eventual challenge to her employer's authority.

The parallel also suggests that Mrs. Bellmont links Frado with Satan, a connection promoted by proslavery writers.[85] Wilson ironically frames the Frado–black snake pairing with Mrs. Bellmont's attempt to prevent her servant from going to "evening [worship] meetings" and her contention that Frado will "turn pious nigger, and preach to white folks" (88). Through Mr. Bellmont's comment that "I thought you Christians held going to church," his sarcastic remarks about his wife's whipping Frado, and the chapter's conclusion with Frado's prayer, "God be merciful to me a sinner" (90), Wilson conveys that it is Mrs. Bellmont, not her servant, who is satanic, indeed, a "she-devil" (17). The author inverts Christian associations of serpents and evil, implying Frado's paradoxically "slender" strength and her endurance. Frado's capability accentuates Mrs. Bellmont's and Mary's incapacity, as Wilson overturns "the usual designation of the black laborer as the 'savage' element to be overseen by white female domesticity."[86] The author accomplishes this inversion by transvaluing the snake, a powerful cultural metaphor and a literal presence in rural southern New Hampshire. In this chapter's complex set of rhetorical moves, Wilson appeals to emotion and ethics. On the one hand, she engenders repugnance and anger toward Mrs. Bellmont's racism and hypocrisy; on the other, she conjures Christian equality and forgiveness. Each response, however, depends upon the embodied rhetoric figured by the snake.

We should turn now to an important, critically elided feature of Frado's labor: her farm work. As the Lowell mill girls discovered after they entered the textile factories, the life that most had left behind could be psychically liberating and physically restorative; one narrative in the *Lowell Offering* conjures "[t]he sunny hill side, with its beautiful grove of tall maple trees, bringing the merry times of sugar-making to remembrance."[87] Wilson exposes pastoral's limitations by depicting Frado's continuous exhaustion. Pastoral, defined by Lawrence Buell as "all literature that celebrates an ethos of rurality or nature or wilderness over against an ethos of metropolitanism," is, as Michael Bennett argues in relation to Frederick Douglass, extremely problematic for antebellum African Americans.[88] Kirkland describes women's frontier hardships, but she does so as an educated, eastern urbanite who, however sympathetic she might be, distinguishes herself from those toiling women by pity or humor. Focusing on work, Wilson expresses a different outlook on environmental stewardship, propounding an ethic of care for humans as well as animals. In a literary context where almost all representations of women's farm chores were idealizations created by middle- or upper-class women, *Our Nig* performs an extraordinary intervention, simultaneously realistic and naturalistic in scope.[89]

To date only R. J. Ellis has taken seriously the rural element of Wilson's novel, observing that "*Our Nig* emerges as both one of the first fictional portraits of farm life produced by a working-class writer and one of the earliest prose accounts of any kind written from the point of view of the rural working class in either the United States or Britain." Possibly uniquely, the novel presents a female perspective. Ellis concludes that "*Our Nig*'s grim economics, whilst rooted in the particularly racist constructions of American life, forcefully exposes [the] labour-intensive side to farm life, otherwise so perfidiously omitted from pastoral discourse on both sides of the Atlantic."[90] Wilson's laboring vision contrasts sharply with Kirkland's satirical sketches of domestic animals, as it does with the amused Thoreau's: "I love to see the domestic animals reassert their native rights, — any evidence that they have not wholly lost their original wild habits and vigor; as when my neighbor's cow breaks out of her pasture in early spring and boldly swims the river, a cold, gray tide, twenty-five or thirty rods wide, swollen by the melted snow. It is the buffalo crossing the Mississippi."[91] As *Our Nig* renders Frado's experiences, this detached, philosophical, and comic standpoint is seldom available to farmworkers.

While virtually all current readers of *Our Nig* focus on Frado's indoor responsibilities and many highlight Wilson's critique of sentimental, white middle-class domesticity, we should thus appreciate how the author illustrates the even more demanding responsibilities of Frado's outdoor labor in the midcentury New England economy:[92]

> Her first work was to feed the hens. She was shown how it was *always* to be done, and in no other way; any departure from this rule to be punished by a whipping. She was then accompanied by Jack to drive the cows to pasture, so she might learn the way. Upon her return she was allowed to eat her breakfast, consisting of a bowl of skimmed milk, with brown bread crusts, which she was told to eat, standing, by the kitchen table, and must not be over ten minutes about it. Mean-

while the family were taking their morning meal in the dining-room. This over, she was placed on a cricket to wash the common dishes; she was to be in waiting always to bring wood and chips, to run hither and thither from room to room.

A large amount of dish-washing for small hands followed dinner. Then the same after tea and going after the cows finished her first day's work. It was a new discipline to the child. She found some attractions about the place, and she retired to rest at night more willing to remain. The same routine followed day after day, with slight variation; adding a little more work, and spicing the toil with "words that burn," and frequent blows on her head. (29–30)

This description is particularly shocking because Frado is about seven years old. In this emotionally intelligent account, Wilson obliterates the idyllic picture of a rural household, substituting a grinding, punishing list, piling task upon task, to generate in her readers an embodied perception of Frado's exhaustion and this environment's injustice.

The environmental historian Chad Montrie points out that farms used "a gendered division of labor, but well into the first half of the nineteenth century the 'women's sphere' . . . included feeding poultry, milking cows, making butter and cheese, tending the garden, berry picking and other gathering, preserving and pickling, shucking corn, apple-paring, making cider and applesauce, cooking, washing, tidying the house, making soap and candles, preparing flax and cleaning fleece, spinning, knitting, weaving, and dying cloth."[93] Yet, while they acknowledged its hardships, rural New England women valued their outdoor work because they profited directly, because such labor was many times communal, and because—like Jemison and her peers—they controlled the pace and content of their activities.[94] Unlike such communal efforts, Frado's solitary work commonly means corporeal and psychic hardship. In an America that prioritized progress, employment ostensibly enabled that end, but *Our Nig* demonstrates that such self-amelioration was sometimes impossible.[95] While farm families of all races relied on children performing age-appropriate duties, Frado's responsibilities far exceed such labor demands in their difficulty and duration; she, and her body, are resources that the Bellmonts regulate and from which they profit. Juxtaposing skimpy food and "small hands" with a "large amount of dish-washing," the author forecloses any prospect of pastoral mooning.

Wilson shows how the blurring of distinctions between indoor, "domestic," and outdoor farm labor ungenders Frado. Contemplating Frado's departure, "Mrs. B. felt that she could not well spare one who could so well adapt herself to all departments—man, boy, housekeeper, domestic, etc." (116). Frado's chores eventually encompass those of adults and children, men and women. Wilson's embodied rhetoric again appeals to feeling and ethics: "There had been additional burdens laid on her. . . . She must now *milk* the cows, she had then only to drive. Flocks of sheep had been added to the farm, which daily claimed a portion of her time. In the absence of the men, she must harness the horse for Mary and her mother to ride, go to mill, in short, do the work of a boy, could one be procured to endure the tirades of Mrs. Bellmont. She was first up in the morning, doing what she could towards breakfast" (52–53). Anyone who has sweated on a farm, especially without mechanized assistance, knows the backbreaking nature of such demands, which allow for little distinctive leisure time. As Ellis points out, in drawing farm labor as she does, Wilson frames a "highly original" counterpoint to pastoral, creating what he calls "apastoral," which works not in opposition to pastoral but "*without* it (in both senses of the word)" (original emphasis).[96] *Our Nig* reveals a grim rural class structure, exacerbated by Frado's race, that is more unremittingly demanding than the urban, indoor care that Berbineau recounts.[97]

Outdoor labor augments Frado's racial difference, literally as well as metaphorically: "At home, no matter how powerful the heat when sent to rake hay or guard the grazing herd, she was never permitted to shield her skin from the sun. She was not many shades darker than Mary now; what a calamity it would be ever to hear the contrast spoken of" (39). This passage recalls Berbineau's nationalist image of farmworkers: "[T]he women were at work as hard as the men their skin was a perfect brown I dont think the women of America could work so." Like Mrs. Bellmont, the white servant separates American women from outdoor laborers who toil like men—or like animals. But Berbineau also distinguishes urban domestic activity from rough rural work, which she suggests has the tendency to ungender women and dehumanize them. Rather than expressing a unified idea of the working class, Berbineau stratifies employment based on place and, perhaps unconsciously, on race. The female laborer's body, and that body's location, matter. If one element of environmental justice is access to nature's pastoral pleasures, *Our Nig* exposes the circumscription of such access for individuals like Frado, in her Milford home and in the nation at large.

WILSON COMPLICATES this labor hierarchy partly by rewriting the various dominant-culture connections between and among African Americans, women, servants, rural people, children, and disabled individuals and nonhuman animals. Compulsory outdoor work offered avenues of escape, especially, and ironically—given the historical deployment of dogs to hunt runaway slaves, vividly illustrated in William Well Brown's *My Southern Home*—for its literal association with animals.[98] Ruffin's observations resonate for *Our Nig*: "Much of [slaves'] work was no doubt grueling and painful; nevertheless, enslavement left people with the task of forging an ecological perspective firmly in the grasp of both the burden and the beauty of being natural. They forged identities as ecological participants based on their work rather than a privileged position in the social fabric."[99] As a farmworker, Frado recognizes, and in some cases respects, animals' individualism and temperament, including the domestic animals that assist with farm labor and provide company.

Nowhere is this outlook more apparent than in her relationship with her dog, Fido, which diverges from Jacobs's association of a dog with degradation. Many readers have pointed out the ironic correspondences between Frado and Fido, beginning with the obvious name echo.[100] In the Bellmonts' (and the North's) economy and psychology, Frado and her dog are merely different versions of domestic animals; each is less than human. Hence, when Frado chooses to eat from Mrs. Bellmont's plate after it is licked clean by Fido rather than dirtied by her employer (71–72), she delivers what Ellis calls "a calculated insult." At the same time, the scene "recapitulates her own social situation: she is literally enduring a dog's life."[101] Julia Stern emphasizes Fido's status as "an unreasoning animal," noting that "the mixed-race child must be made black, defeminized, and turned into an animal" and concluding that "the evil mother's program follows a logic patterned on the hierarchical relationship that exists between humans, beasts, food, and waste."[102] Though less extreme, most criticism reprises some version of this viewpoint.

But as a rural person, Wilson delineates a more complex assessment of

Frado's relationships with animals, particularly Fido. In her first direct reference, Wilson notes, "There were days when Fido was the entire confidant of Frado. She told him her griefs as though he were human; and he sat so still, and listened so attentively, she really believed he knew her sorrows" (41–42). Despite the author's conventionally sentimental description, she confirms that Fido symbolizes more than a sentimental object to the child Frado. He possesses consciousness, intelligence, and kindness and is more humane than humans, as another episode corroborates. When Jack confronts his mother about one of Frado's undeserved whippings, conflict ensues:

> "It is very strange you will believe what others say against your sister," retorted his mother, with flashing eye. "I think it is time your father subdued you."
>
> "Father is a sensible man," argued Jack. "He would not wrong a dog. Where *is* Frado?" he continued.
>
> "Mother gave her a good whipping and shut her up," replied Mary.
>
> Just then Mr. Bellmont entered, and asked if Frado was "shut up yet." (35–36)

The multiple ironies of this encounter explode the ostensible bifurcation between human beings and nonhuman domestic animals and the racism that underwrites the middle-class relegation of servants, especially black servants, to object status. Wilson conjoins Jack's assertion of his father's "sensible" nature—which refers not just to common sense but feeling—to a query about Frado, underlining that although Mr. Bellmont might not wrong a dog, he would indeed wrong Frado, allowing her to be whipped and "shut up." In the Bellmonts' unjust moral economy, Fido ranks more highly.

Although Mrs. Bellmont threatens Jack physical harm and silencing, it is Frado who bears the abuse and being shut up, enclosed and silenced. For the Bellmonts, dog and human being seem interchangeable; in Wilson's penetrating satire, punctuated with gallows humor, the girl suffers being beaten like a dog, as a proxy for Fido and Jack himself. As Lesley Ginsberg points out, "[T]he relationship of pet to pet owner was understood by antebellum Americans as a trope for both slavery and domesticity," and the human-animal relationship figured national debates about "the boundaries and borders of citizenship"; but "antebellum children themselves were noncitizens by definition, a category of the disenfranchised like women, slaves, and animals."[103] Wilson deconstructs multiple social hierarchies, including the romanticized analogies between pet owner/pet and slaveholder/slave, employer/servant, and husband/wife. Additionally, Wilson's depiction of the Frado-Fido relationship challenges hierarchies between humans and nonhuman animals.[104] Her emotionally intelligent, embodied rhetoric confronts readers' own sensibilities and ethics.

Beyond his usefulness to the author as a powerful parallel and cultural touchstone, Fido occupies a central place in her heroine's humane education, demonstrating to Frado that a dog enjoys a more admirable sensibility than Mrs. Bellmont or even Mr. Bellmont. Unlike Frado's mistress, Fido's behavior models the natural kindness with which a child, at least within the middle-class sentimental family, should be treated. Frado naturally gravitates toward this animal sensibility, which enables her to play: "All the leisure moments she could gain were used in teaching him some feat of dog-agility." Wilson affirms, "Fido was the constant attendant of Frado, when sent from the house on errands, going and returning with the cows, out in the fields, to the village. If ever she forgot her hardships it was in his company" (42). Ruffin reflects, "While their work conditions suggested they were subhumans relegated to life with other beasts, much of the voluntary work during enslavement . . . reinforced the outlook that human beings are nature and need to have relationships with nonhuman nature."[105] Although Frado is indentured, not legally enslaved, her happiness depends on Fido's friendship. An open-air companion, not a pampered, sentimentalized pet, he encodes Wilson's satirical rejoinder to the sentimental proslavery contention that slaves (and, by extension, free black laborers) enjoyed "loving bonds" with slave owners like those between humans and pets.[106]

Fido has character, individuality, and loyalty. He even appears to have subjectivity; when Frado runs away after another gratuitous beating, the Bellmont brothers locate her only by bribing her dog, for, as Mr. Bellmont points out, "[W]e shall not be wiser [about her location] unless we can outwit him. He will not do what his mistress forbids him" (49).[107] Noticing that Fido is Frado's lone confidant, James describes her connection with Fido to a sympathetic Aunt Abby:

But to think how prejudiced the world are towards her people; that she must be reared in such ignorance as to drown all the finer feelings.

When I think of what she might be, of what she will be, I feel like
grasping time till opinions change, and thousands like her rise into a
noble freedom. I have seen Frado's grief, because she is black, amount
to agony. It makes me sick to recall these scenes. Mother pretends to
think she don't know enough to sorrow for anything; but if she could
see her as I have, when she supposed herself entirely alone, except her
little dog Fido, lamenting her loneliness and complexion, I think, if
she is not past feeling, she would retract. . . .

   I stepped into the barn, where I could see her. She was crouched
down by the hay with her faithful friend Fido, and as she ceased
speaking, buried her face in her hands, and cried bitterly; then, patting
Fido, she kissed him, saying, "You love me, Fido, don't you? but we
must go to work in the field." She started on her mission; I called her
to me, and told her she need not go, the hay was doing well. (74–75)

Wilson—or Frado at least—attributes sensibility to the nonhuman animal.
What makes this monologue noteworthy, however, is Wilson's emotionally
intelligent juxtaposition of the inhuman, unfeeling Mrs. Bellmont—and
the eloquent but passive James—to the "faithful" companion. Loneliness
and sorrow are Frado's daily lot, and with "[n]o mother, father, brother or
sister to care for me," Fido affords powerful physical and psychological
solace (75).

   That Mrs. Bellmont comprehends Fido's significance becomes clear
when she sadistically sells Frado's "last vestige of earthly joy" and Mr.
Bellmont "by great exertion obtained it again, much to the relief of the
child." Wilson pointedly remarks, "To be thus deprived of all her sources of
pleasure was a sure way to exalt their worth, and Fido became, in her esti-
mation, a more valuable presence than the human beings who surrounded
her" (61, 62). Representing a different kind of "domestic animal," her dog
has individuality and "presence." While the Bellmonts profitably associate
Frado with animals, Fido provides no economic reward for anyone. If servants are less than human to the Bellmonts, Fido is more than human to
Frado (and Wilson). In this household—hardly a home—the author shows
that human nature is unnatural, and animals are more desirable companions, ultimately helping Frado assert her claim for justice and achieve full
self-ownership.

IN THE MID-NINETEENTH century, as the New England population migrated to cities and the west and production moved from the home (principally the farm) to the factory, women's perceptions of their bodies and their relationships to nature transformed correspondingly. Yet many individuals remained in rural locations, where emergent gender ideologies were sometimes less influential than in the city. Experiences of the human body, and its relationship to various animals, diverge radically in urban and rural/farm settings; because rural residents depended on animals in a way that was becoming increasingly invisible to—or elided by—city dwellers, American women's relationship to their corporeality was mediated not only by their race, class, age, and other factors but also by their location. Women workers like Frado depended on their bodies, but social ideals of femininity, influenced by the rising middle class, increasingly stressed consumerism, leisure, and fragility.[108] But the gendered norm of fragility was closely tied to race and class identity.

I have argued that we need to consider how Frado's multiple identities interact and how they function synergistically as well as individually to disadvantage her.[109] In analyzing Wilson's critique of the natural, we should explore another important but neglected perspective on her complex portrait of embodied labor: Frado's increasing disability, which intensifies with her age and self-achievement.[110] By causing this disability, Mrs. Bellmont reinforces Frado's existence as merely a body, for if a black child servant is treated as an animal, how much more so a disabled one?

Disability studies has unpacked the social construction of disability.[111] The concept of normality emerged around 1840, progressing as science, which values measurement and statistics, became a dominant cultural discourse.[112] Expressing an unstable, potentially temporary identity, disability, unlike race or gender (but more like rural status or indentured servitude) is regarded as something with external causes and hence subject to possible remediation.[113] Disability can assume multiple forms, be visible or invisible, and change over time.[114] For Berbineau, disability presents major difficulties, but those difficulties are temporary and the disabilities themselves—the worst of which was probably dysentery—had sources external to her employment, though work probably exacerbated her distress. In Frado's (and presumably Wilson's) case, the Bellmonts' abuse and her demanding labor cause her regular illnesses and physical breakdowns.

Although ethnic studies has historically examined intersections of race with such social identities as gender, class, and sexuality, little scholarship probes how disability and race or ethnicity might be mutually constitutive.[115] The historian Douglas Baynton explains the political purposes that the concept of disability historically underwrites: "[N]onwhite races were routinely connected to people with disabilities, both of whom were depicted as evolutionary laggards or throwbacks."[116] Disability has thus functioned as an overarching disqualification for citizenship—a measure of adulthood, we should notice—that was used to disadvantage women, African Americans and Native Americans, and immigrants; rather than questioning the problematic assumptions surrounding disability, all these groups distanced themselves from it. Disability also dehumanized social outsiders.[117]

Such connections have troubled literary scholarship on African American authors, as Ellen Samuels points out in her discussion of William and Ellen Craft's *Running a Thousand Miles for Freedom*, where she stresses the investment of nineteenth-century writers and current scholars in "wholeness, uprightness, good health, and independence."[118] Through recurrent, if concise, references departing from African American literature's characteristic emphasis on health, Wilson's embodied rhetoric relentlessly portrays Frado's experience as increasingly and variously disabled. Jennifer C. James and Cynthia Wu note, "Arguably the first example of black autopathography, *Our Nig* suggests that the production of black subjectivity and the production of the disabled body are coterminous."[119] Wilson achieves narrative and cultural agency through her genre compression and descriptive reticence; very few scenes are fleshed out for voyeuristic consumption.

Yet the novel's synthetic analysis of corporeality probes beyond this duality, incorporating race and physical capacity with gender via the discourse of beauty and counterdiscourse of ugliness. When Frado's mother, Mag, ponders abandoning her daughter, she takes advantage of Mrs. Bellmont's need and incapacity: "She can't keep a girl in the house over a week; and Mr. Bellmont wants to hire a boy to work for him, but he can't find one that will live in the house with her; she's so ugly, they can't" (18). Wilson subtly compares Mrs. Bellmont's "ugly" temperament to the employer's insistence that Frado is physically ugly, leaving the heroine to wonder if "every one thought her so" and to surmise, as she contemplates her informal indenture's conclusion, that "no one would take her. She was black, no one would love her. She might have to return, and then she would be more in her mistress's power than ever" (108).[120] Disability, racial otherness, ugliness, and labor were linked in midcentury America, and the ugly girl embodied sexual pleasure.[121] Mrs. Bellmont's insistence that Frado is ugly thus supplements the heroine's other forms of social disadvantage and reflects the employer's fears of her servant's emergent sexuality.

Wilson extends this meditation's significance, for she implies that Frado's race conjoins with her youth and femininity ("no one would love her" conjures simultaneously the sentimental woman and the vulnerable child) to render her the perfect servant, obedient as children and women were supposed to be. Mrs. Bellmont tries to transform the child Frado, a "beautiful mulatto, with long, curly black hair, and handsome, roguish eyes, sparkling with an exuberance of spirit almost beyond restraint" into an ungendered servant as she reaches puberty, cutting off the curls that signify her "getting handsome," beating her, and literally muting her (17, 70). By making Frado "ugly," Mrs. Bellmont reiterates the dominant social script, furthering that narrative through disabling whippings. Ironically, Frado's beauty proves her undoing when she meets her future husband, Samuel, who delights to "toy with her shining curls . . . and expose the ivory concealed by thin, ruby lips," in Wilson's ironic parody of romantic fiction. Desexed, she becomes a profitable workhorse; as a feminized heroine, she becomes vulnerable to male hypocrisy and abandonment, undoing the sentimental novel's characteristically triumphant outcome. Reframed from Ecclesiastes, Wilson's bitterly ironic epigraph, "Nothing new under the sun," reinforces her heroine's prospective dead end (126). Mrs. Bellmont transforms Frado into the brown-skinned, outdoor female laborer from whom Berbineau uncomfortably detaches herself.

Wilson pointedly reminds readers, however, that illness and disability were more acceptable—and maybe encouraged—in white middle-class females.[122] Although the dominant culture constructed the female body as "inherently deficient, unhealthy, and abnormal," women like Jane Bellmont exemplified merely the extreme manifestation of the "lady," a concept with which many nineteenth-century women authors, including Lucy Larcom, took issue.[123] Of Jane, Wilson writes, "Although an invalid, she was not excluded from society. Was it strange *she* should seem a desirable companion, a treasure as a wife?" (55). Frado—and Wilson—acknowledges that, in Barbara White's trenchant phrasing, "even a white invalid has more value than a black supergirl."[124] "Invalid" Frado faces a complementary problem: the perception that, ostensibly shirking her responsibilities, she is "playing the lady," defying her assigned race and class roles.[125] Like the relatively privileged Berbineau, Frado counters this assertion; she drudges despite the disability produced by overwork and abuse. Through her character's bodily limitations, Wilson satirically undercuts the medical profession's contention that African Americans could endure hard physical labor.[126]

Price Herndl argues that Wilson downplays disability and illness, and she contends that *Our Nig* is "reticent" and "vague" about Frado's illnesses.[127] But although the author supplies scarce individual details, the embodied rhetoric of health and sickness scaffolds the novel, becoming the bones on which the story uncomfortably rests. Anticipating environmental justice concerns, Wilson uses the idiom of well-being to prioritize individual agency. Mr. Bellmont disallows his wife's greed-informed marriage choice for Jane, telling her suitors that "he could not as a father see his child compelled to an uncongenial union; a free, voluntary choice was of such importance to one of her health" (60). The author contrasts this perspective a few pages later, portraying choiceless Frado:

> From early dawn until after all were retired, was she toiling, overworked, disheartened, longing for relief.
>
> Exposure from heat to cold, or the reverse, often destroyed her health for short intervals. (65)

Wilson's descriptive reticence counterpoints the frequency with which we learn of Frado's incapacity; her restraint allows us painful imaginative freedom. The author's bluntness and formal structuring—each of these sentences is a stark, individual paragraph—combines with her elision of agency to generate shock and distress. Again and again, Wilson synthesizes emotional and ethical appeals, and as Frado's informal indenture ends, terse references to disability accumulate.[128]

Given *Our Nig*'s multiple horrors, it is not surprising that many contemporary readers affirm that Wilson's novel figures triumph over adversity.[129] Triumphalism represented an important discourse for African Americans in mid-nineteenth-century America.[130] Yet Frado never really overcomes her disability, unless we count her eventual attainment of literacy. Mrs. Bellmont attempts desperately to dis-able Frado, to prevent her from voicing her suffering. Her efforts to obstruct the heroine from attending school reinforce Frado's incapacity, for illiteracy encodes another form of disability.[131] Historically, disabled people have been (and continue to be) objectified, serving as objects of sympathy; nondisabled people see the disabled as childlike and dependent, requiring protection.[132] But such standards did not hold for Frado, a vulnerable, black, poor, indentured child. Frado's superimposed muteness parallels, confirms, and augments her other bodily and social disabilities. Responding to contemporary commentators who compared servants to children, Wilson's representation of the "disobedient" child and servant combined with the incapacitated black female intensifies the stakes almost unbearably, illustrating her heroine's social and cultural invalidation while refuting hypocritical narratives of sentimental sympathy based on gender, age, class, and/or ability.[133]

Hungry, embattled, and miserable from the Bellmont household's various toxins, whether Mrs. Bellmont's and Mary's viciousness or the other family members' ineffectual sympathy and cowardly retreat, Frado becomes a parodic heroine in Wilson's environmental justice exposé. Embodying and symbolizing a child, an indentured servant, a female, an African American, a rural worker, and a disabled person, Frado epitomizes outsiderness, advancing Wilson's withering reproach to American citizenship.[134] As a child, Frado should be protected; as a disabled female child—like Stowe's Little Eva—she should be trebly safeguarded. But as a black child in rural, mid-nineteenth-century America, she was considered a profitable, labor-saving status symbol.[135] Recounting Frado's capacity to play, work, and speak, and revealing her identities' superimposed limitations, Wilson creates a complex study of a human being, "still an invalid" but neither "still" nor "invalid," capable of diverse emotional, intellectual, and corporeal experiences (130). As pointedly, she asks her white adult readers to negotiate an emotional tightrope—composed of horror, sympathy, admiration, guilt—as they look in the mirror, regard their own multilayered prejudices, and change their behavior, and their country, accordingly.

BECAUSE OF THE novel's insistence on pain and multiple forms of outsidered identity, it may surprise, even shock, us today that its first readers, primarily white and middle-class from the area around Wilson's Milford home, were mostly young, and more than half were children.[136] Contemporary critics regularly foreground the American child as a symbol of opportunity and resistance to authority, highlighting children's privileged cultural position; readings of *Our Nig*, while acknowledging Frado's obstacles, value "play and even mischief."[137] We have repeatedly seen, however, that the heroine's other identities often undercut her putatively privileged child status. As Stowe's depiction of Topsy denotes, play was reserved for certain children and forbidden to others; without Miss Ophelia's supervision, readers are told, her charge "would hold a perfect carnival of confusion."[138] Rather than a role Frado has to "grow into," her class identity—if not her poverty—is something Wilson argues she must outgrow.[139] And her status as farmworker, not just domestic servant, frames Wilson's portrait. In the farming economy, class is not a matter of pillows—as Karen Sánchez-Eppler observes of middle-class society—it is a matter of cows, and hens, and sheep.[140]

Wilson's reliance on a rural child protagonist strengthens her environmental justice critique. Outdoor play dramatizes not only an assertion of agency but also a claim for justice, as Frado rejects her treatment as an exploitable resource. Wilson describes her heroine's youthful high spirits while questioning how "one spark of playfulness could remain amid such constant toil; but her natural temperament was in a high degree mirthful, and the encouragement she received from Jack and the hired men, constantly nurtured the inclination." Her connection with nonhuman nature confirms her agency: without other people "to be merry with, she would amuse herself with the animals" (54). In one of *Our Nig*'s few overtly humorous episodes, Wilson transforms Kirkland's verbal play and satire—evoking her whimsical linking of Americans and pigs—into Frado's artfully witty behavior. Frado tricks a greedy ram, "a willful leader, who always persisted in being first served . . . many times in his he fury had thrown down Nig, till, provoked, she resolved to punish him" (54). The sheep pasture is enclosed on three sides by a high bank above a river, and when Frado calls him with a "mock repast," he rolls down the bank and, forced to swim across the river, "remained alone until night" (54, 55). Amusing "Mr. Bellmont, with his laborers," she endangers herself by risking drowning, but her cleverness exposes the ram's gluttony and bullying. Frado is more than a clown furnishing comic relief for hardened farmworkers; playing the trickster, she also demonstrates to readers her moral authority and pedagogical skill, foreshadowing her ultimate self-shepherding. Wilson intimates how Frado's outdoor labor will become a liberating force.

Wilson scholars have characterized the sheep as a foil or the means to a lesson.[141] The author's gallows humor suggests that the sheep resembles greedy whites like Mrs. Bellmont, who gives Frado little sustenance and always eats first. He also possesses literal significance, for Wilson shows that he has subjectivity and will, characteristics that underscore his material threat; Ellis rightly argues that the episode stresses the dangers attending farm life.[142] The author also disparages the pastoral genre via the normally reliable sheep metaphor. And because, as Michael Bennett reminds us, "African Americans in the antebellum United States were much more likely to be referred to in the lexicon of slavery as sheep rather than shepherds," Wilson complicates pastoral's affiliated Christian rhetoric.[143] The episode ironically points toward numerous Biblical passages, including Psalms 23:1 ("The Lord is my shepherd; I shall not want"). As the putatively moral adult and spiritual guide, unmotherly Mrs. Bellmont should be supplying a model, shepherding Frado, but instead she steps outside the Christian fold.[144] Combined with its compressed and indirect humor, this episode's embodied and affective rhetoric leads readers to an ethical understanding of Frado's predicament.[145]

In this spiritual economy, death should lead to heaven, or at least rest. In both *Our Nig* and Berbineau's diary, religious practice enables relief from toil; Wilson remarks that youthful Frado "eagerly anticipat[es]" evening prayer meetings as "a pleasant release from labor," while Berbineau praises "the quiet sabbath where man & beast can rest and think of their Maker" (Wilson, 69; Berbineau, 72). But the similarities end there. For the Bostonian, nature holds transcendental meaning, while Wilson problematizes such connections. A merely nominal Christian like Jacobs's Mrs. Flint, Mrs. Bellmont asserts that "[r]eligion was not meant for niggers" (68). When James dies and Frado weeps at the clergyman's prayer, Mrs. Bellmont beats her. Frado should be God's lamb, but her vulnerability increases; as she seeks consolation, Mrs. Bellmont threatens, "if she did not stop trying to be religious, she would whip her to death." Again with gallows humor, Wilson concludes, "Frado pondered; her mistress was a professor of religion; was *she* going to heaven? then she did not wish to go. If she should be near James, even, she could not be happy with those fiery eyes watching her ascending path. She resolved to give over all thought of the future world, and strove daily to put her anxiety far from her" (104).[146] Heaven merely reiterates worldly suffering. Wilson ironizes the Peaceable

Kingdom imagery suffusing midcentury American Christianity: "The wolf also shall dwell with the lamb, and the leopard shall lie down with the kid; and the calf and the young lion and the fatling together; and a little child shall lead them" (Isaiah 11:6). In this world and the next, Wilson avers, the lion (Mrs. Bellmont) will never lie down with the lamb (Frado), and Frado will never inspire Mrs. Bellmont's transformation.[147]

Like Sigourney deploying Christian rhetoric to shame readers, and like Jemison reproving religious hypocrisy, Wilson also invokes a later passage in Isaiah: "He was oppressed, and he was afflicted, yet he opened not his mouth: he is brought as a lamb to the slaughter, and as a sheep before her shearers is dumb, so he openeth not his mouth" (Isaiah 53:7). As it foreshadows Christ's sacrifice, this passage indicates that God's servant takes upon himself the people's sins and uncomplainingly accepts his fate—as Frado repeatedly does, or must do. Wilson must also restrain herself; she notes in the preface that she has "purposely omitted" material that might "provoke shame in our good anti-slavery friends at home."[148] "Home" variously designates New England, the North, and America itself. Regardless of whether Wilson had read *Uncle Tom's Cabin* or learned about it though popular culture, Frado performs an ironic commentary not just on Topsy, but on Stowe's Eva, the "little child" who led family members and readers to Christian goodness through their sentimental sympathy.[149] Ultimately, Wilson's Christian rhetoric—and allusions—share many motivations with Sigourney's maternal sermons or jeremiads: to chastise and thus better America.

These literary alliances gesture toward Frado's recurrent and lifelong struggles to acquire literacy. Like the Lowell mill girls, she combines work and education: "Her school-books were her constant companions, and every leisure moment was applied to them. . . . She had her book always fastened open near her, where she could glance from toil to soul refreshment" (115–16).[150] Later, she occupies "every leisure moment" in self-improvement, individual progress perhaps being the one goal that the beleaguered author could envision (124).[151] Literacy enhances Frado's self-ownership and environmental agency; thus Wilson integrates and esteems *both* embodied experience and cultural activities.

Calling on readers' emotional intelligence to ignite their sympathy, the author alludes to another important cultural reference, this time from children's literature. One of nineteenth-century America's most ubiquitous verses, fostering numerous parodies, Sarah Josepha Hale's "Mary's Lamb" was first published in the *Juvenile Miscellany* in 1830, shortly before Wilson entered the Hayward household.[152] The poem circulated everywhere, and Wilson may have encountered it at school or elsewhere in a *McGuffey's Reader*, where it was published with an illustration beginning with the *Reader*'s initial 1836 appearance.[153] Wilson plays with the verse just as Frado plays with the recalcitrant ram: seriously.

> Mary had a little lamb,
>   Its fleece was white as snow,
> And every where that Mary went
>   The lamb was sure to go;
> He followed her to school one day—
>   That was against the rule,
> It made the children laugh and play
>   To see a lamb at school.
>
> And so the Teacher turned him out,
>   But still he lingered near,
> And waited patiently about,
>   Till Mary did appear.
> And then he ran to her and laid
>   His head upon her arm,
> As if he said—"I'm not afraid—
>   You'll shield me from all harm."
>
> "What makes the lamb love Mary so,"
>   The little children cry;
> "O, Mary loves the lamb you know,"
>   The Teacher did reply,
> "And you each gentle animal
>   In confidence may bind,
> And make them follow at your call,
>   If you are always *kind*."[154]

Wilson's brilliant satire revolves around numerous inversions and revisions. Mary Bellmont, nominally Frado's ("Our Nig's") owner, not only fails to protect her lamb, she actively abuses her. Mary sulks when Frado attends school, seeking to undermine and exclude her. Frado's teacher, unlike Hale's, welcomes her new charge and insists on her equality.[155] Unlike in Hale's poem, school is a liberatory zone, for, as Miss Marsh's "lamb," Frado frees her playful "animal spirits."[156] Mary Bellmont's failure to be "always kind" prompts Wilson to invert the poem's power positions elsewhere: Frado's employment with animals provides her with psychological insight and physical dexterity, and she subjects both the gluttonous ram and selfish Mary to her outdoor pedagogy. Wilson also comments on the problem of whiteness: Frado's innocence contrasts with Mary's culpability, for however much Mary's mother tries to blacken Frado, Mary will never be "white as snow." In her ethical and affective appeal, Wilson parallels the heroine's exclusion from "enlightenment" with she-devil Mrs. Bellmont's attempts to exclude Frado from school and even from heaven.[157]

On a more material level, "Mary's Lamb" occludes "the lamb's agrarian meaning and value." In advocating protecting him from slaughter and consumption, the poem shows that "the classroom is a place not to learn how to care for farm animals but how to treat them as object lessons and to practice gentle command."[158] Rather than maternally shielding Frado "from all harm," Mag, Mrs. Bellmont, and Mary actually engender harm, the first bringing her "as a lamb to the slaughter" and the second flaying her. In her mother's absence, the third literally wields the knife, screaming at the ailing Frado to bring some wood: "'Saucy, impudent nigger, you! is this the way you answer me?' and taking a large carving knife from the table, she hurled it, in her rage, at the defenceless girl. Dodging quickly, it fastened in the ceiling a few inches from where she stood" (64–65). While indirectly acknowledging farming's bloody responsibilities, Wilson simultaneously transforms Hale's sentimental admonitions urging animal kindness into a blistering commentary on the inhuman treatment of human lambs—vulnerable, black, female, disabled servant children—by putative mothers, in a brilliant representation of the synergistic prejudices at work in midcentury America's unjust environments.

WILSON'S USE OF the novel genre—powerfully reinvented—offers her an opportunity for relative expansiveness and, perhaps, expressiveness, unavailable to Berbineau. Writing for publication in a hostile environment nevertheless imposed substantive constraints, propelling her to translate her autobiographical experiences into fictional form. The reception context

Farm woman chopping wood. Image by Jack Delano, June 1914.
Courtesy of the Library of Congress.

also made her value reticence and stylistic compression for some of the same reasons as Jacobs. Unlike Berbineau's explicit and literal travels for self-improvement, Wilson's avatar's journey occurs within a limited scope; yet each author reformulates "homesickness." For Berbineau, travel literally makes her sick, and she longs for Boston. At the same time, "home," represented by the Lowells' moving household, also makes her ill, and sometimes disabled, by its incessant demands. Frado travels between house and field, farm and school, but being "shut up" at home and constrained by work render the Bellmonts' residence a toxic environment. Both Berbineau and Wilson suppress explicit complaints, and their emotionally intelligent accounts advance affective and ethical appeals mediated more by description and ellipsis than explicit demands for equity. Nevertheless, such terse, even telegraphic reports of their labor generate anger, horror, and sympathy for today's readers, if not for their own. The scene of that employment matters: though differently coded, Berbineau's depictions of female agricultural workers and Frado's farm duties manifest clearly the problems of embodied, racialized, and gendered resource exploitation and affirm the desirability of environmental access and agency.

Words, literacy, culture—all are vital to Frado as she seeks "self-improvement." Wilson, who later participated in Boston's Lyceum movement, also prized them.[159] But the author also appreciated corporeal education. Frado appears freest and least endangered in her outdoor incarnations. When her mother and her mother's partner, Seth, state that they intend to give her away, Frado decamps with a companion: "They had climbed fences and walls, passed through thickets and marshes, and when night approached selected a thick cluster of shrubbery as a covert" (20). After the particularly vicious abuse she receives for besting Mary and showing her to be a liar, Jack "took her with him to the field. . . . He resolved to do what he could to protect her from Mary and his mother. He bought her a dog" (37). "Shut up" in the house, she gains solace when "going and returning with the cows, out in the fields" with Fido (117, 42). She achieves mastery over the sheep and Mary outdoors. For Wilson, animals are more than mere metaphors. Rejecting conventional associations between black/female/disabled/child/poor/rural individuals and animals, transvaluing such connections while esteeming literacy and culture, Wilson's environmental novel presents a complex construction of embodiment and of humans' relations to nonhuman nature that contends with supposedly scientific, racialized classification schemes of natural differences. Finally, Frado claims ownership of herself and her resources as she "feels the stirring of free and independent thoughts" outdoors at the woodpile (105). Lacking Jacobs's family support or Berbineau's implied community of servants, Frado escapes from the Bellmonts' tortures and asserts her humanity through literacy and through her access to and agency in unsentimentalized nature.

Idylls of Work and Visions of Leisure:
Lucy Larcom's Working Girls

Harriet Wilson's New England, to cite the title of a recent book, was also Lorenza Stevens Berbineau's and Lucy Larcom's New England. Larcom grew up near the international port city of Salem, Massachusetts, where Milford resident George Blanchard's daughters furnished leadership in its substantial African American community.[160] Larcom also worked in the textile mills of Berbineau's employers. In *Our Nig*, Wilson intimates that

Mag Smith's misfortune occurs partly because she must compete with "foreigners who cheapened toil and clamored for a livelihood" (8).[161] Domestic servants were not the only ones facing such competition; so were factory workers like Larcom, who, in an 1881 reminiscence, cites the "foreigners" who dominate the workers' ranks and make "the toil of the New England woman there every year more difficult and more disagreeable." Yet it is not the immigrants per se that trouble Larcom; it is the "paralyzing caste-ideas crushed into them."[162] Larcom's ethos prioritized connections among women, as one autobiographical essay reveals: "A truism is a truth gone to seed, and perhaps this one is ripe for replanting: that the only just standard by which the worth of any woman's life can be measured is to be found, not in the more or less favorable accidents of her condition, nor yet in the visible amount of labor she may or may not have accomplished, but in the loyalty of her womanhood to the most ennobling instincts and principles of our common humanity."[163]

Best known today for her portrait of factory life in *A New England Girlhood*, Larcom merits closer attention for her representations of nature and the environment in various genres and through different subject positions, such as the child and the older woman. Such breadth makes generalizing about her writing awkward. Of all the women discussed in this chapter, she most nearly approaches nature writing's formal and substantive conventions; her genres include pastoral.[164] Yet she sometimes explores social and environmental justice concerns, and her romantic perspective indirectly critiques industrial capitalism, with its relentless and mechanical emphasis on progress.[165] Like Berbineau and Wilson, she insists on the importance of culture to working women.[166] Like Frado, who "had her book always fastened open near her, where she could glance from toil to soul refreshment," Larcom synthesizes work and education, adding a contemplation of nature that aligns with Berbineau's transcendentalist vision.

Of the three authors, Larcom is most reticent about bodily suffering. While her writing grants the consumption of women's bodies and labor as resources, it also expresses a philosophy of compensation, in the process subduing or eliding the gritty reality of factory work and women's employments more generally. Larcom's concern for respectability demands that her compositions trace a more circuitous course, substantively and formally, than Berbineau's and Wilson's. Not that they were unconcerned with respectability—to the contrary; they too sought to meet middle-class

standards that demanded piety, purity, education, and culture. But corporeal contingencies remained much more urgent for the domestic servants,
especially Wilson, who struggled merely to survive, physically and psychically. At times progressive and other times conservative, Larcom sometimes
engages readers' politics while she elaborates romantic, even sentimental,
representations of nature that encourage our sympathies through pastoral
enjoyment. Embodiment, for Larcom, is potentially pleasurable, and such
pleasure provides leverage. Appreciating her access to and agency in the
environment, Larcom counterpoints Berbineau's and Wilson's accounts of
restriction, making affirmative appeals for environmental justice. Unafraid
of advancing angry entreaties or ironic analyses, she prefers to activate readers' emotional intelligence via companionship and delight.

IN AN 1881 ESSAY in the *Atlantic Monthly*, Larcom explains that labor,
self-improvement, and leisure were much less separate in mid-nineteenth-
century America, and she underscores the changing definitions of *work*
and *class*: "When we talk about 'the working-classes,' we are using very
modern language, which those who formed the great mass of our population forty or fifty years ago would have found it difficult to understand. The
term 'working-people' was then seldom used, because everybody worked."
Employment itself meant respectability, and "the children of that generation were brought up to endure hardness."[167] She could have been speaking
of herself. Reluctant to be stereotyped as a mere "factory-girl," Larcom
was a class migrant, beginning her life in what we would now regard as
the middle class, moving through poverty and millwork, and ultimately
returning to relative—if tenuous—financial security.[168] But her comfortable early childhood strongly affected how she conveyed the relationships
among femininity, nature, and work and her sense of her own environmental agency.

Born on 5 March 1824 in Beverly, Massachusetts, Larcom wandered widely
in her coastal region's natural world, but when her father, Benjamin, died in
January 1832, her childhood's carefree period abruptly concluded. Three years
later, Mrs. Larcom opened a boardinghouse for mill girls in the burgeoning
factory city of Lowell; eleven-year-old Lucy was forced to leave school and
enter the mills, earning a dollar a week. Many other mill girls who came to
Lowell had a more utilitarian attitude toward nature, but Larcom's child-

hood engendered an aesthetic and spiritual appreciation of the natural world akin to Berbineau's.[169] Congenial workmates and a literary life that led to her first publication in the workers' magazine, the *Lowell Offering*, compensated somewhat for unpleasant factory duties, but the machinery's cacophony, combined with the mills' pollution, damaged her health, forcing her to leave Lowell.[170] Unlike Wilson and Berbineau, who tested marriage—and possibly because she enjoyed a supportive family circle—Larcom ended an early engagement, never marrying. In 1857, two years before Wilson published *Our Nig*, the *Crayon*, an elite magazine, published Larcom's poem "Hannah Binding Shoes," which thrust her into the national spotlight and opened all the famous periodicals to her writing.

Numerous publications followed, including her first book of poetry (*Poems*, 1868); two lucrative anthologies, *Roadside Poems for Summer Travelers* (1876) and *Hillside and Seaside in Poetry* (1877); and a blank-verse narrative, *An Idyl of Work* (1875). Her professional life was hardly idyllic. Regularly pressured by financial concerns, she taught at Wheaton College in Massachusetts, at times becoming ill due to overwork. In 1879 she completed a glowingly received critical assessment of major American poets, the beautifully illustrated *Landscape in American Poetry*, which dovetailed with her transcendental perspective and exemplified her commitment to preserving views of the American landscape, as Sigourney had done in *Scenes in My Native Land*.[171] Her most important later publications were *Wild Roses of Cape Ann and Other Poems* (1880), *The Poetical Works of Lucy Larcom* (1884)—which formalized her significance in American literature, appearing in a Household Edition published by the prestigious Houghton Mifflin Company—and her autobiography, *A New England Girlhood* (1889). Along with numerous publications aimed at children and her editorship of the premier children's magazine *Our Young Folks* from 1864 to 1873, the autobiography capped her lifelong commitment to children's literature.[172]

Larcom's most durable and familiar publication, *A New England Girlhood*, affords the best context for estimating her vision of the environment. Though based on her life, the book differs dramatically from Berbineau's diaries and Wilson's novel. First, it recounts the experience of a recognized professional author with a substantial audience on whom she had depended financially for many years; any cultural censure would necessarily be indirect.[173] Because at this point she had more time to write, her volume is much more detailed than her counterparts'. In addition, Larcom was never employed as a servant; her factory labor, and the Lowell community to which she belonged, engendered a very different outlook on independent work. The autobiographical *Atlantic* essay states concisely the motivations that also frame *A New England Girlhood*: "If an excuse is needed for recurring to the scenery of my childhood, it may be said that with most of us nature is only next to religion and the ties of friendship and kindred as a shaping element of life."[174] Perhaps most importantly, Larcom composed her reminiscences near the end of her life, as the subtitle, *Outlined from Memory*, emphasizes. These factors combined with Larcom's relatively comfortable early years to produce a sunny retrospective rooted in place: a magical Beverly home set in a pastoral American past.

Though it reflects an entirely different perception of childhood than *Our Nig*, *A New England Girlhood*, published in the Riverside Library for Young People, also addresses both children and adults, offering distinctive insights and lessons for each audience.[175] It synthesizes the child's immediate delight and the older woman's retrospective pleasure. Like Wilson, Larcom respects the child's experience, and she treasures play, especially outdoor play and unmediated access to the natural world, because it contributes to the child's development.[176] Larcom tacitly acknowledges the fact that many middle-class American women regarded their childhood as a time of unparalleled material and psychological freedom.[177] Displaying this freedom in her own life, she shows that nature's wonders are her first and best teachers and her guides to transcendental meaning.[178]

A New England Girlhood begins by affirming her bond with the Beverly seaside: "It is strange that the spot of earth where we were born should make such a difference to us. People can live and grow anywhere, but people as well as plants have their *habitat*,—the place where they belong, and where they find their happiest, because their most natural life." Larcom's home lies in northeastern Massachusetts, on "this green, rocky strip of shore," where "these gray ledges hold me by the roots, as they do the bayberry bushes, the sweet-fern, and the rock-saxifrage" (17). Connected to place as deeply as plants, individuals flourish or fail because of their roots. Many episodes associate people with natural phenomena or describe them in metaphors based in the environment, as she indirectly critiques a rapidly urbanizing America.

Larcom's white middle-class childhood world, so unlike Frado's, fosters leisured physical and imaginative play. The herbs and flowers, the terrain, the cultivated land all expand the young writer's vision: "Those dandelion fields were like another heaven dropped down upon the earth, where our feet wandered at will among the stars" (90).[179] The water holds a special attraction: "An 'arm of the sea' I was told that our river was, and it did seem to reach around the town and hold it in a liquid embrace. Twice a day the tide came in and filled its muddy bed with a sparkling flood" (32). More maternal than menacing, the river and sea signify possibility, and they are teeming with wonderful creatures:

> One [of the snails] we called a "butter-boat"; it had something shaped like a seat across the end of it on the inside. And the curious sea-urchin, that looked as if he was made only for ornament, when he had once got rid of his spines,—and the transparent jelly-fish, that seemed to have no more right to be alive than a ladleful of mucilage,—and the razor-shells, and the barnacles, and the knotted kelp, and the flabby green sea-aprons,—there was no end to the interesting things I found when I was trusted to go down to the edge of the tide alone. (88)

Nature becomes a character in *A New England Girlhood*, as Larcom's concrete, Thoreauvian rhetoric elaborates embodied experience to elicit a nostalgic, freer past. Depicting "American" childhood, she participates in a nation-building project allied to Sigourney's in *Scenes in My Native Land*, but she is even more ambivalent than her predecessor about progress: privileging the child's perspective, the older Larcom implicitly challenges the unnatural industrial present.

Larcom characterizes the sea as a constant presence. One morning her sister Emilie aroused "very little" Lucy at four o'clock; heading east, Larcom suddenly saw "what looked to me like an immense blue wall, stretching right and left as far as I could see" (85). Awed by this "revelation," she reveals that "I took in at that moment for the first time something of the real grandeur of the ocean" (86). The sea's inhabitants also provoked wonder— and dismay. Unaware that a starfish (which the children called a "five finger") was a living being, she collected one and "hung him on a tree to dry," but when she returned, "he had clasped with two or three of his fingers [around] the bough where I laid him, so that he could not be removed without breaking his hardened shell" (87). Provoking a tender conscience,

this event demonstrates the ethical education that sublimity fosters. Like
Sigourney, Larcom envisions nature's access to divinity within a moral context; for the former, this involved environmental justice activism on behalf
of Native Americans, while for Larcom it would eventually entail antislavery activism. The child tacitly schools the adult's behavior, as the author
invites readers to self-reflection about their relationship to the environment.

Larcom counterbalances such ethical interludes with more mundane
examples of the child's outlook. Many twentieth-century readers (mis)-
understand her as a purely sentimental writer, but her autobiography brims
with humor, often self-directed. As a small child, she tells us, "When the
minister read, 'Cut it down: why cumbereth it the ground?' I thought he
meant to say 'cu-cumbereth.' These vegetables grew on the ground, and I
had heard that they were not very good for people to eat. I honestly supposed that the New Testament forbade the cultivation of cucumbers" (49).
Her literalness causes additional difficulties when she hears an aunt pray,
"Oh Lord, Thou knowest that we are all groveling worms of the dust," and
she returns home, "begging to know whether everybody did sometimes
have to crawl about in the dust" like worms (50). Larcom's humor mirrors
a carefree early childhood that offsets Beverly's Calvinist roots. But this
humor serves a larger purpose, for the author's rhetoric not only appeals to
readers' amusement at childhood's literalness, it also elicits adult desires for
ethical and environmental agency.

This agency extends to domestic environments permeated with the foreign, for her Beverly home incorporates the world. Sketching a heterogeneous mixing of people and exotic natural objects from abroad, she recalls
how "mantel-pieces were adorned with nautilus and conch-shells, and with
branches and fans of coral" (94); how the community was "accustomed to
seeing barrels full of cocoa-nuts rolled about; and there were jars of preserved tropical fruits, tamarinds, ginger-root, and other spicy appetizers,
almost as common as barberries and cranberries, in the cupboards of most
housekeepers" (94–95). Her wonder compares to the adult Berbineau's response to the Great Exhibition. Among the common objects were "many
living reminders of strange lands across the sea": "Green parrots went scold-
ing and laughing down the thimbleberry hedges that bordered the corn-
fields, as much at home out of doors as within. Java sparrows and canaries
and other tropical song-birds poured their music out of sunny windows into

the street, delighting the ears of passing school children long before the robins came" (95). Evoking a delightful sensual embodiment that Wilson almost entirely elides, Larcom synthesizes local and global environments, painting a picture of "a rural Paradise" (107).[180]

This charming history elides the foundation for such home life. The economy that underwrote the Beverly idyll rested on a larger economy that included not just the military (the town claims the first commissioned ship) and the nation's first cotton mill but also the global trade in commodities — and people.[181] One recently authenticated case of 1793 relates to the schooner *Two Friends*, whose "Outward Manifest of October 11, 1791" lists a cargo of "fish, beef, S hooks, [barrel] hoops, oil, candles, and vegetables to the West Indies"; the ship brought sugar and molasses to Beverly, in the interim transporting slaves between Haiti and Cuba.[182] As a child, Larcom was probably unaware of the human commerce that supported Beverly's prosperity, but as an adult and committed abolitionist, she almost certainly discerned these connections. Rather than critiquing this history, her autobiography seeks to reproduce for readers the atmosphere of play and freedom that she enjoyed. Her embodied rhetoric aims to engender delight and nostalgia; she aims at pleasure here, not social remediation.

At the same time, the autobiography's title hints at a potential irony and a determined cheerfulness, given her childhood labor in the Lowell mills and the suffering the country would endure in the Civil War.[183] This politicized perspective on play emerges more explicitly in her children's poem "A Little Old Girl," which rejects domestic social norms while it underscores the physical toil that rural women regularly endured.[184] The protagonist Prudence imitates her adult female counterparts, "knitting stockings, / Sweeping floors, and baking pies"; she occupies "a world that women work in . . . a world where men grow rich" (lines 2–3, 8). In a concise account that resembles Wilson's descriptions of Frado's tasks, each season has its activities, from sewing to gardening to tending animals. Conjuring Larcom's own interrupted outdoor girlhood, Prudence intuits another life:

> Something more has haunted Prudence
>   In the song of bird and bee,
> In the low wind's dreamy whisper
>   Through the light-leaved poplar tree.

> Something lingers, bends above her,
>   Leaning at the mossy well;
> Some sweet murmur from the meadows,
>   On the air some gentle spell. (lines 21–28)

Blaming her distraction on "witches," Prudence ignores nature's beauty and mysteries, but Larcom inserts her own outlook directly in the penultimate stanza, where she intimates that Prudence simply obeys her mother's attitude that "work is good for child or woman." In her own voice she adds, "Childhood's jailer,—'tis a shame!" (lines 30, 35, 36). "A Little Old Girl" attacks the patriarchal status quo, but the poem also excoriates women's collusion, for it is the "gossips," the older women themselves, who smilingly approve of Prudence's efforts: "What a good wife she will make!" (line 40).[185] Her chores exclude her from childhood play and alienate her from nature's transcendent wonders; home symbolizes exploitation, not delight. Unlike Prudence, whose name similarly vibrates with irony, Frado responds to nature's "gentle spell," even with certain punishment. Although for girl readers "A Little Old Girl" may appear to affirm women's status as natural resources, Larcom confronts adults, especially mothers, with a stern question: Am I enforcing my daughters' distance from the natural environment and reproducing laboring female bodies that merely serve as resources for men?

Like many nineteenth-century American women writers, Larcom found children's literature (including *A New England Girlhood*) to afford an amenably indirect method of social analysis and criticism, and she certainly grasped that women's poetry for children enabled women's and children's mutual self-construction.[186] The author could incorporate politicized rhetoric indirectly in children's poetry, but her views emerge explicitly, if briefly, in her autobiography, where she opines, "[I]t was . . . a pity that we were set to hard work while so young."[187] Although throughout *A New England Girlhood* she insists on work's significance, she underlines the need for children to play, addressing mothers at least as much as their children. Elsewhere she avers, "Childhood is short enough, at best; and any abridgement of its freedom is always to be regretted."[188] Ironically, in view of her own youthful aversion to work, Larcom claims that "[c]hildren born half a century ago grew up penetrated through every fibre of thought with the idea that idleness is disgrace."[189] Her idealization of middle-class leisure thus represents a later nineteenth-century conception of childhood.

Leisure, and consequently access to the natural world, was sharply curtailed when her father died. By the time Mrs. Larcom moved her family to Lowell, the city had gained an international reputation, attracting as workers numerous New England farm girls, who entered the factories to support their brothers or save for their own education or marriage. It was they who formed unions to protest the long hours and horrible conditions in the 1830s and 1840s. To attract these independent, mostly white, and largely literate women who regarded themselves as temporarily employed, the mill owners attempted to establish an environment of culture and refinement via Lyceum lectures and regular church attendance.[190] To counter charges of female immorality, they also launched a system of boardinghouses headed by matrons like Mrs. Larcom as guarantors of respectability.[191] The author valued the cultural opportunities and egalitarian social relations that the workers enjoyed, though she essentially elides disputes between them and management, partly because of her bidirectional audience of children and adults. But her autobiography also manifests a sensibility that, however much it appreciates factory labor's economic opportunities and however much it respects Lowell's independent women, retains her childhood era's middle-class principles and experiences, which reflected a more integrated experience of economic activity, where production occurred in the home and did not rely on machinery.[192]

Nature remains central to Larcom's life and aesthetics even when poverty and toil dislodge her rural idyll. Both the autobiography and its precursor essay downplay the losses incurred when her family moved to Lowell, she left school, and she entered millwork. Instead, the writer emphasizes the parallel compensations of culture and her continuing connection with nature. Initially Larcom sees the change as a romantic adventure, and her focus shifts from the sea to the omnipresent Merrimack River and the mountains.[193] Reminding readers that "we were children still," she stresses that "nature still held us close to her motherly heart." Green grass lay close to the mill gates; "violets and wild geraniums grew by the canals." Although mill owners tried to soften the hardscaped Lowell environment by planting flowers and installing tree-lined promenades, Larcom relates how the workers bring inside their outdoor experiences, which helps them "forget the oily smell of the machinery."[194] Here and elsewhere, her embodied rhetoric evokes Berbineau's determination to participate in the natural environment, to assert agency and gain access.

The contingencies of factory work, which left little time to write, led Larcom back to her early love of poetry, which provided a creative outlet and a distraction. With more sustained admission to cultural enrichment than Berbineau and Wilson, Larcom repeatedly draws from romantic and pastoral tradition as a refuge and a means of implicit critique. Less fretful than Berbineau looking out her Paris hotel window, Larcom claims that tasks ease when she focuses on nature: "[W]hen . . . I began to toil at the spindles, with the river rippling past my windows, it brought me more than its own music and beauty; it was a messenger from the hills, from summits touched with the radiance of an invisible heaven." She also describes herself as "a very young spinner, refreshing myself alternately with the blue river and the lovely landscape beyond, and with some scrap of poetry upon the wall beside me, which was also another window, an opening into the unseen."[195] Recalling the outdoor moments in Berbineau's diary, Larcom's retrospective echoes her flight from laboring embodiment to transcendence in nature.[196]

AMONG THE AUTHORS in this chapter, Larcom explores class distinctions the most self-consciously. After she worked in the mills, Larcom revisited the concept of a servant, affirming the old-fashioned idea of interdependent help prevalent in New England households earlier in the nineteenth century: "A girl came into a family as one of the home-group, to share its burdens, to feel that they were her own. The woman who employed her, if her nature was at all generous, would not feel that money alone was an equivalent for a heart's service; she added to it her friendship, her gratitude and esteem. The domestic problem can never be rightly settled until the old idea of mutual help is in some way restored."[197] When she invoked this ideal, she was recalling America's agricultural history, tacitly privileging a communal, interdependent model that, as Wilson dramatizes, was many times unavailable to New England's people of color. Larcom's egalitarian views strengthened after her mill experience and she ultimately insists, "It is the first duty of every woman to recognize the mutual bond of universal womanhood." Demoting individualism, Larcom imagines a community that is necessary in an economic environment in which "[c]hanges of fortune come so abruptly that the millionaire's daughter of to-day may be glad to earn her living by sewing or sweeping to-morrow."[198] Home's comforts were potentially transitory, and hence environmental agency was vital.

Racial and ethnic as well as class differences inform Larcom's communal ethos.[199] Among her important influences was the antislavery activist and poet John Greenleaf Whittier, whom she met during her Lowell experience and who became a mentor, encouraging her political engagement as well as her literary aspirations. Larcom's essentially conservative activism reprises Sigourney's Christian advocacy and white middle-class standards, as we see when her journal records with pleasure meeting one of the Whittiers' guests: "[A]n educated mulatto girl, refined, lady-like in every respect, and a standing reply to those who talk of the 'inferiority of the colored race.'"[200] "Educated," "refined," "lady-like" are disembodied standards of respectability to which, she suggests, all should aspire. Perhaps sensitive to the cultural affiliation between women of color and animals that Wilson deconstructs so effectively, Larcom separates humans from nonhuman nature. This genteel ethos guides much of *A New England Girlhood*'s narrative, as the author struggles to mesh respectability with material life.

Elsewhere in her work, Larcom dispenses with such restrictions. The antebellum period troubled the writer intensely, and she unequivocally supported abolition. In an 1856 letter to Whittier detailing Boston antislavery meetings, she declares, "We are indeed living in a revolution. It makes me ache to think I am doing nothing for the right, for *the holy cause*. What can one do? It is not very agreeable to sit still and blush to be called an American woman."[201] She could, however, compose poems, such as "A Loyal Woman's No," in which a female speaker chastises her lover for refusing to fight for the Union cause in the Civil War.[202] Extending this literary activism, her best-known poem today, "Weaving," emphasizes women's social and moral responsibilities to others in an enlarged vision of America as home.[203]

Nature frames Larcom's insights about troubling interracial bonds, as "Weaving" reveals the network of exploitation that enmeshed Southern slave women and Northern white women factory workers in cotton cloth production. Describing a weaver, the poem's opening lines mingle inside and outside, imagination and reality:

> All day she stands before her loom;
>   The flying shuttles come and go;
> By grassy fields, and trees in bloom,
>   She sees the winding river flow:
> And fancy's shuttle flieth wide,
> And faster than the waters glide. (lines 1–6)[204]

The musing weaver connects culture and nature, and the river symbolizes life itself:

> The river glides along, one thread
>   In nature's mesh, so beautiful!
> The stars are woven in; the red
>   Of sunrise; and the rain-cloud dull.
> Each seems a separate wonder wrought;
> Each blends with some more wondrous thought.
>   (lines 19–24)[205]

The natural elements here are each "a separate wonder" that also "blends" with others; Larcom maintains that only God can perceive the "full pattern" of the "separate shreds" (line 26). She underscores her voice through the weaver's: "nature's mesh" evokes the connections among women embodied literally in the cotton fibers. The river fosters this imaginative link:

> Wind on, by willow and by pine,
>   Thou blue, untroubled Merrimack!
> Afar, by sunnier streams than thine,
>   My sisters toil, with foreheads black;
> And water with their blood this root,
> Whereof we gather bounteous fruit. (lines 37–42)

Nature and the environment mediate conscience for Larcom, as she foregrounds how Northern factory women's livelihoods depend on Southern slave women's toil. In the sunset light, she fancies that the Merrimack's "calm flood / Were changed into a stream of blood" (lines 71–72), as if nature reflects and remarks on human — and here, specifically female — sins. Even more pointedly, it highlights female responsibilities, as she concludes: "Thy sister's keeper know thou art!" (line 78). Guilty as Cain, these Northern white women should ponder their employment's damaging, damning consequences. And so, she implies, should the purchasers of their unholy product.

Larcom stresses "untroubled" nature to censure the exploitative classed and racialized manual labor system that compromises the promise of America and belies the concept of progress. Like Sigourney in "Indian Names" and Wilson in *Our Nig*, she castigates merely nominal Christianity. Yet as she confirms the physical bonds between enslaved women and their white, factory-working Northern counterparts, Larcom gestures toward the sublime and the pastoral to which the Southerners lack access. For them, nature entails suffering, perhaps bloodshed. Testing readers' emotional intelligence, the author invokes distress, sympathy, guilt, and awe and promotes a gendered, community ethos. Unlike nature, human society is not—or should not be—morally neutral. "Weaving" laments black women's embodied confinement and articulates a prescient environmental justice critique.

Notwithstanding this sophisticated understanding of systemic exploitation, Larcom deemphasizes environmental issues closer to home.[206] *A New England Girlhood* appeared many years after Elizabeth Stuart Phelps published her dramatic exposé of the horrors of New England's textile mills, *The Silent Partner* (1871). Imprisoned in her body, the emblematic character Catty Garth, deaf, mute, and blind from cotton-fiber pollution, jumps to her death at Five Falls. Despite Phelps's middle-class point of view, she articulates an important environmental perspective on factory labor, showing how the workers' dirty hands represent profitable golden hands for the mills' owners.[207] Why was Phelps able, or willing, to depict the gritty reality of workers' lives, both at the factory and at home, while Larcom offers a relatively sanitized version? Possibly because of Larcom's Christian work ethic, her feminine tendency to stress positives, or her continuing financial fragility and intended readership (particularly children), her portraits of factory life downplay environmental concerns related to industrial occupations. Her reticence may have also derived from her desire for independence, her unwillingness—like Mag, Frado, and Wilson herself—to receive charity.

But Larcom's published writing provides only glimpses of the physical consequences of long hours, tedium, and noise—health hazards including the recurrent tuberculosis that the author herself periodically endured. After rising at 4:00 a.m., workers would arrive at the factories at 5:00. The historian Thomas Dublin recounts grim early conditions; mill hands "were employed for an average of 12 hours a day, 6 days a week, 309 days a year" and were normally paid between forty and eighty cents a day. Men, of course, earned significantly more.[208] Because company officials believed that air circulation made the threads break more readily, the factories' windows were closed during blistering summer heat and frigid winter cold. "Workers were either sweating or shivering by their machines"; visibility was also poor, causing a high risk of occupational disability. Children were vulnerable to scalping when their hair caught in the equipment, and women who stayed for more than a short period often "suffered from tuberculosis, malnutrition, exhaustion, hearing loss, premature aging, maiming, and death."[209]

To be fair, the conditions in the mills worsened considerably in the decades after Larcom's departure. And Larcom did not entirely ignore such problems, observing that "the noise of machinery was particularly distasteful to me." Nevertheless, she asserts, "I discovered . . . that I could so accustom myself to the noise that it became like silence to me. And I defied the machinery to make me its slave," reiterating the common comparison between Southern chattel slavery and Northern "wage slavery." She also declares that "the regularity enforced by the clangor of the [morning] bell" supplied "good discipline for one who was naturally inclined to dally and to dream, and who loved her own personal liberty with a willful rebellion against control."[210] Willed optimism and her knowledge that she was a moral exemplar for young readers led Larcom paradoxically to diminish the importance of childish play and agency, especially the embodied outdoor pleasure that she prized. Determined partly by bodily self-control, female propriety trumps freedom.

Yet elsewhere the older Larcom challenged confining standards of civility and respectability. "Flowers of the Fallow," one of Larcom's most powerful poems, invokes, then transforms, the traditional association between women and nature. The opening lines resist the romantic ideal of pure, beautiful nature:

> I like these plants that you call weeds, —
>   Sedge, hardhack, mullein, yarrow, —
> That knit their seeds
> Where any grassy wheel-track leads
>   Through country by-ways narrow.[211]

"Lincoln Cotton Mills, Evanston, Ind. Girls at weaving machine; warpers."
Image by Lewis Wickes Hine, October 1908. The mills appear much cleaner
than those in which Larcom worked in the mid-nineteenth century, and many
of the Lowell mill girls were younger than those depicted here.
Courtesy of the Library of Congress.

The harsh, consonantal plant names reinforce the poet's appreciation for a
nature that encompasses "wild" and "cultivated"; the opening stanza also
underscores the powerfully adventitious nature of these "weeds," which
are, paradoxically, linked to culture via the metaphor of "seeds" and the
literal inroads that the technology of wheels ensures. Weeds symbolize un-
controllability, authenticity, and autonomy, evoking Frado's—and young
Larcom's—effervescent energies, energies that contrast with "ladies'" putative "cultivation"—their respectability. If the "wild" weeds signify social
outcasts, the succeeding stanza transvalues these disruptive plants by claiming their precedence to hill farms "grown old with cultivation" (line 7).

When Larcom introduces an ostensibly conventional image of female
nature, here a "matron" and later "Mother Earth" (lines 9, 11), the link that
Candice Bradley has established between weeding and housework seems

salient.[212] This maternal figure resists humans' transformation of the natural world; she fills the spaces that plows produced with "humbler blossoms" that speak through untamed, even erotic, "flowery lips" (line 13).[213] Portraying men's historical role as literal and conceptual creators of the American landscape, Larcom envisions how nature "yielded to your axe, with pain, / Her free, primeval glory" (lines 21–22). Yet the poet counters this perception: she associates postlapsarian nature with the wild, aging woman, who performs a redemptively powerful role:

> You say, "How dull she grows! how plain!"
>   The old, mean, selfish story!
>
> Her wildwood sod you may subdue,
>   Tortured by hoe and harrow;
> But leave her for a year or two,
> And see! she stands and laughs at you
>   With hardhack, mullein, yarrow! (lines 24–30)

This conception of a female, adversarial nature is not new.[214] But Larcom innovates with her insistence on an old, tired Mother Nature. The poem's final stanza describes the weedy flowers as tangible evidence of "heaven's breath," and the speaker imagines herself as intimately, corporeally related to them:

> And I lie down at blessèd ease
>   Among thy weeds and grasses. (lines 34–35)

"Flowers of the Fallow" redeems weeds and their symbolic avatars, older women. Exposing American culture's objectification of Mother Nature and of old women at a time when "redundant women" were being energetically discussed, the writer creates an ecosystem that resists patriarchy in all its forms.[215]

Like Sigourney in "The Cherokee Mother," Larcom invites a reappraisal of metaphoric associations between women and uncivilized nature that reinforce gender hierarchies. Published in the influential *Atlantic Monthly* (as "Fallow," in 1882) and in her own popular collection of poetry *The Poetical Works of Lucy Larcom* (1884), "Flowers of the Fallow" appeared as Americans were increasingly concerned about the exploitation of nature.[216] Larcom's embodied rhetoric, emphasized by her gritty diction, invites readers to a material appreciation of nature's—and women's—social circumscription, and her suggestion of torture engages readers' ethics. Envisioning older women affectionately, ultimately identifying with them, the narrator signals their triumphant escape and their agency. "Flowers of the Fallow" thus indirectly maintains that environmental writing should incorporate age and aging as central analytical categories.

As her life concluded, Larcom continued to explore modernizing America's problems.[217] Another late poem illuminates how human intervention had altered the natural environment. Depicting her native Cape Ann, "My Mariner" begins with a cheerful, romantic ballad about a seafaring husband.[218] But at stanza five the poem's tone and form transform to blank verse that foregrounds a more domesticated and realistic—and consciously nostalgic—portrait of an older landscape. Larcom welcomes readers to share her journey along the shore as it was forty years earlier; admiring hidden pathways, she illustrates the landscape's complex beauties:

> Even now,
> You slip into those rose-roads unaware,
> Just out of reach of landscape gardeners,
> And farmers beauty-blind, whose synonym
> For poison-oak and rose is—underbrush! (lines 55–59)

In this humorous reinvention, beauty means "poison-oak" along with "rose." Larcom decries both purely utilitarian farmers and "landscape gardeners" who have modified the wild landscape for the worse:

> everything
> That hints of Nature closely taken in hand
> By patronizing Wealth, and stroked and smoothed
> Into suburban elegance. (lines 65–68)

Through her radical change in form, voice, and content, the poet satirically signals her denigration—with Sigourney and Kirkland—of American ideals of progress that homogenize the landscape and eradicate wildness; more harshly, Larcom censures conventional norms of beauty, including pastoral. Conceiving of home in nationalist terms, she rejects the domestication of an older, outdoor America and, indirectly, condemns the wealthy women whose consumption has destroyed this environment and the values that it symbolized.

Larcom's diverse genres reveal an environmental sensibility that tackles subjects indirectly and directly. Her child and adult perspectives sometimes clash, and she disciplines her youthful avatar while she celebrates girls' physical freedom in nature. Even as play gives way to respectability and responsibility, her writing evokes romanticized arguments for children's access to and agency in the natural world. In her more political vein, Larcom demands that women recognize their culpability in the exploitation of children and enslaved African American women, and she hopes to inspire ethical action. She critiques American notions of advancement uninformed by appreciation for the environment and argues for a concrete understanding of the natural world that acknowledges older women's authority. Her environmental rhetoric fuses embodiment and aesthetics to arrive at a material transcendentalism more compatible with Thoreau or even Whitman than Emerson. Regardless of her theme or form, Larcom expresses greater optimism and agency than her working-class contemporaries, perhaps because of her middle-class childhood and eventual economic comfort, and because she needed to satisfy middle-class audiences' demands to sustain that comfort. Beyond temperament, experience, or economic exigencies, her approach demonstrates a sophisticated emotional intelligence attuned to a national audience with its own potential for agency.

Ironically, given Larcom's historical moment, reverence for nature, and attachment to her native ground, she conveys less explicit interest in environmental stewardship than either Sigourney or Kirkland. But stewardship requires significant leisure (and possibly a sense of ownership), which none of the working-class women surveyed in this chapter easily or often enjoyed. Pivotal in one of her most important poems, the metaphor of weaving best symbolizes Larcom's ethos and aesthetic. *A New England Girlhood* maintains individuality while it insists upon connections and community; as she draws on her Lowell experience, Larcom concludes, "Every little thread must take its place as warp or woof, and keep in it steadily. Left to itself, it would only be a loose, useless filament. Trying to wander in an independent or disconnected way among the other threads, it would make of the whole web an inextricable snarl. Yet each little thread must be as firmly spun as if it were the only one, or the result would be a worthless fabric. That we are entirely separate, while yet we entirely belong to the Whole, is a truth that we learn to rejoice in."[219] Typifying the moral stance expected of her as a woman and famous children's author, Larcom's elevated, Christian standpoint veils the hands underwriting mill owners' profits, profits that financed Berbineau's European journey, a journey that her own hands enabled. Berbineau's Christianity—like that of Wilson's Frado—is tested by the all-too-concrete reminders of the human needs—food, shelter—that precede elevated visions of "the Whole."

REFUGE AND PRISON, beautiful and frightening, nature and the environment figure diversely in Berbineau, Wilson, and Larcom. Like the Native American women in chapter 1, Berbineau and her peers provide correctives to contemporary ecofeminists' focus on female essentialism. The working-class women offer a stern reality: they must work to survive, as the interrupted childhoods of Wilson and Larcom exemplify. As consumable resources for their employers, they and their labor constructed home in its national as well as local manifestations. Each woman, however indirectly, prioritizes acquiring control over the body and access to the benefits of culture—*and* nature. For all three, their comprehension of the environment was bound to identity and their physical and social place. Reflecting a cross-class perspective, Berbineau prefers to escape from material life's debilitating consequences into aesthetic and spiritual experience, while Wilson and Larcom—though in disparate ways—both deemphasize and embrace corporeal experience. All three women share a fundamental concern with agency and access, touchstones of environmental justice.

Unlike the writers in chapter 1 who promote agency in relation to community identity, for Berbineau, Wilson, and even Larcom, it is relatively individualist.[220] While the two servants speak to questions of national identity, their goals were more personal than political. Berbineau recapitulates a once-in-a-lifetime opportunity for self-improvement; Wilson hopes to support herself and her son while she raises consciousness about Northern racism and indentured wage slavery. Larcom's multigenre writing incorporates more public efforts toward abolition, women's equality, and the conservation of nature.[221] Their writing shows that genre supplies no guarantor of environmental agency, for although all rely on autobiographical elements, their responsibilities, audiences, identities, and locations finally determine that agency. Wilson and Larcom's attention to children and elders should suggest to contemporary ecocritics and activists the importance of including age as an analytical category and these marginalized age groups as crucial audiences. Reading these working-class women's contributions also reminds ecocritics that our bodies themselves are resources and environments, that we must comprehend and value individual as well as collective efforts to achieve environmental justice, and that we should assess all generalizations about the environment in relation to multiform, flexible, and contextualized concepts of class.

Ultimately the circumstances of Berbineau's, Wilson's, and Larcom's literary production shaped their writing, inflecting their choices of genre and rhetoric. Their imagined and actual audiences occupied a continuum: Berbineau's consisted of herself and her fellow servants; Wilson's encompassed African Americans, abolitionists, and children; and Larcom's, the American public. Berbineau presents pastoral views that correspond to the romantic paintings she had doubtless seen in Europe and America; at the same time she reveals pastoral's underside in Europe's hylic laboring women. Her duties affect her rhetoric, as—omitting punctuation, capitalization, and correct orthography—she hurriedly piles image upon image, accumulating beauty to sustain her in its absence. At the same time, her narratives rehearse a superimposed aesthetic of compression, evidenced in the texts' formal irregularities, their substantive elisions, and even their physical size: pocket diaries that would not impede her responsibilities.

At the heart of this chapter and *Fallen Forests* as a whole, Wilson materializes economically and affectively the ways in which women's laboring bodies subsidize class-based consumption. Wilson's antipastoral novel inverts Berbineau's emphasis, providing an implicit judgment of readers— in her time and our own—who focus solely on idealistic representations of nature and offering a complex vision of environmental justice. *Our Nig*'s paucity of natural details mirrors Wilson's contention that pastoral must be apprehended in the context of the work that subsidizes it. Put somewhat differently, in its substance and its shape Wilson's writing tacitly disparages sentimental-romantic rhetorical excess and accounts of female interdependence, including those of predecessors like Kirkland and contemporaries such as Larcom. Reflecting the privileges of relative affluence and education, Larcom uses her prose, and, especially, her poetry, to politicize nature, challenge social hierarchies, and lament the nation's accelerating industrialism and excess individualism, pointing toward the focus of chapter 4: women's attitudes toward respectability, fashion, and consumption.

Coda: Dirty Hands and Golden Hands

Unless they wrote privately or were economically independent, nineteenth-century women writers typically addressed class inequality indirectly. Recognizing indirection's merits, even some who could afford to dissent sometimes chose a more oblique strategy, as Fanny Fern did in the same decade as Berbineau and Wilson. Fern's "The Soliloquy of a Housemaid" exposes elites' demands on laboring women's bodies:

> Oh, dear, dear! Wonder if my mistress *ever* thinks I am made of flesh and blood? Five times, within half an hour, I have trotted up stairs, to hand her things, that were only four feet from her rocking-chair. Then, there's her son, Mrs. George, [*sic*]—it does seem to me, that a great able-bodied man like him, need n't call a poor tired woman up four pair of stairs to ask "what's the time of day?" Heigho!—it[']s "*Sally* do this," and "*Sally* do that," till I wish I never had been baptized at all; and I might as well go farther back, while I am about it, and wish I had never been born.[222]

Lacking an audience, in an isolation that parallels Frado's, the eponymous servant talks merely to herself.

Fern ventriloquizes the housemaid's voice, capturing "the servant problem" from the inside: "Now, instead of ordering me round so like a dray horse, if they would only look up smiling-like, now and then; or ask me how my 'rheumatiz' did; or say good morning, Sally; or show some sort of interest in a fellow-cretur, I could pluck up a bit of heart to work for them. A kind word would ease the wheels of my treadmill amazingly, and would n't cost *them* anything, either" (original emphasis).[223] After losing her first husband and plunging into poverty, Fern knew too well the fragility of social status in mid-nineteenth-century America, as well as the physical vulnerability accompanying such a precipitous fall. "Soliloquy of a Housemaid" goes on to critique middle- and upper-class women's hypocrisy and insensibility from another angle, as the housemaid questions "all the fine glittering things in the drawing room . . . and Miss Clara's diamond ear-rings."[224] Respectability, from Fern's perspective, is a sham enabled by working women's exertions.

Middle-class and affluent Americans' attitudes toward consumption—of objects, of women's bodies—continue to underwrite gender inequality and environmental injustice. The National Labor Committee describes a Haitian woman sewing Pocahontas T-shirts for Disney. Stitching 375 shirts an hour, she averages $10.77 per week; the shirts sell at Wal-Mart for $10.97. This worker embodies the globalization of privilege, earning one-hundredth of the final cost of each T-shirt she produces. The U.S. Department of Labor asserts, "50% of garment factories in the U.S. violate two or more basic labor laws, establishing them as sweatshops."[225] According to the historians Peter Liebhold and Harry Rubenstein, following a 1995 raid on a fenced compound of seven apartments in El Monte, California, where police found seventy-two Thai immigrants who had been "forced to sew in virtual captivity," the Clinton administration, joining representatives in government, labor, industry, and public-interest groups, formed "the White House Apparel Industry Partnership . . . to pursue non-regulatory solutions to sweatshop abuses in the United States and abroad."[226] Such efforts are like fingers in a leaky dike, as Daniel Gross's 2011 exposé of exploited New York food workers documents. He cites as one of the most recent victims "Juan Baten, the 22-year old father of a seven-month old daughter and a devoted husband . . . [who] was crushed and killed in a [tortilla] dough mixing machine. Mr. Baten's workplace did not have a union and had never been inspected by osha, the federal workplace safety authority."[227] What neither account reflects is that sweatshops, especially those common in the garment industry, usually employ women.

On the other end of the supply chain, some female consumers enjoy the greatest power in human history; a recent *Newsweek* story cites a 2010 book on the subject: "American women are responsible for 83 percent of all consumer purchases; they hold 89 percent of U.S. bank accounts, 51 percent of all personal wealth, and are worth more than $5 trillion in consumer spending power—larger than the entire Japanese economy."[228] In the context of a demand for more and cheaper blouses and dresses, skirts and scarves, this power has translated into an efflorescence of sweatshops, both in the United States and abroad. In the past, such working conditions were fueled by middle-class and affluent women's desire for style, represented early on in the fashion plates of *Godey's Lady's Magazine*, which appeared in 1830.[229] The pages of *Vogue*, *Elle*, and *Ebony* predict the future. *Vogue*'s online *Voguepedia* claims that the magazine led the trend we now call "eco fashion," and *Vogue Daily* features an essay entitled "Eco-Minded: Livia Firth Rallies Young London to the Green Carpet Challenge."[230] But as chapter 4 explores, access to fashion, by definition disposable, is unequally distributed, and simple living is sometimes no choice at all.

Fashion plate from *Godey's Lady's Book*, October 1852.
The accompanying description reads, "We would call attention
to the artistic and picturesque grace of this whole engraving,
making it quite as valuable as a picture as a
representative of tasteful fashions."

Chapter 4

Gilt-Edged or "Beautifully Unadorned"

Fashioning Feelings

Mrs Lowells rooms are three Bed chambers a parlour & a dineing room
... the rooms we have a[re] very pleasent & handsomely furneshed they
have very Elegant curtains & Chairs in the Parlour satin damask red and
yellow what they call velvet carpets my room has a handsome carpet two
shades of red blue & Brown paper on the walls blue chintz bed curtains
mahogany bedsted mahogany plush chairs the curtains and paper match.

—LORENZA STEVENS BERBINEAU [in Paris]

We [humans] are affected by climate and locality, by physical, chemical,
electrical forces, as are all animals and plants. With the animals, we farther share the effect of our own activity, the reactionary force of exercise.
... But, beyond these forces, we come under the effect of a third set of
conditions peculiar to our human status; namely, social conditions. In
the organic interchanges which constitute social life, we are affected by
each other to a degree beyond what is found even among the most gre-
garious of animals. ... Throughout all these environing conditions, those
which affect us through our economic necessities are most marked in
their influence.

—CHARLOTTE PERKINS STETSON [GILMAN],
Women and Economics

MERCHANTS OF voluntary simplicity and simple living barrage us today,
as books, magazines, and Internet sites promote a return to "earlier values."
My own history as the daughter of a Depression-era mother who, more
than fifty years later, could relate (with dismay and shame, but also with
pride) having to make her own clothes from others' old garments, resonated with the charge to "use it up, wear it out, make it do, or do without."
As my previous chapters illustrate, Jacobs, Berbineau, Wilson, and Larcom differentially suggest how what Gilman calls "social conditions" and

"economic necessities" profoundly influence one's perspective on the environment. Berbineau's accounting of her hotel's elegant furnishings illuminates how domestic servants underwrote their employers' standards of living with their labor and even their material selves.

Between about 1880 and the turn of the century, disparities—in income, in health, in access to the natural environment—between working people and prosperous Americans exploded. Increased consumption helped ignite the blast. Charlotte Perkins Gilman's extended meditation in *Women and Economics* excoriates her female contemporaries for the selfishness that undergirds this consumption, offering an acid brief for simplicity: "The consuming female, debarred from any free production, unable to estimate the labor involved in the making of what she so lightly destroys, and her consumption limited mainly to those things which minister to physical pleasure, creates a market for sensuous decoration and personal ornament, for all that is luxurious and enervating. . . . As the priestess of the temple of consumption . . . the limitless demander of things to use up, her economic influence is reactionary and injurious."[1] Exposing the connection between consumption and the body, Gilman disparages these comfortable women for their indulgence and ignorant depletion of others' labor and for their self-objectification and self-diminishment: their complicity in social systems that relegate them to the status of lovely objects.

Earlier in *Fallen Forests* I explored how environmental agency depended on such contingencies as an individual's social class, age, racial or ethnic identity, and location. The association of social subordinates (children, white women and women of color, the disabled, and the elderly) with their natural bodies deauthorized them or even relegated them to the status of resources. Here I extend the focus on embodiment with a different emphasis, showing how late nineteenth-century American women writers such as Celia Thaxter, Sarah Orne Jewett, Mary Wilkins Freeman, and Pauline Hopkins negotiate women's place in their individual environments and in American society via respectability, a class-based notion frequently mediated through such concrete necessities as clothing and food. While Berbineau, Wilson, and Larcom speak as the *producers* of wealth and ease, the resources from which the middle class and affluent draw, the writers in this chapter describe the embodied *consumers* of material goods and cultural ideologies. Calibrating their messages to their own consumers—principally prosperous, educated, urban female readers—Thaxter, Jewett, Freeman, and Hopkins map out connections among fashion, social class, respectability, sexuality, and gender identity in order to argue for women's agency over their physical selves and their immediate environments.[2]

Emerging in the late eighteenth century with the development of a sizable middle class, the concept of respectability referenced character or social standing. Cindy S. Aron notes that "[m]iddle-class status rested, in part, on claims to a publicly recognized respectability, a respectability gained by adhering to elaborate and complicated rules of etiquette that governed every minute aspect of life."[3] Respectability and fashion appeared in tandem—*Godey's Lady's Book* emblematizes this correlation—because stylish apparel distinguished its elegant wearer from the embodied laboring woman; it advertised her civility. Related to good breeding, taste, and polished manners, civility, like respectability, segregated the well-heeled from the hoi polloi as surely as elite neighborhoods reinforced geographical distinctions. Middle-class individuals (and aspirants like Jacobs) also linked respectability with physical self-control, especially sexual virtue, supplementing their distance from their rough, unrestrained counterparts.[4] Thus, while male contemporaries such as John Muir and John Burroughs could elevate literal, material wilderness, Thaxter and her cohort struggled to redefine an idea of wilderness that the culture superimposed, though differentially, on women's bodies. How to reconfigure respectability—and their social roles—engaged their attention. By the late nineteenth century, advice writing had long provided avenues for civilizing outsiders and disciplining women's physical selves and their behavior. Reinventing this genre as direct polemic and indirect fictional pedagogy, Thaxter and her contemporaries establish an environmental discourse that situates women's bodies in self-authorized relationships not only to consumer culture but also to material, psychological, community, and national well-being.

In one incarnation, fashion's (and hence, respectability's) antagonist was simplicity; in another, it was simply poverty. Using a complex, hybrid form, Thaxter lambastes ignorant addicts of fashion and advocates unadorned integrity. Jewett and Freeman construct realistic stories that represent women's bodies as symbols of community while they show the practical dimensions of involuntary simplicity. An insider to middle-class African American culture, Hopkins advances a pointed message of Christian humility and material plainness; less directly engaged with the natural world, her story extends her predecessors' concerns with materialism to the city environment. As some American women today experiment with voluntary simplicity and forms of simple living—rejecting their appointment as "priestess[es] of the temple of consumption"—many others struggle toward sufficiency. Jewett, Freeman, and Hopkins anticipate this conflict and offer variously instructive visions of how to negotiate the economic and attitudinal gulf between women and how best to configure relationships between and among individuals and communities. Their conclusions vary, but collectively drawing from an affective ethos, they reveal and sometimes reimagine women's connections to consumption and respectability.

As for earlier writers, form and rhetoric contribute to the authors' environmental messages, their activist predilections, and their ability to spark audiences' emotional intelligence. Critiques of consumption and affiliated class hierarchies appear more indirectly than in their male counterparts' work, often emerging in hybrid or fictional forms illegible as environmental texts. These four women transform and reenergize the feminine genre of advice writing; they also reference the sentimental tradition. Ranging from slapstick to satire, humor, frequently arising from their characters' disjunctive perspectives, emerges as a crucial rhetorical weapon for many late nineteenth-century writers as they address the political and social dimensions of the woman-nature association. As many scholars have argued, however, women's humor renders them more vulnerable to reproach and less likely to be taken seriously in their time and our own.[5] Unlike Kirkland, who prefers nonfiction satire and irony, most of the writers in this chapter prioritize fiction as a more amenable medium for social criticism, perhaps because of its greater indirection. Formal labels aside, these writers blend rhetorical appeals, by turns challenging, amusing, shaming, mirroring, and modeling appropriate responses, whether indirectly through their characters' voices or directly through their own.

All four women were from New England, and all lived at one period in country settings, but Hopkins is most committed to presenting urban views on the questions that this chapter addresses. Perhaps partly because of their personal histories, literary success, and relatively high status, Thaxter and her peers were more able than some, including the working-class women in chapter 3, to censure the later nineteenth century's accelerating industrialism and acquisitiveness.[6] Thaxter, Jewett, Freeman, and Hopkins speak as well to the twenty-first century's gaping class disparities, as environmental activists and theorists attempt to develop alliances that will foster mindful consumption and sustainability.

Green Fashion, Nineteenth-Century Style:
Thaxter's Simple Model

"A charnel house of beaks and claws and bones" seems an unlikely description for a hat. Yet poet and nonfiction writer Celia Thaxter deploys this explosive language in the first issue of *Audubon Magazine*, where she wars on women's barbaric propensity for bird-destroying fashion.[7] She asks her readers, "Does any woman imagine these withered corpses (cured with arsenic) which she loves to carry about, are *beautiful*?" (282). In its frank directness, Thaxter's groundbreaking essay parallels Sigourney's jointly authored "Ladies Circular." More immediately related to the natural environment than the other texts in this chapter, Thaxter's "Woman's Heartlessness" exposes the connections among fashion, nature, home, and women's cultural disadvantage. Thaxter's oeuvre, including her autobiographical narratives and poetry, repeatedly addresses this gendered matrix of concerns.

The isolation of Thaxter's early life prompted her to become a careful observer of nature. She was born in 1835 in the coastal city of Portsmouth, New Hampshire, where her father owned a prosperous business and worked in the custom house. After a political defeat when his daughter was four years old, Thomas Leighton relocated his family to White Island in the nearby Isles of Shoals, where he became the lighthouse keeper. Thaxter's early years with just her parents and two brothers for company were followed by a move to Smutty Nose Island, where the family welcomed paying summer guests. A few years later, her father opened the famous Appledore Hotel with Levi Thaxter, the man who would tutor young Celia and become her husband when she was sixteen.[8] As with many other nineteenth-century American women writers, Thaxter's marriage was frequently unrewarding, and the temperamental and sickly Levi was an uncongenial partner and inadequate provider. After moving the family to Massachusetts, Levi was unwilling to hire housekeeping help for Celia, even as she coped with the demands of her own growing family—including a brain-damaged son for whom she cared throughout her life—and with an active literary career that helped support the family. Celia spent summers with her birth family, when she returned to help run the hotel, a labor-intensive endeavor. During this time she created a renowned garden and hosted a famous salon that attracted eminent artists, musicians, and writers, such as Childe Hassam, Sarah Orne Jewett, Annie and James Fields, Ralph Waldo Emerson, Lucy Larcom, Nathaniel Hawthorne, Thomas Wentworth Higginson, and Samuel Clemens. One frequent guest, John Greenleaf Whittier, was her friend and supporter for many years. As Jane Vallier explains, "The remote Isles of Shoals gave the second generation Transcendentalists a place to contemplate the glories of nature and escape the growing pressures of urban American life."[9]

Such a refuge was limited to the privileged. Problematizing American culture's association of women with nature, Thaxter's autobiographical narrative *Among the Isles of Shoals* reveals a rather different perspective on Thoreauvian simplicity.[10] Strong and attractive, Thaxter's male islanders benefit from outdoor activity, unlike their female counterparts: "It is strange that the sun and wind, which give such fine tints to the complexions of the lords of creation, should leave such hideous traces on the faces of women. When they are exposed to the same salt wind and clear sunshine they take the hue of dried fish, and become objects for men and angels to weep over."[11] Bodily labor takes its toll: "[T]he women, many of whom have grown old before their time with hard work and bitter cares, with hewing of wood and drawing of water, turning of fish on the flakes to dry in the sun, endless household work and the cares of maternity," contrast with their "lords," who "lounged about the rocks in their scarlet shirts in the sun, or 'held up the walls of the meeting-house' . . . with their brawny shoulders." In this supposedly uncomplicated life, the island women are "wrecks of humanity" (66). With its descriptions of relentless, debilitating physical labor, Thaxter's sketch evokes Wilson's portrayals of work in *Our Nig* and Berbineau's reports of female European fieldworkers.

Elsewhere she appreciates a more affirmative, feminized nature's changeability and wildness: "In December the colors seem to fade out of the world. . . . The great, cool, whispering, delicious sea, that encircled us with a thousand caresses the beautiful summer through, turns slowly our sullen and inveterate enemy" (96). "Encircled" and "caresses" imply maternal gestures; the summer sea rocks her as if in amniotic fluid.[12] In another mood, as an ungendered antagonist "raging with senseless fury," nature terrifies (98). As Perry Westbrook suggests, Thaxter "is among the first

American writers to view nature as indifferent, if not downright hostile, to man," an attitude that he avers was unique among American authors of her day.[13] Even in her more cheerful compositions, Thaxter often balances idealism with moments of searing realism that implicitly question the natural paradises of her more well-to-do friends.[14]

Thaxter's adult life, with its physical toil for family, literary friends, and hotel guests, was scarcely simple. Her famous garden provided an escape and alternative feminine creative outlet admired in Victorian America. Leah Glasser claims that writers like Jewett and Thaxter used landscape as a way to "construct their identities in terms that defied traditional gender boundaries. Their imaginative rendering of nature lifted them out of the expectation of service to others within the home, for such writing encouraged and celebrated moments of solitude and self-nurturance."[15] But Thaxter's writing opened a more subversive space both for her creativity and for such public-sphere pursuits as environmental advocacy. Presaging the contemporary concerns of animal welfare activists, Thaxter's depictions of animals, particularly birds, afford her an indirect—and, in light of Levi's avid bird hunting, ironic—means of resisting such subjugation.[16] Thaxter has regularly been cited as a nature writer and is represented in a few contemporary anthologies, principally by selections from her longer nonfiction prose, but her poetry and essays expand current genre definitions for environmental writing and exemplify how emotional intelligence might help foster attitudinal and behavioral transformation.[17]

HOW DOES ONE empathize with a white heron? Returning to hats, we might ponder a *Godey's Lady's Book* Fashion Department illustration for January 1887: "Fig. 34. Hat of beige color felt, turned up in the back, and faced with velvet, high velvet loops in front and jeweled ornament. Feathers at back"; "Fig. 35. Hat of navy blue felt, faced with velvet, trimmed with velvet ribbon and large bunch of feathers upon the left side."[18] Feathers feature prominently in these images, the plumes sometimes adding more than six inches to the wearer's height. Elegant women with carefully arranged hair and discreet expressions model the millinery. Although viewers see only a bust, even a casual reader can grasp the implication of stylish wealth. The next month Thaxter published her fiery essay in *Audubon Magazine* urging women to resist the vogue for wearing birds and feathers. Employing

Detail of illustration from the Fashion
Department in *Godey's Lady's Book*,
January 1887.

several rhetorical modes, she pleads passionately throughout "Woman's
Heartlessness" for an end to such destruction, expressing (and eliciting) sadness, anger, frustration, and bitter humor in an aggressive reinvention of
advice writing.

Thaxter begins quietly, assuming that it was natural for women to have
an affinity with birds; the cultural association between the two was strong.[19]
But the second sentence exposes some women's lack of compassion: "Not
among the ignorant and uncultured so much as the educated and enlightened do we find the indifference and hardness that baffles and perplexes
us." The author's tone remains relatively calm, but her accusations intensify. Recounting several conversations, she lets these affluent women indict
themselves: "One lady said to me, 'I think there is a great deal of sentiment
wasted on the birds. There are so many of them, they will never be missed,
any more than mosquitoes! I shall put birds on my new bonnet.' This was a
fond and devoted mother, a cultivated and accomplished woman. It seemed
a desperate case indeed, but still I strove with it. 'Why do you give yourself
so much trouble,' she asked. 'They will soon go out of fashion and there will
be an end of it.'" Thaxter's satire foregrounds internal splits among women,
exposing fashion's folly. In her fashionista's economy, neither cultivation,
nor accomplishment, nor intelligence can compete with the drive for style.
Because Thaxter's rational reply and appeal to ethics elicit no recognition

in this "desperate case," she attempts to excite readers' horror and disgust. Adorned with what we might call "gallows fashion," her interlocutor departs, "a charnel house of beaks and claws and bones and feathers and glass eyes upon her fatuous head" (281).

Such embodied rhetoric registers birds' physical suffering while simultaneously tendering a dark comedy. Like the other authors I discuss below, Thaxter conveys her message through a substantially greater reliance on humor than many earlier women writers, especially those in chapter 3. Late nineteenth-century women's verbal wit appears more forthrightly than that of their working-class counterparts, who frequently coded or compressed their humor. As Nancy A. Walker explains, women have long been cast in the position of humor's object rather than its subject. The challenge for female humorists is that "humor is at odds with the conventional definition of ideal womanhood. Humor is aggressive; women are passive. The humorist occupies a position of superiority; women are inferior."[20] Women's humor characteristically directs its attention to home and family, whereas male humor typically focuses on the public sphere.[21] Kirkland violates this distinction, encompassing both domestic and natural environments and showing how those boundaries are breached—by flies, by pigs in the kitchen garden. Thaxter and her late nineteenth-century cohort also reject this separation as they test and occasionally transgress the limits of respectable discourse.[22] Ironically, Thaxter deploys her transgressive humor to question the respectability of the bird-wearing women whom she sketches with comic hideousness.

In her reference to a "charnel house," Thaxter scarcely exaggerated. Fashionable women wore not only bird feathers but entire bird bodies, exemplars of the taxidermist's art. An advertisement in an 1875 *Harper's Bazaar* describes the mode without irony: "The entire bird is used, and is mounted on wires and springs that permit the head and wings to be moved about in the most natural manner."[23] Thaxter regards such artifice as ghoulishly unethical, and she was not alone. "Woman's Heartlessness" may have responded to an 1886 letter by American Museum of Natural History ornithologist Frank Chapman about two strolls through New York City's shopping districts. Writing to the editors of *Forest and Stream: A Journal of Outdoor Life, Travel, Nature Study, Shooting*, Chapman enumerates the shocking scene, with 173 birds of forty varieties on display. Nearly 80 percent of the seven hundred women's hats that he counted featured some feathered decoration;

of the remaining number, Chapman notes that more than half were hats "worn by ladies in mourning or elderly ladies," for whom feathers would be inappropriate. He also emphasizes his accounting's incompleteness: "It is evident that, in proportion to the number of hats seen, the list of birds given is very small, but in most cases mutilation rendered identification impossible."[24] Some of the birds were common—robins and grackles—while others seem peculiar, individualistic choices, such as the big yellowlegs and the Acadian owl.[25] Kathy S. Mason notes that "[o]n average, the millinery trade's demand for plumage and skins resulted in the destruction of as many as fifteen million American birds annually, from songbirds to waterfowl."[26] Moreover, many of the birds were killed when they displayed mating plumage, which meant that their hatchlings starved to death. From this perspective, Thaxter's ostensible hyperbole appears understated.

The woman who compared birds with mosquitoes had many compatriots. Thaxter voices shock when another, "mocking, says, 'Why don't you try to save the little fishes in the sea?' and continues to walk the world with dozens of warblers' wings making her headgear hideous" (281–82). Thaxter uses her experience as a poet to advance her message; the repeated *w* sounds add weight to the sentence, which concludes with an image made multiply "hideous" via the transformation of "bonnet" to sterile "headgear" and the doubled *h* sound. She renders the visual audible and registered physically in her readers as embodied knowledge. Many of the women to whom the author speaks promise that when their hats are worn out, they will relinquish wearing birds, but, as Thaxter satirically observes, "alas! birds never 'wear out'" (282).

Providing readers with a little emotional relief as well as a model to emulate, the essay praises "a fine spirit" who acknowledges her own selfishness. As she "recognizes the importance of her own responsibility," she quickly removes the badge of dishonor, sparking Thaxter's exclamation, "And how refreshing is the sight of the birdless bonnet! The face beneath, no matter how plain it may be, seems to possess a gentle charm. She might have had birds, this woman, for they are cheap enough, and plentiful enough, heaven knows! But she has them not, therefore she must wear within things infinitely precious, namely, good sense, good taste, good feeling. Heaven bless every woman who dares to turn her back on Fashion and go about thus beautifully unadorned!" (281). Thaxter underlines her message by repeating her exclamations, expressing excitement and admiration as she redefines beauty, which couples excellent character with an "unadorned" exterior. Fashion gives way to various forms of moral goodness; the writer discredits style as a marker of respectability. Tinged with sentimentality in its excess— for example, the repetition of *good*—the passage contemplates the inter-connection between aesthetics and corporeality.[27] This paragon's simplicity gestures toward the ethical foundation common to mid-nineteenth-century utopian movements, but Thaxter also appeals explicitly to "feeling." Her passion contrasts sharply with Thoreau's affective restraint in *Walden*.

The next paragraph returns to attack mode. Thaxter quotes a Paris news-paper that exploits women's vanity and defines trends ("Birds are worn more than ever"), and she castigates the weak women whose "empty pride" renders them vulnerable to such propaganda. If the fashion paper elides women's agency by its phrasing, the author places the responsibility where it belongs. Shifting pathos again, she assigns the birds sentience and speech. She urges a sea-swallow to fly, comparing "the centre of the storm, the heart of the arctic cold, the winter blast" to female vanity that generates morbid style:

> Do I not see you every day, your mocking semblance writhing as if in agony round female heads—still and stark, sharp wings and tail pointing in stiff distress to heaven, your dried and ghastly head and beak dragged down to point to the face below, as if saying, "She did it?" . . . Yesterday I saw three of you on one hat! Three terns at once, a horrible confusion of death and dismay.
>
> Does any woman imagine these withered corpses (cured with arse-nic) which she loves to carry about, are *beautiful?* Not so; the birds lost their beauty with their lives. To-day I saw a mat woven of warblers' heads, spiked all over its surface with sharp beaks, set up on a bonnet and borne aloft by its possessor in pride! Twenty murders in one! and the face beneath bland and satisfied, for are not "Birds to be worn more than ever"? (282)

Anthropomorphizing the birds, Thaxter ascribes them speech and then articulates her own psychic and physiological horror and disgust, which, she clearly hopes, will provoke a corresponding response.[28] By succumbing to fashion, women risk their respectability, their status as moral exemplars, for this extended image transforms women from beautiful objects to vi-cious murderers. Thaxter's hyperbolic rhetoric and repetition of the pas-sive phrase "birds are worn" render women nauseatingly visible as fashion's immoral agents. She insinuates that by killing birds, women effectively kill themselves.[29]

"Woman's Heartlessness" repeatedly invokes the long-standing correlation between women and evanescent birds to critique both fashion and women's self-reduction. Thaxter shocks readers by contrasting traditional sentimental images with "corpses" and "arsenic," the language of the morgue: "Year after year you come back to make your nest in the place you know and love, but you *shall not* live your humble, blissful, dutiful life, you *shall not* guard your treasured home, *nor* rejoice when your little ones break the silence with their first cry to you for food. You *shall not* shelter and protect and care for them with the same divine instinct you share with human mothers. *No*, some woman wants your corpse to carry on her head" (282–83; emphasis added). Overwriting the emotional comparison, Thaxter heightens the kick of the corpse, a burden literally as well as figuratively carried by women. Environmental devastation that begins with the natural world thus circulates through the public sphere of fashion to the domestic world. Through her parallel of birds with human mothers, the author highlights the endangerment of that privileged private space.

Thaxter's ability to balance emotional and rational responses appears in the two short concluding paragraphs that return to the essay's initial objectivity. She affirms that through the efforts of the Audubon Society and other organizations concerned with animal welfare "still we venture to hope for a better future . . . when women, one and all, will look upon the wearing of birds in its proper light, namely, as a sign of heartlessness and a mark of infamy and reproach" (283). Thaxter forecasts twenty-first-century attitudes toward animals, of which Marianne DeKoven writes, "The strictures against sentimentality that forbid empathy for other animals and that often accompany charges of anthropomorphism are also more and more being replaced by an awareness of the intricate and massive interdependence between humans and other animals."[30] Because of these transformed attitudes, Thaxter's rhetorical sophistication, her ecofeminist objectives, and her emotional intelligence are more legible than ever.

Thaxter's essay was published during a period in which the movement for animal rights was well established. Just after the Civil War, Henry Bergh formed the American Society for the Prevention of Cruelty to Animals on the model of the RSPCA, founded in England four decades earlier. Just a year before "Woman's Heartlessness" appeared, advocates created the American

Ornithologists' Union Bird-Protection Committee; they also formed the first durable U.S. Audubon Society, in Massachusetts, of which Thaxter was a vice president.[31] The society explicitly addressed the problem of fashionable feathers, citing reform as a principal objective.[32] Coupled with the scientific community's efforts, Thaxter's materialist appeals—which she made in several genres, including children's poetry—were at least partly responsible for the passage of the Lacey Act in 1900, which followed earlier efforts to restrict the use of ornamental plumage.[33] Although she is preaching mostly to the converted in "Woman's Heartlessness," Thaxter clearly hopes that her essay will resonate outside Audubon Society circles. By creating resistant fashionistas as characters in a series of embodied encounters, she enables the unconvinced to see themselves from another angle; by pairing sentimental rhetoric with wrenchingly vivid and realistic language and details, she attempts to shock such readers, who might regard themselves as gentle and maternal, into self-awareness.

Ultimately, Thaxter contends with the conventional wisdom—ludicrous, in her view—that presumes women are more moral than men, and she argues that women share men's guilt for environmental destruction and their responsibility for corrective action. Her affective juxtapositions, strategies of repetition and accretion, and synthetic rhetoric exemplify a rationally balanced emotional intelligence fostering ecological intelligence.[34] Participating in a tradition of American women's nature writing that appreciates the small (metaphorically and traditionally feminine) as well as the grand and sublime, Thaxter creates a synesthetic account that combines angry accusation, sentimental sermon, and humor.[35] As she reinvents women's traditional advice writing, Thaxter models authentically respectable behavior that contravenes norms of fashion and the immoral use of nature for human consumption. In her world, nature has independent meaning and value apart from its significance for human beings. Anticipating ecofeminists' emphasis on interspecies equity, Thaxter broadcasts words in much the same way that contemporary animal rights activists spray-paint fur coats.

AS A BRIEF for simplicity, "Woman's Heartlessness" responds to the nation's increasing industrialism and its companion consumerism by rejecting the acquisitive mentality and embracing a modest form of what we today call simple living. Thaxter was a relative latecomer to a long tradition.

Although today the terms *simple living* and *voluntary simplicity* are frequently used interchangeably, the former designates a lifestyle and the latter a philosophy that embraces that lifestyle as a material practice. The historian David Shi describes the complex realizations of simplicity, a concept that, he argues, has always been mutable. Nevertheless, some common characteristics reappear over many centuries, such as the rejection of luxury and materialism, a reverence for nature, and a preference for rural over urban lifeways. The simple life also includes "a desire for personal self-reliance through frugality and diligence, a nostalgia for the past and a skepticism toward the claims of modernity, conscientious rather than conspicuous consumption, and an aesthetic taste for the plain and functional."[36] The American form of this philosophy, he explains, began with the Puritans, continued through the Great Awakening of the 1730s, and developed into the egalitarian and nationalist ethos of republican simplicity. Throughout this time, the Quakers were influential.[37]

A number of the authors in earlier chapters of *Fallen Forests* reference antimaterialist and nature-centered values. The early years of the nineteenth century saw a clash between romantic conceptions of "simple" farming—although Jefferson's practices were anything but—and an emergent industrial economy that relied on consumption. Ironically, the Lowell mills in which Larcom worked and whose profits paid Berbineau's salary were themselves an outgrowth of Jefferson's model of republican industrialism. Francis Cabot Lowell and his colleagues "were possessed of an acute sense of social responsibility and were committed to the ideals of the original Protestant ethic and republican simplicity."[38] Their development of communities of women-headed households where New England farm girls could retain their moral virtues through hard work and church attendance were also, conveniently, profitable. Wilson exposes another side of pastoral's putative simplicity—and its associated respectability. In this context Larcom's account of antebellum rural life in *A New England Girlhood* appears overly optimistic, if not suspect, although as a class migrant and faithful Protestant she shared some values of the dominant class. Sigourney's and Kirkland's arguments in *Scenes in My Native Land* and *Forest Life* recall the republican moment in an effort to counteract, or at least counterpoint, the rush toward materialism.[39] But both these writers acknowledged, one with ambivalent elegy and the other with humorous realism, the obstacles confronting those who desired a more authentic life based upon plainness and community rather than acquisitive individualism.

In the nineteenth century, as before, the simple life embodied what Shi calls "a sentimental ideal" as well as "an actual way of living."[40] Among its idealists were Ralph Waldo Emerson's circle, who took the theory to an extreme. Brook Farm, founded by George Ripley in 1841, was one response to Emersonian philosophy; rejecting capitalist excess and pursuing self-development, participants in the project promulgated an ethic of shared labor and contemplative leisure. The paradigmatic figure for simple living—and the philosophy of voluntary simplicity—is, of course, Thoreau. For many today, Thoreau is the movement's patron saint, and such admonitions as "[s]implicity, simplicity, simplicity! I say, let your affairs be as two or three, and not a hundred or a thousand; instead of a million count half a dozen, and keep your accounts on your thumb-nail" continue to resonate.[41] But for many people, even ostensibly middle-class women, simplicity represented an accommodation rather than a choice. A less successful experiment than Thoreau's individual idyll was Fruitlands, the brainchild of "the tirelessly quixotic" Bronson Alcott, Louisa May Alcott's father.[42] Louisa would satirize the community in her story "Transcendental Wild Oats," highlighting the men's dreaminess and the women's doughtiness. She stresses how women's labor underwrites the experiment; when asked, "Are there any beasts of burden on the place?" the heroine Mrs. Lamb replies, "Only one woman!"[43]

The Civil War loomed as a great divide between Thoreau's era of transcendentalist simplicity and the Gilded Age, when the emergence of the United States as a great industrial power propelled owners of factories, railroads, and mines toward astonishing wealth, simultaneously creating the priestesses at the temple of consumption that Gilman and Thaxter attack. Mark Twain and Charles Dudley Warner's *The Gilded Age: A Tale of Today* (1873) illuminates this era's excess and superficial acquisition. Families like the Vanderbilts, Mellons, Carnegies, Morgans, and Rockefellers consolidated huge fortunes and built enormous "summer cottages" in Newport, Rhode Island. Some women writers, such as María Amparo Ruiz de Burton, whose fiction I consider in chapter 5, endorsed such affluence. Shi foregrounds a group of patrician, Boston-based intellectuals, among them William James, William Dean Howells, Thomas Wentworth Higginson,

Charles Eliot Norton, and Henry Adams, who sought to counter what they regarded as the vulgar pursuit of luxury at the expense of spiritual and cultural development. At the same time that they valued country life and regarded Jeffersonian republicanism with nostalgia, their idea of plain living was acres away from Thoreau's; they proposed "a conservative Emersonian simplicity of the drawing-room and library rather than the garret or hut."[44] Their country retreats had servants. It is this milieu in which Thaxter and her peers composed their domestic fictions and this masculine, elite, urban ethos that they unmasked.

This ethos emerged within a complex national context. The nineteenth century's concluding decades included achievement and conflict, encompassing the completion of the transcontinental railroad (1869), the emergence of the modern labor union movement, the passage of the first Chinese Exclusion Act (1882), the end of Reconstruction and consolidation of Jim Crow in the South, the country's rapid urbanization, and the creation of the Wall Street stock market. These years also marked the establishment of numerous women's colleges, including all the Seven Sisters, and the development of conservation movements that led to the creation of the national park system, beginning in 1872 with Yellowstone. Paralleling 2008's Great Recession, the nineteenth-century's Gilded Age terminated with the Panic of 1893, when the U.S. economy crashed owing to overbuilding, railroad speculation, and questionable financing of business ventures, which sparked a series of bank failures that plunged the country into depression and several years of double-digit unemployment. Yet even after the crash, Thorstein Veblen felt compelled to attack the ongoing problem of conspicuous consumption—purchasing "dwellings, furniture, bric-a-brac, wardrobe and meals" to convey status.[45] In short, the period in which Thaxter and her cohort published was not only a period of xenophobia, racism, and rampant consumption but also—for some—of opportunity and transformation.

Thaxter's essay "Woman's Heartlessness" bespeaks how, in the nineteenth century, fashion advertised a family's respectability and economic status, its female inhabitants' ability to spend and its male residents' ability to provide. Although writers like William Dean Howells (in *The Rise of Silas Lapham*) explored these subjects, women fiction writers addressed them particularly vigorously, attentive to the actual circumstances in which most women, especially rural women, found themselves. Many of the stories I discuss below depict homes *without* men, showing how individuals and communities of women, notably elderly and single women, confront economic success or endure poverty brought on by male extravagance or arrogance. Jewett and Freeman highlight the disastrous convergence for women of age, destitution, and disability.

All of the authors confirm, however, that women regularly collaborate in the dominant culture's material norms, sometimes enforcing (or even, as we have seen with Berbineau, Jacobs, and Larcom, advancing) those norms; Thaxter's feather- and bird-wearing elites were just the extreme examples of this investment in social hierarchy. Shi reminds his readers that the reasons for advocating forms of simplicity are not necessarily benign; they include social control, "preserving the status quo by impressing upon the masses the virtues of hard work, social stability, and personal contentment." He also underscores the fundamentally elite perspective from which current advocates of voluntary simplicity have emerged in the United States.[46] In analyzing Thaxter and her contemporaries, we need to be alert to the potentially conservative and hierarchical implications of their support of simplicity. As we have seen for some of the earlier writers in *Fallen Forests*, a progressive outlook on one issue does not guarantee uniform resistance to social or cultural norms. What does it mean, for example, when "simplicity" is involuntary?

Simple Living Encore:
Consuming Fashions and the Town Poor

In an extended reflection about the bonds between human beings and animals, Sarah Orne Jewett affirms their interdependence and animals' independent consciousness and value:

> It is easy to say that other orders of living creatures exist on a much lower plane than ourselves; we know very little about it, after all. They are often gifted in some way that we are not; they may even carry some virtue of ours to a greater height than we do. But the day will come for a more truly universal suffrage than we dream of now, when the meaning of every living thing is understood, and it is given its rights and accorded its true value: for its life is from God's life, and its limits were fixed by him; its material shape is the manifestation of a thought, and to each body there is given a spirit.[47]

As a whole, Jewett's writing illuminates women's cultural and subjective connections with nonhuman nature. Although she spent substantial portions of her life in cities, Maine—its landscape, its animals, and its rural, frequently impoverished inhabitants—remained foundational to her work even as she lamented the encroachment of consumerist values on Americans outside metropolitan centers. Juxtaposing Thaxter's "Woman's Heartlessness" and Jewett's "A White Heron" helps us to grasp the complicated stances articulated by many nineteenth-century American women fiction writers and to unpack what we should recognize as their ecofeminist rhetoric—ecofeminist because of their awareness of patriarchal societies' combined subordination of nature and women.[48] Thaxter's blistering essay suggests that fashion represents one tool of subordination, while Jewett's famous story about a white heron takes a fictional approach to the quandary of bird-wearing women and environmental destruction. Both texts emphasize the continuity between domestic and wild, culture and nature.

Like her close friend Thaxter, Jewett esteemed the affiliations between humans and nonhuman nature partly because of her personal history. She once observed, "The relationship of untamed nature to what is tamed and cultivated is a very curious and subtle thing to me; I do not know if every one feels it so intensely."[49] Her stories and narratives investigate these tensions, looking backward to her childhood's more natural setting and forward to the increasingly industrialized seacoast region of her mature years. Born in September 1849 in South Berwick, Maine, the young Jewett traveled with her country doctor father on his rounds, absorbing the rural landscape and its plain people, as she did at her paternal grandfather's country store. These early experiences, along with her formal education at the elite Berwick Academy between 1861 and 1865, formed the basis for her vocation. A cosmopolitan adult, Jewett traveled widely in Europe and spent large parts of each year with her long-term companion in a "Boston marriage," Annie Adams Fields, the widow of her publisher, James T. Fields. When she needed to write, however, she returned to her childhood village. Composing in genres ranging from adult and children's fiction to poetry and autobiographical sketches, Jewett published several novels, including the widely praised *Country of the Pointed Firs* (1896).[50]

Jewett oscillates between country and city, but we should not assess her work in bifurcated terms. Despite radical transformations in latter nineteenth-century Maine and the disappearance of Jewett's relatively egalitarian childhood world, class distinctions were still more fluid in her rural settings than in urban locations. To this complexity we need to add, as Alison Easton argues, an appreciation of how Jewett's "personal class perceptions" interfaced with those of her urban, middle-class readers, especially as the author addressed the environment.[51] Although included in some of the same contemporary nature-writing collections as Thaxter, Jewett's work eludes most traditional genre definitions.[52] Her characteristic themes encompass community, rural privation, social class, ethnic outsiders, and the elderly; she often focuses on women's lives, and most contemporary scholarship has examined her gender, class, and racial politics.[53] Yet her commitment to the natural world meshes with her concerns of domesticity and poverty to form a powerful canon of environmental writing, including environmental justice writing that regards nonhuman nature as part of its community.

Published in 1886, Jewett's most famous story, "A White Heron," appeared the year before Thaxter's "Woman's Heartlessness." Pitting country against city, the narrative juxtaposes the perspective of a young girl, Sylvia (a refugee from "a crowded manufacturing town," whose name evokes the woods), living in rural Maine with her grandmother, to that of a young male hunter-ornithologist. The hunter seeks a "rare" white heron to add to his collection, which, he brags, contains "stuffed and preserved [birds], dozens and dozens of them."[54] Sylvia's grandmother tells their visitor that "the wild creatur's counts her one o' themselves," while the hunter seeks the white heron not for food but for a fashionable trophy analogous to the trophy hats of Thaxter's bird-wearing women. Jewett tactfully distinguishes between killing for survival and for amusement through Sylvia's grandmother, who tells the hunter, "Dan, my boy, was a great hand to go gunning. . . . I never wanted for pa'tridges or gray squer'ls while he was to home" (145). The story concludes with Sylvia climbing a huge pine tree to find the bird's nest; the vision the girl acquires provokes her resistant silence in the face of the hunter's desire for knowledge. "A White Heron" has attracted substantial critical attention in the past three decades, with readers arguing that the story dramatizes the conflict between a welcoming, feminized natural world and a violent, grasping masculine cultural realm.[55]

Jewett published "A White Heron" when the bird plumage craze peaked; like Thaxter, she emphasizes the heron's—and nature's—noncommercial, spiritual value. But unlike Thaxter, who excoriates the feather trade's consumers explicitly in "Woman's Heartlessness" (and in children's poems such as "The Great Blue Heron"), Jewett addresses them indirectly by fostering readers' sympathy for Sylvia. As the story alternates between the standpoints of a child and a third-person narrator, it enables her audience to recognize the hunter's allure and what Sylvia's capitulation would mean to her Edenic natural world. Jewett invokes American culture's association between women and nature to advocate preservation of an earlier concept of wildness, also linked with children. Paralleling Thaxter's views, she implies that by enabling the hunter to kill the white heron, Sylvia would murder herself. In an environment in which nature cannot speak for itself, the child must assume agency—ironically, through her silence.

The ambivalent advice that Jewett indirectly offers Sylvia, and thus her readers, bespeaks the author's insight that rural privation poses temptations to exploit environmental resources.[56] Women's knowledge of nature is itself a resource. Revealing the heron's location would bring Sylvia's grandmother relief, for the "handsome stranger" promises what seems to be an enormous bounty of ten dollars for finding the heron: "He can make them rich with money; he has promised it, and they are poor now" (148, 157). Under such circumstances, simple living is poverty with another name. But Sylvia grasps her own bond with sentient nonhuman nature, which represents alternative wealth: "The murmur of the pine's *green* branches is in her ears, she remembers how the white heron came flying through the *golden* air and how they watched the sea and the morning together." As Jewett pits city against country and rich against poor, she questions the attitudes of prodigality and display that enable not only the hunter but her readers to ignore "the sharp report of his gun and the piteous sight of thrushes and sparrows dropping silent to the ground, their songs hushed and their pretty feathers stained and wet with blood" (158; emphasis added). Juxtaposing this concrete image with a romantic conclusion, "A White Heron" translates many of the rhetorical techniques in "Women's Heartlessness" to a fictional format. Jewett values local knowledge that prioritizes reciprocity and a direct relationship between humans and nonhuman nature rather than a potentially distanced attitude of travel, recreation, and resource exploitation.[57]

"A White Heron" also admires economical rural domesticity. The young hunter was surprised "to find so clean and comfortable a little dwelling in this New England wilderness. The young man had known the horrors of

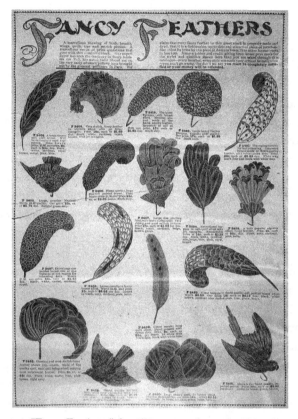

"Fancy Feathers." A millinery supply catalog, 1901,
New York Millinery and Supply Company. Courtesy of the
Smithsonian Institution Libraries, Washington, D.C.

its most primitive housekeeping, and the dreary squalor of that level of
society which does not rebel at the companionship of hens." He appreciates "the best thrift of an old-fashioned farmstead" and "the old woman's
quaint talk" (144–45). Jewett appears to share the young man's position, but
she also pokes fun at his citified ways and superior attitude. Ultimately,
while "A White Heron" advances romantic and emotional—some would
claim sentimental—appeals, it also exposes consumption's economic foundations and preservation's challenges. Its advice for its comfortable readers
is simple, if indirect: your choices dictate how others, especially struggling
rural women, live their lives, so act accordingly.

∽

FIRST PUBLISHED IN the July 1890 *Atlantic Monthly*, Jewett's "The Town Poor" provides another view of women, class, and the environment, criticizing obtuse affluent women and their prideful male counterparts, who fail to understand their individual and community responsibilities.[58] Like "A White Heron," the story gestures toward an economic wilderness endured by poor women in a degraded environment, but it uncovers the consequences of that degradation. At the opening we see Mrs. William Trimble, a prosperous farming widow, traveling home with a poorer neighbor, Miss Rebecca Wright, from the installation of a new minister in the neighboring parish of Parsley, where, as Miss Wright admits, "it's a good deal harder scratchin' . . . they have to git money where they can; the farms is very poor as you go north."[59] They detour to visit friends, two indigent elderly sisters auctioned out by the town's selectmen, as Harriet Wilson may have been. In Jewett's narrative, neediness converges with age and disability to render the ironically named "Bray girls" emblems of distress in a hostile domestic environment.

The sisters Ann and Mandy Bray live in straitened circumstances in a cold garret room owned by the Janes family; as Mrs. Janes confesses to her visitors, "I was put out with Mr. Janes for fetchin' of 'em here, with all I've got to do, an' I own I was kind o' surly to 'em 'long the first of it. He gits money from the town, an' it helps him out; but he bid 'em off for five dollars a month, an' we can't do much for 'em at no such price as that." Mrs. Janes is "pinched and miserable herself, though it was evident that she had no gift at house or home keeping." Despite their concern for the Brays, Miss Rebecca and Mrs. Trimble have little sympathy for Mrs. Janes, with the widow calling their hostess a "poor meechin' body," a triply disparaging phrase. "Poor" indicates impoverished and pathetic, "meechin'" suggests self-effacing and weak, and "body" reduces their hostess to merely physical status. Unlike Wilson's Frado, Jewett's Mrs. Janes seems worthy of no more sympathy than Berbineau's brutalized laborers; she is emphatically not respectable.

Significantly, Mrs. Janes is disabled by "the ague" or the flu, but this illness does not restrain her candor about "the Bray girls": "I do the best for 'em I can, Mis' Trimble, but 'tain't so easy for me as 'tis for you, with all your means to do with." Her outspokenness reinforces her unrespectable status; her mouth is as uncontrolled as her ailing physical form. Jewett calibrates the story's class distinctions carefully. The Bray sisters' reduced gentility is due to the death of their father, a deacon who has donated generously to the church while leaving his daughters penniless. In their current setting, "a small, low room, brown with age, and gray, too, as if former dust and cobwebs could not be made wholly to disappear," "the two elderly women who stood there looked like captives. . . . [T]he room itself was more bare and plain than was fitting to their evident refinement of character and self-respect." The sisters have been wrenched from the domestic comforts of their "neat little village home," with its peach tree and "sprigged chiny cups."[60]

They have also fallen from middle-class standards of "refinement" and respectability. Along with clothing, household possessions could denote character and status. Related to consumption, respectability was an imperative for all women, regardless of their race, social class, or location. Larcom's account in *An Idyl of Work* intimates the dismay of a "town-dame" who laments that

> now even factory-girls
> Shine with gold watches, and you cannot tell,
> Therefore, who are the ladies.[61]

Material objects thus contributed—falsely, in Larcom's view—to perceptions of respectability. In Larcom's girlhood, a central goal of the Lowell mill owners was to establish a morally sound environment for the farm girls whom they employed. Mill girls were expected to be religiously observant, hardworking, and, above all else, physically virtuous. Berbineau's distaste at the European women toiling outdoors on Sundays expresses a slightly different response to this social norm, but it shows the disconnect between laboring embodiment and respectability.

In Jewett's description of the "captives," the Bray girls, their uncomfortable and impoverished domestic environment concretizes their reduced respectability. In this diminished economy, nature becomes an obstacle to be overcome, as it is for Berbineau and for Wilson's Frado: the sisters suffer from cold, Mandy is partially blind, and Ann "carried her right arm in a sling, with piteously drooping fingers." The sisters encode Jewett's awareness of their triple disability: female (and subject to male ineptitude, ignorance, or oblivion), indigent, and aged, they depend entirely on charity for survival. The story ends with Mrs. Trimble resolving to visit the town's selectmen the next day to force them to reinstall the Brays in their former home. Jewett's narrative comments on the rigors of involuntary simplicity and the responsibility of more well-to-do community members, particularly women, to support their poorer and less able neighbors, their responsibility to ensure economic environmental justice. Critiquing both the individuals and the system that has enabled these middle-class women to lose status and health, "The Town Poor" complements Wilson's earlier portrait of rural life, adding the element of community that Frado lacked.

From another perspective, however, the story appears to promote class separation. Mrs. Trimble intends to rescue the fallen middle-class women but not the impoverished and suffering Mrs. Janes or even her own companion, Miss Wright, who is "lame-footed" and who, Jewett intimates, must rely for support on relatives' kindness and generosity.[62] All of the working poor in this story are in fact disabled, unlike Mrs. Trimble, who is "an active business woman, [who] looked after her own affairs herself, in all weathers." Yet despite the Brays' social and physical diminishment, despite the spartan environment of the Janeses' attic, the sisters retain their genteel character, while Mrs. Janes's grudging hospitality and sloppy housekeeping render her suspect, at least for Mrs. Trimble and Miss Wright. Rosemarie Garland Thomson argues that the story centers "on the issue of middle-class women's agency, mobilized by the sentiment generated by the sympathetic spectacle of poverty and legitimated by the seemingly undeniable truth of the body," and she contends that "the rhetoric of reform embedded in the narrative of witness demands an asymmetrical relationship between the agent of reform and the object."[63] "The Town Poor" seeks to mobilize middle-class readers in a reform project via emotional and ethical appeals meticulously attuned to redeeming fallen respectability.

On the other hand, as Jewett makes clear, only the comfortable and successful Mrs. Trimble has the social clout to effect change. The story's turning point arrives near the visit's conclusion, when, after sharing a tiny repast of crackers, a "very small" "piece of hard white cheese," and the last of the sisters' homemade peach preserves, Mrs. Trimble has an epiphany: "Then there was a silence, and in the silence a wave of tender feeling rose high in the hearts of the four elderly women. At this moment the setting sun flooded the poor plain room with light; the unpainted wood was all of a golden-brown, and Ann Bray, with her gray hair and aged face, stood at the head of the table in a kind of aureole. Mrs. Trimble's face was all aquiver as she looked at her; she thought of the text about two or three being gathered together, and was half afraid." Though Jewett withholds the explicitly religious rhetoric that energizes the environmental justice efforts of such earlier writers as Scott and Sigourney, and her reform focus is much narrower, she gestures toward Christian ethics' transformative power. In this moment of revelation, Ann becomes a surrogate Christ.

The plain surroundings coupled with a corporeal experience — sharing food — elicit Mrs. Trimble's recognition of her complicity in the Brays' fall and her awareness that she must assume responsibility for their redemption.[64] As she envisions her own economic comfort and security, she acknowledges her blindness to Rebecca: "I'm ashamed to go home an' see what's set out for supper. I wish I'd brought 'em right along." Mrs. Trimble also admits her own passivity in the sale of the Brays' home, while even Rebecca confides that she has profited, buying the sisters' teacups for a pittance at their property auction. Mrs. Trimble, however, has the resources to buy back the Brays' furniture as well as the horse and wagon to transport it and the influence to lead the project. Sentimental nostalgia propels the reformers and underwrites the story's emphatic references to the Bray *girls*, who embody childlike vulnerability.

But "The Town Poor" goes beyond elaborating middle-class women's complicity in other women's diminished domestic environment, for it comments extensively on the financial mismanagement of the community's and family's males, especially the Brays' father. With misplaced generosity to the parish, he pays for costly, fashionable renovations to the church. Without success, Miss Wright's grandmother has protested: "[S]he riz right up an' said 'twouldn't cost nothin' to let 'em [the old square pews] stay, an' there wa'n't a house carpenter that could do such nice work, an' time would come when the great-grandchildren would give their eye-teeth to have the old meetin'-house look just as it did then." Through a telling natural metaphor Mrs. Trimble — and Jewett — lays such profligacy squarely at the feet of the men in this patriarchal society: "A man ought to provide for his folks he's got to leave behind him, specially if they're women. To be sure, they had their little home; but we've seen how, with all their industrious ways, they hadn't means to keep it. I s'pose he thought he'd got time enough to lay by, when he give so generous in collections; but he didn't lay by, an' there they be. He might have took lessons from the squirrels: even them little wild creatur's makes them their winter hoards, an' men-folks ought to know enough if squirrels does."

Squandering their resources in service to vanity and architectural fashion, "men-folks" have less common sense than squirrels, "little wild creatur's." Charity, Jewett implies, begins at home; given women's dependence on men in this period, the latter should be responsible conservators of resources. Like Louisa May Alcott's "Transcendental Wild Oats," "The Town Poor" deprecates imprudent men. But unlike Alcott's idealistic male pilgrims who "simplify" their families' lives out of misguided principle, Deacon Bray's pride is what forces his daughters to rely on the town's inadequate charity. Although Mrs. Trimble accepts partial responsibility for the situation, at the story's conclusion she declares, "I wish to my heart 'twas to-morrow mornin' a'ready, and I a-startin' for the selec'*men*." Jewett stresses this pronunciation—which occurs twice in the last three paragraphs—reproducing the inflection of rural Maine talk but also underscoring where the final responsibility resides.[65]

The authentic member of the "town poor" in this story is, as I noted earlier, Mrs. Janes, not the elderly Bray girls, who "did use to live so neat and ladylike." The Janes household is tangibly grim, with its "gnawed corner of the door-yard fence," "two or three ragged old hens," and "cheerless kitchen." Significantly, it is Mr. Janes who has committed his wife to care for the sisters with inadequate resources to do so, and it is Mrs. Janes who "went an' dealt with the selec'men, and made 'em promise to find their firewood an' some other things extra." Persistence is required: "They was glad to get rid o' the matter the fourth time I went, an' would ha' promised 'most anything." Equally significantly, Mrs. Janes is herself often abandoned; when the visitors arrive, her husband is away on jury duty, and she tells Mrs. Trimble and Miss Wright that "Mr. Janes don't keep me half the time in oven-wood, he's off so much." Jewett highlights the men's absence and irresponsibility.

Like the Brays' visitors, the narrator appears to sympathize more with the sisters' fallen gentility and diminished respectability than with Mrs. Janes's deprivation and accompanying disability, a bodily suffering reminiscent of Berbineau's misery and Frado's frequent ill health. Ann Bray, however, grasps the contrast, for her insight concludes the informal friends' gathering: "'I believe we ought to 've asked Mis' Janes if she wouldn't come up,' said Ann. 'She's real good feelin', but she's had it very hard, an' gits discouraged. I can't find that she's ever had anything real pleasant to look back to, as we have. There, next time we'll make a good heartenin' time for her too.'" Echoing Stowe's admonition in *Uncle Tom's Cabin* that readers must "feel right," "good feelin'" indicates Jewett's own aim and her project's sentimental inflection. As Wilson does in *Our Nig*, Jewett articulates her characters' humanity through their emotional and corporeal suffering.

However much modern critics like Thomson might castigate the writer's interest in "the performance of bourgeois respectability," which "dictated that the relationship between the middle and the lower classes was one of stewardship" via the mobilization of sympathy, such appeals may have represented the principal avenue for propelling change.[66] Jewett models a complex emotional intelligence in "The Town Poor," for she dramatizes the shared responsibility of care in the characters' rural community and implicitly extends that responsibility to her privileged audience. The author depicts the unnamed village's social environment as a remedy to the uncivilized hardship of neighboring Parsley; she intimates that women, especially elderly and disabled women without men to support them, must bond together. In Jewett's embodied rhetoric, shared food sparks spiritual illumination and community awareness. This material focus combines with Jewett's use of nature imagery in which squirrels furnish a darkly comic yardstick against which to measure human caretaking and justice. Despite the speaker's primary sympathies and her characters' potential blindness to Mrs. Janes's suffering, Jewett herself acknowledges the challenges of systemic poverty, involuntary simplicity, as Freeman also does, though with very different rhetoric.

Gala Dresses and Mistaken Charities:
Old Women, the Body, and Nature

In her famous story "The Revolt of 'Mother,'" Mary Wilkins Freeman explores the connection between humans and nonhuman animals, articulating the patriarchal relations that similarly define men's interactions with women and animals: "[Sarah Penn] threw open another door. A narrow crooked flight of stairs wound upward from it. 'There, father,' said she, 'I want you to look at the stairs that go up to them two unfinished chambers that are all the places our son an' daughter have had to sleep in all their lives. There ain't a prettier girl in town nor a more ladylike one than Nanny, an' that's the place she has to sleep in. It ain't so good as your horse's stall; it ain't so warm an' tight.'" Freeman encodes the standards of respectability that underwrite her avatar Sarah Penn's ethical entreaty as she attempts to dissuade her husband, Adoniram, from building yet another new barn:

> Sarah Penn went back and stood before her husband. "Now, father," said she, "I want to know if you think you're doin' right an' accordin' to what you profess. Here, when we was married, forty year ago, you promised me faithful that we should have a new house built in that lot over in the field before the year was out. You said you had money enough, an' you wouldn't ask me to live in no such place as this. It is forty year now, an' you've been makin' more money, an' I've been savin' of it for you ever since, an' you ain't built no house yet. You've built sheds an' cow-houses an' one new barn, an' now you're goin' to build another. Father, I want to know if you think it's right. You're lodgin' your dumb beasts better than you are your own flesh an' blood. I want to know if you think it's right."
>
> "I ain't got nothin' to say."

The Penns' refined daughter, Nanny, is about to be married, and Sarah fears for her health. There will be no room for Nanny and her new husband in the decrepit old house, but she is incapable of managing her own. Sarah presses Adoniram:

> "Nanny she can't live with us after she's married. She'll have to go somewheres else to live away from us, an' it don't seem as if I could have it so, noways, father. She wa'n't ever strong. She's got considerable color, but there wa'n't never any backbone to her. I've always took the heft of everything off her, an' she ain't fit to keep house an' do everything herself. She'll be all worn out inside of a year. Think of her doin' all the washin' an' ironin' an' bakin' with them soft white hands an' arms, an' sweepin'! I can't have it so, noways, father."

Adoniram condemns himself again, repeating, "I ain't got nothin' to say."[67]

Freeman's Sarah attempts to distinguish her family members, especially Nanny, from their farm animals, though the story's comic conclusion, in which the Penns occupy the new barn, suggests human and nonhuman animals' interdependence in the farming economy. But Freeman's concern with respectability—represented through female embodiment and a comfortable domestic environment—parallels Jewett's in "The Town Poor," where "simple living" merely means indigence marked on the heroines' disabled figures. Sometimes literalizing problems of consumption in struggles over clothing and food, Freeman uses genial humor to signal her affiliation with her elderly, rural, and frequently man-less women characters and to open readers to their dilemmas. Freeman engages with cultural conversations about the links among respectability, female embodiment, simplicity, and poverty. Like the working-class writing in chapter 3, her stories reveal that agency and self-definition are important features of economic environmental justice, in both the local community and the nation.

Freeman was no stranger to economic hardship. When she was in her midteens, her carpenter father, never very successful in business, moved his family from her native Randolph, Massachusetts, to Brattleboro, Vermont, where he opened a dry-goods store. By the time his daughter was twenty-five his business had failed, her mother was forced to become a domestic servant, and the family had moved into the home of a local minister, a humiliating fall in social status. Perhaps because Freeman experienced as an insider the urgencies of neediness and the requirements of paid labor, her publications ponder these themes almost obsessively. She placed a lifelong emphasis on making money in a literary environment increasingly dominated by a paradigm of art for art's sake.[68] Only later in her life was the author liberated from financial necessity, although the shadow of these early life experiences and her own class ambiguity haunted her work.

Like many nineteenth-century American women, Freeman sought to ease her family's economic distress through writing. Her first publication, a children's ballad titled "The Beggar King," appeared in the March 1881 issue of *Wide Awake*. The poem sketches the arrival of the eponymous king and all his subjects in an unnamed village. The townspeople gape, for the newcomers' clothing parodies that of the "real" king: the beggar king is dressed "in mothy ermine" and "a great court-beauty's splendid dress / Was there, all soiled and frayed." The "one dainty thing" in the company is

> A maiden, white as still moonlight,
> Who rode beside the king.
>
> Her hands were full of apple-flowers
> Plucked in the country lanes.

Nature clothes this princess better than her "tattered dress." Invoking a plague of biblical proportions, Freeman's king threatens the "real" king that if he does not marry the princess,

> Like locusts we'll come down,
> And naught that's fair or rich or rare
> We'll leave within the town![69]

Clothing symbolizes status and it creates painful separations. The poem's ostensible happy ending redresses (in both senses) the princess and, the author shows, her father's followers, but he must bid her a tearful farewell. The poem reinvented Freeman's and her mother's sacrifices on behalf of their family at the same time that it translated for children the class conflict fracturing an increasingly unequal United States.

FREEMAN'S WRITING has enjoyed a revival in the past three decades, mostly because of her work's feminist inclinations and its study of rural communities.[70] A few scholars have addressed her nature writing, focusing principally on the gardens and animals in her story collections *Understudies* and *Six Trees*. Yet Terrell Dixon, one of these critics, argues that "nature has figured mostly at the margins of how we understand Freeman's work."[71] As the discussion below shows, I complicate this assessment, even as I shift emphasis to analyze Freeman's complex attitudes toward consumption and her examinations of female agency in domestic and outdoor environments. Appreciating her humor is essential to grasp Freeman's views on the subjects of simple living and respectability. Theories of humor that highlight aggression privilege such modes as satire and irony, while domestic humor, Gregg Camfield argues, prioritizes playfulness and creativity.[72] Unlike Kirkland's barbed remarks about city dwellers' extravagance or satirical stories about foolish western immigrants, Freeman offers readers warm insider accounts of elderly women in challenging material circumstances.[73]

Mixing humor with pathos, two of Freeman's stories explore in particularly noteworthy manner the correlations among respectability, living patterns, corporeality, and consumption.[74] In "A Gala Dress," published in the July 1888 *Harper's Bazaar*, Freeman compares older women of unequal social backgrounds but similar economic status.[75] Magazines such as *Harper's Bazaar* and *Ladies' Home Journal* addressed readers obsessed with fashion and image, and in this framework Freeman's narrative acquires special resonance.[76] Elderly protagonists Emily and Elizabeth Babcock are so financially reduced that they share one good dress and take turns attending events that merit special attire. The story opens with the sisters debating who will wear the dress to the local Fourth of July picnic. With each occasion the sisters change the trimmings to deceive their neighbors; one sister has velvet and the other lace. Gossip threatens to expose their poverty, but shyness, modesty, and pride prevent them from asking for assistance; they seek to preserve their class status—and their respectability—at all costs.

Gesturing toward female embodiment, Freeman pairs fashion and food in "A Gala Dress." Virginia Blum notes the significance of food to Freeman's work, calling it "a central trope in relation to which most of her themes emerge" and adding that "Freeman's characters pay scrupulous attention to the quantity and quality of each other's tables."[77] In "A Gala Dress" the author echoes the sisters' sartorial conflict through literal consumption; in their rural Calvinist economy, material well-being indicates moral superiority. Because "[t]he Babcock sisters guarded nothing more jealously than the privacy of their meals," their neighbor, Matilda Jennings, suspects their straitened finances. One night Matilda barges into their home when the sisters are eating their customary dinner, a cup of weak tea and some bread and butter. As she pretends to regret the interruption, "[a]ll the time her sharp and comprehensive gaze was on the tea-table. She counted the slices of bread, she measured the butter, as she talked." The sisters confront her with dignity, but Matilda is shameless, for when she spots the recently retrimmed black dress, she asks to see both sisters' dresses in a scene of alarming comedy, with nosy Matilda and the decorous Babcocks battling wits.

Freeman conveys the conflict with delicious, fly-on-the-wall humor: "Matilda Jennings, in her chocolate calico, stood as relentlessly as any executioner before the Babcock sisters. They, slim and delicate and pale in their flabby black muslins, leaned toward each other." The writer generates pity for the beleaguered and undernourished Babcocks, but she contrasts them with tasty Matilda, and she gently disparages the sisters' genteel delicacy and their attitude of superiority. Matilda returns home to "her solitary and substantial supper of bread and butter, cold potatoes, and pork and beans." If readers were not hungry before, the "chocolate" appetizer followed by the hearty main course press us to recognize physical desires.

Food and clothing converge to denote class status and confirm femininity. "Matilda . . . was as poor as the Babcocks. She had never, like them, known better days. She had never possessed any fine old muslins nor black silks in her life, but she had always eaten more." In this tenuous economy, Matilda is more willing to acknowledge her bodily existence. Rather than dismiss their family's "faint savor of gentility and aristocracy" and seek common ground with their neighbor, who "had come of wood-sawyers and garden laborers," the sisters "starved daintily and patiently on their little income." This lifestyle may be stubbornly simple and proudly independent, but it is also lonely and deprived.

Tactfully addressing her middle-class readers, Freeman's kindly but pointed criticism unveils the sisters' obsession with outward appearance.[78] For the Babcocks, respectability resides in self-presentation: "[T]hey had an arbitrary conviction that their claims to respect and consideration would be forever forfeited should they appear on state occasions in anything less than black silk. To their notions of etiquette, black silk was as sacred a necessity as feathers at the English court. They could not go abroad and feel any self-respect in those flimsy muslins and rusty woolens." The stolid Matilda's practicality seems much more attractive. When she calls to gather Emily for the Fourth of July picnic and sees her wearing the black silk dress, she exclaims, "My! you ain't goin' to wear that black silk trailin' round the woods, are you?" Elizabeth's protests that Emily has "got to go lookin' decent"—that is, appear respectable—meet with scorn: "Matilda's poor old alpaca had many a threadbare streak and mended slit in its rusty folds, the elbows were patched, it was hardly respectable. But she gave the skirt a defiant switch, and jerked the patched elbows. 'Well, I allers believed in goin' dressed suitable for the occasion,' she said sturdily, as if that was her especial picnic costume out of a large wardrobe." Matilda's reproach reflects Freeman's sympathy. Despite—or perhaps because of—the scene's comedy, readers must appreciate her implicit assertion that "pride goeth before a fall." In contemporary terms, Emily is as out of place at the picnic as if she were wearing a miniskirt and high heels to a beach clambake.[79] Respectability, in Freeman's ethos, means adjusting one's appearance to the occasion and one's circumstances.

Freeman sets the table: food reappears as the festivities conclude and sunset approaches. Matilda has "devoured with relish her brown-bread and cold pork," while "Emily had nibbled daintily at her sweet-cake, and

Harper's Bazaar fashion plate in the same issue as
Freeman's "A Gala Dress." *Harper's Bazaar,* July 1888.

glanced with inward loathing at her neighbor's grosser fare." Here poverty
has physiological dimensions, and the author elicits a physical response of
disgust while she challenges us to contemplate the effects of Emily's pride.
As the neighbors walk home on a wooded path, Matilda steps aside from
a trap into which Emily predictably falls: some boys have set a batch of
firecrackers that blow holes in her hem, and "poor Emily Babcock danced
as a martyr at her fiery trial might have done." Martyred indeed, Emily
rushes home in horror, exclaiming that Elizabeth will never again be able to

appear in public. Freeman revisits the comic vein that bespeaks her simultaneous empathy and critical distance. Her emotional intelligence plays out in the humorous juxtaposition of the Babcocks and Matilda; she stresses the burden of social and economic differences while she invites readers to feel the characters' pride, anguish, and shame. Laughing and crying, we ponder the confining consequences of their tragicomic quest for respectability.

The Babcock sisters' machinations to sustain their status continue when they receive a bonanza from a deceased octogenarian aunt: a trunk full of clothes that contains two black silk dresses. They determine to tell no one and in the subsequent weeks attend various social events and church together, as they have not done for years. Matilda remains suspicious, and by concocting a story that the townspeople thought the sisters were at odds, she infuriates Elizabeth into explosive candor: there is a single silk dress. Matilda is cowed, for in fact only she has suspected the truth and, confronted by Elizabeth's honesty and her willingness to prioritize her bond with Emily over status and pride, Matilda promises to keep the sisters' secret. Ultimately the enemies become allies. Matilda admits, "I s'pose I kinder begretched you that black silk . . . or I shouldn't have cared so much about findin' out. I never had a black silk myself, nor any of my folks that I ever heard of. I ain't got nothin' decent to wear anyway." Like the sisters, Matilda has sustained self-destructive pride, resenting her own involuntary simplicity. In return for this complementary admission, Elizabeth presents the old, mended black silk to Matilda, which sparks a further confession worthy of any contemporary soap opera.

The context is crucial, as Freeman advances an apparently sentimental appeal: Matilda has tears in her eyes, "but she held them unwinkingly." Stepping outdoors, "[s]he reached Emily's flower garden. The peppery sweetness of the nasturtiums came up in her face; it was quite early in the day, and the portulacas were still out in a splendid field of crimson and yellow. Matilda turned about, her broad foot just cleared a yellow portulaca which had straggled into the path, but she did not notice it." Freeman delicately weights this passage with symbolic import. The encounter between the women itself holds "peppery sweetness," with the pain of exposure compensated by the solace of honesty. But Matilda is distracted because she has another revelation: "The homely old figure pushed past the flowers and into the house again. She stood before Elizabeth and Emily. 'Look here,' said she, with a fine light struggling out of her coarse old face, 'I want to tell you—*I see them fire-crackers a-sizzlin' before Em'ly stepped in 'em'*" (original emphasis). Juxtaposing "fine" and "coarse," Freeman prepares readers for this explosive disclosure by paralleling Matilda's unconsciousness of stepping near Emily's "yellow portulaca which had straggled into the path" with Emily's blindness to the holiday firecrackers. Both women become martyrs to their pride. With the shared confessions, the three neighbors establish a small community based on mutual respect, candor, and generosity. Freeman shows finally that even involuntary simplicity can be borne with reliance on these virtues.

Clothing has always served as an overt marker of class and status. As Diana Crane explains, "[C]lothing is an indication of how people in different eras have perceived their positions in social structures and negotiated status boundaries. In previous centuries, clothing was the principal means for identifying oneself in public space." For the Babcock sisters to appear publicly in coarse apparel would have entailed relinquishing their class status (or pretensions). Certainly, for them the black silk dress becomes a "straightjacket, constraining (literally) a person's movements and manners," because one sister is housebound while the other wears it.[80] Although it is difficult for many contemporary Americans to imagine, before industrialized production of cloth and then finished garments, clothes were labor-intensive in creation, scarce, and highly valued, especially in poorer areas. In their rural New England environment, the Babcock sisters' inheritance of a trunkful of clothes from their aunt represents almost inconceivable abundance.[81] Freeman thus tells a cautionary tale, offering advice to women readers. To be poor and low in status, the author insists, does not convey moral superiority or greater respectability; Matilda Jennings is not a standard for emulation. But Freeman also rejects the Babcocks' efforts to maintain their rank and reject their material selves. Simple living does not make one better, it merely confirms one's deprivation and hunger, in every sense, for more. Eager to escape their "natural," embodied social status, elderly women are acutely vulnerable to rejecting their inferior position via fashion, which paradoxically reinforces that position, placing them under house arrest.

Two narrative features bear further attention. First is Freeman's use of the language of flowers, which her readers would have known well. In this nineteenth-century code, nasturtiums imply conquest or victory in battle and patriotism; Emily and Elizabeth putatively triumph as they defend themselves from their neighbors' prying eyes. Freeman also underscores that her story is not just local but national: replete with fireworks, the battle occurs on the Fourth of July, and Matilda and the Babcock sisters all struggle to maintain their independence. Inasmuch as she champions an alliance between the antagonists rather than continued hostilities, Freeman's message is anti-American. In this impoverished economy, prideful autonomy is foolish, potentially dangerous, and patriotism is better served by cooperation. Nasturtiums also symbolize maternal love and charity, which, Freeman intimates, represent a more appropriate approach to interpersonal relationships. The contrasting denotations of this flower language accord with the nasturtium's "peppery sweetness." Portulaca (or moss rose) augments Freeman's dual emphasis, for the flower signifies both superior merit and—showing her humorous vein—voluptuous love, which highlights her interest in female embodiment.[82] As the story ends, moral equality trumps social class difference, and Matilda's cross-class dressing in the Babcock sisters' black silk symbolizes and literalizes the women's reconciliation. Even though it is a "hand-me-down," the dress affirms acceptance of their ostensibly lower-class neighbor and their interdependence with her, in a truce reminiscent of Kirkland's with her less affluent neighbors.[83]

This American drama of war and reconciliation focuses on the protagonists' advanced age. In the United States, the elderly, like women, were affiliated with nature, as Larcom's "Flowers of the Fallow" explicitly acknowledges; corporeal deterioration emblematizes natural processes of decay and death. In "A Gala Dress," the Babcock sisters' obsession with respectable clothing obscures their physicality; genteel social class conceals bodily equality. In appreciating Matilda's plain food and coarse clothing, the author reveals fashion's artificiality. She also deprecates how American society disadvantages older women and dismisses their needs. The Babcocks and Matilda cannot be heroines, because social norms require that such figures be "naturally" young and beautiful; "voluptuous love" should belong to young, heterosexual couples. Despite its occasional poignancy, the story is necessarily comic, not tragic. As she composes fictionalized advice literature, Freeman models emotional intelligence through her combination of realistic narrative, sentimental reconciliation, humorous dialogue, and behavior writing.[84] Disclosing human similarities masked by social artifact, she questions limiting cultural associations among women, the elderly, and the body while she censures social standards that unthinkingly endorse respectability, "simplicity," and "independence."

FREEMAN WROTE at a time when scholars and intellectuals were noting the end of the frontier; the loss of that expanse boded great changes and a fear of what America would become. Responding to the collective anxiety about the loss of nature, many Freeman stories imagine a woman-centered natural world.[85] Perry Westbrook avers that in her work, "Out-of-doors nature is seen and appreciated, but from the kitchen window or during a walk to the village store to replenish the kitchen supplies. The grander aspects of nature—mountains, lakes, the ocean—are almost entirely lacking."[86] But nature's presence and character are everywhere felt in Freeman.[87] Another Freeman story explores the challenges of involuntary simplicity and the social dynamics swirling around women of different classes, but it bears a different message. In "A Mistaken Charity," Freeman rejects the socially constructed images of older, disabled, and poor women, for her heroines possess an intimate rapport with nature like the speaker's in Larcom's "Flowers of the Fallow." "Weeds" in the social garden, linked with savages and children, the heroines reject comfortable women's well-intended benevolence and assert their independence in a rural natural environment.

Aided by their landlord's and neighbors' small charities, sisters Harriet and Charlotte Shattuck eke out a living from their garden and nearby land. As the story opens, Charlotte keeps her sister, Harriet, company while the latter digs dandelion greens for dinner. Freeman depicts the sisters' poverty and their proximity to nature: "There were in a green field a little, low, weather-stained cottage, with a foot-path leading to it from the highway several rods distance, and two old women."[88] Adjacent to but separate from the outside world, the sisters enjoy the natural resources in their own yard. Connected to nature, the house itself is scarcely a human dwelling: "The old wooden door-step was sunk low down among the grasses, and the whole house to which it belonged had an air of settling down and mouldering into the grass as into its own grave." Freeman intimates the decay with which the sisters, Harriet "deaf and rheumatic" and Charlotte blind, are also affiliated. The free rent that their rich landlord provides is not, she explains, a charity: "He might as well have taken credit to himself for not charging a squirrel for his tenement in some old decaying tree in his woods" (235).

Gently humorous, the author accelerates her rhetoric of deterioration: "So ancient was their habitation, so wavering and mouldering . . . that it almost seemed to have fallen below its distinctive rank as a house. Rain and snow had filtered through its roof, mosses had grown over it, worms had eaten it, and birds built their nests under its eaves; nature had almost completely overrun and obliterated the work of man, and taken her own to herself again, till the house seemed as much a natural ruin as an old tree-stump" (235–36). Comfortably inhabited by animals as well as the sisters, the home is organic as nature itself. Freeman reinforces the Shattucks' harmonious coexistence with nonhuman nature and their own "natural ruin." In this corporeal, feminized natural world, nature takes "*her* own to *herself* again," obliterating the "work of man." With its insistent excess, this sketch showcases Freeman's genial humor that turns first toward the sisters and eventually toward readers. The Shattucks' domestic environment synthesizes humans and nonhuman nature in egalitarian familiarity.

Although Freeman pictures nature as inexorably more powerful than human endeavors, the Shattucks' garden reflects its beneficence: "The delight which the two poor old souls took in their own pumpkins, their apples and currants, was indescribable. It was not merely that they contributed *largely* toward their living; they were their own, their private share of the *great wealth* of nature, the *little* taste set apart for them alone out of her *bounty*, and *worth* more to them on that *account*, though they were not conscious of it, than all the *richer* fruits which they received from their neighbors' gardens" (238; emphasis added). Their alliance with nature promotes their well-being, and wealth acquires a different meaning; Freeman reinvents Emersonian notions of self-reliance and translates his transcendent "transparent eyeball" into bodily sustenance.[89] Extending Thoreau's emphasis on simplicity, and combining plenitude and privation, she suggests that sufficiency represents prosperity. Rather than being Christian stewards of nature, the Shattucks depend on and benefit from its bounty.

The sisters are explicitly antiheroines: "Neither of them had ever had a lover; they had always seemed to repel rather than attract the opposite sex," "not merely because they were poor, ordinary, and homely," but because Harriet was considered too blunt spoken and Charlotte too weak minded (236). As they pass from youth to old age, their principal aim is survival by sewing for local families. Freeman comments that they had been for the most part "happy and contented, with that negative kind of happiness and contentment which comes not from gratified ambition, but a lack of ambition itself. All that they cared for they had had in tolerable abundance. . . . The patched, mossy old roof had been kept over their heads, the coarse, hearty food that they loved had been set on their table, and their cheap clothes had been warm and strong" (237). In short, the sisters exemplify authentically simple living or voluntary simplicity, distinctively different than the Babcocks' and Matilda's unhappy plainness in "A Gala Dress" and the Brays' reluctantly reduced domesticity in "The Town Poor."

Freeman's deeply comic yet profoundly sympathetic perspective critiques the culture's attitudes toward these uncivilized, unrespectable elderly women. When the Shattucks' neighbor Mrs. Simonds visits, she gently disparages the sisters' distressing living conditions. Openly hostile, Harriet fears that she and Charlotte will have to "go on the town," but Mrs. Simonds assures them that she will never help send them to the poorhouse. Nevertheless, she and "a rich and childless elderly widow" had begun a "partnership in good works" (242). Performing a role of benevolent maternalism, "the widow was hand in glove with officers of missionary boards and trustees of charitable institutions. There had been an unusual mortality among the inhabitants of the 'Home' this spring, there were several vacancies," and thus finding space for the Shattucks was "very quickly and easily arranged" (243). Affluent women need objects of benevolence to acquire their own agency, and disabled women embody ideal recipients.[90] But even though Harriet is deaf and Charlotte is blind, they resist becoming objects of charity: "The struggle to persuade them to abandon their tottering old home for a better was a terrible one," and Harriet is convinced only by arguments that Charlotte would be more comfortable (243). Freeman's rhetoric problematizes the "Old Ladies' Home": "vacancies" satirically implies not just a high mortality rate but also the inmates' disappearance as persons.

Confronted with "the delight of successful benevolence" of "Mrs. Simonds, the widow, the minister, and the gentleman from the 'Home'" who met the sisters at the depot, Harriet and Charlotte "looked like two forlorn prisoners in their midst." The Home cannot civilize them into respectability, for they resist acculturation: "They did not take kindly to white lace caps and delicate neckerchiefs"; "nothing could transform these two unpolished old women into two nice old ladies" (244). Freeman juxtaposes "women" (physically, biologically defined beings) and "ladies" (socially defined beings), humorously indicating the former's superiority. Disliking the food and their general constraint, Harriet and Charlotte "went to the 'Old Ladies' Home' with reluctance and distress. They stayed for two months, and then—they ran away" (244). The phrasing compares the sisters to children, but the comparison favors children's wildness and independence, evoking Frado's outdoor play, agency, and self-authorization. Unlike the helpless Bray sisters in "The Town Poor," the Shattucks assert agency.

Freeman's stress on fashion in connection with her elderly heroines implies its inherent ludicrousness and inauthenticity. In the Home—as in the middle-class American home—clothing supposedly makes the woman, but unlike the Babcocks in "A Gala Dress," the Shattucks reject cultural constraints, particularly the respectability symbolized by proper clothing. They appreciate "their new black cashmere dresses well enough, but they felt as if they broke a commandment when they put them on every afternoon," preferring their own calico dresses and long aprons, a far plainer attire (244–45). The requirement for literal uniformity includes headwear, and the sisters prefer "to twist up their scanty gray locks into little knots at the back of their heads, and go without caps, just as they had always done": they want to behave naturally. Ironically, it is Charlotte who begs to return to self-sufficiency and simplicity: "O Lord, Harriét . . . let us go home. I can't stay here no ways in this world. I don't like their vittles, an' I don't like to wear a cap; I want to go home and do different" (245). On the road, effusive and "jubilant as two children," they celebrate their "escape," and Harriet reiterates the theme of independence: "I guess they'll see as folks ain't goin' to be made to wear caps agin their will in a free kentry" (246).

America's struggles to define a free country occupied a formative part of Freeman's life; the Civil War was fought during her early teenage years, and by the time *A Humble Romance* (in which the story appeared) was published in 1887, Euramerica had been forced to focus on Native Americans' situation vis-à-vis white culture. Freeman grew up in an era of widely publicized Indian wars and contentious debates about indigenous peoples' humanity— or savagery. The Carlisle Indian Industrial School in Pennsylvania opened in 1879; aiming at Native assimilation, its infamous head, Captain Richard Henry Pratt, promised to "kill the Indian . . . and save the man."[91] Pratt's methods, and his results, were widely publicized and controversial. With prominent accounts appearing in popular print venues, Buffalo Bill's Wild

Fig. 1.—PLAITED STRAW BONNET
Fig. 2.—BLACK LACE BONNET   Fig. 3.—BLACK LACE BONNET
Figs. 1–3.—LADIES' SUMMER BONNETS

Harper's Bazaar fashion plate in the same issue as Freeman's
"A Mistaken Charity." *Harper's Bazaar*, May 1883.

West show began performing in 1883. Freeman's expressed interest in Native Americans appears in at least two publications, her short story "Silence" (1898) and her novel *Madelon* (1896).[92] Her image of the elderly Shattuck sisters being civilized by the Home conjures the "before" and "after" photographs of Native American girls forcibly transported to white-sponsored boarding schools, who were stripped of their familiar clothing and forced to wear conventional white middle-class attire.[93]

Consciously or not, Freeman invokes associations between and among elderly women, children, and Native Americans, all regarded as uncivilized, natural beings.[94] Mrs. Simonds and her prosperous ally epitomize the missionary spirit that swept America in the late nineteenth century, a spirit that more often than not undermined the values of the people such well-intentioned individuals intended to help. These benevolent women enact the psychically, economically, and physically destructive ethic of expansion and colonialism. Most missionary work was conducted by middle-class white women, a fact Freeman would have known; the missionaries aimed to "elevate" their "savage" Indian counterparts, transforming them into servants for Victorian housewives—subordinate mirrors of themselves. Like Wilson—and, as chapter 5 shows, Zitkala-Ša—Freeman exposes the lie of such reform projects. In escaping from the Home, Harriet and Charlotte reestablish a positive balance between women, especially older women, and nature, and they reject charity workers' figurative colonialism.

NATURE PROVIDES more than material provision in "A Mistaken Charity"; it also supplies spiritual sustenance. But this nourishment differs from Berbineau's—or Emerson's—transcendent spirituality. And in contrast to Jewett's "The Town Poor," where Mrs. Trimble's Christian epiphany reveals her failed insight, in "A Mistaken Charity," Freeman's most disabled character, Charlotte, has an epiphany that reconnects her with the natural world. Although blind, she occasionally has moments of second sight that she calls "chinks." Defying the Congregationalist religious tradition from which they, like Freeman herself, emerge—a tradition that privileged the spirit over the body—Freeman's story interweaves spirit and body, which are irrevocably linked for Harriet and Charlotte. Like the Native belief systems that chapter 1 discusses, Charlotte and Harriet's spiritual and physical lives are inseparable. Thus, when Charlotte has visionary moments, they relate not to a "higher" realm but to nature and the body itself. After Mrs. Simonds has departed from her initial visit, Charlotte tells Harriet, "If you had seen the light streamin' in all of a sudden through some little hole you hadn't known of before when you set down on the door-step this mornin', and the wind with the smell of the apple blows in it came in your face, an' when Mis' Simonds brought them hot doughnuts, an' when I thought of the pork an' greens jest now—O Lord, how it did shine in!" (241). While Charlotte's vision privileges sensual, material desires and pleasures, it also encompasses figurative, transcendent significance. Freeman's ironic humor includes Charlotte's use of "O Lord," for the blind woman rejoices in an embodied natural realm.

The passage also evokes literal and figurative inspiration; it re-creates the world in vivid presence. Stacy Alaimo and Susan Hekman's insistence in

Material Feminisms that we respect women's corporeality resonates here.[95] At the Home, Charlotte complains to Harriet about the food: "O Lord, Harriét, when I set down to the table here there ain't no chinks. . . . If we could hev some cabbage, or some pork an' greens, how the light would stream in!" (244). Rejecting Emersonian hierarchies and recalling Thoreauvian simplicity, Freeman's comedy celebrates the reintegration of body and spirit; she literalizes consumption, as the narrative repeatedly breaches artificial barriers that separate natural and domestic environments.

In "A Mistaken Charity," as in "A Gala Dress," Freeman confirms bodies' importance through food. At their new residence, "the fare was of a finer, more delicately served variety than they had been accustomed to; those finely flavored nourishing soups for which the 'Home' took great credit to itself failed to please palates used to common coarser food" (244). The Shattucks desire plain food; echoing Matilda's desire for a "coarse" repast in "A Gala Dress," the sisters' taste for smelly pork and rank greens marks them as impoverished and only too corporeal. Confirming white middle-class Victorian domestic values, the Home attempts to obscure or erase women's—even old women's—sensuality and, more obliquely, their sexuality. Freeman promotes a healthy interest in sensuality through her attention to food and clothing.

Prioritizing respectability, the Home requires the women to conceal and tidy their bodies, but just as Larcom's "weedy" old woman in "Flowers of the Fallow" escapes "cultivation," so do the Shattucks. Their desire to go capless echoes the magnificent erotic scene in *The Scarlet Letter* when Hester releases her hair from under her cap in the woods, the wilderness populated by "savage" Native Americans.[96] In linking Harriet and Charlotte with nature so strongly, Freeman metaphorizes the freedom (and threat) that Native American sexuality posed to Euramericans, a freedom that the author's diction repeatedly emphasizes.[97] The ideal of women as sexually pure echoes notions of racial purity—hence, in its defiance of age- and class-based bodily norms, Freeman's story also figures a dangerous interracial merging in its savage elderly characters. "Captives" in the Home, at home they feel liberated. Freeman's affective, spiritual, and physiological appeals reveal her emotional intelligence, as she evokes these correlations and transvalues gendered and racialized social norms. The advice that Freeman encodes in "A Mistaken Charity" is finally simple: be yourself, authorize your own insights, accept your embodiment—respectability be damned.

At the story's conclusion, Charlotte's inner vision blooms. As they walk up the path to their house, Harriet describes the scene, and Charlotte responds, "'O Lord, Harriét, thar's a chink, an' I do believe I saw one of them yaller butterflies go past it,' cried Charlotte, trembling all over, and nodding her gray head violently" (248). Once inside, Harriet looks out the window:

"The currants air ripe," said she, "*an'* them pumpkins hev run all over everything."

"O Lord, Harriét," sobbed Charlotte, "thar is so many chinks that they air all runnin' together!" (249; original emphasis)

If "chinks" signify light, Freeman implies that Charlotte is no longer blind, though the author hints that she sees through tears. Just as the sisters have claimed their agency, nature has confirmed its power. But the Shattucks are more than its beneficiaries. Ending the story with Charlotte's ecstatic exclamation, Freeman endorses the women's bond with the natural world. Charlotte has in effect become a "transparent eyeball," but her vision inextricably intertwines the divine, the spiritual, and the embodied natural. Simple living, in the sisters' philosophy of voluntary simplicity, translates here to sufficiency in ripeness.

Freeman's narratives complicate standard cultural scripts surrounding women, especially the elderly, the disabled, and the poor. Some of her concern arose from her own experience as a class migrant and some from larger social and demographic issues. Many young men from New England had gone west seeking their fortune before the Civil War, and the war itself decimated the number of marriageable men. Far more than their predecessors, women of her generation faced the prospect of singlehood. These "redundant women" were growing older as Freeman published her accounts of New England village life.[98] Elderly women's greater closeness to nature than their circumscribed youthful counterparts could, she suggests, unsettle social norms surrounding female embodiment; they might "go natural," like Mary Jemison. Responding to so-called scientific debates about gender and race, Freeman's depiction of the Shattuck sisters undercuts stereotypes permeating late nineteenth-century America; it also transvalues the connections between and among women, children, the elderly, the disabled, and the savage. Ultimately, "A Mistaken Charity" materializes nature without idealizing it.

Freeman's stories—not just the two cited here but many others—also speak to contemporary questions surrounding simple living. If plainness is voluntary, as we see with the Shattuck sisters, then it is desirable, but socially enforced hardship is a different matter. While Thaxter's "Woman's Heartlessness" sketches (and addresses) wealthy women—those who possessed the resources to *choose* being "beautifully unadorned"—Freeman's stories characteristically illuminate disadvantaged women's struggles to negotiate between social expectations and personal desires and resources. But Freeman's diverse older women teach us that we should not generalize about a group of people or construct uniform codes of behavior and that perceptions of plenty and want are precisely that. For some women, respectability is intimately linked to consumption—which includes food and fashion—while others reject conformity to arbitrary social norms, preferring sufficiency to superimposed luxury. For those who have always been poor, externally imposed simplicity promises deprivation and resonates with environmental injustice. Freeman shows how such compulsory standards separate people and inhibit or eliminate natural pleasures. Rather than sermonizing or advising readers directly, Freeman uses genial-humored fiction to demonstrate these lessons and engender emotional intelligence that complements her own.

"How strange a thing is nature": Hopkins's Salty Sinners

In her 1905 address at the William Lloyd Garrison Centennial Celebration in Boston, Pauline Hopkins issued a warning:

> Mr. Garrison lived to see his cause triumph in the emancipation of the slave, and died believing that the manhood rights of every citizen of the United States were settled then and forever. But the rise of a younger generation, the influence of an unconquered South, and the acquiescence of an ease-loving north that winks at abuses where commercial relations and manufactures flourish and put money in the purse, have neutralized the effects of the stern policy of these giants of an earlier age. . . . Were Mr. Garrison living in this materialistic age, when the price of manhood is a good dinner, a fine position, a smile of approval and a pat on the back from the man of influence, or a fat

endowment again would he cry aloud, "The apathy of the people is enough to make every statue leap from its pedestal, and to hasten the resurrection of the dead."[99]

Hopkins's resounding critique of Gilded Age consumption and elevation of earlier heroes' moral economy reiterates a theme that informed her life's work. She came of age in an era devoted to materialism and dominated by advertising. At the same time that she sought economic and social uplift and respectability for her fellow African Americans and pressed them toward greater attentiveness to spirituality, she attacked middle-class African Americans' embrace of what she understood as the mainstream society's problematic consumer values.

Those values were everywhere on display. In the June 1889 volume of the *Ladies' Home Journal*, one advertisement for F. Bates & Co. highlights "Dress Reform: Jersey-Fitting Undergarments" "for Men, Women, and Children" "(perfect substitute for corsets)"; another promises "To Purify and Beautify the Skin, Cuticura Remedies Are Simply Infallible"; a third offers time savings with "Instantaneous Chocolate, the Greatest Invention of the Age," noting that "Every Family Should Have It." Saving labor as well as time, the Empire Wringer "turns with half the power required by other machines" ("Back-breakers"). Articles include "Dainties of Ye Olden Times. Piquet and Sweet Wafers," "Interior Decoration: Bed-Rooms," and "Not Too Much Economy," which argues that those who can afford to eat well should do so for their health.[100] Such marketing was not limited to publications addressed to white readers. In addition to plumping such products and services as shoe polish, hotel accommodation, and a flatulence cure, the *Colored American Magazine* from December 1901 also advertised products ranging from Liberty Pure Foods' Oatnuts ("one handful of oatnuts is far better than an equal quantity of beefsteak") to the Shrewsbury Medicine Company's Dande-cura hair tonic ("Long, beautiful, glossy silky hair, always indicates the Spring of Life. Vaselines, pomades and cosmetics ruin the hair and disfigure one for life").[101] As Monika Elbert points out, "American advertising was an attempt to render woman a consumer, one whose powerlessness as an active participant in the marketplace was offset by her buying power within the family itself."[102] Whether in the nineteenth century or the twenty-first, advertisers address personal and family well-being. Reading Hopkins invites us to ask, does the current impulse toward self-improvement advance genuine simplicity or simply transform and accelerate consumerism?

Hopkins's humorous short story "Bro'r Abr'm Jimson's Wedding" provides her readers—then and now—with forceful advice on responsible, ethical living. Hopkins questions mainstream society's reduction of women to beautiful bodies, and she recuperates female respectability for her urban, predominantly African American readers. Hopkins's work underscores the distinctively vexed challenges for those readers of gaining that respectability, because their historical connection with embodiment was far more complex than for their white counterparts. Unlike Freeman's "A Mistaken Charity," "Bro'r Abr'm Jimson's Wedding" situates American women in an urban environment rather than in nature. Even more than Freeman or Jewett, Hopkins values community coherence and interdependent responsibility, and she privileges mature women's centrality to the group's ability to achieve both environmental agency and respectability.

Hopkins experienced firsthand the benefits of a tightly knit community. The descendant of distinguished race activists, religious leaders, and arts visionaries, Pauline Hopkins was born in 1859 to Sarah Allen and Benjamin Northup in Portland, Maine. The family quickly moved to Boston, which had a proud history of African American political, social, cultural, and religious achievement. The author's childhood was marked by two events with opposite significance: the first, her mother's divorce from Benjamin due to his adultery, and the second, Sarah Allen's marriage on Christmas Day 1864 to the hard-working, kind Civil War veteran William A. Hopkins, whose name the writer would adopt. The Hopkins's marriage took place in the historic Twelfth Street Baptist Church, known as the Freeman's Church for its alliance with the Underground Railroad.[103] William Hopkins strongly supported the arts and his stepdaughter's talents, and in 1875, as she completed her education at the city's renowned Boston Girls' High School, she began an acclaimed performance career in Boston's vibrant arts environment. Carol Allen points out, "Hopkins finished high school during a period when most black Americans did not have the opportunity for secondary education."[104] As she considered and then relinquished a longer performing arts career, in the early 1890s Hopkins determined to seek financial security. She obtained stenography training and worked in state government offices, then passed the civil service examination and became a stenographer in the census division of the Massachusetts Bureau of

Statistics of Labor, the groundbreaking agency that compiled the foundational data for Elizabeth Stuart Phelps's reform novel *The Silent Partner*.[105]

Becoming energized by her feminist community's political activism as it
responded to the horrors of southern lynchings and the country's denial of
African American civil rights—and by the courageous efforts of such activists as Ida B. Wells-Barnett and Frances Harper—Hopkins relinquished
her secure civil service position and began a career as a professional author.
When four Virginians established the *Colored American Magazine* in Boston, she joined the venture, which was assertively political and literarily
ambitious. "Hailed as the first, most substantial, and influential African
American periodical of the twentieth century," according to Hopkins biographer Lois Brown, the *Colored American* announced its goals to "offer the
colored people of the United States" a publication that served as "a medium
through which [they] can demonstrate their ability and tastes, in fiction,
poetry, and art, as well as in the arena of historical, social, and economical
literature."[106] On its first anniversary, in May 1901, the journal boasted a
circulation of one hundred thousand; this figure "represented an impressive
35 percent of the nation's literate African American readers." With high
cultural ambitions, it sought an educated and relatively affluent audience,
but the periodical reached a much wider readership through its distribution
in church groups, women's clubs, and reading clubs; and it reached white as
well as black readers.[107]

Hopkins's contributions to the *Colored American* spanned an impressive
array of genres. She published groundbreaking histories in her two series,
"Famous Men of the Negro Race" and "Famous Women of the Negro
Race," as well as short stories, essays, editorials, and three major serial novels.[108] The parent Colored Co-Operative Publishing Company published
her first novel, *Contending Forces*, in 1900. Hopkins's hard work and imaginative pan-African perspective led to her appointment as literary editor in
1903, and the magazine thrived under her visionary stewardship. But intra-
racial politics would intervene, as the magazine increasingly rejected Booker
T. Washington's accommodationist program, instead endorsing a liberal
agenda of civil rights, intellectual growth, and racial uplift.[109] Because the
parent company overextended itself, the owners sought outside financial
assistance, which led to a covert, hostile takeover by Washington's agents.

In the wake of the magazine's transferal to New York, Hopkins departed
from the editorship. Ironically, the new owners, the National Negro Busi-

Cover of the *Colored American Magazine*,
February 1901, during Hopkins's tenure as editor.
Courtesy of the Center for Research Libraries.

ness League, marketed the journal to "an African American entrepreneurial and rising middle-class constituency that embraced the League's mission." Turning away, Brown notes, from "a domestic and international program of high moral racial uplift" and toward an "insular, self-serving promotion" of individual well-being, the magazine quickly lost its quality and ultimately its readership.[110] Although Hopkins joined forces with another progressive magazine, the Atlanta-based *Voice of the Negro*, publishing contributions there and elsewhere, she would never regain the power and authority that she enjoyed during her tenure at the *Colored American*.[111]

ALTHOUGH SCHOLARSHIP on Hopkins has recently flowered, only Barbara McCaskill has appreciated her powerful humor, most visible in "Bro'r Abr'm Jimson's Wedding." Even more than for Freeman, comedy provides a critical tool for Hopkins to dismantle the superstructures of fashion, conspicuous consumption, and bodily excess, including food. McCaskill has argued that "Hopkins reassigns uplift values from Christianity to conjure," observing that "Hopkins's story-within-a-story cheekily unfolds in the dictiest, most pretentious of religious institutions. . . . Where the nativity story emphasizes humility, charity, sacrifice, and innocence, Jimson's wedding day coalesces ambition, competition, peroration, social climbing, opportunism, and greed." She concludes that "instead of attempting to distance itself by checkbook and ballot from the rest of the race, this elite class, Hopkins suggests, must return to the collective advancement and self-respect that uplift purists—or conjurers, for that matter—intend."[112]

Hopkins conveys this message through an intricate rhetorical web that weaves together irony, hyperbole, slapstick, sentimental appeal, modest sermon, and humor to undercut black urban elites' social pretentions. African American women's complex history, in particular their relationship to respectability, required such virtuosity. Respectability demanded adherence to white middle-class gender ideals. In the antebellum period, Jacobs's confession of her liaison with Mr. Sands responded indirectly to sexual norms (and proved her inability, because of her enslavement, to preserve her virtue and her reputation). For women of color and working women throughout the century, purity was essential because the dominant society associated them with sexual licentiousness.[113] Jane E. Dabel explores how, after Reconstruction, respectability retained its importance for black women, with late nineteenth-century elites forming women's clubs to monitor community members: "These clubs carried on the tradition of black women's political activism, but they revealed growing class divisions within the black community. Middle-class black women attempted to impose the standard of respectability on all black women, just as their fathers had attempted to do a generation earlier."[114] Hopkins's dilemma was how to affirm this standard without encouraging black women to become priestesses at the temple of consumption.

"Bro'r Abr'm Jimson's Wedding" iterates characteristic Hopkins themes: strong African American women and an identity mystery. Unlike her longer fictions, where revelations of identity frequently engender tragedy, here they spark comedy, even generating slapstick that nevertheless closes with a serious admonishment. Subtitled "A Christmas Story," her narrative begins with a single-sentence paragraph: "It was a Sunday in early spring the first time that Caramel Johnson dawned on the congregation of —— Church in a populous New England city."[115] The setting is crucial; spring symbolizes rebirth, youth, and sexual renaissance, and this rebirth occurs during Sunday worship. Hopkins's narrator remains relatively impassive. But the next paragraph indicates the author's investment in the debate linking respectability and wealth: "The Afro-Americans of that city are well-to-do, being of a frugal nature, and considering it a lasting disgrace for any man among them, desirous of social standing in the community, not to make himself comfortable in this world's goods against the coming time, when old age creeps on apace and renders him unfit for active business." Hopkins underscores her interest in the community, and she reproaches that community's concern with outward appearances. Respectability (coded as "social standing") and material accumulation represent primary, self-reinforcing goals, but an equally large problem is the group members' competitiveness: "[T]hey vied with each other in efforts to accumulate a small competency." The obverse of simple living, their lifestyles mirror those of the destructive dominant culture, "the constant example of their white neighbors" (469).

Hopkins's satirical edge quickly becomes clear: "Of course, these small *Vanderbilts* and *Astors* of a darker hue must have a place of worship in accord with their worldly *prosperity*, and so it fell out that _____ church was the *richest* plum in the ecclesiastical pudding, and greatly sought by scholarly divines as a resting-place for four years" (emphasis added). More detached, the subsequent paragraph reflects on the unusually large and restless congregation: "How strange a thing is nature; the change of the seasons announces itself in all humanity as well as in the trees and flowers, the grass, and in the atmosphere. Something within us responds instantly to the touch of kinship that dwells in all life" (469). Despite African Americans' characteristic resistance to pastoral, and despite the story's urban location, Hopkins asserts—without apparent humor or irony—humans' rapport with the natural world, foregrounding the spring, a period of luxurious and sensuous growth.[116]

As Hopkins moves indoors, she offers increasingly pointed commentary: "The air, soft and balmy, laden with rich promise for the future, came through the massive, half-open windows, stealing in refreshing waves upon the congregation. The sunlight fell through the colored glass of the windows in prismatic hues, and dancing all over the lofty star-gemmed ceiling, painted the hue of the broad vault of heaven, creeping down in crinkling shadows to touch the deep garnet cushions of the sacred desk, and the rich wood of the altar with a hint of gold" (469). Larded with adjectives, the passage contrasts nature's organic plenitude with humans' artificial wealth. Unlike the authentic night sky, the church interior exhibits a facsimile:

the "star-gemmed ceiling." Hopkins underlines the contradiction between organic spiritual life and social status exemplified in expensive tangible objects. She counterbalances her serious message with genial hyperbolic humor, encouraging her readers to associate material excess with spiritual poverty.

Into this overladen atmosphere she thrusts Caramel Johnson, who inspires admiration and envy, with one bystander gasping, "She's a stunner, and no mistake" (469). As Johnson gives the minister her letter of introduction, the narrator portrays the "pretty girl": "[B]rown of skin, small of feature, with an ever-lurking gleam of laughter in eyes coal black. Her figure was slender and beautifully moulded, with a seductive grace in the undulating walk and erect carriage." Mirroring in human form the church's luxurious beauty, Johnson has more: "[T]he chief charm of the sparkling dark face lay in its intelligence, and the responsive play of a facial expression which was enhanced by two mischievous dimples pressed into the rounded cheeks by the caressing fingers of the god of Love" (470). To muffled laughter the minister announces her absurdly appropriate name: Chocolate Caramel Johnson. A potential Cinderella, the heroine literally embodies the congregation's rejection of simple living and its lust for luxury, for they are so seduced by Caramel's luscious physical form that the minister's request for her character reference appears ludicrous. Hopkins's affectionate and enticing but critical portrait intimates that she rejects superficial standards of respectability. Blending sentimentalism with the insider humor of her character's delicious name, Hopkins enlists readers' sympathies and delight—and their skepticism.

Caramel's attractiveness would have been both amusing and challenging for Hopkins's readers and for the author herself, given the historical connection between verbally and sexually loose women.[117] When moral goodness and purity meant accepting patriarchal standards for female behavior, amusing women, outright funny women—like Fanny Fern, who challenged those standards—were frequently attacked for their lax morals and hence lack of respectability. As the historian E. Frances White and others have detailed, respectability is particularly fraught for African American women. She describes how the emergence of Freud's and Darwin's theories and the metaphors that they employed reinforced the dominant culture's links between women and savages: "[A]nxieties about disease, sexual behavior, and moral development were all expressed in terms of race, gender, and class."[118] Reflecting the fact that "discussions about race and gender were inseparable," White references Freud's famous observation that "the sexual life of adult women is the 'dark continent' for psychology."[119] Within a context that related all women to uncivilized nature—as even Margaret Fuller had done in *Summer on the Lakes*—women writers sought to dissociate themselves from their bodies and to promote respectability, evidenced by asexuality, moral elevation, refined manners, and elegant appearance. As Larcom's wry report of an exchange between distressed "town-dames" dramatizes, gold watches, rather than sartorial simplicity, represented helpful appurtenances when outsiders were confronted with constant social scrutiny.

Hopkins reprises such scrutiny vividly as she develops her male as well as her female characters. The story centers around the eponymous Bro'r Abr'm Jimson, an affluent church member old enough to be Caramel's father, who "owned a house in the suburbs and a fine brick dwelling-house in the city proper" (470). For the congregation, his wealth denotes his social status, and Jimson's female cohort avidly pursues him for a husband. Rumored to be Sister Nash's beau, he discards her for Sister Nash's niece; the narrative wittily undercuts his efforts to steal Caramel from Sister Nash's son Andy (471). As significant as Caramel's name, Jimson's undercuts his desirability and status: Jimsonweed (*Datura stramonium*, also known as Jamestown weed, thorn apple, Devil's Trumpet, and mad apple), a member of the nightshade family, was known since the late seventeenth century as an invasive plant, toxic to humans and animals, that could cause hallucinations.[120] Farmers still practice careful eradication of this widespread and tenacious plant. Hopkins's sly reference conjures Abr'm Jimson's devilish qualities, as she traces the congregation's shared delusions.

Mad for money and the deference it accords, Caramel triangulates between Andy and Jimson and Sister Nash and Jimson; the triangle's legs are money, material social benefits, and respect. When Andy asks if she plans to marry "old Rheumatism . . . come Christmas" and rejects her answer, Caramel retorts, "Andy Nash, you always was a fool, an' as ignerunt as a wil' Injun. I mean to have a sure 'nuff brick house an' plenty of money. That makes people respec' you" (472). Seeking the accoutrements of respectability and fashion—which include a well-built house—Caramel overemphasizes physical well-being, according with her rich embodiment. Because of the longstanding correlation between property ownership, citizenship, and social equality in the United States, Hopkins would not have taken lightly such financial success in the black community.[121] But, although the author clearly admires Caramel's beauty, she rejects the economic ethic that reiterates mainstream society's standards, and she ultimately disciplines both her heroine and Jimson for a consumerist ethic that she delineates as not just comic but immoral and dangerous. Eliciting readers' own lust for Caramel, Hopkins chastises us as well.

The next scene intimates the community's danger, as Hopkins reminds readers of the broader social and cultural environment. Andy's anger and frustration at Caramel's rejection reverberate in a grimly comic encounter at his employer's restaurant, when he clashes with an Irish worker after tripping over her cleaning equipment as he attempts to serve a customer lobster salad. Bridget McCarthy calls him a "wall-eyed, bandy-legged nagur" and her Irish colleagues call out "lynch him!"[122] More than counterbalancing the slapstick of the fallen lobster salad, Hopkins invokes deadly serious conflicts with Irish immigrants. Tensions between black citizens and the Irish had been high since the latter arrived in the United States in significant numbers. As early as 1832, racist Irish mobs in Providence, Rhode Island, attacked its African American community. In Boston, by 1900 "just over 30 percent of registered voters were foreign-born, and approximately half of that number were Irish. Boston's Irish American inhabitants shaped the city emphatically, and its African American population was increasingly overshadowed by the influx of European immigrants."[123] Moreover, the popularity of the minstrel show, where Irish players appeared in blackface, ratcheted up tensions, sometimes unbearably.[124] These ethnic tensions reflected an explosive, unjust environment for cultural and social outsiders.

OTHER STRESSES underlay this comic scene as well. Published in 1901, near the peak of the lynching epidemic, "Bro'r Abr'm Jimson's Wedding" appears to make light of an onerous national problem.[125] Invoking it, Hopkins insists that the ostensibly private relationships on which the story focuses have broad implications for the larger African American community, going well beyond her anonymous city. After Andy's encounter with Bridget, Jimson discusses with Sister Nash an antilynching advocate's approaching visit to the church, but he remains preoccupied by his social position. Jimson and Caramel's self-centeredness and their obsession with money and respect make them neglect pressing political concerns. Hopkins illuminates this myopia: when Jimson reneges on his promise to help release Andy from prison and pontificates on her son's lack of humility, Sister Nash attacks: "[Y]ou ol' rhinocerous-hided hypercrite" (475). Hopkins's hyperbole underscores her emotional intelligence and prompts our own: we may laugh, but we recognize the potentially serious consequences of this accurate evaluation.

Jimson dissembles doubly, for at the wedding his authentic wife and six grown sons appear and challenge his union with Caramel. Again Hopkins exposes the disparity between the materialist "church man" and genuine Christian faith. The concluding section punishes Jimson and Caramel for improper, even immoral behavior. She returns to the opening's descriptiveness: "To a New Englander the season of snow and ice with its clear biting atmosphere, is the ideal time for the great festival. Christmas morning dawned in royal splendor; the sun kissed the snowy streets and turned the icicles into brilliant stalactites." Through her natural images Hopkins foregrounds the holiday's spiritual consequence, which she juxtaposes with the wedding's ostentation: "The presents were many and costly. . . . Brother Jimson's patrons were to be present in a body, and they had sent the bride a solid silver service so magnificent that the sisters could only sigh with envy" (476). Enhanced by the alliteration, the author's irony penetrates the showy façade; unlike the wise men bearing gifts to an impoverished Christ, the visitors bring a superabundance to a grasping and merely nominal Christian. Hopkins's ethos, conveyed by humorous irony as penetrating as Kirkland's, urges her readers toward simplicity—which means rejecting all social fashions—and genuine spirituality.

When she reveals Jimson as a potential bigamist, Hopkins changes rhetorical mode again, as the story oscillates among realistic description, detached narrative, romantic appeal, irony, and comedy. Near the end the story veers again into slapstick. When the minister inquires of the congregation whether "any *man* can show just cause, etc.," the abandoned *wife*, "a woman of ponderous avoirdupois[,] advanced up the aisle," exclaiming, "Hol' on thar, pastor, hol' on! A man cain't have but one wife 'cause it's agin' the law. I'm Abe Jimson's lawful wife, an' hyars his six children—all boys—to pint out their daddy" (emphasis added). Viney Peters speaks for the congregation and the reader when she exclaims, "My soul . . . the ol' sarpen'!" (477). Hopkins heightens the hilarity by imagining the spurned wife as a weighty, uneducated woman who undercuts Jimson's class pretensions and by endowing him with a superfluity of sons. The narrator's educated perspective emerges in the hyperbolic diction ("ponderous avoirdupois").

Despite her obvious pleasure in this entertaining excess, Hopkins reinforces a serious message: Jimson's devilish hypocrisy threatens the community's well-being, as the ensuing row signifies. Caramel threatens to sue Jimson for "breach of promise," while Mrs. Jimson threatens her bodily harm: "Sue him, will you? I'll make a choc'late Car'mel of you befo' I'm done with you, you 'ceitful hussy, hoodooin' hones' men from thar wives" (477). In the subsequent physical battle, Caramel's "satin gown and gossamer veil were reduced to rags" in a reverse Cinderella tale. The church's figurative devil weed, Jimson induces not just hallucinations but madness in the congregation. In the story's happy ending, Jimson vanishes and "Mrs. Jimson came into possession of his property by due process of law," as Hopkins disciplines Jimson and Caramel for unseemly, even sinful conduct (478). Given Sarah Hopkins's early experiences with a respectable but philandering husband, the author's reference to the legal remedy might not surprise us. But given the law's blatant unwillingness to protect African Americans from lynching or sustain their legal rights, this conclusion is more than a little ironic.

Hopkins commends simplicity and redefines respectability, and she conveys her message as much by her rhetoric as by narrative events. Articulating a strong community ethos, she rejects individual advancement, rendering it at once tragic and comic and carefully directing readers' emotions. Much more than an amusing romantic fancy, the story underlines a noteworthy dominant metaphor. When Jimson visits Sister Nash and chastises Andy's behavior, he pompously claims that "[m]y business is with the salt of the earth." Her reply paraphrases scripture: "Salt, of the earth! But ef the salt have los' its saver how you goin' salt it ergin? No, sir, you cain't do it; it mus' be cas' out an' trodded under foot of men." She continues, "That's who's goin' happen you Abe Jimson, hyar me? An' I'd like to trod on you with my foot, an' every ol' good fer nuthin' bag o' salt like you" (475).[126] Hopkins's readers would not have missed the reference to Christ's Sermon on the Mount, nor the fact that it followed the Beatitudes of the persecuted. Sister Nash becomes a comic Christ avatar who challenges Jimson's hypocrisy; she anticipates the revelation of his bigamy and Viney Peters's remark by calling him "a snake in the grass" (475).

Also invoking a purification process, the salt metaphor recurs in the story's last paragraph: "In the home of Mrs. Andy Nash a motto adorns the parlor walls worked in scarlet wool and handsomely framed in gilt. The text reads: 'Ye are the salt of the earth; there is nothing hidden that shall not be revealed'" (478). Presumably Caramel has relinquished her pretensions, and though the motto is "handsomely framed," the "gilt" encodes a two-edged sword. Hopkins conjoins the salt of the earth metaphor with a related allusion to exposure, reminding readers that pretension precedes a fall.[127] Although Freeman's "A Gala Dress" focuses more on individual interactions, "Bro'r Abr'm Jimson's Wedding" too emphasizes how respectability—and conspicuous consumption—destroys community. Like "A Mistaken Charity," though in a very different environment, the story shows how spiritual well-being is incompatible with luxury.[128] Hopkins argues for a morally informed simplicity that will undergird genuine community progress within a fraught national environment of racism and greed. This progress, she submits, will be led by a strong black maternal figure.[129]

As a working African American woman, Hopkins wrote "Jimson" as an insider in a turn-of-the-century America enmeshed in debates about the place of African Americans, most notably women, in the human family. White asserts that for Darwin, "the preeminent scientist of the nineteenth century, discussions about race and gender were inseparable," and she cites the famous case of Saartjie Baartman, known as the Hottentot Venus, who was exported to Europe as a scientific and popular curiosity. With her "savage" anatomy, Baartman purportedly embodied the proof that Africans demonstrated the connection between humans and animals. White underscores how Darwin's metaphors, analogies, and humor (especially that describing Baartman and her cohort) combined with the "disinterested scientist's tone" to create a powerful rhetoric that "was widely read precisely *because* he so effectively defended bourgeois white male power—a power based on the simultaneous control of people of color, white women, and the working classes."[130]

Gesturing toward this larger cultural and political environment, Hopkins's story explores symptoms of dangerous class divisiveness in the black community, exemplified in fashion and elitist behavior, and it critiques superficial assessments of respectability. Hopkins rejects the consumerist escape route that some individuals—both women and men—took to rebut the link between African Americans and nature, a vexed and complex

correlation for black women, for whom this linkage had historically provided a rationale for abuse and rape. As White observes, in the post-
Reconstruction period, which continued to portray black women as "pro-
miscuous by definition," the rape of these women "was no crime at all."[131]
Given this context, respectability possessed central importance for black
women, yet Hopkins pointedly questions its definition. In a sympathetic
narrative that complicates the relationships between nature and culture,
body and spirit, Hopkins depicts individualism's dangers and promotes
community cohesion and responsibility. For all its rollicking humor and
outrageous slapstick, "Bro'r Abr'm Jimson's Wedding" carries a serious message of simplicity and spirituality that resonates in today's new Gilded Age
of flush politicians and megachurches led by millionaire preachers.

"BRO'R ABR'M JIMSON'S WEDDING" appeared in a rich setting. The December 1901 issue of the *Colored American Magazine* opens with William
Stanley Braithwaite's "Holly Berry and Mistletoe: Lyrics," and the holiday
celebration continues with "The Tribute of Beltasar: A Christmas Tale of
the Three Magi." Hopkins's story is immediately preceded by a poem, "The
Gift of the Greatest God," lauding African American James Parker, who
subdued President McKinley's assassin. Conjuring luminaries stretching
from Moses, Plato, and Shakespeare to John Brown and Frederick Douglass, the poet imagines Parker requesting as his reward the freedom to labor
as equals "in fields to us denied— / A chance to toil with willing hands
at work God made us for," "to live as free men; not as half slaves 'mong
the free." The poem comments indirectly on Jimson's social climbing and
conspicuous consumption; at the conclusion a personified "future" promises
to grant this wish for freedom. Bookending Hopkins's story and fostering
Hopkins's message of spiritual union, Flavel Henri Lacques-Waggoner's
"A Vow" fancies a bride's elevated gifting of her soul to her "king, and only
thee."[132]

This poem interrupts Hopkins's political thrust just briefly: three chapters of her serial novel *Hagar's Daughter* and a lengthy installment of "Famous Women of the Negro Race" focusing on Sojourner Truth follow. The
next piece, "The Smoky City: Part III. Social and Business Life," features
Pittsburgh's prominent men and women. Fulsome with praise and lavish
with photographs of homes and people, the essay highlights men's business

success and women's social engagement and activism. Respectability frames the narrative content, with education and work central virtues in this essay that advances racial uplift. The writer's attention to economic success and social achievements appears to compete with Hopkins's message of spirituality and simplicity. But the sketch's emphasis on triumph over adversity moderates this effect. So does the account of Captain Posey's home, which is "what the home of a successful man should be. His parlors are tastefully, but not extravagantly, furnished."[133] The "lovely paintings" were "painted by his wife" rather than (as the author implies) purchased for exorbitant sums. With additional selections such as "The Windy City," the magazine promotes community coherence as central to uplift. In this literary context, "Bro'r Abr'm Jimson's Wedding" negotiates a fine line between reproaching prideful falsehood and celebrating authentic accomplishment.

The literary framework for Hopkins's story suggests the seriousness and thoughtfulness with which she and her cohort regarded problems of consumption. If we take her novels as touchstones, humor is not her characteristic mode, and "Bro'r Abr'm Jimson's Wedding" (along with "General Washington, A Christmas Story" [1900]) seems anomalous. In both her novels and stories, however, Hopkins stresses that morality must accompany material success. Unlike Jacobs and Wilson, who sought a white middle-class audience, Hopkins addressed principally her peers, which enabled her affectionate, though still pointed, humor to include modes ranging from irony to slapstick. Nevertheless, "Bro'r Abr'm Jimson's Wedding" makes a point as serious as any in her longer fiction.

Of the author's novel *Contending Forces* Francesca Sawaya argues, "Hopkins's use of regionalism, her investigation of the local site of Boston, allows for a critique of nationalist myths and their affective claims, at the same time that it enables her to envision a new imagined community, a national community figured through regionalism and its affective claims."[134] "Bro'r Abr'm Jimson's Wedding" too has regional and national as well as personal significance. It reinvents in comic terms her biological father's womanizing while it ironically commemorates her mother's happy marriage to William Hopkins. Even as Hopkins's portrait of "the richest plum in the ecclesiastical pudding" expresses dismay at the corruption of churches' spiritual and political mission, the urban church in "Bro'r Abr'm Jimson's Wedding" reflects indirect pride in her ancestors' involvement in historical institutions like Beacon Hill's African Baptist Church, headed by her maternal great-

Beacon Hill's African Baptist Church, also known as Abolition Church,
where Hopkins's maternal great-granduncle preached. Photograph by
Arthur D. Haskell, February 1937. Courtesy of the Library of Congress.

granduncle, the Reverend Thomas Paul, who welcomed William Lloyd
Garrison and his allies when local white churches timidly rejected his abolitionist zeal.[135]

The story also speaks to Hopkins's struggle to achieve recognition in
Boston's African American community, indirectly honoring the pioneering
achievements of such organizations as the Colored National League and
numerous local female uplift and social circles.[136] Brown points out, "As
her public life in the early 1900s evolved, it would become clear that the
lack of increasingly bourgeois social and educational credentials impeded
Hopkins's access to high respectability." The writer's career as a public per-
former, her outspoken liberal politics, and her unmarried status combined
to effect her "social exclusion . . . at the hands of Boston's and New England's emerging intellectual and social elite"; not least frustrating was her
exclusion from the influential black clubwomen's movement.[137]

Female respectability represented the heart of middle-class black life.
Sigrid Anderson Cordell reminds us, "The early twentieth century was

one of the worst periods of racial oppression and violence in the United States since emancipation."[138] "Bro'r Abr'm Jimson's Wedding" not only commented on the need for black activism to remediate the country's glaring racial inequities, it also underlined the troubling historical affiliations between the black female body and sexuality.[139] Black women's putative lasciviousness had long been the dominant society's excuse for rape, incest, and violence, and African American women remained particularly vulnerable in Hopkins's era.[140] Six years before "Bro'r Abr'm Jimson's Wedding" appeared, Hopkins's contemporaries, distinguished clubwomen leaders Josephine St. Pierre Ruffin and Victoria Earle Matthews, responded forcefully to spurious smears of African American women such as Ida B. Wells-Barnett by a white southern newspaper editor. Matthews asserted, "He has not only slandered the women of negro extraction . . . but the mothers of American morality and virtue," and she insisted that "courageous women should speak through *The Woman's Era* that the world may feel the power of the chaste mentality of the true negro woman."[141]

Within such a background, Chocolate Caramel's materialism is less disturbing than her erotic attractiveness. Unlike Jewett's and Freeman's elderly, white, rural heroines, for whom respectability is not mediated through sexuality, Caramel embodies America's conflicted, racialized environment. Yet, despite the urban setting and her youth, she shares with them a potentially dangerous proximity to the body, material existence, nature itself. Entering the church congregation in the spring, she unsettles the parishioners' prosperous domesticity and comfortable religiosity with her flagrant beauty. Hopkins reinforces her flimsiness through the comic counterpoint of weighty, authentic Mrs. Jimson, and she chastises Caramel's pretensions. But the author does not reject the verdant young woman; instead, she counsels that modesty, humility, and spirituality should accompany a more appropriate bond with her peer, Andy, and a more becoming tutelage by the savvy, maternal Sister Nash. If embodied pleasure is for the young—and sexually active—Hopkins intimates its potential economic and spiritual dangers for African American women. Thus her brief for simplicity, which underlines civilized behavior and castigates the wildness of her money-mad black Bostonians, emerges from a historical and cultural perspective valorizing spiritual over corporeal experience, an earlier ethos more akin to the working-class Sigourney's or Berbineau's than to Jewett's and Freeman's.

EVEN AS THEY censure women's investment in bankrupt ideologies of consumption, Thaxter and her peers illuminate how such factors as age, ability, and race influence social hierarchies. All four writers recognize the problem of female respectability *as* a problem that differentially informs women's moral standpoints, habits of acquisition, and relationships to embodiment. More than her white peers, who privilege individual environmental agency, Hopkins showcases how excess consumption affects the community; she urges cohesion in order to combat pressing contemporary challenges.[142] All four, however, examine ideologies connecting women and nature, explore how various forms of hierarchy interrelate, and complicate conventional formulations of women's transactions with their social environments and nonhuman nature.

Thaxter and her contemporaries' radical transformation of advice writing indicates that in order to better understand American environmental writing ecocritics need to evaluate traditionally feminine, interstitial genres where (transforming Larcom's metaphor) "weeds" persist. Not just the first-person essay and lyric poem but also the sketch—itself a generic hybrid—contribute to this tradition. The authors in this chapter employ diverse rhetorical strategies that establish their emotional intelligence and invoke readers' own. Their periodical publications address audiences that comprised substantial numbers of middle-class, comfortable, urban women disinclined to contemplate the pitfalls of involuntary simplicity or the benefits of material restraint, except by proxy—unless simplicity itself became fashionable. Such readers would likely not be propelled to self-examination or behavioral change, let alone activist engagement, by accusation or sermonizing. Thus Thaxter and her contemporaries create sentimental appeals, indirect sermons, children's literature, and humorous local color sketches that dramatize important issues and permit both sympathy and distance—advice writing transformed into templates for ethical behavior in complex modernizing environments. Ultimately, they undress the priestesses at the temple of consumption—their readers—and urge them to look in the mirror.

During the past several decades the status-conscious attitude that flourished in the late nineteenth century has reappeared with a vengeance in what economist Paul Krugman has called "a new Gilded Age," while social networks, secular and sectarian, have emerged in response to the increasing income disparity and the "affluenza" that have permeated American culture and society.[143] Local efforts address specific, concrete goals like growing sustainable and organic food.[144] What links many initiatives— as in the nineteenth century—is a focus on embodiment and its basic requirements: shelter, clothing, and food. Asserting these needs, nineteenth-century American women writers reframe the interactions among wealth, consumption, and the female body. Their studies of home, fashion, and simple living may not be new, but their indirect approach furnishes alternative avenues for progressive rhetoric. Their work supplies no easy solutions to our current dilemmas, but it makes the challenges of sustainable consumption more transparent, and it demonstrates the complex rhetoric and emotional intelligence needed to confront those challenges.

Coda: Green Fashion Is No Fashion
and Simple Living Is Not

For contemporary American women, nurtured on the froth of advertising and the shine of stuff, consumption is nearly second nature. As in Celia Thaxter's time, "birds are worn." With the emergence of Kate Middleton, the Duchess of Cambridge, as a style icon lauded by fashion magazines, including *Harper's Bazaar* and *Marie Claire*, CNN Money reports that sales of the feather-decorated "fascinator," "a particularly ornate hair accessory," have soared. Frequently made in China, these hats are popular as a substitute for bridal tiaras or veils, and they can cost more than $100.[145] Feathered hats are even appearing on eBay, sometimes fetching hundreds of dollars.[146] Virtually all commentators on Middleton's millinery celebrate its trendiness; the very few critical voices find the hats "ugly."[147] As did their nineteenth-century counterparts, today's buyers emphasize style and beauty. Shopping is serious business, as the princess of consumption has reproduced herself in the millions.

From a more environmentally friendly angle, green fashion (aka eco-fashion) has entered the mainstream; the latest "cruelty-free" fur alternative is human hair. Recently, the designers Stella McCartney and Vivienne Westwood have created sustainable clothing lines.[148] Recognizing the environmental costs of raising cotton, which demands enormous quantities of petroleum-based pesticides and water, many consumers have selected fabrics like hemp or bamboo.[149] Manufacturer Levi Strauss & Co. emblematizes producers' acknowledgment that customers are increasingly demanding environmental accountability; Strauss has "commissioned a scientific life cycle assessment (LCA) to find out the facts about the climate change, water and energy impact of a pair of Levi's® 501® . . . from cotton seed to the landfill."[150] This research indicates that producing a single pair of jeans can require more than six cubic meters of water. On the web, sites like Ecofashionworld.com (efw) promote handmade goods, linking to hundreds of companies, while Ecouterre "is a website devoted to the future of sustainable fashion design."[151] The latest ecofashion is chicken feathers: millions of tons are dumped in landfills, but current research seeks ways to recapture this material for yarns and textiles.[152] Since fashion is by definition disposable, these new products hardly contribute to sustainability, and often only the affluent can afford them.

If shopping is serious business, so is simplicity. *Real Simple* magazine, with its slogan, "life made easier, every day," promotes consumption, regularly featuring self-improvement. An online issue from March 2011 includes as its featured articles "3 Amazing Room Makeovers," "Are You Using the Right Products for Your Skin?" "4 Delicious, Healthy Meals," and "The 15-Minute Full-Body Exercise-Ball Workout," with smaller stories such as "Save Time: 37 Convenience Foods to Keep On Hand."[153] A search on the magazine's website for "sustainable" delivers a single result: "How to Identify Sustainable Seafood."[154] How you look converges with what you eat; the female body remains the focus.

Such improvements may represent, in Andrew Szasz's trenchant phrase, "shopping our way to safety."[155] When environmental awareness merely changes individual purchasing patterns, then it reinforces a lifeboat mentality, where the resource rich believe that they can elude the toxic consequences of world—especially American—production and consumption practices. Such behavior also diminishes the prospect of holistic environmental responsibility and community efforts toward structural change. In this climate of "inverse quarantine," as Szasz defines it, we need the inventive ideas of simplicity and renewed concepts of community that writers like Thaxter, Jewett, Freeman, and Hopkins provide.

Rejecting narrow ideas of respectability and urging collective responsibility for the vulnerable, these authors offer visions of older women that have special resonance today, when, according to the Center for American

Progress, "elderly women are far more likely to be poor than elderly men. *Thirteen percent* of women over 75 years old are poor compared to 6 percent of men" (original emphasis).[156] Given the recent increase in U.S. poverty, citing statistics and appealing to ethics are clearly inadequate, and affective approaches remain vital to sparking progressive change.[157] Thaxter and her peers unconsciously appreciated empathy's biological basis. Their feeling rhetoric fosters empathy with others, including poorer neighbors and nonhuman animals, by evoking emotions such as anger, sympathy, fear, and amusement. Modern brain science reveals that without emotional intelligence we not only lack empathy but are more likely to commit violence, including the psychic violence of removing people and nonhuman animals from their homes. Such consequences suggest that our collective survival may depend on understanding, valuing, and using all our affective skills. But, as the writers in chapter 5 insist we ask, who are *we*?

INDIAN LAND FOR SALE

GET A HOME
OF
YOUR OWN
❋
EASY PAYMENTS

PERFECT TITLE
❋
POSSESSION
WITHIN
THIRTY DAYS

FINE LANDS IN THE WEST
IRRIGATED
IRRIGABLE
GRAZING
AGRICULTURAL
DRY FARMING

IN 1910 THE DEPARTMENT OF THE INTERIOR SOLD UNDER SEALED BIDS ALLOTTED INDIAN LAND AS FOLLOWS:

Location.	Acres.	Average Price per Acre.	Location.	Acres.	Average Price per Acre.
Colorado	5,211.21	$7.27	Oklahoma	34,664.00	$19.14
Idaho	17,013.00	24.85	Oregon	1,020.00	15.43
Kansas	1,684.50	33.45	South Dakota	120,445.00	16.53
Montana	11,034.00	9.86	Washington	4,879.00	41.37
Nebraska	5,641.00	36.65	Wisconsin	1,069.00	17.00
North Dakota	22,610.70	9.93	Wyoming	865.00	20.64

FOR THE YEAR 1911 IT IS ESTIMATED THAT 350,000 ACRES WILL BE OFFERED FOR SALE

For information as to the character of the land write for booklet, "INDIAN LANDS FOR SALE," to the Superintendent U. S. Indian School at any one of the following places:

CALIFORNIA:	MINNESOTA:	NORTH DAKOTA:	OKLAHOMA—Con.	SOUTH DAKOTA:	WASHINGTON:
Hoopa.	Onigum.	Fort Totten.	Sac and Fox Agency.	Cheyenne Agency.	Fort Simcoe.
COLORADO:		Fort Yates.	Shawnee.	Crow Creek.	Fort Spokane.
Ignacio.	MONTANA:	OKLAHOMA:	Wyandotte.	Greenwood.	Tekoa.
IDAHO:	Crow Agency	Anadarko.	OREGON:	Lower Brule.	Tulalip.
Lapwai.	NEBRASKA:	Cantonment.	Klamath Agency.	Pine Ridge.	WISCONSIN:
KANSAS:	Macy.	Colony	Pendleton.	Rosebud.	Oneida.
Horton.	Santee.	Darlington.	Roseburg.	Sisseton.	
Nadeau.	Winnebago.	Muskogee.	Siletz.		
		Pawnee.			

WALTER L. FISHER,
Secretary of the Interior.

ROBERT G. VALENTINE,
Commissioner of Indian Affairs.

U.S. Department of the Interior advertising poster, 1911.

Chapter 5

Domestic and National Moralities

Justice in the West

In that portion of the arid belt which lies within the borders of Idaho between the rich mining-camps of the mountains there is a region whereon
those who occupy it have never labored—the beautiful "Hill-country,"
the lap of the mountain-ranges, the free pastures of the plains. Here,
without help of hands, are sown and harvested the standing crops of wild
grass which constitute the wealth of cattle-men in the valley.

—MARY HALLOCK FOOTE

IN LATE 1888 AND EARLY 1889, the writer and artist Mary Hallock
Foote published "Pictures of the Far West" in the elite eastern monthly
Century Magazine, offering snapshots of the "new" country and illuminating its "wild" character. Quoted above, the first of three sketches, "Looking
for Camp," establishes nature's self-sufficiency; the land provides bounty
without apparent work or cost.[1] Foote's essay underscores humans' insignificance within the West's huge scale and independent presence. "Looking
for Camp" concludes at sunset: "At this hour the stillness is so intense that
the faintest breeze can be heard, creeping along the hill slopes and stirring
the dry, reed-like grasses with a sound like that of a muted string."[2] These
quietly symphonic sounds are both evocative and restful, as Foote balances
an observer's account with the land's own voice. Her rare narrator interventions into these sketches—which resemble animated engravings, reflecting
the author's vocation as a celebrated graphic artist—intimate her appreciation for her surroundings and its creatures but restrain her judgment
and the reader's. Mentioning a settler family and bloody conflicts between
sheep farmers and cattle ranchers, Foote downplays human presence while
creating for eastern audiences what we might call desert pastoral, painting
the savage with a dusting of the civilized.[3]

As the nineteenth century concluded and a new century unfolded, easterners, especially urbanites, continued to regard the West as uncivilized.
Many western writers contested—or, like Bret Harte, banked on—this
dichotomy.[4] Such notions had practical political and economic consequences, as whites continued to appropriate supposedly waste or worthless
land for agriculture, herding, and mining, in effect civilizing it. In several
works published between 1883 and 1924, Sarah Winnemucca (Paiute), María
Amparo Ruiz de Burton, and Zitkala-Ša (Sioux) expose how the savage/
civilized polarity served to dispossess Native peoples and Mexican Americans of their landholdings, arguing for versions of environmental justice.[5]
Using rhetorical tools ranging from sentimentalism and realism to humor
and irony, they question the ethics—including the Christian ethics—of
displacement and consumption. They invert the associations of civilized
and savage, attesting, sometimes through a focus on women and home, that
their people are patriotic and moral, respectable and civilized.

Unlike canonical nature writers such as John Burroughs and John Muir,
Winnemucca, Ruiz de Burton, and Zitkala-Ša have no concern for wilderness preservation per se: they are interested in how humans relate to
nonhuman nature in the context of dominant-society racial, ethnic, and
class hierarchies.[6] They locate people in dynamic and disputed social and
geographical spaces; shaping these conflicts were radically different ideas
about individuals' and communities' relationship to land. The situation in
the turn-of-the-century West was even more complicated than in the early
nineteenth-century east.[7] The competition for land, in particular, had more
varied participants: Native nations, Mexican Americans, whites, the poor
and the rich, Catholics and Protestants, individuals and corporations, and
the federal government all contended for priority. In the Far West, not only
did Native Americans' and whites' views diverge from each other, they
split from those of Mexican Americans.[8] Even internal disparities of class,
education, and status within each group shaped the region's resource wars
for grass, minerals, and water.[9]

The three authors featured in this chapter present an opportunity to
bridge the gap that Charles Waugh has identified between "ecocritics who
pull apart representations of nature in literature and popular culture to
see how they work, and . . . environmental justice critics who examine
public environmental policy." Waugh's assertion that the two perspectives
"rarely . . . come together, either in how cultural representations of nature

influence discriminatory public environmental policy, or conversely in how discriminatory public environmental policy influences how writers represent the environment" requires that we look more closely at Winnemucca's narrative, Ruiz de Burton's novel, and Zitkala-Ša's narratives and exposés, which themselves analyze "discriminatory public environmental policy" and, complementarily, reinvent "cultural representations of nature" in order to transform that policy.[10] When we consider these texts stereoscopically— examining their representations of nature and public policy—elided class-, ethnicity-, and race-based hierarchies and divisions within and between communities click into focus.

These authors understood environmental justice differently and at times problematically. Winnemucca sought to end repeated, forced Paiute removals to unfamiliar land and to find a space for continuing kinship relations; a safe harbor, especially for Paiute women, from white depredations; and ultimately a permanent home possessing adequate natural resources to be self-supporting with occasional U.S. Army assistance. While she affirms Paiute moral and intellectual sovereignty, Winnemucca relinquishes political sovereignty and privileges survival. For Ruiz de Burton, environmental justice demanded that Mexican Americans retain control over their traditional lands, despite other, earlier claims on those lands. Today's readers find her disturbing, for she appeals to an elite white audience, appropriates the image of the Vanishing American for elite Californios, and portrays working-class Mexicans and Indians as savage. Despite her novel's shortcomings, her depictions of sustainable land usage retain some persuasive power, due partly to the Californios' long land tenure in southern California and consequent appreciation of the local ecosystem. Unlike Winnemucca, Zitkala-Ša assumes a pan-Indian identity and argues for intellectual and spiritual sovereignty, but her anti-peyote stance undermines Indian agency. Although she presses Native Americans to retain modest landholdings, she promotes English-language acquisition and values American citizenship.

This chapter explores how Winnemucca, Ruiz de Burton, and Zitkala-Ša necessarily negotiated a maze of competing claims even as they maintained their peoples' right to land tenure and affiliated economic justice. Each of these writers troubles twenty-first-century readers, either because of the claims she makes or the way she makes them. But given the historical and political circumstances, we may be asking too much to expect straightforward avowals of identity, ownership, or belonging, particularly for three women who found themselves in untenable situations no matter which way they turned. Authors such as Winnemucca, Ruiz de Burton, and Zitkala-Ša thus demonstrate that we need to think about environmental justice more expansively.[11] Their sometimes-awkward efforts help illuminate twenty-first-century complexities in both national and transnational terms. In particular, their work reveals that we should assess and respond to internal fractures in communities that may themselves encompass conflicting constituencies. It also indicates that interethnic alliances remain crucial to achieving environmental justice, although forming such alliances may pose significant obstacles.

Constructing a foreign (I use the word deliberately) form of environmental literature, Winnemucca, Ruiz de Burton, and Zitkala-Ša investigate the national and imperial designs differentially superimposed on Native Americans and Mexican Americans during their lifetimes. In an account dominated by resource wars, military and ideological, Winnemucca models a feminine leadership that is—in Jace Weaver's resonant concept—communitist (community + activist).[12] Ruiz de Burton imagines hybrid economic elites who will establish a new California order. Zitkala-Ša's autobiographical narratives contrast civilized Sioux society to savage white culture, while elsewhere she paints devastating portraits of Indian girls ravaged by a corrupt U.S. legal system. Writing against wilderness, the writers dispute stereotypes of the West's inhabitants as savage and reconceptualize the civilized. Through their representations of nature and humans' relationships to it, Winnemucca and her counterparts expose resource wars and contend with discriminatory public policy and laws.

A Moving, Versatile Voice:
Sarah Winnemucca, Nation, and Nature

"The red man, as he appears in effigy and in photograph in this collection, is a hideous demon, whose malign traits can hardly inspire any emotion softer than abhorrence." Responding to the Indian exhibition at the 1876 Philadelphia Centennial Exhibition in his capacity as the *Atlantic Monthly* editor, William Dean Howells goes on to absolve corrupt Indian agents of "malfeasance," commenting, "[P]erhaps we do not sufficiently account for the demoralizing influence of merely beholding those false and pitiless savage faces; moldy flour and corrupt beef must seem altogether too good for them."[13] As Howells's remarks unintentionally reveal, resource wars with Native peoples continued throughout the century, though they attracted less attention from the mainstream media and activists during the years focused on abolition, the Civil War, and Reconstruction than they would later. One individual who ensured the renewed prominence of such conflicts was the nineteenth-century Paiute lecturer and writer Sarah Winnemucca. Speaking to an unethical federal government agent who sells her people's food for profit, Winnemucca exclaims, "Hell is full of just such Christians as you are!"[14] Such comments also indirectly confront eastern urbanites like Howells, underscoring the consequences of colonialism. Noteworthy among the late nineteenth-century activists who fought for environmental justice, Winnemucca published her groundbreaking *Life Among the Piutes* in 1883 to recount her people's tribulations—or, in the words of the volume's trenchant subtitle, *Their Wrongs and Claims*. The author combats unjust public policy and corrupt local officials by representing the Paiute's civility and their harmonious relationship to nature—and by combining affecting images and angry advocacy.[15]

From midcentury onward, the Paiute's traditional homelands, in an area encompassing present-day western Nevada, northern California, and southeastern Oregon, were overrun by whites, initially passing through to make their fortunes in the California Gold Rush. Because the Humboldt River route through the Great Basin area provided a reliable water source, many fortune seekers took this route. Settlement pressures began later, when gold was discovered on Paiute lands.[16] Silver likewise propelled settlement; as Gae Whitney Canfield relates, "The black rocks that the gold miners around Johntown and Gold Hill had been throwing away for months as worthless debris were now recognized to be solid silver."[17] Given that the two societies saw humans' relationships to land, land tenure, and sovereignty so differently, and given the U.S. government's legal, political, and military support for white settlement, discord was as predictable as it had been earlier with the Cherokee and the Seneca.

Intervening forcefully in this period of social upheaval, Winnemucca (Thocmetony, or Shell Flower) was born about 1844 near Humboldt Lake in what is now northwestern Nevada, the granddaughter of a self-appointed Northern Paiute leader.[18] The Paiute's traditionally mobile lifeways frame Winnemucca's narrative. Since food resources were dispersed across their arid lands, bands traveled to find berries, fish, nuts, and small game; the influx of white settlers around the time of Winnemucca's birth disrupted the Paiute's conservative use of the desert's food and water and generated increasing conflict.[19] Fluent in at least three Indian languages as well as English and Spanish, the largely self-educated author emerged as a powerful advocate for Indian rights and a Paiute homeland. As part of her efforts Winnemucca gave more than three hundred public lectures on both coasts, performed on stage as an "Indian Princess," and formed alliances with eastern reformers; her groundbreaking exposé represented the culmination of these activities.[20] *Life Among the Piutes* describes the earliest encounters between Paiutes and whites, outlines her role in the 1878 Bannock Indian War, and details events leading to the creation of a reservation in 1889 within historical Paiute lands, including her extensive experience as a U.S. Army translator and her meetings with government officials in Washington. The book also portrays federal agents' endeavors to transform the traditionally nomadic Paiute into settled farmers—a direct challenge to their sovereignty.

Despite evincing heroic courage and stamina, Winnemucca faced condemnation from her own people, partly because, as a translator, she sometimes conveyed broken promises and misinformation, and partly because some regarded her stance as compromising and assimilationist.[21] Amid continuing debates, Malea Powell highlights Winnemucca's agency and her ability to negotiate between two societies—two nations—by constructing herself "as a *civilized Indian* . . . by textually representing herself as a literate practitioner of Euroamerican discourse at the same time as she clearly represents herself as a Paiute."[22] This self-representation censures dominant-society stereotypes, norms, and behavior, which she contrasts to her nation's moral rectitude and civility. *Life Among the Piutes* has received considerable attention in recent years, with particular emphasis on the writer's gender identity, her activism, and her formal practices. None of its readers, however, considers *Life Among the Piutes* from a specifically ecocritical standpoint. Her appeals to ethics, emotion, and logic demonstrate her self- and community-authorized agency aimed at achieving environmental justice.

Winnemucca depicted corrupt reservation agents, which subjected her to particular calumny, and she confronted government officials' efforts to attack her credibility and prevent her activism.[23] As with all female reformers, her gender rendered her vulnerable to charges of promiscuity, particularly ironic in view of the unrelenting sexual "outrages" (her term) that white men regularly committed against Native women; such abuse, she contends, initiated at least two wars.[24] These character assaults necessitated testimonials corroborating her respectability like those required of Jacobs. Like Ward and Jemison, Winnemucca understood her power within a social system based in gender complementarity rather than hierarchy; her narrative confirms that Paiute women enjoyed more respect and more freedom than their white counterparts.[25] When she died of tuberculosis in 1891, Winnemucca had established herself as an important Native intellectual and reformer.[26]

LIFE AMONG THE PIUTES permits, even encourages, the stereoscopic perspective that Waugh's analysis promotes: the narrative deploys emotionally intelligent rhetoric to synthesize affecting representations of Indian-white relations, evocative images of Paiute relationships with nature, and implicit and explicit attacks on discriminatory public policy. *Life Among the Piutes* anticipates several principles of environmental justice formulated at the 1991 First National People of Color Environmental Leadership Summit. Among them are the condition that "public policy be based on mutual respect and justice for all peoples"; a declaration of "the fundamental right to political, economic, cultural, and environmental self-determination of all peoples"; the recognition of "a special legal and natural relationship of Native Peoples to the U.S. government through treaties, agreements, compacts, and covenants affirming sovereignty and self-determination"; and opposition to "military occupation, repression and exploitation of land, peoples and cultures, and other life forms."[27]

Winnemucca contrasts horrific exploitation—land theft, resource wars, starvation, and sexual abuse of Indian girls—with idyllic portraits of pre-contact life flowering with women. Realizing that attacks on land tenure, gender complementarity, and spiritual sovereignty constituted war on Paiute identity and nationhood, she combats environmental injustice on several fronts. *Life Among the Piutes'* audaciously hybrid account, which includes tribal history, autobiography, ethnography, sentimental appeal, coup tale, myth, testimony, travel narrative, political tract, sermon, adventure story, and oratory, echoes Jemison's and Wilson's inversion of the terms *civilized* and *savage*.[28] We could attribute *Life Among the Piutes'* formal variety to inexperience composing a written text, as editor Mary Mann's introduction intimates, but this variety reproduces the genre hybridity and associative quality of oral speech or conversation.[29] Winnemucca's narrative rehearses in its structure the fast-paced events surrounding the Paiute and her own geographical mobility (and dislocation and exhaustion); "away" and "leave" form constant refrains.[30] To perceive the writer's multiple rhetorical strands, examining her form and the metatextual structuring of voice is as essential as studying content.[31]

The word *justice* appears only seven times in *Life Among the Piutes*, but the book thematizes it so emphatically that Winnemucca does not need to be explicit. The opening lines show the violent effects of white occupation. Winnemucca begins her orally inflected story with an arresting and affecting account of her birth: "I was born somewhere near 1844, but am not sure of the precise time. I was a very small child when the first white people came into our country. They came like a lion, yes, like a roaring lion, and have continued so ever since, and I have never forgotten their first coming" (5). Mirroring the opening structure of traditional European American autobiography, the author appears to claim her life as exceptional, while she also inaugurates a coup tale, which characteristically seeks "to announce one's name, identify one's associates, locate oneself geographically and strategically, list one's achievements, and conclude with an ending formula."[32]

But Winnemucca immediately destabilizes her audience's initial assumptions with qualifiers: "somewhere near 1844, but am not sure of the precise time." Most literate white readers would know their birth year and birth date; like Jemison's indefiniteness, Winnemucca's seems to corroborate her uncivilized beginnings. Yet the writer's vagueness reiterates the uncertainty of her subsequent life. The qualifiers obliquely question customary methods (indeed, even the possibility) of self-construction in this social environment. That is, Winnemucca configures these opening lines to contest authoritative, individualistic white selfhood. The ambiguity bespeaks a story, a spoken rather than written text. Ironically, her refusal to define herself temporally may foster white readers' belief in her story's truthfulness (or authenticity), invoking savage ahistoricity while endorsing for herself and potential Native readers their different, spatial concept of identity.[33]

The next sentence is remarkable for its elision: Winnemucca jumps from an uncertain birth to an equally uncertain childhood, which she remembers for one extraordinary event, white settlers' arrival in traditional Paiute lands. She signifies her difference from her primary audience—"white people"—and her participation in a collective self that is defined partly by its location ("our country"). Wilson's narrative summoned—and satirized —sentimental images of vulnerable, interrupted childhood; similarly invoking this figure, Winnemucca quickly implicates arriving whites in exploitation. "Our country" prefigures the writer's national narrative, a history imagining at least two nations, "the entire Piute nation" and "America" as it was constructed through her people's devastation.[34] David Brumble argues that Winnemucca sees no "*essential* differences" (original emphasis) between "her Indian people and whites"—and on a moral level this argument may be accurate. But on a historical and political plane, the differences, textually marked by aesthetic structure as much as substance, appear enormous.[35]

The third sentence underscores the narrative's self-aware craftedness: beginning with a metaphor ("They came like a lion"), Winnemucca reminds her white auditors of Biblical stories—an ironic reference to Daniel and the lion's den, for here divine assistance emphatically fails the Indians. She enhances these effects with interpolation ("like a lion, *yes*") and augmentation ("like a *roaring* lion") as the sentence unfolds toward a catastrophic conclusion ("I have never forgotten their first coming"). Evoking white settlers' menace and voraciousness, Winnemucca emphasizes the helpless "*very* small child," and she moves from personal history to tribal history. Structurally, these first few sentences progress dynamically from the self, to the whites, back to the Paiute, and then to her grandfather's key role ("I . . . I . . . They . . . My people . . . My grandfather"). As Weaver reminds us, "Natives tend to see themselves in terms of 'self in society'"; that is, the self is part of a larger "we."[36] Winnemucca's self is multiple. She is a tribal member, daughter, and Christian sufferer, but she almost always depicts herself in relation.[37] Offering damning testimony, Winnemucca's account as a whole is animated, participatory, and communitist. It affirms Paiute identity and, through its structure as well as its content, intellectual sovereignty.

WINNEMUCCA UNDERSTANDS that women's social roles, and the exploitation of Paiute women's bodies as resources, form one basis for war. Her ethical and affective appeals repeatedly (and courageously, in Victorian America) expose white settlers' sexual abuse of Paiute women. Early in the narrative, her mother pleads with Winnemucca's brother not to leave her and his sisters alone with the white men, whom she condemns as "beasts" and who "abuse" girls in front of their mother (37).[38] Winnemucca confronts directly the stereotype of the savage, lascivious squaw: wishing to protect their virtue, Indian women are respectable, and white men become the savages, molesting female Indian children. Here and elsewhere, she refers to whites' exploitation of Indian women and girls, coding her allusion to sexual violation as she does later when she cites "outrages." An important rhetorical weapon, this familiar domestic term would have forged direct connections with her white female audience and would have stressed the Paiute's humanity.[39] Moreover, she uses the passive form "outraged," highlighting her own outrage at the women's lack of agency.[40] Expressing her mother's anguish and fear, Winnemucca seeks readers' parallel response through intense, shared language that foregrounds corporeal violation.

Chapter 2, "Domestic and Social Moralities," which addresses white proprieties most directly, possesses kinetic immediacy, again linking orality and literariness and encoding social criticism in ironic textual strategies of indirection and juxtaposition.[41] Winnemucca portrays kinship relations that confirm her people's civilized status and disparage whites' deficient values.[42] Despite its many different meanings, home, a central image from Ward to Jacobs and Wilson, forms Winnemucca's grounds for sympathy. Using her experiences as a lecturer for women-only audiences, the author again carefully attunes her remarks to her predominantly female readers.[43] "Domestic and Social Moralities" mirrors white American women's advice writing while it incorporates autobiography, tribal autobiography, sermon, and ethnography. Her emotionally intelligent strategies range from sentimentalism to accusation and engender feelings that encompass admiration, discomfort, and guilt.[44] White readers, especially women, she insists, should support her project of social and environmental justice.

In Winnemucca's affective calculus, explicitness is sometimes counterproductive. The conversational opening ("Our children are very carefully taught to be good") discreetly distinguishes the admirable Paiute ethos from its white counterpart: "We are taught to love everybody. We don't need to be taught to love our fathers and mothers. We love them without being told to. Our tenth cousin is as near to us as our first cousin; and we don't marry into our relations" (45).[45] The opening's anaphoric structure ("We . . . We . . . We . . . Our") helps make her allegiances transparent to attentive listeners.[46] Her oblique reference to the biblical commandment "honor thy father and mother" ironically implies that Christianity must codify values infrequently practiced in white society that need no formalization among the Paiute. Finally, she counters whites' accusations of (uncivilized) Indian immorality. In an account overwhelmingly concerned with wars, Winnemucca eases readers into her environmental justice plea by framing it in this feminine, domestic context.

"Domestic and Social Moralities" admonishes the dominant society for its failure to comprehend that human and nonhuman nature embody an organic whole and for its ignorance of complementary gender roles. Thus Winnemucca details a married couple's joint responsibility for children, concluding more broadly, "Marriage is a sweet thing when people love each other. If women could go into your Congress I think justice would soon be done to the Indians" (53).[47] The chapter as a whole underlines Paiutes' respect for women by representing their close relationship to nature. During the spring Festival of Flowers, Paiute girls assemble and dance together, accompanied by their "beaux" and families. Gathering the flowers for which most are named, the girls "weave them into wreaths and crowns and scarfs, and dress up in them." Implicitly assessing their white counterparts' subordinate social status, the narrative celebrates women's importance in Paiute society: "They all go marching along, each girl in turn singing of herself; but she is not a girl any more,—she is a flower singing" (47). Appreciating, in George E. Tinker's words, the "interrelatedness . . . balance, and mutual respect among the different species in the world," including flowers, Winnemucca rewrites dominant-society associations of (white) women with delicate embodied objects, merely resources for consumption.[48] Like Ward's and Jemison's accounts, Winnemucca's problematizes contemporary claims that the women-nature connection is essentialist. Emphasizing the entire community's participation in the festival, her critique hinges on rejecting such limiting associations and affirming the Paiute ethos.

Winnemucca's affirmations countered a harsh new reality. As in *Incidents in the Life of a Slave Girl*, sexual abuse threads throughout *Life Among the Piutes*, extending well beyond her mother's plea in the opening chapter.[49] Even in the relatively idyllic "Domestic and Social Moralities," after the author details the Paiute girls' beauty during the Festival of Flowers, she inserts a searing commentary: "My people have been so unhappy for a long time they wish now to *disincrease*, instead of multiply. The mothers are afraid to have more children, for fear they shall have daughters, who are not safe even in their mother's presence" (48; original emphasis). Enclosed by detailed descriptions of community harmony and respect for women, the account of exploitation becomes yet more shocking. For Christian readers, her assertion would have had religious resonances, for protecting their children necessitates that the Paiute must reject God's command to "be fruitful, and multiply, and replenish the earth." The accompanying biblical mandate, to "have dominion over the fish of the sea, and over the fowl of the air, and over every living thing that moveth upon the earth," indicates Winnemucca's irony.[50] Only white men enjoy such mastery, treating the lovely Paiute girls as if they were nonhuman animals.[51] Thus a crucial Paiute goal is separation from whites, owning land where they, and particularly the women, are less vulnerable. Domestic tranquility reflects environmental justice.

Equally attentive to males' roles, Winnemucca criticizes the dominant society directly in the chapter's conclusion, rejecting, as Jemison had done, the stereotype of the belligerent Indian: "It is always the whites that begin the wars, for their own selfish purposes" (51). Winnemucca likewise condemns whites' putative morality when she underscores an ethos of equality and generosity: "Be kind to all, both poor and rich, and feed all that come to your wigwam, and your name can be spoken of by every one far and near. Be kind to both bad and good, for you don't know your own heart." The Paiute have taught their children these customs "for many generations," she attests, concluding with a bald accusation: "I never in my life saw our children rude as I have seen white children and grown people in the streets" (51). Living in balance means respectful interrelationships, not only between human and nonhuman nature but also among persons. Winnemucca portrays Paiute domestic life to humanize her tribe as she attempts to acquire agency over traditional lands. The author's oblique, affective approach demonstrates her emotional intelligence, for "Domestic and Social Moralities" argues powerfully for independent land tenure and environmental justice.

CHAPTER 3, "Wars and Their Causes," features land wars, land loss, and resource deprivation, as Winnemucca exposes the consequences of ill-informed or malicious public policy. By placing it after the engaging account of Paiute domestic social and spiritual practices, Winnemucca invites greater sympathy. First she intimates the Paiute's displacement by white settlers, whose names and families she details, suggesting the size of the immigrant population. But she insists that "[a]ll these white people were loved by my people; we lived there together, and were as happy as could be" (59). The following section again implicitly disparages white norms, for she observes, "[M]y people had not learned to steal. We lived that way in peace for another year." Her sarcasm accumulates by the passage's conclusion: the Paiute traded horses for guns, "yet my people never said, 'We want you to give us something for our land.' Now, there were a great many of our white brothers everywhere through our country, and mines or farms here and there" (59). The narrative stresses both the harmony and peace enjoyed by the Indians and whites and the Paiute's willingness to share their land in an "ethical, balanced, and responsible" manner.[52]

Landownership ensures physical survival. Chapter 5 describes the "Reservation of Pyramid and Muddy Lakes," which is "at first sixty miles long and fifteen wide." Winnemucca highlights the area's beauty and the Indians' sole residency: "No white people lived there at the time it was given us." This resource-rich location initially afforded a good living: "We Piutes have always lived on the river, because out of those two lakes we caught beautiful mountain trout, weighing from two to twenty-five pounds each, which would give us a good income if we had it all, as at first. Since the railroad ran through in 1867, the white people have taken all the best part of the reservation from us, and one of the lakes also" (76). Echoing Jemison's attention to harmonious cultivation and social cooperation, Winnemucca anticipates Weaver's comment that "though land is the central focus of sovereignty and tenure, they also encompass fish, water, air, minerals, timber, game, plant life, and other resources."[53]

In the West, water is especially scarce. The environmental historian Donald Worster avers, "Control over water has again and again provided an effective means of consolidating power within human groups—led, that is, to the assertion by some people of power over others."[54] When they appropriate water, settlers engage in resource wars, as Winnemucca contends when she recounts her brother Natchez's troubles obtaining sufficient irrigation for his farm.[55] Questioning whether this restriction exemplifies public policy, she interjects, "This is the way we are treated by our white brothers. Is it that the government is cheated by its own agents who make these reports?" (77). White readers of conscience, she implies, must join with her to remedy this wrong.

But other resources are equally essential. Having superimposed an economic ethos upon the Paiute, whites appropriate the best natural resources and fail to deliver civilized ways to survive, such as a promised gristmill and sawmill. Their corruption ensures that the $25,000 appropriated for the purpose vanishes, and the Indians are left without lumber to build homes—having relinquished their traditional nomadism—and without means to obtain it: "My people do not own any timber land now. The white people are using the ditch which my people made [for the purpose of building the gristmill and sawmill] to irrigate their land" (77). Long before the acrimonious debate about the Hetch Hetchy Dam, Winnemucca understood that environmental justice requires public policy ensuring equitable resource distribution.[56]

By 1868 four hundred Paiutes were living at the C. F. Smith Army Camp, "taking care of themselves, but under many difficulties, and very destitute. There was no game in that region of any kind, except now and then a hare. They had no land to cultivate, but were living upon anything they could do or gather" (90). Another five hundred lived at Camp McDermitt, to which the first group was later transported. Winnemucca presents cooperation between whites and Indians: here the Indians help maintain themselves; her father requests ammunition and the men "go on hunting excursions in the summer, and bring in dried venison, rabbits, and what other game they could find," while the women "go out and gather grass-seed, and dig roots, and do what they could toward the supplies of next winter" (92). Citing the fairness and conscientiousness of the commanding officer, Colonel McElroy, she augments her credibility with white readers. McElroy supports families with necessary supplies out of his army budget, as well as "good bread,—for they actually baked good bread for them. . . . Every one had enough" (92).

Is her account strategic, we might ask, or is she genuine? In an evaluation that will surprise any viewer of old cavalry-and-Indian films, Winnemucca affirms a feeling that she reiterates repeatedly: "It is this generosity and this kind care and order and discipline that make me like the care of the army for my people" (92). Although she does not depict all army personnel positively, Winnemucca shows that many attempt to relieve the Paiute's suffering, which comes from greedy settlers, unethical individual Indians, corrupt Indian agents, and a remote and grasping federal government indifferent to Indian land claims.[57] Contradicting the contemporary environmental justice principle that opposes military occupation, *Life Among the Piutes* proposes an alternative view in which the military combats discriminatory public policy that fosters resource wars.

Such cooperation between whites and Indians was clearly *not* public policy, as Winnemucca reveals later. As the government slowly delivers more and more of the Paiute's reservation to whites, Winnemucca's father pleads to retain a good federal agent. At another reservation, Pyramid Lake, the Paiute are starving: "My people have nothing to live on there but what little fish they catch, and the best land is taken from them" (121–22).[58] Successive pages show white Indian agents, even the "good" Sam Parrish, consistently calling the Paiute's traditional home "government land." Again Winnemucca cultivates listeners' sympathy for land claims through direct sentimental appeals.[59] One much-cited example, in Powell's words demonstrating the author's "adeptness at negotiating Protestant Christian discourse,"[60] demands sustained attention:

> Oh, for shame! You who are educated by a Christian government in the art of war; the practice of whose profession makes you natural enemies of the savages, so called by you. Yes, you, who call yourselves the great civilization; you who have knelt upon Plymouth Rock, covenanting with God to make this land the home of the free and the home of the brave. Ah, then you rise from your bended knees and seizing the welcoming hands of those who are the owners of this land, which you are not, your carbines rise upon the bleak shore, and your so-called civilization sweeps inland from the ocean wave; but, oh, my God! leaving its pathway marked by crimson lines of blood, and strewed by the bones of two races, the inheritor and the invader; and I am crying out to you for justice,—yes, pleading for the far-off plains of the West, for the dusky mourner, whose tears of love are pleading for her husband, or for their children, who are sent far away from them. Your Christian minister will hold my people against their will; not because he loves them,—no, far from it,—but because it puts money in his pockets. (207)

Echoing early attacks on pseudo-Christians by Jemison, Sigourney, Wilson, and Jacobs, this oratory's most noteworthy feature, the author's indictment of Christian hypocrisy, challenges American nationalist rhetoric, for it is "a Christian government" that has educated settlers "in the art of war."

As they created America, supposedly "the home of the free and the home of the brave," the settlers broke a covenant with God. Winnemucca inscribes the traditional civilized/savage dichotomy to dispute both these terms and their directionality, and she "challenges the notion of white Christianity by naming God as her own—'oh, *my* God.'"[61] Invoking patriotism and virtue, Winnemucca scrutinizes the literal and conceptual foundations of American national identity at Plymouth Rock.

Infused with irony, the reference to "The Star-Spangled Banner" alludes to American independence after the Revolution and the War of 1812 while it stresses Native Americans' embattled situation vis-à-vis the federal government and its privileged white settlers. Violent language resonates throughout the passage. Winnemucca contextualizes bleak, unyielding images and pointed accusations within a sentimental plea aimed to produce shock, shame, and identification. Husbands are slaughtered, children separated from their families and sent to white boarding schools where they are forbidden to use their native languages and commanded to forget their nations' history. Via photographs and newspaper articles white readers would have been well informed about the western Indian wars and "Indian education," but the Indian outlook on these affairs would have been new. Bearing down hard, Winnemucca highlights the centuries-long conflict undergirding America's founding and development. At the same time that she echoes the biblical injunction that whites and Natives are all "of one blood," she pairs "the inheritor" and "the invader," thus probing the land's authentic ownership.[62] The passage as a whole exposes the centuries of laws and public policies that underwrite settlement and land theft. Winnemucca speaks truth to power in this impassioned passage that enlarges the concept of land to comprise citizenship, nationhood—American and Paiute—American geographical territory, and the imaginative, conceptual "land" understood so differently by Indians and whites.[63]

This complex representation of land—as concrete place, as means of sustenance, as source of conflict, as spiritual foundation, and as object and legal entity—resonates throughout the narrative. The author includes a letter from C. Shurtz, the U.S. secretary of the interior, that describes the Malheur Reservation as "their primeval home" and cites the allotment of "one hundred and sixty acres to each head of a family, and each adult male. Such lands they are to cultivate for their own benefit" (223–24). As was true for many tribes during the nineteenth century, the federal government intended that the Paiute, like many other Indian nations, relinquish their traditional lifeways and become sedentary farmers. But worse than whites imposing their legal standards of landownership and their traditions of best use is the government's indifference to physical survival; because wars have displaced them, the Paiute inhabit a wide area and, with winter well established, they are freezing and starving. When Winnemucca asks the secretary for food, he tells her to lead her people back to the Malheur Agency. She acidly observes, "Just think of my taking my people, who were already starving, to go three hundred miles through snow waist-deep" (224–25). The secretary may have an abstract appreciation of land, but he fails entirely to grasp the reality on the ground.

In the lengthy speech cited above the author clearly intends an affective response—anger, guilt, horror—but in addition she seeks corrective action, as the concluding petition, written by Winnemucca, advanced by a Massachusetts congressman, and advocated by editor Mary Mann, indicates. As Powell notes, "White audiences could gain 'salvation' through supporting Winnemucca's cause. And the way to justice was made easy—in the back of *Life Among the Piutes* there was a copy of her petition to Congress on behalf of the Paiutes."[64] Through her structure as well as her voice, the author thus underscores her book's central aim: influencing public policy. Recognizing the complex legal, economic, and political context in which her volume was published, Winnemucca states clearly what the Paiute want:

I, SARAH WINNEMUCCA HOPKINS, grand-daughter of Captain Truckee, who promised friendship for his tribe to General Fremont, whom he guided into California, and served through the Mexican war,—together with the undersigned friends who sympathize in the cause of my people,—do petition the Honorable Congress of the United States to restore to them said Malheur Reservation, which is well watered and timbered, and large enough to afford them homes and support for them all, where they can enjoy lands in severalty without losing their tribal relations, so essential to their happiness and good character, and where their citizenship, implied in this distribution of land, will defend them from the encroachments of the white settlers, so detrimental to their interest and their virtues. (247)

Like Jemison, she criticizes white settlers' introduction of vices, but their physical encroachment is her predominant concern. Her stance on political sovereignty is difficult to assess. She seeks legal ownership of Paiute land, even if that land is held in severalty (individually) rather than in common (collectively).[65] She acknowledges that natural resources, especially water, are fundamental to survival, and she argues for Paiute control. Ostensibly siding with white allies who encouraged allotment, she nevertheless emphasizes the necessity for continuing traditional "tribal relations."

Literacy, and the power to use the dominant society's language to seek defenders and gain redress, was as important to Winnemucca as it was to Wilson.[66] The petition concludes by coupling the language of sentiment— "And especially do we petition for the return of that portion of the tribe arbitrarily removed from the Malheur reservation . . . to the Yakima Reservation . . . in which removal families were ruthlessly separated, and have never ceased to pine for husbands, wives, and children"—with an objective accusation calibrated to provoke audience members' anger: this "restoration was pledged to them by the Secretary of the Interior in 1880, but has not been fulfilled" (247). Revealing such cruel and painful family separations would spark sympathy, but Winnemucca underlines the government's repeatedly broken promises in order to promote equitable public policy through action: readers should, she intimates, sign the petition to Congress. In attempting to retain some traditional Paiute lands and claiming the tribe's agency, Winnemucca battles for environmental justice.[67]

PAIUTE IDENTITY depended on land tenure partly because—as for the Cherokee and the Seneca—place and spiritual traditions were fundamentally interconnected. One of Winnemucca's most emotionally intelligent rhetorical weapons was her appeal to Christians. Because of the author's partial assimilation to white society and her Methodist faith, we cannot be certain how she intends her religious references, and context becomes crucial. Despite her direct pleas to Christians, *Life Among the Piutes* asserts Paiute spiritual sovereignty in several instances. On one occasion she explicitly contrasts traditional Paiute beliefs with Christianity. As a girl in California, she is frightened to illness when she hears "the Methodist minister say that everybody that did wrong was burned in hell forever" and that those in heaven see their friends burning and cannot help (54). But her mother contradicts this view, saying "that it was only here that people did wrong and were in the hell that it made, and that those that were in the Spirit-land saw us here and were sorry for us. But we should go to them when we died, where there was never any wrong-doing, and so no hell. That is our religion" (55). Like Jemison, Winnemucca indicts Christianity's deleterious effects on Native Americans, and she affirms Paiute religious ideas that appreciate the continuity between "Spirit-land" and the everyday world.

Elsewhere Winnemucca materializes—literally grounds—this continuity. When white settlers are rumored to be arriving on Paiute lands, her mother and aunt decide that they must protect their children from capture and perhaps cannibalism: "So they went to work and buried us, and told us if we heard any noise not to cry out, for if we did they would surely kill us and eat us. So our mothers buried me and my cousin, planted sage bushes over our faces to keep the sun from burning them, and there we were left all day" (11). The Paiute believe that the sage plant protects the children; sage features significantly in tribal medicine and ceremony, in particular, to spiritually clean or cure. Thus, as Elizabeth Wilkinson explains, the plant simultaneously prevents sunburn and hides the children from potentially dangerous whites; it also symbolizes the connection between the people and the land, demonstrating "a moment of resistance": "To maintain Piute land-based spirituality is to psychologically resist the white encroachment of Christianity."[68] This scene "shows the land and the people as one; as a child buried in the land with sage 'growing' out of her face, she becomes the land itself, and, because she is in and of the land, [it] saves her from being eaten." Intimating the sage's spiritual and physical protection, Winnemucca exceeds mere self-expression and participates in a ceremonial history that reconnects her with her people.[69]

As the episode develops, the author moves from description to emotion: "Oh, can any one imagine my feelings *buried alive*, thinking every minute that I was to be unburied and eaten up by the people that my grandfather loved so much? With my heart throbbing and not daring to breathe, we lay there all day. It seemed that the night would never come. Thanks be to God! the night came at last. Oh, how I cried and said, 'Oh father, have you forgotten me? Are you never coming for me?' I cried so I thought my very heartstrings would break" (12). For white readers, prospective advocates for and donors to the Paiute cause, the writer invokes a sentimental image: the endangered, possibly abandoned child whose heartrending pleas may go unanswered. But for Native readers the adult Winnemucca challenges "white settlers 'eating up' the land by displacing Piute people. . . . [She] resists her people being 'unburied' from their homeland and 'eaten up' by government peoples and policies."[70] That is, she fights for environmental justice.

The term *father* is ambiguous. When Winnemucca pleads not to be forgotten, does she refer to her father or grandfather? Or does she refer to God, echoing Christ's lament, "My God, my God, why hast Thou forsaken me?"[71] How ironic is this passage? Given her acerbic comments elsewhere and her people's mistreatment, I believe she clearly indicts Christianity, and Christians, for their predatory practices.[72] She concludes, "I was once buried alive; but my second burial shall be for ever, where no father or mother will come and dig me up. It shall not be with throbbing heart that I shall listen for coming footsteps. I shall be in the sweet rest of peace, — I, the chieftain's weary daughter" (12). Winnemucca represents herself not as a Christian God's daughter, nor as her individual father's, but as the child of a generic Paiute leader. Evoking her communal perspective and expressing her weariness, she foregrounds her struggle for Paiute lands as she envisions her identity, even in death, residing in the land itself.[73]

When the Paiute were forced out of their traditional homeland and moved to the Yakima (Yakama) Reservation in present-day Washington State, they faced political, social, and spiritual erasure; to them, removal was genocidal. Continuing to distinguish between community- and place-based spirituality and immoral Christian individualism, Winnemucca repeatedly connects Christians with cash.[74] Perhaps the most egregious example of white corruption occurs when the Paiute are removed to Yakima during the winter. The author recurs repeatedly to economic language. Their supposedly civilized agent, whom she ironically calls Father Wilbur, has no compassion, no Christian charity:

> Well, as I was saying, we were turned over to him as if we were so many horses or cattle. After he received us he had some of his civilized Indians come with their wagons to take us up to Fort Simcoe. They did not come because they loved us, or because they were Christians. No, they were just like all civilized people; they came to take us up there because they were to be paid for it. They had a kind of shed made to put us in. You know what kind of shed you make for your stock in winter time. It was of that kind. Oh, how we did suffer with cold. There was no wood, and the snow was waist-deep, and many died off just as cattle or horses do after travelling so long in the cold. (209–10)

Just as Wilson exposes Mrs. Bellmont's hypocritical Christianity, a faith that denies Frado heaven itself, Winnemucca presents "Father" Wilbur treating the Indians as he would treat "stock," transforming the Paiute into objects to be managed for financial gain. Here again she inverts civilized and savage in an affecting appeal that synthesizes sympathy with Christian ethics. As she has done in her depictions of violated girls and buried children, she promotes embodied reading in order to foster guilt, anger, and responsibility.

Her repeated references to *we* highlight how Winnemucca responded to whites' resource wars not merely as an individual but as a political intermediary; as a consequence, she came under fire from both sides. Defending herself from her community's accusations of betrayal, she distinguishes between her words and whites'. As Carpenter points out, "By translating whites' words but at the same time pointing out the distinction between those words and her own, she demonstrates the failed repetition: the (literal) white lie."[75] Like her contemporary Celia Thaxter, Winnemucca succeeded in influencing opinion, enlisting reformers Mann and her sister Elizabeth Palmer Peabody to help her organize lecture series, raise funds, lobby Congress, create a school with a Paiute-language curriculum, and gain relatively permanent reservation lands.[76] As she contended with discriminatory and dangerous public policy and U.S. law, Winnemucca understood that resource wars were waged not just for land but for identity itself.

LIFE AMONG THE PIUTES emerged in the context of renewed national movements by whites, often sponsored by white women, for Indian rights.[77] To some degree reprising earlier reform movements on behalf of America's indigenous peoples by white women like Sigourney, Lydia Maria Child, and Catharine Beecher—and "aggressively anti-reservation"—these groups promoted assimilation, this time through the profoundly damaging policy of land allotment.[78] As Powell wryly observes, "American discourses of imperialism in the form of anti-tribal pro-private property advocacy were seen as appropriate responses to the problems created by earlier American discourses of imperialism (i.e., Removal)."[79] Underwritten by Christian rhetoric that sought to convert the savage to civilization, such intervention contributed to the Dawes Allotment Act of 1887, with tragic consequences that included further land theft, exploitation of individual Indians, and loss of community identity.[80] Native Americans believed—and many still do—that such acts constituted declarations of war against sovereign nations and thus we should interpret narratives like Winnemucca's and Zitkala-Ša's as anticipating today's environmental justice movements' transnational scope.[81]

As Powell suggests, we should appreciate Winnemucca's performance in *Life Among the Piutes* as "based on an understanding of the discourses about Indians that circulated during the last decades of the nineteenth century and the expectations of the Indian reform groups that comprised Winnemucca's audience."[82] The author develops many emotionally intelligent rhetorical strategies to enlist white readers', especially women's, support. Through vivid representations of the Paiute's relationship to nature and their moral superiority, she asks readers to redefine civilized and savage. Struggling to obtain the fair treatment that the Paiute and all Native peoples deserve from whites and the federal government, she juxtaposes injustice with justice. Her direct addresses foster attention and engagement. She reclaims and reinvents sentimental rhetoric that reductively pronounces Indians to be children, and she invests readers in rescuing those whom she portrays, despite her own counterexample, as relatively helpless, voiceless, and exploited. At the same time, she rejects mainstream, sentimental concepts of femininity and depicts female agency. She generates shock and anger as well as sympathy, but she wants more: action toward informed public policy. Her more objective sketches of traditional, sustainable Paiute practices regarding nature implicitly contrast with white extractive economics. Calling on readers to become authentic Christians, evoking Biblical parallels, and using Biblical language, she attempts to transform Indian-white relations and to gain environmental justice for her people.

Writing against Wilderness:
María Amparo Ruiz de Burton's Civilized Cause

Just two years after Winnemucca published *Life Among the Piutes*, María Amparo Ruiz de Burton issued her own exposé of conditions in the western United States, this time from a Mexican American woman's standpoint. Negotiating with the uncivilized squatters determined to usurp his land and kill his cattle, Don Mariano Alamar, the eponymous hero of Ruiz de Burton's novel *The Squatter and the Don* (1885), addresses readers as a model citizen, forward-thinking, generous, and—unlike his interlocutors—prudent:

"The water is in the sea now, for there we let it go every year; but if we were sensible, judicious men, we would not let it go to waste—we would save it."[83] Ruiz de Burton deploys Don Mariano as a paradigmatic, civilized figure to argue for environmental justice for Mexican Americans in early California. Via her avatar's virtuoso rhetorical appeals to logic, emotion, and ethics, she addresses an audience whom she constructs as progressive, sympathetic, and elite. At the same time, the hero's regressive politics demonstrate her project's internal contradictions, which epitomize for today's readers some central challenges facing projects for social and environmental amelioration.

Taking seriously Waugh's admonition to synthesize the work of eco-critics and environmental justice advocates, we find that Ruiz de Burton's novel presents an exemplary and unsettling antecedent to contemporary debates; *The Squatter and the Don* analyzes "discriminatory public environmental policy" and reinvents "cultural representations of nature" in order to influence that policy.[84] Those representations borrow the rhetoric of the Vanishing American and obscure earlier Native American land claims that writers like Winnemucca so forcefully elaborate. Ruiz de Burton seeks environmental justice for a certain class of Californios, but unlike Winnemucca, she frames her account in fictional form, and, unlike her Paiute contemporary and many current environmental justice advocates, she enjoys a position of relative power and authority.[85] Her unique perspective requires a relatively detailed personal history.

Ruiz de Burton was born in 1832 in Baja California to an aristocratic, landholding military family in a Mexican nation shaped by colonial wars with Spain, the French occupation of Mexico, and an emergent American imperial power engaged in its own wars, including the Mexican-American War.[86] During that conflict, Ruiz de Burton's home came under attack, bringing with it a Vermonter, Captain Henry Burton, with whom Ruiz fell in love. When the war ended in 1848 with the Treaty of Guadalupe Hidalgo and Baja and Alta California were divided, the United States offered U.S. citizenship to Mexicans relocating north. Among the several hundred residents who accepted this arrangement, young Ruiz came north and married Burton.[87] The couple's denominational difference (she was Catholic, he Protestant) produced a stir among Californios—aristocratic Mexican landholders—but they were married in 1849, shortly after Ruiz's seventeenth birthday.

"LOS PENASQUITOS, RESIDENCE OF J. S. TAYLOR, SAN DIEGO CO. CAL.

Rancho de los Peñasquitos, from a drawing published in 1883. This rancho of more
than eight thousand acres was the first Mexican land grant in today's San Diego
County, granted to Francisco Ruiz, Ruiz de Burton's great-uncle. It was probably
similar to Ruiz de Burton's much larger Rancho Jamul. Today it is part of a
San Diego County park. Courtesy of the Library of Congress.

When Burton was assigned the San Diego command in 1852, the couple
purchased a large ranch nearby that would ultimately become the subject
of Ruiz de Burton's second novel, *The Squatter and the Don* (1885), which
delineated the contests over property held by Californios between about
1872 and 1885.[88] When the Civil War began, Burton was transferred east,
and Ruiz de Burton accompanied him with their two children, Nellie and
Henry Halleck. Living on the opposite coast, including Washington, D.C.,
gave Ruiz de Burton a skeptical view of the federal government and eastern white aristocracy; in 1872 she published the satirical novel *Who Would
Have Thought It?* exposing supposedly enlightened New Englanders' racism
and hypocrisy and Yankee politics' corruption and cronyism.[89] Troublingly
for today's readers, Ruiz de Burton insisted that elite Mexican Americans
deserved equal treatment because they were white, not Indian. Her editor
Beatrice Pita concedes that Ruiz de Burton was not without "deeply held
and not easily overcome class, racial, and patriarchal prejudices."[90] José F.
Aranda Jr. similarly cites her status as a "complex, aristocratic, educated,
and elitist white European creole," adding that this novel's publication with

the prominent Philadelphia firm of Lippincott "testifies to her access to the sources of Anglo cultural authority."[91]

Fluent in English, French, and Spanish, Ruiz de Burton began writing, like so many nineteenth-century American women writers, when her husband's 1869 death left her in straitened circumstances.[92] When she and her children returned to California, she discovered that part of their ranch had been sold to pay the family's debts, her landholdings were threatened, and squatters occupied large areas. As *The Squatter and the Don* underscores, although the Treaty of Guadalupe Hidalgo purportedly granted Californios citizenship and its accompanying rights, in 1851 Congress passed the California Land Act, which reneged on treaty conditions by obligating the verification of all land titles' legitimacy through a complicated, corrupt legal process that eventually stripped many Californios, among them Ruiz de Burton, of most or all of their holdings. Squatters were authorized to settle on the allegedly disputed property and establish their own claims.

The novel's racial stereotyping of Indians reveals both the class disparities in Ruiz de Burton's work and the contrast between Native Americans' and elite Mexican Americans' conceptions of land. Yet we should not summarily dismiss her point about land theft. Inveighing against the proposed law during congressional debate, Missouri senator Thomas Hart Benton asserted that its passage would be "perfectly equivalent to a general confiscation of landed property," concluding that it would be "more merciful at once to pass an act of general confiscation, so as to permit the people to go to work in some other way to obtain land, and to save the expenses, anxieties, and I believe I may say the horrors of going through three lawsuits for their property, and one of these lawsuits 3,000 miles from where they live."[93] Patricia Nelson Limerick's broader comment resonates here: "Largely as a consequence of the public lands and relations with conquered people, the West has proved a particularly illuminating case study in state power."[94]

Gender, as well as class, figured significantly in the novel's composition, because Ruiz de Burton emerged from a Spanish and Mexican system that assigned women important legal rights; as Lisbeth Haas explains, they had "the right to control their property and wealth and to litigate on questions related to their person, their families, and their holdings." As a consequence, "Californianas and Indian women had particular burdens as they negotiated more than one gender system in the American period. They were vulnerable as women in U.S. society, where women were not accorded equal status in law or custom, and they were vulnerable to the anti-Mexican prejudices of Anglo-American migrants."[95] Reflecting her Latina heritage, Ruiz de Burton eventually acted as her own counsel as she faced daunting obstacles to clear title to her half-million-acre homestead. Additionally, she engaged in numerous agricultural and commercial enterprises: "She ran cattle, as well as growing wheat and barley on the slopes. Castor beans were also raised, bringing sixty dollars an acre in 1874. The cattle were fed with the leaves and the beans were sold to a paint company. Even the hillsides covered with wildflowers were rented for beehives."[96] The author evinced considerable foresight regarding water conservation issues and the role that water access would play in San Diego's future, planning a large-scale project to supply all the city's needs. Although this ambitious scheme never came to fruition, Ruiz de Burton dammed her ravines to irrigate Rancho Jamul.[97] Although she pursued legal challenges in U.S. and Mexican courts for many years, Ruiz de Burton died without regaining title to all her holdings.

SINCE ROSAURA SÁNCHEZ and Beatrice Pita published their contemporary edition of *The Squatter and the Don* in 1992, Ruiz de Burton has enjoyed considerable critical attention. José F. Aranda Jr. discusses how the author, as an elite, complicates Chicano/a resistance theory. Additional scholarship has analyzed her genres, such as historical romance, while other readers address the writer's sophisticated rhetoric and her affective strategies.[98] Scholars such as Aranda, Sánchez, and Pita contend that "the central story told in *The Squatter and the Don* is not about the illegal dispossession of lands held by Californios but about corporate monopoly and political corruption."[99] Only one scholar, Priscilla Solis Ybarra, has sketched Ruiz de Burton's potential interest to ecocritics.[100] Yet her novel exposes for her contemporaries—and us—the challenges of gaining a particular form of environmental justice when individual, corporate, and governmental forces converge.

Claims that *The Squatter and the Don* represents an environmental justice text pose obstacles because the novel simultaneously affirms Californios' elite and oppressed status. But Ruiz de Burton's nearly forensic study of public policy argues, often explicitly, for agency, for minority populations' ability to decide how their land should be managed. It explores justice literally, by depicting corrupt U.S. court and legislative systems, and indirectly by examining personal morality. Finally, more than any other text in *Fallen Forests*, it articulates an ethic of sustainable, region-appropriate land uses determined by the property owners. Where Winnemucca pursues a secure and separate home, Ruiz de Burton seeks legal ownership and agency. She augments her arguments through representations of certain Mexican Americans as civilized human beings rather than as resources for consumption.

Ruiz de Burton's rhetorical strategies include fictional narrative in which characters, primarily the hero, ventriloquize the author's feelings, as well as direct, orally inflected addresses to readers. Writing against wilderness —and thus against certain mythic formulations of westernness—she highlights for us potential self-divisions that imperil effective change. Late nineteenth- and early twentieth-century environmental justice writers, especially privileged ethnic individuals such as Ruiz de Burton, help us to historicize and complicate our concepts. Appealing to multiple audiences, but principally the powerful Anglos who might exert effective influence on Californios' behalf, she combines stark realism, affecting sentimentalism, and bitter humor to repudiate the ethics of displacement and assert Mexican Americans' humanity, their Americanness, and their citizenship. At the same time, she scrutinizes what counts as justice, and for whom, in the new California.

A short plot summary will indicate the novel's conflicts. Mr. Darrell, a white squatter, is enlisted by other squatters to move to San Diego County to settle on the promising ranch of the major landholder, Don Mariano Alamar, whose title, Darrell has been (wrongly) informed, the local court system has rejected. Ruiz de Burton introduces various community members: Mrs. Darrell, who opposes taking land without payment; Clarence Darrell, Mr. Darrell's kind, educated, and responsible son; and Mercedes, Don Mariano's daughter, whom Clarence eventually marries. Ruiz de Burton directs readers' sympathies by constructing her characters in relatively polarized terms. Although the other squatters are greedy and coarse, Mr. Darrell seems upright, promising his wife that he will not usurp another man's property, but he adheres to the United States' legal definition of ownership rather than taking the moral high ground. Clarence, who, with Mercedes, symbolizes the next generation's potential for reconciliation, upholds a higher standard, believing that land belongs to its Californio owner until proven otherwise. Having made a fortune in stock speculation and mining, he secretly pays his future father-in-law for the land that his father and family occupy. Other primary characters are Don Mariano's neighbors, the Mechlins, especially George, the Mechlins' son, who travels to Washington to counter the squatters' efforts to invalidate the hero's property rights. As John Morán González observes, "Ruiz de Burton retraces the largely untold history of the Californios' dispossession, a collective history based on the disparate legal treatment of Californio citizens to the material advantage of white ones."[101]

The semifeudal seigneurial hacienda tradition informed Ruiz de Burton's representations of nature. In this system, an affluent, Spanish-descended owner controlled the land and oversaw an impoverished peasant community, often of Indian descent, who worked it.[102] The author attempts to enlist readers' backing by eliding ethnic differences and establishing (upper-) class commonality. In this context, agency, especially legal agency, preoccupies her. Don Mariano lacks control over his resources; he cannot prevent squatters from claiming his best property, and the laws that he describes render the Californios passive recipients of remote and uncertain justice. In chapter 2, "The Don's View of the Treaty of Guadalupe Hidalgo," we learn that William Darrell will soon arrive on the Alamar Ranch, bringing his family and other squatters. When his wife questions the ranch's status, Don Mariano replies that "[i]n the matter of our land, we have to await for the attorney general, at Washington, to decide" (17). The hero's, and the author's, restraint here bespeaks the Californios' rationality and invites her audience to share their cause.[103]

Not only has Congress passed laws favoring squatters by assuming faulty Mexican American land title, the newly formed state of California has enacted legislation virtually ensuring that settlers would co-opt Californio holdings.[104] When his future son-in-law, George Mechlin, asks, "Is there no law to punish the thieves who kill your cattle?" Don Mariano articulates the problem:

> There are some enactments so obviously intended to favor one class of citizens against another class, that to call them laws is an insult to law. . . . By those laws any man can come to my land, for instance, plant ten acres of grain, without any fence, and then catch my cattle

which, seeing the green grass without a fence, will go to eat it. Then he puts them in a "*corral*" and makes me pay damages and so much per head for keeping them, and costs of legal proceedings and many other trumped up expenses, until for such little fields of grain I may be obliged to pay thousands of dollars. Or, if the grain fields are large enough to bring more money by keeping the cattle away, then the settler shoots the cattle at any time without the least hesitation, only taking care that no one sees him in the act of firing upon the cattle. (18–19)

As John Ludeke declares, "The 1874 'No-Fence' law passed by the California legislature signaled a victory for the farmer over the cattleman and stands as a symbol of economic change . . . from cattle grazing to cultivation of the soil."[105] Under these provisions, cattle owners were required to corral their animals, an entirely infeasible proposition in desert areas, among them the arid southern California region where large holdings were necessary to sustain herds. Mexican American landowners had no legal recourse when squatters encroached; even more punishingly, they paid taxes on squatter-occupied land. As she confirms the situation's irrationality and excoriates discriminatory laws and public policy, Ruiz de Burton encourages readers' outrage for the Californios' diminished agency. Like Winnemucca, she anticipates the contemporary principle of environmental justice that "considers governmental acts of environmental injustice a violation of international law, the Universal Declaration on Human Rights, and the United Nations Convention on Genocide."[106]

The federal and state legislation that Ruiz de Burton censures clearly violates both the letter and the spirit of the Treaty of Guadalupe Hidalgo, for as Don Mariano tells George, "[T]he American nation pledged its honor to respect our land titles just the same as Mexico would have done." Greed underwrites this betrayal: "Unfortunately . . . the discovery of gold brought to California the riff-raff of the world, and with it a horde of land-sharks, all possessing the privilege of voting, and most of them coveting our lands, for which they very quickly began to clamor" (21). Recalling the opportunism and speculation that Kirkland deplores in Michigan, America's earlier west, Ruiz de Burton outlines how, despite government land being available, the new arrivals covet Mexican holdings; corrupt congressional representatives seeking squatters' votes declare that all California lands open for settlement are subject to an equally corrupt "land commission" that supposedly examines Californios' titles. Ruiz de Burton repeatedly emphasizes the injustice done to Californios, regularly quoting parts of the law.[107] Her "virtually professional exploitation of legal discourse" demonstrates her "deglamorizing the (legal) euphemisms by which the state sanctions its power"; in Anne Goldman's elegant phrasing, "[H]er protracted discussions of legal euphemism, evasion, and abstraction correspondingly tire readers expecting the pleasures of the deus ex machina rather than the pains of habeas corpus."[108]

Although Don Mariano lacks agency, he is dignified and law abiding, reflecting his elite class status and contrasting with the lawless, uncontrolled squatters. Melanie V. Dawson describes how Ruiz de Burton illustrates a range of emotional responses to injustice, including her hero's affective restraint.[109] The author attunes these responses to accord with characters' social power (or lack thereof) as well as to reach white audiences whom she ultimately, like Winnemucca, urges to intervene. Representing Don Mariano as an urbane, civilized advocate, Ruiz de Burton frequently aligns with his perspective, as she does when he tells Clarence, "I don't find it in my heart to blame those people [the squatters] for taking my land as much as I blame all the legislators who turned them loose upon me" (158).[110] She questions fairness, lawfulness, and national character: Don Mariano tells how the legislators "have not only caused me to suffer many outrages," but have also undermined "public morality" and have taught Americans "to lose all respect for their national honor. Because we, *the natives* of California, the Spano-Americans, were, at the close of the war with Mexico, left in the lap of the American nation, or, rather, huddled at her feet like motherless, helpless children, Congress *thought* we might as well be kicked and cuffed as treated kindly" (160; original emphasis). Forcefully assaulting the U.S. legal system with these sentimental images, Ruiz de Burton underscores the legislators' criminality and immorality and their hypocritical betrayal of American ideals. Informed readers, she implies, must respond accordingly.

This corruption extends beyond the government allowing squatters to appropriate Mexican American lands. Even worse, the author contends—paralleling contemporary environmental justice opposition to multinational corporations' destructive behavior—is corporate corruption and bribery, combined with Congress's participation in the railroads' multimillion-dollar land grab.[111] Ruiz de Burton cites the relevant legislation, followed by the narrator's remark, "Here follows a long recital of *frauds* perpetuated by Messrs. Leland Stanford, Huntington, Crocker and Hopkins, under that name of 'Central Pacific Railroad Company' and 'Contract and Finance Company,' etc." (205–6; original emphasis).[112] She concludes the recital with a single, bald paragraph: "The entire statement is a shameful exposure of disgraceful acts, any one of which, were it to be perpetrated by a poor man, would send him to the penitentiary" (206). Ruiz de Burton intermingles actual documents and fiction, contributing to the account's realism, but more importantly she drops the narrative veil, asserting that she is not merely producing a fiction, she is unmasking an actual injustice. Like Winnemucca's direct addresses (as in the "for shame" oratory), such interventions demand that readers take action.[113]

Ruiz de Burton literalizes justice when she depicts the legal system and Californios', and certain San Diegans', lack of agency. "The Fashion of Justice in San Diego" imagines the Goddess of Justice with "bandaged" eyes and "begrimed and soiled" "white robes." Ruiz de Burton's narrator asks angrily, "Who is the poor litigant that would dare arraign an unjust Judge, well sheltered in his judicial ermine, and the entire profession ready to champion him?" (366). Deploring how a particular San Diego jurist wields his power to advance a friend in a congressional race, she highlights how this friendship, coupled with legal chicanery, dispossesses a grieving widow and family of her home: "The answer to Mrs. Mechlin's complaint was a masterpiece of unblushing effrontery that plainly showed it had originated in a brain where brazen falsehoods and other indecencies thrived like water-reptiles growing huge and luxuriating in slimy swamps" (375). The hybrid text incorporates a court document to substantiate this claim. Revealing the author's own voice, Ruiz de Burton's angry hyperbole represents the judicial system and its participants as part of a corrupt wilderness, and she encourages civilized readers to share in her anger and invest in her cause. More than a legal concept, justice forms *The Squatter and the Don*'s ethical center.[114] Legislation provides no guarantee of justice; the reverse is more often accurate. But principled entreaties to corrupt individuals likewise fail. Railroad tycoon Leland Stanford's ethic of profit at all costs—invulnerable to every method of rhetorical appeal—reprises an uncivilized, Wild West morality that Ruiz de Burton repudiates.

THE POLITICAL-LEGAL SYSTEM, minority landownership, and the owners' agency—or helplessness—form central narrative concerns in *The Squatter and the Don*. But the novel addresses environmental justice issues still more concretely, in terms that both her contemporaries and today's readers would recognize and—sometimes—applaud. The California fence laws were passed partly because legislators championed farmers over ranchers. When George Mechlin asks Don Mariano if the cattle owners could not seek legislative action to protect their property, the latter illuminates the underlying ethnic motivations:

> It could be done, perhaps, if our positions were reversed, and the Spanish people—"*the natives*"—were the planters of the grain fields, and the Americans were the owners of the cattle. But as we, the Spaniards, are the owners of the Spanish—or Mexican—land grants and also the owners of the cattle ranchos, our State legislators will not make any law to protect cattle. They make laws "*to protect agriculture*" (they say proudly), which means to drive to the wall all owners of cattle ranchos. . . . [They aim] ostensibly "to protect agriculture," but in reality to destroy cattle and ruin the native Californians. (19; original emphasis)

Who counts as native and what that term expresses for the author are clear. Ruiz de Burton quotes the law itself later, noting precisely its date and discussing its theoretical and practical effects. If, ironically, Don Mariano's cattle were Mexican longhorns, well adapted to harsh and arid conditions, the farmers would have tried "to protect agriculture" yet more aggressively, since these cattle had a reputation for toughness, independence, and the ability "to take care of themselves and their young in the tough company of coyotes, wolves, lions, and grizzlies."[115]

By enacting such unjust laws, the author suggests, legislators ignore the land's best natural uses. Don Mariano's initial meeting with the squatters sketches him confronting the conflict between agriculture and ranching, as Ruiz de Burton critiques public policy via her representations of nature. In offering the squatters their own land and assistance developing ranches, Don Mariano attempts to envision a sustainable land management plan for San Diego County.[116] Although he appeals to their greed, he articulates a civilized land-use ethic that will assure everyone long-term prosperity. This stewardship ethic, as Vincent Pérez observes, invokes the diversity of the hacienda system—"a Mexican agrarian (colonial) past."[117] This history has given Californios valuable knowledge of the land and local ecosystem; thus Don Mariano stresses the region's erratic rainfall and presses the squatters to take a sustainable approach: "It is a mistake to try to make San Diego County a grain-producing county. It is not so, and I feel certain it never will be, to any great extent. This country is, and has been and will be always, a good grazing county—one of the best counties for cattle-raising on this coast, and the very best for fruit-raising on the face of the earth. God intended it should be. Why, then, not devote your time, your labor and your money to raising vineyards, fruits and cattle, instead of trusting to the uncertain rains to give you grain crops?" (52).

Evoking divinely authorized stewardship not incompatible with twenty-first-century Christian ecology, Ruiz de Burton's argument would have resonated with her peers, both Anglo and Latino, because the concrete situation for San Diego and California agriculture was tenuous. Although droughts were frequent earlier occurrences, in the novel's 1870s time frame particularly grim conditions meant that some regions lost huge proportions of their cattle. In 1870 and 1872, nearly one-fourth of southern California herds perished, 1873 was another dry year, and in 1876–77 "the San Joaquin Valley and the south central coast areas were devastated." Beginning in the early 1870s, Texas fever threatened to further devastate cattlemen's herds.[118]

The squatters' response privileges short-term profit over long-term prosperity; fruit trees need time to root. But Don Mariano proposes a solution: selling them cattle interest-free with a four- or five-year payback, by which time the orchard ventures would be profitable. He generously offers each squatter a quitclaim deed to his holding—160 acres per family—if they accept his plan, requiring merely that they fence their orchards and vineyards to protect his cattle. He confronts their skepticism with faith in San Diego County's fruitfulness, citing the "superior quality" of "our figs, oranges, apricots, and . . . all semi-tropical fruits" and affirming that "an orchard of forty acres or vineyard of twenty will pay better after three years' growth than one hundred and sixty acres of wheat or barley in good seasons, and more than three hundred acres of any grain in moderately good seasons, or one thousand acres in bad seasons" (54). Reemphasizing the proper use of natural resources, he explains that, unlike grain in large fields, young fruit trees could be irrigated and that after they were established, they would not need additional water. California readers would have nodded in acknowledgment when Don Mariano reminds his interlocutors that "the bad seasons were [all over California], and only in a few places, moderately good crops were harvested; in the southern counties none at all. We had rains enough to get sufficiently good grazing, but not to raise grain" (56). Practical and realistic, the intelligent and ostensibly enlightened Don Mariano thus represents the author's persuasive, civilized avatar. Democratizing landownership and providing agency over resources, his solutions are attractive both for Ruiz de Burton's contemporaries and for current advocates of sustainability and environmental justice.

As Winnemucca similarly indicates, water resources provoked conflicts in the western United States; this blue gold shaped the area's development and will determine its future. The San Diego area occupies a coastal strip typically receiving ten to thirteen inches of rain annually; in the foothills, rainfall is normally seventeen inches, while "in the higher mountains, it might be as much as forty-five inches a year."[119] Paralleling Ruiz de Burton's own foresight, Don Mariano creates a plan for building reservoirs to prevent wasted rainfall, agreeing to pay for half the expense (54–55). A conservationist rather than a preservationist, he again urges proper land usage: "Believe me, it will be a great God-send to have a thriving, fruit-growing business in our county. To have the cultivated land well fenced, and the remainder left out for grazing. Then there would not be so many thousands of useless acres as now have to be. . . . Is it not a pity to impoverish our county by making the bulk of its land useless? The foolishness of letting all of the rainfall go to waste, is an old time folly with us" (55). His focus on agricultural productivity conveys a concept of progress that would have been familiar to Ruiz de Burton's eastern audience; as we shall see, it has ethnic resonances. Showing the squatters' resistance, which culminates in tragedy for animals, humans, and the land, the author summons readers — whom she constructs as thoughtful, forward thinking, and informed and who would be well aware of actual conditions on the ground — to help advance her cause. Far from wilderness, she promises a fruitful, farmed state.

THUS FAR I HAVE referred to *The Squatter and the Don* as a novel, but this choice is dictated mostly by convenience. Genre, particularly Ruiz de

Burton's response to pastoral, frames environmental justice and ecocritical considerations.[120] Dawson foregrounds how the novel lacks actual scenery: "Rather than allow the alluring landscape to serve as a means of justifying material ambitions, Ruiz de Burton replaces imperialist descriptions of the land with a language of feeling."[121] Revisiting the definition of pastoral as "all literature that celebrates an ethos of rurality or nature or wilderness over against an ethos of metropolitanism," we should ask how it connects here to herding and contemplative escape.[122]

Ironically, *The Squatter and the Don* rejects traditional pastoral in virtually every respect, for its cattle herding references economics rather than spirituality or pleasurable retreat.[123] Ruiz de Burton takes far more delight in recounting sophisticated indoor activities than actual tending of cattle: such activities are left to vaqueros and Indians. When squatter Mathews protests that he cannot manage cattle ranching, Don Mariano replies, "You will not have to be a vaquero. I don't go '*busquering*' around *lassoing*, unless I wish to do so. . . . You can hire an Indian boy to do that part. They know how to handle *la reata* and *echar el laso* to perfection" (56). The novel's most detailed account of herding merely gestures toward pastoral, portraying a drive under duress to Clarence's property. Ruiz de Burton gives a single paragraph interlude: "A good day's journey was made that day, and night overtook them as they descended into a small valley, which seemed to invite them to rest within its pretty circumference of well-wooded mountain slopes, from which merry little brooks ran singing and went to hide their music among the tall grasses that grew in rank solitude" (325). Self-conscious and barely rescued from preciousness by its concluding words, this passage forecloses nearly all the book's pastoral possibility.[124] By midnight the bucolic dream has turned nightmarish, with a storm that awakens Don Mariano, who rightly fears that the snow "will be a winding-sheet for my poor cattle" (326).

In contrast to this eclipsed pastoral, Ruiz de Burton luxuriates in long legal discourses, family encounters, and domestic details such as the visit by the Alamar sisters Elvira and Mercedes to the Mechlins' east coast "cottage." Mrs. Mechlin relishes the sartorial pleasures available to her young visitors: "We will order some summer things to be made immediately. But I feel quite sure that we can find some imported dresses ready made that will suit. I saw some lovely batists [*sic*] and grenadines at Arnold & Constable's, just from Paris, also beautifully embroidered muslins at Stewart's" (180).

Just as Thaxter's fashionistas demand fashionable millinery, these heroines expect style and beauty. Situated in Long Branch, New Jersey, the cottage symbolizes the Mechlins' wealth and social status, for the historic beach community was the resort of U.S. presidents and power brokers.[125] Many miles separate the Californias' luxury and the involuntary simplicity of Jewett's Bray girls or Freeman's elderly Babcock sisters. Even the voluntary simplicity of Thaxter's ethical, "beautifully unadorned" women is foreign to Ruiz de Burton's privileged ladies.

Ruiz de Burton conjoins Long Branch with New York, Saratoga, Washington, and Newport: "The Mechlin villa, shaded by tall elms and poplars, and surrounded by shrubbery and flowers, with a beautiful lawn and fountains in front, facing the ocean, and well-kept walks and arbors in different places on the grounds, was certainly a charming abode, fit to please the most fastidious taste" (181). Although Mercedes ultimately returns to her family, Clarence, and California, Ruiz de Burton develops an alluring account of the eastern high society life with which she was intimately familiar. In this environment, money enables the Californias to enjoy a detached, appreciative spectatorship of nature, a distance that guarantees (disembodied) female respectability.[126] Scarcely pastoral, such lifestyles demanded huge fortunes and armies of servants and gardeners. Ruiz de Burton's rendering emphasizes the Californias' civilized status, their ease in America's highest social circles. Nature signifies a refuge and amusement but not a cause—or, as it is for Freeman's Shattuck sisters, a source of tangible and transcendental well-being. If the estates of the eastern elite denote pastoral, it is indeed tamed, domesticated.

Genre matters, since claiming *The Squatter and the Don* as an environmental justice narrative requires that we acknowledge its gendered affiliations with urbanism and cosmopolitanism as necessary substitutes for pastoralism; it departs dramatically from more nature-focused contemporaries and successors, including *Life Among the Piutes*, *Ramona*, and Gertrude Atherton's *The Californians*.[127] Dawson believes that the author's refusal "to treat the landscape with detailed attention" inhibits readers' "desire for possession" of that landscape, that "the novel's avoidance of the scenic California vista . . . makes it impossible to attach a hospitable or comforting dimension to material realities."[128] But the text is actually quite attached to certain material realities, which encompass, especially for its women characters—and readers—the pleasures of Long Branch and Newport. What it circumvents is the economic basis for those pleasures: the wealth that comes from unchallenged landownership, agency over that property, and the physical labor, like Wilson's and Berbineau's, that underwrites comfort. Thus the story avoids landscape—and pastoral—not to forestall readers' desires to possess that landscape but because the author rejects associations between Mexican Americans and nature. This intention seems particularly pertinent given the novel's elision of the Californias' embodiment; Ruiz de Burton sketches her respectable Mexican American heroines as lovely and even fun-loving but always chaste, obedient, and cultured: civilized, never savage. In this sense, she reinvents the West as feminine and marries it to eastern order.[129]

WE SHOULD FINALLY reconsider Ruiz de Burton's complex perspective and its relation to contemporary environmental justice concerns, for this perspective determines how she represents character—in both senses. Unlike Winnemucca (or Jemison, Ward, Jacobs, and Wilson), who came from an economically marginalized community, Ruiz de Burton enjoys family and personal connections that comprise Mrs. Abraham Lincoln and Mrs. Jefferson Davis, bespeaking her adjacency to the core of American power.[130] As Aranda remarks, "[S]he is not a Dolores Huerta of the United Farm Workers Union or a Gloria Anzaldúa of the borderlands in nineteenth-century clothes."[131] Moreover, unlike Winnemucca, Jemison, and Ward, who conceptualize their and their nations' identities in relation to place, she comprehends land within a seigneurial hacienda tradition that valued property's productive possibilities. Although family connections certainly affected Ruiz de Burton, economic imperatives figured significantly, perhaps more significantly, and she was an ardent capitalist.[132] Her novel depicts her hero's exploitation of Indian and mestizo labor to subsidize his family's aristocratic lifestyle. Unlike Our Nig, which promotes class-based environmental justice, The Squatter and the Don furthers elites' interests. Ruiz de Burton's justice, moreover, elides the claims of California's Native Americans, whose population declined by more than one hundred thousand in the two decades following the Treaty of Guadalupe Hidalgo.[133] Citing that treaty, Timothy Deines observes of Article XI that "[h]ere,

'Indian' simply represents the *savage* condition of possibility for the *civilized* political recognition of Mexicans as persons capable of owning property, among other rights and liberties" (original emphasis).[134]

As Aranda points out, "The critiques and contradictions that surface in [Ruiz de Burton's and her peers'] writings about U.S. colonialism do so not from newly subordinated subject positions but from enraged and embittered equals who in losing the material trappings of elite society resort to words to set the record straight on the Colossus of the North."[135] Notwithstanding the text's elitism, we should take seriously Rosaura Sánchez's contention: "Although [the] novel represents an aggressive attempt to speak for the Californio and Mexicano collectivity, her struggle is more inclusive, and her work attempts to speak for all 'citizens,' Californios as well as those subject to domination by monopolies and to deception by corrupt legislatures and Congress."[136] Reading Ruiz de Burton's novel thus obliges twenty-first-century readers to complicate how we understand environmental justice and to assess various minoritized communities' interlocking—and sometimes competing—rights.

Recognizing Ruiz de Burton's hierarchical views, we can furthermore read *The Squatter and the Don*'s environmental justice thrust as a rejection of *human* pollution. Squatters appear in an almost uniformly negative light, as types of savages. Immoral, uneducated, greedy, and illiterate, they contaminate and threaten the Alamar land, family, and way of life. As the squatters consider Don Mariano's proposal to share his cattle and land, they engage in coarse conversation. In contrast, the Alamar men "look like Englishmen" (49), and they have gentlemen's deportment; like their female counterparts, they are entirely respectable. When Miller rudely announces his early departure to collect his milk cows before dark, Ruiz de Burton intimates Don Mariano's intelligence, refinement, and good humor through his reply: "Exactly, we want to look after our cows, too." As she advances her satire, Ruiz de Burton underscores the hero's wit in moving from milk cows to the contested issue of beef cattle: "All saw the fine irony of the rejoinder, and laughed heartily. Miller scratched his ear, as if he had felt the retort there, knowing well, that with the exception of Mathews and Gasbang, he had killed and '*corraled*' more of the Don's cattle than any other settler" (51). The author's urbane humor compares with Kirkland's as the latter encounters rough western settlers. But unlike Kirkland, whose satire often contains affectionate elements, Ruiz de Burton sees no redeeming qualities in the interlopers on the Alamar ranch. Here environmental justice means ridding the land of the unrespectable squatters' polluting and declassing influence.

Soliciting readers' alliances with the Californios, Ruiz de Burton places them—and us—in a disturbing position vis-à-vis her less privileged characters, whether Mexican American, Native American, or Anglo. *The Squatter and the Don* sidesteps the long-disputed history of western land tenure. González outlines how the ranchero economy demanded indentured Indian labor and how, after the Treaty of Guadalupe Hidalgo—and ultimately joined by Anglos—Californios ensured cheap labor: they endorsed laws that blocked Indian citizenship and maintained their affiliation with privileged whiteness.[137] Ruiz de Burton repeatedly distinguishes Mexican American elites from disgusting squatters. Landownership, and thus agency, depends on concepts of waste that metonymically associate property and people. Don Mariano explains the land-grab history to Clarence:

> The cry was raised that our land grants were too large; that a few, lazy, thriftless, ignorant natives, holding such large tracts of land, would be a hindrance to the prosperity of the State, because such lazy people would never cultivate their lands, and were even too sluggish to sell them. . . . The settlers want the land of the lazy, the thriftless Spaniards. Such good-for-nothing, helpless wretches are not fit to own such lordly tracts of land. It was wicked to tolerate the waste, the extravagance of the Mexican Government, in giving such large tracts of land to a few individuals. The American Government never could have been, or ever could be, guilty of such thing. No, never! (161)

Deeply ironic, the passage conjures the "Americans'" fallacious conflation of "the lazy, thriftless" Mexicans with similarly stereotyped Indians.[138] Ruiz de Burton reinforces the point when Victoriano reminds a servant to tend his horses: "'Yes, *patroncito*, I'll do it right away,' said the lazy Indian, who first had to stretch himself and yawn several times, then hunt up tobacco and cigarette paper, and smoke his cigarette. This done, he, having had a heavy supper, shuffled lazily to the front of the house" (296). Ruiz de Burton lards on qualifiers that foreground the shiftless Indian, subtly invoking African American stereotypes as well. Elsewhere she makes explicit the dominant society's perception that "the native Spaniards are lazy and stupid and thriftless" (396). Don Mariano's speech additionally ventriloquizes white Americans' hypocritical outrage about ostensibly unused—and, it is insinuated, empty—land, a rationale historically used to dispossess Native Americans, whose ownership history remains unnarrated in *The Squatter and the Don*.[139] The earlier argument about productive land bespeaks these associations, obliquely indicating the Californios' efforts to civilize the wilderness.

Ironically, in light of her apparent contempt for Native Americans, Ruiz de Burton deploys an image that aligns her Californio elites with them: the Vanishing American.[140] The author harnesses romantic, emotional rhetoric that had for many decades elaborated narratives of Indian, not Mexican, disappearance, and she piggybacks on Indians' claims for justice. A new kind of endangered species, the elite Californios could benefit from this association without necessarily enduring its most negative consequences. This connection appears particularly canny when we acknowledge the profound religious difference between Ruiz de Burton's Catholic and (presumably) Protestant romantic pairings. Despite the romance in her own life story—reportedly inspiring the ballad "The Maid of Monterey"—the reality on the ground would have been more problematic for ordinary Californians or, for that matter, Americans elsewhere.[141] By downplaying religion—though one chapter title incorporates the word *Christian*, it appears just twice more, and *Catholic* appears on merely three pages—Ruiz de Burton negotiates tactfully between readers of different denominations.

Unlike *Life Among the Piutes* or Helen Hunt Jackson's *Ramona*, *The Squatter and the Don*'s impact appears to have been modest in the centers of eastern power, although it attracted an avid western audience. Finally, it advocates justice for vulnerable Mexican Americans both by exposing unjust laws and inequitable public policy and by representing civilized character(s). Ruiz de Burton formulates a new, composite, elite Californian identity that resists Californios' "vanishing." This privileged, hybrid identity is, she insists through her interethnic romances, the only tenable, and perhaps just, route to a future state (in both senses) of concord. To achieve this end, she converts the contested West into a civilized, affluent California bride.

WHO SHOULD have agency, who counts as a person, and who counts as a citizen are questions that *The Squatter and the Don* repeatedly requires readers to consider. If environmental justice means understanding group disadvantage and advocating political and legal solutions, Ruiz de Burton's novel merits the label, ending with Doña Josepha's plea for truth, justice, and corrective action on behalf of its Mexican American landowners.[142] Yet the author's characters and rhetoric ask audience members to identify with the novel's Californio elites, and the book's diminishment of working Mexican Americans and Native Americans offends and burdens twenty-first-century readers. We might grant that ethnic and gender stereotypes virtually compelled Ruiz de Burton to write against wilderness, especially as she envisaged solving ethnic (and legal) conflicts via marriage. Her novel nevertheless obligates us to face some challenging questions, such as: Can only "practical and realistic, intelligent and progressive" figures—as I have described Don Mariano above—represent the environmental justice movement? How can they do so if they incorporate class bias and/or racism? Who is best situated to argue effectively for environmental equity? Contemporary analyses of environmental justice and ecocriticism can benefit by examining vexed projects such as Ruiz de Burton's, which illuminates for us the challenges of alliances, the complexity of identity analysis, and the heterogeneity of communities that we may conceptualize too narrowly. Ruiz de Burton's rhetorical tactics, including sentimentalism, affective restraint, humor, and anger, urge educated, elite readers to take up Californios', and sometimes San Diegans', cause. Within this historical and literary framework, environmental justice acquires a decidedly different resonance.

"A Kinship to Any and All": Zitkala-Ša's Resourceful Rhetoric

Assessing the results of a 1918 conference of the Society of American Indians in the *American Indian Magazine*, Zitkala-Ša highlights the disparity between American ideals and reality in light of World War I: "American Indians are watching democracy, baptized in fire and blood overseas. They are watching the christening with mingled feelings of deepest concern,—the thing lies so close to their hearts it is difficult to give it expression. Indian soldiers lie dead on European battlefields, having intermingled their blood with that of every other race in the supreme sacrifice for an ideal." The next paragraph heightens the rhetoric: "Surely, the flaming shafts of light typifying political and legal equality and justice,—government by the people, now penetrating the dark cloud of Europe are a continuous

"Educating the Indians—a Female Pupil of the
Government School at Carlisle Visits Her Home at
Pine Ridge Agency." *Frank Leslie's Illustrated Newspaper*,
15 March 1884. Courtesy of the Library of Congress.

revelation. The light grows more effulgent, emanating as it does from the greatest of democracies,—America."[143] The triumphant language invites questions: Is Zitkala-Ša serious or satirical? Both? Her tone is unclear, but the dark and light imagery pointing toward Christian salvation culminates with the passage's conclusion: "The sunburst of democratic ideals cannot bring new hope and courage to the small people of the earth without reaching the remotest corners within America's own bounds." The author alludes to Lincoln's Gettysburg Address, perhaps hoping to inspire her dual audience—

educated Indians and sympathetic whites—to help her realize an indigenous vision of "democratic ideals." As P. Jane Hafen (Taos Pueblo) observes, the author's "published works were sentimental, lyrical, and often attuned to her audience of mainstream Americans, whom she hoped to educate about American Indian issues."[144]

Zitkala-Ša's writing career, encompassing literary essays and stories in America's most prestigious periodicals, the *Atlantic Monthly* and *Harper's*, extended to activist journalism. The author sought equality and justice for Native Americans, but like Winnemucca and (in a different way) Ruiz de Burton, she created an ambiguous legacy. On the one hand, she dedicated her life to helping Indians gain access to education and economic resources, and she promoted efforts to obtain Native sovereignty. But even as she celebrated traditional intellectual and spiritual beliefs—explaining, in one prominent essay, "Why I Am a Pagan"—she undercut those efforts toward sovereignty with her anti-peyote stance, testifying against peyote use in Congress. As James Cox contends, "[H]er relationship to both Native and non-Native cultural and intellectual traditions was a constant negotiation characterized by many shifts between acceptance of, resistance to, and compromise with those traditions."[145] Hafen maintains that, despite the writer's embrace of many of the dominant culture's ideologies, "she remained firmly committed to her tribal sovereignty" and argues that she "impeaches the dominant culture with its own tools and . . . appeals emotionally for recognition of her Indian voice."[146] Her rhetorical strategies and personal example offer powerful models for today's activists fighting resource wars, fostering Native agency, and seeking environmental justice.

With formal education at such institutions as White's Manual Labor Institute (a Quaker-run boarding school in Indiana) and Earlham College, Zitkala-Ša (Gertrude Bonnin) was born in America's centennial year, the daughter of a full-blooded Sioux mother and a white father whom she never met. She worked as a teacher at the Carlisle Indian Industrial School in Pennsylvania from 1897 to 1899.[147] As a Boston Conservatory of Music student between 1899 and 1901, she visited Paris in 1900, where she performed as a violin soloist for Carlisle. Oddly, as Ruth Spack notes, she had just published her *Atlantic* essays, which revealed her dislocation and criticism of the school, much to the dismay of Carlisle's leaders, who publicly attacked her work and privately derided the author.[148] After serving as a clerk on the Standing Rock Reservation in the Dakotas, Zitkala-Ša married the Sioux activist Ray Bonnin. The pair moved to the Uintah and Ouray Reservation in Utah, where for many years they engaged in activist efforts, seeking land settlements and negotiating with government officials. Having been elected the secretary-treasurer of the Society of American Indians (SAI) in 1916, she moved with her husband to Washington, D.C., where she eventually became the editor of the SAI's *American Indian Magazine*.[149]

Zitkala-Ša exploded on the mainstream literary scene with three fictionalized autobiographical narratives in the *Atlantic Monthly*.[150] "Impressions of an Indian Childhood," "The School Days of an Indian Girl," and "An Indian Teacher among Indians" collectively introduced the *Atlantic*'s affluent eastern white readers to her western childhood, Sioux traditions, and outsider's perspective on the dominant society, especially its Christian norms.[151] Zitkala-Ša's literary work has been the subject of numerous essays and book chapters, which address issues ranging from her social intermediation to her analysis of gender and her powerful rhetoric; almost none of the scholarship on her writing has considered her oeuvre in an ecocritical context.[152] But her *Atlantic* pieces, short fiction, essays in periodicals such as the *American Indian Magazine*, and, especially, her later coauthored publication, *Oklahoma's Poor Rich Indians: An Orgy of Graft and Exploitation of the Five Civilized Tribes, Legalized Robbery*, range from tactful briefs to forceful, overt testimony for environmental justice. Using gendered rhetorical strategies, Zitkala-Ša's contributions encompass several modes and genres. Her earliest work, personal narratives for a principally white audience, issue relatively indirect argument; addressing educated Indians and sympathetic whites, her journalism of the 1910s speaks more directly; and the exposé in *Oklahoma's Poor Rich Indians* reveals harsh realities for an audience of powerful U.S. elites. These diverse forms cohere and their arguments gain authority from her affective rhetoric, her representations of nature, and her sustained, analytical critique of public and government policy.

ALTHOUGH ITS OUTLOOK is pan-Indian, Zitkala-Ša's writing articulates a specifically Sioux ethos. Elizabeth Cook-Lynn (Crow Creek Sioux) stresses that the Sioux valorize the "continuous overtracing of personal histories within the *tiospaye* concept (defined as a societal/cultural/tribal organizational construct), which is based upon blood and ancestral ties and lineage." Cook-Lynn foregrounds "the *tiospaye* concept *as a nationalistic*

forum for the people" (original emphasis): "the appropriate interpretation of traditional literatures suggests that nationalism is a major reason for their existence." Such literatures hence form the "foundations for native political insight and action."[153] Paralleling this insight, Jeffrey Myers points out that for Zitkala-Ša "to preserve her culture—and by extension all Native American cultures, which as a pan-Indian advocate was her explicit political cause—Zitkala-Ša must argue for the preservation of the land that her culture holds sovereign and sacred."[154] Reading Zitkala-Ša, then, we must remember that even writing that (from a western standpoint) appears to be personal has larger political implications.[155]

Zitkala-Ša's work particularly emphasized American Indian women. Ruth Spack reminds us that U.S. government–sponsored anthropologists imparted most of the information about Native Americans available to the author's contemporaries; virtually all these researchers were male and received their information from a male elder through a translator. The dominant disciplinary paradigm separated groups into civilized and primitive, and the anthropologists placed American Indians in the latter category. As we have seen, Winnemucca's enemies constructed her as a squaw, who supposedly symbolized savagery, drunkenness, and lasciviousness. But the princess/squaw stereotypes of American Indian women predominant since settlers' arrival in the New World continued well into the twentieth century.[156] Responding to these images, Zitkala-Ša humanizes her Native women through carefully modulated syntheses of personal and others' experiences that allowed the writer an expressiveness possibly intended to counter anthropologists' supposedly objective outsider accounts.[157] The first three *Atlantic* essays, ostensibly romantic views of tribal life, encompass the author's childhood, removal to a white-run school, and position as an Indian teacher in the government-subsidized Carlisle. Countering male scientists' descriptions, these engaging essays establish an insider's corrective outlook, critical of the dominant society but presented in emotionally intelligent ways that render the harsh appraisal more palatable to white—especially female—readers.[158]

"Impressions of an Indian Childhood" opens with a section titled "My Mother," which provides a pastoral glimpse of Zitkala-Ša's childhood home that elicited—and rebutted—eastern audiences' expectations about the Wild West and its ostensibly uncivilized inhabitants: "A wigwam of weather-stained canvas stood at the base of some irregularly ascending hills. A footpath wound its way gently down the sloping land till it reached the broad river bottom." Zitkala-Ša suspends the elegiac tone as she portrays work—gathering water three times a day "from the muddy stream" of the Missouri River. This account combats the stereotype of Indian women as beasts of burden, for, as Spack avers, water gathering "is shown to be an activity of high status, to which a young girl can aspire."[159] The plangent mood resumes as the author accompanies her mother on these journeys and observes her carefully: "Often she was sad and silent, at which times her full arched lips were compressed into hard and bitter lines, and shadows fell under her black eyes." Begging her mother to disclose the reasons for her sadness, the daughter, "a wild little girl of seven," "was as free as the wind that blew my hair, and no less spirited than a bounding deer."[160] Larcom's independent—and interrupted—childhood idyll resonates here, as Zitkala-Ša combines natural images and sentimental rhetoric invoking youthful freedom in order to spark *Atlantic* readers' sympathies.[161] She also inaugurates the theme of environmental agency that Winnemucca's and Ruiz de Burton's narratives insistently analyze.

We quickly learn that Zitkala-Ša's mother is sad because she fears dispossession: "[T]he paleface [might] . . . take away from us the river we drink" (37). Buried beneath this metonymic image is the federal government's military actions enforcing removal. Unlike Winnemucca's explicit account of wars—and her praise for the U.S. Army's just treatment—Zitkala-Ša's initial approach is more obliquely judgmental. Her mother exposes the history of Sioux displacement and land theft. Pointing to the nearby hill "where my uncle and my only sister lay buried," the mother becomes her daughter's proxy, enabling a blunt, angry accusation: "There is what the paleface has done! Since then your father too has been buried in a hill nearer the rising sun. We were once very happy. But the paleface has stolen our lands and driven us hither. Having defrauded us of our land, the paleface forced us away" (38). In this context, the opening pastoral is deceptive. Myopically individualist, such accounts elide both the underlying conflict between nations and diminished Indian sovereignty. Like Winnemucca, Zitkala-Ša deploys the image of the child—here, the orphan—to engage readers' emotional intelligence, and she fosters anger as well as compassion. This history of resource wars and removal frames "Impressions of an Indian Childhood" and the entire narrative sequence in the *Atlantic*.

Many of the successive stories employ rhetorical strategies similar to

Winnemucca's. In "Impressions of an Indian Childhood," Zitkala-Ša recounts her own version of domestic and social moralities; educating her readers, she simultaneously humanizes her family and community members and elevates them into heroes. Unlike anthropological and popular accounts that discussed Indian women's burdensome home life, "Impressions of an Indian Childhood" conveys the author's awe at elders' stories, relates her mother's precise aesthetics as she teaches her daughter traditional beadwork, and conveys the Lakota Sioux ethos of hospitality and respect in a humorous episode in which the youthful Zitkala-Ša brews muddy "coffee" for an elder.[162] Such accounts combat stereotypes of Indian savages and advance the argument for environmental justice.

Pastoral recurs in a delicately cautionary story. Some missionaries give little Zitkala-Ša marbles of various sizes and colors, and she recalls them as she accompanies her mother along the river; seeing "great chunks of ice piled all along the bank," she notices "the colors of the rainbow in the crystal ice": "Immediately I thought of my glass marbles at home. With my bare fingers I tried to pick out some of the colors, for they seemed so near the surface. But my fingers began to sting with the intense cold, and I had to bite them hard to keep from crying. From that day on, for many a moon, I believed that glass marbles had river ice inside of them" (45). The deceptively desirable marbles, which seem miraculous, cause suffering, and they forecast Zitkala-Ša's encounters with missionaries who lure her from her happy home and take her to a punitive Christian school. Divorced from her history and her community, she travels an inverted journey, not only from west to east but also from civilization to savagery. As the narrative culminates, we learn of Zitkala-Ša's friend Judéwin, who "had told me of the great tree where grew red, red apples; and how we could reach out our hands and pick all the red apples we could eat" (46). Christian readers would not have missed the symbolism of temptation nor the implication that leaving home entailed losing Eden.[163] With political, national, and geographical resonances, home in these *Atlantic* narratives encompasses the spiritual dimensions that predecessors such as Ward and Winnemucca underline. Zitkala-Ša intimates that by deceiving the innocent, the Christian story secures whites' spiritual sovereignty. At the same time, by rejecting pastoral, she indirectly condemns the public policy that separates children from their homes, their nations.[164]

Embodied rhetoric frequently enhances the effectiveness of Zitkala-Ša's narratives; like Wilson and Winnemucca, she elicits readers' sympathies and sparks anger through material means. In "The School Days of an Indian Girl," whether she describes the discomfort and shame of tight clothing, the physical violence of a forced haircut (which symbolized cowardice for the Sioux), being forced to relinquish her comfortable moccasins, the delight of creating snow angels, or her own angry mashing of hated turnips, the author conveys her sensibility, and enlists our emotional intelligence, through embodied experiences. Unlike Ruiz de Burton, who emphatically elides her Californias' corporeal presence, Zitkala-Ša tenders charged, concrete images to excoriate the removal policy that placed Native children in government- and Christian-sponsored schools. These images foreground not just the savage Christians' actions but the writer's resistance, perfumed with the sweet smell of turnips.

A fourth *Atlantic* essay, "Why I Am a Pagan" (1902), extends the earlier pieces' romantic perspective and sentimental rhetoric while it proclaims Zitkala-Ša's spiritual sovereignty by focusing on Indian access to non-human nature.[165] Although her more "respectable" contemporaries continued to obscure their embodiment, Zitkala-Ša revels in sensual pleasures. The opening evokes the relationship between Indian spirituality and the natural world: "When the spirit swells my breast I love to roam leisurely among the green hills; or sometimes, sitting on the brink of the murmuring Missouri, I marvel at the great blue overhead. With half closed eyes I watch the huge cloud shadows in their noiseless play upon the high bluffs opposite me, while into my ear ripple the sweet, soft cadences of the river's song. . . . My heart and I lie small upon the earth like a grain of throbbing sand" (801–2).[166] As Sigourney does in "Niagara," the author urges humility. But this vision is emphatically not Christian, for Zitkala-Ša represents "the wild prairie flowers" as "lovely little folk" with "quaint little faces." As she recalls a Sioux legend, the writer reveals her goal: "I fain would trace a subtle knowledge of the native folk which enabled them to recognize a kinship to any and all parts of this vast universe" (802).[167] Paralleling the ethos of Ward, Jemison, and Winnemucca, Zitkala-Ša paints her nation's appreciation of human interconnectedness with the flowers, and she offers her white contemporaries a moment of shared joy, even exhilaration.

Zitkala-Ša uses sentimental, feminine rhetoric to counterbalance the potential affront that the title (and contents) presented the *Atlantic*'s Christian readers.[168] Augmenting her miniaturizing description of the flowers, she

Clothes-mending class. Carlisle Indian School, Carlisle, Pennsylvania. Image by
Frances Benjamin Johnston, c. 1901. Courtesy of the Library of Congress.

depicts visiting a "log cabin whither I am strongly drawn by the tie of a
child to an aged mother." The cabin has multiple functions: it evokes for
urban white audience members a pleasingly separate, uncivilized lifestyle;
it resonates with rustic, pastoral pleasures; it conjures the "American" pioneer spirit; and—showing kinship ties modulated by gender—it encodes
Sioux national identity. Zitkala-Ša's nostalgic return to childhood includes
a sentient "black shaggy dog," Chan, whose "articulation is quite beyond
my ear." Like Larcom evoking almost Emersonian transcendence, the author reiterates her overarching perception: "I feel in keen sympathy with
my fellow creatures, for I seem to see clearly again that all are akin" (802).
As George E. Tinker explains, Indian intellectual traditions emphasize a
broad understanding of community, where "human beings are not privileged over the rest of the world, nor are individuals privileged over the good
of the whole community."[169] In conveying her connection to Chan, the
writer asserts Sioux spiritual sovereignty; simultaneously, she stimulates
white readers' emotional intelligence in a portrait sparking interest, sympathy, and warmth, even if those readers do not share her egalitarian ethos
or appreciate her nationalist thrust.

Having established this affective link, Zitkala-Ša deftly shifts to a critique that echoes Jemison's. She acknowledges that her sense of kinship
should encompass a "native preacher," an Indian missionary who requires
the respect demanded of "God's creature, though he mouth most strangely
the jangling phrases of a bigoted creed." In the context of the essay's opening paragraphs extolling nature's transcendent virtues—and embodied
pleasures—the missionary's insistence that Zitkala-Ša attend church to
avoid "the deep pit below, [where] the sinful ones dance in torturing flames"
would appear almost comic, were it not for the author's painful recollection
that her own mother "is now a follower of the new superstition." As for
many women of color, such as Jacobs, Wilson, and Winnemucca, satire is
the dominant humorous form. As the essay culminates, Zitkala-Ša reflects
that "the pale-faced missionary and the hoodooed aborigine are both God's
creatures. . . . A wee child toddling in a wonder world, I prefer to their
dogma my excursions into the natural gardens where the voice of the Great
Spirit is heard in the twittering of birds, the rippling of mighty waters, and
the sweet breathing of flowers" (803). Her sentimental language speaks out
of (in both senses) the mainstream ethos; here she becomes a word warrior who entered enemy strongholds like the *Atlantic Monthly*. Recalling
Winnemucca's account of Christian hypocrisy and Paiute women's bonds
with the natural environment, Zitkala-Ša's meditation affirms her spiritual
sovereignty, a central feature of environmental justice.

ZITKALA-ŠA's personal essays and literary short fiction represent the initial phase of her writing career; the second, based partly on her personal
experience on the Uintah and Ouray Reservation, was more explicitly political. Like Winnemucca, she had lived through tumultuous times for her
people. Born in the year of the Battle of the Little Big Horn, part of the
Lakota War of 1876–77, she grew up in an atmosphere swirling with conflict. According to the 1868 Treaty of Fort Laramie, the U.S. government
had reserved the sacred Black Hills exclusively for Sioux use, but after General George Custer led prospectors into the Black Hills—and they found
gold in 1874—this treaty was increasingly breached.[170] The Oglala leader
Crazy Horse was assassinated in 1877, the same year that the U.S. Congress formally reneged on the Fort Laramie agreement, confiscating Sioux
lands and withdrawing economic assistance.[171] In 1887 Congress passed the

Dawes (General Allotment) Act, a powerful blow to Native sovereignty. In 1890 the Hunkpapa Lakota leader Sitting Bull was murdered, just prior to the Wounded Knee Massacre; both these events occurred while Zitkala-Ša was "at home on the Yankton reservation on a school break."[172] Such events powerfully affected her writing and her life's work.

After this bloody period, in the aftermath of Wounded Knee a pan-Indian movement began to gather force. One vital outgrowth was the Society of American Indians, founded in 1911, "whose major theme was accommodation to and acceptance of white society as permanent," according to Hazel Hertzberg.[173] The reservation and government school system (including Carlisle), and the English-only imperative in such schools, mirrored this assimilationist standard. Hertzberg observes, "For many students . . . Pan-Indian movements provided a psychological home, a place where they belonged. A large segment of the Pan-Indian leadership was educated in the eastern boarding schools."[174] According to Robert Allen Warrior (Osage), this organization marked "the first time Native intellectuals had joined in a common organization." Partly through its *American Indian Magazine*, the SAI sought to build bridges between Native nations and the dominant society while it forwarded Indian interests. One problem with the organization's activists, Warrior suggests, was their failure "to recognize that the ideals that they sought for U.S. society and Natives were far from realizable and that the Indian situation at the turn of the century was a battle of community values versus individualistic chaos rather than a battle of one set of cohesive, livable values against another."[175] At the heart of these values were conflicting beliefs about individuals' and communities' relationships to land and nation.

Unlike Zitkala-Ša's *Atlantic* essays (and the stories she published in *Harper's*), her contributions to the *American Indian Magazine* express her environmental justice aims more explicitly. In its initial incarnation, the magazine was relatively conservative; it encompassed personal, reservation, and national political concerns, and it endorsed "the basic precepts of the allotment era: improved education, concrete legal status, and citizenship for Indians."[176] But under Zitkala-Ša's editorship, Cox indicates, the magazine's tone changed, becoming "less conciliatory, but more romanticized"; she "advanced her interest in literature and community activism" and highlighted women's (both Native and non-Native) roles in "local, national, and global affairs."[177] While she addressed a primarily pan-Indian audience, she also appealed to progressive whites. A key goal in her journalism was to influence federal Indian policy.

A story titled "Chipeta, Widow of Chief Ouray, with a Word about a Deal in Blankets" epitomizes her multiple editorial emphases. Zitkala-Ša addresses two issues. The first is Ute peyote use, which she sought to discourage by visiting Chipeta and her brother—and by writing about that visit. The second is how the federal government treated Native Americans who had historically been loyal. From the opening, the author encourages readers' skepticism and courts their angry complicity, but she attacks U.S. policy indirectly. The second part of the narrative begins casually, almost as an aside: "[W]hile conversing with a friend who had been interested in my visit I heard an amazing story. It was about my friend Chipeta. It was like a tale in a night-mare and I could hardly believe it."[178] Her disbelief quickly turns to indignation and anger, and through her friend's account she conveys her own censure. The government, her friend relates, planned to give a gift to Chipeta in recognition of "Chief Ouray, faithful friend of the border settlers and loyal advocate of obedience to Federal orders" (336). In an aside, Zitkala-Ša voices delight ("light streamed into my heart") and imagines great possibilities: "What if the gift should be a genuine guarantee of water rights to the Ute Indians, or the title to their 250,000 acres of grazing lands to be held intact for the future unallotted children, or a message from the Great White Father giving news of Federal action against the peyote drug?" (336).

Within the framework proposed by contemporary environmental justice advocates and Native activists, this vision exemplifies a mixed message. On the one hand, Zitkala-Ša pursues reparations and Indian sovereignty; on the other, she seeks public policy or legislation that would regulate peyote, thus diminishing Native agency and sovereignty.[179] This topic was hotly contested in the author's time, and her sponsorship of efforts banning peyote—ironically bringing her together with her bitter adversary, Colonel Richard H. Pratt, Carlisle's founder—made her vulnerable to attacks, especially after her 1918 Senate testimony for anti-peyote forces.[180] Because she believed that peyote had destructive effects similar to alcohol, she constructs her heroine through the "conventional social reform discourses of Indian inferiority and helplessness," representing Chipeta, in Cox's words, "as an infantile and abused loyalist to the government and an uninformed abuser of peyote."[181]

However, Zitkala-Ša's broader—and, given its placement, I believe more important—message in "Chipeta, Widow of Chief Ouray," invites readers' sense of disproportion and outrage over the putative gift to Chief Ouray's elderly widow: "a pair of trading store shawls" (336). Not even handmade or personally selected, the shawls denote her status as a squaw, though Zitkala-Ša never articulates this idea directly. Chipeta shows her gratitude by sending "a large and expensive Navajo blanket. It was a free will offering, paid for by personal money" (337). In contrast, the government's gift is a sham, for, her interlocutor tells Zitkala-Ša, it is ultimately funded by Ute money—that is, by Chipeta herself. Conveying these events principally through a secondary narrator, the author distances herself, but her own voice finally reemerges; the sentimental image of the vulnerable widow helps enlist readers' outrage and underlines the writer's own. As she closes the story, she praises Chipeta's "faithful service": "No shawl is big enough to obscure or cover the gifts you have given freely and for which no material thing will ever repay you" (337). This conclusion suggests that Native American generosity extends well beyond the individual widow's, and it gestures toward Indians' need for justice and sovereignty, however mediated.

Zitkala-Ša's journalism illustrates her belief that acquiring U.S. citizenship will help Indians achieve environmental justice. Like Winnemucca, she underscores Native American loyalty and patriotism, and she promotes citizenship within a global context.[182] Many Indians served in the U.S. military during World War I, and Zitkala-Ša lauds their selfless service with angry but tactful irony. Arguing for authentic democracy in "America, Home of the Red Man," she combines factual narrative, subtle satire, and—again—sentimental rhetoric. As she moves through a sequence of "rapidly shifting pictures of individual sacrifices of Indians, both young and old," she tells first of an "old grandmother, whom someone dubbed a 'Ute squaw' [who] now appeared [in my mind] wonderously glorified. Her furrowed face was aglow with radiance. Her bent form, clad in pitiful rags, changed in a twinkling to an eye of strength and grace. Her spirit shining through earthly misfortunes, revealed an angel in disguise."[183] The elder woman's transformation occurs because her sacrifice is enormous: she has donated $500, nearly all her life savings, to support the war effort. Consonant with the author's other portraits of strong Indian women, this image augments her powerful rhetoric to foreground Native women's contributions to American national well-being.

Zitkala-Ša envisions another patriot, a machine gunner wounded in France, who continues to serve America. He joins the cavalry, and when he is injured and can no longer contribute there performs garden work; he writes, "I am digging spuds to help win the war." For readers not yet disarmed by disabled and elderly individuals' sacrifices or convinced of their civility, the writer conjures a more detached image: a Native American U.S. senator filing a bill—unopposed by "a single [Indian] voice"—to divert all Indian funds to the U.S. government if it needed more war funding.[184] Here her direct petition evokes Jacobs's and Winnemucca's approaches: "America! Home of the Red Man! How dearly the Indian loves you! America! Home of Democracy, when shall the Red Man be emancipated? When shall the Red Man be deemed worthy of full citizenship, if not now?" (340). While she advances no explicit claim for environmental justice or Native sovereignty, her affectively weighted rhetoric proposes, at the very least, Indian equality and agency.

Zitkala-Ša's other essays make explicit her belief that citizenship would foster Native Americans' ability to obtain environmental justice. In "Letter to the Chiefs and Head-men of the Tribes," she writes formally as secretary of the Society of American Indians to address two issues: "English-speaking and retaining ownership of a portion of our Indian lands."[185] She advocates that all Native Americans learn English as a means to establish pan-Indian communication and community. Cox points out that "[i]n contemporary intellectual contexts, Bonnin's defense of Indian land would take high precedence, while her insistence on speaking English would militate against efforts . . . to maintain Native languages."[186] As we have seen, "The School Days of an Indian Girl" confirms the physical dangers of *not* learning English, while it condemns forced language acquisition.[187] Reaching two audiences and cultivating cross-ethnic alliances must have presented imposing challenges; as Hafen attests, "Often [Zitkala-Ša] seemed caught between validating her indigenous beliefs and seeking public approval."[188]

"Letter to the Chiefs and Head-men of the Tribes" demonstrates Zitkala-Ša's mixed legacy. While the first half, endorsing English acquisition, undercuts Indian sovereignty, the second part mirrors Ward's and the Cherokee women's much earlier pleas to the Cherokee National Council to retain traditional lands. She too attempts to influence Indian nations' public policy with a direct appeal to chiefs: "I fear they [Indians] are selling their lands too fast and without consideration for the future children of our race. Indians are an out-of-doors people, and though we may become educated in the White man's way and even acquire money, we cannot really be happy unless we have a small piece of this Out-of-Doors to enjoy as we please. For the sake of our children's children we must hold onto a few acres that they may enjoy it as we have. —" (341). Although she lacks her predecessors' focus on women's connection with the land, Zitkala-Ša indicates Native Americans' different worldview; whites' money economy is particularly foreign to an Indian ethos. Like the Cherokee women, she affirms her transgenerational perspective. Indians themselves, she urges, possess some agency over their future, and they are responsible for ensuring environmental justice for their children by retaining traditional lands.

Again like her Cherokee counterparts, Zitkala-Ša speaks as an insider to insiders with a shared history. Her rhetoric stresses the *we* and forwards modest claims to "a *small* piece of this Out-of Doors" and "a *few* acres" while it argues for sovereignty. She reinforces this stance, adding a nostalgic tone in the penultimate paragraph, which juxtaposes whites' urban—and, she implies, economically grasping—lifestyles to her outdoor childhood: "Many times as I walk on the paved streets of the city, I long for the open Indian country in which I played as a child." The spiritual link between humans and the natural world requires respect. The paragraph concludes with a resonant image: "The White man is a wonderful builder of stone houses, which to me are better to look upon from the outside than to live in, as they shut out the sky and sunshine" (341). Tactfully but satirically conjuring a cave, she hints that whites' claustrophobic lifeways are savage, not civilized, just as Winnemucca had done. Home, largely construed (and mirroring the outdoor images that animate her earlier *Atlantic* essays), again symbolizes environmental justice for her nation.

ZITKALA-ŠA's intellectual work, her autobiographical narratives, her political engagements with the SAI, and her public performances reflected her commitment to activism; so did her leadership roles in both white and Indian groups. This activism involved the exposure of "wrongs and claims" endured by other Native nations. Perhaps her most significant attempt to intervene in U.S. law and public policy was *Oklahoma's Poor Rich Indians: An Orgy of Graft and Exploitation of the Five Civilized Tribes, Legalized Robbery* (1924).[189] Working with Charles H. Fabens, representative of the

American Indian Defense Association, and Matthew K. Sniffen, secretary of the Indian Rights Association, Zitkala-Ša represented the General Federation of Women's Clubs and its Indian Welfare Committee in the trio's investigative visit to Oklahoma.[190] Their report blasted the Oklahoma Closure Act of 1908, which assigned jurisdiction over members of the Five Civilized Tribes to a corrupt network of influential individuals and groups such as the county probate courts, judges, guardians, attorneys, bankers, and merchants.[191] At risk were nearly ten million acres of Indian land.[192] Clara Sue Kidwell observes, "By 1923, the situation of Indian guardianship in Oklahoma had reached the proportions of a national scandal."[193] As earlier with the Cherokee, the Iroquois, and the Paiute, valuable resources motivated these new Indian wars: Kidwell explains that "the discovery of oil in the great Glen Pool in 1904 and the Cushing Pool in 1913" helped destroy the coal-based economy that provided the Choctaws' primary wealth.[194] Resource wars quickly followed.

Paralleling Ruiz de Burton's exposure of racist legislation and public policy and her quest for legal reform, the sensational *Oklahoma's Poor Rich Indians* "shocked the public and led to further investigation and attempts at reform."[195] A prefatory note by Herbert Welsh, the president of the Indian Rights Association, reveals the stakes: the authors' "report discloses a situation that is almost unbelievable in a civilized country," he exclaims, adding that nothing short of "radical and immediate change" in the existing system will save the Five Civilized Tribes from "pauperization and virtual extermination."[196] More than any of Zitkala-Ša's works, the jointly authored narrative exemplifies how the literary representation of nature and public environmental policy converge: *Oklahoma's Poor Rich Indians* illuminates how dominant-society conceptions of Indian girls and women as "natural resources" have created discriminatory and unethical policies and laws. Zitkala-Ša likely composed the most moving sections that detail the exploitation of a woman and two girls.[197] Her affective rhetoric combines sentimental images with angry attacks; the text upends conventional definitions of civilized and savage, contrasting the predatory guardians with their vulnerable, innocent victims. An argument for justice rather than a brief for sovereignty—indeed, it demands federal protection and oversight—*Oklahoma's Poor Rich Indians* makes all too palpable the consequences of resource "extraction": Natives' destitution, rape, murder, and perhaps even genocide.

The narrative proper begins with a summary that evokes Ruiz de Burton's legal rhetoric. Fabens, Sniffen, and Zitkala-Ša studied "14,229 probate cases in six counties where the Indian population is the largest" and discovered that probate administration costs ranged between 20 and 70 percent of the total estate. Listing the many injustices that the Five Civilized Tribes had suffered from the U.S. Congress, the Oklahoma Supreme Court, and the local courts, the writers broaden the scope of their blame: "[I]n many of the Counties the Indians are virtually at the mercy of groups that include the county judges, guardians, attorneys, bankers, merchants—not even overlooking the undertaker—all regarding the Indian estates as legitimate game" (4–5). But the corruption extends beyond economics, for white guardians allow Indian children to starve. Their treatment of girls is especially cruel: "[Y]oung Indian girls (mere children in size and mentality) have been robbed of their virtue and their property through kidnapping and a liberal use of liquor" (6). In this matrix of economic, legal, and material injustice, gender matters. Like Winnemucca, who depicts the violated girl and the villainous male tempter, traditional images in white-authored texts, the writers foster sympathy and outrage. Such exploitation, they insist, demands ameliorative action.

This passage anticipates Zitkala-Ša's sentimental rhetoric in her blistering exposés "Regardless of Sex or Age," "A Seven Year Old Victim," and "In Osage County." Augmenting Winnemucca's and her own earlier accounts of Indian childhood interrupted, she demonstrates how Indian women and girls are exploited as natural resources. As Tanis C. Thorne submits, "*Oklahoma's Poor Rich Indians* was a particularly powerful political weapon because it gave the statistical evidence of corruption and attendant Indian suffering a human face."[198] In the guardianship system, "young women and girls were particularly vulnerable to being murdered due to Section 9" of the act, which provided that the death of a landowner without full- or half-blood heirs removed restrictions on the sale of her land.[199] Coupling sentimental descriptions with hair-raising details of corruption and violence, including rape, Zitkala-Ša draws readers' attention to female orphans, whose plight would likely inspire the greatest outrage. Tiny Millie Neharkey, who is eighteen but looks more like a thirteen- or fourteen-year-old, is the "victim of an unscrupulous, lawless party, and whose little body was mutilated by a drunken fiend who assaulted her night after night," despite her screams for help (26).[200] Consciously intensifying the rhetoric, Zitkala-Ša intimates that, given the viciousness of the crimes, hyperbole is impossible; indeed, she repeatedly emphasizes, as she embraces the girl, that "[t]here was nothing I could say" (26).

In another egregious example, the seven-year-old orphan Ledcie Stechi was starved to death and her land stolen. According to Kidwell, "a virtual poster child for . . . charges of graft and corruption," Stechi was targeted after gold was discovered on her land.[201] At one point, Zitkala-Ša describes how the "rich little Choctaw girl, with her feeble grandmother, came to town carrying their clothes, a bundle of faded rags, in a flour sack. Ledcie was dirty, filthy, and covered with vermin. She was emaciated and weighed about 47 pounds" (27). The guardian's abuse continued until the girl's murder by "grafters" whose "greed . . . made them like beasts surrounding their prey" (28). Zitkala-Ša holds nothing back. She forces our gaze to "the little dead body—its baby mouth turned black, little fingernails turned black, and even the little breast all turned black!" and then turns to the devastated grandmother, who will be the next "sheep for slaughter by ravenous wolves in men's forms unless the good people of America intervene immediately" (28). Poisoned by her putative guardian, Ledcie's body uncovers his crime's horrific consequences. Zitkala-Ša's embodied rhetoric nearly surpasses the bounds of propriety and respectability, revealing the depth of her outrage and seeking a complementary response. As Winnemucca had done, Zitkala-Ša asks, who is the savage?

Oklahoma's Poor Rich Indians exhibits how object status transferred from land to person and back again: if the land symbolized "natural resources," property, so did the Native Americans who were its merely nominal owners. Zitkala-Ša's depictions of orphaned Indian girls and women who are "legally bound and gagged" echoes Wilson's portrait of abandoned, motherless Frado (32). Zitkala-Ša's interpretation of resources reprises Winnemucca's; herself labeled a loose woman for her free speech, Winnemucca condemned the objectification and exploitation of Indian women's and girls' bodies. Ruiz de Burton's women occupy an entirely different environment, for economic privilege buffers them from being regarded as merely bodies. Like many of her predecessors, Zitkala-Ša outlines how the United States' resource wars inverted the terms of the civilized/savage dichotomy. But *Oklahoma's Poor Rich Indians* relentlessly indicts the white predators for supreme heinousness. It elicits sympathy, pain, and anger, confronting the U.S. government's avatars, eager for Indian gold.

For Ledcie Stechi, Millie Neharkey, and many others, their embodiment meant not only starvation and torture but rape and death, for their "alienable" land, in the era's too-resonant legalese, was where their value resided. Mined for money and cast aside as waste, these girls and their land found a courageous spokesperson in Zitkala-Ša, whose volume was published, ironically, the same year that all Native Americans were granted U.S. citizenship.[202] Confronting lawful exploitation, *Oklahoma's Poor Rich Indians* foregrounds a pan-Indian predicament that was too often gendered, arguing—through embodied rhetoric and affecting representations of Indian children and women—for Indian agency and radical changes in federal law and public policy.

DESPITE THE substantial differences among *Life Among the Piutes*, *The Squatter and the Don*, and Zitkala-Ša's narratives, stories, journalism, and exposés, all three writers seek redress for communities as well as individuals; the Indian women speak for their nations. If environmental justice literature requires comprehending group exploitation and demanding political and legal solutions, these authors' texts warrant the rubric. Showing how representations of nature and the natural converge with unjust public policy and law, they also underscore readers' responsibility: *Life Among the Piutes* concludes with a petition, *The Squatter and the Don* ends with Doña Josepha's (and the author's) plea for truth and justice, and *Oklahoma's Poor Rich Indians* announces repeatedly that "[t]his is an appeal for *action, immediate action*" (26; original emphasis).

Though differently, Sarah Winnemucca, María Amparo Ruiz de Burton, and Zitkala-Ša afford exemplary models and cautionary tales. As many of their predecessors had done, they demonstrate the troubling results of humans dominating nature. Those who separate themselves from nonhuman animals, for example, are more likely to brutalize others and risk becoming savages themselves. Marshaling affective resources to connect with readers, they model messages of justice that encompass humans' many homes, whether individual, local, or national, whether spiritual or natural. Their writing reveals the awkward truth of humans' material vulnerability, and it promotes humility as we relate to our many environments. Offering touchstones to emulate and to contest, their work finally illuminates our need to reimagine family, kinship, home, and nation—not just for now, but for the future.

Female homesteader in Oklahoma.
Courtesy of the Research Division of the Oklahoma Historical Society.

Coda: Redeeming Futures

How to advance environmental justice in the U.S.—especially through
public policy and law—continues to elicit controversy. The blockbuster film
Avatar (2009) is one example of how such controversy plays out. When the
film appeared, some members of the U.S. armed forces protested, claiming
that *Avatar* villainized the military (a central character, Miles Quatrich, a
cowboy colonel with scarred face and southern accent, is literally a killing
machine) and that it would hurt overseas American troops. As in Jemison's, Winnemucca's, and Zitkala-Ša's texts, nature features as a primary
character. Some indigenous groups and nations expressed cautious support,
partly because the film extends planetary citizenship rights to living entities
beyond human beings.[203]

The film features an American experiment in 2154 on the planet Polyphe-
mus's moon Pandora, where a team of RDA corporation scientists and private
military personnel seeks the rare element unobtainium, for the Earth's resources have been depleted and the planet contaminated. The RDA project
director, who is all about the money, claims that the invaders have tried to
reach—we might say assimilate—the indigenous Na'vi people by building
homes and schools, but the latter have no interest in learning the newcomers' ways. Ostensibly formulating a social bridge, the scientists develop
a genetic engineering procedure that combines Na'vi and human DNA, ex-
tracorporeally growing indigenous forms with which certain team members

can link via placement in a high-tech casket. The tall, blue-skinned Na'vi avatars' mission: learn the nature-centered humanoid indigenes' traditions and language and convince the controlling clan to agree to peaceful removal from their animate forest homeland.

Avatar, which I have mentally subtitled "The Indians (and Nature) Get Even," retells familiar American stories, such as the Pocahontas–John Smith tale. For early white settlers the Indian princess story reassured fearful investors and potential immigrants that the indigenous population was fundamentally civilizable. It figuratively tamed and humanized the wilderness she embodied. Finally, it foregrounded an alluring and racy (for the seventeenth century) romance, reinvented in the eponymous Walt Disney cartoon film. *Avatar*'s romance between the protagonists Jake and Neytiri derives directly from this plot, but here the civilized man turns savage. Like Jemison's captivity narrative, this story has had durable, sensational interest; but men's return to nature has always been more acceptable than women's.[204] When measured by their compassion, dignity, social complexity, connection to nature, and peacefulness, *Avatar*'s savages are civilized and its civilized more often savage.

Avatar reprises another critical narrative in mainstream America, Adam and Eve in the Garden of Eden. The Na'vis' trees suggest the biblical Tree of Life; all three of their primary trees, in fact, sustain life. But the Tree of Knowledge of Good and Evil does not exist on Pandora. Although she guides him from innocence to experience, Neytiri does not cause Jake's fall from goodness. Instead, he *begins* as fallen—both literally and psychically crippled—and ascends into goodness and life through her agency. Neytiri herself destroys the evil forces that satanic Quatrich symbolizes, and she saves Jake's human life, enabling him eventually to become fully Na'vi when he connects to the Tree of Souls. Females, including the scientist Grace, represent life givers and spiritual guardians. But more than preservers of home and bringers of life, women are courageous fighters who possess strong bodies. For many twenty-first-century viewers, these empowered women create a tempting tale.

The RDA forces' giant bulldozer levels the Hometree and the Tree of Voices, sparking the great mourning and dislocation that parallel the Trail of Tears, the removal of Native Americans from their traditional southeastern homelands. The Na'vi suffer forced removal from their Hometree, which the intruders raze for the unobtainium below it, just as Cherokee removal quickly followed the discovery of gold in Georgia. Although their battles have different outcomes, the Na'vis' fight to retain their homeland reenacts Cherokee resistance and symbolizes a parallel demand, when confronting rapacious colonialism, for environmental justice. As a whole, the Na'vi are the most sympathetic among the film's cartoonish characters; the filmmakers invite viewers to take their side and cheer their triumph.

The Cherokee, Seneca, Paiute, and Sioux nations whose writers *Fallen Forests* discusses have endured war on numerous fronts beyond literal battlefields. Resource wars sought not simply precious extractable commodities such as gold but also orchards, grain fields, and lakes. Other battles contested religion, gender roles, language, political sovereignty. *Avatar* shows analogous indirect sites of conflict; the invaders interpenetrate Na'vi society via a romance, though—as Winnemucca and Zitkala-Ša emphasize—such connections are much more likely to exploit indigenous women than to foster social bonds. While it represents the Na'vi, especially the women, as thinking heroes, *Avatar* luxuriates in battle scenes; explosions are plentiful. Despite the protests that the film demonizes the Earth warriors—and to some extent it does—it invests their actions with glamour and excitement. Though the Earth soldiers' high-tech weapons ultimately fail against the Na'vis' natural environment and integrated, cooperative society, diabolism like Quatrich's and the violence he sponsors are doubtless alluring for some. Contemporary viewers must ask whether *Avatar*'s emotional reenactment, with its sentimental and triumphant conclusion, merely assuages white guilt or appeals to cultural nostalgia for lost innocence. Who are "our" agents, our avatars? Are satisfied moviegoers the only ones redeemed? What actions, if any, are required? And what, finally, constitutes environmental justice?

After Words

Toward Common Ground

Now, said she, in the heart of the woods,
 The sweet south-winds assert their power,
And blow apart the snowy snoods
 Of trilliums in their thrice-green bower.
 Now all the swamps are flushed with dower
 Of viscid pink, where, hour by hour,
 The bees swim amorous, and a shower
 Reddens the stream where cardinals tower.
Far lost in fern of fragrant stir
Her fancies roam, for unto her
 All Nature came in this one flower.

—HARRIET PRESCOTT SPOFFORD,
 from "Pomegranate-Flowers"

 these hips are big hips.
 they need space to
 move around in.

 —LUCILLE CLIFTON,
 from "homage to my hips"

PUBLISHED IN THE May 1861 *Atlantic Monthly*, Harriet Prescott Spofford's erotic fantasy, which depicts a seamstress contemplating the pomegranate bloom on her windowsill, needs little interpretation. Even in the mid-nineteenth century, a few American women found ways to explore—and sometimes celebrate—their connection to nature. As we have seen repeatedly, nonelite women faced particular challenges surrounding their embodiment, but even elites like Emily Dickinson were frequently forced to convert themselves into "Nobody," no-body. Unapologetically affirming her size and animation, Lucille Clifton's contemporary poem illuminates some of the past century's social transformations. Unlike earlier "small"

329

women who, as Fanny Fern reminds us, corseted themselves into illness and showcased birdlike appetites, Clifton escapes such confinement.

As the contemporary authors whom I'll discuss below demonstrate, many of the nineteenth-century writers' rhetorical strategies retain their power. Though these contemporaries may not be familiar with their predecessors' work, their emotionally intelligent appeals reveal the tenacity and cultural embeddedness of their precursors' performances, including forms as well as stance and language. In debates about nature and the natural, we've seen that genre matters, but it neither determines nor forecloses writers' participation in such debates. Nineteenth-century romantic and pastoral poetry offered women amenable, well-established modes for investigating their relationships to nature. Writers such as Sigourney, Larcom, Thaxter, Rose Terry Cooke, Helen Hunt Jackson, Ina Coolbrith, and Lizette Woodworth Reese — not to mention Dickinson — created optimistic, awe-inspiring, and intimate portraits of the nation's landscapes without necessarily advancing conservation or reform agendas. Some poets did effectively merge conventional aesthetics and political rhetoric: many of Sigourney's supposedly sentimental Indian poems fall into this category, as does "Fallen Forests." Travel writing such as Kirkland's *Forest Life* or Fuller's *Summer on the Lakes* may be more legible as nature writing than a text like *Incidents in the Life of a Slave Girl*, not just because Jacobs portrays nature less often but also because her perspective extends beyond an individual persona. Community-representative or jointly authored earlier texts (like Jacobs's and the Cherokee oratories) are nevertheless hospitable to an ecocritical framework. Novels such as Wilson's *Our Nig* and Ruiz de Burton's *The Squatter and the Don* argue for environmental justice, though Wilson's spartan style contrasts vividly with Ruiz de Burton's assertive, juridical thrust; both speak for beleaguered communities, but the authors' positions diverge dramatically.

Regardless of their genres, writers may express ambivalence toward progress (Sigourney, Kirkland, Larcom), while others (Berbineau, Ruiz de Burton) may embrace it, though sometimes with qualifications. Many value community over individualism (the Cherokee women, Hopkins, Jewett, Winnemucca), while others appreciate individual choice and fear superimposed values (Ruiz de Burton, Freeman). Nineteenth-century American women writers variously reject, negotiate, or escape the dominant society's nature/culture dichotomy; some provide models that enable critique of contemporary ecofeminists' essentialism debates. Race, ethnicity, and class frequently matter less than aspirations: though each author establishes her own standards, Scott, Berbineau, Wilson, and Hopkins, like Ruiz de Burton, write against wilderness, against concepts of the savage.

LIKE THEIR PRECURSORS, many contemporary women writers connect the domination of nature with colonialism, imperialism, and the exploitation of women, working-class and rural people, and people of color. They similarly tailor their environmental projects to their ethos, audiences, and occasions. Though more readily apprehended as environmental writing than some nineteenth-century writers' work, the texts to which I now turn, Barbara Kingsolver's *Animal, Vegetable, Miracle*, Jamaica Kincaid's *My Garden (Book):*, Annie Dillard's *Teaching a Stone to Talk*, and Winona LaDuke's *All Our Relations*, amuse, instruct, admonish, and inspire. I have ordered the first three on a continuum (admittedly arbitrary) from less to more self-consciously literary; I end with LaDuke to suggest the difference between her and Dillard and to close the narrative circle. As Clifton's "homage to my hips" indicates, contemporary women authors articulate variously embodied perspectives. Many affirm an affiliation or partnership with nature; sometimes this connection remains rooted in the body, while other times it elicits spiritual flights. Writing about home in distinctive ways, they, like their predecessors, contemplate such subjects as domestic and wild, native and immigrant, civilized and savage; they reprise and revise earlier authors' hybrid genres and complex rhetorical approaches incorporating emotional, logical, and ethical appeals.

With contributions from her chef-artist elder daughter Camille and scientist husband Steven L. Hopp, Barbara Kingsolver combines autobiography, travel writing, food writing, science writing, natural history, philosophy, and local history in *Animal, Vegetable, Miracle*, which documents the family's year of eating locally but also promotes simple living and sustainability.[1] *Animal, Vegetable, Miracle* led the *New York Times* best-seller list for many weeks. With an ample seasoning of humor to accompany her bitter greens, Kingsolver elaborates an affable and self-disparaging jeremiad-pastoral that updates Kirkland's *Forest Life* and turns toward modern science. Although Kingsolver's journey counterpoints Kirkland's—she travels east, toward family, home, and a more sustainable lifestyle than is possible in arid Tucson—it also returns her to a wilder domesticity.

The story begins with the family piling in the car for a classic American road trip: "We'd sold our house and stuffed the car with the most crucial things: birth certificates, books-on-tape, and a dog on drugs. (Just for the trip, I swear.)"[2] Kingsolver's voice colludes with readers, grants us intimacy, and sparks sympathy. After describing the move's motivations—such as concern over Arizona's scarce resources and its un-self-reliance ("Rob Mexico's water or guzzle Saudi Arabia's gas?")—she ponders Americans' traditional reasons for relocation, affirming her family's goal of "realigning our lives with our food chain," then announcing bluntly and self-mockingly, "Naturally, our first stop was to buy junk food and fossil fuel" (6). The author's home-building links directly to resource shortages and global trade; the tension between domestic and foreign threads through the volume.

But the trouble begins at home. Despite a six-month drought, the Tucson gas station attendant frowns and growls at clouds that threaten rain on her day off, when she hoped to wash her car. Kingsolver sympathizes, but she admires the waitress at the restaurant near their destination, the family's Virginia farm, who hopes for just-right rain. The lesson is modest: "It's not my intention here to lionize country wisdom over city ambition. I only submit that the children of farmers are likely to know where food comes from, and that the rest of us might do well to pay attention" (8). Such philosophy—some might call it didacticism, mirroring nineteenth-century women's advice writing—is tempered by the author's genial humor; she admits she and her family are among the guilty.

Quietly questioning how Americans understand progress, Kingsolver uncovers the links between it, nature, food, and the body, observing that "[t]he baby boom psyche embraces a powerful presumption that education is a key to moving *away* from manual labor, and dirt—two undeniable ingredients of farming" (9; original emphasis). Ironically, as preceding chapters have shown, many of Kingsolver's predecessors, including working-class writers like Wilson and Larcom, shared this "baby boom" assumption. But their accounts help to illuminate the privilege of Kingsolver's readers, who have the education necessary to recognize healthy food and the economic resources to choose "simplicity"—organic and locally grown produce— without getting their hands dirty.

Kingsolver occasionally offers glimpses of her own working-class history, but she carefully avoids alienating more-affluent audience members, using humor (and, like Kirkland and Freeman, local color) to soften the blow when she links modern middle-class Americans' attitudes toward nature with female embodiment: "I used to take my children's friends out to the garden to warm them up to the idea of eating vegetables, but this strategy sometimes backfired: they'd back away slowly saying, 'Oh *man*, those things touched *dirt!*' Adults do the same by pretending it all comes from the clean, well-lighted grocery store. We're like petulant teenagers rejecting our mother. We *know* we came out of her, but *ee-ew*" (10; original emphasis). Like Kirkland's and Larcom's "ladies" (and "gentlemen"), contemporary people elide or reject connection with ostensibly contaminated (mother) earth as the domestic slides uncomfortably into the uncivilized. Echoing a child's voice, the author proposes that readers grow up.

Kingsolver's narrative affords direct as well as indirect lessons in biology, nutrition, capitalism, and globalization. One section chastises Americans' discomfort with farmers; we dehumanize them, spending eighty-five cents per food dollar on "the processors, marketers, and transporters" and then complaining about the price of organic products "that might send back more than three nickels per buck to the farmers: those actual humans putting seeds in the ground, harvesting, attending livestock births, standing in the fields at dawn casting their shadows upon our sustenance" (13). She portrays how our impoverished food culture and industrial food production make Americans fat and sick. Hopp's accompanying text dispels the myth that the world's people will starve without industrial agriculture (18).

At the same time rejecting political correctness, Kingsolver explains realistically and affectingly that many families have benefited from tobacco farming, which "paid our schoolteachers and blacktopped our roads." Beyond effecting improvements, tobacco farming framed family and community life: "It was the sweet scent of the barn loft where I hid out and read books on summer afternoons. . . . It was the reason my first date had to end early on a Friday night: he had to get up early on Saturday to work the tobacco." Though it causes cancer and uses chemicals, "it sends people to college. It makes house payments, buys shoes, pays doctor bills" (74). Lacking an economic alternative in food production, family farms will disappear. Although she does not say so directly, access to resources and agency loom large, in a class-based environmental justice argument that elsewhere becomes explicit.

Kingsolver's maternal scoldings include attacks on agribusiness, which colludes with marketers and "Late Capitalism" to ensure that Americans consume the former's calorie overproduction, but her most effective consciousness-raising couples her predecessors' sentimental rhetoric with wit: "Children have been targeted especially; food companies spend over $10 billion a year selling food brands to kids, and it isn't broccoli they're pushing. Overweight children are a demographic in many ways similar to minors addicted to cigarettes, with one notable exception: their parents are usually their suppliers" (15). The gallows humor here (more comic elsewhere, when she describes her children conducting "blindfolded color-taste contests" for rainbow Swiss chard "when deprived of ready access to M&Ms") only enhances Kingsolver's contention that Americans' ignorance of farming and despisal of dirt mean that children are the ultimate victims (56). As Wilson's novel grimly depicts, middle-class and affluent Americans' desire to distance themselves from farm labor and laborers is hardly recent.

Children embody the tension between wild and civilized, and many affecting and hilarious passages underline this conjunction. Kingsolver shares her daughter Lily's adventures raising poultry, which begin at the post office: "Lily quickly turned to the box with *her* name on it: a small cardboard mailing crate with dime-sized holes on all sides and twenty-eight loud voices inside: the noise-density quotient of one kindergarten packed in a shoebox. Lily picked it up and started crooning like a new mother" (87; original emphasis). Occupying a cultivated, domestic, intermediate space, humans are continuous with nonhuman nature, and a child's perspective illuminates this continuity. The author shows Lily's response when she disparages her daughter's feelings for a dead hen; Kingsolver has "made the mistake of pointing out that it was *just a chicken*":

> "You don't understand, Mama," she said, red-eyed. "I love my chickens as much as I love *you*."
>
> Well, shut me up.

Sensing her mother's hurt feelings, Lily returns an hour later to rectify the slight, claiming, "I'm sorry. If I love my chickens six, I love you seven." Kingsolver's wry, unspoken response resonates: "Oh, good. I'm not asking who's a ten" (93–94; original emphasis). The episode's intimacy and humor enlist readers in the chicken cause while we share the mother's mock dismay. Later, Kingsolver confirms Lily's feelings as her own turkey "babies" arrive: "I can't claim I felt emotionally neutral as I took these creatures in my hands, my fingers registering downy softness and a vulnerable heartbeat. I felt maternal, while at the same time looking straight down the pipe toward the purpose of this enterprise. These babies were not pets" (89). Sentimentalism gives way to realism, but the embodied link between people and animals remains palpable.

Evoking Kirkland's laugh-out-loud account of Michigan pig-citizens, Kingsolver's description of turkey sex comically combines economics and natural history lessons to deplore agribusiness's unnatural creation: "[T]he Broad-Breasted White, a quick fattening monster bred specifically for the industrial-scale setting. These are the big lugs so famously dumb, they can drown by looking up at the rain." Because the turkeys are top-heavy, deformed, and idiotic, they cannot have turkey sex. ("Poor turkeys," Kingsolver comments.) To reproduce requires "a professional turkey sperm-wrangler" who artificially inseminates the hens: "If you think they send the toms off to a men's room with little paper cups and *Playhen Magazine*, that's not how it goes. I will add only this: if you are the sort of parent who threatens your children with a future of unsavory jobs when they ditch school, here's one more career you might want to add to the list" (90). Coupling advice writing, humor, and down-home philosophy, Kingsolver exposes how Americans' departure from the farm, reliance on cheap food, and infatuation with disembodied progress have concrete consequences. Nature, she implies, will always resist rough handling, here coming to a literal dead end without human intervention.

Kingsolver reprises her nineteenth-century predecessors' rhetorical strategies and tropes, among them appeals to motherhood and vulnerable children, revealing the degree to which such rhetoric has become naturalized in much contemporary American women's nature writing and environmental writing. These parallels continue, though with different emphases, in Jamaica Kincaid's work. Kingsolver's project addresses local, national, and international concerns from a different perspective than Kincaid's *My Garden (Book):*. The former is a "native" returning to home ground, but in her Vermont setting the Afro-Caribbean American Kincaid is a distinctive and, she stresses, deliberately flamboyant immigrant. Telling the imperial tale from an outsider's perspective, her essay collection represents a mirror image to Sigourney's *Scenes in My Native Land* and a privileged complement to Wilson's *Our Nig*. Unlike Winnemucca's or Kirkland's, Kincaid's displacement is voluntary; unlike Ruiz de Burton's, her privilege is not inherited, but her volume offers a subtle, cumulative argument for environmental justice.

She shares with her precursors—and with Kingsolver—a multigenre framework, here combining garden writing, humor, history, local color sketch, philosophy, social commentary, and pastoral. More explicitly literary than Kingsolver—like Thoreau, she has a chapter on "Reading"—her essays incorporate texts that include Gertrude Jekyll's gardening advice, *Mrs. Beeton's Guide to Household Management*, and William Prescott's *Conquest of Mexico*. Kincaid begins with a multilayered origin story: "My attachment in adult life to the garden begins in this way: shortly after I became a mother for the first time, my husband gave me a hoe, a rake, a spade, a fork, some flower seeds to mark the occasion of that thing known as Mother's Day."[3] She plants them and admits that "nothing grew," because "the ground was improperly prepared, it was in the shade of a big oak tree and a big maple tree (those two trees really did grow in the same vicinity and I did not appreciate them then; so annoying, their leaves falling down in the autumn and dirtying up the yard, I thought then)" (4). Motherhood does not confer natural knowledge (nor, as she shows in a later account of a friend's racist mother, does it guarantee humaneness). Resisting dirt—which denotes backwardness—she learns, and teaches readers, to appreciate its merits. At the same time, she refuses the Hallmark sentimentalism that Mother's Day symbolizes.

Demystifying motherhood elsewhere, she locates herself in America by portraying her own mother's situation. Dirt (and its significance) varies depending on location. In Antigua, "[m]y mother would preside over the yard with an agitation that is perhaps endemic to people in her situation. The dishes are clean, then they are dirty, and then they are clean and then they are dirty. The stone heap will not stay in its immaculate mound. . . . Nothing behaves, nothing can be counted on to do so" (44–45). Though she rejects sentiment, the author is not without feeling: she elicits in us her mother's emotions of despair and frustration. Like Kirkland, and similarly humorous, Kincaid depicts the disparities between people in different places and of different classes; like her predecessor, she interprets them with an insider's and outsider's eye. She also accepts that disparate standards apply, suggesting ironically that those of the people in her past are "on a level I can never meet, and even more deeply, fervently hope never to meet," because "the inside of my house looks like my yard; it is smudged with dirt, it is disorderly for the inside of a house" (45). Housekeeping, like gardening, involves proper ordering, putting things in their appropriate location; here—as for Freeman's Shattuck sisters—dirt emblematizes agency, the freedom to choose one's location, and genuinely voluntary simplicity.

Kincaid's genial, self-mocking voice shepherds readers through a carefully constructed thicket of reflections, apparently casual but everywhere planned. More than in *Forest Life* or even in *Animal, Vegetable, Miracle*, the domestic resonates with polyvalence. Like Kingsolver, Kincaid emphasizes home's embodied ground: "All small events are domestic events, and domestic events are those events that can occur in any area in which it seems quite all right to expel saliva. If I were asked to make a definition of domestic space, I would say that domestic space is any space in which anyone might feel comfortable expelling any bodily fluid" (36). She flaunts her exclusion of "spit" and "pee" (for example) from the highfalutin' passage, mimicking "adult" writers' distance from such bodily fluids. But a later episode underscores that those bodies and their fluids are natural. Emblematizing this false detachment, her supposedly civilized adulthood means that she does not know "the names of the plants in the place I am from (Antigua)." This ignorance has consequences; not only is she unable to appreciate "the white lily that blooms in July, opening at night, perfuming the air with a sweetness that is almost sickening," but she also cannot specify "a bush called whitehead bush; it was an important ingredient in the potions my mother and her friends made for their abortions" (119). If one chooses to be foreign, then being civilized may entail alienation from an earlier home and more innocent self.

Approaching readers' education indirectly elsewhere, Kincaid, like Kingsolver (and, though very differently, Wilson), uses a child's eyes to expose constructions of the natural. Her four-year-old daughter, Annie, is nearby while her parents, assuming Annie's invisibility, discuss an acquaintance whom they decide is "a homophobe." When their daughter's unexpected voice asks what the term means, her father quietly explains, ending with two men getting married. Annie's final question—"who wears the veil"—and her father's response—"they decide"—conclude the dialogue, but Kincaid has gracefully conveyed the complex resonances of home, to which the narrative immediately returns (47–48). The chapter closes with a more philosophical definition: "[T]he place in which the mystical way of maneuvering through the world in an ethical way, a way universally understood to be honorable and universally understood to be ecstatic and universally understood to be the way we would all want it to be, carefully balanced between our own needs and the needs of other people, people we do not know and may never like" (48). Home is not a place of being but a way of being that respects the self and others equally.

Elsewhere, Kincaid ponders a larger field, expanding how we comprehend the domestic. As a foreigner visiting famous English gardens, she reflects, "I was in a country whose inhabitants (they call themselves subjects, not citizens) do not know how to live in the present and cannot imagine living in the future, they can live only in the past, because it, the past, has such a clear outcome, a winning outcome. A subdued nature is part of this worldview in which everything looks beautiful" (111–12). Symptomatic of a larger problem, "this ignorance of the botany of the place I am from (and am of) really only reflects the fact that when I lived there, I was of the conquered class and living in a conquered place; a principle of this condition is that nothing about you is of any interest unless the conqueror deems it so" (121). Naming is the conqueror's prerogative, signifying his ownership; he can unnaturally re-create the world, bringing to Antigua a botanical garden full of foreign plants, just as Kincaid herself can bring such plants to Vermont.

Kincaid acknowledges the complexities of joining the conquering class: "In the place I am from, I would have been a picture of shame: a woman covered in dirt, smelling of manure, her hair flecked with white dust (powdered lime), her body a cauldron of smells pleasing to her, and her back crooked with pain from bending over." Humorously moving from the natural to the erotic, she concedes, "In the place I am from, I would not have allowed a man with the same description as such a woman to kiss me" (121). Transplantation means asking awkward, uncomfortable questions: "[W]hat is the relationship between gardening and conquest? Is the conqueror a gardener and the conquered the person who works in the field?" (116). This episode tactfully extends Kingsolver's (and Jewett's, and Freeman's) reproof of many Americans for their class blindness (Kincaid's primary audience is also middle class), for Kincaid gardens for pleasure and beauty, not, as her family did, for medicine and sustenance. More explicitly aware of her transclass journey than Larcom, the author also dramatizes, through her transnational movements—imaginative as well as physical—how location frequently transforms gender roles, particularly as those roles relate to the natural world.

As Wilson, Larcom, and Winnemucca demonstrate, literacy empowers. Kincaid structures her book through a rhetorical device that twines through the essays: "What to do?" flowers repeatedly and pointedly. In pastoral reflections that relish plants' names and genealogies and evoke a lost Edenic past, Kincaid invites readers to share her reflections about the future. As the volume's title implies, the creative activities of gardening and writing both provoke inspiration and frustration: "How agitated I am when I am in the garden, and how happy I am to be so agitated. How vexed I often am when I am in the garden and how happy I am to be so vexed. What to do? Nothing works just the way I thought it would, nothing looks just the way I had imagined it." When it does work, "I am startled that my imagination is so ordinary" (14).

More introspective than Kingsolver's volume, Kincaid's also contemplates —and exposes—her own "unnatural" situation in frigid, alien—*and* flowering, familiar—Vermont. This fractured pastoral generates ambivalence: "The naming of things is so crucial to possession—a spiritual padlock with the key thrown irretrievably away—that it is a murder, an erasing, and it is not surprising that when people have felt themselves prey to it (conquest), among their first acts of liberation is to change their names" (122). As she composes these words, the author contemplates her own situation, looking out the window at her own beguilingly beautiful garden. "And I thought how I had crossed a line; but at whose expense? I cannot begin to look, because what if it is someone I know? I have joined the conquering class: who else could afford this garden—a garden in which I grow things it would be much cheaper to buy at the store?" (123). Who enables "simple living," "voluntary simplicity"?

Part natural history, part exhortation, part vision quest, Annie Dillard's autobiographical essay collection *Teaching a Stone to Talk* is fascinated by simplicity, though it seldom speaks directly of gender. Always grounded in the nonhuman natural world, the essays launch everywhere into metaphoric flights that sizzle and explode in overtly aesthetic performances. Seeing and feeling mesh in this ecstatic aesthetic home; logic is excluded and ethics are admitted through a back door, in glimpses. Among *Fallen Forests'* writers,

Dillard's closest relative is probably the poet Sigourney, who shares her descendant's focus on the romantic sublime and the spiritual. Do the essays in *Teaching a Stone to Talk*, which accords with virtually all current definitions of nature writing, preclude the political? Or do they explore alternative ideas of simplicity or environmental justice?

The volume opens with "Living Like Weasels," which begins, "A weasel is wild. Who knows what he thinks?" In Dillard's postlapsarian vision —shared with Kincaid—humans are inevitably alienated from wilderness, fallen into culture. The weasel operates by bodily need, by instinct: "he bites his prey at the neck, either splitting the jugular vein at the throat or crunching the brain at the base of the skull, and he does not let go." She recounts how a naturalist refuses to kill a weasel "socketed into his hand deeply as a rattlesnake. The man could in no way pry the tiny weasel off, and he had to walk half a mile to water, the weasel dangling from his palm, and soak him off like a stubborn label."[4] Small but deadly, the weasel possesses an enviable obstinacy, and his attachment to the man identifies their homological relationship as animals. A second anecdote, in which a man shoots an eagle and "found the dry skull of a weasel fixed by the jaws to his throat," illustrates this small animal's fierce tenacity (12).

Like Kincaid, Dillard incorporates an intertextual element; she has been reading about weasels because she has met one, and she shares the excursion to that meeting. The venue is Hollins Pond, aka Murray's Pond, two acres wide and six inches deep. "In winter, brown-and-white steers stand in the middle of it, merely dampening their hooves; from the distant shoreline they look like miracle itself, complete with miracle's nonchalance." Although the pastoral cattle are missing in this encounter, their winter water walk predicts the impending epiphany, all the more startling since "this is, mind you, suburbia" (12). Lest we fly too far too fast, Dillard returns us to earth: "There's a 55 mph highway at one end of the pond, and a nesting pair of wood ducks at the other. Under every bush is a muskrat hole or a beer can" (13). Her sketch refuses exceptionalism and foregrounds an ordinary landscape, more like Kirkland dropping her rose-tinted glasses than Sigourney exalting Niagara Falls. Humans are, for better or worse, part of nature; it is their first and last home. Nevertheless, Dillard's language begs simultaneously literal and metaphorical readings.

Coming face to face with an actual wild weasel jolts Dillard, in one of her favorite locutions, awake, and a narrative space performs a gasp before the vision: "Weasel! I'd never seen one wild before. He was ten inches long, thin as a curve, a muscled ribbon, brown as fruitwood, soft-furred, alert. His face was fierce, small and pointed as a lizard's; he would have made a good arrowhead. There was just a dot of chin, maybe two hairs' worth, and then the pure white fur began that spread down his underside." The naturalist needs metaphor to convey the animal's essence: its movement, its solidity, its sharpness—and its foreignness: "He had two black eyes I didn't see, any more than you see a window" (13). Dillard's metaphors both foster intimacy and underscore alienation. Insistently figurative, the description struggles toward explanation: "Our eyes locked, and someone threw away the key"; "our look was as if two lovers, or deadly enemies, met unexpectedly on an overgrown path when each had been thinking of something else: a clearing blow to the gut." Love and hate, violence and abstraction collide viscerally, as the author wrestles with words to capture for herself, and for readers' reperformance, her feeling response: "It was also a bright blow to the brain, or a sudden beating of brains, with all the charge and intimate grate of rubbed balloons. It emptied our lungs. It felled the forest, moved the fields, and drained the pond." An apocalyptic exchange of selfhoods, the encounter affirms humans' intimacy with animals and elegizes our forever-distanced state: "If you and I looked at each other that way, our skulls would split and drop to our shoulders. But we don't. We keep our skulls. So" (14).

The return to personhood, to thinking, to logic begins slowly, like surfacing from a profound sleep. Dillard's Thoreauvian meditation detaches her from the weasel: "I would like to learn, or remember, how to live." From wild animals, she wishes to "learn something of mindlessness, something of the purity of living in the physical senses and the dignity of living without bias or motive. The weasel lives in necessity and we live in choice" (15). Writers such as Berbineau, Wilson, and Freeman contradict this view, suggesting, like Kincaid and Kingsolver, that only those who have already exceeded subsistence enjoy such choice. Perhaps Dillard captures simplicity's essence, a mind-free (not mindless) concern for survival; perhaps Freeman's Harriet and Charlotte represent her unacknowledged precursors, escaped from social norms and, as we might say, closer to nature. "Yielding at every moment to the perfect freedom of a single necessity" means the freedom of not having to choose (16). Dillard's conclusion circles back to the eagle's flight, invoking for each weasel-reader her "one necessity" and picturing it pulling her "aloft even, till your eyes burn out and drop . . . let your very bones unhinge and scatter, loosened over fields, over fields and woods, lightly, thoughtless, from any height at all, from as high as eagles" (16). Seduced by her vision and uplifted by her "you," even knowing the story's ending, I always lose myself in this encounter.

But my response is visceral as much as intellectual, emotional as much as logical. Dillard makes the world strange and, in doing so, makes readers strangers to themselves. Sublimity, awe, wonder: these are my reactions. But, I imagine skeptics asking, can they be shared by everyone? And isn't this view sentimental, a reaching back to a prelapsarian past in which humans are relieved of ethical responsibility for others, including nonhuman animals? Many of Dillard's other essays respond to these questions. "The Deer at Providencia" depicts the author on a trip to Ecuador; her accidental companions are four older city men, Americans. "At the village called Providencia we saw a sight which moved us, and which shocked the men": a tiny deer bound around its neck and feet, injuring itself in the struggle to get free. Here the writer detaches herself from the sentimental: "It was 'pretty,' delicate of bone like all deer, and thin-skinned for the tropics" (60, 61). She reports the animal's struggles and the men's reactions to her apparent impassivity ("I looked detached, apparently, or calm, or focused, still"), noting, "I have thought a great deal about carnivorousness; I eat meat. These things are not issues; they are mysteries." Because she is the youngest, and female, the men expect her to be emotional, but she announces—to them and us—"Gentlemen of the city, what surprises you? That there is suffering here, or that I know it?" (64). Dillard rejects ostensibly feminine sentiment and privileges rationality—or some deeper, unreachable feeling.

Yet in its very extremity and excess Dillard's diction conjures her predecessors', which prioritizes affective appeals over reason and ethics. Contextualizing Dillard's rejection of sentimental rhetoric illuminates this different perspective. The conclusion of "God in the Doorway" invokes nineteenth-century language surrounding Christian suffering, love, and redemption (141). "On a Hill Far Away" highlights human vulnerability through the author's encounters with a newly born foal and a little boy (77–83). Perhaps most intimately, the volume ends with Dillard's elegiac account of a holiday weekend in the country with her daughter. While explicitly rejecting nostalgia—close kin to sentimentalism due to her daughter's presence—she succumbs to it, as the child teaches her how to live mindfully once more. She confides that on the Sunday morning return trip "we will visit my sister, as we did on the way—my sister, whom I love" (176). Home comprises not just nature, which can be inscrutable, but also family.

Like Kingsolver and many of the earlier writers, Dillard counterbalances elegy with humor: "I am trying to tell the child a few of the principles by which I live. A good gag is worth any amount of time, money, and effort; never draw to fill an inside straight; always keep score in games, never in love; always keep them guessing; . . . and (this is the hard part) listen to no one." The author wonders, as her daughter leaves the kitchen and goes to her room, if she is being obedient or rebellious: "She is this obedient. I have never detected a jot of rebellion in her. If she stays this way she is doomed. On the other hand, I wonder: did she do it for the gag?" (170). Wittily mirroring her own advice, Dillard negotiates affect and logic through the image of the vulnerable child. The story concludes with a poignant "ripple of wind": "It is an entirely misplaced air—fall, that I have utterly forgotten, that could be here again, *another* fall, and here it is only July. I thought I was younger, and would have more time. The gust crosses the river and blackens the water where it passes, like a finger closing slats" (177).

The sole balm or release for such loss, and for the suffering she witnesses in Providencia, Dillard contends—echoing Emily Dickinson—is language elevated by imagination: "All those things for which we have no words are lost. The mind—the culture—has two little tools, grammar and lexicon: a decorated sand bucket and a matching shovel. With these we bluster about the continents and do all the world's work. With these we try to save our very lives" (99). The body is easily corrupted: "The mind wants to live forever, or to learn a very good reason why not. . . . The mind wants to know all the world, and all eternity, and God. The mind's sidekick, however, will settle for two eggs over easy" (99). The pastoral, even the sublime (figured in a total eclipse of the sun), yield to and necessarily complement embodiment's comedy. But embodiment enables perception of the transcendent.

Comprising a series of detailed essays grounded in place, Winona LaDuke's *All Our Relations* offers a grimmer view. Although the book examines problems facing several Native nations, the title expresses the author's broader understanding of home and family, which encompasses the world and all its inhabitants. The narrative's jeremiad combines stories of individuals and their communities, opening apocalyptically: "The last

150 years have seen a great holocaust. There have been more species lost
in the past 150 years than since the Ice Age. During the same time, Indigenous peoples have been disappearing from the face of the earth. Over
2,000 nations of Indigenous peoples have gone extinct in the western hemisphere, and one nation disappears from the Amazon rainforest every year."[5]
LaDuke translates Dillard's transcendent vision to the political and the
social, combining forensic and scientific with emotionally evocative diction:
"lost," "disappearing," "extinct," and, most pointedly, "holocaust," which
underlines the human agency that authorizes this vanishing act, an extension, perhaps deliberate, of earlier efforts to "kill the Indian and save the
man."[6] If we are not shocked, she implies, we should be.

LaDuke makes her argument transparent: "There is a direct relationship between the loss of cultural diversity and the loss of biodiversity."[7]
The disappearance of salmon in the U.S. Northwest connects with human
loss: "The stories of the fish and the people are not so different. Environmental destruction threatens the existence of both" (1). Sounding an
elegiac note, the author educates, or reminds, readers about the traditional
connection between human and nonhuman nature in Native American
teachings, which affirm our family relations with "animals, fish, trees, and
rocks . . . our brothers, sisters, uncles, and grandpas." To ostensibly modern Americans, such relations may seem naïve or even sentimental. But
LaDuke affirms their power and Native nations' determined "struggle to
preserve that which remains and the struggle to recover," indicting industrialism as the destructive agent (2).

Echoing the voices of Cherokee women, Jemison, and Winnemucca,
LaDuke speaks for a pan-Indian community; her volume lauds outsized
heroism in the face of daunting challenges:

> While Native peoples have been massacred and fought, cheated,
> and robbed of their historical lands, today some of their lands are sub-
> ject to some of the most invasive industrial interventions imaginable.
> According to the Worldwatch Institute, 317 reservations in the United
> States are threatened by environmental hazards, ranging from toxic
> wastes to clearcuts.
>
> Reservations have been targeted as sites for 16 proposed nuclear
> waste dumps. Over 100 proposals have been floated in recent years to
> dump toxic waste in Indian communities. Seventy-seven sacred sites

have been disturbed or desecrated through resource extraction and development activities. (2–3)

The catalog of horrors continues, as LaDuke reprises Wilson's rhetorical mode: she lards the introduction with crushing details, assaulting the reader's sensibility. The author combines scientific facts with charged language that accentuates her outrage ("massacred," "cheated," "desecrated"), evoking emotions to engage our ethics.

Hardly traditional nature writing, *All Our Relations* shares many of the methods that Wilson, Winnemucca, and Ruiz de Burton adopt in their struggles for environmental justice. The volume proper opens with a powerful address to and on behalf of mothers. Chapter 1, "Akwesasne: Mohawk Mothers' Milk and PCBs," portrays an individual, Katsi Cook, "Mohawk midwife turned environmental activist," who protects and nurtures her community. The author's rhetoric reprises Katsi's own: "Katsi is alternating between singing and explaining to me the process of bioaccumulation of polychlorinated biphenyls (PCBS) in breast milk. A combination of Mother Theresa and Carl Sagan" (11). Traditional and modern, Cook uses the theme of motherhood to undercut contemporary definitions of progress; LaDuke indirectly invokes the most vulnerable individuals, babies, appealing to readers' feeling, logic, and ethics. The author's grim wit helps us swallow some bitter pills.

Beginnings extend beyond individual births. Re-creating and expanding the concept of home, LaDuke retells the Haudenosaunee origin story of the Woman Who Fell from the Sky, depicting the turtle's role as earth bearer and concluding, "As a result, North America is known today by the name *Turtle Island.*" Then she shifts emphatically to the present: "As in the creation legend, the turtle remains the bedrock of many ecosystems. But snapping turtles found at so-called Contaminant Cove on the Akwesasne reservation contained some 3,067 parts per million (ppm) of PCB contamination; others were found with 2,000 ppm PCB contamination. (According to EPA guidelines, 50 ppm PCBS in soil is considered to be 'contaminated')" (12). History lesson follows science lesson, as the author highlights the Haudenosaunee principles of government, one of which, the Great Law of Peace and the Good Mind, "upholds principles of kinship, women's leadership, and the value of the widest possible community consensus." American leaders (such as Washington and Franklin, she reminds us) studied those principles, yet they participated, through "land speculation over territory held by these peoples," in the resource wars that continue today (13).

Paralleling Jemison's and Winnemucca's rhetorical strategies, LaDuke interrupts her pedagogical mode and angrily assesses these wars and their consequences: "Mohawk lands were ceded through force, coercion, and deceit until fewer than 14,600 acres remained in New York State. By 1889, 80 percent of all Haudenosaunee land in New York State was under lease to non-Indian interests and individuals" (13). These transfers ultimately meant that General Motors and other industries became Akwesasne neighbors and contaminated the Great Lakes waters. Like Kingsolver's, LaDuke's (and Katsi Cook's) story focuses on food and its impact on the body—especially women's bodies: "'The fact is that women are the first environment,' says Katsi. 'We accumulate toxic chemicals like PCBS, DDT, Mirex, HCBS, . . . dumped into the waters by various industries. They are stored in our body fat and are excreted primarily through breast milk'" (18). Because of these dangerous levels of industrial chemicals, Mohawk mothers have been forced to alter their traditional fish-based diet to protect themselves and their children. While Kingsolver sometimes softens the truth, LaDuke exposes the individual and community consequences of ongoing resource wars. Winnemucca's entreaties on behalf of mothers and families, combined with her rational accounting of "wrongs and claims," anticipate her contemporary counterpart's rhetorical strategy: LaDuke juxtaposes sentimental images—motherhood and children—with industrial contamination. Her scientific facts prohibit a merely sympathetic response, but she marshals that emotional connection toward ethical responsibility and, she clearly hopes, action.

Home encompasses more than the local or even the national. The problem's transnational scope augments the challenge of achieving environmental justice, for many of the global corporations implicated reside in numerous jurisdictions, involving the U.S. and Canada, New York State and the province of Quebec, several different Mohawk jurisdictions, and the Mohawk government (20). But *All Our Relations* writes out of elegy and jeremiad to tell success stories, coup tales of individuals who have fought false progress despite great odds. The "collaborative epidemiological research" that Katsi Cook's achievements with the Akwesasne Mother's Milk Project sparked was "one of a scant 11 Superfund studies funded by the U.S.

Congress, and the only one focused on human health" (19). The chapter finishes with another sketch of the physical, social, and spiritual consequences of Cook's efforts and recurs to the jeremiad mode. Headway with General Motors is slow, but Cook has met with EPA representatives, and some cleanup has begun. The Mohawks are a first front in the war against the planet: "As the Mohawks would say, when the turtle dies, the world unravels. Instead of letting that happen, the Mohawks are determining their history . . . [and] [r]ebirthing their nation" (23).[8]

The rebirthing continues, in the Mohawk nation and beyond. In various ways direct and indirect, these contemporary authors ask, How can individuals and communities rebirth our nation(s), connecting past and future in authentic and transformative ways? What kind of stories have succeeded, and what are those we might tell, in our current planetary emergency, that will wake us to action? Perhaps most pertinently, following their predecessors' path, their writing requires *readers'* emotional intelligence, simultaneously insisting that we consider who's speaking, to whom, when, and why. Kingsolver's *Animal, Vegetable, Miracle* employs genial nudging; the author uses ethical, logical, and emotional approaches. The book is well-seasoned with facts, science: appeals to rationality and ethics. We may like our Cheetos, but they make us sick, and she shows us why. Alternatively, her humor invites us for a family visit and treats us as valued neighbors in an expanded community. Kincaid demands we think and throws us off balance. Concluding our joint excursion, she reminds us that the root of *travel* is *travail*, work: "Eden is . . . so rich in comfort, it tempts me to cause discomfort; I am in a state of continual discomfort and I like this state so much I would like to share it" (229). Dillard believes that "Nature's silence is its one remark, and every flake of the world is a chip off that old and immutable block" (69). With flamboyant metaphoric flights, she evokes a lost nature and urges us to follow. Most explicitly political, LaDuke circles back in her final chapter ("The Seventh Generation") to history, synthesizing U.S. constitutional law and indigenous teachings: "The challenge at the cusp of the millennium is to transform human laws to match natural laws, not vice versa. And to correspondingly transform wasteful production and voracious consumption. America and industrial society must move from a society based on conquest to one steeped in the practice of survival" (197).

IT MAY SEEM STRANGE to think of caring for a river. The mighty Merrimack, which powered the Lowell mills, empties in my birthplace city of Newburyport, Massachusetts; at the main harbor where U.S. Route 1 crosses on a modern bridge, the water is roughly a quarter-mile wide. When I was a child, my grandfather regaled me with stories of winter passings during his childhood fifty years earlier: before the metal bridge was built, men drove teams of horses and oxen pulling sledges loaded with supplies across the frozen water to neighboring Salisbury. When I looked at the river with five-year-old eyes, its broad black flow skirted by automobile-sized ice cakes, I thought the story was fabricated, mere make-believe. Today, fifty years later, the river is ice-free, or iceless, depending on your perspective. Drivers on the bridge can look down and watch the braided current rushing to Plum Island and the Atlantic beyond.

The river waters will endure, whether the sea level rises and the city is engulfed or whether the ice returns with an even deeper burden of cold. In the end, without the future, memory is meaningless, and history vanishes.

Newburyport iron bridge over the Merrimack River, looking toward Salisbury, Massachusetts, c. 1902. Author's collection.

Notes

Grounding the Texts

1. These plants are all native to the western hemisphere.

2. Morse and Parish, *A Compendious History of New England*, 85; "The Merrimack River."

3. Quascacunquen signifies "waterfall"; Native Americans named the area for the falls on the eponymous river, which was renamed the Parker River after one of the first settlers' leaders, the minister Thomas Parker. See Coffin, *A Sketch of the History*, 9; "Newbury—A Brief History"; "The Landing at Parker River"; and "The History of Old Town Hill."

4. Quoted in Awiakta, *Selu*, 92.

5. As chapter 1 outlines, Cherokee and Seneca societies esteemed women, and their traditional male counterparts understood nature as women did. Thus Ward and Mary Jemison present particular challenges for gendered analysis. This problem inheres (though to a much lesser extent) with Sarah Winnemucca and Zitkala-Ša, whom I discuss in chapter 5. My argument focuses, however, on how the women's perspectives deviate from the dominant society's masculine ethos.

6. "American" and "U.S." are not synonymous, but I use the terms interchangeably for narrative variety and economy. Readers should remain aware of the umbrella term's appropriativeness. Coined by the British historian Eric Hobsbawm, the term "long nineteenth century" encompasses the 1780s to 1914. *The Age of Extremes*, 6. As my title indicates, my long nineteenth century stretches forward to 1924, when all Native Americans were granted full U.S. citizenship.

7. Kollin, "The Wild, Wild North," 44.

8. In order to extend these contestations into the present, each chapter engages strategically in what Scott Slovic has called "narrative scholarship," which embeds critical reflection in stories. See Slovic, "Ecocriticism with or without Narrative."

9. On the roots of the environmental movement, see Adamson and Slovic, "Guest Editors' Introduction," 5–6.

10. To a greater or lesser degree, my discussion also draws from and converses with such academic disciplines as environmental history, regional studies, disability studies, whiteness theory, sexuality studies, history of the book, cultural studies, feminist theory, literary history, humor studies, and Native Studies. On the tensions between individualism and community in the recent United States, see Putnam, *Bowling Alone*.

Inevitably, *Fallen Forests* omits important environmentally inflected concerns, perhaps most notably animal rights, a subject on which I have too much to say. For a framework on Animal Studies that leads to other resources (including the *PMLA* special issue that it introduces), see DeKoven, "Guest Column." My project also elides many important nineteenth-century American women writers, including Emily Dickinson. I exclude Dickinson because I understand her work as closer to nature writing than environmental writing.

11. Classic scholarship on nineteenth-century American women's writing also includes Baym, *Woman's Fiction*; Shirley Samuels, *The Culture of Sentiment*; Frances Smith Foster, *Written by Herself*; Romero, *Home Fronts*; and Merish, *Sentimental Materialism*. Ecocriticism focusing on nineteenth-century American women's writing includes: Kolodny, *The Land Before Her*; Norwood, *Made from This Earth*; and Gianquitto, *"Good Observers of Nature."*

12. On the public/private-sphere dichotomy, see Easton et al., "Introduction: Becoming Visible." For a discussion of sentimentalism's continuing resonance in the contemporary United States, see Berlant, *The Female Complaint*.

13. Lunsford, "On Reclaiming Rhetorica," 6; Ritchie and Ronald, *Available Means*. Ritchie and Ronald cite a number of *topoi*, or rhetorical themes, that distinguish feminine rhetoric (xxii–xxvii). See also Glenn, *Rhetoric Retold*; Wertheimer, *Listening to Their Voices*; Campbell, *Man Cannot Speak for Her*. For critical work in rhetoric related to earlier American women, see Kolodny, "Inventing a Feminist Discourse"; Bean, "Conversation as Rhetoric"; Mattingly, *Well-Tempered Women*; Nan Johnson, *Gender and Rhetorical Space*; Mattingly, *Appropriate[ing] Dress*; Powell, "Princess Sarah, the Civilized Indian"; Powell, "Sarah Winnemucca Hopkins"; Elizabeth Wilkinson, "Story as a Weapon." For essays on feminist rhetorical theory, methodology, and pedagogy, see, for example, Ratcliffe, *Anglo-American Feminist Challenges*; Foss, Foss, and Griffin, *Feminist Rhetorical Theories*; Ronald and Ritchie, *Teaching Rhetorica*; Schell and Rawson, *Rhetorica in Motion*; Buchanan and Ryan, *Walking and Talking Feminist Rhetorics*.

Daniel C. Payne cites the "rhetorical skill" of many canonical environmental writers, including such writers as Emerson, Thoreau, George Perkins March, and John Burroughs. *Voices in the Wilderness*, 4.

14. Cokinos, "What Is Ecocriticism?"

15. On expansion of the field, see Murphy, *Literature, Nature, and Other*; Murphy, *Farther Afield*; Armbruster and Wallace, *Beyond Nature Writing*; Branch, *Reading the Roots*; Buell, *The Future of Environmental Criticism*. Genre distinctions are Western, as Murphy notes (*Farther Afield*, 8) and as such feminist theorists as Paula Gunn Allen and Gloria Anzaldúa have repeatedly emphasized. Paula Gunn Allen (Laguna Pueblo), *The Sacred Hoop*; Paula Gunn Allen, introduction to *Spider Woman's Granddaughters*, 1–25; Anzaldúa, *Borderlands/La Frontera*. Murphy argues for a distinction between genre and mode. *Farther Afield*, 49. He also shows that the nonfiction essay, which has provided the touchstone for American nature writing and the basis for the construction of a canon of such writing, has a number of problems, including its foundation in a Eurocentric, Judeo-Christian Enlighten-

ment perspective that specifies observer detachment and assumes alienation from nature; its emphasis on the individual; and its refusal of "political" themes (52–54). But his advocacy of a consciously environmental perspective in literature, while politically meaningful, skews the discussion of environmental writing toward more recent literature and unintentionally devalues many earlier women writers. On the possibility for women's nature writing to question social norms, see Buell, "American Pastoral Ideology Reappraised," 18–19. On the problem of "nonliterary" genres, see Sweet, "Projecting Early American Environmental Writing," 426–27.

16. Glotfelty, "Introduction."

17. Bracke, "Redrawing the Boundaries," 766.

18. Sturgeon, *Environmentalism in Popular Culture*, 23. For an overview of three characteristic ecocritical approaches to "nature," see Sweet, "Projecting Early American Environmental Writing," 419. Sweet argues for an "eco-economic" model that "provides a critique of the growth paradigm's denial of the real environmental basis and costs of growth" (421). As Philippon observes, Sweet's model elides the discontinuities between earlier and later periods, particularly "the pace and scale of technological change" that has underwritten our current crisis. "Is Early American Environmental Writing Sustainable?" 435. As will become evident, especially in chapter 3, my approach to the women writers has some affinities with Sweet's emphasis on the georgic mode, which "manifests our labouring, information-gathering, productive behavior" and hence our continuity with nature (422). See also Sweet, *American Georgics*, 6.

19. Philippon, *Conserving Words*, 8.

20. A number of years ago John Elder described traditional nature writing as "a form of personal, reflective essay, grounded in attentiveness to the natural world and an appreciation of science but also open to the spiritual meaning and intrinsic value of nature"; recognizing the limitations of this description, particularly in relation to urban nature and Americans of color, he called for an expansion of its boundaries. Quoted in Armbruster and Wallace, *Beyond Nature Writing*, 2–3.

21. Ulman, "Thinking like a Mountain," 49.

22. McKibben, *American Earth*, xxii.

23. Slovic, "Epistemology and Politics," 84.

24. Ibid., 84–85. Slovic also formulates two rhetorical modes: "embedded persuasive rhetoric" and "discrete persuasive rhetoric" (86); the first combines pastoral with jeremiad while the second isolates or sequences them.

25. Ibid., 93, 105, 83.

26. Ibid., 85, 83.

27. Killingsworth and Palmer, "Millennial Ecology," 41.

28. I omit quotation marks around most terms from this point forward, since they distract from the analysis. Terms and concepts are italicized when they first appear. For some of the terms central to ecocriticism and related definitional challenges, see Irene Diamond and Orenstein, *Reweaving the World*; Lyon, "A Taxonomy of Nature Writing"; Buell, *The Environmental Imagination*, 7–8; Branch et

al., *Reading the Earth*; Gaard and Murphy, *Ecofeminist Literary Criticism*; Mazel, *American Literary Environmentalism*; Murphy, *Farther Afield*; Rochelle Johnson, *Passions for Nature*, xiii; Buell, *The Future of Environmental Criticism* (esp. chapters 1 and 2); Barnhill, "Surveying the Landscape," 273–90. Rochelle Johnson also gives an exemplary account of the history of the term *nature* in the United States; see *Passions for Nature*, 1–23. See also Myers, *Converging Stories*, 8ff., for an account of debates surrounding definitions of *ecology*, *ecocentricity*, and *race*. I seldom use the term *ecology*, preferring to retain its biological resonance, although I sometimes quote texts that use it as a cognate for *the environment*.

29. See Ulman, "Thinking like a Mountain," 47.

30. Goleman, *Emotional Intelligence*. The term has a historical resonance; see Thorndike, "Intelligence and Its Uses." A Columbia University psychology professor, Thorndike calls "social intelligence" "the ability to understand and manage men and women, boys and girls—to act wisely in human relations" (228). Contemporary researchers disagree about even such fundamentals as the concept's denomination. They also distinguish between "ability emotional intelligence," which signifies "the ability to perceive emotion, integrate emotion to facilitate thought, understand emotions and to regulate emotions to promote personal growth" (including others' emotions and growth) and which is measured by performance-based tests, and "trait emotional intelligence," which represents self-reported emotional efficacy, a personality trait rather than an ability. Petrides, Pita, and Kokkinaki, "The Location of Trait Emotional Intelligence," 273; Salovey and Grewal, "The Science of Emotional Intelligence," 281–85.

31. Goleman, *Emotional Intelligence*, 43–44. For a popular perspective on EI's application to business and everyday life, see, for example, Bradberry and Greaves, *Emotional Intelligence 2.0*. This application corroborates its potential for manipulative purposes. The characteristics of EI and its measurability continue to be energetically debated in worldwide psychological, business, and educational scholarship. See, for example, Sánchez-Ruiz, Pérez-González, and Petrides, "Trait Emotional Intelligence Profiles"; Pauline Parker and Sorenson, "Emotional Intelligence and Leadership Skills."

32. Initiated by Ann Douglas and Jane Tompkins, the debate on sentimentalism's meaning and value has generated numerous responses. Douglas, *The Feminization of American Culture*; Jane Tompkins, *Sensational Designs*. See, for example, Howard, "What Is Sentimentality?"; Dillon, "Sentimental Aesthetics." Feminist scholarship has long been engaged with research on gender differences in handling emotions and relationships; see, for example, Gilligan, *In a Different Voice*. On sentiment and sentimentalism's roots, see Dillon, "Sentimental Aesthetics"; see also Camfield, *Sentimental Twain*. Segregating sentimentalism from its stylistic and affective companions has impoverished our understanding of the complex emotional-intellectual transactions sparked by these affiliations. See Kilcup, *Robert Frost and Feminine Literary Tradition*; Cari M. Carpenter, *Seeing Red*; Mielke, *Moving Encounters*.

33. See Kilcup, "Essays of Invention."

34. Goleman, *Emotional Intelligence*, 103, 105, 115. Although literary and cultural scholars often insist on the difference between sympathy and empathy, they may have similar biological foundations. See Wexler, *Tender Violence*.

35. Goleman, *Emotional Intelligence*, 6–7. Accounts of emotion in relation to nineteenth-century American women's writing tend to be limited in affective scope, while EI research encompasses a broad emotional range. On the physical effects of sentimental sympathy, see Dillon, "Sentimental Aesthetics"; Sánchez-Eppler, *Touching Liberty*; Noble, *The Masochistic Pleasures of Sentimental Literature*. We should observe that emotional responses are based in biology, specifically in the amygdala, which occupies "a privileged position as an emotional sentinel, able to hijack the brain." Goleman, *Emotional Intelligence*, 17. Hence emotional responses always override rationality; the more stress an individual feels, the more likely she or he is to revert to biology—and be susceptible to manipulation.

36. Goleman, *Emotional Intelligence*, 9.

37. Ibid., 116.

38. An obvious danger is the traditional essentialist affiliation of emotion with women and reason with men and the valorization of one over the other.

39. Many feminists cite Françoise D'Eaubonne's work as foundational to ecofeminism; others add the simultaneous activism of women at Love Canal and the Chipko movement in India, among others. See Barbara T. Gates, "A Root of Ecofeminism," 7–16. Some critics of ecofeminism cite its essentialism, while others—often activists—regard such debates themselves as abstractions that detract from actions for social change. See Moore, "Imagining Feminist Futures." Karen J. Warren's taxonomy delineates some of the movement's major strands. *Ecofeminist Philosophy*, 21–38.

40. Sturgeon, *Environmentalism in Popular Culture*, 9. Sturgeon observes that many contemporary environmental justice advocates are women (10), an observation that I extend backward into the nineteenth century, with particular emphasis on women of color and working-class writers. See also Merchant, *Radical Ecology*, 193–222.

41. Mack-Canty, "Third-Wave Feminism," 175.

42. Some critics, such as Simon C. Estok, have distinguished between ecofeminism, which places gender at the center of its project, and ecocriticism, which includes but does not privilege gender in its commitment to the natural world. At the same time, he suggests, the two approaches share an ethical commitment to praxis. "Bridging the Great Divide," 197–200.

43. This perspective has some contemporary credence; Laurel Kearns argues that "activism is . . . what we do every day when we teach and learn." "Afterword: Teaching Indoors," 222.

44. Gaard and Murphy, "A Dialogue on the Role," 2, 3.

45. Several of these volumes concentrate in whole or in part on nineteenth-century American women's writing. Kolodny and Johnson center on their writers'

commitment to metaphor, while Norwood and Gianquitto address women scientists' more concrete affiliations with nature. Focused principally on contemporary texts, Alaimo's, Ruffin's, and Sturgeon's volumes describe important links with historical precedents. Merchant's work in environmental history grounds my account from a different perspective.

46. Sturgeon, *Environmentalism in Popular Culture*, 11.

47. Philippon, *Conserving Words*, 6–7ff.

48. Because of the historically debilitating associations between women and nature, hostility to materiality remains particularly strong in some quarters; as Stacy Alaimo and Susan Hekman point out, "The guiding rule of procedure for most contemporary feminisms requires that one distance oneself as much as possible from the tainted realm of materiality by taking refuge within culture, discourse, and language." "Introduction: Emerging Models," 1. Gaard discusses a related problem for ecofeminists in "Ecofeminism Revisited."

49. Killingsworth and Palmer, *Ecospeak*, 32. Killingsworth and Palmer cite René Dubos's accounting of the Bible's overwhelmingly negative representation of wilderness.

50. Pearce provides the exemplary account of this dynamic. *Savagism and Civilization*.

51. Alaimo, *Bodily Natures*, 5, 9.

52. Killingsworth and Palmer, "Millennial Ecology," 23.

53. Kolodny, *The Lay of the Land*, 67–68. On the continued dominance of the economic growth paradigm, see Sweet, "Projecting Early American Environmental Writing," 421.

54. Killingsworth and Palmer, *Ecospeak*, 1. Herndl and Brown propose a rhetorical model for environmental discourse that affiliates corners of the classical rhetorical triangle with different modes. The ethnocentric model (ethos) constructs nature as a resource to be managed; regulatory discourse fits this model. The anthropocentric perspective (logos) regards nature as an object of knowledge; scientific discourse occurs in this framework. The ecocentric model (pathos) conceptualizes nature as spirit, and it sponsors poetic discourse. *Green Culture*, 10–12. While Herndl and Brown's model has some explanatory power, it is unwieldy in the nineteenth-century context. Throughout *Fallen Forests* I use variants of the classical rhetorical triad of ethos (ethics), logos (logic), and pathos (emotion) to assess the writers' perspectives and approaches.

55. On the significance of discourse contexts, see Philippon, "Is Early American Environmental Writing Sustainable?" 435.

56. Sam McKegney's discussion of the difficulties facing non-Native scholars of Native literatures offers analogues for all identity-based criticism. "Strategies of Ethical Engagement," 56–67. Like many New Englanders whose family members arrived in America early, I have Native ancestry.

57. As Buell, Johnson, and many others indicate, seeing nature as a constructed concept is not incommensurate with understanding it as a concrete presence. See

Rochelle Johnson, *Passions for Nature*, 1–22. Myers usefully describes the tension between constructivist and essentialist perspectives and, as I do, attempts to mediate between the two. *Converging Stories*, 8ff.

58. Emphasizing the restoration of the literal and the material and rejecting "the mentality of domination enacted in literature and literary criticism," *Fallen Forests* seeks to extend Josephine Donovan's work. "Ecofeminist Literary Criticism," 164.

59. DeGraaf, Wann, and Naylor, *Affluenza*.

60. McKibben, *Deep Economy*, 1–2. See also Murphy, *Ecocritical Explorations*, 20.

61. Also an activist and American Indian spiritual leader, Tinker has produced influential scholarly work, including *American Indian Liberation*, *Spirit and Resistance*, and *Missionary Conquest*.

62. Although the writers' location figures centrally in *Fallen Forests*, I only indirectly address regionalism as a genre. For a discussion of the scholarly history of regionalism, see Fetterley and Pryse, *Writing Out of Place*, 34–65. See also Joseph, *American Literary Regionalism*; Lutz, *Cosmopolitan Vistas*; Stephanie Foote, *Regional Fictions*; Robert Jackson, *Seeking the Region*.

63. Paralleling writers such as Andrea Smith, Philippon urges ecocritics to consider whether "religious conviction" might be "a basis for environmental action." "Is Early American Environmental Writing Sustainable?," 436.

64. Kirkland, *Forest Life*, 1:147; Sigourney, *Scenes in My Native Land*, 117.

65. Murphy, *Farther Afield*, 86.

66. Helfand and Gold, *Blue Vinyl*.

67. Celia Thaxter, "The Sandpiper's Nest."

Chapter 1. "We planted, tended, and harvested our corn"

The epigraphs are taken from Catesby, "Of the Soil of Carolina," 135; Cherokee Indian Women, "Letter from Cherokee Indian Women"; see Justice, "Katteuha (Cherokee)." Justice notes that although the speaker may have been Nancy Ward, it could also have been another Beloved Woman who represented a group of Cherokee women.

1. Klare, *Resource Wars*, 25. Echoing Klare, Jared Diamond observes (and Al Gore points out) that societies have long warred over resources. Jared Diamond, *Collapse*, 6; Gore, *An Inconvenient Truth*.

2. Klare, *Resource Wars*, 19, 190. See also Dinar, "Resource Scarcity and Environmental Degradation," 1; Renner, *The Anatomy of Resource Wars*, 9; Le Billon, "The Geopolitical Economy of 'Resource Wars,'" 1, 2–3.

3. Gedicks, *The New Resource Wars*, 13–38, 39–43. We must distinguish between current conflicts and the historical ones referenced in this chapter. The terminology itself tells the tale: although some applications of *resource* suggest its interpretation as a source of assistance or "means of supplying a deficiency or need," in the plural the term conveys an understanding of objects, including "money, materials,

people, or some other asset" that can be exploited for economic or material gain, or "the collective means possessed by a country or region for its own support, enrichment, or defense." *Natural resources* signifies "those materials or substances of a place which can be used to sustain life or for economic exploitation." *Oxford English Dictionary*, online.

4. In making this contention I am not asserting that Native women and Euramerican women's emotional landscapes were identical; indeed, as the account that follows indicates, the circumstances and valences of affective appeals varied even within cultures, as we see with the Cherokee women.

5. Ritchie and Ronald, introduction to *Available Means*, xxii.

6. I provide specific citations in discussions of the individual writers.

7. In an excellent overview of ecocritical history and current challenges, Ursula Heise argues that the environmental justice movement needs to formulate a transnational perspective. Her argument elides an important feature of U.S. history, namely, the internal transnationality represented by Native American nations. Heise, "Ecocriticism and the Transnational Turn." Far from being "domestic dependent nations," as the U.S. Congress and Supreme Court denominated them in the nineteenth century, these groups were initially recognized as sovereign nations. See Merchant, *The Columbia Guide*, 141. See also Sweet's call for "a reexamination of the American nature-writing and regionalist canons in historical, global context." "Projecting Early American Environmental Writing," 426. I agree with Glen A. Love's assertion that both environmentalists and ecocritics need to incorporate local and global perspectives. "Et in Arcadia Ego," 197–98.

8. "Principles of Environmental Justice."

9. Weaver, introduction to *Defending Mother Earth*, 10. The anthropologist Shepard Kretch III coined the concept of the "Ecological Indian." *The Ecological Indian*, 22. Kretch's work has been widely discussed, defended, and criticized; see, for example, Harkin and Lewis, *Native Americans and the Environment*. See also Weaver, introduction to *Defending Mother Earth*, 3, 4. Rifkin issues a salient caution about using the (Euramerican) concept of "nation" to describe Native social-organizational-familial systems, expressing particular concern about the erasure of questions of class and literacy in such superimpositions; see "Representing the Cherokee Nation," 47–51.

10. Sze, "Environmental Justice Literature to Literature of Environmental Justice," 163.

11. See Buell, *Writing for an Endangered World*, 8–9. Buell's (and before him, Leo Marx's) accounts of disrupted pastoral focus on Western tradition.

12. Andrea Smith makes perhaps the most prominent connection between resource wars and gender; see *Conquest*.

13. Ward, [Speech to U.S. Treaty Commissioners], 28.

14. This argument contrasts with Stacy Alaimo's assertion of American women's search for "undomesticated ground"; her early writers are Euramerican. See Alaimo, *Undomesticated Ground*, 16–18, 27–37.

15. Mankiller, *Mankiller*, 55.

16. Le Billon, "The Geopolitical Economy of 'Resource Wars,'" 2.

17. Commentators such as Mark Catesby, William Bartram, and J. Hector St. John de Crèvecoeur—now commonly regarded as part of the nature writing canon—in varying degrees repeat a pattern established with Columbus: celebrating America's beauty, appreciating its sustaining features, and acknowledging its potential for profit. All three writers are included in Branch, *Reading the Roots*; see Catesby, *The Natural History of Carolina* (1731); Bartram, *Travels through North and South Carolina*; Crèvecoeur, *Letters from an American Farmer*.

18. See, for example, Merchant, *The Death of Nature*; Lynn White Jr., "The Historical Roots." White's essay has undergone sustained critique; see Ruether, "Ecological Theology," 226–34; Whitney, "Christianity and Changing Concepts of Nature," 26–51. For a theological-philosophical perspective on recovering connections between humans and the nonhuman natural world, see Wirzba, *The Paradise of God*. Wirzba emphasizes agrarian tradition as a central feature of this renewal; responding to the Lynn White thesis, he argues that the domination perspective misinterprets the Genesis story (125ff.). Gary Fick connects farming, stewardship, and faith, with attention to specific Biblical passages; he addresses gender issues as well in his chapter "Abuse, Poverty, and Women." *Food, Farming, and Faith*, 129–50.

19. Bauman, Bohannon, and O'Brien, introduction to *Grounding Religion*, 2.

20. On contemporary interpretations of Genesis and for some explanation of the resonances of the original Hebrew, see Fick, *Food, Farming, and Faith*, 15–42.

21. Tinker, "An American Indian Theological Response," 157; see Deloria, *God Is Red*, 79.

22. Tinker, "An American Indian Theological Response," 158; see Deloria, *God Is Red*, 88–90.

23. Tinker, "An American Indian Theological Response," 158, 159; see Deloria, *God Is Red*, 95.

24. Tinker, "An American Indian Theological Response," 162.

25. See Deloria, *God Is Red*, 63, 67, chapter 4.

26. Tinker, "An American Indian Theological Response," 163; Deloria, *God Is Red*, 145. Gellately and Kiernan offer statistics and cite explicit statements by U.S. government agents and officials urging the extermination of Native peoples. "The Study of Mass Murder," 21–24; see also Stannard, *American Holocaust*, ix–x, 128, 145.

27. Deloria, *God Is Red*, 67.

28. Perdue, *Cherokee Women*, 64, 95ff.

29. Ibid., 97–98.

30. Ibid., 111–13, 118–19. On Jefferson's attitude toward and role in the appropriation of Native lands, see Rifkin, *Manifesting America*, 10–12, 88–89.

31. Alaimo, *Undomesticated Ground*, 3–4; see 2.

32. See Alaimo, *Undomesticated Ground*, 11ff. One problem with this account, as mentioned earlier, is its assumption of the application of dominant-society values to all women.

33. Pearce, *Savagism and Civilization*, 127; see 91–120.

34. Ritchie and Ronald, introduction to *Available Means*, xvii.

35. For more details on Ward's life, see Perdue, "Nancy Ward." On Cherokee women's roles, I am indebted throughout to Perdue's groundbreaking work; see also *Cherokee Women*. In their section introduction "Many Revolutions," Barker-Benfield and Clinton note the negative impact of the fur trade on the Cherokee in the eighteenth century, which kept men away from home hunting and required extra labor from women; as they sought furs for European goods, Indians may have destroyed their ecosystems (57).

36. For some Cherokees, Ward represents not a heroic intermediary but a cultural traitor. For a discussion of Ward's interventions on behalf of whites, see Perdue, "Nancy Ward," 90ff.

Jeffrey Myers and Elizabeth Ammons are among the scholars who underscore the "strong connections between racial oppression and destructive attitudes toward the land" in the work of nineteenth-century Native American writers like Sarah Winnemucca. Myers, *Converging Stories*, 4; Ammons, *Brave New Words*, 93.

37. Of course, resource wars also occurred between Indian nations, including the encounter between Cherokees and Creeks in which Ward acquired her honorific.

38. For additional discussion of the figures of the War Woman and the Beloved Woman, see Perdue, *Cherokee Women*, 38–39; Perdue, "Nancy Ward," 85ff.; Miles, "Circular Reasoning," 224–25. Elizabeth Cook-Lynn avers that Native Americans have long been at war with the U.S. federal government. *Anti-Indianism in Modern America*, 151, 154.

39. Over time, perhaps no resource has sparked more violence than gold. The skein of gold threads through Columbus's journal, forming a repeated pattern through which he anticipates his benefactors' desires, as when, for example, he relates that "[o]ne of the indians told the Admiral that he had ordered his statue to be made of gold as large as life." Columbus, "Journal of the First Voyage." More recently, as a *60 Minutes* segment has documented, the vicious conflicts over gold in the Congo that have caused about five million casualties continue. CBSNews.com, "How Gold Pays for Congo's Deadly War"; "Gold Addiction Fuels Brutal Congo War." See also Klare, *Resource Wars*, 209.

40. "Memorial in Behalf of the Cherokees," 60.

41. For further details on this land grab, see Hershberger, "Mobilizing Women, Anticipating Abolition," 16ff. See also Merchant, *The Columbia Guide*, 141–42. Much later, even "progressives" like Lucy Lowry Hoyt Keys and Narcissa Owen would angrily recount the cruelty of the Trail of Tears, continuing the Cherokee women's tradition of dissent. See Kilcup, "The art spirit," 11–12.

42. Miles, "Circular Reasoning," 222. Miles points out how "the national issue of land exchange was also a women's issue" (223).

43. Weaver, introduction to *Defending Mother Earth*, 19; see also Cook-Lynn, *New Indians, Old Wars*, xi, 73. For a discussion of the U.S. government's legal and

rhetorical reshaping of Cherokee sovereignty and leadership in order to advance removal, see Rifkin, *Manifesting America*, chapter 1.

44. Ward, [Letter to U.S. Treaty Commissioners], quoted in Samuel Cole Williams, *Tennessee during the Revolutionary War*, 201. Ward's words could have been mistranscribed, but the sentiments she expresses dovetail with Cherokee tradition. See also Kilcup, *Native American Women's Writing*, 27, 28–30.

45. Perdue, *Cherokee Women*, 61–62. On Republican Motherhood, see Kerber, "The Republican Mother"; Matthews, *"Just a Housewife,"* 21, 26, 45. By 1841 Catharine Beecher would claim that "American democracy rose or fell on the efforts of its female members." Matthews, *"Just a Housewife,"* 46. See also Sklar, *Catharine Beecher*, 161.

46. Perdue, *Cherokee Women*, 55.

47. For a cogent discussion of the use of "children" in Apess and in Euramerican discourses, see Cheryl Walker, *Indian Nation*, 56, 187, 188.

48. War Women also decided the fate of war captives, a significant right in this context. The white men's response to Ward seems to demonstrate a certain level of insight into Cherokee culture and women's significance in it, although we cannot help but read their equally double (but possibly disingenuous) language with profound unease: "Mothers: We have listened well to your talk; it is humane. . . . No man can hear it without being moved by it. Such words and thoughts show the world that human nature is the same everywhere. Our women shall hear your words, and we know how they will feel and think of them. We are all descendants of the same woman. We will not quarrel with you, because you are our mothers. We will not meddle with your people if they will be still and let us live in peace." Colonel William Christian, quoted in Samuel Cole Williams, *Tennessee during the Revolutionary War*, 201.

49. Miles, "Circular Reasoning," 226.

50. Perdue, *Cherokee Women*, 119–20; Weaver, introduction to *Defending Mother Earth*, 19; Rifkin, "Representing the Cherokee Nation," 47–80.

51. Cherokee Women, "Petitions of the Women's Councils." Like many of her Native American successors, Ward participates in both—to use Cheryl Walker's terms—"transpositional" and "subjugated" discourses. Walker's terms possess considerable explanatory power, but because applying them would require lengthy explanations, I have chosen not to employ them here. *Indian Nation*, 16–17.

52. Miles, "Circular Reasoning," 226.

53. Ritchie and Ronald, introduction to *Available Means*, xxi, xxii.

54. Weaver, introduction to *Defending Mother Earth*, 8.

55. Perdue, *Cherokee Women*, 13. Perdue remarks that in practice gender roles were less rigid than in theory and that men and women often helped each other (18). See Miles, "Circular Reasoning," 227.

56. For one version of the Selu and Kana'tī narrative, see Mooney, *Myths of the Cherokee*, 340; see also Perdue, *Cherokee Women*, 13–15. On gender complementarity, see Paula Gunn Allen (Laguna Pueblo), "The Sacred Hoop."

57. Awiakta, *Selu*, 9. Awiakta emphasizes gender complementarity (23–26). See also Miles, "Circular Reasoning," 226.

58. Perdue, *Cherokee Women*, 13.

59. Ibid., 25, 24; see Miles, "Circular Reasoning," 227.

60. Roderick Nash, *Wilderness and the American Mind*, 29. The Indians were associated with "unimproved" land (33). For a discussion of the Cherokee and land "improvements," see Sweet, *American Georgics*, chapter 6.

61. John Ridge to Albert Gallatin, 27 February 1826, John Howard Payne Papers, Newberry Library, Chicago, Ill., quoted in Perdue, "Nancy Ward," 96. See Perdue, *Cherokee Women*, 62; Fassett, "Afterword," 178–79.

62. "Cherokee Mission Schools." As Elspeth Whitney suggests in her refutation of the Lynn White thesis, "Christianity and Changing Concepts of Nature," consideration of Christianity's cultural influence must be grounded in place and in historical moment. For the Cherokee, two of the greatest impacts arrived in the form of Moravian and ABCFM missionaries. For an overview of the three-pronged efforts—encompassing "Christianization, education, and the instilling of private property"—by whites to "civilize" Indians, see Grinde, "Taking the Indian out of the Indian," 25ff.

63. Miles, "Circular Reasoning," 228.

64. The speech emblematizes "the link between literature and social relationships that is a natural part of the oral tradition" and language's transformative power in effecting social change. Womack, *Red on Red*, 16; see 17, 66–67. See also Bruchac, *Roots of Survival*, 91; Armstrong, "Land Speaking," 183.

65. Miles, "Circular Reasoning," 231.

66. The petition concludes, "There are some white men among us who have been raised in this country from their youth, are connected with us by marriage, & have considerable families, who are very active in encouraging the emigration of our nation. These ought to be our truest friends but prove our worst enemies. They seem to be only concerned how to increase their riches, but do not care what becomes of our Nation, nor even of their own wives and children." Cherokee Women, "Petitions of the Women's Councils."

67. Miles argues that "the women's rhetoric shifted to better target an entrenched white and male opposition," which is accurate, but she deemphasizes the loss of Cherokee culture, especially of women's authority, with their assimilation to Christian norms. "Circular Reasoning," 231.

68. Perdue, *Cherokee Women*, 62 and passim; see Miles, "Circular Reasoning," 225. We should note that "grants" of land by the Indians, particularly in the early years of the American republic, indicated not exclusive or individual ownership in the English sense but the right to *use* land.

69. For more on the timing, authorship, and effects of these petitions, see Miles, "Circular Reasoning," 227ff.; Perdue, "Nancy Ward," 97; Awiakta, *Selu*, 95–97.

70. Perdue, "Cherokee Women and the Trail of Tears," 97; see Mihesuah, *Cultivating the Rose Buds*, 10. A third petition, published in the *Phoenix* on 12 November

1831, demonstrates a further degree of diminution in Cherokee women's status, assuming an entirely supplicant stance more common among their white counterparts. For the continued transformation in Cherokee women's roles, see Carolyn Ross Johnson, *Cherokee Women in Crisis*, 36–55.

71. Awiakta, *Selu*, 120.

72. Ibid., 92; see Perdue, *Cherokee Women*, 55.

73. See Wiley and de Klerk, "Common Myths and Stereotypes," 35.

74. On egalitarian Cherokee education, see Stremlau, *Sustaining the Cherokee Family*, 99. Stremlau and others focus principally on postremoval education, but some of the later practices reflect traditional values; see Perdue, *Cherokee Women*, 161–62. On the ethnocidal effects of whites' education campaigns, see Grinde, "Taking the Indian out of the Indian."

75. "Constitution of the Cherokee Nation," 2.

76. Gold had been found much earlier, but it entered into the public consciousness more broadly in 1828; see About North Georgia, "North Georgia's Gold Rush," http://ngeorgia.com/history/goldrush.html. See also the numerous articles listed under "Gold" in the *Cherokee Phoenix* index via the Sequoyah Research Center, American Native Press Archives, http://www.anpa.ualr.edu/.

77. David Williams, "Gold Rush."

78. Portnoy, *Their Right to Speak*, 5.

79. Paula Gunn Allen suggests that Indians have themselves long been at war with the U.S. government. Introduction to *Spider Woman's Granddaughters*, 8; see Cook-Lynn, *Anti-Indianism in Modern America*, 151, 154.

80. McKibben, *American Earth*, xxii.

81. Glen A. Love provides a useful summary of Lawrence Buell's overview of pastoral in American literary tradition. "Et in Arcadia Ego," 195–207; Buell, "American Pastoral Ideology Reappraised." One problem with pastoral theory for ecocriticism, as my discussion reveals, is its inapplicability to earlier Native literatures.

82. We can more readily appreciate the connection between peace and the environment if we consider the obliteration of many Cherokee towns (sites of corn cultivation) during the Revolutionary War. These depredations prompted many Cherokees to abandon their traditional forms of residence in towns and to live more widely separated in individual homesteads. Perdue, *Cherokee Women*, 105–6. More recently, the Nobel Peace Prize Committee has underscored this connection by awarding the prize to environmental activist Wangari Maathai (2004).

As Heise points out regarding contemporary environmental justice advocates, the Cherokee women were more concerned with "community betterment" than with "alone-with-nature experiences." Referring to Lawrence Buell, Heise also observes that contemporary environmental justice discourse "tends both to presuppose the existence of tightly knit historical communities with long traditions, and to fashion communities that seem to have coherence only in the face of risk." Heise, *Sense of Place*, 38, 155; Buell, *Writing for an Endangered World*, 41. Risk, however, in both Buell's and Heise's conceptions, relates principally to modern, technologically generated toxics and pollutants; a far greater risk for the Cherokee and other Native tribes in early America was dispossession.

83. Sigourney, "The Cherokee Mother," 7.

84. Miles, "Circular Reasoning," 224; see 323ff.

85. Ibid., 231ff; Andrea Smith, *Native Americans and the Christian Right*, xi. Alliance politics focus on commonalities rather than differences, enabling groups with disparate, even clashing, beliefs to work together for a common cause.

86. Although the Second Great Awakening was polymorphic, assuming different forms in different regions and within various denominations, in one manifestation it rejected centralized religious authority and assigned power to individuals, while in another it signified efforts by churches to reestablish their power and authority in the face of enormous, anxiety-provoking social, economic, and cultural transformation. See Hatch, *The Democratization of American Christianity*.

87. Finseth, "The Second Great Awakening."

88. See, for example, Lodge and Hamlin, *Religion and the New Ecology*; Gibson, *Eco-Justice*; Engel, "Democracy, Christianity, Ecology," 217; Pearson, "Electing to Do Ecotheology"; Kirkpatrick, "For God So Loved the World"; Neville, "Response to Thomas Berry's *The Great Work*"; James A. Nash, "The Bible vs. Biodiversity"; Wright, "Christianity and Environmental Justice"; Gottlieb, *The Oxford Handbook*.

Contemporary ecofeminist theologian Rosemary Radford Ruether argues that "eco-justice" should be central to "the Church's mission." "Conclusion: Eco-justice"; see also Bohannon and O'Brien, "Environmental Justice and Eco-Justice," 171. Bohannon and O'Brien distinguish between the two terms, suggesting that the former is more concerned with specific human communities, while the latter envisions a global community invested in "an ideal of harmonious coexistence throughout the community of life" (173).

Even among Christian fundamentalists, what Bill Moyers has called "Green Christianity," which emphasizes stewardship of the earth, is becoming prominent. See, for example, Moyers on America, "Is God Green?" See also Goodstein, "Evangelical Leaders Join Global Warming Initiative"; Kearns, "Noah's Ark Goes To Washington."

89. For example, Bryant's "Thanatopsis" and "The Prairies" sound elegiac notes for Native American mound builders that differ substantially from Sigourney's interventions. Bryant's "Indian at the Burial-Place of His Fathers," which gives voice to an Indian, sounds a register more like Sigourney's, but it lacks her ethical commitment to legal and social change.

90. If one counts newspaper reprints—for copyright legislation had yet to smother poetry's free circulation—Sigourney's annual poetry publications totaled well into the hundreds. See Kilcup, "Lydia Sigourney."

91. Paula Bernat Bennett and Kilcup, "Rethinking Nineteenth-Century American Poetry," 1–10. In *Ecocritical Explorations*, Patrick D. Murphy affirms the po-

tential for popular genres such as science fiction to intervene in environmental debates. In nineteenth-century America, poetry enjoyed analogous currency.

92. Baym, "Reinventing Lydia Sigourney." See also Egan, "Poetic Travelers." Cheryl Walker argues that Sigourney belongs to a category of nationalist poets. "Nineteenth-Century American Women Poets Revisited." Many other women poets, from Margaret Fuller to Lucy Hooper, addressed similar public, ostensibly indecorous subjects for women; one famous example is Lucy Larcom's powerful abolitionist poem "Weaving," which I discuss in chapter 3.

93. Baym, "Reinventing Lydia Sigourney," 391.

94. Lauter, "Teaching Lydia Sigourney," 117.

95. Baym, "Reinventing Lydia Sigourney," 396.

96. Sigourney, *Traits of the Aborigines*, 171.

97. Zagarell, "Expanding 'America.'"

98. See Dippie, *The Vanishing American*, xii. Dippie contends that "a fully rounded version of the Vanishing American won public acceptance after 1814," and he describes how American writers such as Bryant "helped define the Vanishing American theme" (10, 13).

99. Baym, "Reinventing Lydia Sigourney," 394.

100. Sigourney, *Traits of the Aborigines*, 274–75n3. For further discussion of *Traits of the Aborigines*, see Paula Bernat Bennett, "Was Sigourney a Poetess?," 274–76.

101. Sigourney, *Letters of Life*, 327.

102. Pearce describes Sigourney's advocacy for "noble savages" in *Traits of the Aborigines* and her plea to Christianize them. *Savagism and Civilization*, 190.

103. We should acknowledge the period's bidirectional publishing activity; Native Americans published in Christian periodicals and white Christians in Native American periodicals. See Hershberger, "Mobilizing Women, Anticipating Abolition," 19.

104. Miles, "Circular Reasoning," 232–33.

105. "Circular: Addressed to Benevolent Ladies." Subsequent quotes from the circular are all taken from this source. See Hershberger, "Mobilizing Women, Anticipating Abolition," 25ff.

106. Lauter, "Teaching Lydia Sigourney," 118. Hershberger, "Mobilizing Women, Anticipating Abolition," explores the possible reasons for Beecher's decision to keep the circular's authorship anonymous, as well as the catastrophic health consequences for Beecher.

107. Sturgeon addresses the problematics of the frontier myth. *Environmentalism in Popular Culture*, 54–57. See also Slotkin, *The Fatal Environment*.

108. Interestingly, the Christian appeal to abstract principles is based on concrete, place-based problems. Deloria critiques Christianity's reliance on such principles in comparison to Native religions' contextualized perspective. *God Is Red*, 69.

109. Hershberger, "Mobilizing Women, Anticipating Abolition," 17, 16.

110. Opposition to removal came from every region, including the South itself. Hershberger, "Mobilizing Women, Anticipating Abolition," 20ff.; see Portnoy,

Their Right to Speak. On the Cherokee and slavery, see Yarbrough, *Race and the Cherokee Nation.*

111. Stephen Brandon claims that the letter was never sent but appeared in the *Phoenix* as part of a concerted national strategy by white Indian reformers to spark action through emotion. "Sacred Fire and Sovereign Rhetorics," 189. Brandon also claims that Sigourney's publications authorized and inaugurated women's participation in public-sphere activities; both the circular and the letter address this issue explicitly. See also Hershberger, "Mobilizing Women, Anticipating Abolition," 26ff.

112. Ritchie and Ronald, introduction to *Available Means*, xxiv.

113. Paula Bernat Bennett, *Nineteenth-Century American Women Poets*, 7n4.

114. Paula Bernat Bennett, "Was Sigourney a Poetess? The Aesthetics of Victorian Plenitude in Lydia Sigourney's Poetry," draft essay, private communication, 30 March 2006. See also Paula Bernat Bennett, "Was Sigourney a Poetess?"; Brandon, "Sacred Fire and Sovereign Rhetorics," 190.

115. Sigourney, "The Cherokee Mother." Sigourney also published similar poems in the Euramerican press; see Jordan, "The Source."

116. Brandon, "Sacred Fire and Sovereign Rhetorics," 206.

117. Ibid., 209.

118. Paula Bernat Bennett, *Nineteenth-Century American Women Poets*, 8.

119. In another, related, poem, "Indian Girl's Burial," published after removal, Sigourney steps back and assumes a sympathetic observer's perspective, perhaps indirectly inscribing a national elegy. First published in the journal *Western Adventurer* in 1837, the poem was repeatedly reprinted in Sigourney's collections and in various anthologies.

120. The juxtaposition of these two poems highlights the necessity of what I have called "situated criticism" for appreciating nineteenth-century American women nature writers; that is, we are more likely to err about a writer's stance if we fail to apprehend her writing as a holistic network of conversing ideas and concerns. Kilcup, "I Like These Plants," 51.

121. Lauter, "Teaching Lydia Sigourney," 117.

122. Sigourney, "Indian Names."

123. Baym comments, "Unwilling to adopt a tragic or ironic stance toward history (though she could not always avoid doing so), Sigourney could not accept the palliating conviction found in so many writings of the time that the destruction of the Indians was merely inevitable." "Reinventing Lydia Sigourney," 395. "Indian Names" goes well beyond the nostalgic construction of the noble savage that Roy Harvey Pearce discusses vis-à-vis *Traits of the Aborigines* and a matrix of similar works: "[T]he inevitable destruction of the noble savage is not explained; it is merely accepted. The fact of destruction serves only further to ennoble the savage." *Savagism and Civilization*, 189.

124. Heise, *Sense of Place*, 139. Buell discusses "toxic discourse," which he calls "expressed anxiety arising from perceived threat of environmental hazard due to

chemical modification by human agency." *Writing for an Endangered World*, 31; see 30ff. Two important elements of this discourse are the "mythography of betrayed Edens" (*Writing for an Endangered World*, 37) and what Heise identifies as "the moral passion of the weak and politically repressed against those perceived to be strong and politically powerful" (139), both of which apply in this earlier context.

125. Here I diverge from Ken Egan Jr.'s reading of Sigourney, though I agree with his point about the ideological force of much nineteenth-century American women's nature poetry. "Imperial Strains," 501, 506.

126. "Indian Names" appears vulnerable to Laura Wexler's critique (in "Tender Violence") of nineteenth-century sentimental fiction. But this critique is problematic for several reasons. See Kilcup, *Robert Frost and Feminine Literary Tradition*, 266.

127. Lauter, "Teaching Lydia Sigourney," 117.

128. Sigourney, "The Western Home," 252, lines 31–39.

129. Jemison, *A Narrative of the Life*, 128. All references are to the 1990 Syracuse edition, which I have chosen because it retains the appendices of Seaver's 1824 edition. My practice is to cite Seaver when discussing the editorial materials such as the introduction and appendix and to cite Jemison for the main text.

130. For an introduction to Jemison's life, see Namias, "Editor's Introduction." Laura L. Mielke calls the narrative "the year's bestseller." *Moving Encounters*, 78. According to Scheckel, Jemison's narrative was one of four books (with three Cooper novels) that sold over one hundred thousand copies in the United States in the period between 1823 and 1827. *The Insistence of the Indian*, 70, 164. Adoption practices and gender norms among the Iroquois (of which the Seneca were a member nation) require brief explanation. The Iroquois practiced the blood feud, in which a family member's murder was avenged by capturing and killing the murderer or his relative. Jemison emphasizes that such practices were conducted only as part of a system of justice. In part due to the population losses sustained via disease and earlier resource conflicts with whites and other Indians, by Jemison's time the Iroquois often adopted captives rather than killing them, and at the behest of the clan mothers such individuals became integral members of the adoptive family. Jemison herself eventually became a clan mother, a person of influence. Judith K. Brown explains, "Iroquois matrons enjoyed unusual authority in their society, perhaps more than women have ever enjoyed anywhere at any time." "Iroquois Women," 243. Although the member tribes of the Iroquois Confederacy spoke related but different languages, they were united in many cultural practices, including matrilineality and matrilocality. Because much of the research conducted on these tribes refers to the Iroquois, I use the umbrella term when citing it.

131. Kolodny, *The Land Before Her*, 73.

132. Rifkin, *When Did Indians Become Straight?*, 53. In chapter 1, Rifkin focuses on the relationship between the dominant society's concept of the family and Indian land policy, exploring in detail the "translation of the geopolitics of indigenous self-determination into the biopolitics of race" (48). My discussion focuses

on Jemison's gendered Seneca cultural affiliations and relationship to nature as the means through which her (indirect) argument for environmental justice emerges. Numerous commentators have explored the racialized quality of Jemison's narrative; see, for example, Tawil, *The Making of Racial Sentiment*, 100ff. As I have argued, and as accounts by Rifkin, Susan Walsh, Scheckel, and others indicate, we need to scrutinize Seaver's role in the narrative's construction far more than Tawil's discussion suggests. Walsh, "With Them Was My Home"; Scheckel, *The Insistence of the Indian*, chapter 4.

133. See Walsh, "With Them Was My Home," 49–51. On the complexities of reading Native American texts, see Krupat, introduction to *Ethnocriticism, Ethnography, History*. For an analysis of some of the significant changes made to the narrative over the years of its publication and how those changes enhance the representation of Jemison as white, see Mielke, *Moving Encounters*, 81–85. Many readers before Walsh, Kolodny included, focused on Jemison's status as a *white* woman, even though, according to June Namias, the "Iroquois saw her as one of their own and still do." *White Captives, Gender and Ethnicity*, 149. As Rifkin's work amply demonstrates, the relationship between race and ethnicity is a particularly vexed question. Namias uses the latter term because she believes it conveys an identity comprising cultural practices and perspectives as well as physical appearance. While corporeality and ethnicity can often be strongly correlated, such correlations are themselves culturally defined. Given the Seneca's common practice of adopting whites, embodied qualities were not essential to their self-definition. I find the term *race* equally problematic because of its implication in constantly shifting and historically mutable cultural norms. Nineteenth-century Euramericans and Native Americans were necessarily aware of Jemison's difference—she had blond hair—but, while the former identified her as "The White Woman" (Seaver, *A Narrative of the Life*, xxiv, xxv; Namias, "Editor's Introduction," 4), the Seneca noted her physical characteristics but acknowledged her and her children as Seneca. For further discussion of the problematics of Walsh's and Namias's accounts, see Oakes, "We planted, tended and harvested," 45–51.

134. Seaver, *A Narrative of the Life*, xxx. Seaver packed her story with his own interpretations, as I discuss.

135. Not to attempt to separate Jemison's and Seaver's voices, according to Walsh, "would be to dismiss the very idea of an Indian subject position, to ignore the possibility of voices, perspectives, and narrative traditions in opposition to the progressivist ideology of well-intentioned white editors." "With Them Was My Home," 51. I obviously question Seaver's progressivism and good intentions. Because of the difficulty of distinguishing between Seaver's and Jemison's voices, in the discussion that follows I emphasize the effects of the text's rhetoric and deemphasize the writer's emotional intelligence.

136. On the contrast between Euramerican and Native American understandings of nature and between the concepts of the Corn Mother and the moral mother in early New England, see Merchant, *Earthcare*, 27–29, 91–108.

137. For more detail on this transaction, see Rifkin, *When Did Indians Become Straight?*, 53, 57–58.

138. Red Jacket indicates the importance of land to the Seneca: "Once the Six Nations were a great people and had a large council fire which was held at Onondaga, but now at Buffaloe, and soon may be removed from there. Now the Onondagas are nobody, have no lands of their own, but we ever hospitable to our bretheren, let them sit down on our lands. We are still a great people and much respected by all the Western Indians, which is allowing to our having land of our own. You wish to buy all our lands, except such reservations as you might make for us to raise corn on. It will make us nobody to accept such reservations, and where you may think proper—if this should be the case we could not say we were a free people. Brothers, we mentioned before that our fore fathers had sold their lands and had eat up all the money they got for them." *The Collected Speeches of Sagoyewatha*, 88.

139. The Treaty of Big Tree excludes Jemison's land; see "The Treaty of Big Tree" (summary and transcription); The Treaty of Big Tree, "Agreement with the Seneca, 1797"; and Norman B. Wilkinson, "Robert Morris and the Treaty," 257–78.

140. As Rifkin argues, whites' efforts to undermine sovereignty and obtain land relied on the superimposition of European legal standards of identity and land tenure on indigenous peoples; in order successfully to alienate commonly held Seneca land, they had to define Jemison as white and hence able to sell her land individually. Such a definition would, of course, deny her status as a Seneca matron. See Rifkin, *When Did Indians Become Straight?*, 49 and chapter 1.

141. Seaver, *A Narrative of the Life*, x.

142. Jemison, *A Narrative of the Life*, 111.

143. See also Jemison's account of Ebenezer Allen in *A Narrative of the Life*, chapter 8, especially 74–75; on Allen and the threat to Seneca land tenure and lifeways, see Dennis, *Seneca Possessed*, 40–49.

144. See, for example, Jemison, *A Narrative of the Life*, 39ff, 47ff.

145. On Sullivan's notorious campaign, see Lisa Brooks, *The Common Pot*, 116–18; Joseph R. Fischer, *A Well-Executed Failure*, 2. Adamiak cites General Sullivan's estimate that he and his troops destroyed at least 160,000 bushels of corn. "The 1779 Sullivan Campaign."

146. As Gretchen M. Bataille and Kathleen Mullen Sands comment, "[F]emale Indian autobiographies tend to integrate some elements of historic, ceremonial, and social importance into the narratives but concentrate on everyday events and activities and family crisis events." *American Indian Women*, 8; see 6.

147. Jemison, *A Narrative of the Life*, 59. Ironically, Seaver's appendix conveys the whites' depredations on the Indians at least as thoroughly as Jemison's own narrative; see 130–41. Jemison's emphasis becomes even more evident when we recognize the structural technique that Seaver uses to diminish it; he seeks an additional account of the Sullivan expedition from a European American man. The editor is unapologetic about his goal: "It has been thought expedient to publish in

this volume, the following account of Gen. Sullivan's expedition, in addition to the facts related by Mrs. Jemison, of the barbarities which were perpetrated upon Lieut. Boyd, and two others. . . . it is presumed that it will be received with satisfaction" (134–35). The placement of this lengthy account, in a formal appendix, encloses Jemison's own Seneca female perspective within a dominant-culture, male one. In unsettlingly affirmative terms, a contemporary website also describes the destruction; see "General John Sullivan."

148. Underscoring the frequency of Euramericans' massacres of Native Americans, Stannard makes an observation that bears repeating: "No matter how numbed—or even, shamefully, bored—we might become at hearing story after story of the mass murder, pillage, rape, and torture of America's native peoples, we can be assured that, however much we hear, we have heard only a small fragment of what there was to tell." *American Holocaust*, 126.

For a discussion of the challenges of defining genocide, see Destexhe, former secretary general of Doctors without Borders, *Rwanda and Genocide*, 3–7. Destexhe addresses the 1948 UN Convention for the Prevention and the Punishment of the Crime of Genocide, offering a definition that applies to Native Americans in the nineteenth century: genocide is a criminal act with the intent of destroying an ethnic, national, or religious group targeted as such. Robert Gellately and Ben Kiernan also address the definition, with particularly useful attention to legal and analytical concepts. "The Study of Mass Murder." Larry May argues that genocidal crimes should include cultural genocide and ethnic cleansing. *Genocide*, 1; see also Lawrence Davidson, *Cultural Genocide*, 1–2, 22–23; "Appendix II: On Racism and Genocide," in Stannard, *American Holocaust*, 269–81.

Rensink provides an overview of recent scholarship; he argues that "while using genocidal terminology too liberally can prove equally damaging to useful scholarship, excessive definitionalism must not come at the cost of moving scholarship forward." "Genocide of Native Americans," 16; 15–36). See also Schabas, "Convention on the Prevention and Punishment."

Although the term itself is of recent origin (1944), from Native Americans' perspective, the United States conducted genocidal activities from before its formal inception; see Tinker's remark above, page 27. For discussions of Native Americans and forms of genocide, including education, land appropriation, and assaults on gender and gender identity, see, for example, Tinker, *Missionary Conquest*; Churchill, *Struggle for the Land*; Deloria, *Custer Died for Your Sins*; Andrea Smith, *Conquest*; Frey, "Focus on the United States"; and Stannard, *American Holocaust*, especially part 3, "Sex, Race, and Holy War," 147–246. For a critical response to some of this scholarship, see Barkan, "Genocides of Indigenous Peoples," 120–27.

149. Converse, "The Iroquois Creation." One of many versions, Converse's was published posthumously in *Myths and Legends of the New York State Iroquois*, edited by Arthur C. Parker. See Parker's version, "How the World Began." For a contemporary retelling, see "The Woman Who Fell from the Sky," in Paula Gunn Allen, *Spider Woman's Granddaughters*, 65–68.

150. Brooks, *The Common Pot*, 2.

151. Thomas, "The Three Sisters."

152. For another relevant Seneca story, see Kelsey, "Natives, Nation, Narration," 152.

153. Martha Harroun Foster, "Lost Women of the Matriarchy," 123. Foster's essay contains a compendium of scholarship on Iroquois women, from which many of my remarks are drawn. According to anthropologist Phyllis Rogers (Cherokee), at one time Iroquois women cultivated no fewer than three hundred varieties of corn. "The Role of Women in the Creation of the Iroquois Confederacy: A Reinterpretation" (paper presented at Women's Studies Colloquium, Colby College, Waterville, Maine, March 1990); personal communications, fall 1989–fall 1993. See also Arthur C. Parker, *The History of the Seneca Indians*, 75–76. Despite this history, concepts of property ownership that had been changing from the time of first contact to Jemison's era were becoming increasingly homogenized and Europeanized, with an emphasis on individual, male control. See also Rifkin, *When Did Indians Become Straight?*, 51–51, 97.

154. Martha Harroun Foster, "Lost Women of the Matriarchy," 123. Matthew Dennis cites Red Jacket's and other Seneca leaders' insistence that their cultivation practices required fallow land, necessitating significant holdings. *Seneca Possessed*, 187–88.

155. Jemison unconsciously counteracts Seaver's introductory remark that goes beyond praising Franklinian work habits to suggesting Indian women's beast-of-burden status: "Industry is a virtue which she has uniformly practised from the day of her adoption to the present. She pounds her samp, cooks for herself, gathers and chops wood, feeds her cattle and poultry, and performs other laborious services. Last season she planted, tended and gathered corn—in short, she is always busy." *A Narrative of the Life*, xxvii–xxviii. Later in the narrative, Seaver's voice emerges plainly: "It is well known that the squaws have all the labor of the field to perform, and almost every other kind of hard service, which, in civil society, is performed by the men" (160). Jemison's emphasis on community work efforts reinforces her assertion of Seneca identity. Paula Gunn Allen observes that a "concentration on the negative effect of individuality forms a major theme in the oral literatures of all tribes" and that "individualism (as distinct from autonomy or self-responsibility) becomes a negatively-valued trait." Introduction to *Spider Woman's Granddaughters*, 5, 9. For a related discussion of how gender functions for white readers and of Jemison's resistance to cooptation, see Scheckel, *The Insistence of the Indian*, chapter 4.

156. Kolodny, *The Land Before Her*, 75; see Bataille and Sands, *American Indian Women*, 18–19.

157. Such distinctions are in themselves Western; as Brian Swann quotes Lame Deer, "We Indians live in a world of symbols and images where the spiritual and the commonplace are one." *Smoothing the Ground*, xii; see Walsh, "With Them Was My Home," 55; Namias, "Editor's Introduction," 28–29.

158. See Judith K. Brown, "Iroquois Women," 247; Namias, "Editor's Introduction," 22; F. W. Waugh, *Iroquois Foods and Food Preparation*, 13–14.

159. Given her attitude elsewhere, it seems likely that "prisoner" is Seaver's word, although given Seneca capture and adoption practices, it could be Jemison's, but drained of its negative connotations. On these practices, see Wallace, *The Death and Rebirth*, 44ff.

160. Despite the Native American norm of modesty for women (Bataille and Sands, *American Indian Women*, 18), one wonders if the references to Jemison's two sisters and herself might not be a reference to "The Three Sisters" and hence to her own female power (and Seaver's obtuseness). If the image of corn functions on a variety of levels to express Jemison's individual identity as a Seneca woman, it also affirms communal cultural values and tribal solidarity, which, according to Bataille and Sands, are another characteristic of Native American women's autobiography. Paula Gunn Allen declares that "right relationship, or right kinship, is fundamental to Native aesthetics." Introduction to *Spider Woman's Granddaughters*, 8. The representation of such values reappears in Jemison's description of her family. *A Narrative of the Life*, 40–42. It is possible also that Jemison might have envisioned the speech in terms that Seaver could understand; as Walsh notes, she had plainly rehearsed what she would say. "With Them Was My Home," 51.

161. See Cox, Maxwell, and Thomas, *This Well-Wooded Land*, 7–8, 40.

162. Slotkin, *Regeneration through Violence*, 94–95. See Demos, *The Unredeemed Captive*.

163. Merchant, *American Environmental History*, 35.

164. Ibid., 35, 36.

165. Seaver, *A Narrative of the Life*, 145.

166. Ibid., 144–45.

167. Ibid., 146.

168. Seaver's introduction presents Jemison as thoroughly "Indianized" in relation to religion: "Her ideas of religion, correspond in every respect with those of the great mass of the Senecas. She applauds virtue, and despises vice. She believes in a future state, in which the good will be happy, and the bad miserable; and that the acquisition of that happiness, depends primarily upon human volition, and the consequent good deeds of the happy recipient of blessedness." He concludes, "The doctrines taught in the Christian religion, she is a stranger to." Although he affirms her paganism and depicts her as the noble savage, he also attempts to seduce his audience with an account of a woman whose beliefs and values corresponded to their own, even if she lacked Christian "doctrines." *A Narrative of the Life*, xxx–xxi.

169. Rifkin, *When Did Indians Become Straight?*, 48–49.

170. I have explored this point at more length elsewhere; see Oakes, "We planted, tended and harvested"; Mielke, *Moving Encounters*; and Tawil, *The Making of Racial Sentiment*, also discuss the sentimental language in Jemison's narrative.

171. Among the victims of alcohol were two of Jemison's sons.

172. See Buckley, "The Jesuits and the Iroquois"; Richter, "Iroquois versus Iro-

quois." Nancy C. Unger observes, "Understanding native women's reluctance to relinquish their respected position within their traditional cultures helps solve the puzzle of why missionaries intent on imposing patriarchal values frequently complained that it was easier to convert men than women." "Women, Sexuality, and Environmental Justice," 47.

173. Marilyn Holly, "Handsome Lake's Teachings," 80–94.

174. Jefferson's 1802 letter to Handsome Lake applauds the latter's determination to preach temperance and promises emphatically that land shall not be taken from the Seneca: "The right to sell is one of the rights of property." Jefferson, "To Brother Handsome Lake." See also Wallace's account of Jefferson's relationship with Handsome Lake, which urged land cessions. *Jefferson and the Indians*, 291–92.

175. Tinker, *American Indian Liberation*, 28–33; see also Tinker, *Missionary Conquest*.

176. Unger, "Women, Sexuality, and Environmental Justice," 49. See Andrea Smith, "Malthusian Orthodoxy," 126–27.

177. Martha Harroun Foster, "Lost Women of the Matriarchy," 129. On Handsome Lake's investment in witch-hunting, see Dennis, *Seneca Possessed*, especially chapter 3.

178. Martha Harroun Foster, "Lost Women of the Matriarchy," 129–30; see Marilyn Holly, "Handsome Lake's Teachings," 85. Matthew Dennis confirms that in Handsome Lake's lifetime "[t]he troubled post-Revolutionary years were marked by an outbreak of Seneca witch-hunting that particularly targeted women." *Seneca Possessed*, 82.

179. "Principles of Environmental Justice."

180. See Rifkin, *When Did Indians Become Straight?*, 49.

181. On the pollution and recent cleanup efforts, see Dowty, "Working to Clean Onondaga Lake"; Nojiri, "Haudenosaunee Ceremony Celebrates Onondaga Lake"; "Onondaga Lake Superfund Site."

182. Slovic, "Epistemology and Politics," 84.

183. "Maria Gunnoe."

184. Journalist Jonathan Hiskes writes, "After she began working against coal companies in 2004, 'wanted' posters of Gunnoe appeared in local convenience stores, and her daughter's dog was shot." "An Interview with 'Green Nobel' Winner."

185. Hiskes, "An Interview with 'Green Nobel' Winner." See also Fletcher, "Interview of Cherokee Woman."

186. Awiakta, *Selu*, 95.

187. Ibid., 6.

Chapter 2. "Such Progress in Civilization"

Epigraphs: Hawthorne, "Sketches from Memory," 2:492; Hawthorne describes traveling beside the Erie Canal. Greeley, *Glances at Europe*, 39.

1. Sigourney, *Scenes in My Native Land*, 120. For a later response to New England elms, see Holmes, *The Autocrat of the Breakfast-Table*, 233–39.

2. Some might argue that the more appropriate term here is ethnocide, which refers to the systematic and deliberate destruction of an ethnic group's culture, but Sigourney emphatically supported Native Americans' Christianization and "civilization"; what she systematically protested were policies of removal and violence by the U.S. government. See chapter 1, note 148.

3. Other European colonial powers, such as France and Spain, were equally eager to exploit the New World's resources, including timber, but I focus here on Britain.

4. Emerson, "The Progress of Culture."

5. See William W. Stowe, who focuses on Margaret Fuller's *Summer on the Lakes* as a combination of travel writing and vacation writing. "Busy Leisure."

6. Lunsford, "On Reclaiming Rhetorica," 6.

7. On women's roles in contemporary forest defense actions, see Gaard, "Ecofeminism Revisited," 38–39.

8. Stradling, *The Nature of New York*, 84. For a discussion of nature writing's romantic roots, the sublime, and nineteenth-century American male writers, see Branch, "Indexing American Possibilities." Sigourney also highlights the putatively silent voice of nature; see Manes, "Nature and Silence"; McDowell, "The Bakhtinian Road"; Eric Todd Smith, "Dropping the Subject."

9. See "Explore the Roar."

10. According to Ginger Strand, in its first well-known version, the story was published by Lewis Henry Morgan in his early ethnology, *League of the Hodé-no sau-nee or Iroquois*. See Strand, *Inventing Niagara*, 35ff., for an accounting of some of Morgan's shortcomings. Strand also relates how distinguished scholar and writer Joseph Bruchac (Abenaki) attributes the story to Ely Parker (38ff.).

11. Both Paula Bennett and I have explored, in different contexts, the work of women nature poets. See Paula Bernat Bennett, "Late Nineteenth-Century American Women's Nature Poetry"; Kilcup, *Robert Frost and Feminine Literary Tradition*. See also Mary V. Davidson, "What We've Missed." On Sigourney's subjectivity, see Annie Finch, "The Sentimental Poetess in the World"; see also Murphy, *Literature, Nature, and Other*, on the "I" of romantic poetry. Buell notes the "self-relinquishment" of some nature writers. *The Environmental Imagination*, 156ff. It is worth recalling that Sigourney's father was an estate manager for a wealthy Connecticut family and that his responsibilities may have included gardening. Critics' reluctance to consider Sigourney and others like her in a tradition of women's nature writing or environmental writing may emerge from the characterization of her work as entirely sentimental and the denigration of sentimental attitudes toward nature and pastoralism. See Marx, *The Machine in the Garden*, 5; Rosenthal, *City of Nature*, 67; Buell, *The Environmental Imagination*, 199. John Gatta discusses a few nineteenth-century Euramerican women writers (Thaxter and Fuller among them), but his focus remains with how male writers understood the relationship between nature and religion. See *Making Nature Sacred*, 106–10.

12. Sigourney, "Niagara," 43.

13. Matthew 14:35–36: "And when the men of that place had knowledge of him, they sent out into all that country round about, and brought unto him all that were diseased; And besought him that they might only touch the hem of his garment: and as many as touched were made perfectly whole." King James version, http://kingjbible.com/matthew/14.htm; see also Luke 8:43–44.

14. As Roderick Nash points out, national self-examination about wilderness began early, with Audubon, Caitlin, Parkman, and Cole among the prompters. *Wilderness and the American Mind*. On nationalism and ethnicity, see Pearce, *Savagism and Civilization*; Maddox, *Removals*; and Nelson, *The Word in Black and White*. On nature and nationalism, see Stein, *Shifting the Ground*; Stephen May, "A beautiful and thrilling specimen"; Mazel, *American Literary Environmentalism*, xviii–xx and passim; Turner, "Cultivating the American Garden"; Pfaelzer, "Nature, Nurture, and Nationalism"; and Bishop, "A Feeling Farmer." Buell (*Writing for an Endangered World*), Murphy (*Farther Afield*), and Heise (*Sense of Place*) argue for an international perspective on nature-oriented literature.

15. Buell, *The Environmental Imagination*, 50.

16. Morgan noted that the Iroquois council fires extended from the Hudson to Niagara. *League of the Ho-dé-no sau-nee*, 36, 37–38. His nostalgic/sentimental description contrasts with Sigourney's in "Indian Names." *League of the Ho-dé-no sau-nee*, 135. See also Arthur C. Parker, *The History of the Seneca Indians*, 28–31. See also the Seneca Nation website, sni.org.

17. Seaver, *A Narrative of the Life*, appendix, 91. Jemison's discussion of conflicts include *A Narrative of the Life*, 53ff; chapter 8, regarding Ebenezer Allen and Fort Niagara; and chapter 5, which cites the Indians and French preparing for battle to retake Fort Ne-a-gaw (Neagaw), 39.

18. Morgan, *League of the Ho-dé-no sau-nee*, 97–98; see William W. Canfield, *The Legends of the Iroquois*, 47–50, 208. On the conflicts at Niagara, see Arthur C. Parker, *The History of the Seneca Indians*, 56, 93–95, 98–99, 103–4, 107–9. Currently the Seneca Nation of Indians owns and operates a gaming casino in Niagara Falls, N.Y. On the Iroquois and the Niagara region, see Aquila, *The Iroquois Restoration*, 117–19. The Seneca were a member tribe of the Iroquois Confederacy and the Keepers of the Western Door. See Seneca Nation of Indians, sni.org.

19. Ken Egan Jr. has suggested, "The poem could test the imperial self's claim for dominion over the wild." "Poetic Travelers," 49.

20. James B. Brown, *Views of Canada*, 236.

21. Sigourney begins with "the Table-Rock, where the great flood / Reveals its fullest glory" and ends with a chapter titled "Farewell to Niagara," where the writer asserts that if she had no other responsibilities, "it were sweet / To linger here, and be thy worshipper, / Until death's footstep broke this dream of life." *Scenes in My Native Land*, 318, lines 32–34.

22. Sivils, "William Bartram's *Travels*"; Hallock, *From the Fallen Tree*, 158.

23. The few resources include: William W. Stowe, "Busy Leisure"; Kollin, "The First White Woman"; Pagh, "An Indescribable Sea"; and Eacker, "Gender in

Paradise." See also Hallock on earlier texts by Jane Colden and Anne Grant. *From the Fallen Tree*, chapters 5, 7.

24. I am not arguing the status of autobiographical nature writing in the conventional literary canon; rather, I am suggesting that one of nature writing's internally canonical forms is the autobiographical essay. See Murphy's *Farther Afield*, which also emphasizes the nebulous line between fiction and nonfiction (28).

25. Schriber, *Writing Home*.

26. As previous chapters outline, contemporary feminist theory struggles to reconnect women, nature, and the material body without essentialism. For example, Stacy Alaimo advises that we should imagine "human corporeality as transcorporeality, in which the human is always intermeshed with the more-than-human world." *Bodily Natures*, 2. See also Alaimo, *Undomesticated Ground*, 1–23. Alaimo offers a useful analysis of Catharine Maria Sedgwick's *Hope Leslie*; see *Undomesticated Ground*, chapter 1, 27–37.

27. Kollin, "The First White Woman," 106.

28. "Big Tree Treaty Centennial." Following this notice—indicating its relative insignificance—is another noting the arrival of three "sparrers" (boxers) in the city.

29. Arthur C. Parker, "Certain Iroquois Tree Myths and Symbols."

30. See, for example, Jemison, *A Narrative of the Life*, 46, 48, 28.

31. Stradling, *The Nature of New York*, 19.

32. Lisa Brooks, *The Common Pot*, 169. See chapters 4 and 5 for a discussion of the Mashpee Indians' and William Apess's treatment (in multiple senses) of the forest. William Cronon discusses English settlers' delight at the forests (in the context of English deforestation), pointing out that "scarcity colored the way they reacted to New England forests." Cronon, *Changes in the Land*, 21.

33. For more on the King's Mark, see "Why the Name King's Mark," http://ccrpa.org/km/King's%20Mark%20Why%20The%20Name%20King's%20Mark.htm. Calculations of currency conversion vary widely, depending on the index and variables used. One calculator estimates that £100 in 1691 would be the equivalent of between £13,800 and £187,000 in 2010. See Lawrence H. Office and Samuel H. Williamson, "Purchasing Power of British Pounds from 1245 to Present," MeasuringWorth, 2011, www.measuringworth.com/ppoweruk, via R. Davies's website at the University of Exeter, http://projects.exeter.ac.uk/RDavies/arian/current/howmuch.html. See also Merchant, *The Columbia Guide*, 30.

34. Merchant, *The Columbia Guide*, 29; see 28–33.

35. Stairs, "Design and Deforestation," 273. See also Cronon, *Changes in the Land*, chapter 6 (108–26).

36. Cox, Maxwell, and Thomas, *This Well-Wooded Land*, 12.

37. Stairs, "Design and Deforestation," 275. On the forests' naval and military uses, see also Cox, Maxwell, and Thomas, *This Well-Wooded Land*, 11.

38. Le Billon, "The Geopolitical Economy of 'Resource Wars,'" 3.

39. Hagenstein, review of *This Well-Wooded Land*, 417.

40. Hobbs, "The Beginnings of Lumbering," 17ff.

41. Merchant, *The Columbia Guide*, 29.

42. The environmental historian Chris J. Magoc notes that by the mid-eighteenth century, farmers and scientists "began to suspect that deforestation was disrupting the hydrogeological cycle, causing changes in climate." Farmers in all regions of the country contributed to deforestation; prior to 1850, 114 million acres had been cleared for agriculture, but in the next decade nearly 40 million additional acres were cut. *Environmental Issues in American History*, 54. Vermonter George Perkins Marsh was among the first to articulate connections between clear-cutting, climate change, and declining land health. See Marsh, *Address Delivered before the Agricultural Society*, also available in Magoc, *Environmental Issues in American History*, 59–60; Marsh, *Man and Nature*.

43. Sigourney, *Pleasant Memories of Pleasant Lands*, 387.

44. Such hope was expressed in the founding of the *Dial* in 1840 under Margaret Fuller's editorship and of Brook Farm in 1841.

45. Probably not coincidentally, *Scenes in My Native Land* represented a genre for which the public was hungry, a project that could make money for a writer who supported both her husband and children and her parents.

46. The purpose of Sigourney's rhetoric here—unlike most of her writing that I discuss in chapter 1—is not classical persuasion but the creation of community, a purpose allied with female/feminine rhetorical practice. Lunsford, "On Reclaiming Rhetorica," 6; see also Ritchie and Ronald, *Available Means*.

47. Stradling, *The Nature of New York*, 82.

48. Sigourney, *Scenes in My Native Land*, 117–19. In 1838 the *Southern Literary Messenger* published a series of essays by "J. F. O." focusing on poems about trees; see, for example, "Yet More about Trees," "Another Tree Article," and "The Last Tree Article." Ironically, given the Southern publication context, the author writes from Newburyport, Massachusetts.

49. Bryant's "Among the Trees," which announces to the tree, "Ye have no history," opens a 1918 collection in which it appears. See Dwight, *Travels in New-England and New-York*, 1:18. Dwight was for many years the president of Yale College; an excerpt from his work appears in Branch, *Reading the Roots*, 230–35. Dwight frames his work as a defense of America against the "aspersions" of European travelers (18–19).

50. Hindle, "The Artisan," 11. See Stairs, "Design and Deforestation," 275.

51. Hindle, "The Artisan," 11.

52. Stairs, "Design and Deforestation," 275.

53. "What Is Clearcutting?"

54. Rochelle Johnson outlines writer Susan Fenimore Cooper's and painter Thomas Cole's complex reactions to such "progress." *Passions for Nature*, 103, 73–74, 83.

55. Paula Bennett identifies the "rage" inflecting Sigourney's "raw, infuriated description of what nineteenth-century forestry practices were doing to a land given to us by God in trust." Paula Bernat Bennett, "Emily Dickinson and Her Peers,"

306. Bennett cites Sigourney's 1854 version, which she argues is even harsher than the 1844 version (307).

56. Sigourney was hardly unique in regarding her Christianity as a touchstone for citizenship; see, for example, Rochelle Johnson, *Passions for Nature*, 166–69. See also Cooper, introduction to *The Rhyme and Reason*.

57. This passage may also encode a sectarian comment from Sigourney on Cromwell's Puritanism and the revolutionaries' regicide of King Charles I. Mary Ellis Gibson, e-mail communication, 12 January 2012.

58. As Rochelle Johnson observes, following Emerson, Sigourney's contemporaries understood nature as divinely granted to humans. *Passions for Nature*, chapter 4.

59. Unlike Susan Fenimore Cooper, whose *Rural Hours* (published in 1850, a few years after *Scenes in My Native Land*) focuses on the natural history of a particular locale, Sigourney often concentrates on the larger picture.

60. See "After Words," this volume.

61. According to Geneseo, New York's, current website, "[O]ne particularly large specimen of oak . . . gave the original Indian village here its name of Big Tree. The tree in question stood on the banks of the Genesee and was thought to be more than 300 years old when erosion of the river bank finally caused its downfall on November 8, 1857." "History of Geneseo." "Legend has it that Seneca Indians, the original inhabitants of our favorite piece of the planet, called this place jo-nis-hi-yuh, meaning the pleasant or beautiful valley." The site credits the Seneca for their aesthetic sensibilities, but it erases the long history of conflict between Indians and whites in its account of white land acquisition and settlement—not surprisingly, since it aims to attract tourists. Its historical section claims that the influential whites who founded the community, the Wadsworths, "had great love and appreciation for the wondrous oak trees standing on our land. In clearing the wilderness, they left many and when leasing land required that tenants maintain the great oaks. Most are still standing in even greater grandeur than when they were first encountered."

62. Proposed in 1808 and begun in 1817, the Erie Canal, which connects the Hudson River to Lake Erie, was completed in 1825, not long before Sigourney's journey. Containing eighteen aqueducts and eighty-three locks, it rises 568 feet over its 363-mile course. See "Clinton's Big Ditch"; "Erie Canal—175th Anniversary."

63. Stradling, *The Nature of New York*, 26.

64. Ibid., 45.

65. In addition to celebrating the famous tree and demonstrating the connections between the two ancient trees, the poem also highlights the careers of the Wadsworth brothers, who were closely related to Sigourney's patron, Daniel Wadsworth. For the family history, see Horace Andrew Wadsworth, *Two Hundred and Fifty Years*, which contains an engraving of the Charter Oak at Hartford (86; see 87). See also "William Wadsworth (patriarch)," *Wikipedia*, http://en.wikipedia.org/wiki/William_Wadsworth_%28patriarch%29.

66. Sigourney's response parallels that expressed in William Wordsworth's "Yew-Trees." As Mary Ellis Gibson points out, Sigourney's "romantic focus on a single tree reveals her debt to British romanticism, a set of poetic tropes and themes developed in a largely deforested country . . . where ancient trees therefore assumed an outsized presence." E-mail communication, 4 December 2011.

67. Stradling, *The Nature of New York*, 20.

68. Watters, " As Soon as I Saw," 87.

69. "The Washington Elm."

70. This nationalist outlook persists, typified in the historical society's closing affirmation: "Americanism was not forced upon the public by its leaders. Americanism, like the Revolution itself, emerged from meetinghouses, merchant houses, farmhouses, and state houses, and from a complex, rocky relationship between the different regions. Although we now take it for granted, the very basic ideas upon which our government and our identity as Americans is based were envisioned, fought for, and implemented by our not-so-distant ancestors. Monuments, like the Washington Elm, were a part of this process, contributing to the creation of a uniquely American identity." Ibid.

71. Sears, *Sacred Places*, 29.

72. Ibid., 142. On Cole's romanticism, see Nash, *Wilderness and the American Mind*, 78–82; Stradling, *The Nature of New York*, 79–80.

73. Sears, *Sacred Places*, 142.

74. Sigourney describes many places she considers key to American history, including such chapters as "First Church at Jamestown," "Bunker Hill Monument," "Montpelier," and "Autumn on Staten Island." On American pastoral's nationalism, see Buell, "American Pastoral Ideology Reappraised," 21.

75. Representing an important strategy of rhetorica, such rhetorical and formal diversity presents challenges for today's readers. The chapters' miscellaneous character may derive in part from the fact that several originated as separate essays, but other travel writing shared *Scenes in My Native Land*'s grab-bag qualities. Ritchie and Ronald, introduction to *Available Means*, xxiv.

76. See, for example, "The Charter-Oak at Hartford," in Sigourney, *Scenes in My Native Land*, 77ff.

77. Fuller, Review of *Scenes*, 1:52. Another critic comments, "On the whole, this is an elegant and variously interesting volume; one which, if not of the highest class, is of the kind that never fails to please, from the delicacy of sentiment and the refined tone of mind which it indicates." Review of *Scenes*, in *Atheneum*, 302. See also review of *Scenes*, in *Hunt's Merchant's Magazine*. For a discussion of Fuller's attitudes toward the wilderness, see Egan, "Poetic Travelers."

78. Cronon, *Changes in the Land*, 24–30.

79. Hobbs, "The Beginnings of Lumbering," 22–23. Dwight comments that "the white pine is the noblest forest tree in New-England, and probably in the world." *Travels in New-England and New-York*, 36.

80. Stairs, "Design and Deforestation," 275.

81. "Lumber Industry."

82. Philip, *Robert Fulton*, 310.

83. Hunter and Hunter, *Steamboats on the Western Rivers*, 266.

84. Ibid.

85. Isenberg, *The Destruction of the Bison*, 93.

86. Quoted in Paula Bernat Bennett, " Was Sigourney a Poetess?," 280–81.

87. Paula Bernat Bennett, " Was Sigourney a Poetess?," 281. Bennett points out that, later in life, Sigourney reluctantly reconciled herself to the steamboat because it made travel to Europe so much easier. E-mail communication, 10 January 2012. Bennett's cogent assessment of the closing lines observes that they "partake of elegy, eulogy, and encomium at once." Was Sigourney a Poetess?," 279, 282–83.

88. Matthew 22:21, King James version, http://kingjbible.com/Matthew/22.htm.

89. Although my focus differs slightly from Bennett's, we arrive at similar conclusions; see Paula Bernat Bennett, "Was Sigourney a Poetess?," 282–83. Bennett's primary purpose is to argue for the problematics of labeling Sigourney a "poetess," not to explore her environmentalism. Sigourney departs from the views expressed by Emerson; see Egan, "Imperial Strains," 499.

90. Fuller, *Summer on the Lakes*, 18. Fuller's narrative parallels Sigourney's bellicose language in *Scenes in My Native Land*, but Fuller seems more resigned.

91. Quoted in Stairs, "Design and Deforestation," 274.

92. Ibid., 273. Stairs notes, "Old Hickory's vision of a technological utopia signaled impending doom for the forests of the Upper Middle West" (274).

93. Ibid., 275.

94. Ibid., 275.

95. Ibid., 276; Cox, Maxwell, and Thomas, *This Well-Wooded Land*, 105–6, 156.

96. Stairs, "Design and Deforestation," 276.

97. Zagarell, introduction to *A New Home*, xv.

98. Kirkland, *A New Home*, 5–6.

99. Buell, *The Environmental Imagination*, 68.

100. Zagarell, introduction to *A New Home*, xxx, xxxii.

101. Caroline Gebhard explores Kirkland's humor in "Caroline M. Kirkland's Satire."

102. Ibid., 159.

103. See Barnes, "The Politics of Vision," 67.

104. Gebhard, " Caroline M. Kirkland's Satire," 175.

105. For more information on Kirkland, see Nancy A. Walker, "Caroline Kirkland"; Bouma, "Caroline Kirkland"; Fink, "Antebellum Lady Editors"; Fetterley, "Caroline Kirkland"; "Caroline Kirkland."

106. Barnes, "The Politics of Vision," 62–63.

107. See Jeffrey, *The Great Silent Army*, 130; Bowma, "Caroline Kirkland," 228–29; Kirkland, *The Helping Hand*, quoted in Freedman, *Their Sisters' Keepers*, 34; Mabbott and Jordan, "The Prairie Chicken," 157–58. On Kirkland and John Sartain's *Union Magazine*, see Frank Luther Mott, *A History of American Magazines*, 1:347,

769–72. On Kirkland's criticism of English pretentions and class disparities, see Kirkland, *Forest Life*, 1:203–7.

108. Barnes, "The Politics of Vision," offers the only extended discussion of *Forest Life*. See also Kolodny, *The Land Before Her*, 148–54.

109. See Obuchowski, "Murdered Banquos of the Forest." Obuchowski cites Kirkland's awareness of human overconsumption and its consequences for the future, calling her "an environmentalist, an unusual stance among mid-nineteenth-century writers in the Midwest" (78).

110. Kirkland, *Forest Life*, 1:143–44.

111. Bartram, *Travels through North and South Carolina, Georgia, East and West Florida . . .*, quoted in Bruce Silver, " William Bartram's and Other Eighteenth-Century Accounts," 607–9.

112. Meeker, "The Comic Mode," 165, 168; see Turner, "Cultivating the American Garden," 45.

113. Ritchie and Ronald, introduction to *Available Means*, xxvi–xxvii.

114. On the significance of home to nature writing, see Mazel, *American Literary Environmentalism*, 136–42; on its meaning to working-class women, see Kilcup, "Introduction: A Working-Class Woman's View," 2–3. On bioregionalism, see, for example, Merchant, *Radical Ecology*, 217–22.

115. Kirkland's satire suggests the garden writing of Gail Hamilton. Hamilton, "My Garden." On the tradition of American women's humor, see Nancy A. Walker's classic study *A Very Serious Thing*. David Mazel discusses Kirkland briefly, emphasizing her juxtaposition of domestic (female) and economic (male) values. *American Literary Environmentalism*, 137–39. Less obviously situated in the category of travel literature is a set of sketches that I cite briefly in chapter 5, Mary Hallock Foote's 1888–89 series for the widely distributed *Century Magazine*, "Pictures of the Far West," which anticipates such writers as Mary Austin and Annie Dillard. See Kilcup, *Nineteenth-Century American Women Writers: An Anthology*, 359–61.

116. On the relationship between pastoral and wilderness, see Love, "Et in Arcadia Ego," 202–3. See also Buell, "American Pastoral Ideology Reappraised."

117. See Kirkland, *Forest Life*, 1:37–38, 1:154ff.

118. María Carla Sánchez, *Reforming the World*, 83.

119. Kirkland, *Forest Life*, 1:43. I depart from Ken Egan Jr. and Nathaniel Lewis, who believe that "Kirkland advocated the transformation of the Michigan wilderness through technology." Egan, "Poetic Travelers," 59; see Lewis, *Unsettling the Literary West*, 54ff. Egan suggests that "Kirkland frets the direction of change on the frontier, the possibilities for building a meaningful, sustainable culture" ("Poetic Travelers," 60), but he does not pursue this idea. Lewis contends that in *A New Home* "Kirkland held settlement deforestation to be a civilizing good." *Unsettling the Literary West*, 54; see 50ff.

120. Luke 13:6–9, King James version, http://kingjbible.com/luke/13.htm.

121. Kirkland, *Forest Life*, 1:44. We should recall the traditional use of the white pine for warships' masts.

122. Although I do not have space to consider it here, Kirkland's episodes about gardens and gardening deserve attention; see Kirkland, *Forest Life*, 1:50–56.

123. See Rochelle Johnson, *Passions for Nature*, 51–52, on Cooper's perspective on tree loss.

124. Karen A. Weyler points out that the rhetoric of spartan republicanism had burned itself out by the 1790s. Personal communication, 30 November 2011.

125. See Buell, "American Pastoral Ideology Reappraised," 12.

126. Jack Temple Kirby discusses hogs in Southern forests in *Mockingbird Song*, 119–24.

127. Byrd, *A Journey to the Land of Eden*, 47–48. Kirkland's passage also suggests Thoreau's account of domestic animals gone wild. See Thoreau, "Walking," 197. I cite this reference in a different connection in chapter 3.

128. Elsewhere in *Forest Life*, Kirkland showcases her considerable powers as a humorist to expose the hypocrisy and racism of Americans, even in the supposedly freedom-loving west, vis-à-vis Native Americans and African Americans; see chapter 15, 1:156–57, 204–6.

129. Kirkland appears in John S. Hart's stunningly popular volume *The Female Prose Writers of America*, where the headnote asserts, "For racy wit, keen observation of life and manners, and a certain air of refinement which never forsakes her, even in the roughest scenes, these sketches of western life were entirely without a parallel in American literature. Their success determined in a great measure Mrs. Kirkland's course of life, and she has since become an author by profession." Hart, "Caroline M. Kirkland," 116.

130. In his 1846 review of her work in *Godey's Lady's Book*—which also considers Margaret Fuller—Edgar Allan Poe comments that *A New Home* "wrought an undoubted sensation" in the literary world, "not so much in picturesque description, in racy humor, or in animated individual portraiture, as in *truth* and novelty" in representing the west. Poe, "The Literati of New York City," 75.

131. Other reasons for Kirkland's disappearance include the lack of copyright protections for books by American authors and the more lucrative format of magazine publishing for authors—where Kirkland directed most of her subsequent efforts.

132. Jacobs, *Incidents in the Life of a Slave Girl*, 16.

133. Kimberly N. Ruffin describes how the Jena Six, a group of black students in Louisiana, were confronted with nooses when they attempted to enjoy the shade of their high school's "white tree." Ruffin points to the ongoing resonance, metaphorical and literal, of trees in African American (and American) society. *Black on Earth*, 1–4. Focusing on contemporary literature, Ruffin's *Black on Earth* contributes to the emerging project of inserting African American literary texts into ecocritical discussions.

A local reporter has written an alternative account of the Jena Six story that complicates the narrative significantly; see Franklin, "Media Myths about the Jena 6." While Franklin's piece offers compelling evidence to deconstruct the standard media version, the public outcry surrounding the case indicates the continuing and sometimes racialized resonance of trees in American society.

134. Ruffin, *Black on Earth*, 27.

135. Finseth, *Shades of Green*, 30. Jacobs's responses to nature rarely figure in critical assessments; see, for example, Fleischner, *Mastering Slavery*; Frances Smith Foster, *Written by Herself*; and Carla L. Peterson, *Doers of the Word*. References to Jacobs's work are too numerous to cite. Additional classic studies include Yellin, "Written by Herself"; Foreman, "The Spoken and the Silenced"; and Sánchez-Eppler, *Touching Liberty*. More recent work includes Stone, "Interracial Sexual Abuse"; and Warner, "Harriet Jacobs at Home."

136. Ritchie and Ronald, introduction to *Available Means*, xvii.

137. For a perspective on Frederick Douglass's slave narrative that complements my remarks on Jacobs, see Michael Bennett, "Anti-Pastoralism, Frederick Douglass, and the Nature of Slavery." As Murphy observes of contemporary literature, many marginalized writers explore nature as part of a matrix of struggle (against colonialism, war, or racism, for example) and hence may be silenced by normative expectations about nature writing. Lacking a fully articulated and coherent tradition of "American nature writing" on which to look back, nineteenth-century women would not have been so constrained—rather, they are delimited and silenced by contemporary *critical* norms. Discussing contemporary African literature, Murphy notes that in such literature the environment cannot be treated without "attention to violence, warfare, government corruption, and transnational corporate greed"; elsewhere he emphasizes the need to "appreciate cultural diversity as a physical manifestation of biological diversity." *Farther Afield*, 68, 74. In *Writing for an Endangered World*, modeling one way in which our perspectives and formal categories might be expanded, Buell submits Jane Addams's description of a neighborhood garbage dump as an example of environmental writing (15–16).

138. Roorda, *Dramas of Solitude*, 5.

139. Ruffin, *Black on Earth*, 10. As Ruffin points out, "the concept of ecological burden and beauty informs a number of literary styles" and genres (16).

140. On Jacobs's story as a travel text, see Hardack, "Water Rites." Hardack is principally concerned with issues of authenticity and realism; his concerns and his conclusions differ substantially from mine.

141. Mart A. Stewart, "Slavery and African American Environmentalism."

142. See, for example, Stein, *Shifting the Ground*; Paula Gunn Allen, *The Sacred Hoop*; Norwood, *Made from This Earth*; Sturgeon, *Ecofeminist Natures*; and Gaard and Murphy, *Ecofeminist Literary Criticism*.

143. Joni Adamson and Scott Slovic have affirmed, "The roots of the environmental movement can be traced back to the abolition movement, which revealed the connections between colonization, slavery, resource exploitation, and capital," and many historical social justice movements modeled strategies for "early environmentalism." "Guest Editors' Introduction," 5–6.

144. Melvin Dixon, *Ride Out the Wilderness*, 17. Dixon focuses on male writers' slave narratives; as my analysis indicates, the situation may have been somewhat more complicated for women slave narrators.

145. Ibid., 26. Merchant also points out the dual valences of the forest (often construed as wilderness) for enslaved persons, observing that on the one hand, "[s]laves sought safe haven in the forest from excessive labor and harsh treatment" and that "the forest also offered routes to the North and way stations along the underground railway." *American Environmental History*, 76. See also Elizabeth D. Blum, "Power, Danger, and Control," 251–53, 255ff. For example, enslaved women cited their pharmacological knowledge, a source of agency and power, including power "over their reproductive lives" (260).

146. Melvin Dixon, *Ride Out the Wilderness*, 4–5.

147. Kirby, *Poquosin*, xiii.

148. Carpio, *Laughing Fit to Kill*, 66.

149. See Slicer, "The Body as Bioregion"; Ritchie and Ronald, introduction to *Available Means*, xxvi–xxvii.

150. See Carpio, *Laughing Fit to Kill*, 67.

151. This passage echoes two, by Henry Bibb and Frederick Douglass, that may contain African elements: "In African beliefs water, as well as the wilds, was a place of divine power." Melvin Dixon, *Ride Out the Wilderness*, 24.

152. Hershberger, "Mobilizing Women, Anticipating Abolition," 35; see 36ff.

153. Quoted in ibid., 38; see 38ff. Hershberger argues that the anti-removalists' disappointment with their efforts' outcome fueled a surge of antislavery activism in the early 1830s (40).

154. Portnoy, *Their Right to Speak*, 3. See Portnoy's introduction for further connections between antislavery and anti-removal activists.

155. Barbara Cook writes, "The parallels between the antebellum culture of slavery and today's racist politics of urban enclosure suggest that slave narratives can be considered an extended metaphor for environmental racism as it operates today." "Enclosed by Racist Politics," 33.

156. Mart A. Stewart, "Slavery and African American Environmentalism," 10.

157. Carolyn Merchant observes that "African Americans presented more difficult problems for European colonizers than did Indians. Although both Indians and blacks were regarded as savage, Africans and Indians were constructed differently and treated differently. White-black differences seemed more pronounced than those between Indians and whites." "Shades of Darkness."

158. Mart A. Stewart, "Slavery and African American Environmentalism," 10.

159. See Finseth, *Shades of Green*, 257; Elizabeth D. Blum, "Power, Danger, and Control," 249. See also Bayley, *A Narrative of Some Remarkable Incidents*.

160. Finseth, *Shades of Green*, 257.

161. Mart A. Stewart, "Slavery and African American Environmentalism," 20.

162. Ruffin, *Black on Earth*, 27.

163. Timothy Silver, *A New Face on the Countryside*, 116.

164. For a discussion of enslaved persons' central role in the production of naval stores, including the grueling manufacture of turpentine, and the particular forms of exploitation workers endured, see Cassandra Y. Johnson and McDaniel, "Turpentine Negro." See also Cox, Maxwell, and Thomas, *This Well-Wooded Land*, 17–18.

165. Cox, Maxwell, and Thomas, *This Well-Wooded Land*, 13, 129.

166. Timothy Silver, *A New Face on the Countryside*, 117, 121. See Kirby, *Mockingbird Song*, 125.

167. Marzio, "Carpentry in the Southern Colonies," 238–44.

168. Kirby, *Poquosin*, 29.

169. Timothy Silver, *A New Face on the Countryside*, 129. For two wonderful contemporary accounts of America's forests, see Janisse Ray on Georgia's forest ecology (and loss) in *Ecology of a Cracker Childhood* and Joan Maloof on Maryland's eastern shore in *Teaching the Trees*.

170. Kirby, *Poquosin*, 33.

171. Saillant, "Wipe away All Tears."

172. On Benjamin and Phillip, see Jacobs, *Incidents in the Life of a Slave Girl*, 41–43; on Harriet and Phillip, see 167, 169, 170, 174, 185, 188, 192, 193, 196, 211, 227, 231, 237. The name Benjamin appears frequently in the Bible, but Jacobs surely chose the name in reference to the Benjamin of Deuteronomy, who is the beloved of God and whom Moses blessed before his death: *"And* of Benjamin he said, The beloved of the LORD shall dwell in safety by him; *and the* LORD shall cover him all the day long, and he shall dwell between his shoulders. King James version, Deuteronomy 33:12, http://kingjbible.com/deuteronomy/33.htm; original emphasis. Like Phillip, Benjamin represents protection and power.

173. For Jacobs's references to Africanist traditions and her criticism of Christianity, see Warner, "Harriet Jacobs at Home," 40–43; Connor, *Conversions and Visions*.

174. Jacobs, *Incidents in the Life of a Slave Girl*, 111, 154, 278, 284, 294.

175. Quoted in Ruffin, *Black on Earth*, 6–7.

176. John 14:1–2, 13–18, King James version, http://kingjbible.com/john/14.htm.

177. Kirkland, *A New Home*, 28.

178. One of Ritchie and Ronald's *topoi* for rhetorica is an expanded definition of "woman." Introduction to *Available Means*, xxv.

179. Jewett, "A Winter Drive," 167, 180. Jewett's essay emerged in a national climate of concern over American forests that culminated in a variety of congressional acts preserving (or seeking to conserve) them. See "Chronology of Selected Events." Among the signal events were the founding of the American Forestry Association (1875) and the initial publication of *Forest and Stream* (1873). The environmental historian Jamie H. Eves catalogs the numerous early commentators on the environmental consequences of overzealous cutting. "Shrunk to a Comparative Rivulet," 38–39.

180. Acheson, "Maine," 126.

181. Muir, "The American Forests."

182. Concerns encompass quality as well as quantity; see Acheson, "Maine."

183. On the Maine woods debate as reported in the *Boston Globe*, see Daley, "A Race to Save Maine Woods"; Daley, "Paul Bunyan on Trial."

184. Rimer, "In Clear-Cutting Vote."

185. Nancy Allen, "Cutting Out Clear-Cutting."

186. Buell, *Writing for an Endangered World*, chapter 1.

187. See Rimer, "In Clear-Cutting Vote."

188. Tinker offers a provocative critique of sustainable development. *Spirit and Resistance*, 1–27.

189. Rimer, "In Clear-Cutting Vote." See also Passell, "On Clear-Cutting, Economists Can't See."

190. White, "Are You an Environmentalist."

Chapter 3. Golden Hands

1. Jacobs, *Incidents in the Life of a Slave Girl*, 98–102.

2. See Cassandra Y. Johnson and McDaniel, "Turpentine Negro," 51–62.

3. To date I have located only two works that address earlier working-class women's writing from an ecocritical perspective; both focus on eighteenth-century British women poets as nature writers: Milne, "Gender, Class, and the Beehive"; and Milne, *Lactilla Tends Her Fav'rite Cow*. For some examples of texts about women and work, see Frances Harper, "Fancy Etchings"; Mary Mapes Dodge, "Miss Maloney on the Chinese Question"; Mary Hallock Foote, "The Fate of a Voice"; Sarah Orne Jewett, "The Passing of Sister Barsett"; and Laura Jacobson, "The Wooing of Rachel Schlipsky," in Kilcup, *Nineteenth-Century American Women Writers: An Anthology*, 170–71, 242–43, 341–59, 391–97, and 478–86, respectively. See also Thomson, "Benevolent Maternalism"; Hapke, *Labor's Text*.

4. Quoted in Ruffin, *Black on Earth*, 6–7. Much scholarship on working-class identity has focused on the body's significance, but, as Rita Felski warns, focusing on embodiment alone has serious risks. "Nothing to Declare," 34–35. Although he focuses on male writers and male experience, Sweet points out that traditional pastoral literature "elides various relations among land, labor, and capital." "Projecting Early American Environmental Writing," 423. See also Philippon, "Is Early American Environmental Writing Sustainable?," 437.

5. Of all the authors discussed thus far in *Fallen Forests*, by virtue of her birth Sigourney most nearly approximates a working-class outlook as it is traditionally understood. Writing unabashedly for money rather than for self-expression or aesthetic achievement, Sigourney anticipates later working-class women writers. See Paula Bernat Bennett, "Was Sigourney a Poetess?" 266–67. We can also understand Jacobs's *Incidents in the Life of a Slave Girl* in a tradition of working-class women's writing. As Laura Hapke has noted, Jacob's text "is permeated with the realization that slave women were excluded from cultural concepts of femi-

nine behaviour." Hapke, *Labor's Text*, 82; see Becker, "Harriet Jacobs's Search for Home."

6. Defining "working-class" for the mid-nineteenth century presents numerous impediments. See Dimock and Gilmore, introduction to *Rethinking Class*, 2; Kaplan, "Introduction: Millennial Class," 13; Lauter, "Working-Class Women's Literature," 110, 111. Despite the growth of education for girls and women by mid-century, occupational opportunities were limited: laundress, domestic servant, seamstress, milliner, factory worker, schoolteacher, writer, governess. With the possible exception of the last two, all involved manual labor. See Clinton and Lunardini, *The Columbia Guide*, 3–8; see also chapter 2. Respectability circumscribed possibilities for women workers; as I describe below, even factory work was initially suspect.

7. Thompson, *The Making of the English Working Class*, 9–11.

8. Ritchie and Ronald emphasize "physicality as a *topoi* from which to write." Introduction to *Available Means*, xxvi–xxvii. Claiming embodied rhetoric as a source of authority, of course, does not mean that *only* women write embodied rhetoric or that women use *only* embodied rhetoric, but it allows for the possibility that such rhetoric is gendered.

On ecofeminism and the body, see, for example, Slicer, "Towards an Ecofeminist Standpoint Theory"; Alaimo, "Skin Dreaming." Although corporeality could be a delicate subject for nineteenth-century American women writers, many explored it, though in coded form. See Paula Bernat Bennett, "The Pea that Duty Locks"; Paula Bernat Bennett, "Pomegranate-Flowers." See also Paula Bernat Bennett, *Nineteenth-Century American Women Poets*, 158–59, 49–51. The sexual body that white women were seeing as a prospective means of liberation remained for Harriet Jacobs, Sarah Winnemucca, and others a potential source of confinement and exploitation.

9. Scharff, *Seeing Nature through Gender*, 30.

10. Wilson, *Our Nig*, 17.

11. Thoreau, "The Ponds," 182, and "Brute Neighbors," 217.

12. Berbineau, *From Beacon Hill to the Crystal Palace*, 58, 78.

13. Dulles, *Americans Abroad*, 66.

14. Ibid., 1; Schriber, *Writing Home*, 13. See also Steadman, *Traveling Economies*.

15. Taylor, "A Beacon Hill Domestic," 96. I am indebted to this work for much of my background material.

16. The diaries reveal payments ranging from $10 to $55. At her death, her estate was worth about $800. See Taylor, "A Beacon Hill Domestic," 95–96n20. Thomas Dublin suggests that in 1866 Berbineau earned $98; in 1867, $140; and in 1868, $224. He also notes that in the same period she received payments totalling $260 from Georgina Lowell that he speculates were dividends from shares in textile mills. *Transforming Women's Work*, 189. Dublin's figures reflect the years during which Berbineau's health was failing, confirming Taylor's assertions about the exceptional treatment she received from the Lowells.

17. Taylor, "A Beacon Hill Domestic," 99; see Dublin, *Transforming Women's Work*, 188–90.

18. In England in 1851, the largest plurality of working women (37 percent) were domestic servants, while across the Atlantic in Boston, 60 percent fell into this category. The vast majority worked in private homes rather than, for example, in hotels. Most were young and single, and most disliked their occupation, which, while it often provided a measure of autonomy and financial independence, not only required separation from family and hard physical work but to many seemed to compromise their pride and even, in some sense, to enslave them. In the "democratic" United States in particular, servants' status and their proper relation to their employers were fraught, full of potential friction on both sides. Dudden, *Serving Women*, 94–96, 108–14; Dublin, *Transforming Women's Work*, 154–56; Seccombe, *Weathering the Storm*, 32.

19. Sutherland, *Americans and Their Servants*, 141; Dudden, *Serving Women*, 44–103.

20. Taylor, "A Beacon Hill Domestic," 103–4. Given how much the Beechers and others complained about Irish servants, much of Berbineau's value to the Lowells probably came from her Protestant American status. Karen A. Weyler, personal communication, 17 January 2012.

21. Taylor, "A Beacon Hill Domestic," 107.

22. Ibid., 90. Even though her diaries explicitly reflect few contemporary occurrences and we must read between the lines to infer their influence, Berbineau's travel diaries should also be contextualized within the period of intense social change in which they were written, which included (in the United States) the Seneca Falls convention, unionist strikes in the Lowell mills, and the formation of various reform groups. Additionally, the Irish famines of the late 1840s and early 1850s propelled a large number of individuals to the United States; most of the women who immigrated became servants.

For another discussion of Lowell mill girls, see Dublin, "Women, Work, and Protest." For a discussion of the larger industrial environment and its relationship to domestic ideology, see Kessler-Harris, "Industrial Wage Earners." The situation was somewhat different in New York City, as Christine Stansell documents; see *City of Women*.

23. With the midcentury rise of the middle class and increasing wealth of the upper class, the desire for servants — for practical household assistance and as status symbols — mushroomed. In this context, the "servant problem" — finding and retaining "good" servants — was a popular topic in England and the United States, engendering numerous advice books for both employers and domestic workers. See Ryan, introduction to *Love, Wages, Slavery*, 1–14.

24. On Americans' motivations for travel, see Schriber, *Writing Home*, 19ff.; Dulles, *Americans Abroad*, 104–7; Lockwood, *Passionate Pilgrims*, 92; Mulvey, *Anglo-American Landscapes*, 6–8.

25. Schriber, *Writing Home*, 134; see Caesar, *Forgiving the Boundaries*.

26. Schriber, *Writing Home*, 27.

27. As Janet Zandy points out, "home" also possesses a psychic dimension. Introduction to *Calling Home*, 1.

28. Sharer, "Going Into Society," 173; Watson, "The facts which go to form this fiction," 12.

29. We can only speculate whether this double vision occurred because of her closeness to the family, because of her travels, or because it was prevalent among her fellow servants.

30. Stacy Alaimo's work is helpful in this context; see *Bodily Natures*, 2.

31. Alaimo and Hekman, "Introduction: Emerging Models," 4.

32. Berbineau also comments on the beauty of Europe's art, antiques, and architecture, seemingly aware of the virtual requirement of self-improvement imposed on U.S. travelers. Schriber, *Writing Home*, 20.

33. The highest mountain in Europe (about 15,800 feet), Mont Blanc provided an early goal for alpinists; it also inspired pilgrimages by artists and writers of the nineteenth century, including Percy Bysshe Shelley and Harriet Beecher Stowe, for its sublime appearance. In speaking of the mountains here and below, Berbineau follows an established literary tradition.

34. Many women writers, usually nonprofessionals, asserted their inability to capture the landscape in language. Pagh, "An Indescribable Sea," 4.

35. Leighton, *American Gardens*, 83–100; Mulvey, *Anglo-American Landscapes*, 15–16, 126.

36. See Schriber, *Writing Home*, 88–89.

37. As I comment elsewhere, her perceptions about European poverty are complex; see Kilcup, "Introduction: A Working-Class Woman's View." For many women, diaries were themselves objects of sentiment, coming as gifts from husbands, friends, or family members; see McCarthy, "A Pocketful of Days," 292.

38. Alaimo and Hekman, "Introduction: Emerging Models," 5. Berbineau's observations echo dominant-culture associations that remain in force, "contaminating" ecofeminist scholarship itself. See Gaard, "Ecofeminism Revisited," 28, 41.

39. Margaret Fuller falls into the position of stereotyping Native American women as beasts of burden in her travel narrative. Fuller, *Summer on the Lakes*. See especially chapter 6, "Mackinaw." For a discussion of the covertly racialized content of some nineteenth-century fiction on the working class, see Schocket, "Discovering Some New Race."

Lockwood remarks on the embarrassment engendered by Hiram Powers's prize-winning statue "The Greek Slave," which suggested to many viewers the injustice of slavery in America (*Passionate Pilgrims*, 262–67); she also discusses the connections often made between slavery and the English factory system (208–26, 236–45). On Americans' sense of superiority, see Dulles, *Americans Abroad*, 5.

40. Schriber, *Writing Home*, 6, 34, 52–53, 77ff., 85.

41. Felski, "Nothing to Declare," 35.

42. Even among native-born servants, distinctions flourished. See Jacobs, *Incidents in the Life of a Slave Girl*, 264–67.

43. Stowe, *Sunny Memories of Foreign Lands*, 2:22. Many critics have written about Americans defining themselves against the Old World; see Strout, *The American Image*, 1–2. David Spurr's discussion of the tropes and interpretive strategies commonly applied by travelers to the colonial "other" resonates for European travelers like Stowe and Berbineau. *The Rhetoric of Empire*, 3–4.

44. Dudden, *Serving Women*, 5, 12–43.

45. For two different perspectives on the subject of European poverty, see my analysis of the diaries of Georgina Lowell and another family member, Katherine Bigelow Lawrence. Kilcup, "Introduction: A Working-Class Woman's View," 25–26, 34–35.

46. This expectation was not always a reality; see Dudden, *Serving Women*, 178–82. Farm women almost always worked on Sundays, even in the twentieth century. See Riney-Kehrberg, *Waiting on the Bounty*, 84.

47. On the other hand, Berbineau's distinctively Protestant sympathies are strained by the Catholics whom she encounters; she refers to them as "poor deluded people." *From Beacon Hill to the Crystal Palace*, 93. As with Stowe, Berbineau's anti-Catholic remarks may have been inflected by the fact that a huge number of Irish Catholic women emigrating to America came to Boston as servants. See Dudden, *Serving Women*, 60, 67–71; Stowe, *Sunny Memories of Foreign Lands*, 2:330–33; Berbineau, *From Beacon Hill to the Crystal Palace*, 93.

48. It is unclear whether Berbineau took opium for pain or in order to sleep; either possibility suggests the stress of hard work. On servants' health concerns, see Dudden, *Serving Women*, 194, 208.

49. On Berbineau's lingering illness, see Taylor, "A Beacon Hill Domestic," 94. Berbineau suffered virtually no seasickness on the return voyage. See Berbineau, *From Beacon Hill to the Crystal Palace*, 117–23 (20 November–5 December).

50. See Kilcup, "Introduction: A Working-Class Woman's View," 13, 18–19, 25–26.

51. Ibid., 28–36.

52. Alaimo and Hekman, "Introduction: Emerging Models," 15.

53. Middle-class standards were often imposed on working-class people; see Sharer, "Going Into Society"; Watson, "The facts which go to form this fiction"; and Thomson, "Benevolent Maternalism."

54. Barbara A. White, "'Our Nig' and the She-Devil," 21. White's account indicates the difficulty of distinguishing between the fictional Frado and the autobiographical Wilson, whose experiences overlap significantly. See also Ellis, "What Happened to Harriet E. Wilson?"

55. Wilson, *Our Nig*, 134. All references are to this edition.

56. Lang discusses Wilson's challenges in finding language to describe home. *The Syntax of Class*, 43; see 63–68.

57. Many Wilson critics have commented on Milford, New Hampshire's, status as a station on the Underground Railroad and its numerous abolitionist undertakings. I am not arguing for the divorce between rural and urban spheres; what I am suggesting is that however cosmopolitan such activities may have been, their (national) interventions do not negate Wilson's (or Frado's) situation on a farm. Although Berbineau herself came from Maine—virtually all of which was rural in 1851—she acculturated, we might even say assimilated, to her employers' cosmopolitan perspective.

58. See Leveen, "Dwelling in the House of Oppression," 565. Lesley Ginsberg cites George Fitzhugh's assertion allying slaves, women, and children in their inability for self-care; see "Of Babies, Beasts, and Bondage," 91–92. Gretchen Short describes Frado as an unalterably "foreign" touchstone against which the "domesticity of the community and its members are defined." "Harriet Wilson's *Our Nig*," 12. As my account explores, Frado's—and Wilson's—identities do not merge seamlessly; in many instances they conflict. Even as proslavery advocates disparaged so-called white wage slavery in the industrializing North, arguing that chattel slavery was more humane, midcentury American white workers sought to elevate their status by distinguishing themselves from slaves and immigrants, gaining status via a rejection of "foreign," ethnic, and "colored." See Roediger, *The Wages of Whiteness*.

59. Jacobs, *Incidents in the Life of a Slave Girl*, 76; Short, "Harriet Wilson's *Our Nig*," 9.

60. Finseth, *Shades of Green*, 2, 137–48.

61. On African Americans and the environment, see Melvin Dixon, *Ride Out the Wilderness*; Glave and Stoll, *"To Love the Wind and the Rain"*; Kimberly K. Smith, *African American Environmental Thought*; Glave, *Rooted in the Earth*.

62. Ruffin, *Black on Earth*, 10, 19, 27, 31.

63. Criticism on the novel has flourished. In addition to the critics cited elsewhere in the notes, see, for example, Ryan, *Love, Wages, Slavery*, 126–27; Kyla Wazana Tompkins, "Everything 'Cept Eat Us," 216; Santamarina, "The View from Below"; Lovell, "By Dint of Labor and Economy," 1–32.

64. Cynthia J. Davis, "Speaking the Body's Pain," 393, 400. Davis points out that pain is often conceived as having an external source and the potential for relief (398; see 400).

65. Foreman, "Recovered Autobiographies and the Marketplace," 126, 127. Ellis takes issue with Foreman's contention concerning Mag's habitual drunkenness. "What Happened to Harriet E. Wilson?," 166.

66. Cassandra Jackson, "Beyond the Page."

67. "Principles of Environmental Justice"; see also U.S. Environmental Protection Agency, "Environmental Justice." Absent from the EPA definition is the global context for environmental justice, where nations share benefits and responsibilities. See also Matsuoka, "Building Healthy Communities."

68. On the Haywards' abolitionist links, see Barbara A. White, "'Our Nig' and

the She-Devil," 37–38; Foreman, *Activist Sentiments*, 44–45; Foreman, "Recovered Autobiographies and the Marketplace," 125–26.

69. See Barbara A. White, "'Our Nig' and the She-Devil," 46–47n9. As Thomson remarks, in a slave economy, disabled children were liabilities. "Benevolent Maternalism," 560. Wilson shows how, for the poor, *all* children, whether or not disabled, were considered liabilities.

70. White describes terrible conditions in the county poorhouse, especially for African Americans. Barbara A. White, "'Our Nig' and the She-Devil," 23–27.

71. Barbara A. White, "'Our Nig' and the She-Devil," 21; Henry Louis Gates Jr. and Ellis, introduction to *Our Nig*, xl.

72. Barbara A. White, "'Our Nig' and the She-Devil," 23. Since *Our Nig*'s 1983 recovery and authentication by Henry Louis Gates Jr., critics have framed it in various genre contexts. Other critical concerns have included slavery, Wilson's attainment of selfhood and authority, her attitude toward Christianity, and nationalism and citizenship. Appreciating the book's complexity, I call it a novel for convenience's sake. See, for example, Barbara A. White, "'Our Nig' and the She-Devil"; Henry Louis Gates Jr., "Parallel Discursive Universes"; Doriani, "Black Womanhood in Nineteenth-Century America"; Breau, "Identifying Satire"; Carby, "Hear My Voice, Ye Careless Daughters," 94; Stern, "Excavating Genre in *Our Nig*"; King, "The Demystification of Sentiment"; Ellis, "Traps Slyly Laid"; Dowling, *Capital Letters*, 29; Ernest, "Economies of Identity"; Foreman, "Recovered Autobiographies and the Marketplace"; Frink, "Fairy Tales and *Our Nig*"; Elizabeth J. West, "Reworking the Conversion Narrative"; Bassard, "I Took a Text"; Ellis, "Body Politics and the Body Politic." For one of the most comprehensive discussions, see Ellis, *Harriet Wilson's "Our Nig."*

73. Lang, *The Syntax of Class*, 67.

74. Neither Frado nor Berbineau, for all the latter's relative privilege, ever enjoyed the sentimentalized family membership enjoined in mid-nineteenth-century advice writing. Ryan, introduction to *Love, Wages, Slavery*, 1–2. As Taylor observes of Berbineau and the Lowells, she never did "join them at table." "A Beacon Hill Domestic," 115.

75. See Short, "Harriet Wilson's *Our Nig*," 3–4, 6.

76. Valerie Cunningham, "New Hampshire Forgot," 99. See Leveen, "Dwelling in the House of Oppression," 564. For a discussion of indenture and benevolent practices in New Hampshire during Wilson's childhood, see Foreman, *Activist Sentiments*, 54–55. Harriet Beecher Stowe's family employed black indentured servants during her youth, and, as Joan Hedrick notes, Stowe herself "expressed in 1863 a desire to dismiss her household servants in favor of a bound girl she could train to her liking." *Harriet Beecher Stowe*, 311.

77. Thomson, "Benevolent Maternalism," 568.

78. Thomson, "Crippled Girls and Lame Old Women," 132.

79. Of Mrs. Bellmont, White notes, "Rebecca's father may have been a child

beater. . . . [C]hild abusers have usually been abused themselves when they were children." Barbara A. White, "'Our Nig' and the She-Devil," 31.

80. Marianne DeKoven suggests, "Analyzing the use of animal representation can clarify modes of human subjugation that ideology might otherwise obscure." "Guest Column," 363.

81. Cynthia J. Davis, "Speaking the Body's Pain," 400; see 392. See Kyla Wazana Tompkins, "Everything 'Cept Eat Us," 215; Stern, "Excavating Genre in *Our Nig*," 453–54.

82. We see this motif throughout nineteenth-century American women's fiction, independent of the author's race. For example, in Rose Terry Cooke's "Dely's Cow," the heroine finds solace, companionship, and understanding from Biddy during her husband's absence during the Civil War. Cooke's story is fundamentally comic, while Wilson's is tragic.

83. See Price Herndl, "The Invisible (Invalid) Woman," 567; Ginsberg, "Of Babies, Beasts, and Bondage," 91; Ellen Samuels, "A Complication of Complaints," 40; see also McCaskill, "Yours Very Truly," 517. Only three years after *Our Nig*'s publication, Rebecca Harding Davis, in her fictionalized account of the autistic savant Thomas Bethune (Thomas Wiggins; 1849–1908), underscores his "strong appetites and gross bodily health," which she cites as characteristic of "the lowest Guinea type." Rebecca Harding Davis, "Blind Tom," 582. Glenda Carpio offers a brief account of the novel's satire. *Laughing Fit to Kill*, 32–33, 67–71.

84. For more information, see "Snakes of Massachusetts"; New Hampshire Fish and Game, "Black Racer." Nineteenth-century journal articles sometimes affirmed the value of this reptile; see, for example, "Antagonism of Harmless Serpents"; "King Snakes and Rattle Snakes."

85. Price Herndl, "The Invisible (Invalid) Woman," 567.

86. Short, "Harriet Wilson's *Our Nig*," 13.

87. E. E. T., "Childhood's Home"; see "Betsey," "Recollections of My Childhood"; Montrie, "I Think Less of the Factory," 282–85.

88. Buell, *The Environmental Imagination*, 439; Michael Bennett, "Anti-Pastoralism, Frederick Douglass, and the Nature of Slavery."

89. On the novel's realism, see Joyce W. Warren, "Performativity and the Repositioning," 14–18.

90. Ellis, "*Our Nig*: Fetters," 66, 80. See also Ellis, introduction to *Harriet Wilson's "Our Nig,"* 6–7, chapter 5 (125–58).

91. Thoreau, "Walking," 197.

92. See, for example, Leveen, "Dwelling in the House of Oppression," 573, 569; Santamarina, "The View from Below," 71–72; Thomson, "Benevolent Maternalism." Though women were sometimes responsible for milking and then for making butter and cheese or feeding hens, the more strenuous work was usually left to men.

93. Montrie, "I Think Less of the Factory," 278.

94. Montrie specifically discusses the Lowell mill girls. Ibid.

95. Ellis, *Harriet Wilson's "Our Nig,"* 102–3.

96. Ellis, *"Our Nig*: Fetters," 65. Borrowing from Sweet's georgic paradigm, we might also call Wilson's approach antigeorgic. "Projecting Early American Environmental Writing."

97. See Kete, "Slavery's Shadows," 116, 119.

98. William Wells Brown, *My Southern Home*, 80, 82.

99. Ruffin, *Black on Earth*, 29.

100. See, for example, Barbara A. White, "'Our Nig' and the She-Devil," 22; Ellis, "Traps Slyly Laid," 65, 66.

101. Ellis, "Traps Slyly Laid," 66; see Barbara A. White, "'Our Nig' and the She-Devil," 34. However, this expression of Frado's own agency also entertains the heroine — and Wilson herself.

102. Stern, "Excavating Genre in *Our Nig*," 448, 453; see 448–54.

103. Ginsberg, "Of Babies, Beasts, and Bondage," 101, 102.

104. See ibid.

105. Ruffin, *Black on Earth*, 36.

106. Ginsberg, "Of Babies, Beasts, and Bondage," 89; see Leveen "Dwelling in the House of Oppression," 573.

107. I interpret this passage differently than Foreman. *Activist Sentiments*, 55.

108. Consumerism "requires playfulness, appetite, and taste." Gray, *Race and Time*, 190.

109. See Ellen Samuels, "A Complication of Complaints," 18.

110. See Ellis, *Harriet Wilson's "Our Nig,"* 138.

111. Thomson, *Extraordinary Bodies*. Thomson remarks elsewhere on the subjective experience of disability versus disability as a social identity. "Benevolent Maternalism," 578–79n4.

112. Davis connects this trend to the development of bourgeois hegemony and middle-class ideology (11ff.) as well as eugenics (18). Lennard J. Davis, "Constructing Normalcy."

113. Of course, the past twenty years of theory has suggested the fluidity and social construction even of racial and gender identity, as well as the performative elements of various identities. See Ellen Samuels, "A Complication of Complaints," 22. See also Couser, "Signifying Bodies," 112.

114. James and Wu cite Henri-Jacques Striker's *A History of Disability* for the connection between "environmentally instigated forms of disability" and various types of corrective intervention. "Editors' Introduction," 4.

115. James and Wu, "Editors' Introduction," 4.

116. Baynton, "Disability and the Justification of Inequality," 36. For another literary example, see Rebecca Harding Davis, "Blind Tom," 581. Davis compares her hero, Thomas Bethune's "instinct" to that of "a dog's or an infant's" (582).

117. Baynton, "Disability and the Justification of Inequality," 36. See also Watson, "The facts which go to form this fiction," 16ff. Diane Price Herndl observes

that Wilson, Jacobs, and Harper establish their humanity through their disability. "The Invisible (Invalid) Woman," 567, 568. Given the associations outlined above, it was doubtless profoundly disturbing to Wilson that the environment in which her son George lived much of his life, the county poor farm, was filled with disabled individuals, including the violent insane. Barbara A. White, "'Our Nig' and the She-Devil," 23–27.

118. Ellen Samuels, "A Complication of Complaints," 18. See Price Herndl, "The Invisible (Invalid) Woman," 554.

119. James and Wu, "Editors' Introduction," 7.

120. See Leveen, "Dwelling in the House of Oppression," 575. The use of *ugly* for ill-tempered was common in the early nineteenth century; see, for example, Eliza Leslie, "Incorrect Words," in Kilcup, *Nineteenth-Century American Women Writers: An Anthology*, 21–24.

121. Bauer, "In the Blood," 61; see Thomson, "Benevolent Maternalism," 573ff. Elizabeth Stuart Phelps demonstrates these associations vividly via the character of millworker Catty in her labor novel *The Silent Partner* (1871).

122. See Price Herndl, "The Invisible (Invalid) Woman," 554–55; Ellen Samuels, "A Complication of Complaints," 34; see also Baynton, "Disability and the Justification of Inequality." 42; Price Herndl, *Invalid Women*, 78; Price Herndl, "The Invisible (Invalid) Woman," 567; Thomson, "Feminist Theory, the Body, and the Disabled Figure," 279.

123. Ellen Samuels, "A Complication of Complaints," 34. On playing the lady, see Price Herndl, "The Invisible (Invalid) Woman," 565.

124. Barbara A. White, "'Our Nig' and the She-Devil," 34.

125. Illness also confirmed the notion advanced by proslavery advocates that African American women required the "care" provided by slavery. Price Herndl, "The Invisible (Invalid) Woman," 560, 564–65, 558. Kyla Wazana Tompkins notes that disability was a class as well as a race marker. "Everything 'Cept Eat Us," 37. Jacobs addresses related issues in her loving (and pointedly ironic) portrait of her aunt Nancy and in her description of her period in her grandmother's attic. See Price Herndl, "The Invisible (Invalid) Woman," 561–63.

126. Price Herndl, "The Invisible (Invalid) Woman," 564, 565.

127. Ibid., 559, 564.

128. See, for example, Wilson, *Our Nig*, 118, 122, 123.

129. This impulse represents a particular temptation for disabled life-writers, since it suggests that "success in overcoming adversity, is . . . not available to many disabled people." Couser, "Signifying Bodies," 111.

130. Jacobs was scarcely unique in celebrating even a "small" and temporary "triumph over my tyrant." Jacobs, *Incidents in the Life of a Slave Girl*, 85. Observing black leaders' insistence that blacks participated in their own subjugation by their unwillingness to "rise" from menial occupations, Santamarina argues that Wilson exposes the structural inequalities in Northern labor that necessitated African

Americans' self-reliance and resistance within, rather than movement outside of, racist work relations, and she values Wilson's realistic depiction of Frado's efforts merely to survive. Santamarina, "The View from Below."

131. Ellen Samuels discusses literacy and illiteracy as a disability (in other writers' work). "A Complication of Complaints," 24–26; see Kyla Wazana Tompkins, "Everything 'Cept Eat Us," 212–13.

132. Klages, *Woeful Afflictions*, 2. Even the adult Berbineau receives such protection: Francis Lowell returns her home to America, first class. In first class Berbineau would have been guaranteed the care of a steward if she had become more ill.

133. "Maids and Mistresses"; Thomson, "Benevolent Maternalism," 561.

134. Levander contends that "the child . . . has historically helped to constitute and buttress the nation." *Cradle of Liberty*, 6.

135. See Foreman, *Activist Sentiments*, 55.

136. Eric Gardner suggests that "the book's purchasers either interpreted or deployed *Our Nig* as a book geared toward the moral improvement of young readers," perhaps because it principally concerns a child's search for self and God. "This Attempt of Their Sister," 227–28, 238, 239, 246; see also Gardner, "Of Bottles and Books." Deborah C. De Rosa argues that because it conformed to norms of femininity, children's literature provided a "nonthreatening" venue for women to enter political discourse, but one way to interpret Wilson's relative lack of sales is that readers may not have perceived her narrative in this way. *Domestic Abolitionism*, 7.

137. See Sánchez-Eppler, *Dependent States*, 40–41, 44, 51, 45, 46, 51. Lisa E. Green offers a related argument. "The Disorderly Girl." See also Levander and Singley, introduction to *The American Child*, 4.

138. Harriet Beecher Stowe, *Uncle Tom's Cabin*, 325. According to Gillian Avery, the American work ethic was much stronger than that in England, and children's literature reflects that difference. In this context, Frado's playfulness becomes even more challenging to social norms. Avery, *Behold the Child*, 69.

139. Sánchez-Eppler, "Playing at Class."

140. See ibid., 44, 58.

141. See Doriani, "Black Womanhood in Nineteenth-Century America," 216; Ernest, "Economies of Identity," 435.

142. Ellis, "*Our Nig*: Fetters," 79. Such dangers were registered much later by Robert Frost in "Out, Out—."

143. Michael Bennett, "Anti-Pastoralism, Frederick Douglass, and the Nature of Slavery," 196.

144. See Psalms 23:1, 80:1; Ecclesiastes 12:11; Isaiah 40:4, 63:14.

145. Carpio suggests that satire offers Wilson both a means to inspire reform and a way to cope with her rage. *Laughing Fit to Kill*, 33.

146. Ellis questions Frado's conversion to Christianity. Introduction to *Harriet Wilson's "Our Nig,"* 84–88. Wilson's account foreshadows Huckleberry Finn's determination to separate himself from the harsh Miss Watson.

147. The idea that "the lion shall lie down with the lamb" represents a misquotation of two verses from Isaiah. The first is Isaiah 11:6, cited in the chapter text; the second is, "The wolf and the lamb shall feed together, and the lion shall eat straw like the bullock: and dust *shall* be the serpent's meat." Isaiah 65:25, King James version, http://kingjbible.com; original emphasis. The concept of enemies at peace remains accurate. Some of the most familiar representations of the concept belong to Quaker painter Edward Hicks (1780–1849), who composed more than a hundred versions of *The Peaceable Kingdom*. Hicks's work incorporates both Biblical imagery and contemporary events; in many, he displays European settlers and Native Americans signing a treaty. Worcester Art Museum, "Edward Hicks." Ellis notes Wilson's consistent reference to Old Testament sources or her ironic use of New Testament ones. Introduction to *Harriet Wilson's "Our Nig,"* 91.

148. Wilson, preface to *Our Nig*, n.p.

149. Ellis, introduction to *Our Nig*, xxiv–xxv, xxviii.

150. Raimon, "Miss Marsh's Uncommon School Reform," 177. Raimon names Wilson's teacher as Abigail Kent Marsh; see Ellis's cautions about this attribution, first made by Foreman and Pitts in their 2005 edition of *Our Nig*. "What Happened to Harriet E. Wilson?," 164.

151. Ellis outlines Wilson's considerable literary accomplishments. Introduction to *Harriet Wilson's "Our Nig."*

152. Hale, "Mary's Lamb."

153. McGuffey, *Old Favorites*, 3–4.

154. Janet Gray argues that "Mary's Lamb" "entered the popular imagination by way of the seriously didactic project of republican motherhood." See Gray, *Race and Time*, 193, 197.

155. See Raimon, "Miss Marsh's Uncommon School Reform," 173, 175.

156. On African Americans' access to and treatment in schools, see Watters, "As Soon as I Saw," 79; Valerie Cunningham, "New Hampshire Forgot," 103. For background on New Hampshire education and its potential effects on Wilson (and Frado), see Ellis, *Harriet Wilson's "Our Nig,"* 107–10.

An idea common in the eighteenth century (and still common in the nineteenth), the doctrine of "animal spirits" refers to the "(supposed) agent responsible for sensation and movement, originating in the brain and passing to and from the periphery of the body through the nerves; nervous action or force." *Oxford English Dictionary* online. I obviously use the term ironically in relation to Frado.

157. Gray points out the problems Hale's religious symbolism creates for her. *Race and Time*, 198–99.

158. Ibid., 198.

159. Wilson, *Our Nig*, 124. See Raimon, "Miss Marsh's Uncommon School Reform," 174; Henry Louis Gates Jr. and Ellis, introduction to *Our Nig*, xlix–lxvi.

160. George Blanchard, one of two Milford-area African Americans, was a member of the New Hampshire state militia when General John Sullivan called

it out during the American Revolution; as Jemison describes, Sullivan was the leader whose troops destroyed the Seneca settlements. Pitts, "George and Timothy Blanchard," 43, 51.

161. See Dublin, *Women at Work*, 145–64. Thomas B. Lovell notes that "Mag's self-sufficiency is threatened by what many of her contemporaries called 'white slavery,' the employment of predominantly immigrant workers in the North to perform menial tasks at or below subsistence wages." "By Dint of Labor and Economy," 20–21. See Robinson, *Loom and Spindle*, 6.

162. Larcom, "Among Lowell Mill Girls," 611. Larcom reflects similar attitudes in another autobiographical essay that emphasizes education to acculturate immigrants toward "the idea of American citizenship." Larcom, "III. American Factory Life." This essay suggests Larcom's separation from immigrants (she conceives of them as children), but it also stresses their moral equality (145).

163. Larcom, "Among Lowell Mill Girls," 612.

164. Little scholarship has been done on Larcom's poetry, and contemporary critics like Rose Norman stress the crucial role of poetry and poetry writing in Larcom's autobiography. "New England Girlhoods." On Larcom's poetry, see Jessica Lewis, "Poetry Experienced." Larcom's work often complicates the sentimental mode with which she is still often affiliated. See Marchalonis, *The Worlds of Lucy Larcom*; Kilcup, "Something of a Sentimental Sweet Singer"; Kilcup, "I Like These Plants." Early reviewers acknowledged the realism of Larcom's poetry—one praised her "perfect simplicity and self-control" and the "life-like" quality of "Hannah Binding Shoes"—and her originality, referring to her as a "genius." Review of *Poems*. See also Spofford, "Lucy Larcom's Poems." Larcom herself advises aspiring young women poets to avoid sentimentality and to be concrete. *A New England Girlhood*, 215. Larcom had earlier outlined her childhood memories; see "Autobiography"; "III. American Factory Life."

165. See Montrie, "I Think Less of the Factory," 290.

166. See Loeffelholz, "A Strange Medley-Book," 22.

167. Larcom, "Among Lowell Mill Girls," 600, 596.

168. Norman, "New England Girlhoods," 108. For the most detailed account of Larcom's life, see Marchalonis, *The Worlds of Lucy Larcom*.

169. On mill girls' transformed attitudes toward nature after their arrival in Lowell, see Montrie, "I Think Less of the Factory," 277.

170. Larcom, *A New England Girlhood*, 175–79. For some contemporary reprintings of *Lowell Offering* selections, see Eisler, *The Lowell Offering*; Foner, *The Factory Girls*.

171. See, for example, "Illustrated Books," *Literary World*, 20 December 1879, 436; "Notes in Season," *Publishers' Weekly*, 1 November 1879, 521; "Literary Notices," *Eclectic Magazine*, n.s., 31, no. 1 (January 1880): 123.

172. On the role of children's literature in nineteenth-century American culture, see Kilcup and Sorby, "Pretty New Moons." On the Larcom-Whittier relationship,

see Kilcup, "Lucy Larcom"; Marchalonis, "A Model for Mentors?" On Larcom's publications, see Loeffelholz, "A Strange Medley-Book," 8–9.

173. On Larcom's relationship with her readers, see Carol Holly, "Nineteenth-Century Autobiographies of Affiliation," 224. Larcom may have trusted her readers to be sympathetic, as Holly suggests (225–26), but she still had to consider the economic consequences of her writing.

174. Larcom, "Among Lowell Mill Girls," 601.

175. Marchalonis, *The Worlds of Lucy Larcom*, 252; Kort, "Lucy Larcom's Double-Exposure," 25–28.

176. Norman, "New England Girlhoods," 108, 110; see Jessica Lewis, "Poetry Experienced," 184–86. Both Norman and Lewis focus on genre.

177. MacLeod, *American Childhood*, 6.

178. Jessica Lewis, "Poetry Experienced," 185.

179. Larcom follows in the tradition of Susan Fenimore Cooper's *Rural Hours* (1850), Henry David Thoreau's *Walden* (1854), and Celia Thaxter's *Among the Isles of Shoals* (1873) and anticipates Thaxter's *An Island Garden* (1894) and Sarah Orne Jewett's *The Country of the Pointed Firs* (1896).

180. Larcom's fall into poverty would prompt her years later to ask her publisher, James T. Fields, to make one book "as inexpensive as possible" so that more people could afford it. Addison, *Lucy Larcom*, 160.

181. "First Cotton Mill in America"; Larcom, "Among Lowell Mill Girls," 594–95; Braudo, "Navy Birthplace Still up for Debate."

182. See "Outward Manifest of the *Two Friends*." S-hooks are forged iron hangers in the eponymous shape; the cook attached them to a crane overhanging a fireplace in order to raise, lower, and move various pots.

183. Norman, "New England Girlhoods," 108.

184. Larcom, *The Poetical Works*, 154–55. See Santamarina, "The View from Below," 71 (section epigraph).

185. Larcom was never directly involved in the woman's rights movement. Marchalonis, *The Worlds of Lucy Larcom*, 9, 63, 180. But see her poems "Getting Along," "Unwedded," "Her Choice," "Sylvia," and "A Gambrel Roof." Larcom, *The Poetical Works*, 25–26, 26–28, 28–29, 206–8, 218–21.

186. Gray, *Race and Time*, 188.

187. Larcom, *A New England Girlhood*, 9; see also Larcom, "Among Lowell Mill Girls," 600–602.

188. Larcom, "Among Lowell Mill Girls," 602; see *A New England Girlhood*, 67.

189. Larcom, "Among Lowell Mill Girls," 596.

190. Ibid., 594–95.

191. Larcom also projects the moral health of the enterprise. Ibid., 595.

192. See ibid.

193. Ibid., 598.

194. Larcom, *A New England Girlhood*, 163; see Montrie, "I Think Less of the Factory," 285, 283, 275.

195. Larcom, "Among Lowell Mill Girls," 598–99, 605.

196. Larcom translates the flight from a factory environment literally in her oxymoronically titled, book-length poem *An Idyl of Work*.

197. Larcom, *A New England Girlhood*, 199. Louisa May Alcott's *Work* may have provided one antecedent for such an attitude. Karen A. Weyler, personal communication, 15 January 2012.

198. Larcom, *A New England Girlhood*, 200.

199. In *A New England Girlhood* this theme forms a subtle narrative undercurrent; see, for example, 96. In an account of John Greenleaf Whittier's visit to Lowell, Larcom highlights the mill girls' antislavery views, noting that women were not expected to give—or even have—opinions on public matters. *A New England Girlhood*, 255.

200. Quoted in Addison, *Lucy Larcom*, 147.

201. Shepard, "Letters of Lucy Larcom," 506, 507.

202. Appearing in the *Atlantic Monthly* in 1863, the Browningesque poem was widely approved for its "strong statement of true womanly nobility and patriotic feeling"; it also reflects her disdain for her fiancé, Frank, and those like him who avoided conflict. Marchalonis, *The Worlds of Lucy Larcom*, 148.

203. In a letter to Whittier, Larcom asserts the necessity for morality—but without preachiness—in poetry. Shepard, "Letters of Lucy Larcom," 511.

204. Larcom, *The Poetical Works*, 93. The poem transforms Tennyson's poem "The Lady of Shalott," in which the romantic heroine-weaver dies and floats down a river, into a political meditation with overtones of a sermon. Of course, Larcom inverts Tennyson's trajectory in several respects, insisting (for example) that her narrator-weaver should look—and act—beyond the confines of the mill in which she works.

205. See also Larcom, "Among Lowell Mill Girls," 607.

206. See Larcom, *A New England Girlhood*, 183, 226. On the factories' pollution and workers' consequent health problems, see, for example, Chrostek, "Occupational Health & Safety in Textile." Larcom was not alone in presenting such a cheerful view and obscuring health issues; editorials in the *Lowell Offering* frequently disputed charges of an unhealthy environment. See, for example, Robinson, *Loom and Spindle*, 33; Kort, "Lucy Larcom's Double-Exposure," 36. Montrie explores how the workers articulated both sides of the discussion. "I Think Less of the Factory," 282–84.

207. Most current critical attention to the novel has focused on class and gender issues. See Thomson, "Benevolent Maternalism"; Watson, "The facts which go to form this fiction"; Bauer, "In the Blood"; Lang, "The Syntax of Class."

208. Dublin, *Women at Work*, 59, 66.

209. Chrostek, "Occupational Health & Safety in Textile."

210. Larcom, *A New England Girlhood*, 183; see 226. When she is teaching at

Wheaton College, the writer confides in a letter to her friend Elizabeth Whittier, John Greenleaf Whittier's sister, that the birds and flowers of spring help restore her health, which had been compromised by her time in the factories. See Shepard, "Letters of Lucy Larcom," 513.

211. Larcom, "Flowers of the Fallow," in *The Poetical Works*, 296–97, lines 1–5; also in Kilcup, *Nineteenth-Century American Women Writers: An Anthology*, 180.

212. Bradley, "Keeping the Soil in Good Heart."

213. On the connections between flowers and eroticism in Dickinson, see Paula Bernat Bennett, "The Pea that Duty Locks."

214. Kolodny, *The Lay of the Land.*

215. Vicinus, *Independent Women, Work and Community*; Chambers-Schiller, *Liberty, a Better Husband.*

216. The poem was published soon after the inauguration of the national park system with the setting aside of Yellowstone in 1872. David Mazel reminds us that the primary victims in the creation of national parks in the western United States were Native Americans, while in the East they were poor whites. He also notes that some scholars regard Yosemite, which was set apart by the federal government in 1864 and ceded to the state of California before its return to the national park system in 1890, as the world's first national park. *American Literary Environmentalism*, xix, 166n5, 167n7.

217. Larcom's later work in particular joins that of regionalists like Jewett and Freeman, who rejected the conceptualization of local people and places as premodern and antiprogress. See Marjorie Pryse, "Literary Regionalism and Global Capital."

218. Larcom, *The Poetical Works*, 183–85.

219. Larcom, *A New England Girlhood*, 184–85.

220. I distinguish between class consciousness (a sense of group identity, which Larcom and, to a lesser degree, Berbineau express) and class awareness (an understanding of one's individual position on the social ladder, experienced by Wilson). Blumin, *The Emergence of the Middle Class*, 9–11.

221. Slovic's nature-writing continuum—epistemological to political—is relevant here. Berbineau lies at the epistemological end of this continuum, Wilson in the middle, Larcom at other end. See Grounding the Text, 7.

222. Fern, "Soliloquy of a Housemaid," 85.

223. Ibid.

224. Ibid., 86.

225. Woolf, "Women and Sweatshops." See also Liebhold and Rubenstein, "Between a Rock and a Hard Place."

226. Liebhold and Rubenstein, "Between a Rock and a Hard Place." For a discussion of some of the causes of sweatshop resurgence, see also Cockburn and St. Clair, "How the Labor Dept. Helps."

227. Gross, "The Killing of Juan Baten."

228. Jessica Bennett and Ellison, "Women Will Rule the World." Bennett and Ellison cite Dychtwald, *Influence.*

229. See Blumin on women and consumption. *The Emergence of the Middle Class*, 185.

230. "Eco Fashion," *Voguepedia;* Mower, "Eco-Minded." In 2011, an online issue of *Ebony* included a link to "Sustainable Clothing 101: Eco-Fashion"; the link has disappeared.

Chapter 4. Gilt-Edged or "Beautifully Unadorned"

The epigraphs are taken from Berbineau, *From Beacon Hill to the Crystal Palace*, 73–74; Gilman, *Women and Economics*, 2.

1. Gilman, *Women and Economics*, 120.

2. Ellen Garvey argues that "the advertising-supported magazine as an institution has buttressed the interests of advertisers and the commercial discourse as a whole, and constructed the reader—especially the female reader—as a consumer." *The Adman in the Parlor*, 4. My account below demonstrates how some women resisted this superimposed identity.

3. Aron, "The Evolution of the Middle Class," 185. See also Scott, *Natural Allies*, 82–83.

4. Aron, "The Evolution of the Middle Class," 185.

5. The touchstone study for women's humor is Nancy A. Walker, *A Very Serious Thing*. Thaxter and her cohort have also been diminished by their commitment to regionalism. For a history of debates about literary regionalism, see Fetterley and Pryse, *Writing Out of Place*, chapter 2. More recently, claiming that the label "regionalist" distorts perceptions of the texts it ostensibly encompasses, Mark Storey has argued for an alternative conception of "rural fiction," which "can challenge the urban-centric tendency of postbellum American literary history." "Country Matters," 194, 213.

6. Marjorie Pryse discusses the commitment of regionalist writers, including Jewett and Freeman, to a critique of an earlier version of global capitalism. "Literary Regionalism and Global Capital."

7. Thaxter, "Woman's Heartlessness," in Kilcup, *Nineteenth-Century American Women Writers: An Anthology*, 281. On Thaxter's life, see Fields, *Authors and Friends*; Stubbs, "Celia Laighton Thaxter"; Rosamond Thaxter, *Sandpiper*; Laighton, *Ninety Years*; Simpson and Lambert, *From Isles of Shoals*; Barbara A. White, "Legacy Profile"; Older, *The Island Queen*; Vallier, *Poet on Demand*; Mandel, *Beyond the Garden Gate*; Kilcup, "Celia Laighton Thaxter."

For women's roles in the creation of the modern Audubon Society, see Kathy S. Mason, "Out of Fashion"; Merchant, "George Bird Grinnell's Audubon Society"; and Price, "Hats Off to Audubon." See also Lutts, *The Nature Fakers*. Recent *Audubon* issues have cited Thaxter's work; see "Teeny Terns" and "Plumed Hunters." Nova Scotia Museum of Natural History, "Hats Off to Birds!" cites shocking orders for feathers. Bird Wicks, "Ethno-Ornithology Sunday (on a Monday)," offers a contemporary blogger's account with two illuminating illustrations.

8. Westbrook, "Celia Thaxter's Controversy with Nature," 500ff. Westbrook attributes to Levi a positive effect on Thaxter's writing (501–2), though her letters sometimes demonstrate the psychological hardships she endured. On the Appledore Hotel, see Stephen May, "An Island Garden."

9. Vallier, *Poet on Demand*, 18. On Thaxter's independent religious ideas, see Westbrook, "Celia Thaxter's Controversy with Nature," 503–10.

10. See Littenberg, "From Transcendentalism to Ecofeminism."

11. Celia Thaxter, *Among the Isles of Shoals*, 61–62.

12. See Woodward, "Celia Thaxter's Love Poems."

13. Westbrook, "Celia Thaxter's Controversy with Nature," 492, 495. See also Westbrook, *Acres of Flint*, chapter 9; Cary, "Multi-Colored Spirit"; Westbrook, "Celia Thaxter: Seeker"; Oakes, "Colossal in Sheet-Lead"; Littenberg, "From Transcendentalism to Ecofeminism"; Fetterley, "Theorizing Regionalism"; Glasser, "The Sandpiper and I"; and Pryse, "Reading Regionalism."

14. While Thaxter was ostensibly a member of the middle class by virtue of her family connections, the shape of her life suggests her affinity with working-class women.

15. Glasser, "The Sandpiper and I," 1.

16. Wolfe, "Human, All Too Human," 567; Glasser, "The Sandpiper and I," 5. In the context of Thaxter's attentiveness to animals, Marianne DeKoven's assertion is useful: "Analyzing the uses of animal representation can clarify modes of human subjugation that ideology might otherwise obscure." "Guest Column," 363.

17. Thaxter is represented in the following collections and criticism: Anderson, *Sisters of the Earth*; Anderson and Edwards, *At Home on This Earth*; Strom, *Birdwatching with American Women*; Robert Finch and Elder, *The Norton Book of Nature Writing*; Fetterley and Pryse, *American Women Regionalists*; Patterson, Thompson, and Bryson, *Early American Nature Writers*; and Spretnak, "Ecofeminism." Glasser points to Thaxter's innovative structuring of *Among the Isles of Shoals*. "The Sandpiper and I," 8–9.

18. "Fashion Department."

19. Merchant, "George Bird Grinnell's Audubon Society," 6.

20. Nancy A. Walker, *A Very Serious Thing*, 12.

21. Ibid., 44.

22. Here I depart from Walker, who emphasizes Kirkland's domestic interests. Nancy A. Walker, *A Very Serious Thing*, 49.

23. Quoted in Haug, "Wings, Breasts, and Birds."

24. Quoted in Merchant, "George Bird Grinnell's Audubon Society," 12–13.

25. Price lists 174 birds mentioned by Chapman; see *Flight Maps*, 57–110.

26. Kathy S. Mason, "Out of Fashion," 3.

27. As Elizabeth Maddock Dillon observes, "from its inception, aesthetics has been focused on bodily sensation." "Sentimental Aesthetics," 499.

28. Thaxter translates for readers a bird's bodily experience, and although ecocritics have long questioned anthropomorphization as a superimposition of human

sensibilities on nonhuman nature, a kind of colonialism, nineteenth-century writers frequently adopted this strategy.

29. See Kilcup, "I Like These Plants," 43; DeKoven, "Guest Column," 363.

30. DeKoven, "Guest Column," 366.

31. Westbrook, "Celia Thaxter's Controversy with Nature," 512. George Bird Grinnell, publisher of *Field and Stream*, created the first Audubon Society. See Kathy S. Mason, "Out of Fashion," 1–4, 7; Merchant, "George Bird Grinnell's Audubon Society."

32. "To discourage the buying and wearing for ornamental purposes the feathers of any wild bird, and to further otherwise the protection of our native birds. We would awaken the community to the fact that this fashion of wearing feathers means the cruel slaughter of myriads of birds, and that some of our finest birds are already decimated." Quoted in *Feathers and Facts*, 7–8.

33. The Lacey Act formed the foundation for a constellation of later animal-protection legislation, including the Endangered Species Act. Cart, "The Lacey Act," 12, 13; see Merchant, "George Bird Grinnell's Audubon Society," 18.

34. All rhetoric is, of course, synthetic, but Thaxter's essay exemplifies a particularly self-conscious usage of rhetorical variety.

35. See Paula Bernat Bennett, "The Pea That Duty Locks."

36. Shi, *The Simple Life*, 3.

37. Shi describes American writers visiting Europe and commenting on the older cultures' extravagance and corruption. Ibid., 54–55.

38. Ibid., 93ff.

39. Shi comments briefly on Kirkland; see ibid., 115–16.

40. Ibid., 7.

41. Thoreau, *Walden*, 101.

42. Shi, *The Simple Life*, 136.

43. Alcott, "Transcendental Wild Oats," 252.

44. Shi, *The Simple Life*, 157, 159.

45. Veblen, *The Theory of the Leisure Class*, 47.

46. Shi, *The Simple Life*, 6, 7.

47. Jewett, "River Driftwood." Frederick Turner's caution about the continuity between nature and culture resonates for a discussion of Jewett's fiction. "Cultivating the American Garden," 40–41. See also Armbruster and Wallace, *Beyond Nature Writing*, 4ff. For two provocative applications of ecocriticism to nineteenth-century American women's writing, see Hoyer, "Cultivating Desire, Tending Piety"; Terrell Dixon, "Nature, Gender, and Community."

48. Mazel, *American Literary Environmentalism*, 153.

49. Jewett, "An October Ride," 100. All of Jewett's work is available online at The Sarah Orne Jewett Text Project at Coe College, http://www.public.coe.edu/~theller/soj/sj-index.htm.

50. Alice Brown, Review of *The Country of the Pointed Firs*; Cather, preface, 11.

51. Easton, "How Clearly the Gradations," 208–10; see also Sherman, "Party Out of Bounds."

52. Jewett is included in Anderson, *Sisters of the Earth*, and Anderson and Edwards, *At Home on This Earth*, but not in Robert Finch and Elder, *The Norton Book of Nature Writing*. See also Lupfer, "Before Nature Writing," 177; Donovan, "Women's Masterpieces," 113; McMurry, "In Their Own Language"; Sherman, *Sarah Orne Jewett*; Alaimo, *Undomesticated Ground*, 38–62.

53. For an overview of work on Jewett, see Kilcup and Edwards, "Confronting Time and Change." See also Donovan, "Women's Masterpieces"; Sherman, "Jewett and the Incorporation"; Donovan, "Jewett on Race"; Zagarell, "Narrative of Community"; Sandilands, "The Importance of Reading Queerly"; Rust, "The Old Town of Berwick"; Bill Brown, "Regional Artifacts"; Easton, "Outdoor Relief."

54. Jewett, "A White Heron," 147.

55. Elsewhere in her work Jewett questions Americans' bifurcated and gendered notions of humans and nonhuman nature. Recent essays include Brault, "Silence as Resistance"; and Paton, "Furry Soul Mates." Earlier considerations include, Donovan, *Sarah Orne Jewett*, 69–72; Roman, *Sarah Orne Jewett*, 197–205; Renza, *"A White Heron,"* 116–22; and Donovan, "Silence or Capitulation."

56. Pryse observes that "regionalist fiction is always covertly and often overtly about economic conditions." "Literary Regionalism and Global Capital," 71; see 77.

57. See Brault, "Silence as Resistance," 86–87.

58. The *Atlantic* understood itself as a serious magazine for intellectuals. The issue in which "The Town Poor" was published includes essays ranging from "Science and the African Problem" and "An American Definition of Gothic Architecture" to biographical portraits and serial fiction. *Atlantic Monthly* 66, no. 393 (July 1890).

59. Jewett, "The Town Poor," at The Sarah Orne Jewett Text Project, http://www.public.coe.edu/~theller/soj/saw/poor.htm. Terry Heller's note reads, "'The Town Poor' first appeared in *Atlantic Monthly* (66:71–78) in July 1890, and was collected that year into *Strangers and Wayfarers*. This text is from the 1969 Garrett Press reprinting of the 1890 edition of *Strangers and Wayfarers*. Errors have been corrected and indicated with brackets." All references to the story are from this source.

60. The sentimentalized teacups emblematize what Lori Merish has identified as the commodification of sympathy; see *Sentimental Materialism*.

61. Larcom, *An Idyl of Work*, 20.

62. Ironically, it is Miss Wright who notes of the Janeses, "They always had the name of bein' slack an' poor-spirited, an' they [took the Brays] just for what they got out o' the town."

63. Thomson, "Crippled Girls and Lame Old Women," 135. Thomson discusses "The Town Poor" and Mary Mapes Dodge's "Sunday Afternoon in a Poor-House," reprinted in Kilcup, *Nineteenth-Century American Women Writers: An Anthology*, 243–46.

64. Jewett may also be ironically invoking Thoreau here: "Simplify, simplify. Instead of three meals a day, if it be necessary eat but one; instead of a hundred dishes, five; and reduce other things in proportion." Thoreau, *Walden*, 89.

65. Interestingly, Miss Rebecca invokes the possibility that the new doctor might be able to ameliorate the sisters' disabilities; perhaps Jewett is suggesting that poverty has exacerbated bodily incapacity and that restoration to their former home will enable its remediation.

66. Thomson, "Crippled Girls and Lame Old Women," 134.

67. Freeman, "The Revolt of 'Mother,'" 457

68. See Virginia L. Blum, "Mary Wilkins Freeman," 73.

69. Freeman, "The Beggar King."

70. Studies of Freeman include: Koppelman, "About 'Two Friends'"; Cutter, "Beyond Stereotypes"; Glasser, *In a Closet Hidden*; Reichardt, *Mary Wilkins Freeman*; Camfield, "I Never Saw Anything." See also Camfield, *Necessary Madness*, 135–49.

71. Terrell Dixon, "Nature, Gender, and Community," 162. See Mann, "Gardening as 'Women's Culture'"; Marchalonis, "Another Mary Wilkins Freeman," 93; Griffin, "Understudies." See also Luscher, "Seeing the Forest for the Trees"; and Alaimo, *Undomesticated Ground*, 58–62. For another view that does not discuss Freeman, see Jennifer Mason, *Civilized Creatures*.

72. Camfield, *Necessary Madness*, 4–6.

73. Kirkland, *Forest Life*, 1:63–64.

74. In *Necessary Madness*, Camfield underscores Freeman's combination of "comedy and pathos" (139).

75. Freeman, "A Gala Dress." Because the story occupies little more than a single page, I omit page references in my discussion. See Pryse, "Literary Regionalism and Global Capital," 84–85.

76. As Monika M. Elbert points out, Freeman's sophisticated depictions of rural women show how they were as invested in fashion as their urban counterparts. "The Displacement of Desire," 192. Some of Freeman's later works foreground the interconnection between nature and culture, borrowing less from Emerson than from the contemporary passion for the occult. In *Six Trees* and *Understudies*, humans and nature have many kinds of intercourse; stories such as "The Great Pine" and "The Cat" dramatize these links.

77. Virginia L. Blum, "Mary Wilkins Freeman," 73, 75.

78. Elbert suggests that the author consistently undermines the "love affair with the commodity" that her country women shared with socialite readers, presenting a sometimes extreme counterpoint to the luxurious depictions featured in *Harper's Bazaar*. "Mary Wilkins Freeman's Devious Women," 253, 254, 258.

79. For related examples, see Rose Terry Cooke, "Miss Beulah's Bonnet" and Jewett's "Dulham Ladies."

80. Diana Crane, *Fashion and Its Social Agendas*, 1, 2. See also Kriebl, "From Bloomers to Flappers"; Gayle V. Fisher, *Pantaloons and Power*; Patricia A. Cunningham, *Reforming Women's Fashion*.

81. Diana Crane, *Fashion and Its Social Agendas*, 2. Although the sewing machine was invented in the late eighteenth century, it did not achieve production feasibility until well into the nineteenth century; in rural areas, it would have been a luxury item. See "History of the Sewing Machine."

82. For a historical sketch of the language of flowers, see Sheley, "The 'Language of Flowers'"; see also Laufer, *Tussie Mussies*, 4–25. On nasturtium, see Rhoads, "The Floral Calendar": "The generic name . . . is derived from a Greek word signifying 'a warlike Trophy.' In the emblematic language of flowers, the T. Majus means 'Honor to the brave.' A very singular phenomenon is sometimes exhibited by the nasturtium. During twilight, and before sunrise . . . it is said to emit sparks or flashes of light from the petals of its flowers" (347). See also Strong, *The American Flora*, 186; the entry reads, "*Darkness flies at your approach.* In the darkness of mid-summer's night, it is said, that the electrical sparks may be seen emanating from the flowers of this plant" (original emphasis). Nasturtium is also said to mean: jest (Seaton, *The Language of Flowers*, 185); splendor (*The Language of Flowers*, 289, 312); patriotism (Ildrewe, *The Language of Flowers*, 136, 166). Moss rose represents: voluptuous love (Seaton, *The Language of Flowers*, 108); superior merit, voluptuousness (Ildrewe, *The Language of Flowers*, 44); confession of love (Dumont, *The Language of Flowers*, 69); voluptuous love, voluptuous pleasure (*The Language of Flowers*, 78, 309); voluptuousness, love (Tyas, *The Language of Flowers*, 142, 222, 224). See also "Meanings of Flowers"; Harten, "The Language of Flowers"; "The Complete Herbal A–Z Guide."

83. Clearly it is possible to read the conclusion differently, with Matilda retaining her secondary status via the old dress. But to me Freeman's tone and rhetoric suggest otherwise. I differ here from Elbert, who emphasizes the competitive element in this story and more generally in Freeman's early work. "Mary Wilkins Freeman's Devious Women," 261.

84. On women writers' genre hybridity, see Kilcup, "Essays of Invention."

85. See Donovan, *New England Local Color Literature*, 119; Brand, "Mary Wilkins Freeman."

86. Westbrook, *Mary Wilkins Freeman*, 32; see Van Wyck Brooks, *New England*, 466, 467.

87. Unlike Westbrook, Donovan points out that Freeman was among the writers in whom we see "a *fear* that the female sanctuary [or paradise] may be destroyed— not so much by male sexuality per se but by the forces of masculine knowledge, by industrialism, by patriarchal governmental and educational institutions." *New England Local Color Literature*, 121.

88. Freeman, "A Mistaken Charity," 234.

89. Luscher notes that Freeman was "well-read in Emerson." "Seeing the Forest for the Trees," 364; see 365.

90. Thomson, "Benevolent Maternalism."

91. Pratt, "The Advantages of Mingling Indians."

92. "Silence" reinvents the 1704 Raid on Deerfield as a romantic Euramerican

love story. In *Madelon*, Freeman explores women's sexuality, propensity for violence, and cultural associations with nonhuman nature—their "savage" elements—
through the eponymous racially and ethnically mixed Native American heroine
and Madelon's domesticated white alter ego, Dorothy Fair. Glasser reminds readers that Freeman's stereotypes were part of nineteenth-century aesthetics; whether
we should perceive this work as intellectual colonialism is a matter for another
discussion. *In a Closet Hidden*, 248n22. It is worth noting, however, that the author's
presentation of Madelon is far more affirmative than that of the anemic Dorothy.
Though troubling for modern readers, this bifurcation and stereotyping suggest
the affinities between female and Native American perspectives for Freeman and
her contemporaries. In addition to her engagement in the broader cultural scene,
Freeman may have encountered Native Americans during her youth and young
adulthood in Brattleboro, Vermont (not far from Deerfield, Massachusetts), which
was near one of the first permanent white settlements in Vermont, Fort Dummer.
See U.S. Department of the Interior, "Vermont History." The town was one of the
historical centers of the Abenaki.

93. See, for example, the image of Native American girls from the Omaha
tribe photographed at the Carlisle School in Pennsylvania between 1876 and 1896,
"Omaha Girls"; see also the images of Tom Torlino on the website California Indian Education (CALIE), "Indian Boarding Schools." Photographic enhancement
of "appropriate" skin color was one technique used to dramatize the difference
between "savage" and "civilized" individuals. But forms of assimilation were not
necessarily seen as negative by all Native Americans, as the resources on this site
describe; see also Ora Eddleman Reed's series in *Twin Territories*, "Types of Indian
Girls."

94. The analysis that follows draws from my earlier work with the anthropologist Phyllis Rogers (Cherokee). Kilcup and Rogers, "Brave with Flowers."

95. Alaimo and Hekman, "Introduction: Emerging Models," 4.

96. Pearce, *Savagism and Civilization*.

97. The mainstream culture's association between nature, sexuality, and Native Americans is longstanding and uneasy. See D'Emilio and Freedman, *Intimate
Matters*, 3, 6–9, 63, 86–93, 107–8.

98. See Turkes, "Must Age Equal Failure?," 198.

99. Quoted in Lois Brown, *Pauline Elizabeth Hopkins*, 538.

100. *Ladies' Home Journal* 6, no. 7 (June 1889): 12, 14, 15, 15, 15, 9, 21.

101. These ads appear in the same issue as "Bro'r Abr'm Jimson's Wedding."
Colored American Magazine 4, no. 2 (December 1901): 170–75. For the relationships
among advertising, fiction, and gender in nineteenth-century American magazines, see Garvey, *The Adman in the Parlor*.

102. Elbert, "Mary Wilkins Freeman's Devious Women," 252. On women's consumerism, see Blumin, *The Emergence of the Middle Class*, 141, 185.

103. Lois Brown, *Pauline Elizabeth Hopkins*, 45. For biographical details in this
section, I rely on Brown's account. See also Wallinger, *Pauline E. Hopkins*.

104. Carol Allen, *Black Women Intellectuals*, 15.

105. Watson, "The facts which go to form this fiction."

106. Lois Brown, *Pauline Elizabeth Hopkins*, 263–64; "Editorial and Publishers' Announcements," *Colored American Magazine* (May 1900): 60, cited in Lois Brown, *Pauline Elizabeth Hopkins*, 264.

107. Lois Brown, *Pauline Elizabeth Hopkins*, 271; see also Carby, *Reconstructing Womanhood*, 127; Carol Allen, *Black Women Intellectuals*, 20; Gruesser, "Pauline Hopkins' *Of One Blood.*"

108. On Hopkins's innovative histories, see Doreski, "Inherited Rhetoric and Authentic History."

109. Jill Bergman suggests that gender politics rather than race politics was the reason for Hopkins's dismissal from her editorial position. "Everything we hoped she'd be." See also Cordell, "The Case Was Very Black"; Alisha R. Knight, "Furnace Blasts"; Wallinger, "Pauline E. Hopkins as Editor"; Bergman, "A New Race of Colored Woman."

110. Lois Brown, *Pauline Elizabeth Hopkins*, 438, 439, 455ff.; Wallinger, "Pauline E. Hopkins as Editor," 162.

111. One of Hopkins's models was the famous black woman activist Frances Harper, whose outspoken public speeches combined with powerful poetry, fiction, and nonfiction to capture social problems and energize her audiences toward action; Hopkins featured Harper in the series "Famous Women of the Negro Race." See Ammons, *Conflicting Stories*, 78; Lois Brown, *Pauline Elizabeth Hopkins*, 305–6, 19, 175; Kilcup, "Essays of Invention," 192, 193, 194.

112. McCaskill "'To Labor . . . and Fight," 171, 173.

113. See chapter 3, 166–67; Bauer, "In the Blood," 61.

114. Dabel, *A Respectable Woman*, 158.

115. Hopkins, "Bro'r Abr'm Jimson's Wedding: A Christmas Story," in Kilcup, *Nineteenth-Century American Women Writers: An Anthology*, 469. All subsequent references are to this source.

116. As in my earlier discussion of Wilson, I qualify Michael Bennett's contention that "a main current within African American culture has, from Frederick Douglass to Toni Morrison, expressed a profound antipathy toward the ecological niches usually focused on in ecocriticism: pastoral space and wilderness." "Anti-Pastoralism, Frederick Douglass, and the Nature of Slavery," 208.

117. Barreca, *They Used to Call Me Snow White*. Barreca writes of the twentieth century, but her observations hold true here. In *Gossip*, Patricia Meyer Spacks connects gossip's oral freedom with female sexual licentiousness.

118. E. Frances White cites Nancy Stepan's idea here. *Dark Continent of Our Bodies*, 88.

119. Ibid., 97; White quotes Freud in her chapter epigraph (81). White's account of the social and intellectual context for this issue resonates for all women.

120. *Oxford English Dictionary* online; see also "Datura stramonium L." in GRIN (Germplasm Resources Information Network) database; "Datura spp." in Cornell

University Department of Animal Science, "Plants Poisonous to Livestock and Other Animals."

121. In this connection, see Nerad, "So strangely interwoven."

122. Hopkins, "Bro'r Abr'm Jimson's Wedding," in Kilcup, *Nineteenth-Century American Women Writers: An Anthology*, 473. Hopkins's stance toward the Irish is unclear here; whether she uses them as a mere foil or whether she is invested in the stereotype depicted is peripheral to my discussion.

123. Lois Brown, *Pauline Elizabeth Hopkins*, 38, 254.

124. As Paula Bennett and Lott indicate, the connections between African Americans and Irish Americans were complex. See Paula Bernat Bennett, "Mill Girls and Minstrels"; Lott, *Love and Theft*, 21, 79, 88, and passim.

125. See Lois Brown, *Pauline Elizabeth Hopkins*, 164.

126. See Matthew 5:13.

127. Luke 8:16–17: "16 No one lights a lamp and hides it in a jar or puts it under a bed. Instead, he puts it on a stand, so that those who come in can see the light. 17 For there is nothing hidden that will not be disclosed, and nothing concealed that will not be known or brought out into the open." New International Version, http://www.biblegateway.com/passage/?search=Luke+8&version=NIV. See Matthew 10:26: "Fear them not therefore: for there is nothing covered, that shall not be revealed; and hid, that shall not be known"; Luke 12:2–3: "2 For there is nothing covered, that shall not be revealed; neither hid, that shall not be known. 3 Therefore whatsoever ye have spoken in darkness shall be heard in the light; and that which ye have spoken in the ear in closets shall be proclaimed upon the housetops." King James Version, www.kingjbible.com.

128. At the same time, Hopkins's writing often investigates other elements of nature and the natural, including her complicated response to social Darwinist–related ideologies that, as Martin Japtok argues, celebrate wealth and technological achievement. "Pauline Hopkins's *Of One Blood*."; see also Nickel, "Eugenics and the Fiction of Pauline Hopkins."

129. On Hopkins's emphasis on (and creation of) the black maternal New Woman, see Bergman, "A New Race of Colored Woman."

130. E. Frances White, *Dark Continent of Our Bodies*, 97–98.

131. Ibid., 34.

132. Corrothers, "The Gift of the Greatest God," 102; Lacques-Waggoner, "A Vow," 112.

133. Ewell, "The Smoky City," 138.

134. Sawaya, "Emplotting National History," 85.

135. Lois Brown, *Pauline Elizabeth Hopkins*, 9.

136. Ibid., 168–69. See Carol Allen, *Black Women Intellectuals*, 27.

137. Lois Brown, *Pauline Elizabeth Hopkins*, 18, 19; 174–75; 194; see 20; see 67–69 for the revisionary genealogy that the author created for herself.

138. Cordell, "The Case Was Very Black," 60.

139. In its pan-African emphasis, the *Colored American* encompassed a global

perspective as well. See Lois Brown, *Pauline Elizabeth Hopkins*, 387–89, 399–406, 432–35, 475–79. For a view of the interrelationship between domestic and international relations, see Bernardi, "Narratives of Domestic Imperialism." See also Carla L. Peterson, "Unsettled Frontiers."

140. See Cordell's analysis of "Talma Gordon" in "The Case Was Very Black"; see also Putzi, "Raising the Stigma."

141. Quoted in Lois Brown, *Pauline Elizabeth Hopkins*, 171; see 170–73.

142. Hopkins's emphasis on community responsibility more nearly approaches Jacobs's and Larcom's perspective (particularly in "Weaving") than Wilson's.

143. Krugman, "For Richer." Ironically, the Alternatives for Simple Living group (www.simpleliving.org) and the Simple Living Network (www.simpleliving .net) recently discontinued operation, though for different reasons. Archives for the Alternatives for Simple Living group are available at http://web.archive.org/ web/20110716011612/http://www.simpleliving.org/, while the latter network continues through the Simple Living forums, http://www.simplelivingforum.net/. See also DeGraaf, Wann, and Naylor, *Affluenza*.

144. See "What Is the Difference"; Simple Living Institute, "News"; Siegel, *The Politics of Simple Living*. For some foundational and recent texts, see Gregg, *The Value of Voluntary Simplicity*; Schumacher, *Small Is Beautiful*; Elgin, *Voluntary Simplicity*; Dominguez and Robin, *Your Money or Your Life*; McKibben, *Deep Economy*.

145. Parija Kavilanz, "Kate Middleton 'Fascinator' Hats"; see also "Kate Middleton's Princess Style Diary."

146. Hat Millinery, eBay Canada, http://stores.ebay.ca/HatMillinery.

147. Brewington, "William and Kate Appear in Wales."

148. See Fox, "Ethical Labels Take to the Catwalk"; National Association of Sustainable Fashion Designers, http://www.sustainabledesigners.org/; Sustainable Cotton Project, "About Us"; Hebblethwaite and Ethirajan, "Sandblasted Jeans"; Jenkins, "Sustainable Fashion Design Courses"; Rissanen, "Zero-waste with Loomstate."

149. Chapagain et al., "The Water Footprint of Cotton Consumption." See also "Water Use: From Fibre to Fashion," which notes the disparate impacts of cotton farming on various world regions and also underscores consumers' water footprint in washing clothes.

150. Levi Strauss & Co., "Life Cycle of a Jean"; Levi Strauss & Co., "Levi Strauss & Co. Life Cycle Approach." Levi Strauss is also aware of chemical contamination endemic to its production; see Levi Strauss & Co., "Chemicals."

151. See Ecofashionworld.com, "Eco Fashion Guide"; Ecouterre, "About Us." See also Sass Brown, *Eco Fashion*; Black, *Eco-Chic*; Matheson, *Green Chic*.

152. DuFault, "Chicken Feathers!"

153. See *Real Simple*, www.realsimple.com. The magazine represents a modernization of *Ladies' Home Journal* for a more affluent and educated audience.

154. RealSimple, "How to Identify Sustainable Seafood."

155. Szasz, *Shopping Our Way to Safety*.

156. Cawthorne, "The Straight Facts."

157. Statistics on this trend are legion; see, for example, World Hunger Education Service, "Hunger in America."

Chapter 5. Domestic and National Moralities

1. Mary Hallock Foote, "Pictures of the Far West," 109. The essay is accompanied by a Foote drawing of a man leading a reluctant horse through a hilly, grassy landscape with a crescent moon on the horizon; the essay shrinks this human/domestic animal presence substantially.

2. Ibid.

3. These sketches elide the numerous Native Americans who peopled this vast region. On the historical deployment of the terms *civilized* and *savage*, see Pearce, *Savagism and Civilization*, 200ff., 229ff.

4. Writers such as Ora Eddleman Reed (Cherokee) insisted on the West's civilized qualities in such editorial columns as "What the Curious Want to Know" and photoessays like "Types of Indian Girls," which appeared in the turn-of-the-century territorial magazine that she edited, *Twin Territories*. See note 20 below.

5. As chapter 1 points out, with some notable exceptions, ecocritical scholarship and environmental justice advocacy have, for historical, theoretical, and practical reasons, tended to focus principally on much more recent texts and contexts. Greta Gaard argues for a more historically informed approach. "New Directions for Ecofeminism," 647–48, 660. Most notable among the exceptions is Jeffrey Myers's *Converging Stories*. I use the name Zitkala-Ša instead of Gertrude Bonnin because the author chose to write under this name and because most contemporary readers use it.

6. We should recall Ian Frederick Finseth's admonition about the antebellum period: "In talking about race or nature . . . we are always talking, at some level, about the other." *Shades of Green*, 2, 137–48.

7. Limerick, "Region and Reason."

8. Kolodny, among others, reminds us of the West's moving boundaries. Kolodny, *The Land Before Her*, xii.

9. A reminder from chapter 1: Resource wars represent "conflict over vital materials." Klare, *Resource Wars*, 25. The term *resource wars* is recent, but it has historical resonances, as some observers acknowledge. Like other contemporary commentators—among them geographers, political scientists, sociologists, and military historians—Klare focuses on current contexts, paying particular attention to struggles for oil and water that concern nation-states (19). See also Dinar, "Resource Scarcity and Environmental Degradation," 1; Renner, *The Anatomy of Resource Wars*, 9; Le Billon, "The Geopolitical Economy of 'Resource Wars,'" 1, 2–3.

10. Charles Waugh, "Only You Can Prevent a Forest," 114. I take seriously Robert T. Hayashi's caution against limiting ecocritical study of multiethnic literature

to environmental justice. As the analysis below indicates, I concur with his call for more attention to "the historical link between the social and natural realms." "Beyond Walden Pond," 61.

11. I include writers such as Susette LaFlesche and Ida B. Wells-Barnett in this group.

12. Weaver, *"That the People Might Live,"* 43.

13. Howells, "A Sennight of the Centennial," 103.

14. Winnemucca, *Life Among the Piutes*, 239. Winnemucca published under the name Sarah Winnemucca Hopkins, but I use the name more familiar to twenty-first-century audiences.

15. Although less invested in justice for other Native nations than Zitkala-Ša, Winnemucca advocates for them as well; see, for example, Winnemucca, *Life Among the Piutes*, 244–45.

16. Gae Whitney Canfield, *Sarah Winnemucca*, 10. For a discussion of some environmental consequences, see also Elizabeth Wilkinson, "Story as a Weapon," 155–56.

17. Gae Whitney Canfield, *Sarah Winnemucca*, 19. See also Zanjani, *Sarah Winnemucca*, 43.

18. I base this sketch of Winnemucca's life on Powell, "Sarah Winnemucca Hopkins," 72–80; for more detail, see Gae Whitney Canfield, *Sarah Winnemucca*; Zanjani, *Sarah Winnemucca*.

19. Gae Whitney Canfield, *Sarah Winnemucca*, 4–5; see also Schwantes, *The Pacific Northwest*, 37. On the effects of the gold rush on Sierran Native peoples, see Beesley, *Crow's Range*, 35–43.

20. Winnemucca furthermore presented herself as an Indian princess via photographs, which were often enclosed in or attached to copies of *Life Among the Piutes*. See Scherer, "The Public Faces of Sarah Winnemucca"; Bolton, "The Native Eloquence," 127, 152. Cherokee editor and writer Ora Eddleman Reed and Cherokee socialite and writer Narcissa Owen similarly used photographs to overturn the civilized/savage dynamic. See Alexia Kosmider's discussion of Cherokee author and editor Ora Eddleman Reed, "Strike a Euroamerican Pose"; and Kilcup, "The True American Woman."

21. Powell values Winnemucca's "display of notions of 'good Indianness'" and assesses her narrative's performative qualities and activist intentions. Powell, "Sarah Winnemucca Hopkins," 75; Powell, "Rhetorics of Survivance," 406. Powell also underscores the importance of representing Indian writers like Winnemucca as "complete human being[s] with problems and shortcomings as well as strengths and victories," not just as heroes or mythic figures. "Sarah Winnemucca Hopkins," 73–74. Cari M. Carpenter outlines the debate surrounding Winnemucca's contributions ("Tiresias Speaks," 72), while Senier offers evidence for Winnemucca's views opposing allotment and assimilation (*Voices of American Indian Assimilation*, 80ff.).

22. Powell, "Rhetorics of Survivance," 406. For a range of views on Winnemucca's narrative and cultural stances, see Krupat, "The Indian Autobiography," 24;

Senier, *Voices of American Indian Assimilation*, chapter 2; Cheryl Walker, *Indian Nation*, 22; Cari M. Carpenter, "Sarah Winnemucca and the Rewriting of Nation," 121–24; Murray, *Forked Tongues*, 3 and passim. On the problematics of the concept of mediation in relation to American Indian literatures, see Weaver, *"That the People Might Live,"* 34–35; he notes, for example, that "Natives . . . often express scant interest in bridging their worldview with that of the dominant culture" (35). Mary Louise Pratt argues that indigenous people sometimes compose what can best be called "autoethnography." *Imperial Eyes*, 9.

23. Powell discusses the smear campaign against the author after her book's publication and her forceful responses. "Sarah Winnemucca Hopkins," 83–88; see also Cari M. Carpenter, "Tiresias Speaks," 74–76.

24. See Powell, "Rhetorics of Survivance," 411–12. Winnemucca replies to these charges. *Life Among the Piutes*, 258; see appendix.

25. On gender complementarity, see chapter 1; see also Hollrah, *"The Old Lady Trill,"* chapter 3; Knack, "The Dynamics of Southern Paiute Women's Roles."

26. Winnemucca's ill health in her last years was brought on in part by an unfortunate marriage to Lewis Hopkins, who frequently gambled away her income, and by the unremitting physical demands of her earlier years as a translator and intermediary. With assistance from Nathaniel Hawthorne's sisters-in-law, the well-known reformers Elizabeth Palmer Peabody and Mary Mann, Winnemucca eventually created an innovative, Indian-run school, the Peabody Indian School, that (unlike government- and missionary-sponsored institutions) promoted bilingualism and celebrated Paiute traditions; after the Dawes Act was passed, she fought to be able to maintain this bilingual education. Senier points to Winnemucca's "more dispersed notion of agency than that achieved in [Helen Hunt] Jackson's works," and she emphasizes the former's communitism. *Voices of American Indian Assimilation*, 103.

27. "Principles of Environmental Justice."

28. On Winnemucca's genre inclusivity, see, for example, Powell, "Rhetorics of Survivance," 406; Brumble, *American Indian Autobiography*, 66, 68; Ruoff, "Early Native American Women Authors"; Georgi-Finlay, "The Frontiers of Native American Women's Writing," 224, 226, 239; and McClure, "Sarah Winnemucca," 35–39. Cari M. Carpenter notes Winnemucca's "simultaneous adoption and troubling of ethnographic conventions." "Tiresias Speaks," 73.

On the inversion of *civilized* and *savage*, see Powell, "Sarah Winnemucca Hopkins" 80. See also Ruoff, "Three Nineteenth-Century American Indian Autobiographers," 252; Cari M. Carpenter, "Tiresias Speaks," 74; Cari M. Carpenter, "Sarah Winnemucca and the Rewriting of Nation," 113.

29. It is difficult to know to what degree Winnemucca's editor, Mary Mann, intervened in structuring the narrative, although she asserts in her "Editor's Preface" that she has only corrected spelling and punctuation, and there is no reason to believe otherwise. Powell, "Rhetorics of Survivance," 406; McClure, "Sarah Winnemucca," 50n5. As Wilson's *Our Nig* and Ruiz de Burton's *The Squatter and*

the Don demonstrate, genre hybridity occurs in novels as well as autobiography. See S. Alice Callahan's (Muscogee/Creek) *Wynema* (1891).

30. See Cari M. Carpenter, "Tiresias Speaks," 77–78. For an extended discussion of Winnemucca's movement, see Gioia Woods, "Sarah Winnemucca." Although I take seriously Powell's point that critics often distinguish too sharply between oral and written productions—and that such distinctions are not value-neutral—we should acknowledge that *Life Among the Piutes* emerged from Winnemucca's lecture tours and that part of its impact resides in the immediacy and presence conveyed by such oral gestures as direct address. Powell, "Sarah Winnemucca Hopkins," 76–77; see also Tisinger, "Textual Performance and the Western Frontier," 177–85.

We could read *Life Among the Piutes* as another form of enforced travel writing, akin to Jacobs's *Incidents in the Life of a Slave Girl*.

31. The difficulties inherent in conducting an aesthetic approach—not least the separation of features that would not be separated in Native tradition—may be offset by the potential benefits, admittedly political, of recuperating value for these texts in a Western tradition that Winnemucca herself was trying to negotiate. Conducting such an investigation does not necessarily privilege art for art's sake; rather, it can reveal the means by which political, social, or moral goals are accomplished. See Cook-Lynn, "American Indian Intellectualism," 131, 132; Sequoyah, "How (!) Is an Indian?," 453. McClure tackles an important issue: the "discomfort" that many critics have "for Indian writers like Winnemucca who seem to be overly assimilated and sympathetic with the dominant culture." "Sarah Winnemucca," 29. See Krupat, introduction to *Native American Autobiography*, 13; Cheryl Walker, *Indian Nation*, 139; Cari M. Carpenter, "Tiresias Speaks," 72. Weaver assesses the drawbacks of seeking "authentic" Indianness. *"That the People Might Live,"* chapter 1 (3–45).

The term *survivance* (survival + resistance) was invented by Gerald Vizenor. See *Manifest Manners*.

32. Wong, "Native American Life Writing," 128. Some critics have claimed that Winnemucca probably had no knowledge of the dominant society's literary traditions, but her years of contact with whites and her public performances should convince us otherwise. McClure, "Sarah Winnemucca," 40; Brumble, *American Indian Autobiography*, 63; Tisinger, "Textual Performance and the Western Frontier," 173–74; Powell, "Sarah Winnemucca Hopkins," 76.

33. Tinker, "An American Indian Theological Response," 163; Deloria, *God Is Red*, 63, 67, chapter 4.

34. Winnemucca, *Life Among the Piutes*, 5; see Cheryl Walker, *Indian Nation*; Senier, *Voices of American Indian Assimilation*; Powell, "Rhetorics of Survivance," 407–8.

35. Brumble, *American Indian Autobiography*, 64; see Cheryl Walker, *Indian Nation*, 45, 139. Elsewhere Winnemucca suggests that good whites, like some of the soldiers she describes, can lose their whiteness, becoming, as Cari M. Carpenter sug-

gests, "honored as a member of the Paiute family and nation." "Sarah Winnemucca and the Rewriting of Nation," 118–19. *Life Among the Piutes* also demonstrates clearly, and repeatedly, that not all Indians act properly, in defense of their community and nation.

36. Weaver, *"That the People Might Live,"* 39; Weaver is citing Donald Fixico.

37. Georgi-Finlay argues that Winnemucca's text represents "the collaboration, or . . . dialogue of voices, female and male, eastern and western, Indian and white," although she emphasizes the "collaboration between women of two cultures." "The Frontiers of Native American Women's Writing," 230. See also Powell, "Rhetorics of Survivance," 407–8.

38. In a later situation of threat to herself and her female counterparts, Winnemucca reflects on the power of "two women with knives, for I know what an Indian woman can do. She can never be outraged by one man; but she may be by two." *Life Among the Piutes*, 228; see 228–44.

39. Cari M. Carpenter, "Tiresias Speaks," 76–77. In an allied perspective, Senier points out that Winnemucca's narrative is "crammed with the voices of her readers (real and anticipated)." *Voices of American Indian Assimilation*, 145. As Powell notes, the author repeatedly differentiates between white men's and white women's treatment of the Indians and, in her depiction of the latter as "'angels' who bring gifts," appeals affectingly to her largely female white audience. Powell, "Sarah Winnemucca Hopkins," 77–78, 8off.

40. See Winnemucca, *Life Among the Piutes*, 183, 228, 244.

41. For a discussion of indirection, see Radner and Lanser, "Strategies of Coding."

42. On Winnemucca's domestic discourse, see Cari M. Carpenter, "Tiresias Speaks," 75; Cari M. Carpenter, "Sarah Winnemucca and the Rewriting of Nation," 120; Cheryl Walker, *Indian Nation*, 139–41.

43. Powell, "Sarah Winnemucca Hopkins," 81–82.

44. Because Senier, Carpenter, and Mielke all offer extended analyses of the uses of sentimental discourse in Native American literature, I emphasize other elements here. Mielke, *Moving Encounters*; Senier, *Voices of American Indian Assimilation*; Cari M. Carpenter, *Seeing Red*. Carpenter argues that Winnemucca offers "a sustained sentimental critique of colonialism" (105).

45. See Cheryl Walker, *Indian Nation*, 139–41.

46. This indirect testimony is allied to the formal testimony given by Susette LaFlesche to Congress on the removal of the Poncas. See Kilcup, *Native American Women's Writing*, 172–74. Later writers, including Zitkala-Ša, deploy a similar rhetorical stance that both praises and accuses; these later writers would struggle perhaps even more with the internal conflict between a community-based ethic reflecting Indian nationhood and the requirements of an individualistic, Eurocentric literary tradition.

47. See Senier on the parallel between Winnemucca's statement and one of Elizabeth Palmer Peabody's remarks. *Voices of American Indian Assimilation*, 109.

48. Tinker, "An American Indian Theological Response," 158, 159; see Deloria, *God Is Red*, 95.

49. See, for example, Winnemucca, *Life Among the Piutes*, 34, 102, 116, 139, 228, 244.

50. Genesis 1:28, King James version.

51. On some of the animalistic terminology that whites used to describe Native Americans, see Stannard, *American Holocaust*, 145.

52. "Principles of Environmental Justice."

53. Weaver, introduction to *Defending Mother Earth*, 20. Martha C. Knack and Omer C. Stewart focus on whites' appropriation of Paiute water rights. *As Long as the River Shall Run*, xii.

54. Worster, *Rivers of Empire*, 20.

55. Gae Whitney Canfield, *Sarah Winnemucca*, 221ff.; Zanjani, *Sarah Winnemucca*, 268ff.

56. Winnemucca becomes an important part of early public discourse on this crucial (and still current) topic of water distribution; see Spurgeon, "Miracles in the Desert." As Timothy Silver observes, " 'Conservation' and 'waste' are modern concepts that Indians would not have understood," but they clearly grasped the notion of resource scarcity. *A New Face on the Countryside*, 66.

57. See Winnemucca's comments about newspaper propaganda regarding Indians. Winnemucca, *Life Among the Piutes*, 97–98.

58. See Winnemucca, *Life Among the Piutes*, 124, 133, 134, 144, 146.

59. Powell, "Rhetorics of Survivance," 408.

60. Ibid., 409.

61. Elizabeth Wilkinson, "Story as a Weapon," 176. For additional readings, see Powell, "Rhetorics of Survivance," 408–9; Cari M. Carpenter, "Sarah Winnemucca and the Rewriting of Nation," 114–15.

62. Acts 17:26; see Elizabeth Wilkinson, "Story as a Weapon," 177. Pauline Hopkins deployed this allusion powerfully; see *Of One Blood*.

63. We see Christian economics at work slightly later, when Winnemucca tells us of "the working time," in which men, women, and boys "were set to work clearing land . . . for wheat," completing about sixty acres in ten days. "Father" Wilbur, a corrupt government agent, "hired six civilized Indians to plough" the land, but only these individuals were paid (three dollars a day) "because they were civilized and Christian." Winnemucca, *Life Among the Piutes*, 211. Elsewhere Wilbur threatens to put Winnemucca in jail and sells Paiute supplies (238ff.).

64. Powell, "Sarah Winnemucca Hopkins," 409–10.

65. In Winnemucca's era, Native Americans stood on both sides of the allotment debate; some believed that assimilation to white norms was the single route to survival, while others held that such assimilation was cultural suicide. It is unclear to which group Winnemucca belonged. See Gae Whitney Canfield, *Sarah Winnemucca*, 203; see note 21 above.

66. Powell, "Rhetorics of Survivance," 413–14. Bolton points out that even the

term *Paiute* represented an identity superimposed on Winnemucca's people; in this sense, language itself encodes an injustice. "The Native Eloquence," 155.

67. As Cari M. Carpenter reminds us, Elizabeth Palmer Peabody herself emphasized the significance of Winnemucca's agency. "Tiresias Speaks," 77.

68. Elizabeth Wilkinson, "Story as a Weapon," 167.

69. Ibid., 169, 168.

70. Ibid., 169. In addition, Winnemucca conjures two taboos, cannibalism and incest, for a "bifurcated audience": "[I]t is both an indication to whites of their barbarity and, in borrowing from the cannibalism theme of origin stories, a Paiute-centered take on this encounter." Cari M. Carpenter, "Sarah Winnemucca and the Rewriting of Nation," 117.

71. Matthew 27:46; Mark 15:34, King James version, http://kingjbible.com.

72. Elizabeth Wilkinson argues that the passage that concludes this episode echoes Christian rhetoric and signifies Winnemucca's "resistance to white encroachment" on Paiute lands and traditions. "Story as a Weapon," 170.

73. Ibid., 172. Wilkinson also focuses on Winnemucca's attention to the Paiute's traditional hunting and gathering practices and how she "uses her rhetoric to simultaneously chastise and appeal to her white audience" (173).

74. Winnemucca relates how one corrupt Christian reservation agent responsible for distributing government supplies profits from stealing Paiute resources, attacking him directly when this federal agent attempts to show off before a visitor. Winnemucca, *Life Among the Piutes*, 86–87.

75. Cari M. Carpenter, "Sarah Winnemucca and the Rewriting of Nation," 125.

76. For another angle on the relationship between Winnemucca and the Peabody sisters and a discussion of Mary Mann's participation in the composition of *Life Among the Piutes*, see Rodier, "Authorizing Sarah Winnemucca?"

77. In 1879, Amelia Stone Quinton began the initiative that would become formalized in the Women's National Indian Association; by 1882, this group had presented its third petition to Congress supporting the rights of Native Americans and urging the honoring of government treaties with the tribes, a petition that contained one hundred thousand signatures. In the same period, the famous writer Helen Hunt Jackson completed her study condemning federal Indian policy and its broken treaties. She sent her exposé, *A Century of Dishonor* (1881), to every member of the U.S. Congress, hoping that its catalog of outrages, in particular the pattern of land theft, would cease. Although Jackson liberally employed the Euramerican rhetoric of civilized and savage—the former referencing whites and the latter Indians—she sought to redress years of broken treaties, violence, and wars and the simultaneous neglect of America's indigenous peoples. Goldman comments, "After being appointed Commissioner of Indian Affairs by President Chester Arthur in 1883, she devoted much of the latter half of her life to Indian policy reform." "I think our romance is spoiled," 68. When *A Century of Dishonor* failed to engender a satisfactory response, Jackson published her novel *Ramona* (1884), which fictionalized the exploitation and abuse of California's Native Americans and sought,

through a sentimental interracial romance, to provoke sympathy, anger, and action among her white readers over Indian land expropriation. Although Jackson hoped her book would have the impact for Indians that *Uncle Tom's Cabin* had had for African Americans, it too contributed toward the devastating Dawes Act, which allotted traditionally community-held land to individual Indians in severalty, resulting in the loss of millions of acres to white settlers and speculators. Jackson included in the appendix to *A Century of Dishonor* a letter from Winnemucca to an army officer. See Rodier, "Authorizing Sarah Winnemucca?," 110–11.

78. Powell, "Sarah Winnemucca Hopkins," 70.

79. Powell, "Rhetorics of Survivance," 404. However well-meaning some reformers may have been, many of their efforts proceeded from the "anti-Indianism" that continues today. Cook-Lynn, *Anti-Indianism in Modern America.*

80. Powell observes that President Grant's 1870 "peace policy" not only forced all Indians onto reservations "for their own protection" but also appointed religious groups, such as the Quakers, Catholics, and Methodists, to control "both Bureau of Indian Affairs (BIA) appointed offices and the Board of Indian Commissioners in an attempt to disrupt the unfair policies visited upon reservation communities by corrupt BIA officials. Christian agents were also to provide the 'proper' example of piety, private property, and agrarian work ethic necessary to convince Native peoples of the value of civilization"; she points out that they argued for allotment. "Rhetorics of Survivance," 402–4. See Senier's historicized account of Jackson's resistance to assimilation. *Voices of American Indian Assimilation*, chapter 1. Other white activist organizations included the Indian Rights Association and the Lake Mohonk Conference of the Friends of the Indian; see Hertzberg, *The Search for an American Indian Identity*, 21–22. Cook-Lynn argues that the denigration of Indians is not limited to non-Indians and highlights "one of the major techniques of Anti-Indianism": "the *use and misuse* of historical events of Indian life and experience in order to blame, denigrate, shame, or dehumanize Indians." *Anti-Indianism in Modern America*, 16.

81. Such white-led reform groups and individuals addressed America's ongoing resource wars periodically over the nineteenth century, but Indians themselves had long gathered together for self-protection and resistance to the U.S. government. See Hertzberg, *The Search for an American Indian Identity*, 6–10. On Susette LaFlesche (Tibbles; Inshta Theamba, or Bright Eyes; Omaha, 1854–1903), see Johansen, "Susette LaFlesche." For a selection of LaFlesche's oratory and writing, see Kilcup, *Native American Women's Writing*, 169–87.

82. Powell, "Sarah Winnemucca Hopkins," 70.

83. Ruiz de Burton, *The Squatter and the Don*, 54.

84. Charles Waugh, "Only You Can Prevent a Forest," 114.

85. As John Morán González observes, the novel "complicates received notions of how resistance may inhere in texts simply because of perceived racial alterity." *The Troubled Union*, 87.

86. The biographical outline that follows relies on the following sources: Aranda,

"María Amparo Ruiz de Burton"; Pita, "María Amparo Ruiz de Burton"; Rosaura Sánchez and Pita, "María Amparo Ruiz de Burton." John-Michael Rivera underscores that this white, landed elite defined themselves as the "gente de razon." *The Emergence of Mexican America*, 74, 103. See also Pérez, *Remembering the Hacienda*, 52ff.

87. Aranda, "María Amparo Ruiz de Burton," 312.

88. Rosaura Sánchez and Pita, "María Amparo Ruiz de Burton," 77.

89. Although space prohibits a discussion of Ruiz de Burton's first novel, *Who Would Have Thought It?* addresses a number of important issues relevant to this project, including consumerism and female embodiment. See, for example, Rivera, *The Emergence of Mexican America*, chapter 3 (82–109); Bost, "West Meets East."

90. Pita, "Engendering Critique," 135. See also Rosaura Sánchez and Pita, "María Amparo Ruiz de Burton," 79–80; María Carla Sánchez, "Whiteness Invisible"; Haas, *Conquests and Historical Identities*, 80.

91. Aranda, "Contradictory Impulses," 563, 557.

92. As Sánchez and Pita point out, "[T]he novel was as much a commercial venture as a literary and ideological undertaking. She lived on a meager army widow's pension, while engaged in costly litigation to validate her claim to her Rancho Jamul lands, and she was sorely in need of income." Rosaura Sánchez and Pita, "María Amparo Ruiz de Burton," 77.

93. Bancroft, *History of California*, 6:634, cited in Clare B. Crane, "The Pueblo Lands."

94. Limerick, "Region and Reason," 90.

95. Haas, *Conquests and Historical Identities*, 86, 85; see Ruiz, "From Out of the Shadows," 15.

96. Crawford, "María Amparo Ruiz Burton." See also Haas, *Conquests and Historical Identities*, 77ff.

97. See Crawford, "María Amparo Ruiz Burton."

98. In their introduction Sánchez and Pita define the novel as a historical romance; other critics have confirmed and contended with this assessment. For an example of the former, see González, *The Troubled Union*, chapter 4 (85–106). Jesse Alemán and Anne E. Goldman have argued variously for the author's dynamic use of historical, legal, and romance forms in conjunction with the novel genre; see Alemán, "Novelizing National Discourses"; Goldman, "I think our romance is spoiled." See also Montes, "María Amparo Ruiz de Burton Negotiates"; Warford, "An Eloquent and Impassioned Plea"; Dawson, "Ruiz de Burton's Emotional Landscape." Dawson offers the most extended argument for the text's literary realism. See also Deines, "Interrogating the Moral Contract."

99. Aranda, "Contradictory Impulses," 558–59; Aranda cites Rosaura Sánchez and Pita, "María Amparo Ruiz de Burton." González augments this perspective, arguing that Ruiz de Burton shows how the Central Pacific Railroad had become an empire within a nation "that threatened to replace the nation's white citizenship with the corporate empire's white slavery. Delinking class difference from

racial difference, corporations made white Californios into Indians, white workers into the structural equivalent of black or Chinese workers, and U.S. citizens into colonial subjects." *The Troubled Union*, 103.

100. Ybarra, "Erasure by U.S. Legislation." While it stresses Californios' "knowledge of California ecology" (142) and discusses the Don's proposals for land use in *The Squatter and the Don*, Ybarra's essay, to which I had access only after *Fallen Forests* had gone to press, emphasizes Mexican Americans' ecological knowledge, while my account focuses on how Ruiz de Burton's ethical and affective rhetoric seeks to engage readers in her (problematic) project of environmental justice.

101. González, *The Troubled Union*, 93.

102. For an account of the historical background, see Pérez, *Remembering the Hacienda*, esp. chapters 1 and 2.

103. On the characters' feelings about their property, see Dawson, "Ruiz de Burton's Emotional Landscape," 42.

104. The first fence laws, enacted in 1851, rendered rancheros liable for damages done by their cattle to others' property; the even more ruinous 1872 version required cattle owners to fence their fields. See Ludeke, "The No Fence Law," 98–115; Engstrand and Ward, "Rancho Guajome." See also Engstrand and Scharf, "Rancho Guajome."

105. Ludeke, "The No Fence Law," 98. Although Ludeke writes of the San Joaquin Valley, the changes he documents were not limited to that region. Ruiz de Burton skims over another exacerbating factor in the demise of cattle ranching: the punishing droughts of the 1860s and 1870s, which I discuss below. See Pulling, "California's Cattle-Range Industry."

106. "Principles of Environmental Justice."

107. See, for example, Ruiz de Burton, *The Squatter and the Don*, 37, 48–49.

108. Goldman, "I think our romance is spoiled," 74.

109. Dawson, "Ruiz de Burton's Emotional Landscape," 44–45.

110. See Ruiz de Burton, *The Squatter and the Don*, 159ff., 231.

111. Ruiz de Burton, *The Squatter and the Don*, 203ff., 340ff.

112. With evident disgust, Ruiz de Burton repeatedly censures owner Henry Huntington's bribery of Congress to ensure his railroad's success. *The Squatter and the Don*, 121ff., 156, 199, 206, 331–32, 337–57 passim, 379.

113. See Deines, "Interrogating the Moral Contract," 288; Goldman, "I think our romance is spoiled," 79–80; Warford, "An Eloquent and Impassioned Plea," 6; Pita, "Engendering Critique," 129, 133, 135.

114. See Deines, "Interrogating the Moral Contract," for an extended argument.

115. *Visalia (Calif.) Times-Delta*, 25 June 1959, cited in Ludeke, "The No Fence Law," 105. As Ludeke asserts, the growth of the farm population by the early 1870s virtually ensured the passage of the no-fence laws requiring cattlemen to enclose their stock (115).

116. Ybarra, "Erasure by U.S. Legislation," 142–44. Ybarra observes, "The real

bit of wisdom to gather from Ruiz de Burton's depiction of this historical moment is the fact that Mexican Americans and their environmental knowledge were factored out of the land-management equation" (145).

117. Pérez, *Remembering the Hacienda*, 71; see 6.

118. See Pulling, "California's Cattle-Range Industry."

119. Pourade, "Water Is King."

120. Goldman alludes briefly to pastoral. "I think our romance is spoiled," 66.

121. Dawson, "Ruiz de Burton's Emotional Landscape," 47.

122. Buell, *The Environmental Imagination*, 439.

123. Beyond farming and cattle ranching, *The Squatter and the Don* addresses other forms of resource usage, including the continually contested activity of mining; Clarence derives millions from his investment in Arizona mines. There is substantial criticism on mining, including attention to American women's writing by Foote, Austin, and others, but I do not have the space to consider this topic in detail. See, for example, Cella, "The Ambivalent Heritage of Mining"; Floyd, "Mining the West"; and Floyd, "A Sympathetic Misunderstanding?"

124. One other noteworthy paragraph, describing Yosemite, appears at the beginning of chapter 15. *The Squatter and the Don*, 148.

125. The community's website cites its history: "The town of Long Branch NJ, is one of the largest cities on the Jersey Shore. From the period of the 1860's through the First World War, it was also the most glamorous. Long Branch's early years as a resort town was a virtual 'Who's Who' of society, including such names as Astor, Fisk, & Drexel." "Long Branch, NJ, Brief History."

126. As writers from Merchant, Kolodny, and Norwood to Alaimo and Stein have amply documented, this association of women with nature presents significant challenges and opportunities. Merchant, *Earthcare*; Kolodny, *The Lay of the Land*; Kolodny, *The Land Before Her*; Norwood, *Made from This Earth*; Alaimo, *Undomesticated Ground*; Stein, *Shifting the Ground*.

127. See Dawson, "Ruiz de Burton's Emotional Landscape," 57–60.

128. Ibid., 47, 56–57.

129. Kolodny, *The Lay of the Land*, 136. If pioneer women sought "the proverbial Garden of the West," so did their successors, even late nineteenth-century cosmopolitan women like Ruiz de Burton herself, who reached toward "a complete integration of home and community made possible by that fertility." Kolodny, *The Land Before Her*, 12.

130. Pérez discusses Ruiz de Burton's sympathies for the Confederacy and southern aristocracy. *Remembering the Hacienda*, 60–61; chapter 2 passim; see Bost, "West Meets East." Aranda also notes Ruiz de Burton's connections with President and Mrs. Lincoln and Mr. and Mrs. Jefferson Davis. "Contradictory Impulses," 560–62.

131. Aranda, "Contradictory Impulses," 555.

132. See, for example, Pita "Engendering Critique," 135; Rosaura Sánchez and Pita, "María Amparo Ruiz de Burton," 79; Rosaura Sanchez, "Dismantling the

Colossus," 126. Pérez explores Ruiz de Burton's "claims to pre-bourgeois seigneur-ial (Mexican) society as a means of contesting injustice under U.S. rule and the intrusion of modernity into their native region." *Remembering the Hacienda*, 50.

133. Cited in Deines, "Interrogating the Moral Contract," 283; see also Stannard, *American Holocaust*, 145.

134. Deines, "Interrogating the Moral Contract," 283; see 287. Ruiz de Burton's husband had been responsible for Native American displacement, and her attitude toward Native Americans (and African Americans) in the novel is at least implic-itly racist. Aranda, "Contradictory Impulses," 566. Several recent accounts cite the genocidal language of California governor Pete Burnett in 1851; see, for example, Rensink, "Genocide of Native Americans," 20; Gellately and Kiernan, "The Study of Mass Murder," 23.

135. Aranda, "Contradictory Impulses," 573–74.

136. Rosaura Sánchez, "Dismantling the Colossus," 118. In a similar vein, Mon-tes contends that although "[m]any critics have recoiled at the anti-Indian senti-ment in her work . . . I argue that it is important to study this in order to look at how we still perpetuate such sentiments in the twentieth century." "María Amparo Ruiz de Burton Negotiates," 216.

137. González, *The Troubled Union*, 88–91.

138. On Ruiz de Burton's attitude toward Indians and the antipathy between Mexicans and Native Americans, see Rivera, *The Emergence of Mexican America*, 103. See also Ruiz de Burton, *The Squatter and the Don*, 271.

139. Ruiz de Burton further complicates our task by presenting squatter John Gasbang as cheating "poor Indians" in gambling. *The Squatter and the Don*, 367.

140. As Goldman points out, the story "invokes the 'plight' of native Califor-nians by mourning their downward slide," while Warford asserts that "Ruiz de Burton argues that the Alamar family and the Californio culture are *not* destined to die out, as opposed to their stereotypical portrayal by other California writers such as Atherton." Goldman, "I think our romance is spoiled," 68; Warford, "An Eloquent and Impassioned Plea," 8.

141. On "The Maid of Monterey," see Rivera, *The Emergence of Mexican America*, 88; Montes, "María Amparo Ruiz de Burton Negotiates," 214ff. The period's viru-lent anti-Catholicism (anti-Irish in some areas, anti-Italian in others) emerged vividly in Thomas Nast's cartoons. See, for example, Nast, "The American River Ganges." For a discussion of the image, see Freese, "American National Identity."

142. See Pearce, *Savagism and Civilization*, 223. Ruiz de Burton was not the only elite to contemplate such issues; her contemporary, Narcissa Owen (Cherokee), who likewise moved at the centers of U.S. national power, offers another kind of performance in *Memoirs of Narcissa Owen* (1907). See Owen, *A Cherokee Woman's America*.

143. "Zitkala-Ša, "Editorial Comment," in Kilcup, *Native American Women's Writing*, 338.

144. Hafen, "Zitkala-Ša," 31.

145. James H. Cox, "Yours for the Indian Cause," 173; see Cathy N. Davidson and Norris, introduction to *American Indian Stories*, xiii.

146. Hafen, "Zitkala-Ša," 31, 32.

147. For an analysis of Zitkala-Ša's boarding school experience, see Katanski, *Learning to Write "Indian,"* 95–130. For a thumbnail biography and timeline, see Hollrah, *"The Old Lady Trill,"* 29–30.

148. Spack, "Zitkala-Ša, *The Song of Hiawatha,*" 213–14.

149. Cathy N. Davidson and Norris, introduction to *American Indian Stories*, xxv. See also Regier, *Masterpieces of American Indian Literature*, 201–3. On Native American periodical literature during these years, see Peyer, "Non-fiction Prose." Some of Zitkala-Ša's many essays and editorials in *American Indian Magazine* and other Native American periodicals have been reprinted in Kilcup, *Native American Women's Writing*, 333–49; see also the generous selection of essays and speeches reprinted in Cathy N. Davidson and Norris, *American Indian Stories*, 164–264.

150. Spack argues that the narratives present a kind of composite autobiography. "Re-visioning Sioux Women."

151. See Cathy N. Davidson and Norris, introduction to *American Indian Stories*, xxxi–xxxiv; Hafen, "Zitkala-Ša," 34.

152. One noteworthy exception is Jeffrey Myers, who argues for the author's environmental justice work in texts as diverse as her traditional oral tales collected in *Old Indian Legends* (1901); various essays collected later as *American Indian Stories* (1921), which include the *Atlantic* and *Harper's* contributions; and magazine writing. Myers, *Converging Stories*. Although I focus below on her early political publications, I do not address *Indian Truth*, the magazine of the National Council of American Indians, which Zitkala-Ša founded in 1926 after the demise of the SAI and of which she was president until her death in 1938.

For recent work on the author, see, for example, Winter, *American Narratives*, chapter 3 (30–88); Burt, "Death Beneath This Semblance of Civilization"; Chiarello, "Deflected Missives"; Cari M. Carpenter, "Detecting Indianness"; Reynolds, "Mother Times Two"; Stromberg, "Resistance and Mediation"; Enoch, "Resisting the Script of Indian Education"; Lukens, "The American Story of Zitkala-Ša"; Carden, "The Ears of the Palefaces"; Bernardin, "The Lessons of a Sentimental Education"; Spack, "Translation Moves"; Kelsey, *Tribal Theory in Native American Literature*, 62–75; Velikova, "Troping in Zitkala-Sa's Autobiographical Writings"; Newmark, "Writing (and Speaking) in Tongues"; Ron Carpenter, "Zitkala-Ša and Bicultural Subjectivity." In one of the few discussions of Zitkala-Ša's periodical literature, Charles Hannon explores the author's rejection of racialized discourse. "Zitkala-Ša and the Commercial Magazine Apparatus," 192–96.

153. Cook-Lynn, "The American Indian Fiction Writers," 93.

154. Myers, *Converging Stories*, 115. See also Hafen, "Zitkala-Ša," 32.

155. As we saw in chapter 1, Native American versions of nationalism and national identity are much broader than their Western counterparts.

156. Spack, "Re-visioning Sioux Women," 26–28.

157. Okker, "Native American Literatures and the Canon," 95.

158. Carlisle supporters attacked Zitkala-Ša viciously, however. For some of their responses, see Katanski, *Learning to Write "Indian,"* 123–29.

159. Spack, "Re-visioning Sioux Women," 29. Spack points out that women's farming activities resonate differently in Sioux society than in the dominant society (29–30), as we saw for Jemison and her Cherokee counterparts.

160. Zitkala-Ša, "Impressions of an Indian Childhood," 37.

161. Numerous critics have commented on the author's use of sentimentalism; see, for example, Wexler, "Tender Violence"; Bernardin, "The Lessons of a Sentimental Education." On Zitkala-Ša and autobiography, see Bernardin, "The Lessons of a Sentimental Education"; Cutter, "Zitkala-Ša's Autobiographical Writings"; Spack, "Re-visioning Sioux Women."

162. On the education that the author receives from her mother, see Katanski, *Learning to Write "Indian,"* 117–18.

163. Katanski, *Learning to Write "Indian,"* 119.

164. In an essay critiquing the superimposition of dominant-society critical frameworks (specifically regionalism) on Native American literature, Gary Totten observes, "Perhaps the greatest drawback of attempting to reconcile Zitkala-Ša's work with dominant national history through a regionalist aesthetic is the way such an approach ignores issues of Indigenous nationalism." "Zitkala-Ša and the Problem of Regionalism," 99. For a discussion of how compulsory heterosexuality superimposed on Native kinship systems advanced the goal of appropriating tribal lands, see Rifkin, "Romancing Kinship" and *When Did Indians Become Straight?*, especially chapter 3.

165. Zitkala-Ša, "Why I Am a Pagan"; this essay was reprinted in Zitkala-Ša, *American Indian Stories*. See Spack, "Re-visioning Sioux Women," 33–34.

166. Several critics underscore Zitkala-Ša's stylistic mastery in this passage; see Myers, *Converging Stories*, 119; Meisenheimer, Jr., "Regionalist Bodies/Embodied Regions," 117–18.

167. Observing how this essay responds to John Muir's *Our National Parks*, Myers notes that Zitkala-Ša "addresses the separation, in the dominant culture, of the self from the nonhuman world." *Converging Stories*, 121.

Here we should return to Native theologian George E. Tinker: "Christianity and its sacred texts regularly impute to God attributes that are intrinsically human-like. . . . [while Indian tribal spiritualities understand God] as a spiritual force that permeates the whole of the world and is manifest in countless ways in the world around us at any given moment and especially in any given place." Tinker, "An American Indian Theological Response," 157; see Deloria, *God Is Red*, 79.

168. See Myers, *Converging Stories*, 117. When she collected the story in *American Indian Stories*, she renamed it "The Great Spirit."

169. Tinker, "An American Indian Theological Response," 159; see Deloria, *God Is Red*, 90, 95.

170. Greene, *Lakota and Cheyenne*, xv.

171. "Treaty of Fort Laramie."

172. Cathy N. Davidson and Norris, introduction to *American Indian Stories*, xii; James H. Cox, "Yours for the Indian Cause," 175.

173. Hertzberg, *The Search for an American Indian Identity*, 14, 26; see Warrior, *Tribal Secrets*, 5–14.

174. Hertzberg, *The Search for an American Indian Identity*, 18; see 20. The founders and early Indian supporters of the Society of American Indians included Charles Alexander Eastman (Sioux) and the Reverend Sherman Coolidge (Arapaho). These Indian intellectuals, along with Charles Daganett (Peoria), Dr. Carlos Montezuma (Yavapai), Thomas Sloan (Omaha), Henry Roe Cloud (Winnebago), and, most importantly, Arthur C. Parker (Seneca) formed the core founders. The founding conference, held symbolically in Columbus, Ohio, on Columbus Day (12 October 1911), articulated a series of shared principles held by most participants. Hertzberg, *The Search for an American Indian Identity*, 42–57, 73–75. Hertzberg also cites Fayette McKenzie, a non-Indian, as one of the founders (24).

As many scholars have pointed out, the boarding schools were profoundly problematic, constituting ethnocide or genocide; see, for example, Grinde, "Taking the Indian out of the Indian"; Churchill, "Genocide by Any Other Name"; Rensink, "Genocide of Native Americans"; Adams, *Education for Extinction*.

175. Warrior, *Tribal Secrets*, 6, 7. Warrior explains, "[These SAI founders represented] a generation [that] was the integrationist legacy of post–Wounded Knee existence. They were adults at the time of the transition to reservation life, the federal allotment policy, and the land and lease swindles that came along with allotment and western expansion. . . . [They] believed strongly in doing away with special educational and health programs for Natives, abandonment of Native traditional government structures, and full participation in U.S. life" (7). James H. Cox cites a number of issues that Native scholars and creative writers have addressed or continue to address. "Yours for the Indian Cause," 174–75.

176. Peyer, "Non-fiction Prose," 110. Peyer points out that Carlos Montezuma created "a private monthly newsletter," the *Wassaja* (1916–22), "partly in response to the prevailing moderate stand of the SAI journal."

177. James H. Cox, "Yours for the Indian Cause," 179. Cox describes Zitkala-Ša's resistance, both in her work as editor and in her capacity as an SAI member, to Arthur C. Parker's assimilationist stance.

178. Zitkala-Ša, "Chipeta, Widow of Chief Ouray," 336.

179. See James H. Cox, "Yours for the Indian Cause," 182; Cathy N. Davidson and Norris, introduction to *American Indian Stories*, xxii–xxiv.

180. Edmunds, *The New Warriors*, 44–47; see Lee D. Baker, *Anthropology and the Racial Politics of Culture*, 18–19; Hollrah, *"The Old Lady Trill,"* 41–44.

181. James H. Cox, "Yours for the Indian Cause," 182. Even within the SAI, peyote use proved divisive. Hafen, "Pan-Indianism and Tribal Sovereignties," 9, cited in Hollrah, *"The Old Lady Trill,"* 39. For more on the debate, see Aberle, *The*

Peyote Religion among the Navajo; Omer Call Stewart, *Peyote Religion*; Maroukis, *The Peyote Road*; and Huston Smith and Snake, *One Nation under God*.

Peyote use for religious purposes was ultimately approved by an act of the U.S. Congress, which identified it as part of traditional Indian religious practices. Traditional Indian Religious Use of Peyote, 42 U.S.C. § 1996a, http://www.law.cornell.edu/uscode/text/42/1996a.

182. James H. Cox, "Yours for the Indian Cause," 186–87. See, for example, Zitkala-Ša, "Indian Gifts to Civilized Man," *The Indian Sentinel* (July 1918), reprinted in Kilcup, *Native American Women's Writing*, 337–38; and "Editorial Comment," *American Indian Magazine* (July–September 1918), reprinted in Kilcup, *Native American Women's Writing*, 338–39.

183. Zitkala-Ša, "America, Home of the Red Man," 339.

184. As I suggest in *Native American Women's Writing*, this individual was probably Robert L. Owen (Cherokee, 1856–1947), who was one of the first Oklahoma senators. Elected to Congress in 1907, he was reelected in 1912 and 1918 (340n6).

185. Zitkala-Ša, "Letter to the Chiefs and Head-Men," 340.

186. James H. Cox, "Yours for the Indian Cause," 190.

187. Katanski, *Learning to Write "Indian*,*"* 122.

188. Hafen, *Dreams and Thunder*, xx.

189. Bonnin, Fabens, and Sniffen, *Oklahoma's Poor Rich Indians*. According to Thorne, John D. Rockefeller paid for printing *Oklahoma's Poor Rich Indians*. "Poor Rich Indians," 251n29. Thorne describes how "two other muckraking studies" reinforced the message of *Oklahoma's Poor Rich Indians*. One was composed by lawyer Marshall Mott, the Creek national attorney, whose report was funded by the American Home Missionary Society. "Poor Rich Indians," 115; see Marshall Mott, *The Act of May 27, 1908*.

190. The American Indian Defense Association, founded in 1923 by social worker John Collier, the future commissioner of Indian affairs, fought the Dawes Act's assimilationist policies and "aggressively assailed the entire system of [Indian] administration, which it equated with a 'dungeon.'" "Association on American Indian Affairs Records." The Indian Rights Association was founded in Philadelphia in 1882. For a discussion of the interaction of these groups and the Society of American Indians, see Hertzberg, *The Search for an American Indian Identity*, 201ff.

191. Thorne, "Poor Rich Indians," 115.

192. Bonnin, Fabens, and Sniffen, *Oklahoma's Poor Rich Indians*, 11.

193. Kidwell, *The Choctaws in Oklahoma*, 191.

194. Ibid., 194.

195. Nancy M. Peterson, "From the Heart of Chaos," 230.

196. Herbert Welsh, "In Explanation," in Bonnin, Fabens, and Sniffen, *Oklahoma's Poor Rich Indians*, 3.

197. The text states, "There are some phases of our investigation that can be presented best by a feminine mind, and we leave it to Mrs. Bonnin to describe the

following three cases." Bonnin, Fabens, and Sniffen, *Oklahoma's Poor Rich Indians*, 23. Millie Neharkey, Ledcie Stechi, and Martha Axe Roberts are the three cases. See Elizabeth Wilkinson, "Story as a Weapon," 219–32; Hollrah, *"The Old Lady Trill,"* 47–51.

198. Thorne, "Poor Rich Indians," 115.

199. Elizabeth Wilkinson, "Story as a Weapon," 216; see Kidwell, *The Choctaws in Oklahoma*, 190ff., for a detailed account. See Elizabeth Wilkinson ("Story as a Weapon," 190–237) for a fuller exploration of Zitkala-Ša's rhetoric and its concrete consequences. Neither Wilkinson, Kidwell, nor other commentators presents *Oklahoma's Poor Rich Indians* as an environmental justice narrative, but Wilkinson frames both Winnemucca's and Zitkala-Ša's writing (more broadly) within concerns about land preservation. See also Reed, "The Indian Orphan."

200. See Hollrah, *"The Old Lady Trill,"* 43ff.; Elizabeth Wilkinson, "Story as a Weapon," 225ff.

201. Kidwell, *The Choctaws in Oklahoma*, 192.

202. Before this time, individual tribes had been granted citizenship, but the Indian Citizenship Act of 1924 extended it to Native Americans born in the United States. For a discussion of the act and the complexity of Indians' response to it, see Bruyneel, "Challenging American Boundaries." Cook-Lynn notes the problematic status of Indians' dual U.S.–tribal nation citizenship. *New Indians, Old Wars*, 136.

203. Adamson, "Indigenous Literatures, Multinationalism, and *Avatar*," 144–46. For two conflicting views, see Good Fox, "Avatars to the Left of Me," cited in Adamson, "Indigenous Literatures, Multinationalism, and *Avatar*," 161; Justice, "James Cameron's *Avatar*."

204. Popular culture as well as literary examples abound: for example, the hagiography surrounding Davy Crockett and Daniel Boone; and James Fenimore Cooper's Leatherstocking novels. Even the television cartoon series *The Flintstones* depicts Wilma and Betty as domesticated and Fred and Barney as wild.

After Words

Epigraphs are from Spofford, "Pomegranate-Flowers," 575; Clifton, "homage to my hips," 6. On Spofford's poem, see Paula Bernat Bennett, "Pomegranate-Flowers."

1. Anticipating Dillard, Sigourney describes her youth: "There was a rural independence in our style of living which pleased us all. Our poultry and eggs were abundant and fine, our cow furnished an overflow of the richest milk, cream, and butter, and our hams, etc., preserved by a recipe of my father's, were proverbial for their delicacy. It is something to know what you are eating. More than this, we knew what *they* had eaten, upon whom we fed, and their aliment had been healthful and ample." *Letters of Life*, 114.

2. Kingsolver, *Animal, Vegetable, Miracle*, 2.

3. Kincaid, "Wisteria," *My Garden (Book):*, 3.

4. Dillard, *Teaching a Stone to Talk*, 11.

5. LaDuke, *All Our Relations*, 1. LaDuke's book discusses male as well as female activists.

6. These are Captain Richard H. Pratt's famous words, framing his founding of the U.S. Training and Industrial School for Native Americans at Carlisle, Pennsylvania, in 1879. Pratt, "The Advantages of Mingling Indians," 261; see Grinde, "Taking the Indian out of the Indian."

7. LaDuke's argument here anticipates (and counters) Sweet's criticism of such connections. "Projecting Early American Environmental Writing," 426.

8. Since LaDuke's volume was published, General Motors has continued to resist cleanup requirements. The Haudenosaunee Environmental Task Force website relates that a new challenge faces the Mohawk Nation: a proposal by the U.S. Army Corps of Engineers to widen and deepen the St. Lawrence River, which would dramatically impact the environment, stirring up contaminated sediments; creating lower water levels harmful to fish, birds, and other animals; and fostering the growth of invasive species. "Haudenosaunee Environmental Restoration"; see also International Joint Commission, "International Joint Commission Makes Recommendations"; and International Joint Commission, "St. Lawrence River Area of Concern."

Bibliography

Aberle, David F. *The Peyote Religion among the Navajo.* 2nd ed. Norman: University of Oklahoma Press, 1991.

About North Georgia. "North Georgia's Gold Rush." http://ngeorgia.com/ history/goldrush.html.

Acheson, James M. "Maine: On the Cusp of the Forest Transition." *Human Organization* 67, no. 2 (Summer 2008): 125–36.

Adamiak, Stanley J. "The 1779 Sullivan Campaign: A Little-Known Offensive Strategic to the War Breaks the Indian Nations' Power." Archiving Early America. http://www.earlyamerica.com/review/1998/sullivan.html.

Adams, David Wallace. *Education for Extinction: American Indians and the Boarding School Experience, 1875–1928.* Lawrence: University Press of Kansas, 1995.

Adamson, Joni. "Indigenous Literatures, Multinationalism, and *Avatar*: The Emergence of Indigenous Cosmopolitics." *American Literary History* 24, no. 1 (2012): 143–62.

Adamson, Joni, and Scott Slovic. "Guest Editors' Introduction: The Shoulders We Stand On: An Introduction to Ethnicity and Ecocriticism." *MELUS* 34, no. 2 (Summer 2009): 5–24.

Addison, Daniel Dulany. *Lucy Larcom: Life, Letters, and Diary.* Boston: Houghton Mifflin, 1894.

Alaimo, Stacy. *Bodily Natures: Science, Environment, and the Material Self.* Bloomington: Indiana University Press, 2010.

———. "'Skin Dreaming': The Bodily Transgressions of Fielding Burke, Octavia Butler, and Linda Hogan." In Gaard and Murphy, *Ecofeminist Literary Criticism,* 123–38.

———. *Undomesticated Ground: Recasting Nature as Feminist Space.* Ithaca, N.Y.: Cornell University Press, 2000.

Alaimo, Stacy, and Susan Hekman. "Introduction: Emerging Models of Materiality in Feminist Theory." In *Material Feminisms,* edited by Stacy Alaimo and Susan Hekman, 1–19. Bloomington: Indiana University Press, 2008.

Alcott, Louisa May. "Transcendental Wild Oats." *Independent* 25 (18 December 1873): 1569–71. Reprinted in Kilcup, *Nineteenth-Century American Women Writers: An Anthology,* 247–56. Page references are to the Kilcup anthology.

Alemán, Jesse. "Novelizing National Discourses." In *Recovering the U.S. Hispanic Literary Heritage,* vol. 3, edited by Maria Herrera-Sobek and Virginia Sánchez Korrol, 38–49. Houston: Arte Publico Press, 2000.

Allen, Carol. *Black Women Intellectuals: Strategies of Nation, Family, and Neighborhood in the Works of Pauline Hopkins, Jessie Fauset, and Marita Bonner*. New York: Routledge, 1998.

Allen, Nancy. "Cutting Out Clear-Cutting." *Synthesis/Regeneration* 10 (Spring 1996). www.greens.org/s-r/10/10-17.html.

Allen, Paula Gunn. "The Sacred Hoop: A Contemporary Perspective." In Allen, *The Sacred Hoop*, 54–75.

———. *The Sacred Hoop: Recovering the Feminine in American Indian Traditions*. Boston: Beacon Press, 1986.

———, ed. *Spider Woman's Granddaughters: Traditional Tales and Contemporary Writing by Native American Women*. Boston: Beacon Press, 1989.

Alternatives for Simple Living. Site discontinued; archives available at http://web.archive.org/web/20110716011612/http://www.simpleliving.org/.

Ammons, Elizabeth. *Brave New Words: How Literature Will Save the Planet*. Iowa City: University of Iowa Press, 2010.

———. *Conflicting Stories: American Women Writers at the Turn into the Twentieth Century*. New York: Oxford University Press, 1992.

Anderson, Lorraine. *Sisters of the Earth: Women's Prose and Poetry about Nature*. New York: Vintage, 2003.

Anderson, Lorraine, and Thomas S. Edwards. *At Home on This Earth: Two Centuries of U.S. Women's Nature Writing*. Hanover, N.H.: University Press of New England, 2004.

"Antagonism of Harmless Serpents to Poisonous Ones." In "Editor's Scientific Record," *Harper's New Monthly Magazine* 45, no. 266 (July 1872): 308.

Anzaldúa, Gloria. *Borderlands/La Frontera: The New Mestiza*. 2nd ed. San Francisco: Aunt Lute, 1999.

Aquila, Richard. *The Iroquois Restoration: Iroquois Diplomacy on the Colonial Frontier, 1701–1754*. Detroit: Wayne State University Press, 1997.

Aranda, José F., Jr. "Contradictory Impulses: María Amparo Ruiz de Burton, Resistance Theory, and the Politics of Chicano/a Studies." *American Literature* 70, no. 3 (1998): 551–79.

———. "María Amparo Ruiz de Burton." In *American Prose Writers, 1870–1920*, edited by Sharon M. Harris, 310–16. Detroit: Gale, 2000.

Armbruster, Karla M., and Kathleen R. Wallace, eds. *Beyond Nature Writing: Expanding the Boundaries of Ecocriticism*. Charlottesville: University Press of Virginia, 2001.

Armstrong, Jeannette C. "Land Speaking." In *Speaking for the Generations: Native Writers on Writing*, edited by Simon Ortiz, 174–94. Tucson: University of Arizona Press, 1998.

Aron, Cindy S. "The Evolution of the Middle Class." In *A Companion to 19th-Century America*, edited by William L. Barney, 178–91. Malden: Blackwell 2006.

"Association on American Indian Affairs Records, 1851–2010 (bulk 1922–1995): Finding Aid." Princeton University Library. http://diglib.princeton.edu/ead/getEad?id=ark:/88435/z316q159f.

Avery, Gillian. *Behold the Child: American Children and Their Books, 1621–1922.* Baltimore: Johns Hopkins University Press, 1995.

Awiakta, Marilou. *Selu: Seeking the Corn Mother's Wisdom.* Golden, Colo.: Fulcrum, 1993.

Baker, Lee D. *Anthropology and the Racial Politics of Culture.* Durham, N.C.: Duke University Press, 2010.

Barkan, Elazar. "Genocides of Indigenous Peoples: Rhetoric of Human Rights." In *The Specter of Genocide: Mass Murder in Historical Perspective,* edited by Robert Gellately and Ben Kiernan, 117–39. New York: Cambridge University Press, 2003.

Barker-Benfield, G. J., and Catherine Clinton. "Many Revolutions." In *Portraits of American Women: From Settlement to the Present,* edited by G. J. Barker-Benfield and Catherine Clinton, 55–63. New York: Oxford University Press, 1998.

Barnes, Elizabeth. "The Politics of Vision in Caroline Kirkland's Frontier Fiction." *Legacy* 20, no. 1–2 (2003): 62–75.

Barnhill, David Landis. "Surveying the Landscape: A New Approach to Nature Writing." *ISLE: Interdisciplinary Studies in Literature and Environment* 17, no. 2 (Spring 2010): 273–90.

Barreca, Regina. *They Used to Call Me Snow White . . . But I Drifted: Women's Strategic Use of Humor.* New York: Penguin, 1991.

Bartram, William. *Travels through North and South Carolina, Georgia, East and West Florida. . . .* Philadelphia: James and Johnson, 1791. Documenting the American South. University Library, University of North Carolina at Chapel Hill. http://docsouth.unc.edu/nc/bartram/menu.html.

Bassard, Katherine Clay. "'I Took a Text': Itinerancy, Community, and Intertextuality in Jarena Lee's Spiritual Narratives." In *Spiritual Interrogations: Culture, Gender, and Community in Early African American Women's Writing,* 87–107. Princeton, N.J.: Princeton University Press, 1999.

Bataille, Gretchen M., and Kathleen Mullen Sands. *American Indian Women: Telling Their Lives.* Lincoln: University of Nebraska Press, 1987.

Bauer, Dale M. "'In the Blood': Sentiment, Sex, and the Ugly Girl." *differences* 11, no. 3 (1999–2000): 57–75.

Bauman, Whitney A., Richard R. Bohannon II, and Kevin J. O'Brien, eds. *Grounding Religion: A Field Guide to the Study of Religion and Ecology.* New York: Routledge, 2011.

Bayley, Solomon. *A Narrative of Some Remarkable Incidents, in the Life of Solomon Bayley, Formerly a Slave. . . .* In Branch, *Reading the Roots,* 242–46.

Baym, Nina. *American Women of Letters and the Nineteenth-Century Sciences: Styles of Affiliation.* New Brunswick, N.J.: Rutgers University Press, 2002.

————. *American Women Writers and the Work of History, 1790–1860.* New Brunswick, N.J.: Rutgers University Press, 1995.

————. "Reinventing Lydia Sigourney." *American Literature* 62, no. 3 (September 1990): 385–404.

————. *Woman's Fiction: A Guide to Novels by and about Women in America, 1820–70.* Ithaca, N.Y.: Cornell University Press, 1978.

Baynton, Douglas. "Disability and the Justification of Inequality in American History." In *The New Disability History: American Perspectives*, edited by Paul K. Longmore and Laurie Umansky, 33–57. New York: New York University Press, 2001.

Bean, Judith Mattson. "Conversation as Rhetoric in Margaret Fuller's *Woman in the Nineteenth Century.*" In *In Her Own Voice: Nineteenth-Century American Women Essayists*, edited by Sherry Lee Linkon, 27–40. New York: Garland, 1997.

Becker, Elizabeth C. "Harriet Jacobs's Search for Home." *CLA Journal* 35, no. 4 (1989): 411–21.

Beesley, David. *Crow's Range: An Environmental History of the Sierra Nevada.* Reno: University of Nevada Press, 2004.

Bennett, Jessica, and Jesse Ellison, "Women Will Rule the World." In "The Future of Work." *Newsweek*, 5 July 2010. http://www.newsweek.com/2010/07/06/women-will-rule-the-world.html.

Bennett, Michael. "Anti-Pastoralism, Frederick Douglass, and the Nature of Slavery." In Armbruster and Wallace, *Beyond Nature Writing*, 195–210.

Bennett, Paula Bernat. "Emily Dickinson and Her Peers." In *A Companion to American Literature and Culture*, edited by Paul Lauter, 284–315. Malden, Mass.: Wiley-Blackwell, 2010.

————. "Late Nineteenth-Century American Women's Nature Poetry and the Evolution of the Imagist Poem," *Legacy* 9, no.2 (1992): 89–103.

————. "Mill Girls and Minstrels: Working-Class Poetry in the Nineteenth Century." In Bennett, Kilcup, and Schweighauser, *Teaching Nineteenth-Century American Poetry*, 51–66.

————, ed. *Nineteenth-Century American Women Poets: An Anthology.* Malden, Mass.: Blackwell, 1998.

————. "'The Pea that Duty Locks': Lesbian and Feminist-Heterosexual Readings of Emily Dickinson's Poetry." In *Lesbian Texts and Contexts: Radical Revisions*, ed. Karla Jay, Renee Vivien, and Allen Young, 104–25. New York: New York University Press, 1990.

————. *Poets in the Public Sphere: The Emancipatory Project of American Women's Poetry, 1800–1900.* Princeton, N.J.: Princeton University Press, 2003.

————. "'Pomegranate-Flowers': The Phantasmic Productions of Late-Nineteenth-Century Anglo-American Women Poets." In *Solitary Pleasures: The Historical, Literary, and Artistic Discourses of Autoeroticism*, edited by Paula Bennett and Vernon A. Rosario II, 189–213. New York: Routledge, 1995.

———. "Was Sigourney a Poetess? The Aesthetics of Victorian Plenitude in Lydia Sigourney's Poetry." *Comparative American Studies* 5, no. 3 (September 2007): 265–89.

Bennett, Paula Bernat, and Karen L. Kilcup. "Rethinking Nineteenth-Century American Poetry." In Bennett, Kilcup, and Schweighauser, *Teaching Nineteenth-Century American Poetry*, 1–10.

Bennett, Paula Bernat, Karen L. Kilcup, and Philipp Schweighauser, eds. *Teaching Nineteenth-Century American Poetry*. New York: MLA, 2007.

Berbineau, Lorenza Stevens. *From Beacon Hill to the Crystal Palace: The 1851 Travel Diary of a Working-Class Woman*. Edited by Karen L. Kilcup. Iowa City: University of Iowa Press, 2002.

Bergman, Jill. "'Everything we hoped she'd be': Contending Forces in Hopkins Scholarship." *African American Review* 38, no. 2 (2004): 181–99.

———. "'A New Race of Colored Woman': Pauline Hopkins at the *Colored American Magazine*." In *Feminist Forerunners: New Womanism and Feminism in the Early Twentieth Century*, edited by Ann Heilmann, 87–100. London: Pandora, 2003.

Bernardi, Debra. "Narratives of Domestic Imperialism: The African-American Home in the *Colored American Magazine* and the Novels of Pauline Hopkins, 1900–1903." In *Separate Spheres No More: Gender Convergence in American Literature, 1830–1930*, edited by Monika M. Elbert, 203–24. Tuscaloosa: University of Alabama Press, 2000.

Bernardin, Susan. "The Lessons of a Sentimental Education: Zitkala-Ša's Autobiographical Narratives." *Western American Literature* 32, no. 3 (1997): 212–38.

Berlant, Lauren. *The Female Complaint: The Unfinished Business of Sentimentality in American Culture*. Durham, N.C.: Duke University Press, 2008.

"Betsey" [pseud. Betsey Chamberlain?]. "Recollections of My Childhood." *Lowell Offering*, ser. 2, no. 1 (1841): 79.

"Big Tree Treaty Centennial." *New York Times*, 16 September 1897, 4.

Bird Wicks. "Ethno-Ornithology Sunday (on a Monday): Bird Hats." 29 September 2008. *Something Clever: Ponderings of a Wandering Mind* (blog). http://birdcolibri.blogspot.com/2008/09/ethno-ornithology-sunday-on-monday-bird.html.

Bishop, James E. "A Feeling Farmer: Masculinity, Nationalism, and Nature in Crèvecoeur's Letters." *Early American Literature* 43, no. 2 (2008): 361–77.

Black, Sandy. *Eco-Chic: The Fashion Paradox*. London: Black Dog, 2008.

Blum, Elizabeth D. "Power, Danger, and Control: Slave Women's Perceptions of Wilderness in the Nineteenth Century." *Women's Studies* 31 (2002): 247–65.

Blum, Virginia L. "Mary Wilkins Freeman and the Taste of Necessity." *American Literature* 65, no. 1 (March 1993): 69–94.

Blumin, Stuart. *The Emergence of the Middle Class: Social Experience in the American City, 1760–1900*. New York: Cambridge University Press, 1989.

Boggis, JeriAnne, Eve Allegra Raimon, and Barbara A. White, eds. *Harriet Wilson's New England*. Hanover, N.H.: University Press of New England, 2007.

Bohannon, Richard R., II, and Kevin J. O'Brien. "Environmental Justice and Eco-Justice." In Bauman, Bohannon, and O'Brien, *Grounding Religion*, 163–80.

Bolton, Linda. "The Native Eloquence of Frederick Douglass and Sarah Winnemucca." In *Facing the Other: Ethical Disruption and the American Mind*, 124–71. Baton Rouge: Louisiana State University Press, 2004.

Bonnin, Gertrude [Zitkala-Ša], Charles H. Fabens, and Matthew K. Sniffen. *Oklahoma's Poor Rich Indians: An Orgy of Graft and Exploitation of the Five Civilized Tribes, Legalized Robbery*. Philadelphia: Office of the Indian Rights Association, 1924.

Bost, Suzanne. "West Meets East: Nineteenth-Century Southern Debates on Mixture, Race, Gender, and Nation." *Mississippi Quarterly* 56, no. 4 (Fall 2003): 647–56.

Bouma, Jana A. "Caroline Kirkland (1801–1864)." In *Writers of the American Renaissance: An A-to-Z Guide*, edited by Denise D. Knight, 227–34. Westport, Conn.: Greenwood, 2003.

Bracke, Astrid. "Redrawing the Boundaries of Ecocritical Practice." *ISLE: Interdisciplinary Studies in Literature and Environment* 17, no. 4 (Autumn 2010): 765–68.

Bradberry, Travis, and Jean Greaves. *Emotional Intelligence 2.0.* San Francisco: TalentSmart, 2009.

Bradley, Candice. "Keeping the Soil in Good Heart: Women Weeders, the Environment, and Ecofeminism." In *Ecofeminism: Women, Culture, Nature*, edited by Karen J. Warren, 290–99. Bloomington: Indiana University Press, 1997.

Branch, Michael P. "Indexing American Possibilities: The Natural History Writing of Bartram, Wilson, and Audubon." In Glotfelty and Fromm, *The Ecocriticism Reader*, 282–302.

———, ed. *Reading the Roots: American Nature Writing before Walden*. Athens: University of Georgia Press, 2004.

Branch, Michael P., Rochelle Johnson, Daniel Patterson, and Scott H. Slovic, eds., *Reading the Earth: New Directions in the Study of Literature and the Environment*. Moscow: University of Idaho Press, 1998.

Brand, Alice Glarden. "Mary Wilkins Freeman: Misanthropy as Propaganda." *New England Quarterly* 50, no. 1 (March 1977): 83–100.

Brandon, Stephen. "Sacred Fire and Sovereign Rhetorics: Cherokee Literacy and Literature in the Cherokee and American Nations, 1790–1841." PhD diss., University of North Carolina, Greensboro, 2003. Dissertation Abstracts International, Section A: The Humanities and Social Sciences, May 2004 [64 (11): 4049].

Braudo, Britt. "Navy Birthplace Still up for Debate." *Salem (Mass.) Gazette*, 17 October 2010. http://www.wickedlocal.com/salem/news/x115386463/Navy-birthplace-still-up-for-debate#axzz1G29rEZ8A.

Brault, Rob. "Silence as Resistance: An Ecofeminist Reading of Sarah Orne Jewett's 'A White Heron.'" In *New Directions in Ecofeminist Literary Criticism*, edited by Andrea Campbell, 74–89. Newcastle upon Tyne: Cambridge Scholars Press, 2008.

Breau, Elizabeth. "Identifying Satire: Our Nig." *Callaloo* 16, no. 2 (Spring 1993): 455–65.

Brewington, Autumn. "William and Kate Appear in Wales." *Washington Post*, February 24, 2011. http://voices.washingtonpost.com/royal-wedding-watch/2011/02/william_and_kate_in_wales.html.

Brooks, Lisa. *The Common Pot: The Recovery of Native Space in the Northeast*. Minneapolis: University of Minnesota Press, 2008.

Brooks, Van Wyck. *New England: Indian Summer 1865–1915*. New York: E. P. Dutton, 1940.

Brown, Alice. Review of *The Country of the Pointed Firs* (1897). In *Critical Essays on Sarah Orne Jewett*, edited by Gwen L. Nagel, 39. Boston: G. K. Hall, 1984.

Brown, Bill. "Regional Artifacts (The Life of Things in the Work of Sarah Orne Jewett)." *American Literary History* 14, no. 2 (Summer 2002): 195–226.

Brown, James B. *Views of Canada and the Colonists*. Edinburgh: Adam and Charles Black, 1851.

Brown, Judith K. "Iroquois Women: An Ethnohistoric Note." In *Toward an Anthropology of Women*, edited by Rayna R. Reiter, 235–51. New York: Monthly Review Press, 1975.

Brown, Lois. *Pauline Elizabeth Hopkins: Black Daughter of the Revolution*. Chapel Hill: University of North Carolina Press, 2008.

Brown, Sass. *Eco Fashion*. London: Laurence King, 2010.

Brown, William Wells. *My Southern Home; or, The South and Its People*. Boston: A. G. Brown, 1880.

Bruchac, Joseph. *Roots of Survival: Native American Storytelling and the Sacred*. Golden, Colo.: Fulcrum, 1996.

Brumble, H. David, III. *American Indian Autobiography*. Berkeley: University of California Press, 1988.

Bruyneel, Kevin. "Challenging American Boundaries: Indigenous People and the 'Gift' of U.S. Citizenship." *Studies in American Political Development* 18, no. 1 (Spring 2004): 30–43.

Bryant, William Cullen. "Among the Trees." In *The Message of the Trees: An Anthology of Leaves and Branches*, edited by Maud Cuney-Hare, 3–5. Boston: Cornhill, 1918.

Buchanan, Lindal, and Kathleen J. Ryan, eds. *Walking and Talking Feminist Rhetorics: Landmark Essays and Controversies*. Anderson, S.C.: Parlor Press, 2010.

Buckley, Cornelius Michael, S. J. "The Jesuits and the Iroquois" [Foreword]. In *Jesuit Missionaries to North America: Spiritual Writings and Biographical Sketches*, by Francois Roustang, S.J. San Francisco: Ignatius Press, 2006. http://www .ignatiusinsight.com/features2006/buckley_jesuitsna_mar06.asp.

Buell, Lawrence. "American Pastoral Ideology Reappraised." *American Literary History* 1, no.1 (1989): 1–29.

———. *The Environmental Imagination: Thoreau, Nature Writing, and the Formation of American Culture*. Cambridge, Mass.: Harvard University Press, 1995.

———. *The Future of Environmental Criticism: Environmental Crisis and Literary Imagination*. Malden, Mass.: Wiley-Blackwell, 2005.

———. *Writing for an Endangered World: Literature, Culture, and Environment in the U.S. and Beyond*. Cambridge, Mass.: Harvard University Press, 2001.

Burt, Ryan. "'Death Beneath This Semblance of Civilization': Reading Zitkala-Ša and the Imperial Imagination of the Romantic Revival." *Arizona Quarterly* 66, no. 2 (2010): 59–88.

Byrd, William. *A Journey to the Land of Eden and Other Papers*. 1841. Reprint, New York: Macy-Masius, 1928. Documenting the American South. University Library, University of North Carolina at Chapel Hill. http://docsouth.unc .edu/nc/byrd/byrd.html.

Caesar, Terry. *Forgiving the Boundaries: Home as Abroad in American Travel Writing*. Athens: University of Georgia Press, 1995.

California Indian Education (CALIE). "Indian Boarding Schools." http://www .californiaindianeducation.org/indian_boarding_schools.

Camfield, Gregg. "'I Never Saw Anything at Once So Pathetic and Funny': Humor in the Stories of Mary Wilkins Freeman." *American Transcendental Quarterly* 13, no. 3 (September 1999): 215–31.

———. *Necessary Madness: The Humor of Domesticity in Nineteenth-Century American Literature*. Oxford: Oxford University Press, 1997.

———. *Sentimental Twain: Samuel Clemens in the Maze of Moral Philosophy*. Philadelphia: University of Pennsylvania Press, 1994.

Campbell, Karlyn Kohrs, comp. *Man Cannot Speak for Her: Key Texts of the Early Feminists*. 2 vols. Westport, Conn.: Greenwood, 1989.

Canfield, Gae Whitney. *Sarah Winnemucca of the Northern Paiutes*. Norman: University of Oklahoma Press, 1983.

Canfield, William W. *The Legends of the Iroquois: Told by "The Cornplanter."* New York: A. Wessels, 1902.

Carby, Hazel V. "'Hear My Voice, Ye Careless Daughters': Narratives of Slave and Free Women before Emancipation." In *Black Women's Intellectual Traditions: Speaking Their Minds*, edited by Kristin Waters and Carol B. Conaway, 91–112. Hanover, N.H.: University Press of New England, 2007.

———. *Reconstructing Womanhood: The Emergence of the Afro-American Woman Novelist*. New York: Oxford University Press, 1987.

Carden, Mary Paniccia. "'The Ears of the Palefaces Could Not Hear Me':

Languages of Self-Representation in Zitkala-Ša's Autobiographical Essays."
In *Diversifying the Discourse: The Florence Howe Award for Outstanding Feminist Scholarship, 1990–2004*, edited by Mihoko Suzuki and Roseanna Lewis Dufault, 124–41. New York: Modern Language Association, 2006.

"Caroline Kirkland." Scribbling Women. Public Media Foundation. http://www.scribblingwomen.org/ckbio.htm.

Carpenter, Cari M. "Detecting Indianness: Gertrude Bonnin's Investigation of Native American Identity." *Wicazo Sa Review* 20, no.1 (2005): 139–59.

———. "Sarah Winnemucca and the Rewriting of Nation." In *Racially Writing the Republic: Racists, Race Rebels, and Transformations of American Identity*, edited by Bruce Baum and Duchess Harris, 112–27. Durham, N.C.: Duke University Press, 2009.

———. *Seeing Red: Anger, Sentimentality, and American Indians*. Columbus: Ohio State University Press, 2008.

———. "Tiresias Speaks: Sarah Winnemucca's Hybrid Selves and Genres." *Legacy* 19, no. 1 (2002): 71–80.

Carpenter, Ron. "Zitkala-Ša and Bicultural Subjectivity." *Studies in American Indian Literatures* 16, no. 3 (2004): 1–28.

Carpio, Glenda. *Laughing Fit to Kill: Black Humor in the Fictions of Slavery*. New York: Oxford University Press, 2008.

Cart, Theodore Whaley. "The Lacey Act: America's First Nationwide Wildlife Statute." *Forest History* 17, no. 3 (October 1973): 4–13.

Cary, Richard. "The Multi-Colored Spirit of Celia Thaxter." *Colby Library Quarterly* 6, no. 12 (1964): 512–36.

Catesby, Mark. *The Natural History of Carolina, Florida, and the Bahama Islands*. London, 1731–47. E-text by Kristy Amacker. http://xroads.virginia.edu/~ma02/amacker/etext/pre.htm.

———. "Of the Soil of Carolina." In Branch, *Reading the Roots*, 133–35. Originally published in *The Natural History of Carolina, Florida, and the Bahama Islands*.

Cather, Willa. Preface to *The Country of the Pointed Firs and Other Stories*, by Sarah Orne Jewett. Garden City, N.Y.: Doubleday-Anchor, 1956.

Cawthorne, Alexandra. "The Straight Facts on Women in Poverty." Center for American Progress. October 2008. http://www.americanprogress.org/issues/2008/10/pdf/women_poverty.pdf.

CBSNews.com. "How Gold Pays for Congo's Deadly War." *60 Minutes*. 30 November 2009. http://www.cbsnews.com/2100-18560_162-5774127.html.

Cella, Matthew J. C. "The Ambivalent Heritage of Mining in Western American Literature: Wheeler's Dime Novels and Austin's *The Land of Little Rain*." *ISLE: Interdisciplinary Studies in Literature and Environment* 16, no. 4 (Autumn 2009): 761–78.

Chambers-Schiller, Lee Virginia. *Liberty, a Better Husband: Single Women of America: The Generations of 1780–1840*. New Haven, Conn.: Yale University Press, 1984.

Chapagain, A. K., A. Y. Hoekstra, H. H. G. Savenije, and R. Gautam. "The Water Footprint of Cotton Consumption." Value of Water Research Report Series, no. 18. UNESCO-IHE Institute for Water Education, Delft, Netherlands. September 2005. http://www.waterfootprint.org/Reports/Report18.pdf.

Cherokee Indian Women. "Letter from Cherokee Indian Women, to Benjamin Franklin, Governor of the State of Pennsylvania." In *The Heath Anthology of American Literature*, 6th ed., vol. A, edited by Paul Lauter et al., 828–29. Boston: Wadsworth, 2009.

"Cherokee Mission Schools." *North Carolina History: A Digital History.* LEARN North Carolina. http://www.learnnc.org/lp/editions/nchist-newnation/5305. Originally published in Edmund Schwarze, *History of the Moravian Missions among Southern Indian Tribes of the United States* (Bethlehem, Pa.: Times, 1932): 112–15.

Cherokee Women. "Petitions of the Women's Councils, 1817, 1818." In *The Cherokee Removal: A Brief History with Documents*, edited by Theda Perdue and Michael D. Green, 125–26. Boston: Bedford Books of St. Martin's Press, 1995. Original is in Papers of the American Board of Commissioners for Foreign Missions (ABCFM), Houghton Library, Harvard University.

Chiarello, Barbara. "Deflected Missives: Zitkala-Ša's Resistance and Its (Un) Containment." *Studies in American Indian Literatures* 17, no. 3 (2005): 1–26.

"Chronology of Selected Events in the Development of the American Conservation Movement, c. 1850–1920." The Evolution of the Conservation Movement, 1850–1920. Library of Congress. http://memory.loc.gov/ammem/amrvhtml/conshome.html.

Chrostek, Alina. "Occupational Health & Safety in Textile." Yale–New Haven Teachers Institute. http://www.yale.edu/ynhti/curriculum/units/1996/2/96.02.07.x.html.

Churchill, Ward. "Genocide by Any Other Name: North American Indian Residential Schools in Context." In *Genocide, War Crimes and the West: History and Complicity*, edited by Adam Jones, 78–115. London: Zed Books, 2004.

———. *Struggle for the Land: Native North American Resistance to Genocide, Ecocide, and Colonization*. San Francisco: City Lights, 2002.

"Circular: Addressed to Benevolent Ladies of the U. States." *Christian Advocate and Journal and Zion's Herald*, December 25, 1829, 4, 17. APS Online, 65.

Clifton, Lucille. "homage to my hips." In *two-headed woman*, 6. Amherst: University of Massachusetts Press, 1980.

Clinton, Catherine, and Christine Lunardini. *The Columbia Guide to American Women in the Nineteenth Century*. New York: Columbia University Press, 2000.

"Clinton's Big Ditch." The Erie Canal. http://www.eriecanal.org/.

Cockburn, Alexander, and Jeffrey St. Clair. "How the Labor Dept. Helps the INS Keep Sweatshops Profitable." *Counterpunch.* June 15, 1998. http://www.counterpunch.org/dolsweats.html.

Coffin, Joshua. *A Sketch of the History of Newbury, Newburyport, and West Newbury, from 1635 to 1845.* Boston: Samuel G. Drake, 1845.

Cokinos, Christopher. "What Is Ecocriticism?" Paper presented at "Narrative Scholarship: Storytelling in Ecocriticism," Western Literature Association Annual Meeting, Vancouver, B.C., October 1995. Association for the Study of Literature and Environment. http://www.asle.org/site/resources/ecocritical-library/intro/defining/cokinos/.

Columbus, Christopher. "Journal of the First Voyage of Columbus." Transcribed by Bartolome de Las Casas. Early Americas Digital Archive. http://mith2 .umd.edu/eada/html/display.php?docs=columbus_journal.xml. Originally published in Julius E. Olson and Edward Gaylord Bourne, eds., *The Northmen: Columbus and Cabot, 985–1503, Original Narratives of Early American History* (New York: Charles Scribner's Sons, 1906).

"The Complete Herbal A–Z Guide to the Language of Flowers." The Complete Herbal. http://www.complete-herbal.com/atoz/atozoflanguageofflowers.html.

Connor, Kimberley Rae. *Conversions and Visions in the Writings of African American Women.* Knoxville: University of Tennessee Press, 1994.

"Constitution of the Cherokee Nation [continued]." *Cherokee Phoenix,* 28 February 1828, 2. Georgia Historic Newspapers. http://neptune3.galib.uga.edu/ssp/cgi-bin/tei-news-idx.pl?sessionid=7f000001&type=issues&id=chrkphnx&yr=1828.

Converse, Harriet Maxwell (Ya-ie-wa-noh). "The Iroquois Creation." In *Myths and Legends of the New York State Iroquois,* edited by Arthur C. Parker, 31–33. New York State Museum Bulletin 125. Albany: University of the State of New York, 1908.

Cook, Barbara. "Enclosed by Racist Politics: Space, Place, and Power Dynamics in the Slave Narrative of Harriet Jacobs and in Environmental Justice Activism." In *Restoring the Connection to the Natural World: Essays on the African American Environmental Imagination,* edited by Sylvia Mayer, 31–44. New Brunswick, N.J.: Transaction, 2003.

Cook-Lynn, Elizabeth. "The American Indian Fiction Writers: Cosmopolitanism, Nationalism, the Third World, and First Nation Sovereignty." In *Why I Can't Read Wallace Stegner and Other Essays: A Tribal Voice,* 78–96. Madison: University of Wisconsin Press, 1996.

———. "American Indian Intellectualism and the New Indian Story." In *Natives and Academics: Researching and Writing about American Indians,* edited by Devon A. Mihesuah, 111–38. Lincoln: University of Nebraska Press, 1998.

———. *Anti-Indianism in Modern America: A Voice from Tatekeya's Earth.* Urbana: University of Illinois Press, 2001.

———. *New Indians, Old Wars.* Urbana: University of Illinois Press, 2007.

Cooper, Susan Fenimore. Introduction to *The Rhyme and Reason of Country Life,* 18–34. New York: Putnam, 1854.

Cordell, Sigrid Anderson. "'The Case Was Very Black against Her': Pauline Hopkins and the Politics of Racial Ambiguity at the *Colored American Magazine*." *American Periodicals* 16, no. 1 (2006): 52–73.

Cornell University Department of Animal Science. Plants Poisonous to Livestock and Other Animals. "Datura spp." http://www.ansci.cornell.edu/plants/ jimsonweed/jimsonweed.html.

Corrothers, James D. "The Gift of the Greatest God." *Colored American Magazine* 4, no. 2 (December 1901): 101–3.

Couser, G. Thomas. "Signifying Bodies: Life Writing and Disability Studies." In *Disability Studies: Enabling the Humanities*, edited by Sharon L. Snyder, Brenda Jo Brueggemann, and Rosemarie Garland Thomson, 109–17. New York: MLA, 2002.

Cox, James H. "'Yours for the Indian Cause': Gertrude Bonnin's Activist Editing at *The American Indian Magazine*, 1915–1919." In Harris, *Blue Pencils and Hidden Hands*, 173–97.

Cox, Thomas R., Robert S. Maxwell, and Phillip Drennon Thomas. *This Well-Wooded Land: Americans and Their Forests from Colonial Times to the Present*. Lincoln: University of Nebraska Press, 1985.

Crane, Clare B. "The Pueblo Lands: San Diego's Hispanic Heritage." *Journal of San Diego History* 37, no. 2 (Spring 1991). http://www.sandiegohistory.org/ journal/91spring/pueblo.htm.

Crane, Diana. *Fashion and Its Social Agendas: Class, Gender, and Identity in Clothing*. Chicago: University of Chicago Press, 2001.

Crawford, Kathleen. "María Amparo Ruiz Burton: The General's Lady." *Journal of San Diego History* 30, no. 3 (Summer 1984). http://www.sandiegohistory.org/ journal/84summer/burton.htm.

Crèvecoeur, J. Hector St. John. *Letters from an American Farmer*. 1782. University of Virginia American Studies Program hypertexts. http://xroads.virginia.edu/ ~hyper/crev/contents.html.

Cronon, William. *Changes in the Land: Indians: Indians, Colonists, and the Ecology of New England*. Rev. ed. New York: Hill and Wang, 2003.

Cunningham, Patricia A. *Reforming Women's Fashion, 1850–1920: Politics, Health, and Art*. Kent, Ohio: Kent State University Press, 2003.

Cunningham, Valerie. "New Hampshire Forgot: African Americans in a Community by the Sea." In Boggis, Raimon, and White, *Harriet Wilson's New England*, 97–105.

Cutter, Martha J. "Beyond Stereotypes: Mary Wilkins Freeman's Radical Critique of Nineteenth-Century Cults of Femininity." *Women's Studies: An Interdisciplinary Journal* 21, no. 4 (1992): 383–95.

———. "Zitkala-Ša's Autobiographical Writings: The Problems of a Canonical Search for Language and Identity." *MELUS* 19, no. 1 (1994): 31–44.

Dabel, Jane E. *A Respectable Woman: The Public Roles of African American Women in 19th-Century New York*. New York: New York University Press, 2008.

Daley, Beth. "Paul Bunyan on Trial: The State That Timber Built Debates the Future of Logging." *Boston Globe*, 19 September 2000. Available at http://www.bio.net/bionet/mm/ag-forst/2000-September/015637.html.

———. "A Race to Save Maine Woods: Development Threat Spurring Push to Buy Land." *Boston Globe*, 18 September 2000. Available at http://www.bio.net/bionet/mm/ag-forst/2000-September/015636.html.

Davidson, Cathy N., and Ada Norris, eds. *American Indian Stories, Legends, and Other Writings.* By Zitkala-Ša. New York: Penguin, 2003.

Davidson, Lawrence. *Cultural Genocide.* New Brunswick, N.J.: Rutgers University Press, 2012.

Davidson, Mary V. "What We've Missed: Female Romantic Poets and the American Nature Writing Tradition." *CEA Critic* 54, no. 1 (1991): 110–18.

Davis, Cynthia J. "Speaking the Body's Pain: Harriet Wilson's *Our Nig.*" *African American Review* 27, no. 3 (Fall 1993): 391–404.

Davis, Lennard J. "Constructing Normalcy: The Bell Curve, the Novel, and the Invention of the Disabled Body in the Nineteenth Century." In *The Disability Studies Reader*, edited by Lennard J. Davis, 9–28. New York: Routledge, 1997.

[Davis, Rebecca Harding.] ("The author of 'Margaret Howth.'") "Blind Tom." *Atlantic Monthly* 10, no. 61 (November 1862): 580–85.

Dawson, Melanie V. "Ruiz de Burton's Emotional Landscape: Property and Feeling in *The Squatter and the Don.*" *Nineteenth-Century Literature* 63, no. 1 (June 2008): 41–72.

DeGraaf, John, David Wann, and Thomas H. Naylor. *Affluenza: The All-Consuming Epidemic.* San Francisco: Berrett-Koehler, 2001.

Deines, Timothy. "Interrogating the Moral Contract in Ruiz de Burton's *The Squatter and the Don.*" *REAL: The Yearbook of Research in English and American Literature* 22 (2006): 269–89.

DeKoven, Marianne. "Guest Column: Why Animals Now?" *PMLA* 124, no. 2 (2009): 361–69.

Deloria, Vine, Jr. *Custer Died for Your Sins: An Indian Manifesto.* New York: Macmillan, 1969.

———. *God Is Red: A Native View of Religion.* Updated ed. Golden, Colo.: Fulcrum, 1994.

D'Emilio, John, and Estelle B. Freedman. *Intimate Matters: A History of Sexuality in America.* New York: Harper and Row, 1988.

Demos, John. *The Unredeemed Captive: A Family Story from Early America.* New York: Knopf, 1994.

Dennis, Matthew. *Seneca Possessed: Indians, Witchcraft, and Power in the Early American Republic.* Philadelphia: University of Pennsylvania Press, 2011.

De Rosa, Deborah C. *Domestic Abolitionism and Juvenile Literature, 1830–1865.* Albany: State University of New York Press, 2003.

Destexhe, Alain. *Rwanda and Genocide in the Twentieth Century.* New York: New York University Press, 1995.

Diamond, Irene, and Gloria Feman Orenstein, eds. *Reweaving the World: The Emergence of Ecofeminism*. San Francisco: Sierra Club, 1990.

Diamond, Jared. *Collapse: How Societies Choose to Fail or Succeed*. New York: Viking Penguin, 2005.

Dillard, Annie. *Teaching a Stone to Talk: Expeditions and Encounters*. New York: Harper Colophon, 1982.

Dillon, Elizabeth Maddock. "Sentimental Aesthetics." *American Literature* 76, no. 3 (September 2004): 495–523.

Dimock, Wai-chee, and Michael T. Gilmore. Introduction to *Rethinking Class: Literary Studies and Social Formations*, edited by Wai-chee Dimock and Michael T. Gilmore, 1–14. New York: Columbia University Press, 1994.

Dinar, Shlomi. "Resource Scarcity and Environmental Degradation: Analyzing International Conflict and Cooperation." In *Beyond Resource Wars: Scarcity, Environmental Degradation, and International Cooperation*, edited by Shlomi Dinar, 3–22. Cambridge, Mass.: MIT Press, 2011.

Dippie, Brian W. *The Vanishing American: White Attitudes and U.S. Indian Policy*. Middletown, Conn.: Wesleyan University Press, 1982.

Dixon, Melvin. *Ride Out the Wilderness: Geography and Identity in Afro-American Literature*. Urbana: University of Illinois Press, 1987.

Dixon, Terrell. "Nature, Gender, and Community: Mary Wilkins Freeman's Ecofiction." In Armbruster and Wallace, *Beyond Nature Writing*, 162–76.

Dominguez, Joe, and Vicki Robin. *Your Money or Your Life*. New York: Penguin, 1999.

Donovan, Josephine. "Ecofeminist Literary Criticism: Reading the Orange." *Hypatia* 11, no. 2 (Spring 1996):161–84.

———. "Jewett on Race, Class, Ethnicity, and Imperialism: A Reply to Her Critics." *Colby Quarterly* 38, no. 4 (December 2002): 403–16.

———. *New England Local Color Literature: A Women's Tradition*. New York: Frederick Ungar, 1983.

———. *Sarah Orne Jewett*. New York: Frederick Ungar, 1980.

———. "Silence or Capitulation: Prepatriarchal 'Mothers' Gardens' in Jewett and Freeman." *Studies in Short Fiction* 23, no. 1 (1986): 43–48.

———. "Women's Masterpieces." In *Challenging Boundaries: Gender and Periodization*, edited by Joyce W. Warren and Margaret Dickie, 26–38. Athens: University of Georgia Press, 2000.

Doreski, C. K. "Inherited Rhetoric and Authentic History: Pauline Hopkins and the *Colored American Magazine*." In *The Unruly Voice: Rediscovering Pauline Elizabeth Hopkins*, edited by John Cullen Gruesser, 71–97. Urbana: University of Illinois Press, 1996.

Doriani, Beth Maclay. "Black Womanhood in Nineteenth-Century America: Subversion and Self-Construction in Two Women's Autobiographies." *American Quarterly* 43, no. 2 (June 1991): 199–222.

Douglas, Ann. *The Feminization of American Culture*. New York: Knopf, 1977.

Dowling, David. *Capital Letters: Authorship in the Antebellum Literary Market.* Iowa City: University of Iowa Press, 2009.

Dowty, Douglass. "Working to Clean Onondaga Lake a Sacred Task for Haudenosaunee." *Syracuse (N.Y.) Post-Standard.* 19 April 2010. http://www.syracuse.com/news/index.ssf/2010/04/clean_onondaga_lake_a_sacred_t.html.

Dublin, Thomas H. *Transforming Women's Work: New England Lives in the Industrial Revolution.* Ithaca, N.Y.: Cornell University Press, 1994.

———. *Women at Work: The Transformation of Work and Community in Lowell, Massachusetts, 1826–1860.* New York: Columbia University Press 1981.

———. "Women, Work, and Protest in the Early Lowell Mills: 'The Oppressing Hand of Avarice Would Enslave Us.'" In *The Working Class and Its Culture,* edited by Neil Larry Shumsky, 127–44. New York: Garland, 1996.

Dudden, Faye E. *Serving Women: Household Service in Nineteenth-Century America.* Middletown, Conn.: Wesleyan University Press, 1983.

DuFault, Amy. "Chicken Feathers!" EcoSalon. 17 February 2009. http://ecosalon.com/chicken-feathers/.

Dulles, Foster Rhea. *Americans Abroad: Two Centuries of European Travel.* Ann Arbor: University of Michigan Press, 1964.

Dumont, Henrietta. *The Language of Flowers: The Floral Offering; A Token of Affection and Esteem; Comprising the Language and Poetry of Flowers.* Philadelphia: Peck and Bliss, 1851.

Dwight, Timothy. *Travels in New-England and New-York.* 4 vols. New Haven, Conn.: Timothy Dwight/S. Converse, 1821.

Dychtwald, Maddy. *Influence: How Women's Soaring Economic Power Will Transform Our World for the Better.* New York: Voice-Hyperion, 2010.

Eacker, Susan A. "Gender in Paradise: Harriet Beecher Stowe and Postbellum Prose on Florida." *Journal of Southern History* 64, no. 3 (1998): 495–512.

Easton, Alison. "'How Clearly the Gradations of Society Were Defined': Negotiating Class in Sarah Orne Jewett." In Kilcup and Edwards, *Jewett and Her Contemporaries,* 207–22.

———. "'Outdoor Relief': Sarah Orne Jewett, Annie Adams Fields, and the Visit in Gilded Age America." In Floyd et al., *Becoming Visible,* 129–51.

Easton, Alison, R. J. Ellis, Janet Floyd, and Lindsey Traub. "Introduction: Becoming Visible." In Floyd et al., *Becoming Visible,* 1–14.

"Eco Fashion." *Voguepedia.* http://www.vogue.com/voguepedia/Eco_Fashion.

Ecofashionworld.com. "Eco Fashion Guide." http://www.ecofashionworld.com/.

Ecouterre. "About Us." http://www.ecouterre.com/about.

Edmunds, R. David. *The New Warriors: Native American Leaders since 1900.* Lincoln: University of Nebraska Press, 2001.

E. E. T. "Childhood's Home." *Lowell Offering,* ser. 2, no. 1 (1841): 69.

Egan, Ken, Jr. "Imperial Strains: Poetry and Empire in the Nineteenth-Century United States." *ISLE: Interdisciplinary Studies in Literature and Environment* 17, no. 3 (Summer 2010): 498–508.

———. "Poetic Travelers: Figuring the Wild in Parkman, Fuller, and Kirkland." *Western American Literature* 44, no. 1 (Spring 2009): 49–62.

Eisler, Benita, ed. *The Lowell Offering: Writings by New England Mill Women.* New York: Norton, 1997.

Elbert, Monika M. "The Displacement of Desire: Consumerism and Fetishism in Mary Wilkins Freeman's Fiction." *Legacy* 19, no. 2 (2002): 192–215.

———. "Mary Wilkins Freeman's Devious Women, *Harper's Bazaar*, and the Rhetoric of Advertising." *Essays in Literature* 20, no. 2 (September 1993): 251–72.

Elgin, Duane. *Voluntary Simplicity: Toward a Way of Life That Is Outwardly Simple, Inwardly Rich.* 2nd, rev. ed. New York: HarperCollins, 2010.

Ellis, R. J. "Body Politics and the Body Politic in William Wells Brown's *Clotel* and Harriet Wilson's *Our Nig*." In Kilcup, *Soft Canons*, 99–122.

———, ed. *Harriet Wilson's "Our Nig": A Cultural Biography of a 'Two-Story' African American Novel.* Amsterdam: Rodopi, 2003.

———. Introduction to *Our Nig*, edited by R. J. Ellis, vii–xxxvii. Nottingham, UK: Trent Editions, 1998.

———. "*Our Nig*: Fetters of an American Farmgirl." In *Special Relationships: Anglo-American Affinities and Antagonisms, 1854–1936*, edited by Janet Beer and Bridget Bennett, 65–88. Manchester: Manchester University Press, 2002.

———. "Traps Slyly Laid: Professing Autobiography in Harriet Wilson's *Our Nig*." In *Representing Lives: Women and Auto/Biography*, edited by Alison Donnell and Pauline Polkey, 65–76. New York: Macmillan–St. Martin's, 2000.

———. "What Happened to Harriet E. Wilson, *née* Adams? Was She Really Hattie Green?" *Transition: An International Review* 99 (2008): 162–68.

Emerson, Ralph Waldo. "The Progress of Culture." 18 July 1867. In *The Complete Works of Ralph Waldo Emerson.* Vol. 8, *Letters and Social Aims.* Also available at RWE.org, Complete Works of RWE, http://www.rwe.org/complete-works/viii-letters-and-social-aims/progress-of-culture.

Engel, J. Ronald. "Democracy, Christianity, Ecology: A Twenty-First-Century Agenda for Eco-Theology." *Cross Currents* 61, no. 2 (2011): 217–31.

Engstrand, Iris H. W., and Mary F. Ward. "Rancho Guajome: An Architectural Legacy Preserved." *Journal of San Diego History* 41, no. 4 (Fall 1995). http://www.sandiegohistory.org/journal/95fall/guajome.htm.

Engstrand, Iris Wilson, and Thomas L. Scharf. "Rancho Guajome: A California Legacy Preserved." *Journal of San Diego History* 20, no. 1 (Winter 1974). http://www.sandiegohistory.org/journal/74winter/legacy.htm.

Enoch, Jessica. "Resisting the Script of Indian Education: Zitkala-Ša and the Carlisle Indian School." *College English* 65, no. 2 (2002): 117–41.

"Erie Canal—175th Anniversary." The Erie Canal. http://www.eriecanal.org/UnionCollege/175th.html.

Ernest, John. "Economies of Identity: Harriet E. Wilson's Our Nig." *PMLA*, 109, no. 3 (1994): 424–38.

Estok, Simon C. "Bridging the Great Divide: Ecocritical Theory and the Great Unwashed." *ESC* 31, no. 4 (December 2005): 197–200.

Eves, Jamie H. "'Shrunk to a Comparative Rivulet': Deforestation, Stream Flow, and Rural Milling in 19th-Century Maine." *Technology and Culture* 33, no. 1 (January 1992): 38–65.

Ewell, Thomas S. "The Smoky City: Part III. Social and Business Life." *Colored American Magazine* 4, no. 2 (December 1901): 133–48.

"Explore the Roar: Adventure Guide." Maid of the Mist. http://www.maidofthe mist.com/en/.

"Fashion Department" [illustration]. *Godey's Ladies' Book*, January 1887, 114, 679. APS Online, 86.

Fassett, Thom White Wolf. "Afterword: Where Do We Go from Here?" In Weaver, *Defending Mother Earth*, 177–90.

Feathers and Facts: A Reply to the Feather-Trade, and Review of Facts with Reference to the Persecution of Birds for Their Plumage. London: Royal Society for the Protection of Birds, 1911.

Felski, Rita. "Nothing to Declare: Identity, Shame, and the Lower Middle Class." *PMLA* 115, no. 1 (2000): 33–45.

Fern, Fanny. "Soliloquy of a Housemaid." In *Fern Leaves from Fanny's Portfolio*, ser. 2. Auburn, N.Y.: Buffalo, Miller, Orton, & Mulligan, 1854. Available at Pat Pflieger, Voices from 19th-Century America. http://www.merrycoz.org/voices/fanny/FANNY03.HTM.

Fetterley, Judith. "Caroline Kirkland." In *The Heath Anthology of American Literature*, 5th ed., edited by Paul Lauter. Cengage Learning. http://college.cengage .com/english/lauter/heath/4e/students/author_pages/early_nineteenth/ kirkland_ca.html.

———. "Theorizing Regionalism: Celia Thaxter's *Among the Isles of Shoals*." In Inness and Royer, *Breaking Boundaries*, 38–53.

Fetterley, Judith, and Marjorie Pryse, eds. *American Women Regionalists, 1850–1910*. New York: Norton, 1995.

———. *Writing Out of Place: Regionalism, Women, and American Literary Culture*. Urbana: University of Illinois Press, 2003.

Fick, Gary W. *Food, Farming, and Faith*. Albany: State University of New York Press, 2008.

Fields, Annie Adams. *Authors and Friends*. Boston: Houghton Mifflin, 1897.

Finch, Annie. "The Sentimental Poetess in the World: Metaphor and Subjectivity in Lydia Sigourney's Nature Poetry." *Legacy: A Journal of American Women Writers* 5, no. 2 (1988): 3–18.

Finch, Robert, and John Elder. *The Norton Book of Nature Writing*. New York, Norton, 2003.

Fink, Steven. "Antebellum Lady Editors and the Language of Authority." In Harris, *Blue Pencils and Hidden Hands*, 205–21.

Finseth, Ian Frederick. "The Second Great Awakening and Rise of Evangelicalism." In "'Liquid Fire Within Me': Language, Self and Society in Transcendentalism and Early Evangelicalism, 1820–1860." M.A. thesis, University of Virginia, 1995. http://xroads.virginia.edu/~ma95/finseth/evangel.html.

———. *Shades of Green: Visions of Nature in the Literature of American Slavery, 1770–1860*. Athens: University of Georgia Press, 2009.

"First Cotton Mill in America." Beverly (Mass.) Community History. http://www.globalindex.com/nsbol/1municip/beverly/his_cott.htm.

Fischer, Joseph R. *A Well-Executed Failure: The Sullivan Campaign against the Iroquois, July–September 1779*. Columbia: University of South Carolina Press, 1997.

Fisher, Gayle V. *Pantaloons and Power: A Nineteenth-Century Dress Reform in the United States*. Kent, Ohio: Kent State University Press, 2001.

Fleischner, Jennifer. *Mastering Slavery: Memory, Family, and Identity in Women's Slave Narratives*. New York: New York University Press, 1996.

Fletcher, Matthew L. M. "Interview of Cherokee Woman Opposing W. Va. Coal Mining." 22 August 2010. *Turtle Talk* (blog). Indigenous Law and Policy Center at Michigan State University College of Law. http://turtletalk.wordpress.com/2010/08/22/interview-of-cherokee-woman-opposing-w-va-coal-mining/.

Floyd, Janet. "Mining the West: Bret Harte and Mary Hallock Foote." In Kilcup, *Soft Canons*, 202–18.

———. "A Sympathetic Misunderstanding? Mary Hallock Foote's Mining West." *Frontiers* 22, no. 3 (2001): 148–67.

Floyd, Janet, Alison Easton, R. J. Ellis, and Lindsey Traub, eds. *Becoming Visible: Women's Presence in Late Nineteenth-Century America*. Amsterdam: Rodopi, 2010.

Foner, Philip S., ed. *The Factory Girls: A Collection of Writings on Life and Struggles in the New England Factories of the 1840s*. Urbana: University of Illinois Press, 1977.

Foote, Mary Hallock. "Pictures of the Far West: Looking for Camp." *Century Magazine* 37, no. 1 (November 1888): 108–9. Reprinted as "Pictures of the Far West" in Kilcup, *Nineteenth-Century American Women Writers: An Anthology*, 359–61. Page references refer to the *Century Magazine* edition.

Foote, Stephanie. *Regional Fictions: Culture and Identity in Nineteenth-Century American Literature*. Madison: University of Wisconsin Press, 2001.

Foreman, P. Gabrielle. *Activist Sentiments: Reading Black Women in the Nineteenth Century*. Urbana: University of Illinois Press, 2009.

———. "Recovered Autobiographies and the Marketplace: *Our Nig*'s Gendered Genealogies and Harriet Wilson's Entrepreneurial Enterprise." In Boggis, Raimon, and White, *Harriet Wilson's New England*, 123–38.

———. "The Spoken and the Silenced in *Incidents in the Life of a Slave Girl* and *Our Nig*." *Callaloo* 13, no. 2 (Spring 1990): 313–24.

Foreman, P. Gabrielle, and Reginald Pitts, eds. *Our Nig; or, Sketches from the Life of a Free Black*. By Harriet E. Wilson. New York: Penguin, 2005.

Foss, Karen A., Sonja K. Foss, and Cindy L. Griffin. *Feminist Rhetorical Theories*. Thousand Oaks, Calif.: Sage, 1999.

Foster, Frances Smith. *'Til Death or Distance Do Us Part: Love and Marriage in African America*. New York: Oxford University Press, 2010.

———. *Written by Herself: Literary Production by African American Women, 1746–1892*. Bloomington: Indiana University Press, 1993.

Foster, Martha Harroun. "Lost Women of the Matriarchy: Iroquois Women in the Historical Literature." *American Indian Culture and Research Journal* 19, no. 3 (1995): 121–40.

Fox, Imogen. "Ethical Labels Take to the Catwalk at London Fashion Week." *Guardian*, 17 September 2010. http://www.guardian.co.uk/lifeandstyle/2010/sep/17/ethical-labels-london-fashion-week.

Franklin, Craig. "Media Myths about the Jena 6." *Christian Science Monitor*, 24 October 2007. www.csmonitor.com/2007/1024/p09s01-coop.html.

Freedman, Estelle B. *Their Sisters' Keepers: Women's Prison Reform in America, 1830–1930*. Ann Arbor: University of Michigan Press, 1981.

[Freeman], Mary E. Wilkins. "The Beggar King." *Wide Awake* 12, no. 3 (March 1881): 160–66. http://home.comcast.net/~wilkinsfreeman/Short/OnceUponATime.htm#v49.

———. "A Gala Dress." *Harper's Bazaar* 21, no. 28 (14 July 1888): 470–71.

———. "A Mistaken Charity." In *A Humble Romance and Other Stories*, 234–49. New York: Harper & Brothers, 1887.

———. "The Revolt of 'Mother.'" In *A New England Nun and Other Stories*, 448–68. New York: Harper & Brothers, 1891.

Freese, Peter. "American National Identity in a Globalized World as a Topic in the Advanced EFL-Classroom." *American Studies Journal* 51 (2008). http://asjournal.zusas.uni-halle.de/103.html.

Frey, Rebecca Joyce. "Focus on the United States." In *Genocide and International Justice*, 33–65. New York: Facts on File, 2009.

Frink, Helen. "Fairy Tales and *Our Nig*." In Boggis, Raimon, and White, *Harriet Wilson's New England*, 183–200.

Fuller, Margaret. Review of *Scenes in My Native Land*, by Lydia H. Sigourney (1845), *New-York Daily Tribune*, 28 January 1845, 1. Reprinted in *Margaret Fuller, Critic: Writings from the "New-York Tribune," 1844–1846*, edited by Judith Mattson Bean and Joel Myerson, 1:46–53. New York: Columbia University Press, 2000.

———. *Summer on the Lakes, in 1843*. Edited by Susan Belasco Smith. Urbana: University of Illinois Press, 1991.

Gaard, Greta. "Ecofeminism Revisited: Rejecting Essentialism and Re-placing Species in a Material Feminist Environmentalism." *Feminist Formations* 23, no. 2 (Summer 2011): 26–53.

———. "New Directions for Ecofeminism: Toward a More Feminist Eco-criticism." *ISLE: Interdisciplinary Studies in Literature and Environment* 17, no. 4 (2010): 643–65.

Gaard, Greta, and Patrick D. Murphy. "A Dialogue on the Role and Place of Literary Criticism within Ecofeminism." *ISLE: Interdisciplinary Studies in Literature and Environment* 3, no. 1 (Summer 1996): 1–6.

———, eds. *Ecofeminist Literary Criticism: Theory, Interpretation, Pedagogy.* Urbana: University of Illinois Press, 1998.

Gardner, Eric. "Of Bottles and Books: Reconsidering Harriet Wilson's *Our Nig.*" In Boggis, Raimon, and White, *Harriet Wilson's New England*, 3–26.

———. "'This Attempt of Their Sister': Harriet Wilson's *Our Nig* from Printer to Readers." *New England Quarterly* 66, no. 2 (June 1993): 226–46.

Garvey, Ellen Gruber. *The Adman in the Parlor: Magazines and the Gendering of Consumer Culture.* New York: Oxford University Press, 1996.

Gates, Barbara T. "A Root of Ecofeminism: *Ecoféminisme.*" *ISLE: Interdisciplinary Studies in Literature and Environment* 3, no. 1 (Summer 1996): 7–16.

Gates, Henry Louis, Jr. "Parallel Discursive Universes: Fictions of the Self in Harriet E. Wilson's *Our Nig.*" In *Figures in Black: Words, Signs, and the "Racial" Self*, 125–63. New York: Oxford University Press, 1989.

Gates, Henry Louis, Jr., and R. J. Ellis. Introduction to *Our Nig; or, Sketches from the Life of a Free Black*, edited by Henry Louis Gates and R. J. Ellis, xiii–lxviii. New York: Vintage, 2011.

Gatta, John. *Making Nature Sacred: Literature, Religion, and the Environment in America from the Puritans to the Present.* New York: Oxford University Press, 2004.

Gebhard, Caroline. "Caroline M. Kirkland's Satire of Frontier Democracy in *A New Home, Who'll Follow?*" In *Women, America, and Movement: Narratives of Relocation*, edited by Susan L. Roberson, 157–75. Columbia: University of Missouri Press, 1998.

Gedicks, Al. *The New Resource Wars: Native and Environmental Struggles against Multinational Corporations.* Montreal: Black Rose Books, 1994.

Gellately, Robert, and Ben Kiernan. "The Study of Mass Murder and Geno-cide." In *The Specter of Genocide: Mass Murder in Historical Perspective*, edited by Robert Gellately and Ben Kiernan, 3–26. New York: Cambridge University Press, 2003.

"General John Sullivan." http://www.sonofthesouth.net/revolutionary-war/general/john-sullivan.htm.

Georgi-Finlay, Brigitte. "The Frontiers of Native American Women's Writing: Sarah Winnemucca's *Life Among the Piutes.*" In Krupat, *New Voices*, 222–52.

Gianquitto, Tina. *"Good Observers of Nature": American Women and the Scientific Study of the Natural World, 1820–1885.* Athens: University of Georgia Press, 2007.

Gibson, William E., ed. *Eco-Justice — The Unfinished Journey.* Albany: State University of New York Press, 2004.

Gilligan, Carol. *In a Different Voice: Psychological Theory and Women's Develop-ment*. Cambridge, Mass.: Harvard University Press, 1982.

[Gilman], Charlotte Perkins Stetson. *Women and Economics: A Study of the Eco-nomic Relation between Women and Men as a Factor in Social Evolution*. Boston: Small, Maynard, 1898.

Ginsberg, Lesley. "Of Babies, Beasts, and Bondage: Slavery and the Question of Citizenship in the Antebellum American Children's Literature." In Levander and Singley, *The American Child*, 85–105.

Glasser, Leah Blatt. *In a Closet Hidden: The Life and Work of Mary E. Wilkins Freeman*. Amherst: University of Massachusetts Press, 1996.

———. "'The Sandpiper and I': Landscape and Identity on Celia Thaxter's Isles of Shoals." *American Literary Realism* 36, no. 1 (Fall 2003): 1–21.

Glave, Dianne D. *Rooted in the Earth: Reclaiming the African American Environ-mental Heritage*. Chicago: Lawrence Hill, 2010.

Glave, Dianne D., and Mark Stoll, eds. *"To Love the Wind and the Rain": African Americans and Environmental History*. Pittsburgh: University of Pittsburgh Press, 2005.

Glenn, Cheryl. *Rhetoric Retold: Regendering the Tradition from Antiquity through the Renaissance*. Carbondale: Southern Illinois University Press, 1997.

Glotfelty, Cheryll. "Introduction: Literary Studies in an Age of Environmental Crisis." In Glotfelty and Fromm, *The Ecocriticism Reader*, xv–xxxvii.

Glotfelty, Cheryll, and Harold Fromm, eds. *The Ecocriticism Reader: Landmarks in Literary Ecology*, Athens: University of Georgia Press, 1996.

"Gold." *Cherokee Phoenix* Index. Sequoyah Research Center, American Native Press Archives. http://www.anpa.ualr.edu/indexes/cherokee_phoenix_index /g.htm.

"Gold Addiction Fuels Brutal Congo War." Huffington Post. March 18, 2010. http://www.huffingtonpost.com/2009/11/25/60-minutes-gold-addiction _n_370905.html.

Goldman, Anne E. "'I think our romance is spoiled'; or, Crossing Genres." In *Over the Edge: Remapping the American West*, edited by Valerie J. Matsumoto and Blake Allmendinger, 65–84. Berkeley: University of California Press, 1999.

Goleman, Daniel. *Emotional Intelligence: Why It Can Matter More Than IQ*. New York: Bantam, 1995.

González, John Morán. *The Troubled Union: Expansionist Imperatives in Post-Reconstruction America*. Columbus: Ohio State University Press, 2010.

Good Fox, Julia. "Avatars to the Left of Me, Pandora to the Right: An Indig-enous Woman Considers James Cameron's *Avatar*." 21 January 2010. *Good Fox: Culture, Politics, Indian Country* (blog). http://juliagoodfox.com/avatar/.

Goodstein, Laurie. "Evangelical Leaders Join Global Warming Initiative." *New York Times*. 8 February 2006. http://www.nytimes.com/2006/02/08/ national/08warm.html.

Gore, Al. *An Inconvenient Truth*. Directed by Davis Guggenheim. Hollywood: Paramount, 2006. DVD.

Gottlieb, Roger S., ed. *The Oxford Handbook of Religion and Ecology*. New York: Oxford University Press, 2009.

Gray, Janet. *Race and Time: American Women's Poetics from Antislavery to Racial Modernity*. Iowa City: University of Iowa Press, 2004.

Greeley, Horace. *Glances at Europe: In a Series of Letters from Great Britain, France, Italy, Switzerland, &c. during the Summer of 1851*. New York: Dewitt & Davenport, 1851.

Green, Lisa E. "The Disorderly Girl in Harriet E. Wilson's *Our Nig*." In Boggis, Raimon, and White, *Harriet Wilson's New England*, 139–54.

Greene, Jerome A. *Lakota and Cheyenne: Indian Views of the Great Sioux War, 1876–1877*. Norman: University of Oklahoma Press, 1994.

Gregg, Richard B. *The Value of Voluntary Simplicity*. Wallingford, Pa.: Pendle Hill, 1936.

Griffin, Susan M. "Understudies: Miming the Human." *PMLA* 124, no. 2 (2009): 511–19.

GRIN (Germplasm Resources Information Network) database. USDA, ARS, National Genetic Resources Program. National Germplasm Resources Laboratory. http://www.ars-grin.gov/cgi-bin/npgs/html/taxon.pl?13323.

Grinde, Donald A. "Taking the Indian out of the Indian: U.S. Policies of Ethnocide through Education." *Wicazo Sa Review* 19, no. 2 (Fall 2004): 25–32.

Gross, Daniel. "The Killing of Juan Baten: Death in a New York Food Sweatshop." *Counterpunch*. 3 February 2011. http://www.counterpunch.org/gross02032011.html.

Gruesser, John. "Pauline Hopkins' *Of One Blood*: Creating an Afrocentric Fantasy for a Black Middle-Class Audience." In *Modes of the Fantastic: Selected Essays from the Twelfth International Conference on the Fantastic in the Arts*, edited by Robert A. Latham and Robert A. Collins, 74–83. Westport, Conn.: Greenwood, 1995.

Haas, Lisbeth. *Conquests and Historical Identities in California, 1769–1936*. Berkeley: University of California Press, 1995.

Hafen, P. Jane, ed. *Dreams and Thunder: Stories, Poems, and "The Sun Dance Opera."* By Zitkala-Ša. Lincoln: University of Nebraska Press, 2001.

——. "Pan-Indianism and Tribal Sovereignties in *House Made of Dawn* and *The Names*." *Western American Literature* 34, no. 1 (Spring 1999): 6–24.

——. "Zitkala-Ša: Sentimentality of Sovereignty." *Wicazo Sa Review* 12, no. 2 (Fall 1997): 31–41.

Hagenstein, W. D. Review of *This Well-Wooded Land: Americans and Their Forests from Colonial Times to the Present*, by Thomas R. Cox, Robert S. Maxwell, and Phillip Drennon Thomas. *Oregon Historical Quarterly* 87, no. 4 (Winter 1986): 416–19.

Hale, Sarah Josepha. "Mary's Lamb." *Juvenile Miscellany*, n.s., 5 (September–

October 1830): 64. https://tspace.library.utoronto.ca/html/1807/4350/poem911
.html.

Hallock, Thomas. *From the Fallen Tree: Frontier Narratives, Environmental Politics, and the Roots of a National Pastoral, 1749–1826*. Chapel Hill: University of North Carolina Press, 2003.

Hamilton, Gail. "My Garden." In *Gail Hamilton: Selected Writings*, edited by Susan Coultrap-McQuin, 31–54. New Brunswick, N.J.: Rutgers University Press, 1992.

Hannon, Charles. "Zitkala-Ša and the Commercial Magazine Apparatus." In *"The only efficient instrument": American Women Writers and the Periodical*, edited by Aleta Feinsod Cane and Susan Alves, 179–201. Iowa City: University of Iowa Press, 2001.

Hapke, Laura. *Labor's Text: The Worker in American Fiction*. New Brunswick, N.J.: Rutgers University Press, 2001.

Hardack, Richard. "Water Rites: Navigating Passage and Social Transformation in American Slave and Travel Narratives." In *Multiculturalism: Roots and Realities*, edited by C. James Trotman, 49–73. Bloomington: Indiana University Press, 2002.

Harkin, Michael E., and David Rich Lewis, eds. *Native Americans and the Environment: Perspectives on the Ecological Indian*. Lincoln: University of Nebraska Press, 2007.

Harris, Sharon M., ed. *Blue Pencils and Hidden Hands: Women Editing Periodicals, 1830–1910*. Boston: Northeastern University Press, 2004.

Hart, John S. "Caroline M. Kirkland." In *The Female Prose Writers of America*, edited by John S. Hart, 116–17. Philadelphia: E. H. Butler, 1851.

Harten, Chrissie. "The Language of Flowers." A Flower Arranger's Garden. http://www.thegardener.btinternet.co.uk/flowerlanguage.html.

Hatch, Nathan O. *The Democratization of American Christianity*. New Haven, Conn.: Yale University Press, 1991.

Haudenosaunee Environmental Task Force. "Haudenosaunee Environmental Restoration: An Indigenous Strategy for Human Sustainability." http://hetf
.org/index.php/about-us.

Haug, Joanne. "Wings, Breasts, and Birds." Victoriana: Resources for Victorian Living. http://www.victoriana.com/Victorian-Hats/birdhats.htm.

Hawthorne, Nathaniel. "Sketches from Memory." In *The Complete Works of Nathaniel Hawthorne*, 2:476–95. Boston: Houghton Mifflin, 1882.

Hayashi, Robert T. "Beyond Walden Pond: Asian American Literature and the Limits of Ecocriticism." In *Coming into Contact: Explorations in Ecocritical Theory and Practice*, edited by Annie Merrill Ingram, Daniel J. Philippon, and Adam W. Sweeting, 58–75. Athens: University of Georgia Press, 2007.

Hebblethwaite, Cordelia, and Anbarasan Ethirajan. "Sandblasted Jeans: Should We Give up Distressed Denim?" BBC News Magazine. 30 September 2011. http://www.bbc.co.uk/news/magazine-15017790.

Hedrick, Joan. *Harriet Beecher Stowe: A Life*. New York: Oxford University Press, 1994.

Heise, Ursula. "Ecocriticism and the Transnational Turn in American Studies." *American Literary History* 20, no. 1–2 (2008): 381–409.

———. *Sense of Place and Sense of Planet: The Environmental Imagination of the Global*. New York: Oxford University Press, 2008.

Helfand, Judith, and Daniel B. Gold. *Blue Vinyl*. New York: Blue Vinyl Toxic Comedy Pictures, 2002. DVD.

Herndl, Carl G., and Stuart C. Brown. *Green Culture: Environmental Rhetoric in Contemporary America*. Madison: University of Wisconsin Press, 1996.

Hershberger, Mary. "Mobilizing Women, Anticipating Abolition: The Struggle against Indian Removal in the 1830s." *Journal of American History* 86, no. 1 (June 1999): 15–40. www.historycooperative.org/journals/jah/86.1/hershberger.html.

Hertzberg, Hazel W. *The Search for an American Indian Identity: Modern Pan-Indian Movements*. Syracuse, N.Y.: Syracuse University Press, 1982.

Hindle, Brooke. "The Artisan during America's Wooden Age." In *Technology in America*, edited by Carroll W. Pursell Jr., 8–16. Cambridge, Mass.: MIT Press, 2000.

Hiskes, Jonathan. "An Interview with 'Green Nobel' Winner Maria Gunnoe." *Grist*. 25 April 2009. http://www.grist.org/article/2009-04-24-interview-with-maria-gunnoe.

"History of Geneseo." Geneseo, N.Y. http://www.geneseony.com/community/index.asp.

"The History of Old Town Hill." The Sons and Daughters of the First Settlers of Newbury, Massachusetts. http://www.sonsanddaughtersofnewbury.org/.

"History of the Sewing Machine." Museum of American Heritage. http://www.moah.org/exhibits/virtual/sewing.html.

Hobbs, John E. "The Beginnings of Lumbering as an Industry in the New World, and First Efforts at Forest Protection: A Historical Study." *Forestry Quarterly* 4, no. 1 (March 1906): 14–23.

Hobsbawm, Eric J. *The Age of Extremes: A History of the World, 1914–1991*. New York: Vintage, 1994.

Hollrah, Patrice. *"The Old Lady Trill, the Victory Yell": The Power of Women in Native American Literature*. New York: Routledge, 2003.

Holly, Carol. "Nineteenth-Century Autobiographies of Affiliation: The Case of Catharine Sedgwick and Lucy Larcom." In *American Autobiography: Retrospect and Prospect*, edited by John Paul Eakin, 216–34. Madison: University of Wisconsin Press, 1991.

Holly, Marilyn. "Handsome Lake's Teachings: The Shift from Female to Male Agriculture in Iroquois Culture; An Essay in Ethnophilosophy." *Agriculture and Human Values* 7, no. 3–4 (1990): 80–94.

Holmes, Oliver Wendell. *The Autocrat of the Breakfast-Table*. New York: Thomas Y. Crowell, 1900.

Hopkins, Pauline. *Of One Blood; or, The Hidden Self*. Edited by Deborah McDowell. New York: Washington Square Press, 2004. Serialized in *Colored American Magazine*, November 1902–November 1903. Reprinted in Hazel V. Carby, ed., *The Magazine Novels of Pauline Hopkins*. New York: Oxford University Press, 1988.

Howard, June. "What Is Sentimentality?" *American Literary History* 11, no. 1 (Winter 1999): 63–81.

Howells, W. D. "A Sennight of the Centennial." *Atlantic Monthly* 38 (July 1876): 92–107.

Hoyer, Mark T. "Cultivating Desire, Tending Piety: Botanical Discourse in Harriet Beecher Stowe's *The Minister's Wooing*." In Armbruster and Wallace, *Beyond Nature Writing*, 111–25.

Hunter, Louis C., and Beatrice Jones Hunter. *Steamboats on the Western Rivers: An Economic and Technological History*. Cambridge, Mass.: Harvard University Press, 1949. Reprint, Mineola, N.Y.: Dover, 1993. Page references are to the Dover edition.

Ildrewe, Miss, ed. *The Language of Flowers*. Boston: Lee and Shepard, 1874.

Inness, Sherrie A., and Diana Royer, eds. *Breaking Boundaries: New Perspectives on Women's Regional Writing*. Iowa City: University of Iowa Press, 1997.

International Joint Commission. "International Joint Commission Makes Recommendations on Government Cleanup Efforts in the St. Lawrence River Area of Concern." News release, 14 May 2003. http://www.ijc.org/rel/news/030514.html.

———. "St. Lawrence River Area of Concern: Status Assessment." May 2003. http://www.ijc.org/php/publications/html/stlawrence/index.html.

Isenberg, Andrew C. *The Destruction of the Bison: An Environmental History, 1750–1920*. New York: Cambridge University Press, 2001.

Jackson, Cassandra. "Beyond the Page: Rape and the Failure of Genre." In Boggis, Raimon, and White, *Harriet Wilson's New England*, 155–65.

Jackson, Robert. *Seeking the Region in American Literature and Culture: Modernity, Dissidence, Innovation*. Baton Rouge: Louisiana State University Press, 2005.

Jacobs, Harriet. *Incidents in the Life of a Slave Girl*. Edited by L. Maria Child. Boston: Published for the Author, 1861.

James, Jennifer C., and Cynthia Wu. "Editors' Introduction: Race, Ethnicity, Disability, and Literature; Intersections and Interventions." *MELUS* 31, no. 3 (Fall 2006): 3–13.

Japtok, Martin. "Pauline Hopkins's *Of One Blood*, Africa, and the 'Darwinist Trap.'" *African American Review* 36, no. 3 (Fall 2002): 403–15.

Jefferson, Thomas. "To Brother Handsome Lake." 3 November 1802. Papers of

Thomas Jefferson. Indian Addresses. The Avalon Project, Yale Law School. http://avalon.law.yale.edu/19th_century/jeffind2.asp.

Jeffrey, Julie Roy. *The Great Silent Army of Abolitionism: Ordinary Women in the Antislavery Movement*. Chapel Hill: University of North Carolina Press, 1998.

Jemison, Mary. *A Narrative of the Life of Mrs. Mary Jemison*. Edited by James E. Seaver. Syracuse, N.Y.: Syracuse University Press, 1990.

Jenkins, Brian. "Sustainable Fashion Design Courses: What's Available?" 14 March 2011. *Miss Malaprop* (blog). http://nola.humidbeings.com/posts/detail/207425/Sustainable-Fashion-Design-Courses-Whats-Available-Guest-Post-by-Brian-Jenkins.

Jewett, Sarah Orne. "An October Ride." In *Country By-Ways*, 92–115. Boston: Houghton Mifflin, 1881.

———. "River Driftwood." 1881. The Sarah Orne Jewett Text Project. http://www.public.coe.edu/~theller/soj/cbw/river.htm.

———. "A White Heron." In *Tales of New England*, 138–58. Boston: Houghton Mifflin, 1879, 1894.

———. "A Winter Drive." In *Country By-Ways*, 163–85. Boston: Houghton Mifflin, 1881.

J. F. O. "Another Tree Article." *Southern Literary Messenger* 4, no. 9 (September 1838): 563–65.

———. "The Last Tree Article." *Southern Literary Messenger* 4, no. 12 (December 1838): 796–800.

———. "Yet More about Trees." *Southern Literary Messenger* 4, no. 7 (July 1838): 474–75.

Johansen, Bruce E. "Susette LaFlesche (Inshta Theamba, Bright Eyes)." In *Native Americans Today: A Biographical Dictionary*, 155–57. Santa Barbara, Calif.: Greenwood, 2010.

Johnson, Carolyn Ross. *Cherokee Women in Crisis: Trail of Tears, Civil War, and Allotment, 1838–1907*. Tuscaloosa: University of Alabama Press, 2003.

Johnson, Cassandra Y., and Josh McDaniel. "Turpentine Negro." In Glave and Stoll, *"To Love the Wind and the Rain,"* 51–62.

Johnson, Nan. *Gender and Rhetorical Space in American Life, 1866–1910*. Carbondale: Southern Illinois University Press, 2002.

Johnson, Rochelle. *Passions for Nature: Nineteenth-Century America's Aesthetics of Alienation*. Athens: University of Georgia Press, 2009.

Jordan, Philip D. "The Source of Mrs. Sigourney's 'Indian Girl's Burial.'" *American Literature* 4, no. 3 (November 1932): 300–305.

Joseph, Philip. *American Literary Regionalism in a Global Age*. Baton Rouge: Louisiana State University Press, 2007.

Justice, Daniel Heath. "James Cameron's *Avatar*: Missed Opportunities." 20 January 2010. *First Peoples: New Directions in Indigenous Studies* (blog). http://www.firstpeoplesnewdirections.org/blog/?p=169/.

————. "Katteuha (Cherokee)." In *The Heath Anthology of American Literature*, 6th ed., vol. A, edited by Paul Lauter, et al., 827. Boston: Wadsworth, 2009.

Kaplan, Cora. "Introduction: Millennial Class." *PMLA* 115, no. 1 (January 2000): 9–19.

Katanski, Amelia V. *Learning to Write "Indian": The Boarding-School Experience and American Indian Literature*. Norman: University of Oklahoma Press, 2005.

"Kate Middleton's Princess Style Diary." HarpersBazaar.com. http://www .harpersbazaar.com/fashion/fashion-articles/kate-middleton-feathered -hat#fbIndex40.

Kavilanz, Parija. "Kate Middleton 'Fascinator' Hats a Hit in the U.S." 29 April 2011. CNN Money. http://money.cnn.com/2011/04/25/smallbusiness/kate _middleton_fascinator/index.htm.

Kearns, Laurel. "Afterword: Teaching Indoors, but Not Business as Usual." In Bauman, Bohannon, and O'Brien, *Grounding Religion*, 222–27.

————. "Noah's Ark Goes to Washington: A Profile Of Evangelical Environ-mentalism." *Social Compass* 44, no. 3 (1997): 349–66.

Kelsey, Penelope M. "Natives, Nation, Narration: Reading Roanoke in the American Renaissance." *ESQ: A Journal of the American Renaissance* 49, no. 1–3 (2003): 149–60.

————. *Tribal Theory in Native American Literature: Dakota and Haudenosaunee Writing and Indigenous Worldviews*. Lincoln: University of Nebraska Press, 2008.

Kerber, Linda. "The Republican Mother: Women and the Enlightenment—An American Perspective." *American Quarterly* 28, no. 2 (Summer 1976): 187–205.

Kessler-Harris, Alice. "Industrial Wage Earners and the Domestic Ideology." In *Out to Work: A History of Wage-Earning Women in the United States*, 45–73. New York: Oxford University Press, 1982.

Kete, Mary Louise. "Slavery's Shadows: Narrative Chiaroscuro and *Our Nig*." In Boggis, Raimon, and White, *Harriet Wilson's New England*, 109–22.

Kidwell, Clara Sue. *The Choctaws in Oklahoma: From Tribe to Nation, 1855–1970*. Norman: University of Oklahoma Press, 2007.

Kilcup, Karen L. "'The art spirit remains in me to this day': Contexts, Con-temporaries, and Narcissa Owen's Political Aesthetics." In Owen, *A Cherokee Woman's America*, 1–43.

————. "Celia Laighton Thaxter." In Denise D. Knight and Nelson, *Nineteenth-Century American Women Writers*, 426–32.

————. "Essays of Invention: Transformations of Advice in Nineteenth-Century American Women's Writing." In Kilcup, *Nineteenth-Century American Women Writers: A Critical Reader*, 184–205.

————. "'I Like These Plants That You Call Weeds': Historicizing American Women's Nature Writing." *Nineteenth-Century Literature* 58, no. 1 (2003): 42–74.

———. "Introduction: A Working-Class Woman's View of Europe." In Berbineau, *From Beacon Hill to the Crystal Palace*, 1–49.

———. "Lucy Larcom." In *American Writers*, edited by Jay Parini, 137–57. New York: Scribner's, 2003.

———. "Lydia Sigourney, 1791–1865." In Denise D. Knight and Nelson, *Nineteenth-Century American Women Writers*, 361–67.

———, ed., *Native American Women's Writing c. 1800–1924: An Anthology*. Malden, Mass.: Blackwell, 2000.

———, ed. *Nineteenth-Century American Women Writers: A Critical Reader*. Malden, Mass.: Blackwell, 1998.

———, ed. *Nineteenth-Century American Women Writers: An Anthology*. Cambridge: Blackwell, 1997.

———. *Robert Frost and Feminine Literary Tradition*. Ann Arbor: University of Michigan Press, 1997.

———, ed. *Soft Canons: American Women Writers and Masculine Tradition*. Iowa City: University of Iowa Press, 1999.

———. "'Something of a Sentimental Sweet Singer': Robert Frost, Lucy Larcom, and 'Swinging Birches.'" In *Roads Not Taken: Rereading Robert Frost*, edited by Earl J. Wilcox and Jonathan Barron, 11–31. Columbia: University of Missouri Press, 2000.

———. "'The True American Woman': Narcissa Owen's Embodied National Narrative." In Floyd et al., *Becoming Visible*, 239–59.

———. *See also* Oakes, Karen.

Kilcup, Karen L., and Thomas S. Edwards. "Confronting Time and Change: Jewett, Her Contemporaries, and Her Critics." In Kilcup and Edwards, *Jewett and Her Contemporaries*, 1–30.

———, eds. *Jewett and Her Contemporaries: Reshaping the Canon*. Gainesville: University Press of Florida, 1999.

Kilcup, Karen L., and Phyllis Rogers. "'Brave with Flowers': Nature, Inner Vision and Freeman's Allegories of the Native American." Paper presented at the Northeast Modern Language Association Convention, Hartford, Conn., 6 April 1991.

Kilcup, Karen L., and Angela Sorby. "'Pretty New Moons': Contact Zones in Nineteenth-Century American Children's Poetry." In *Over the River and through the Woods: An Anthology of Nineteenth-Century American Children's Poetry*, edited by Karen L. Kilcup and Angela Sorby. Baltimore: Johns Hopkins University Press, forthcoming.

Killingsworth, M. Jimmie, and Jacqueline S. Palmer. *Ecospeak: Rhetoric and Environmental Politics in America*. Carbondale: Southern Illinois University Press, 1992.

———. "Millennial Ecology: The Apocalyptic Narrative from *Silent Spring* to *Global Warming*." In Herndl and Brown, *Green Culture*. 21–45.

Kincaid, Jamaica. *My Garden (Book):*. New York: Farrar, Straus and Giroux, 1999.

King, Debra Walker. "The Demystification of Sentiment." In *Recovered Writers/Recovered Texts: Race, Class, and Gender in Black Women's Literature*, edited by Dolan Hubbard, 31–45. Knoxville: University of Tennessee Press 1997.

King James Bible. http://kingjbible.com.

"King Snakes and Rattle Snakes." *Scientific American* 10, no. 2 (23 September 1854): 10.

Kingsolver, Barbara. *Animal, Vegetable, Miracle: A Year of Food Life*. New York: HarperCollins, 2007.

Kirby, Jack Temple. *Mockingbird Song: Ecological Landscapes of the South*. University of North Carolina Press, 2006.

———. *Poquosin: A Study of Rural Landscape and Society*. University of North Carolina Press, 1995.

Kirkland, Caroline. *Forest Life*. 2 vols. New York: C. S. Francis, 1842.

———. [Mrs. C. M. Kirkland]. *The Helping Hand: Comprising an Account of the Home for Discharged Female Convicts and an Appeal on Behalf of That Institution*. New York: Scribner, 1853.

———. [Pseud. Mrs. Mary Clavers]. *A New Home—Who'll Follow?; or, Glimpses of Western Life*. New York: C. Francis, 1839.

Kirkpatrick, Martha. "'For God So Loved the World': An Incarnational Ecology." *Anglican Theological Review* 91, no. 2 (2009): 191–212.

Klages, Mary. *Woeful Afflictions: Disability and Sentimentality in Victorian America*. Philadelphia: University of Pennsylvania Press, 1999.

Klare, Michael T. *Resource Wars: The New Landscape of Global Conflict*. New York: Henry Holt-Metropolitan, 2004.

Knack, Martha C. "The Dynamics of Southern Paiute Women's Roles." In *Women and Power in Native North America*, edited by Laura F. Klein and Lillian A. Ackerman, 146–58. Norman: University of Oklahoma Press, 2000.

Knack, Martha C., and Omer C. Stewart. *As Long as the River Shall Run: An Ethnohistory of Pyramid Lake Indian Reservation*. Berkeley: University of California Press, 1984.

Knight, Alisha R. "Furnace Blasts for the Tuskegee Wizard: Revisiting Pauline Elizabeth Hopkins, Booker T. Washington and the *Colored American Magazine*." *American Periodicals* 17, no. 1 (2007): 41–64.

Knight, Denise D., and Emmanuel S. Nelson, eds. *Nineteenth-Century American Women Writers: A Bio-Bibliographical Critical Sourcebook*. Westport, Conn.: Greenwood, 1997.

Kollin, Susan. "'The First White Woman in the Last Frontier': Writing Race, Gender, and Nature in Alaska Travel Narratives." *Frontiers: A Journal of Women's Studies* 18, no. 2 (1997): 105–24.

———. "The Wild, Wild North: Nature Writing, Nationalist Ecologies, and Alaska." *American Literary History* 12, nos. 1–2 (2000): 44.

Kolodny, Annette. "Inventing a Feminist Discourse: Rhetoric and Resistance in

Margaret Fuller's *Woman in the Nineteenth Century*." *New Literary History* 25, no. 2 (Spring 1994): 355–82.

———. *The Land Before Her: Fantasy and Experience of the American Frontiers, 1630–1860*. Chapel Hill: University of North Carolina Press, 1984.

———. *The Lay of the Land: Metaphor as Experience and History in American Life and Letters*. Chapel Hill: University of North Carolina Press, 1984.

Koppelman, Susan. "About 'Two Friends' and Mary Eleanor Wilkins Freeman." *American Literary Realism* 21, no. 1 (Fall 1988): 43–57.

Kort, Amy. "Lucy Larcom's Double-Exposure: Strategic Obscurity in 'A New England Girlhood.'" *American Literary Realism* 31, no. 1 (Fall 1998): 25–40.

Kosmider, Alexia. "Strike a Euroamerican Pose: Ora Eddleman Reed's 'Types of Indian Girls.'" *American Transcendental Quarterly* 12, no. 2 (June 1998): 109–31.

Kretch, Shepard, III. *The Ecological Indian: Myth and History*. New York: Norton, 2000.

Kriebl, Karen J. "From Bloomers to Flappers: The American Women's Dress Reform Movement, 1840–1920." PhD diss., Ohio State University, 1998. Dissertation Abstracts International, Section A: The Humanities and Social Sciences, February 1999 [59 (8): 3171].

Krugman, Paul. "For Richer." *New York Times*, 20 October 2002. http://www.nytimes.com/2002/10/20/magazine/20INEQUALITY.html; http://www.pkarchive.org/economy/ForRicher.html.

Krupat, Arnold. "The Indian Autobiography: Origins, Type, and Functions." *American Literature* 53, no. 1 (1981): 22–42.

———. Introduction to *Ethnocriticism, Ethnography, History, Literature*, 3–45. Berkeley: University of California Press, 1992.

———. Introduction to *Native American Autobiography: An Anthology*, edited by Arnold Krupat, 3–17. Madison: University of Wisconsin Press, 1994.

———, ed. *New Voices in Native American Literary Criticism*. Washington, D.C.: Smithsonian Institution Press, 1993.

Lacques-Waggoner, Flavel Henri. "A Vow." *Colored American Magazine* 4, no. 2 (December 1901): 112.

Ladies' Home Journal. www.lhj.com.

LaDuke, Winona. *All Our Relations: Native Struggles for Land and Life*. Cambridge, Mass.: South End Press, 1999.

Laighton, Oscar. *Ninety Years at the Isles of Shoals*. Boston: Star Island Corporation, 1971.

"The Landing at Parker River." The U. S. GenWeb Project. http://newbury.essexcountyma.net/landing.htm.

Lang, Amy Schrager. *The Syntax of Class: Writing Inequality in Nineteenth-Century America*. Princeton, N.J.: Princeton University Press, 2003.

———. "The Syntax of Class in Elizabeth Stuart Phelps's *The Silent Partner*." In *Rethinking Class: Literary Studies and Social Formations*, ed. Wai-chee Dimock and Michael T. Gilmore, 267–85. New York: Columbia University Press, 1994.

The Language of Flowers. 2nd ed. Philadelphia: Carey, Lea and Blanchard, 1835.

Larcom, Lucy. [Miss Lucy Larcom]. "III. American Factory Life—Past, Present and Future." *Journal of Social Science* 16 (1882): 141–46.

———. "Among Lowell Mill Girls." *Atlantic Monthly* 48 (November 1881): 593–612.

———. "Autobiography,—No. II. Recollections of L. L." *Lowell Offering* 5 (1845): 211–23.

———. *An Idyl of Work.* Boston: James R. Osgood, 1875.

———. *A New England Girlhood: Outlined from Memory.* Boston: Houghton Mifflin, 1889.

———. *The Poetical Works of Lucy Larcom.* Household ed. Boston: Houghton Mifflin, 1884.

Laufer, Geraldine Adamich. *Tussie Mussies: The Language of Flowers.* New York: Workman, 1993.

Lauter, Paul. "Teaching Lydia Sigourney." In Bennett, Kilcup, and Schweighauser, *Teaching Nineteenth-Century American Poetry*, 109–24.

———. "Working-Class Women's Literature: An Introduction to Study." In *Politics of Education: Essays from "Radical Teacher"*, edited by Susan Gushee O'Malley, Robert C. Rosen, and Leonard Vogt, 110–39. Albany: State University of New York Press, 1990.

Le Billon, Philippe. "The Geopolitical Economy of 'Resource Wars.'" In *The Geopolitics of Resource Wars*, edited by Philippe Le Billon, 1–28. New York: Frank Cass, 2005.

Leighton, Ann. *American Gardens of the Nineteenth Century: "For Comfort and Affluence".* Amherst: University of Massachusetts Press, 1987.

Levander, Caroline F. *Cradle of Liberty: Race, the Child, and National Belonging from Thomas Jefferson to W. E. B. Du Bois.* Durham, N.C.: Duke University Press, 2006.

Levander, Caroline F., and Carol J. Singley, eds. *The American Child: A Cultural Studies Reader.* New Brunswick, N.J.: Rutgers University Press, 2003.

Leveen, Lois. "Dwelling in the House of Oppression: The Spatial, Racial, and Textual Dynamics of Harriet Wilson's *Our Nig.*" *African American Review* 35, no. 4 (2001): 561–80.

Levi Strauss & Co. "Chemicals." http://www.levistrauss.com/sustainability/planet/chemicals.

———. "Levi Strauss & Co. Life Cycle Approach to Examine the Environmental Performance of Its Products." http://www.levistrauss.com/sites/levistrauss.com/files/librarydocument/2012/6/e-valuate-web-content-2012-05-23.pdf.

———. "Life Cycle of a Jean." http://www.levistrauss.com/sustainability/product/life-cycle-jean.

Lewis, Jessica. "'Poetry Experienced': Lucy Larcom's Poetic Dwelling in *A New England Girlhood*." *Legacy* 18, no. 2 (2001): 182–92.

Lewis, Nathaniel. *Unsettling the Literary West: Authenticity and Authorship*. Lincoln: University of Nebraska Press, 2008.

Liebhold, Peter, and Harry Rubenstein. "Between a Rock and a Hard Place: A History of American Sweatshops, 1820–Present." *History Matters: The U.S. Survey Course on the Web*. http://historymatters.gmu.edu/d/145.

Limerick, Patricia Nelson. "Region and Reason." In *All Over the Map: Rethinking American Regions*, edited by Edward L. Ayers, 83–104. Baltimore: Johns Hopkins University Press, 1996.

Littenberg, Marcia. "From Transcendentalism to Ecofeminism: Celia Thaxter and Sarah Orne Jewett's Island Views Revisited." In Kilcup and Edwards, *Jewett and Her Contemporaries*, 137–52.

Lockwood, Allison. *Passionate Pilgrims: The American Traveler in Great Britain, 1800–1914*. New York: Cornwall, 1981.

Lodge, David M., and Christopher Hamlin, eds. *Religion and the New Ecology: Environmental Responsibility in a World in Flux*. Notre Dame, Ind.: University of Notre Dame Press, 2006.

Loeffelholz, Mary. "'A Strange Medley-Book': Lucy Larcom's *An Idyl of Work*." *New England Quarterly* 80, no. 1 (March 2007): 5–34.

"Long Branch, NJ, Brief History" Long Branch, New Jersey, Website of New Jersey Shore. http://www.long-branch.net/.

Lott, Eric. *Love and Theft: Blackface Minstrelsy and the American Working Class*. New York: Oxford University Press, 1995.

Love, Glen A. "Et in Arcadia Ego: Pastoral Theory Meets Ecocriticism." *Western American Literature* 27, no. 3 (1992): 195–207.

Lovell, Thomas B. "By Dint of Labor and Economy: Harriet Jacobs, Harriet Wilson, and the Salutary View of Wage Labor." *Arizona Quarterly* 52, no. 3 (1996): 1–32.

Ludeke, John. "The No Fence Law of 1874: Victory for San Joaquin Valley." *California History* 59, no. 2 (Summer 1980): 98–115.

Lukens, Margaret A. "The American Story of Zitkala-Ša." In *In Her Own Voice: Nineteenth-Century American Women Essayists*, edited by Sherry Lee Linkon, 141–55. New York: Garland, 1997.

"Lumber Industry." In Gale Group, *Encyclopedia of American History*, 2006. http://www.answers.com/topic/lumber-industry.

Lunsford, Andrea A. "On Reclaiming Rhetorica." In *Reclaiming Rhetorica: Women in the Rhetorical Tradition*, edited by Andrea A. Lunsford, 3–8. Pittsburgh: University of Pittsburgh Press, 1995.

Lupfer, Eric. "Before Nature Writing: Houghton, Mifflin and Company and the Invention of the Outdoor Book, 1880–1900." *Book History* 4 (2001): 177–204.

Luscher, Robert M. "Seeing the Forest for the Trees: The 'Intimate Connection' of Mary Wilkins Freeman's Six Trees." *American Transcendental Quarterly* 3, no. 4 (1989): 363–81.

Lutts, Ralph H. *The Nature Fakers: Wildlife, Science, and Sentiment.* Charlottesville: University Press of Virginia, 1990.

Lutz, Tom. *Cosmopolitan Vistas: American Regionalism and Literary Value.* Ithaca, N.Y.: Cornell University Press, 2004.

Lyon, Thomas J. "A Taxonomy of Nature Writing." In Glotfelty and Fromm, *The Ecocriticism Reader,* 276–81.

Mabbott, Thomas O., and Philip D. Jordan. "The Prairie Chicken: Notes on Lincoln and Mrs. Kirkland." *Journal of the Illinois State Historical Society* 25, no. 3 (October 1932): 154–66.

Mack-Canty, Colleen. "Third-Wave Feminism and the Need to Reweave the Nature/Culture Duality." *NWSA Journal* 16, no. 3 (Fall 2004): 154–79.

MacLeod, Anne Scott. *American Childhood: Essays on Children's Literature of the Nineteenth and Twentieth Centuries.* Athens: University of Georgia Press, 1994.

Maddox, Lucy. *Removals: Nineteenth-Century American Literature and the Politics of Indian Affairs.* New York: Oxford University Press, 1991.

Magoc, Chris J. *Environmental Issues in American History: A Reference Guide with Primary Documents.* Westport, Conn.: Greenwood, 2006.

"Maids and Mistresses." *Scribner's Monthly Magazine* 6 (September 1873): 628.

Maloof, Joan. *Teaching the Trees: Lessons from the Forest.* Athens: University of Georgia Press, 2007.

Mandel, Norma H. *Beyond the Garden Gate: The Life of Celia Laighton Thaxter.* University Press of New England, 2004.

Manes, Christopher. "Nature and Silence." In Glotfelty and Fromm, *The Ecocriticism Reader,* 15–29.

Mankiller, Wilma Pearl. *Mankiller: A Chief and Her People.* New York: St. Martin's, 1993.

Mann, Susan Garland. "Gardening as 'Women's Culture' in Mary E. Wilkins Freeman's Short Fiction." *New England Quarterly* 71, no. 1 (March 1998): 33–53.

Marchalonis, Shirley. "Another Mary Wilkins Freeman: *Understudies* and *Six Trees.*" *American Transcendental Quarterly* 9, no. 2 (June 1995): 89–101.

———. "A Model for Mentors?: Lucy Larcom and John Greenleaf Whittier." In *Patrons and Protégées: Gender, Friendship, and Writing in Nineteenth-Century America,* edited by Shirley Marchalonis, 94–121. New Brunswick, N.J.: Rutgers University Press, 1988.

———. *The Worlds of Lucy Larcom, 1824–1893.* Athens: University of Georgia Press, 1989.

"Maria Gunnoe." The Goldman Environmental Prize. http://www.goldman prize.org/2009/northamerica.

Maroukis, Thomas C. *The Peyote Road: Religious Freedom and the Native American Church.* Norman: University of Oklahoma Press, 2010.

Marsh, George Perkins. *Address Delivered before the Agricultural Society of Rutland County, Sept. 30, 1847.* Rutland, Vt.: Herald Office, 1847.

———. *Man and Nature; or, Physical Geography as Modified by Human Action.* New York: C. Scribner, 1864.

Marx, Leo. *The Machine in the Garden: Technology and the Pastoral Ideal in America.* London: Oxford University Press, 1964.

Marzio, Peter C. "Carpentry in the Southern Colonies during the Eighteenth Century with Emphasis on Maryland and Virginia." *Winterthur Portfolio* 7 (1972): 229–50.

Mason, Jennifer. *Civilized Creatures: Urban Animals, Sentimental Culture, and American Literature, 1850–1900.* Baltimore: Johns Hopkins University Press, 2005.

Mason, Kathy S. "Out of Fashion: Harriet Hemenway and the Audubon Society, 1896–1905." *Historian* 65, no. 1 (December 2002): 1–14.

Matheson, Christie. *Green Chic: Saving the Earth in Style.* Napierville, Ill.: Sourcebooks, 2008.

Matsuoka, Martha, comp. "Building Healthy Communities from the Ground Up: Environmental Justice in California." September 2003. http://www.cbecal .org/wp-content/uploads/2012/05/Building-Healthy-Communities-from-the -Ground-Up.pdf.

Matthews, Glenna. *"Just a Housewife": The Rise and Fall of Domesticity in America.* New York: Oxford University Press, 1987.

Mattingly, Carol. *Appropriate[ing] Dress: Women's Rhetorical Style in Nineteenth-Century America.* Carbondale: Southern Illinois University Press, 2002.

———. *Well-Tempered Women: Nineteenth-Century Temperance Rhetoric.* Carbondale: Southern Illinois University Press, 1998.

May, Larry. *Genocide: A Normative Account.* New York: Cambridge University Press, 2010.

May, Stephen. "'A beautiful and thrilling specimen': George Caitlin, the Death of Wilderness, and the Birth of the National Subject." In Branch, Johnson, Patterson, and Slovic, *Reading the Earth,* 129–43.

———. "An Island Garden, a Poet's Passion, a Painter's Muse." *Smithsonian* 21, no. 9 (December 1990): 69–79, 150.

Mazel, David. *American Literary Environmentalism.* Athens: University of Georgia Press, 2000.

McCarthy, Molly. "A Pocketful of Days: Pocket Diaries and Daily Record-Keeping among Nineteenth-Century New England Women." *New England Quarterly* 73, no. 2 (2000): 274–96.

McCaskill, Barbara. "'To Labor . . . and Fight on the Side of God': Spirit, Class, and Nineteenth-Century African American Women's Literature." In Kilcup, *Nineteenth-Century American Women Writers: A Critical Reader,* 164–83.

———. "'Yours Very Truly': Ellen Craft—The Fugitive as Text and Artifact." *African American Review* 28, no. 4 (1994): 509–29.

McClure, Andrew. "Sarah Winnemucca: [Post]Indian Princess and the Voice of the Paiutes." *MELUS* 24, no. 2 (Summer 1999): 29–51.

McDowell, Michael J. "The Bakhtinian Road to Ecological Insight." In Glotfelty and Fromm, *The Ecocriticism Reader*, 371–91.

McGuffey, William Holmes. *Old Favorites from the McGuffey Readers, 1836–1936.* N.p.: American Book Co., 1936.

McKegney, Sam. "Strategies of Ethical Engagement: An Open Letter Concerning Non-Native Scholars of Native Literatures." *Studies in American Indian Literatures* 20, no. 4 (Winter 2008): 56–67.

McKibben, Bill, ed. *American Earth: Environmental Writing since Thoreau.* New York: Library of America, 2008.

———. *Deep Economy: The Wealth of Communities and the Durable Future.* New York: Times/Henry Holt Books, 2007.

McMurry, Andrew. "'In Their Own Language': Sarah Orne Jewett and the Question of Non-human Speaking Subjects." *ISLE: Interdisciplinary Studies in Literature and Environment* 6, no. 1 (Winter 1999): 51–63.

"Meanings of Flowers." Flowerstoturkey.com. http://www.flowerstoturkey.com/about-flowers/flower-meanings.asp.

Meeker, Joseph W. "The Comic Mode." In Glotfelty and Fromm, *The Ecocriticism Reader*, 155–69.

Meisenheimer, D. K., Jr. "Regionalist Bodies/Embodied Regions: Sarah Orne Jewett and Zitkala-Ša." In Inness and Royer, *Breaking Boundaries*, 109–23.

"Memorial in Behalf of the Cherokees." Edited by Samuel Hazard. *The Register of Pennsylvania* 5, no. 4 (23 January 1830): 60.

Merchant, Carolyn. *American Environmental History.* New York: Columbia University Press, 2007.

———. *The Columbia Guide to American Environmental History.* New York: Columbia University Press, 2002.

———. *The Death of Nature: Women, Ecology, and the Scientific Revolution.* New York: HarperOne, 1990.

———. *Earthcare: Women and the Environment.* New York: Routledge, 1996.

———. "George Bird Grinnell's Audubon Society: Bridging the Gender Divide." *Environmental History* 15 (January 2010): 3–30.

———. *Radical Ecology: The Search for a Livable World.* New York: Routledge, 1992.

———. "Shades of Darkness: Race and Environmental History." *Environmental History* 8, no. 3 (July 2003): 380–94.

Merish, Lori. *Sentimental Materialism: Gender, Commodity Culture, and Nineteenth-Century American Literature.* Durham, N.C.: Duke University Press, 2000.

"The Merrimack River." Merrimack River Watershed Council. http://www.merrimack.org/watershed-resources/the-merrimack-river/.

Mielke, Laura. *Moving Encounters: Sympathy and the Indian Question in Antebellum Literature.* Amherst: University of Massachusetts Press, 2008.

Mihesuah, Devon A. *Cultivating the Rose Buds: The Education of Women at the Cherokee Female Seminary, 1851–1909.* University of Illinois Press, 1993.

Miles, Tiya. "'Circular Reasoning': Recentering Cherokee Women in the Anti-removal Campaigns." *American Quarterly* 61, no. 2 (2009): 221–43.

Milne, Anne. "Gender, Class, and the Beehive: Mary Collier's 'The Woman's Labour' (1739) as Nature Poem." *ISLE: Interdisciplinary Studies in Literature and Environment* 8, no. 2 (2001): 109–29.

———. *Lactilla Tends Her Fav'rite Cow: Ecocritical Readings of Animals and Women in Eighteenth-Century British Labouring-Class Women's Poetry.* Lewisburg, Pa.: Bucknell University Press, 2008.

Montes, Amelia María de la Luz. "María Amparo Ruiz de Burton Negotiates American Literary Politics and Culture." In *Challenging Boundaries: Gender and Periodization,* edited by Joyce W. Warren and Margaret Dickie, 202–25. Athens: University of Georgia Press, 2000.

Montrie, Chad. "'I Think Less of the Factory than of My Native Dell': Labor, Nature, and the Lowell 'Mill Girls.'" *Environmental History* 9, no. 2 (2004): 275–95.

Mooney, James, comp. *Myths of the Cherokee and Sacred Formulas of the Cherokees.* Washington, D.C.: Government Printing Office, 1900. Reprinted from Bureau of American Ethnology, *Nineteenth Annual Report, 1897–98.* Washington, D.C., 1900. http://www.sacred-texts.com/nam/cher/motc/.

Moore, Niamh. "Imagining Feminist Futures: The Third Wave, Postfeminism, and Eco/feminism." In *Third Wave Feminism: A Critical Exploration,* 2nd ed., edited by Stacy Gillis, Gillian Howie, and Rebecca Munford, 125–41. New York: Palgrave Macmillan, 2007.

Morgan, Lewis Henry. *League of the Ho-dé-no sau-nee or Iroquois.* Vol. 1. New York: Dodd, Mead, 1851.

Morse, Jedidiah, and Elijah Parish. *A Compendious History of New England: Designed for Schools and Private Families.* Newburyport, Mass.: Thomas and Whipple, 1809.

Mott, Frank Luther. *A History of American Magazines.* 5 vols. Cambridge, Mass.: Belknap Press of Harvard University Press, 1957.

Mott, Marshall. *The Act of May 27, 1908 Placing in the Probate Courts of Oklahoma Indian Jurisdiction: A National Blunder.* Washington, D.C., 1925.

Mower, Sarah. "Eco-Minded: Livia Firth Rallies Young London to the Green Carpet Challenge." *Vogue Daily.* 14 September 2012. http://www.vogue.com/vogue-daily/article/eco-minded-livia-firth-rallies-young-london-to-the-green-carpet-challenge/#1.

Moyers on America. "Is God Green?" http://www.pbs.org/moyers/moyerson america/green/.

Muir, John. "The American Forests." *Atlantic Monthly* 80, no. 478 (August 1897): 145–57. http://www.theatlantic.com/magazine/archive/1897/08/the-american-forests/5017/.

Mulvey, Christopher. *Anglo-American Landscapes: A Study of Nineteenth-Century Anglo-American Travel Literature.* Cambridge: Cambridge University Press, 1983.

Murphy, Patrick D. *Ecocritical Explorations in Literary and Cultural Studies: Fences, Boundaries, and Fields.* Lanham, Md.: Lexington, 2010.

———. *Farther Afield in the Study of Nature-Oriented Literature.* Charlottesville: University Press of Virginia, 2000.

———. *Literature, Nature, and Other: Ecofeminist Critiques.* Albany: State University of New York Press, 1995.

Murray, David. *Forked Tongues: Speech, Writing, and Representation in Native American Texts.* Bloomington: Indiana University Press, 1991.

Myers, Jeffrey. *Converging Stories: Race, Ecology, and Environmental Justice in American Literature.* Athens: University of Georgia Press, 2005.

Namias, June. "Editor's Introduction." In *A Narrative of the Life of Mrs. Mary Jemison by James E. Seaver,* edited by June Namias, 3–45. Norman: University of Oklahoma Press, 1992.

———. *White Captives, Gender and Ethnicity on Successive American Frontiers.* Chapel Hill: University of North Carolina Press, 1993.

Nash, James A. "The Bible vs. Biodiversity: The Case against Moral Argument from Scripture." *Journal for the Study Of Religion, Nature & Culture* 3, no. 2 (2009): 213–37.

Nash, Roderick. *Wilderness and the American Mind.* 4th ed. New Haven, Conn.: Yale University Press, 2001.

Nast, Thomas. "The American River Ganges: The Priests and the Children." *Harper's Weekly,* 30 September 1871, 916. Reprinted in Morton Keller, "The World of Thomas Nast," http://cartoons.osu.edu/nast/keller_web.htm, fig. 16.

National Association of Sustainable Fashion Designers. http://www.sustainable designers.org/.

Nelson, Dana D. *The Word in Black and White: Reading "Race" in American Literature, 1638–1867.* New York: Oxford University Press, 1993.

Nerad, Julie Cary. " 'So strangely interwoven': The Property Inheritance, Race, and Sexual Morality in Pauline E. Hopkins's *Contending Forces.*" *African American Review* 35, no. 3 (2001): 357–73.

Neville, Robert Cummings. "Response to Thomas Berry's *The Great Work.*" *Worldviews: Environment, Culture, Religion* 5, no. 2–3 (2001): 136–41.

"Newbury—A Brief History." The U.S. GenWeb Project. http://newbury .essexcountyma.net/history.htm.

New Hampshire Fish and Game. "Black Racer." http://www.wildlife.state.nh.us/ Wildlife/Nongame/snakes/profile_black_racer.htm.

Newmark, Julianne. "Writing (and Speaking) in Tongues: Zitkala-Ša's American Indian Stories." *Western American Literature* 37, no. 3 (2002): 335–58.

Nickel, John. "Eugenics and the Fiction of Pauline Hopkins." *American Transcendental Quarterly* 14, no. 1 (2000): 47–60.

Noble, Marianne. *The Masochistic Pleasures of Sentimental Literature*. Princeton, N.J.: Princeton University Press, 2000.

Nojiri, Matthew. "Haudenosaunee Ceremony Celebrates Onondaga Lake." *Syracuse (N.Y.) Post-Standard*, 3 October 2009. http://www.syracuse.com/news/index.ssf/2009/10/haudenosaunee_ceremony_celebra.html.

Norman, Rose. "New England Girlhoods in Nineteenth-Century Autobiography." *Legacy* 8, no. 2 (Fall 1991): 104–17.

Norwood, Vera. *Made from This Earth: American Women and Nature*. Chapel Hill: University of North Carolina Press, 1993.

Nova Scotia Museum of Natural History. "Hats Off to Birds!" East Coast Birds. http://museum.gov.ns.ca/mnh/nature/nsbirds/feat05.htm.

Oakes, Karen. "'Colossal in Sheet-Lead': The Native American and Piscataqua Region Writers." In *A Noble and Dignified Stream: The Piscataqua Region in the Colonial Revival, 1860–1930*, edited by Sarah M. Giffen and Kevin M. Murphy, 165–76. York, Maine: Old York Historical Society, 1992.

———. "'We planted, tended and harvested our corn': Gender, Ethnicity, and Transculturation in *A Narrative of the Life of Mrs. Mary Jemison*." *Women and Language: Women and the Language of Race and Ethnicity* 18, no. 1 (1995): 45–51.

Obuchowski, Mary DeJong. "'Murdered Banquos of the Forest': Caroline Kirkland's Environmentalism." *Midwestern Miscellany* 33 (2005): 73–79.

Okker, Patricia. "Native American Literatures and the Canon: The Case of Zitkala-Ša." In *American Realism and the Canon*, edited by Tom Quirk and Gary Scharnhorst, 87–101. Newark: University of Delaware Press, 1994.

Older, Julia. *The Island Queen: Celia Thaxter of the Isles of Shoals*. Hancock, N.H.: Appledore Books, 1994.

"Omaha Girls." C. 1876–96. CorbisImages. http://www.corbisimages.com/Enlargement/NA005894.html.

"Onondaga Lake Superfund Site: Onondaga Lake Cleanup." New York State Department of Environmental Conservation. http://www.dec.ny.gov/chemical/8668.html.

"Outward Manifest of the *Two Friends*" (transcript). 1791. National Archives and Records Administration, Waltham, Mass. Available at Essex LINCs, "Primary Resources for the *Introduction to Primary Sources* lesson, February, 2009." http://www.essexlincs.org/pdfs/narafeb09/outwardmanifest1791.pdf.

Owen, Narcissa. *A Cherokee Woman's America: Memoirs of Narcissa Owen, 1821–1907*. Edited by Karen L. Kilcup. Gainesville: University Press of Florida, 2005.

Pagh, Nancy. "An Indescribable Sea: Discourse of Women Traveling in the Northwest Coast by Boat." *Frontiers: A Journal of Women's Studies* 20, no. 3 (1999): 1–26.

Parker, Arthur C. "Certain Iroquois Tree Myths and Symbols." *American Anthropologist* 14, no. 4 (October–December 1912): 608–20.

———. *The History of the Seneca Indians*. Long Island, N.Y.: Ira J. Friedman, 1967.

———. "How the World Began: A Seneca Creation Myth." In *Seneca Myths and Folk Tales*, edited by Arthur C. Parker, 59–73. Publications of the Buffalo Historical Society, vol. 27. Buffalo, N.Y.: Buffalo Historical Society, 1923. http://www.pitt.edu/~dash/senecacreation.html. Reprinted in *Seneca Myths and Folk Tales*. Lincoln: University of Nebraska Press, 1989.

Parker, Pauline, and John Sorenson. "Emotional Intelligence and Leadership Skills among NHS Managers: An Empirical Investigation." *International Journal of Clinical Leadership* 16 (2008): 137–42.

Passell, Peter. "On Clear-Cutting, Economists Can't See the Forest or the Trees." *New York Times*, 31 October 1996. http://www.nytimes.com/1996/10/31/business/on-clear-cutting-economists-can-t-see-the-forest-or-the-trees.html.

Paton, Priscilla. "Furry Soul Mates, Aloof Birds, Pesky Rodents: Liminality, Animal Rescue Films, and Sarah Orne Jewett." In *Of Mice and Men: Animals in Human Culture*, edited by Nandita Batra and Vartan Messier, 28–41. Newcastle, UK: Cambridge Scholars Press, 2009.

Patterson, Daniel, Roger Thompson, and Scott Bryson, eds. *Early American Nature Writers: A Biographical Encyclopedia*. Westport, Conn.: Greenwood, 2008.

Payne, Daniel C. *Voices in the Wilderness: American Nature Writing and Environmental Politics*. Hanover, N.H.: University Press of New England, 1996.

Pearce, Roy Harvey. *Savagism and Civilization: A Study of the Indian and the American Mind*. Berkeley: University of California Press, 1988.

Pearson, Clive. "Electing to Do Ecotheology." *Ecotheology* 9, no. 1 (2004): 7–28.

Perdue, Theda. *Cherokee Women: Gender and Culture Change, 1700–1835*. Lincoln: University of Nebraska Press, 1998.

———. "Cherokee Women and the Trail of Tears." In *Unequal Sisters: A Multicultural Reader in U.S. Women's History*, 3rd ed., edited by Vicki L. Ruiz and Ellen Carol DuBois, 93–104. New York: Routledge, 2000.

———. "Nancy Ward." In *Portraits of American Women: From Settlement to the Present*, edited by G. J. Barker-Benfield and Catherine Clinton, 83–100. New York: Oxford University Press, 1998.

Pérez, Vincent. *Remembering the Hacienda: History and Memory in the Mexican American Southwest*. College Station: Texas A&M University Press, 2006.

Peterson, Carla L. *Doers of the Word: African American Women Speakers and Writers in the North (1830–1880)*. New Brunswick, N.J.: Rutgers University Press, 1998.

———. "Unsettled Frontiers: Race, History, and Romance in Pauline Hopkins's *Contending Forces*." In *Famous Last Words: Changes in Gender and Narrative Closure*, edited by Alison Booth, 177–96. Charlottesville: University Press of Virginia, 1993.

Peterson, Nancy M. "From the Heart of Chaos: Finding Zitkala-Ša." In *The

Way West: True Stories of the American Frontier, edited by James A. Crutchfield, 223–32. New York: Forge, 2005.

Petrides, K. V., Ria Pita, and Flora Kokkinaki. "The Location of Trait Emotional Intelligence in Personality Factor Space." *British Journal of Psychology* 98, no. 2 (2007): 273–89.

Peyer, Bernd. "Non-fiction Prose." In *The Cambridge Companion to Native American Literature*, edited by Joy Porter and Kenneth M. Roemer, 108–11. New York: Cambridge University Press, 2005.

Pfaelzer, Jean. "Nature, Nurture, and Nationalism: 'A Faded Leaf of History.'" In Kilcup, *Nineteenth-Century American Women Writers: A Critical Reader*, 112–27.

Phelps, Elizabeth Stuart. *The Silent Partner*. Boston: Houghton Mifflin, 1871.

Philip, Cynthia Owen. *Robert Fulton: A Biography*. Lincoln, Nebr.: iUniverse, 2002.

Philippon, Daniel J. *Conserving Words: How American Nature Writers Shaped the Environmental Movement*. Athens: University of Georgia Press, 2004.

———. "Is Early American Environmental Writing Sustainable?: A Response to Timothy Sweet." *American Literary History* 22, no. 2 (2010): 432–38.

Pita, Beatrice. "Engendering Critique: Race, Class, and Gender in Ruiz de Burton and Martí." In *José Martí's "Our America": From National to Hemispheric Cultural Studies*, edited by Jeffrey Belknap and Raúl Fernández, 129–44. Durham, N.C.: Duke University Press, 1998.

———. "María Amparo Ruiz de Burton." In *Chicano Writers: Third Series*, edited by Francisco A. Lomelí and Carl R. Shirley, 251–55. Detroit: Gale, 1999.

Pitts, Reginald H. "George and Timothy Blanchard: Surviving and Thriving in Nineteenth-Century Milford." In Boggis, Raimon, and White, *Harriet Wilson's New England*, 41–57.

"Plumed Hunters." Earth Almanac. *Audubon*, March–April 2001. http://www.audubonmagazine.org/earthalmanac/almanac0103.html.

Poe, Edgar A. "The Literati of New York City.—No. IV: Some Honest Opinions at Random Respecting Their Authorial Merits, with Occasional Words of Personality." *Godey's Lady's Book* 33 (August 1846): 72–78. http://www.eapoe.org/works/misc/litratb4.htm.

Portnoy, Alisse. *Their Right to Speak: Women's Activism in the Indian and Slave Debates*. Cambridge, Mass.: Harvard University Press, 2005.

Pourade, Richard R. "Water Is King." In *The Rising Tide, 1920–1941*. Vol. 6 of *The History of San Diego*. San Diego: Union-Tribune, 1967. http://www.sandiegohistory.org/books/pourade/rising/risingchapter3.htm.

Powell, Malea D. "Princess Sarah, the Civilized Indian: The Rhetoric of Cultural Literacies in Sarah Winnemucca Hopkins's *Life Among the Piutes*." In *Rhetorical Women: Roles and Representations*, edited by Hildy Miller and Lillian Bridwell-Bowles, 63–80. Tuscaloosa: University of Alabama Press, 2005.

———. "Rhetorics of Survivance: How American Indians Use Writing." *College Composition and Communication* 53, no. 3 (February 2002): 396–434.

———. "Sarah Winnemucca Hopkins: Her Wrongs and Claims." In *American Indian Rhetorics of Survivance: Word Medicine, Word Magic*, edited by Ernest Stromberg, 69–94. Pittsburgh: University of Pittsburgh Press, 2006.

Pratt, Mary Louise. *Imperial Eyes: Travel Writing and Transculturation*. 2nd ed. New York: Routledge, 2008.

Pratt, Richard H. "The Advantages of Mingling Indians with Whites." In *Americanizing the American Indians: Writings by the "Friends of the Indian" 1880–1900*, edited by Francis P. Prucha, 260–71. Cambridge, Mass.: Harvard University Press, 1973.

Price, Jennifer. *Flight Maps: Adventures with Nature in Modern America*. New York: Basic Books, 2000.

———. "Hats Off to Audubon." *Audubon*, December 2004. http://audubon magazine.org/features0412/hats.html.

Price Herndl, Diane. *Invalid Women: Figuring Feminine Illness in American Fiction and Culture, 1840–1940*. Chapel Hill: University of North Carolina Press, 1993.

———. "The Invisible (Invalid) Woman: African American Women, Illness, and Nineteenth-Century Narrative." *Women's Studies* 24, no. 6 (1995): 553–72.

"Principles of Environmental Justice." http://www.ejnet.org/ej/principles.html.

Pryse, Marjorie. "Literary Regionalism and Global Capital: Nineteenth-Century U.S. Women Writers." *Tulsa Studies in Women's Literature* 23, no. 1 (Spring 2004): 65–89.

———. "Reading Regionalism: The 'Difference' It Makes." In *Regionalism Reconsidered: New Approaches to the Field*, edited by David Jordan, 47–64. New York: Garland, 1994.

Pulling, Hazel Adele. "California's Cattle-Range Industry: Decimation of the Herds, 1870–1912." *Journal of San Diego History* 11, no. 1 (January 1965). http://www.sandiegohistory.org/journal/65january/cattle.htm.

Putnam, Robert D. *Bowling Alone: The Collapse and Revival of American Community*. New York: Simon and Schuster, 2001.

Putzi, Jennifer. "'Raising the Stigma': Black Womanhood and the Marked Body in Pauline Hopkins's *Contending Forces*." *College Literature* 31, no. 2 (Spring 2004): 1–21.

Radner, Joan N., and Susan S. Lanser. "Strategies of Coding in Women's Culture." In *Feminist Messages: Coding in Women's Folk Culture*, edited by Joan Newlon Radner, 1–29. Urbana: University of Illinois Press, 1993.

Raimon, Eve Allegra. "Miss Marsh's Uncommon School Reform." In Boggis, Raimon, and White, *Harriet Wilson's New England*, 167–81.

Ratcliffe, Krista. *Anglo-American Feminist Challenges to the Rhetorical Traditions: Virginia Woolf, Mary Daly, Adrienne Rich*. Carbondale: Southern Illinois University Press, 1996.

Ray, Janisse. *Ecology of a Cracker Childhood*. Minneapolis: Milkweed Editions, 2000.

Real Simple. www.realsimple.com.

———. "How to Identify Sustainable Seafood." http://www.realsimple.com/food-recipes/shopping-storing/food/how-identify-sustainable-seafood-10000001707996/index.html.

Red Jacket. *The Collected Speeches of Sagoyewatha, or Red Jacket*. Edited by Graham Ganter. Syracuse, N.Y.: Syracuse University Press, 2006.

Reed, Ora Eddleman. "The Indian Orphan." *Twin Territories*, January 1908. Reprinted in Kilcup, *Native American Women's Writing*, 394–95.

———. "Types of Indian Girls" (series). *Twin Territories*.

Regier, Willis Goth, ed. *Masterpieces of American Indian Literature*. Lincoln: University of Nebraska Press, 2005.

Reichardt, Mary R. *Mary Wilkins Freeman: A Study of the Short Fiction*. New York: Twayne, 1997.

Renner, Michael. *The Anatomy of Resource Wars*. Washington, D.C.: Worldwatch Institute, 2002.

Rensink, Brenden. "Genocide of Native Americans: Historical Facts and Historiographical Debates." In *Genocide of Indigenous Peoples*, edited by Samuel Totten and Robert K. Hitchcock, 15–36. New Brunswick, N.J.: Transaction, 2011.

Renza, Louis A. *"A White Heron" and the Question of Minor Literature*. Madison: University of Wisconsin Press, 1984.

Review of *Poems*, by Lucy Larcom. *Atlantic Monthly* 23 (January 1869): 136.

Review of *Scenes in My Native Land*, by Lydia H. Sigourney. *Atheneum: Journal of English and Foreign Literature, Science, and the Fine Arts* 909 (29 March 1855): 302–3.

Review of *Scenes in My Native Land*, by Lydia H. Sigourney. *Hunt's Merchant's Magazine* 13, no. 2 (August 1845): 207.

Reynolds, Margot. "Mother Times Two: A Double Take on a Gynocentric Justice Song." In *Cultural Sites of Critical Insight: Philosophy, Aesthetics, and African American and Native American Women's Writings*, edited by Angela L. Cotton and Christa Davis Acampora, 171–90. Albany: State University of New York Press, 2007.

Rhoads, Professor James. "The Floral Calendar" and "Tropaeolum Majus (Nasturtium)." *Sartain's Union Magazine of Literature and Art* 4, no. 5 (1849): 347–48.

Richter, Daniel K. "Iroquois versus Iroquois: Jesuit Missions and Christianity in Village Politics, 1642–1686." *Ethnohistory* 32, no. 1 (Winter 1985): 1–16.

Rifkin, Mark. *Manifesting America: The Imperial Construction of U.S. National Space*. New York: Oxford University Press, 2009.

———. "Representing the Cherokee Nation: Subaltern Studies and Native American Sovereignty." *boundary 2* 32, no. 3 (2005): 47–80.

————. "Romancing Kinship: A Queer Reading of Indian Education and Zitkala-Ša's *American Indian Stories*." *GLQ: A Journal of Lesbian and Gay Studies* 12, no.1 (2006): 27–59.

————. *When Did Indians Become Straight?: Kinship, the History of Sexuality, and Native Sovereignty*. New York: Oxford University Press, 2011.

Rimer, Sara. "In Clear-Cutting Vote, Maine Will Define Itself." *New York Times*, 25 September 1996. http://www.nytimes.com/1996/09/25/us/in-clear-cutting -vote-maine-will-define-itself.html.

Riney-Kehrberg, Pamela. *Waiting on the Bounty: The Dust Bowl Diary of Mary Knackstedt Dyck*. Iowa City: University of Iowa Press, 1999.

Rissanen, Timo. "Zero-Waste with Loomstate." *560* (online magazine, Parsons' School of Fashion). August 16, 2010. http://fashion.parsons.edu/2010/08/16/ zero-waste-with-loomstate/.

Ritchie, Joy, and Kate Ronald, eds. *Available Means: An Anthology of Women's Rhetoric(s)*. Pittsburgh: University of Pittsburgh Press, 2001.

Rivera, John-Michael. *The Emergence of Mexican America: Recovering Stories of Mexican Peoplehood in U.S. Culture*. New York: New York University Press, 2006.

Robinson, Harriet H. *Loom and Spindle; or, Life among the Early Mill Girls*. New York: Crowell, 1898. http://libweb.uml.edu/clh/All/han.pdf.

Rodier, Katharine. "Authorizing Sarah Winnemucca? Elizabeth Peabody and Mary Peabody Mann." In *Reinventing the Peabody Sisters*, edited by Monika M. Elbert, Julie E. Hall, and Katharine Rodier, 108–25. Iowa City: University of Iowa Press, 2006.

Roediger, David. *The Wages of Whiteness: Race and the Making of the American Working Class*. New York: Verso, 1991.

Roman, Margaret. *Sarah Orne Jewett: Reconstructing Gender*. Tuscaloosa: University of Alabama Press, 1992.

Romero, Lora. *Home Fronts: Domesticity and Its Critics in the Antebellum United States*. New York: Oxford University Press, 1997.

Ronald, Kate, and Joy Ritchie, eds. *Teaching Rhetorica: Theory, Pedagogy, Practice*. Portsmouth, N.H.: Boynton/Cook, 2006.

Roorda, Randall. *Dramas of Solitude: Narratives of Retreat in American Nature Writing*. Albany: State University of New York Press, 1998.

Rosenthal, Bernard. *City of Nature: Journeys to Nature in the Age of American Romanticism*. Newark: University of Delaware Press and Associated University Press, 1980.

Rowlandson, Mrs. Mary [White]. *The sovereignty & goodness of God, . . . being a narrative of the captivity and restauration of Mrs. Mary Rowlandson, . . . [Narrative of the Captivity and Ransom of Mrs. Mary Rowlandson]*. Cambridge, Mass.: Samuel Green, 1682. http://digital.library.upenn.edu/webbin/gutbook/ lookup?num=851.

Ruether, Rosemary Radford. "Conclusion: Eco-justice at the Center of the

Church's Mission." In *Christianity and Ecology: Seeking the Well-Being of Earth and Humans*, edited by Dieter T. Hessel and Rosemary Radford Ruether, 603–14. Cambridge, Mass.: Harvard University Center for the Study of World Religions, 2000.

———. "Ecological Theology: Roots in Tradition, Liturgical and Ethical Practice for Today." *Dialog: A Journal of Theology* 42, no. 3 (Fall 2003): 226–34.

Ruffin, Kimberly N. *Black on Earth: African American Ecoliterary Traditions*. Athens: University of Georgia Press, 2010.

Ruiz, Vicki L. "From Out of the Shadows: Mexican Women in the United States." *Magazine of History* 10, no. 2 (Winter 1996): 15–18.

[Ruiz de Burton, María Amparo]. Loyal, C. *The Squatter and the Don: A Novel Descriptive of Contemporaneous Occurrences in California*. San Francisco, 1885.

Ruoff, A. LaVonne Brown. "Early Native American Women Authors: Jane Johnston Schoolcraft, Sarah Winnemucca, S. Alice Callahan, E. Pauline Johnson, and Zitkala-Ša." In Kilcup, *Nineteenth-Century American Women Writers: A Critical Reader*, 81–111.

———. "Three Nineteenth-Century American Indian Autobiographers." In *Redefining American Literary History*, edited by A. LaVonne Brown Ruoff and Jerry W. Ward Jr., 251–69. New York: MLA, 1990.

Rust, Marion. "'The Old Town of Berwick,' by Sarah Orne Jewett." *New England Quarterly* 73, no. 1 (March 2000): 122–58.

Ryan, Barbara. *Love, Wages, Slavery: The Literature of Servitude in the United States*. Urbana: University of Illinois Press, 2006.

Saillant, John. "'Wipe away All Tears from Their Eyes': John Marrant's Theology in the Black Atlantic, 1785–1808." *Journal of Millennial Studies* 1, no. 2 (Winter 1999). http://www.bu.edu/mille/publications/winter98/saillant.PDF.

Salovey, Peter, and Daisy Grewal, "The Science of Emotional Intelligence." *Current Directions in Psychological Science* 14, no. 6 (2005): 281–85.

Samuels, Ellen. "'A Complication of Complaints': Untangling Disability, Race, and Gender in William and Ellen Craft's *Running A Thousand Miles for Freedom*." *MELUS* 31, no. 3 (Fall 2006): 15–47.

Samuels, Shirley, ed. *The Culture of Sentiment: Race, Gender, and Sentimentality in 19th-Century America*. Oxford: Oxford University Press, 1992.

Sánchez, María Carla. *Reforming the World: Social Activism and the Problem of Fiction in Nineteenth-Century America*. Iowa City: University of Iowa Press, 2009.

———. "Whiteness Invisible: Early Mexican American Writing and the Color of Literary History." In *Passing: Identity and Interpretation in Sexuality, Race, and Religion*, edited by Linda Schlossberg and María Carla Sánchez, 64–91. New York: New York University Press, 2001.

Sánchez, Rosaura. "Dismantling the Colossus: Martí and Ruiz de Burton on the Formulation of Anglo América." In *José Martí's "Our America": From National to Hemispheric Cultural Studies*, edited by Jeffrey Belknap and Raúl Fernández, 115–28. Durham, N.C.: Duke University Press, 1998.

Sánchez, Rosaura, and Beatrice Pita. "María Amparo Ruiz de Burton and the Power of Her Pen." In *Latina Legacies: Identity, Biography and Community*, edited by Vicki L. Ruiz and Virginia Sánchez Korrol, 72–83. New York: Oxford University Press, 2005.

Sánchez-Eppler, Karen. *Dependent States: The Child's Part in Nineteenth-Century American Culture*. Chicago: University of Chicago Press, 2005.

———. "Playing at Class." In Levander and Singley, *The American Child*, 40–62.

———. *Touching Liberty: Abolition, Feminism, and the Politics of the Body*. Berkeley: University of California Press, 1993.

Sánchez-Ruiz, María José, Juan Carlos Pérez-González, and K. V. Petrides. "Trait Emotional Intelligence Profiles of Students from Different University Faculties." *Australian Journal of Psychology* 62, no. 1 (March 2010): 51–57.

Sandilands, Catriona. "The Importance of Reading Queerly: Jewett's *Deephaven* as Feminist Ecology." *ISLE: Interdisciplinary Studies in Literature and Environment* 11, no. 2 (Summer 2004): 57–77.

Santamarina, Xiaomara. "The View from Below: Menial Labor and Self-Reliance in Harriet Wilson's *Our Nig*." In *Belabored Professions: Narratives of African American Working Womanhood*, 64–100. Chapel Hill: University of North Carolina Press, 2009.

The Sarah Orne Jewett Text Project. Coe College. http://www.public.coe.edu/~theller/soj/sj-index.htm.

Sawaya, Francesca. "Emplotting National History: Regionalism and Pauline Hopkins's *Contending Forces*." In Inness and Royer, *Breaking Boundaries*, 72–87.

Schabas, William A. "Convention on the Prevention and Punishment of the Crime of Genocide." United Nations Audiovisual Library of International Law. http://untreaty.un.org/cod/avl/ha/cppcg/cppcg.html.

Scharff, Virginia J. *Seeing Nature through Gender*. Lawrence: University Press of Kansas, 2003.

Scheckel, Susan. *The Insistence of the Indian: Race and Nationalism in Nineteenth-Century American Culture*. Princeton, N.J.: Princeton University Press, 1996.

Schell, Eileen E., and K. J. Rawson, eds. *Rhetorica in Motion: Feminist Rhetorical Methods and Methodologies*. Pittsburgh: University of Pittsburgh Press, 2010.

Scherer, Joanna Cohan. "The Public Faces of Sarah Winnemucca." *Cultural Anthropology* 3, no. 2 (May 1998): 178–204.

Schocket, Eric. "'Discovering Some New Race': Rebecca Harding Davis's 'Life in the Iron Mills' and the Literary Emergence of Working-Class Whiteness." *PMLA* 115, no. 1 (2000): 46–59.

Schriber, Mary Suzanne. *Writing Home: American Women Abroad, 1830–1920*. Charlottesville: University Press of Virginia, 1997.

Schumacher, E. F. *Small Is Beautiful: Economics as If People Mattered*. London: Blond and Briggs, 1973.

Schwantes, Carlos A. *The Pacific Northwest: An Interpretive History*. Rev. and enl. ed. Lincoln: University of Nebraska Press, 1996.

Schwarze, [Pastor] Edmund. *History of the Moravian Missions among Southern Tribes of the United States.* Bethlehem, Pa.: Times Publishing, 1923.

Scott, Anne Firor. *Natural Allies: Women's Associations in American History.* Urbana: University of Illinois Press, 1992.

Sears, John F. *Sacred Places: American Tourist Attractions in the Nineteenth Century.* New York: Oxford University Press 1989.

Seaton, Beverly. *The Language of Flowers: A History.* Charlottesville: University Press of Virginia, 1996.

Seaver, James E., ed. *A Narrative of the Life of Mrs. Mary Jemison.* Syracuse, N.Y.: Syracuse University Press, 1990.

Seccombe, Wally. *Weathering the Storm: Working-Class Families from the Industrial Revolution to the Fertility Decline.* London: Verso, 1993.

"Selu and Kana'tī." In Mooney, *Myths of the Cherokee*, 340.

Seneca Nation of Indians. sni.org.

Senier, Siobhan. *Voices of American Indian Assimilation and Resistance: Helen Hunt Jackson, Sarah Winnemucca, and Victoria Howard.* Norman: University of Oklahoma Press, 2001.

Sequoyah, Jana. "How (!) Is an Indian?" In Krupat, *New Voices*, 453–73.

Sharer, Wendy B. "'Going Into Society' or 'Bringing Society In'?: Rhetoric and Problematic Philanthropy in *The Silent Partner.*" *American Transcendental Quarterly* 11, no. 3 (September 1997): 171–90.

Sheley, Nancy Strow. "The 'Language of Flowers' as Coded Subtext: Conflicted Messages of Domesticity in Mary Wilkins Freeman's Short Fiction." *WPD: Working Papers on Design* 2 (2007): 5–14. http://sitem.herts.ac.uk/artdes _research/papers/wpdesign/wpdvol2/sheley.pdf.

Shepard, Grace Florence, ed. "Letters of Lucy Larcom to the Whittiers." *New England Quarterly* 3, no. 3 (1930): 501–18.

Sherman, Sarah Way. "Jewett and the Incorporation of New England: 'The Gray-Mills of Farley.'" *American Literary Realism* 34, no. 3 (Spring 2002): 191–216.

———. "Party Out of Bounds: Gender and Class in Jewett's 'The Best China Saucer.'" In Kilcup and Edwards, *Jewett and Her Contemporaries*, 223–48.

———. *Sarah Orne Jewett, an American Persephone.* Hanover, N.H.: University Press of New England, 1989.

Shi, David E. *The Simple Life: Plain Living and High Thinking in American Culture.* New York: Oxford University Press, 1985. Reprint, Athens: University of Georgia Press, 2007.

Short, Gretchen. "Harriet Wilson's *Our Nig* and the Labor of Citizenship." *Arizona Quarterly* 57, no. 3 (Autumn 2001): 1–27.

Siegel, Charles. *The Politics of Simple Living: A New Direction for Liberalism.* Berkeley, Calif.: Preservation Institute, 2008. http://www.preservenet.com/ simpleliving/PoliticsOfSimpleLiving.html.

Sigourney, Lydia H. "The Cherokee Mother." In Paula Bernat Bennett, *Nineteenth-Century American Women Poets*, 7–8.

———. "Indian Names." In *The Female Poets of America*, edited by Rufus Wilmot Griswold, 99. Philadelphia: Parry and McMillan, 1854. Reprinted in Kilcup, *Nineteenth-Century American Women Writers: An Anthology*, 46–47.

———. [Mrs. L. H. Sigourney]. *Letters of Life*. New York: Appleton, 1866.

———. "Niagara." In Kilcup, *Nineteenth-Century American Women Writers: An Anthology*, 43–44.

———. *Pleasant Memories of Pleasant Lands*. Boston: James Munroe and Company, 1842.

———. [Mrs. L. H. Sigourney]. *Scenes in My Native Land*. Boston: James Munroe and Company, 1844.

———. *Traits of the Aborigines of America: A Poem*. Cambridge: University Press, 1822.

———. "The Western Home." Chadwyck-Healey Literature Collections, American Poetry.

Silver, Bruce. "William Bartram's and Other Eighteenth-Century Accounts of Nature." *Journal of the History of Ideas* 39, no. 4 (October–December 1978): 597–614.

Silver, Timothy. *A New Face on the Countryside: Indians, Colonists, and Slaves in the South Atlantic Forests, 1500–1800*. New York: Cambridge University Press, 1990.

Simple Living Institute. "News." http://www.simplelivinginstitute.org/index.html.

Simple Living Network. www.simpleliving.net. Forums continued at http://www.simplelivingforum.net/.

Simpson, Gary, and Deborah Lambert. *From Isles of Shoals, Celia Thaxter*. Durham, N.H.: University of New Hampshire, 1984. Videocassette, 58 min.

Sivils, Matthew Wynn. "William Bartram's *Travels* and the Rhetoric of Ecological Communities." *ISLE: Interdisciplinary Studies in Literature and Environment* 11, no. 1 (Winter 2004): 57–70.

Sklar, Kathryn Kish. *Catharine Beecher: A Study in American Domesticity*. New York: Norton, 1976.

Slicer, Deborah. "The Body as Bioregion." In Branch, Johnson, Patterson, and Slovic, *Reading the Earth*, 107–16.

———. "Towards an Ecofeminist Standpoint Theory: Bodies as Grounds." In Gaard and Murphy, *Ecofeminist Literary Criticism*, 49–73.

Slotkin, Richard. *The Fatal Environment: The Myth of the Frontier in the Age of Industrialization, 1800–1890*. New York: Macmillan, 1985.

———. *Regeneration through Violence: The Mythology of the American Frontier, 1600–1860*. Norman: University of Oklahoma Press, 1973.

Slovic, Scott. "Ecocriticism with or without Narrative: The Language of Con-

scious Experience versus the Language of Freefall." Paper presented at
"Narrative Scholarship: Storytelling in Ecocriticism," Western Literature
Association Annual Meeting, Vancouver, B.C., October 1995. Association for
the Study of Literature and Environment. http://www.asle.org/site/resources/
ecocritical-library/intro/narrative/slovic/.

———. "Epistemology and Politics in American Nature Writing: Embedded
Rhetoric and Discrete Rhetoric." In Herndl and Brown, *Green Culture*, 82–110.

Smith, Andrea. *Conquest: Sexual Violence and American Indian Genocide.* Cambridge, Mass.: South End Press, 2005.

———. "Malthusian Orthodoxy and the Myth of ZPG: Population Control as
Racism." In Weaver, *Defending Mother Earth*, 122–43.

———. *Native Americans and the Christian Right: The Gendered Politics of Unlikely
Alliances.* Durham, N.C.: Duke University Press, 2008.

Smith, Eric Todd. "Dropping the Subject: Reflections on the Motives for an
Ecological Criticism." In Branch, Johnson, Patterson, and Slovic, *Reading the
Earth*, 29–39.

Smith, Huston, and Reuben Snake. *One Nation under God: The Triumph of the
Native American Church.* Santa Fe, N.M.: Clear Light, 1995.

Smith, Kimberly K. *African American Environmental Thought: Foundations.*
Lawrence: University Press of Kansas, 2007.

"Snakes of Massachusetts: Black Racer Snake." *Massachusetts Snakes: A Guide.*
University of Massachusetts, Amherst, Natural Resources and Environmental
Conservation. 1993. http://web.archive.org/web/20100402124605/http://www
.umass.edu/nrec/snake_pit/pages/bracer.html.

Spack, Ruth. "Re-visioning Sioux Women: Zitkala-Ša's Revolutionary American
Indian Stories." *Legacy* 14, no.1 (1997): 25–42.

———. "Translation Moves: Zitkala-Ša's Bilingual Indian Legends." *Studies in
American Indian Literatures* 18, no. 4 (2006): 43–62.

———. "Zitkala-Ša, *The Song of Hiawatha*, and the Carlisle Indian School Band:
A Captivity Tale." *Legacy* 25, no. 2 (2008): 211–24.

Spacks, Patricia Meyer. *Gossip.* New York: Knopf, 1985.

[Spofford, Harriet Prescott.] H. P. S. "Lucy Larcom's Poems." *Galaxy* 7 (1869): 299.

———. "Pomegranate-Flowers." *Atlantic Monthly* 7, no. 43 (May 1861): 573–79.
Reprinted in Paula Bernat Bennett, *Nineteenth-Century American Women Poets*,
215–22.

Spretnak, Charlene. "Ecofeminism: Our Roots and Flowering." In Diamond and
Orenstein, *Reweaving the World*, 3–14. San Francisco: Sierra Club Books, 1990.

Spurgeon, Sara L. "Miracles in the Desert: Literature, Water, and Public Discourse in the American West." *ISLE: Interdisciplinary Studies in Literature and
Environment* 16, no. 4 (Autumn 2009): 743–59.

Spurr, David. *The Rhetoric of Empire: Colonial Discourse in Journalism, Travel
Writing, and Imperial Administration.* Durham, N.C.: Duke University Press,
1993.

Stairs, David C. "Design and Deforestation." *Leonardo* 32, no. 4 (1999): 273–79.

Stannard, David. *American Holocaust: The Conquest of the New World.* New York: Oxford University Press, 1992.

Stansell, Christine. *City of Women: Sex and Class in New York, 1789–1860.* New York: Knopf, 1986.

Steadman, Jennifer Bernhardt. *Traveling Economies: American Women's Travel Writing.* Columbus: Ohio State University Press, 2007.

Stein, Rachel. *Shifting the Ground: American Women Writers' Revisions of Nature, Gender, and Race.* Charlottesville: University Press of Virginia, 1997.

Stepan, Nancy. "Race and Gender: The Role of Analogy in Science." In *The "Racial" Economy of Science: Toward a Democratic Future,* ed. Sandra Harding, 359–76. Bloomington: Indiana University Press, 1993.

Stern, Julia. "Excavating Genre in *Our Nig.*" *American Literature* 67, no. 3 (Fall 1995): 439–66.

Stewart, Mart A. "Slavery and African American Environmentalism." In Glave and Stoll, *"To Love the Wind and the Rain,"* 9–20.

Stewart, Omer Call. *Peyote Religion: A History.* Norman: University of Oklahoma Press, 1993.

Stone, Andrea. "Interracial Sexual Abuse and Legal Subjectivity in Antebellum Law and Literature." *American Literature* 81, no. 1 (March 2009): 65–92.

Storey, Mark. "Country Matters: Rural Fiction, Urban Modernity, and the Problem of American Regionalism." *Nineteenth-Century Literature* 65, no. 2 (September 2010): 192–213.

Stowe, Harriet Beecher. *Sunny Memories of Foreign Lands.* 2 vols. Boston: Phillips, Sampson, and Company, 1854.

———. *Uncle Tom's Cabin.* Edited by Mary R. Reichardt. San Francisco: Ignatius Press, 2009.

Stowe, William W. "'Busy Leisure': Margaret Fuller, Nature, and Vacation Writing." *ISLE: Interdisciplinary Studies in Literature and Environment* 9, no. 1 (Winter 2002): 25–43.

Stradling, David. *The Nature of New York: An Environmental History of the Empire State.* Ithaca, N.Y.: Cornell University Press, 2010.

Strand, Ginger. *Inventing Niagara: Beauty, Power, and Lies.* New York: Simon & Schuster, 2008.

Stremlau, Rosemarie. *Sustaining the Cherokee Family: Kinship and the Allotment of an Indigenous Nation.* Chapel Hill: University of North Carolina Press, 2001.

Strom, Deborah. *Birdwatching with American Women: A Selection of Nature Writings.* New York: Norton, 1986.

Stromberg, Ernest. "Resistance and Mediation: The Rhetoric of Irony in Indian Boarding School Narratives by Francis La Flesche and Zitkala-Ša." In *American Indian Rhetorics of Survivance: Word Medicine, Word Magic,* edited by Ernest Stromberg, 95–109. Pittsburgh: University of Pittsburgh Press, 2006.

Strong, Asa B., M.D. *The American Flora; or, History of Plants and Wild Flowers.* 4 vols. New York: Green & Spencer, 1845–50.

Strout, Cushing. *The American Image of the Old World.* New York: Harper and Row, 1969.

Stubbs, M. Wilma. "Celia Laighton Thaxter, 1835–1894." *New England Quarterly* 8, no. 4 (December 1935): 518–33.

Sturgeon, Noël. *Ecofeminist Natures: Race, Gender, Feminist Theory, and Political Action.* New York: Routledge, 1997.

———. *Environmentalism in Popular Culture: Gender, Race, Sexuality, and the Politics of the Natural.* Tucson: University of Arizona Press, 2009.

Sustainable Cotton Project. "About Us: Cleaning Up Cotton in California." http://www.sustainablecotton.org/pages/show/about-us.

Sutherland, Daniel E. *Americans and Their Servants: Domestic Service in the United States from 1800 to 1920.* Baton Rouge: Louisiana State University Press, 1981.

Swann, Brian. *Smoothing the Ground: Essays on Native American Oral Literature.* Berkeley: University of California Press, 1983.

Sweet, Timothy. *American Georgics: Economy and Environment in Early American Literature.* Philadelphia: University of Pennsylvania Press, 2002.

———. "Projecting Early American Environmental Writing." *American Literary History* 22, no. 2 (2010): 419–31.

Szasz, Andrew. *Shopping Our Way to Safety: How We Changed from Protecting the Environment to Protecting Ourselves.* Minneapolis: University of Minnesota Press, 2009.

Sze, Julie. "From Environmental Justice Literature to the Literature of Environmental Justice." In *The Environmental Justice Reader: Politics, Poetics, and Pedagogy,* edited by Joni Adamson, Mei Mei Adams, and Rachel Stein, 163–80. Tucson: University of Arizona Press, 2002.

Tawil, Ezra. *The Making of Racial Sentiment: Slavery and the Birth of the Frontier Romance.* New York: Cambridge University Press, 2006.

Taylor, P. A. M. "A Beacon Hill Domestic: The Diary of Lorenza Stevens Berbineau." *Proceedings of the Massachusetts Historical Society* 98 (1986): 90–115.

"Teeny Terns." Earth Almanac. *Audubon,* July–August 2009. http://www.audubonmagazine.org/earthalmanac/almanac0907.html.

Thaxter, Celia. *Among the Isles of Shoals.* Boston: James R. Osgood, 1873. Reprint, Sanbornville, N.H.: Wake-Brook House, 1962. Page references are to the Osgood edition.

———. *Poems.* New York: Hurd and Houghton, 1871.

———. "The Sandpiper's Nest." *Our Young Folks* 3, no. 7 (July 1867): 433. Reprinted in Kilcup, *Nineteenth-Century American Women Writers: An Anthology,* 280–81.

Thaxter, Rosamond. *Sandpiper: The Life and Letters of Celia Thaxter, and Her Home on the Isles of Shoals, Her Family, Friends, and Favorite Poems.* Rev. ed. Francestown, N.H.: M. Jones, 1963.

Thomas, Lois. "The Three Sisters." In *Indian Legends of Eastern Canada*. Compiled by students at Centennial College. Toronto: Education Division, Indian Affairs Branch, 1969, 1971. http://www.birdclan.org/threesisters.htm.

Thompson, E. P. *The Making of the English Working Class*. Rev. ed. Harmondsworth: Penguin, 1978.

Thomson, Rosemarie Garland. "Benevolent Maternalism and Physically Disabled Figures: Dilemmas of Female Embodiment in Stowe, Davis, and Phelps." *American Literature* 68, no. 3 (September 1996): 555–86.

———. "Crippled Girls and Lame Old Women: Sentimental Spectacles of Sympathy in Nineteenth-Century American Women's Writing." In Kilcup, *Nineteenth-Century American Women Writers: A Critical Reader*, 128–45.

———. *Extraordinary Bodies: Figuring Disability in American Culture and Literature*. New York: Columbia University Press, 1997.

———. "Feminist Theory, the Body, and the Disabled Figure." In *The Disability Studies Reader*, edited by Lennard J. Davis, 279–92. New York: Routledge, 1997.

Thoreau, Henry David. "Brute Neighbors." In *Walden*, 214–27.

———. "The Ponds." In *Walden*, 168–93.

———. *Walden; or, Life in the Woods*. Edited by Jeffrey S. Cramer. New Haven, Conn.: Yale University Press, 2004.

———. "Walking." In *Excursions*, 161–214. Boston: Ticknor and Fields, 1863.

Thorndike, Edward L. "Intelligence and Its Uses." *Harper's* 140 (December 1919–May 1920): 227–35.

Thorne, Tanis C. "'Poor Rich Indians' and the Turning Political Tide." In *The World's Richest Indian: The Scandal over Jackson Barnett's Oil Fortune*, 103–20. New York: Oxford University Press, 2003.

Tinker, George E. *American Indian Liberation: A Theory of Sovereignty*. Maryknoll, N.Y.: Orbis Books, 2008.

———. "An American Indian Theological Response to Ecojustice." In Weaver, *Defending Mother Earth*, 153–76.

———. *Missionary Conquest: The Gospel and Native American Genocide*. Minneapolis: Fortress Press, 1993.

———. *Spirit and Resistance: Political Theology and American Indian Liberation*. Minneapolis: Fortress Press, 2004.

Tisinger, Danielle. "Textual Performance and the Western Frontier: Sarah Winnemucca Hopkins's *Life Among the Piutes: Their Wrongs and Claims*." *Western American Literature* 37, no. 2 (Summer 2002): 171–94.

Tompkins, Jane. *Sensational Designs: The Cultural Work of American Fiction, 1790–1860*. New York: Oxford University Press, 1985.

Tompkins, Kyla Wazana. "'Everything 'Cept Eat Us': The Antebellum Black Body Portrayed as Edible Body." *Callaloo* 30, no. 1 (Winter 2007): 201–24.

Totten, Gary. "Zitkala-Ša and the Problem of Regionalism: Nation, Narratives, and Critical Traditions." *American Indian Quarterly* 29, no. 1–2 (Winter/Spring 2005): 84–123.

"The Treaty of Big Tree." 1794. Summary and treaty transcription. The Erastus Granger Papers: A Digital Library. http://www.oswego.edu/library2/archives/ digitized_collections/granger/bigtree.html.

[The Treaty of Big Tree.] "Agreement with the Seneca, 1797." In *Indian Affairs: Laws and Treaties*, vol. 2, *Treaties*, compiled and edited by Charles J. Kappler. Washington, D.C.: Government Printing Office, 1904. http://digital.library .okstate.edu/kappler/vol2/treaties/sen1027.htm.

"Treaty of Fort Laramie" 1868. *Our Documents: 100 Milestone Documents from the National Archives*. National Archives and Records Administration. http:// www.ourdocuments.gov/doc.php?flash=true&doc=42.

Turkes, Doris J. "Must Age Equal Failure?: Sociology Looks at Mary Wilkins Freeman's Old Women." *American Transcendental Quarterly* 13, no. 3 (September 1999): 197–214.

Turner, Frederick. "Cultivating the American Garden." In Glotfelty and Fromm, *The Ecocriticism Reader*, 40–51.

Tyas, Robert. *The Language of Flowers; or, Floral Emblems of Thoughts, Feelings and Sentiments*. London: George Routledge, 1869.

Ulman, H. Lewis. "'Thinking like a Mountain': Persona, Ethos, and Judgment in American Nature Writing." In Herndl and Brown, *Green Culture*, 46–81.

Unger, Nancy C. "Women, Sexuality, and Environmental Justice in American History." In *New Perspectives on Environmental Justice: Gender, Sexuality, and Activism*, edited by Rachel Stein, 45–60. New Brunswick, N.J.: Rutgers University Press, 2004.

U.S. Department of the Interior, National Park Service. "Vermont History." http://www.nps.gov/nr/travel/centralvermont/vhistory1.htm.

U.S. Environmental Protection Agency. "Environmental Justice." Last updated 10 December 2012. http://www.epa.gov/oecaerth/environmentaljustice/.

Vallier, Jane. *Poet on Demand: The Life, Letters, and Works of Celia Thaxter*. Portsmouth, N.H.: Peter Randall, 1994.

Veblen, Thorstein. *The Theory of the Leisure Class*. Edited by Martha Banta. 1899. Reprint, New York: Oxford University Press, 2008.

Velikova, Roumiana. "Troping in Zitkala-Ša's Autobiographical Writings, 1900–1921." *Arizona Quarterly* 56, no. 1 (2000): 49–64.

Vicinus, Martha. *Independent Women, Work and Community for Single Women, 1850–1920*. Chicago: University of Chicago Press, 1985.

Vizenor, Gerald. *Manifest Manners: Narratives on Postindian Survivance*. Lincoln: University of Nebraska Press, 1999.

Wadsworth, Horace Andrew. *Two Hundred and Fifty Years of the Wadsworth Family in America*. Lawrence, Mass.: Eagle Steam Job Printing Rooms, 1883.

Walker, Cheryl. *Indian Nation: Native American Literature and Nineteenth-Century Nationalisms*. Durham, N.C.: Duke University Press, 1997.

———. "Nineteenth-Century American Women Poets Revisited." In Kilcup, *Nineteenth-Century American Women Writers: A Critical Reader*, 231–44.

Walker, Nancy A. "Caroline Kirkland (1801–1864)." In Denise D. Knight and Nelson, *Nineteenth-Century American Women Writers*, 286–92.

———. *A Very Serious Thing: Women's Humor and American Culture*. Minneapolis: University of Minnesota Press, 1988.

Wallace, Anthony F. C. *The Death and Rebirth of the Seneca*. New York: Vintage, 1972.

———. *Jefferson and the Indians: The Tragic Fate of the First Americans*. Cambridge, Mass.: Belknap Press of Harvard University Press, 1999.

Wallinger, Hanna. *Pauline E. Hopkins: A Literary Biography*. Athens: University of Georgia Press, 2005.

———. "Pauline E. Hopkins as Editor and Journalist: An African American Story of Success and Failure." In Harris, *Blue Pencils and Hidden Hands*, 146–72.

Walsh, Susan. "'With Them Was My Home': Native American Autobiography and *A Narrative of the Life of Mrs. Mary Jemison*." *American Literature* 64, no. 1 (1992): 49–70.

Ward, Nancy. [Letter to U.S. Treaty Commissioners]. Nathaniel Green Papers, Library of Congress, Washington, D.C. Reprinted in *American State Papers*, class 2: *Indian Affairs*, 1:41. Washington, D.C., 1832.

———. [Speech to U.S. Treaty Commissioners, 1781, 1785]. In Kilcup, *Native American Women's Writing*, 27, 28.

Warford, Elisa. "'An Eloquent and Impassioned Plea': The Rhetoric of Ruiz de Burton's *The Squatter and the Don*." *Western American Literature* 44, no. 1 (Spring 2009): 5–21.

Warner, Anne Bradford. "Harriet Jacobs at Home in *Incidents in the Life of a Slave Girl*." *Southern Quarterly* 45, no. 3 (Spring 2008): 30–47.

Warren, Joyce W. *Ecofeminist Philosophy: A Western Perspective on What It Is and Why It Matters*. Lanham, Md.: Rowman & Littlefield, 2000.

———. "Performativity and the Repositioning of American Literary Realism." In *Challenging Boundaries: Gender and Periodization*, edited by Joyce W. Warren and Margaret Dickie, 3–25. Athens: University of Georgia Press, 2000.

Warrior, Robert Allen. *Tribal Secrets: Recovering American Indian Intellectual Traditions*. Minneapolis: University of Minnesota Press, 1995.

"The Washington Elm." *Cambridge and the American Revolution* (online exhibit). Cambridge Historical Society. http://cambridgehistory.org/discover/Cambridge-Revolution/Washington%20Elm.html.

"Water Use: From Fibre to Fashion." Modint corporate social responsibility factsheet. October 2010. Available at http://www.modint.nl/cms/showpage.aspx?id=1027 (link at bottom of page).

Watson, William Lynn. "'The facts which go to form this fiction': Elizabeth Stuart Phelps's *The Silent Partner* and the *Massachusetts Bureau of Labor Statistics Report*." *College Literature* 29, no. 4 (2002): 6–25.

Watters, David H. "'As Soon as I Saw My Sable Brother, I Felt More at Home':

Sampson Battis, Harriet Wilson, and New Hampshire Town History." In Boggis, Raimon, and White, *Harriet Wilson's New England*, 67–96.

Waugh, Charles. "'Only You Can Prevent a Forest': Agent Orange, Ecocide, and Environmental Justice." *ISLE: Interdisciplinary Studies in Literature and Environment* 17, no. 1 (2010): 113–32.

Waugh, F. W. *Iroquois Foods and Food Preparation*. Department of Mines, Geological Survey, Memoir 86, no. 12, Canada Anthropological Series. Ottawa: Government Printing Bureau, 1916. http://www.archive.org/stream/cu31924101546921/cu31924101546921_djvu.txt.

Weaver, Jace, ed. *Defending Mother Earth: Native American Perspectives on Environmental Justice*. Maryknoll, N.Y.: Orbis Books, 1996.

———. *"That the People Might Live": Native American Literatures and Native American Community*. New York: Oxford University Press, 1997.

Wertheimer, Molly Meijer, ed. *Listening to Their Voices: The Rhetorical Activities of Historical Women*. Columbia: University of South Carolina Press, 1997.

West, Elizabeth J. "Reworking the Conversion Narrative: Race and Christianity in *Our Nig*." *MELUS* 24, no. 2 (1999): 3–27.

Westbrook, Perry. *Acres of Flint: Writers of Rural New England, 1870–1900*. Washington, D.C.: Scarecrow Press, 1951.

———. "Celia Thaxter: Seeker of the Unattainable." *Colby Library Quarterly* 6, no. 12 (1964): 499–512.

———. "Celia Thaxter's Controversy with Nature." *New England Quarterly* 20, no. 1–4 (December 1947): 492–515.

———. *Mary Wilkins Freeman*. Rev. ed. New York: Twayne, 1988.

Wexler, Laura. *Tender Violence: Domestic Visions in an Age of U.S. Imperialism*. Chapel Hill: University of North Carolina Press, 2000.

———. "Tender Violence: Literary Eavesdropping, Domestic Fiction, and Educational Reform." In Shirley Samuels, *The Culture of Sentiment*, 9–38.

"What Is Clearcutting?" National Resources Defense Council. http://www.nrdc.org/land/forests/fcut.asp.

"What Is the Difference between Simple Living and Voluntary Simplicity?" *Choosing Voluntary Simplicity* (blog). http://www.choosingvoluntarysimplicity.com/what-is-the-difference-between-simple-living-voluntary-simplicity/.

White, Barbara A. "Legacy Profile: Celia Thaxter (1835–1894)." *Legacy* 7, no. 1 (1990): 59–64.

———. "'Our Nig' and the She-Devil: New Information about Harriet Wilson and the 'Bellmont' Family." *American Literature* 65, no. 1 (March 1993): 19–52.

White, E. Frances. *Dark Continent of Our Bodies: Black Feminism and the Politics of Respectability*. Philadelphia: Temple University Press, 2001.

White, Lynn, Jr. "The Historical Roots of Our Ecologic Crisis." In Glotfelty and Fromm, *The Ecocriticism Reader*, 3–14.

White, Richard. "Are You an Environmentalist or Do You Work for a Living?" In *Uncommon Ground: Rethinking the Human Place in Nature*, edited by William Cronon, 171–85. New York: Norton, 1996.

Whitney, Elspeth. "Christianity and Changing Concepts of Nature: An Historical Perspective." In *Religion and the New Ecology: Environmental Responsibility in a World in Flux*, edited by David M. Lodge and Christopher Hamlin, 26–51. Notre Dame, Ind.: University of Notre Dame Press, 2006.

"Why the Name King's Mark." King's Mark Resource Conservation and Development Project, Inc. Last updated 24 February 2011. http://ccrpa.org/km/King's%20Mark%20Why%20The%20Name%20King's%20Mark.htm.

Wiley, Terrence G., and Gerda de Klerk. "Common Myths and Stereotypes Regarding Literacy and Language Diversity in the Multilingual United States." In *Ethnolinguistic Diversity and Education: Language, Literacy, and Culture*, edited by Lisya Seloni and Juyoung Song, 23–43. New York: Routledge, 2010.

Wilkinson, Elizabeth. "Story as a Weapon in Colonized America: Native American Women's Transrhetorical Fight for Land Rights." PhD diss., University of North Carolina, Greensboro, 2008. Dissertation Abstracts International, Section A: The Humanities and Social Sciences, February 2009 [69 (8): 3155-3156].

Wilkinson, Norman B. "Robert Morris and the Treaty of Big Tree." *Mississippi Valley Historical Review* 40, no. 2 (September 1953): 257–78.

Williams, David. "Gold Rush." *New Georgia Encyclopedia*. www.georgiaencyclopedia.org/nge/Article.jsp?id=h-785.

Williams, Samuel Cole. *Tennessee during the Revolutionary War*. Knoxville: University of Tennessee Press, 1974.

[Wilson, Mrs. H. E.] *Our Nig; or, Sketches from the Life of a Free Black, in a Two-Story White House, North*. Boston: Rand & Avery, 1859. http://etext.lib.virginia.edu/toc/modeng/public/WilOurn.html.

Winnemucca [Hopkins], Sarah. *Life Among the Piutes: Their Wrongs and Claims*. Boston: Cupples, Upham, 1883.

Winter, Molly Crumpton. *American Narratives: Multiethnic Writing in the Age of Realism*. Baton Rouge: Louisiana State University Press, 2007.

Wirzba, Norman. *The Paradise of God: Renewing Religion in an Ecological Age*. New York: Oxford University Press, 2003.

Wolfe, Cary. "Human, All Too Human: 'Animal Studies' and the Humanities." *PMLA* 124, no. 2 (2009): 564–75.

Womack, Craig. *Red on Red: Native American Literary Separatism*. Minneapolis: University of Minnesota Press, 1999.

Wong, Hertha D. Sweet. "Native American Life Writing." In *The Cambridge Companion to Native American Literature*, edited by Joy Porter and Kenneth M. Roemer, 125–44. New York: Cambridge University Press, 2005.

Woods, Gioia. "Sarah Winnemucca: Multiple Places, Multiple Selves." In

Moving Stories: Migration and the American West 1850–2000, edited by Scott E. Casper and Lucinda M. Long, 51–70. Reno: Nevada Humanities Committee/ University of Nevada Press, 2001.

Woodward, Pauline. "Celia Thaxter's Love Poems." *Colby Library Quarterly* 23, no. 3 (September 1987): 144–53.

Woolf, Linda M. "Women and Sweatshops." http://www.webster.edu/~woolflm/ sweatshops.html.

Worcester Art Museum. "Edward Hicks: The Peaceable Kingdom." http://www .worcesterart.org/Collection/American/1934.65.html.

Wordsworth, William. "Yew-Trees." In *The Poetical Works of William Wordsworth*, 2:53–54. London: Longman, Rees et al., 1827.

World Hunger Education Service. "Hunger in America: 2011 United States Hunger and Poverty Facts." *Hunger Notes*. Last updated 22 November 2011. http://www.worldhunger.org/articles/Learn/us_hunger_facts.htm.

Worster, Donald. *Rivers of Empire: Water, Aridity, and the Growth of the American West*. New York: Pantheon, 1985.

Wright, Nancy G. "Christianity and Environmental Justice." *Cross Currents* 61, no. 2 (2011): 161–90.

Yarbrough, Fay A. *Race and the Cherokee Nation: Sovereignty in the Nineteenth Century*. Philadelphia: University of Pennsylvania Press, 2007.

Ybarra, Priscilla Solis. "Erasure by U.S. Legislation: Ruiz de Burton's Nineteenth-Century Novels and the Lost Archive of Mexican American Environmental Knowledge." In *Environmental Criticism for the Twenty-First Century*, edited by Stephanie LeMenager, Teresa Shewry, and Ken Hiltner, 135–47. New York: Routledge, 2010.

Yellin, Jean Fagan. "Written by Herself: Harriet Jacobs' Slave Narrative." *American Literature* 53, no. 3 (November 1981): 479–86.

Zagarell, Sandra A. "Expanding 'America': Lydia Sigourney's *Sketch of Connecticut*, Catharine Sedgwick's *Hope Leslie*." *Tulsa Studies in Women's Literature* 6, no. 2 (1987): 225–45.

———. Introduction to *A New Home: Who'll Follow; or, Glimpses of Western Life*, by Caroline Kirkland, xi–xlvi. New Brunswick, N.J.: Rutgers University Press, 1990.

———. "Narrative of Community: The Identification of a Genre." In *Narratives of Community: Women's Short Story Sequences*, edited by Roxanne Harde, 449–79. Newcastle, UK: Cambridge Scholars Press, 2007.

Zandy, Janet. Introduction to *Calling Home: Working Class Women's Writings, An Anthology*, edited by Janet Zandy, 1–13. New Brunswick, N.J.: Rutgers University Press, 1990.

Zanjani, Sally. *Sarah Winnemucca*. Lincoln: University of Nebraska Press, 2001.

Zitkala-Ša. "America, Home of the Red Man." *American Indian Magazine*, Winter 1919. Reprinted in Kilcup, *Native American Women's Writing*, 339–40. Page references are to the Kilcup edition.

————. *American Indian Stories*. Washington: Hayworth, 1921.

————. "Chipeta, Widow of Chief Ouray, with a Word about a Deal in Blankets." *American Indian Magazine*, July–September 1917. Reprinted in Kilcup, *Native American Women's Writing*, 335–37. Page references are to the Kilcup edition.

————. "Impressions of an Indian Childhood." *Atlantic Monthly* 85, no. 507 (January 1900): 37–47. http://etext.virginia.edu/toc/modeng/public/ZitImpr.html.

————. "Letter to the Chiefs and Head-Men of the Tribes." *American Indian Magazine*, Winter 1919. Reprinted in Kilcup, *Native American Women's Writing*, 340–41. Page references are to the Kilcup edition.

————. "Why I Am a Pagan." *Atlantic Monthly* 90 (1902): 801–3. http://etext.lib.virginia.edu/toc/modeng/public/ZitPaga.html.

Index